CSWE's Core Competencies and Practice Behavior Examples in This Text

Competency	Chapter
Professional Identity	
Practice Behavior Examples...	
Serve as representatives of the profession, its mission, and its core values	2, 7, 8, 9
Know the profession's history	2
Commit themselves to the profession's enhancement and to their own professional conduct and growth	4
Advocate for client access to the services of social work	2, 4, 7, 8, 9, 13, 14
Practice personal reflection and self-correction to assure continual professional development	4, 6, 7, 13, 14
Attend to professional roles and boundaries	3, 4, 6, 7, 9, 11, 13, 14
Demonstrate professional demeanor in behavior, appearance, and communication	3, 6, 7, 9, 10, 11, 12, 13, 14
Engage in career-long learning	6
Use supervision and consultation	4, 8, 13, 14
Ethical Practice	
Practice Behavior Examples...	
Obligation to conduct themselves ethically and engage in ethical decision making	4, 9, 12, 14
Know about the value base of the profession, its ethical standards, and relevant law	4, 9
Recognize and manage personal values in a way that allows professional values to guide practice	4
Make ethical decisions by applying standards of the National Association of Social Workers Code of Ethics and, as applicable, of the International Federation of Social Workers/International Association of Schools of Social Work Ethics in Social Work, Statement of Principles	4, 9, 12
Tolerate ambiguity in resolving ethical conflicts	4, 9, 14
Apply strategies of ethical reasoning to arrive at principled decisions	4, 9, 12
Critical Thinking	
Practice Behavior Examples...	
Know about the principles of logic, scientific inquiry, and reasoned discernment	8, 9, 10, 12
Use critical thinking augmented by creativity and curiosity	4, 6, 7, 10, 11, 12, 13, 14
Requires the synthesis and communication of relevant information	4, 7, 8, 10, 11, 12, 14
Distinguish, appraise, and integrate multiple sources of knowledge, including research-based knowledge, and practice wisdom	3, 4, 6, 9, 10, 11, 12, 13, 14
Analyze models of assessment, prevention, intervention, and evaluation	3, 6, 7, 8, 9, 10, 12, 13, 14
Demonstrate effective oral and written communication in working with individuals, families, groups, organizations, communities, and colleagues	4, 6, 7, 8, 9, 10, 11, 12, 13, 14

Adapted with the permission of Council on Social Work Education

CSWE's Core Competencies and Practice Behavior Examples in This Text

Competency	Chapter
Diversity in Practice	
Practice Behavior Examples...	
Understand how diversity characterizes and shapes the human experience and is critical to the formation of identity	2, 4, 6, 7, 8, 9, 11, 12, 14
Understand the dimensions of diversity as the intersectionality of multiple factors including age, class, color, culture, disability, ethnicity, gender, gender identity and expression, immigration status, political ideology, race, religion, sex, and sexual orientation	4, 6, 8, 9, 10, 11, 12
Appreciate that, as a consequence of difference, a person's life experiences may include oppression, poverty, marginalization, and alienation as well as privilege, power, and acclaim	2, 3, 4, 6, 8, 9, 11, 12, 14
Recognize the extent to which a culture's structures and values may oppress, marginalize, alienate, or create or enhance privilege and power	4, 5, 6, 9, 11
Gain sufficient self-awareness to eliminate the influence of personal biases and values in working with diverse groups	3, 4, 6, 7, 11, 14
Recognize and communicate their understanding of the importance of difference in shaping life experiences	3, 6, 8, 9, 11, 12, 14
View themselves as learners and engage those with whom they work as informants	4, 6, 7, 9, 12
Human Rights & Justice	
Practice Behavior Examples...	
Understand that each person, regardless of position in society, has basic human rights, such as freedom, safety, privacy, an adequate standard of living, health care, and education	1, 2, 4, 7, 9, 10, 12, 13, 14
Recognize the global interconnections of oppression and are knowledgeable about theories of justice and strategies to promote human and civil rights	3, 6, 11
Incorporates social justice practices in organizations, institutions, and society to ensure that these basic human rights are distributed equitably and without prejudice	1, 2, 6, 9
Understand the forms and mechanisms of oppression and discrimination	4, 6, 7, 13, 14
Advocate for human rights and social and economic justice	4, 6, 9
Engage in practices that advance social and economic justice	4, 6, 9, 14
Research-Based Practice	
Practice Behavior Examples...	
Use practice experience to inform research, employ evidence-based interventions, evaluate their own practice, and use research findings to improve practice, policy, and social service delivery	2, 7, 8, 10, 12, 13, 14, 4, 9, 10
Comprehend quantitative and qualitative research and understand scientific and ethical approaches to building knowledge	7, 8, 9, 10, 12, 14
Use practice experience to inform scientific inquiry	2, 7, 9, 10
Use research evidence to inform practice	2, 7, 8, 9, 10, 11, 12, 13, 14

CSWE's Core Competencies and Practice Behavior Examples in This Text

Competency	Chapter
Human Behavior	
Practice Behavior Examples...	
Know about human behavior across the life course; the range of social systems in which people live; and the ways social systems promote or deter people in maintaining or achieving health and well-being	1, 2, 6, 9, 10, 11, 12, 14
Apply theories and knowledge from the liberal arts to understand biological, social, cultural, psychological, and spiritual development	6, 7, 8, 10, 11, 12, 13
Utilize conceptual frameworks to guide the processes of assessment, intervention, and evaluation	9, 10, 11, 12, 13, 14
Critique and apply knowledge to understand person and environment.	2, 3, 7, 10, 11, 12, 13, 14
Policy Practice	
Practice Behavior Examples...	
Understand that policy affects service delivery and they actively engage in policy practice	2
Know the history and current structures of social policies and services; the role of policy in service delivery; and the role of practice in policy development	1, 2, 9
Analyze, formulate, and advocate for policies that advance social well-being	3, 4, 14
Collaborate with colleagues and clients for effective policy action	3
Practice Contexts	
Practice Behavior Examples...	
Keep informed, resourceful, and proactive in responding to evolving organizational, community, and societal contexts at all levels of practice	2, 6, 9, 13
Recognize that the context of practice is dynamic, and use knowledge and skill to respond proactively	3, 9, 10, 12, 13, 14
Continuously discover, appraise, and attend to changing locales, populations, scientific and technological developments, and emerging societal trends to provide relevant services	6, 9, 10, 11, 13, 14
Provide leadership in promoting sustainable changes in service delivery and practice to improve the quality of social services	3, 8

CSWE's Core Competencies and Practice Behavior Examples in This Text

Competency	Chapter
Engage, Assess Intervene, Evaluate	
Practice Behavior Examples...	
Identify, analyze, and implement evidence-based interventions designed to achieve client goals	5, 7, 8, 9, 10, 12, 13, 14
Use research and technological advances	5, 7, 8, 9, 10
Evaluate program outcomes and practice effectiveness	8
Promote social and economic justice	4, 6, 9, 14
A) ENGAGEMENT	
Substantively and effectively prepare for action with individuals, families, groups, organizations, and communities	10, 11, 12, 13, 14
Use empathy and other interpersonal skills	4, 5, 6, 7, 8, 11, 12, 13, 14
Develop a mutually agreed- on focus of work and desired outcomes	4, 5, 6, 7, 8, 9, 11, 12, 13, 14
B) ASSESSMENT	
collect, organize, and interpret client data	4, 5, 6, 7, 8, 9, 11, 12, 13, 14
Assess client strengths and limitations	4, 5, 6, 7, 9, 10, 11, 12, 13, 14
Develop mutually agreed-on intervention goals and objectives	4, 5, 6, 7, 8, 9, 11, 12, 13, 14
Select appropriate intervention strategies	4, 5, 6, 7, 8, 9, 10, 11, 12, 13, 14
C) INTERVENTION	
Implement prevention interventions that enhance client capacities	3, 8, 10, 11, 13
Help clients resolve problems	4, 5, 6, 7, 10, 11, 12, 13, 14
Negotiate, mediate, and advocate for clients	4, 5, 7, 9, 11, 12, 13, 14
Facilitate transitions and endings	4, 5, 7, 9, 10, 12, 13, 14
D) EVALUATION	
Critically analyze, monitor, and evaluate interventions	2, 8, 9, 10, 12, 13, 14

Interventions for Serious Mental Disorders

Working with Individuals and Their Families

Christina E. Newhill

University of Pittsburgh

PEARSON

Boston Columbus Indianapolis New York San Francisco Upper Saddle River
Amsterdam Cape Town Dubai London Madrid Milan Munich Paris Montréal Toronto
Delhi Mexico City São Paulo Sydney Hong Kong Seoul Singapore Taipei Tokyo

Editor in Chief: Ashley Dodge
Editorial Assistant: Amandria Guadalupe
Managing Editor: Denise Forlow
Program Manager: Carly Czech
Editorial Project Manager: Doug Bell, PreMediaGlobal, Inc.
Executive Marketing Manager: Kelly May
Marketing Coordinator: Jessica Warren
Digital Media Director: Brian Hyland
Digital Media Project Manager: Tina Gagliostro
Senior Operations Supervisor: Mary Fischer
Operations Specialist: Eileen Corallo
Creative Art Director: Jayne Conte
Cover Designer: Karen Noferi
Interior Design: Joyce Weston Design
Cover Art: Shutterstock / AlexAnnaButs
Full-Service Project Management: Murugesh Rajkumar Namasivayam /PreMediaGlobal
Printer/Binder: RR Donnelley
Cover Printer: RR Donnelley

Credits and acknowledgments borrowed from other sources and reproduced, with permission, in this textbook appear on appropriate page within text.

Library of Congress Cataloging-in-Publication Data

Newhill, Christina E.
Interventions for serious mental disorders: working with individuals and their families / Christina E. Newhill, professor, University of Pittsburgh.
pages cm
Includes index.
ISBN-13: 978-0-205-73065-0 (alk. paper)
ISBN-10: 0-205-73065-5 (alk. paper)
1. Mentally ill—Rehabilitation. 2. Mentally ill—Family relationships. 3. Community mental health services. 4. Mental health services. I. Title.
RC480.53. N485 2015
616.89—dc23

2013037936

10 9 8 7 6 5 4 3 2 1

PEARSON

ISBN-10: 0-205-73065-5
ISBN-13: 978-0-205-73065-0

Contents

Preface

For Dean, Tiffany, Eva, and David

Social workers are the primary providers of mental and behavioral health care services to individuals with severe and persistent mental illness and their families in the United States today, particularly in resource-poor areas and with those clients who are the most disadvantaged. Critical to providing appropriate and effective treatment and services is having the right knowledge base and skill repertoire. The overall purpose of this book is to prepare the beginning social work practitioner to work with some of the most challenging clients commonly seen at public community mental/behavioral health care services. The serious mental illnesses addressed in this text include schizophrenia and related psychotic disorders, major mood disorders (bipolar disorder, major depressive disorder), paranoid disorders and conditions, severe personality disorders, and alcohol and/or other substance use problems in combination with mental illness.

The philosophy underlying the text includes a number of basic assumptions:

1. Work with severely mentally ill clients and their families is intellectually and emotionally challenging and profoundly rewarding.
2. Severely mentally ill clients and their families differ from one another in important and complex ways with regard to personal strengths and challenges, social assets, manifestations of illness, and prospects for future functioning and recovery.
3. Effective intervention requires a *collaborative* approach to working with the individual and his or her family along with proactive efforts to support and enhance the client's ability to move forward toward personal recovery.
4. Awareness, acceptance, and understanding of the clinician's own strengths, challenges, and emotional reactions is important for understanding the needs of severely mentally ill clients and their families and to maintain practice excellence and avoid frustration, boredom, and burnout.

Features

There are many features of this text that will enhance your learning experience, however, they are only as useful as you make them. By engaging with this text and its resources, you'll gain a variety of practice-based competencies including:

- **How to manage legal and ethical issues relevant to practice with individuals with severe mental illness (SMI) and their families.** The text covers the basic principles of community mental/behavioral health practice, professional and personal values and ethics, and how to manage legal issues including involuntary civil commitment, psychiatric advance directives, HIPAA, confidentiality, and the duty to warn.
- **Overcoming potential and actual barriers to engagement in treatment.** The text includes how to develop and maintain a therapeutic alliance with individuals with serious mental illness; how to manage and overcome the impact of stigma; how to manage a client's lack of insight and facilitate illness awareness; and how to work with and engage involuntary and resistant clients.

- **Engaging and treating individuals across a range of serious mental disorders.** The text provides ample case illustrations and client–clinician dialogues to enhance understanding of how such disorders present and to facilitate clinical skill development.
- **Practice with individuals with serious mental illness from diverse client groups.** The text provides clinical guidance and multiple case illustrations representing differences in race, ethnicity, culture, gender, sexual orientation, and religious affiliation.
- **Guidelines and evidence-based interventions for working with families of individuals with serious mental illness.** The text illustrates and describes the phases families go through when mental illness emerges in a loved one and presents a detailed overview of family psychoeducation, how to work with families proactively in a supportive collaborative manner, and a review of self-help and advocacy resources for families.

Several areas of specialized practice knowledge for working with individuals with serious mental illness. The text covers case management in mental/behavioral health practice, social work practice and psychopharmacology, suicide risk assessment, and a range of evidence-based psychosocial interventions.

Learning Outcomes

After completing the text, students will have achieved a number of learning outcomes, including:

- **Understanding Historical Context** – students will possess an understanding of how the history and current context of practice has shaped how services are provided to individuals with serious mental illness and their families and be able to draw from history to capitalize on past successes and avoid repeating past mistakes to forge a better future for mental health care and services.
- **CSWE Core Competencies** – students will develop their comprehension and application of CSWE's core competencies and practice behaviors for
  - Effective engagement, assessment, and intervention with individuals with severe and persistent mental illness and their families utilizing a biopsychosocial holistic approach.
  - Providing disorder-specific evidence-based psychosocial interventions to individuals with schizophrenia, major mood disorders, personality disorders, paranoid disorders, co-occurring disorders, and individuals who are suicidal.
  - Discussing the role of psychotropic medication in treating serious mental illness and how psychosocial strategies can enhance medication adherence.
- **Analyzing Diversity in Context** – students will be able to analyze how various aspects of diversity characterize and shape the experience of living with serious mental illness and affect what individuals and families need and want from social workers and other providers of services.
- **Oral Communication Skills** – students can develop their oral communication skills by engaging with others in and out of class to discuss their comprehension of the chapter based on the chapter's learning objectives.
- **Assessment and Writing Skills** – students can develop their assessment and writing skills in preparation for future licensing exams by completing topic-based and chapter review assessments for each chapter.

Acknowledgements

Writing a textbook as a single author is a formidable and challenging process, and thus, the support, encouragement, and guidance from those I worked most closely with was particularly invaluable. I want to especially thank Carly Czech, Program Manager, Social Work/Human Services/Family Therapy at Pearson Education, and Doug Bell, Senior Project Manager with PreMedia Global. Both Carly and Doug were vitally instrumental in bringing this project to completion. I also want to thank my husband, Dean, for his unfailing support and putting up with all the hours, days, weeks, and months of writing I had to do. Finally, I must thank the many clients who must remain unnamed whose stories and experiences are reflected throughout the various chapters and whose lives provided me with the insights and commitment to write this text and hopefully will inspire future generations of clinicians to commit to careers working with individuals with severe and persistent mental illness and with their families. A special recognition goes to the consumer account contributors who shared their beautiful essays describing their experiences living with mental illness for this text—thank you.

This text is available in a variety of formats—digital and print. To learn more about our programs, pricing options, and customization, visit www.pearsonhighered.com.

Chapter 1

Understanding How Societies Have Cared for and Treated Individuals with Severe Mental Illness

Ancient Times to the Rise of the Asylum to Community-Based Mental Health Care

INTRODUCTION

As we review the history of how diverse societies have cared for and treated individuals with mental illness, we will see repeated over the centuries certain approaches that have been helpful and others that have been harmful and tragic. Today, as we close the doors of our state hospitals, embrace evidenced-based practice, and emphasize the importance of recovery, we must approach these efforts with a dose of caution and look back at the history of our efforts to care for and treat individuals with serious mental illness to see where similar endeavors worked and where they did not work. For example, there were many aspects of state hospital care that were harmful to their patients, but—as many consumers who lived in the state hospital will tell you—there were parts of the asylum that were good. Is it possible to eliminate what was bad and harmful, but retain what was good about the hospital in some way? For many patients, for example, the state hospital provided support, continuity of treatment, and a sense of community and purpose. How can we replicate that piece today as we provide services? Living in the community does not necessarily mean having a sense of being part of that community. To be a fully prepared clinician, one must be competent in the practices of today but also knowledgeable about the journey humankind has taken over the centuries as we have struggled to care for those who are most vulnerable and disadvantaged in our societies, in particular, individuals with severe mental illness.

Understanding how social work practice evolved in providing care and treatment for individuals with mental illness and their families requires that we first have an appreciation of the early history of how people have viewed mental illness, which provides insights into how and why mental illness, in contrast to many other types of illness, continues to carry a heavy burden of stigma (Sharfstein, 2012; Hinshaw, 2007).

An examination of this history certainly shows that we have made significant progress from the views and approaches to "treatment" characteristic of ancient times, but it also illustrates how some of our so-called progressive scientific concepts and treatments had parallel counterparts long ago. Over time, however, our general collective understanding of and beliefs about abnormal behavior has shifted from beliefs based on superstition and supernatural causes to beliefs based on scientific inquiry and natural causes. However, in spite of significant progress in understanding the etiology of mental illness and the development of more effective interventions to treat mental disorders, it is important to recognize that we still are not free of many of the culturally conditioned constraints of our past with regard to our attitudes toward individuals who exhibit symptoms of mental illness. The sheer presence of large numbers of mentally ill individuals who are homeless and living in our streets and parks today is a clear indicator of the continued problems of stigma, exclusion, and community indifference (Schutt & Goldfinger, 2011). To begin our historical journey, we will start by addressing how abnormal behavior was viewed and responded to in ancient times.

THE EARLY HISTORY OF THE CARE AND TREATMENT OF INDIVIDUALS WITH MENTAL ILLNESS/ABNORMAL BEHAVIOR

Abnormal Behavior in Ancient Times

Human life has presumably existed for over 3 million years on our earth, although written records extend back only a few thousand years (Butcher, Mineka, & Hooley, 2007). These existing records suggest that from earliest times our ideas about mental illness were confounded with notions of demon possession, believing that symptoms of mental illness were caused by a demon or deity possessing the individual's mind or soul. The earliest known treatment of abnormal behavior was that practiced by Stone Age cave dwellers some half million years ago. Human skulls from that period show evidence that such people—probably at the instruction of a shaman—drilled holes in an individual's head to allow the demon or deity possessing the person to escape. This process was called trephining (Walker, 1997). What is amazing about this phenomenon is that some of the skulls from this period show evidence of healing, suggesting that some people actually survived the process and lived for some years afterward. Given that such crude surgeries did not have the benefit of sanitary conditions or medications to treat infection, the fact that some individuals survived is remarkable (Selling, 1943). In addition, the fact that trephining targeted the afflicted individual's skull suggests that people may have identified symptoms of mental illness as residing in the individual's head and may even have had a rudimentary notion of the existence of the brain as the source of one's mind where emotions and behaviors are rooted (Selling, 1943).

Later, two Egyptian papyri from the sixteenth century B.C. were discovered that contained written evidence of the treatment of diseases and behavior disorders. For example, these papyri contained detailed descriptions of the treatment of traumatic injuries to various parts of the body and other surgical procedures, and provided the first recorded description of the brain (Okasha & Okasha, 2000). However, these early writings often used words like "driving out" and "banishing" when describing treatment of conditions suggesting the presence of mental illness, indicating that in spite of a beginning understanding of scientific medicine, beliefs in demon or spirit possession predominated. During this period of history, the art of healing was practiced primarily by shamans or members of the priesthood. Their treatments generally used various herbs and ointments that were believed to have healing properties. Amulets, such as certain stones and gems, were also believed to have magical medicinal powers and were used in the treatment of medical and emotional ills (Stone, 1937). For example, the semiprecious gemstone lapis lazuli, which is colored a vivid ultramarine blue with streaks of gold pyrites, was prized for its beauty and its purported ability to heal.

Early writings of the Chinese, Egyptians, Hebrews, and Greeks show they generally attributed abnormal behavior to a demon or god who had taken possession of the individual. This is really not surprising since people at that time also thought that evil spirits caused natural occurrences such as thunderstorms, earthquakes, pestilence, and so forth. People could not believe that natural causes could explain such catastrophic events and, when they occurred, people would desperately attempt to appease the angry spirit or god believed to be the cause. People also attributed many positive occurrences, such as a particularly bountiful harvest, to good spirits or gods and would express their thanks in return via various rituals.

Now, whether it was believed that a good spirit or an evil spirit was causing an individual's abnormal behavior depended upon the person's symptoms (Butcher, Mineka, & Hooley, 2007). A "good spirit" was likely if the person spoke with religious or mystical content consistent with the majority beliefs of the society in which the individual lived, and the person was basically calm and not troublesome. In such cases, the person may have been treated with awe and respect by others. Some historians, for example, have speculated that some ancient mystics and prophets might have met criteria for the diagnosis of a mental disorder in today's times, but at the time they lived, their behavior was viewed as a spiritual gift. For example, Saint Joan of Arc, a French national heroine who was instrumental in preventing the defeat of France during the Hundred Years War in 1429, began having religious visions and hearing the voices of saints at the age of 13. These voices told Joan that God had chosen her to help the king drive the English out of France (Pernoud, 1969; Warner, 1981). Within Joan's devout Catholic family and community, she was viewed as possessing unique spiritual gifts, and she went on to save France from defeat through her strong, courageous leadership. If Joan, however, had been seen in a typical psychiatric emergency room in the twenty-first century, she most likely would have been diagnosed with a psychotic illness and given psychotropic medication to suppress her symptoms. If Joan had been medicated in 1429, would that have derailed her career as a successful military strategist along with her future canonization? On the other hand, would an appropriate medication have succeeded in preventing her death via being burned at the stake? It is food for thought.

In contrast, an "evil spirit" was considered likely if the afflicted person was excited, overactive and troublesome, and engaged in behavior contrary to accepted religious teachings and social norms. People thought to be possessed by evil spirits were often treated with fear and loathing by others, banished from their communities, and sometimes incarcerated, particularly if their behavior involved aggression. This suggests that social norms play a strong role in determining whether a particular individual's behavior is within the realm of normal behavior or not, and those parameters can differ across time and culture.

The ancient Hebrews believed that deranged behavior reflected the wrath of God and that God could inflict madness as punishment for misdeeds by withdrawing His protection from evil. For example, there is a passage in the Bible, Deuteronomy 28:28, which relates that Moses said, "*The Lord shall smite thee with madness*, and blindness and astonishment of heart." "Astonishment of heart" has been interpreted as panic, akin to the "irritable heart" syndrome conceptualized by Jacob Mendes DaCosta during the American Civil War in the nineteenth century, which we now classify as an anxiety disorder (DaCosta, 1871). Another story in the New Testament section of the Bible relates that Jesus cured a man with an "unclean spirit" by transferring the devils in his body to a herd of swine. The possessed pigs then ran violently down the steep side of a cliff into the sea (Mark 5:1–13). This story clearly supports the supernatural model, which has been the predominant model throughout recorded history for explaining abnormal behavior and emphasizes human existence as a continual battle between good and evil (Millon, 2004). In addition, this passage illustrates the most common treatment in early times for such supernaturally caused afflictions, which is the use of exorcism. Exorcism (from the Late Latin word *exorcismus*, and from the Greek word *exorkizein*, to abjure) utilizes various techniques to cast out demons or other evil spirits from a person who is believed to be possessed. The practice of exorcism has been used since ancient times across many different cultures, continues even to this day, and is usually conducted by a member of the clergy. The exorcism process may extend over many hours or days, and the exorcist uses a range of tools including prayers, religious symbols, or other tangible materials believed to facilitate the exorcism process (Martin, 1976).

The Golden Age of Greece and Hippocrates

The period of history known as the Classical Period or the Golden Age of Greece (500–300 B.C.) included great advancements in the arts, philosophy architecture, literature, government, and medicine, including progressive ideas about the causes of and treatment for mental illness. These advancements occurred, in large part, because it was a politically and socially stable time under beneficent leadership, including the Athenian leader Pericles (495–429 B.C.), who ruled during the time between the Persian and Peloponnesian wars (Sarton, 1993).

During this time, priests assumed the duty of performing exorcisms to rid people of evil spirits. These priests functioned as a mix of clergy, physician, psychologist, and magician. This was also, however, the beginning of more humane treatment for individuals suffering from mental illness because, generally, the priests were very kind. For example, one of the common procedures used to treat emotional disturbances was "temple sleep treatment" in which the priest allowed the disturbed individual to sleep in the temple, and the dreams they had while in the temple would reveal what would be needed to cure them (Menting, 2007). Over two thousand years later, Freud resurrected these ideas as a key therapeutic technique, explicated in his book *The Interpretation of Dreams* (Freud, 1915).

During this time, Hippocrates (460–377 B.C.), who is often referred to as the father of modern medicine, was trained as a physician, and through his practice and research, knowledge about human anatomy and physiology was significantly advanced. Hippocrates also contributed some very progressive ideas to the treatment of those with mental illness. Hippocrates rejected the idea that the intervention of deities, spirits, and demons was central to the development of disease, both mental and physical (Stone, 1937). In a famous quote, he states: "For my own part, I do not believe that the human body is ever befouled by a God." Instead, Hippocrates insisted that disease, including mental disorders, had natural causes and required treatment on that basis. He emphasized that the brain was center of intellectual activities and thus, mental disorders were due to brain pathology along with the influence of heredity and predisposition (Goldberg, 2006).

Hippocrates conceived of three general categories of mental disorder: (1) mania, (2) melancholia, and (3) "phrenitis" (brain fever). Although our current nosology differs and is greatly expanded from his, Hippocrates's ideas about the treatment of mental disorders were far in advance of the typical remedy of exorcism. Hippocrates explained mental illness as being caused by "humoral pathology" similar to other diseases. In this model, he proposed that disease is caused by disproportions of the four "humors" essential to the body's balance of health. These four humors were black bile, yellow bile, phlegm, and blood, and each affected the heat, cold, dryness, and moistness of the body, respectively.

Hippocrates believed that mental disorders that were caused by bile and phlegm differed from each other. Those individuals suffering from so-called "depravements of the brain" from phlegm presented as quiet, depressed, and withdrawn. In contrast, those suffering from a disproportion of bile presented as excited, noisy, and mischievous.

Common treatments for both included bloodletting and purging by instructing the afflicted person to ingest vile concoctions such as a mixture of pureed vulture liver cooked in blood and administered in honey, which the patient was instructed to take for three weeks (Selling, 1943).

Hippocratic advancements, however, also included treating afflicted individuals with emotional kindness, light, massage, and utmost comfort. Such kindly treatment was not representative of the times, however, and was only afforded by the affluent. Impoverished individuals with mental illness benefitted little from these progressive approaches. Hippocrates also had theories about illnesses in women that were testament to the fact that he knew little about female physiology. For example, he theorized that hysteria (which involves symptoms of physical illness in the absence of any identified physical cause) was caused by the woman's uterus wandering to various parts of her body pining for children. The treatment for hysteria, according to Hippocrates, was marriage.

Another influential individual in the theory of mental disorders was the Greek philosopher Plato (429–347 B.C.). One of Plato's most significant contributions to the understanding of mental disorder was his view that psychological phenomena represent reflections of the inner state of the whole organism, with symptoms as indicators of an underlying disorder. Plato's ideas about mental illness were rooted in his theory of the human soul. Plato believed that the soul consisted of three parts: (1) the rational part, (2) the spiritual part, and (3) the part reflecting appetite or desire. This model is similar to Sigmund Freud's structural model of mental life, that is, that mental life consists of the id, ego, and superego (Freud, 1923). Often these parts were in conflict with each other, and such conflict could produce psychological distress. Plato wrote extensively about ethics, politics, and the law, and addressed the problem of how society should manage mentally disordered individuals who commit crimes. Plato strongly believed that such individuals should not be held responsible for their actions and, thus, should not receive punishment in the same way as normal people: "[S]omeone may commit an act when mad or afflicted with disease. . . . [If so,] let him pay simply for the damage; and let him be exempt from other punishment" (Plato, n.d.). Plato also believed mentally ill individuals should be cared for in the community humanely. These are issues, of course, that we are still grappling with today. However, in spite of his progressive thinking, Plato still believed there was some divine influence with mental disorders.

Hippocrates's work and ideas continued with the work of later Greek and Roman physicians; however, as time went on and Rome fell, society fell into disarray, and the intense belief in demon possession resurfaced. The only exception was the survival of Greek thought in some Islamic countries, and "nowhere during the medieval period did the mentally ill find more understanding and better treatment than in the hands of . . . Moslems (sic)" (Deutsch, 1949, p. 15). In fact, the first mental hospital was built in Baghdad in A.D. 792. One of the most outstanding figures in Islamic medicine was the Arabian physician Avicenna (A.D. 980–1037), who wrote a book called *The Canon of Medicine*, which is considered to be the most widely studied medical work ever written. Avicenna insisted that people with mental illness should be treated as sick persons, not as if possessed (Deutsch, 1949).

The following is a case reported in *The Canon of Medicine*, which illustrates Avicenna's humane approach to treating individuals with mental illness, in this case, a prince suffering from the delusion that he had been transformed into a cow.

> A certain prince . . . was afflicted with melancholia and suffered from the delusion that he was a cow . . . he would low like a cow, causing annoyance to everyone . . . crying "Kill me so that a good stew may be made of my flesh" . . . finally he would eat nothing . . . Avicenna was persuaded to take the case . . . first of all he sent a message

> to the patient bidding him to be of good cheer because the butcher was coming to slaughter him where at the sick man rejoiced. Sometime afterwards Avicenna, holding a knife in his hand, entered the sickroom saying, "Where is this cow that I may kill it?" The patient lowed like a cow to indicate where he was. By Avicenna's orders he was laid on the ground bound hand and foot. Avicenna then felt him all over and said "He is too lean, and not ready to be killed. He must be fattened." Then they offered him suitable food of which he now partook eagerly, and gradually he gained strength, got rid of his delusion, and was completely cured. (Browne, 1921)

This case illustrates the use of what we now call the "therapeutic paradox" (Rohrbaugh, Tennen, Press, & White, 1981), that is, employing a treatment strategy that appears on the surface to be in opposition to desired therapeutic goals but which actually facilitates reaching the goals, coupled with the therapeutic use of food (Newhill, 2003). Unfortunately, such advances had little impact on Western practices. This brings us to the Middle Ages.

The Middle Ages (approximately A.D. 500–1500)

During the Middle Ages, particularly the middle and late eras, progress with regard to the scientific inquiry into causes and treatment for mental illness was limited, and the treatment of psychiatrically disturbed individuals was generally characterized by ritual, superstition, punishment, and exclusion from society, rather than by attempts to understand the person's condition. Treatments generally utilized a mixture of astrology, alchemy, theology, magic rites, exorcism, healing wells, and shrines without much basis in research or guidance from theory. Mental disorders, however, were very prevalent during the Middle Ages, especially toward the end, when medieval institutions, social structures, and beliefs began to change drastically and there was widespread famine and disease, social and political turmoil, diminished expectations, loss of confidence in institutions, and feelings of helplessness in the face of forces beyond human control (Tuchman, 1978).

One unusual type of disorder during this time was mass madness, which was a peculiar trend during last half of Middle Ages and involved the widespread occurrence of group hysteria. These episodes of group hysteria took a number of forms including dance manias, which manifested in the form of epidemics of jumping, dancing, and convulsions and were reported as early as the tenth century. In Italy, such dance manias were known as "tarantism" and were blamed on suffering a bite from a tarantula spider (Stone, 1937). The true origin of such episodes of mass madness or mass hysteria has been a subject of debate. Some scholars have argued that such occurrences represent the phenomenon called "emotion contagion," in which a strong emotion, such as fear, sadness, or joy, spreads to others, who begin to feel the same way (Wang, 2006), an explanation invoked to explain more recent cases of mass hysteria (Rockney & Lemke, 1992). Others have concluded that the behavior at that particular historical time was similar to the ancient frenetic rites people engaged in when worshipping the pagan god Dionysus. With the advent of Christianity, such rites were forbidden by the Catholic Church; however, they were still deeply engrained in the culture and, thus, emerged in the form of the dance manias. Such occurrences peaked during fourteenth and fifteenth centuries, a period particularly characterized by oppression, famine, and pestilence (Stone, 1937).

This was also the time of the Black Death, which was a pandemic of two forms of plague that wiped out over a quarter of Europe's population in the 1300s. Today, doctors can cure plague, if caught early enough, with antibiotics; but in those days antibiotics did not exist and the outcome was inevitably death within four to five days. Not understanding the origin of these horrible diseases only increased superstition and belief in evil spirits.

Browne, E.G. (1921). Arabian medicine. NY: MacMillan.

People simply could not believe that such a frightening catastrophe could have natural causes and, thus, could be within their power to control, prevent, and spread.

The doom and gloom that permeated the general psyche during this time provided a backdrop for the development of unusual forms of mental illness. For example, the disorder of lycanthropy was a relatively common affliction during this time. Lycanthropy involves a disorder in which the person has the delusion that he or she can shape-shift into the form of an animal. Cases of lycanthropy during the Middle Ages usually involved people believing they could turn into a wolf, an animal that elicited great fear in people at that time. Such cases were probably the source for the emergence of the belief in werewolves. Interestingly, there is evidence that lycanthropy is not an extinct syndrome but has been reported in modern times, although patients with the disorder report delusions involving a wide range of animals, not just wolves (Keck, Pope, Hudson, et al., 1988; Moselhy, 1999).

In the early centuries of medieval times, in contrast to the later centuries, the treatments provided to individuals with mental illness were at least tolerable and even kind and humane. Those mentally ill individuals viewed as "mildly insane" and nonviolent were allowed to wander about the community and beg for food, although mentally ill people who were aggressive or violent were treated as criminals and usually incarcerated.

Monasteries opened the first asylums in Europe for custody of people with mental illness as early as 1369. In the late fourteenth century, Bethlehem Hospital in London opened, and later its name was corrupted to "Bedlam" because of the chaotic conditions in the wards. Treatment was very harsh, as documented in the Bedlam inventory taken in 1403, which described how to restrain a patient: "[First], a collar, encircling the neck and confined by a chain to a pole fixed at the head of the patient's bed, [then] an iron frame, the lower part of which encircled the body, and the upper part of which passed over the shoulder, having on either side apertures for the arms, which encircled them over the elbows." (Stone, 1937, p. 136).

Throughout the Middle Ages, an important continuing influence was the theological notion of dualism, that is, good versus evil, light versus darkness. It was a time of great fear and superstition, and people believed that everywhere, Satan and his demons were at work and ready to dive into human souls and possess them. Stemming from this, in the fifteenth and sixteenth centuries, exorcism was once again the treatment of choice for individuals considered to be insane.

The Witch Hunts, Exorcisms, and Executions

During the second half of the Middle Ages, things took a turn for the worse, and fifteenth and sixteenth century Europe witnessed extensive witch hunts in which hundreds of people were accused and executed as witches. Possessed persons were believed to have made a pact with the Devil, with this pact consummated by signing a book in blood that gave the person supernatural powers. It was believed that such people then could cause pestilence, storms, floods, sexual impotence, and injuries to their enemies; that they could turn milk sour and could rise through the air, ruin crops, and turn themselves into animals—in short, they were witches (Nemec, 1974). Furthermore, these beliefs were held by many members of the high clergy. Even Martin Luther, the German leader of the Protestant Reformation, believed in witches and advocated for their execution.

Although we used to believe that most of the so-called witches were mentally ill people, recently discovered historical evidence questions the extent of this, suggesting that many, if not most, of the accused witches were impoverished elderly women who were viewed by the community as having "sharp tongues" and bad tempers (Schoeneman, 1984). They were not mentally ill, but they were people that many members of the community did not like and did not value and, thus, were viewed as expendable. This issue, however, is still being debated.

As time went on during this period, the hysteria over witches grew so great that even highly regarded competent physicians subscribed to these beliefs. Only a few cried out in protest—for example, the physician Paracelsus, Reginald Scot, and Agrippa—and "at the danger of their lives, tried to convince their frenzied contemporaries of their fallacies in burning innocent people" (Stone, 1937, p. 139). Finally, some physicians spoke out publicly in criticism of the witch hunts and execution of witches, notably Johann Weyer (1515–1588), who wrote a book entitled *The Deception of Demons* (1563), which, point by point, refuted each claim made in the primary witch-hunting manual of the time, *Malleus Maleficarum. Malleus Maleficarum* (translation: Witches' Hammer) was written in 1486 by two theologians, Heinrich Kramer and James Sprenger, who had been appointed by the pope to act as papal inquisitors into incidents of witchcraft (Colp, 2005). Weyer argued that the witch hunts had harmed many innocent people, and that individuals targeted as witches were simply ill in mind or body and, thus, should be provided care, not punishment (Weyer, 1563). Finally, the advocates of science and medicine began to prevail over superstition and demonology, which paved the way for the development of more humanitarian approaches for the care of individuals with mental illness and, eventually, improvements in treatment strategies.

Assess your comprehension of *the care and treatment of individuals with mental illness in ancient times through the early to mid-Middle Ages* by completing this quiz.

The Establishment of Early Shrines and Asylums for the Care of Individuals with Mental Illness

From the sixteenth century on, the care of mentally ill individuals gradually became the task of special social institutions. Most, however, were no better than concentration camps and were referred to by lay people as "madhouses." Residents lived and died amid conditions of incredible filth and cruelty. Violent mentally ill people were put on display in cages for the public to gawk at and tease at a penny a look, while nonviolent ones were allowed to roam the streets and beg for basic necessities (Selling, 1940).

In the colonies of the United States, the first public hospital devoted solely to the care and treatment of individuals with mental illness was opened in the fall of 1773 in Williamsburg, Virginia. The hospital was built to care for "these miserable Objects, who cannot help themselves," to quote Virginia governor Francis Fauquier in 1766 (as cited in Zwelling, 1985). However, treatment in the United States proved to be no better than in Europe, and the techniques used were extremely aggressive and primarily designed to intimidate the patient. These so-called treatments included powerful drugs, water treatments, bleeding and blistering, electric shocks, and the generous use of physical restraints (Zwelling, 1985; Deutsch, 1949). In fact, the period 1773–1835 is often referred to as the "Age of Restraint" (The Public Hospital 1773–1885, n.d.).

There were a few bright spots, however. Gradually, a few shrines developed in which kindness and offers of comfort were extended to those who came to the shrine for help. One of the most famous examples of a shrine for individuals with mental illness was the shrine near the town of Gheel, in Belgium, which has been visited by mentally ill pilgrims since the thirteenth century and, during the nineteenth century, was used as a model for reforming asylums in America (Grob, 1994). The story behind the Gheel Shrine, which honors Saint Dymphna, is dramatic and compelling, although it is not clear how much is truth and how much is fable. The following account is based on material published by the St. Dymphna Devotion Society, which is a subgroup of the Franciscan Mission Associates.

> The Gheel Shrine commemorates Saint Dymphna, who is the Catholic patron saint "of those afflicted with nervous and emotional illness". The story relates that Dymphna was the only child of an Irish pagan king of Oriel who lived sometime around the 12th Century. Her mother was a devout Christian of extraordinary

character and beauty and, without her husband's knowledge, had Dymphna baptized as a Christian when she was a young child.

Following his wife's untimely death, the king began to search for a new wife who was as beautiful and kind as Dymphna's mother had been. When he was unsuccessful in his quest, his advisors suggested that he consider marrying his own daughter, given that she was as beautiful as his late wife. Initially, the king was horrified, but the idea grew in his mind until he decided to approach his daughter who was by then 14 years old. Dymphna refused to abide by her father's request, and fled the kingdom with the priest who had baptized her. They reached Belgium, and traveled to the town of Gheel, where they decided to stay to rest after their long journey.

When the king heard what had happened, he was furious and set out with companions to find Dymphna. Upon finding her and the priest, the king tried to persuade his daughter to reconsider the request to marry him. When the priest tried to defend Dymphna, the king ordered him to be put to death immediately. One final time, the king ordered his daughter to obey him and "when she refused, he drew back his sword and struck off the head of his own child, who fell prostate at his feet. She was barely fifteen years of age. . . . [I]t was quite some time before the inhabitants of Gheel came to remove them for burial in a cave, which was the prevalent custom at that time. Years later, when workmen removed the earth at the entrance of the cave to give the priest and Dymphna a more appropriate burial, they were astonished to find two white tombs carved from stone. Then, opening the girl's coffin, they saw on her breast a red tile bearing the words "Here lies the holy virgin and martyr, Dymphna". Later, legend has it, five mentally ill individuals spent the night in the forest near Dymphna's tomb, and woke up the next morning to find themselves cured and restored to sanity. People believed it was Dymphna's spirit that cured them. (Franciscan Mission Associates, n.d.)

Since the twelfth century when, supposedly, these events took place, thousands of mentally ill people have made pilgrimages to visit Gheel and Dymphna's tomb in hopes of receiving a cure. The town of Gheel eventually developed a large system of dozens of foster homes in which residents provided shelter for the mentally ill pilgrims in exchange for help with farming. Gheel became a welcoming, inclusive community to mentally ill people over the course of many generations. The town of Gheel continues the work today, with over two thousand mentally ill individuals living in residents' homes and working with the inhabitants. This brings us to the time of humanitarian reform.

Humanitarian Reform and the Era of Moral Treatment/Management

By the eighteenth century, asylums that cared for the mentally ill were in great need of reform. The first great reformist whose policies and actions significantly improved the situation for people with mental illness was French physician Philippe Pinel (1745–1826), who was instrumental in the development of the treatment approach and philosophy called moral treatment (Grob, 1994). Pinel's interest in mental illness stemmed from a personal tragedy when a friend, who suffered from "nervous melancholy" that evolved into mania, committed suicide. Pinel believed that his friend's psychiatric care had been mismanaged, and this spurred his desire to understand mental illness and work toward developing more effective treatments for the afflicted.

In 1793, after the first phase of French revolution, Pinel was placed in charge of La Bicêtre hospital in Paris, which housed mentally ill men. The following is a description

---

Franciscan Mission Associates (no date). St. Dymphna's Story. The St. Dymphna Devotion, Franciscan Mission Associates, P.O. Box 598, Mount Vernon, New York.

of the conditions that the patients lived in at La Bicêtre, which was typical of treatment at that time.

> These chronic insane were treated like animals. They were shackled to the walls of their cells by iron collars which held them flat against the wall and permitted little movement. They could not lie down at night, as a rule, although occasionally the collars were opened and the patients were permitted to lie down on straw pallets if their hands and feet could still be kept shackled. Oftentimes there was a hoop of iron around the waist of the patient, and in addition to this hoop there were chains on both the hands and the feet. It was usually the custom to permit these chains to be sufficiently long so that the patient could feed himself out of a bowl, the food usually being a mushy gruel—bread soaked in a weak soup. Since little was known about dietetics, naturally no attention at all was paid to the type of diet given to the patients. They were presumed to be animals and as such they would have no discrimination, and would not care whether the food was good or bad. No attempt was made to diagnose nor to classify them accurately . . . the cells [the patients lived in] were box-like, dark, unlighted, with almost no ventilation. . . . No one visited the patient except to feed him. Not even the most elementary gestures of humanity were in vogue at that time. (Selling, 1943, pp. 54–55)

Pinel was shocked and deeply disturbed by the situation at La Bicêtre and firmly believed this type of so-called "treatment" was wrong. After much effort, Pinel received grudging permission from the French government to remove the chains from the inmates to test his views that mentally ill individuals should be treated with kindness and consideration as sick people, not as vicious beasts or criminals. Some patients at La Bicêtre had been chained for 30 years or more without ever being able to venture past the walls, breathe fresh air, or see the sun. However, Pinel took a great chance in making his plea, and could have literally lost his head courtesy of the guillotine. However, his plan worked—the chains were removed, the vast majority of the patients evidenced no aggressive behavior, and the atmosphere became one of peace and calmness, even amongst those considered to be most intractable. It is important to recognize that Pinel's new approach to the treatment of hospitalized mentally ill patients evolved, was allowed, and occurred in the context of a society undergoing massive upheaval, including revolutionary activities aimed at supporting the rights of the oppressed and most destitute of the population in France (Neely, 2008), and, thus, keeping mentally ill people in chains represented yet another group suffering under the status quo and deserving of basic human rights.

Soon after his appointment at La Bicêtre, Pinel became an apprentice to Jean-Baptiste Pussin (1745–1811), who had been employed as a caretaker at the hospital for many years. He observed that Pussin's technique was a noncoercive and kind management of the mentally ill patients, and this approach came to be called moral treatment. Pinel and Pussin emphasized the importance of kindness and compassion toward the patients, along with an emphasis on talking to the patient and getting to know his or her personality and background—the first example of what social workers call psychosocial assessment and development of a therapeutic alliance. Pinel developed great empathy toward his patients, as illustrated in the following quote from *A Treatise on Insanity* (Pinel, 1806):

> I cannot here avoid giving my most decided suffrage in favour of the moral qualities of maniacs. I have nowhere met, excepting in romances, with fonder husbands, more affectionate parents, more impassioned lovers, more pure and exalted patriots, than in the lunatic asylum, during their intervals of calmness and reason. A man of

---

Selling, L.S. (1943). Men against madness. N.Y.: Greenberg.

Pinel, P. (1806). A Treatise on Insanity: In which are Contained the Principles of a New and More Practical Nosology of Maniacal Disorders Than Has Yet Been Offered to the Public. London, UK: Oxford University Press.

> sensibility may go there every day of his life, and witness scenes of indescribable tenderness associated to a most estimable virtue. (Pinel, 1806, p. 16)

Based on his observations, Pinel developed a new classification of mental disorders that included mania, melancholia, idiocy, and dementia, and argued that such disorders were caused by a combination of heredity and environmental factors. With the success he achieved, Pinel was then placed in charge of the Salpêtrière hospital in 1795, which housed mentally ill women in France, and he continued his mission to remove the chains and provide moral treatment. As an interesting side note, Pinel himself was once saved from a mob that accused him of antirevolutionary activities during the Reign of Terror by a soldier whom he had freed from asylum chains several years earlier.

At the same time as Pinel was reforming the hospitals in France, an English Quaker named William Tuke established the York Retreat in England in 1796 under the premise that caring and humane treatment could cure insanity (Rothman, 1990). The York Retreat was a pleasant country house where patients lived and worked in a kindly religious atmosphere. Charland (2007), in a historical analysis of the York Retreat, argues that the moral treatment provided at York was somewhat different from Philippe Pinel's moral treatment in large part because it was rooted in Tuke's Quaker values. Tuke's approach was guided by "benevolent theory," which proposes that one can facilitate a patient's return to sanity by appealing to their inner capacity for affection toward others. Charland (2007) comments that there "were clearly two 'moral' aspects to the treatment and management practices of the Retreat. They were moral in a wide, mental, psychological sense, as opposed to more physical methods and interventions. But they were also moral in a narrower ethical sense that derived from Quaker values and morality and the doctrine of inner light" (p. 69). Although most historians have concluded that the York Retreat achieved significant humanitarian goals in the care of individuals with mental illness, Foucault (1972) argues that the retreat was a "duplicitous exercise in religious internment" (p. 600), and merely substituted physical restraint with mind control and religious indoctrination.

There is no question that moral treatment was driven by the values of its practitioners and may have even involved the imposition of practitioner values onto patients, yet it certainly also provided a more kindly and humane environment that was a vast improvement from what patients endured in earlier times. In addition, one must bear in mind that the achievements of moral treatment were accomplished without the assistance of the psychotropic medications that are available today. Furthermore, many of the individuals who were hospitalized in the retreats or asylums at the time had physical disorders with psychological manifestations for which there were no existing treatments. Some patients had brain tumors, some were in the third stage of syphilis (general paresis), some had forms of dementia, and some had other types of physical brain disorders.

Tuke encountered much initial opposition to his ideas due to the fact that the societal belief in demonology was still quite strong in England at that time. However, one of Tuke's colleagues, Dr. Samuel Hitch (who was the founder of the Association of Medical Officers of Asylums and Hospitals for the Insane), was successful in introducing improvements in staffing at Gloucester Asylum in England, replicating what was done at York, by employing trained nurses and nurse supervisors, which significantly improved patient care. Thus, in general, there was movement toward a greater emphasis on improving patient care, enhancing patients' spiritual and moral development, and improving patients' character, which, it was believed, would serve to restore the person's sanity.

Tuke's and Pinel's successes with moral treatment soon reached America and served to inspire physician Benjamin Rush (1745–1813), who is considered to be the founder of American psychiatry, to institute reforms to how people with mental illness were treated in the United States. With "a capacity for assimilating knowledge, keen observation, and inductive reasoning" (Deutsch, 1949, p. 72), Rush rejected superstition and beliefs in demonology and brought scientific rigor—such as it was—to the treatment of the mentally ill. Rush also believed that mentally ill patients should be treated humanely, and he was the first to advocate heating patients' cells (for a long time it was believed that people with mental illness could not feel heat or cold); however, he still believed in astrology as a possible cause of mental illness and advocated the use of bloodletting and purgatives. Thus, his approach was a mixture of advancement and status quo.

In 1844, the superintendents of 13 of the asylums in the United States banded together to form the Association of Medical Superintendents of American Institutions for the Insane, which later continued as the American Psychiatric Association. Its formal periodical, originally called the *American Journal of Insanity*, is now the *American Journal of Psychiatry*. This group of asylum superintendents was confident that they could cure insanity and, if they pooled their efforts, mental illness could be eradicated (Colp, 2005). This brings us to the contributions of pioneering reformer Dorothea L. Dix.

Dorothea Dix: Tireless Advocate for the Welfare of People with Mental Illness

Dorothea Dix (1802–1887) was a strong and persistent advocate for the rights of poor and marginalized people living in poorhouses, mental hospitals, and prisons, and was particularly a champion of the needs of individuals with serious mental illness. Her empathy for human suffering was probably rooted in her difficult and unhappy childhood. Her mother was rumored to be mentally ill and her father, a Methodist preacher, suffered from alcoholism. When two more children were born into the family, Dix took on the role of parent for her younger brothers. She often commented that she "never knew childhood." Her father did spend time teaching Dix to read and write, and this led to considerable success in school and spurred her interest in teaching. Like many women of her day who worked outside of the home, Dix was a schoolteacher for much of her life, until she was forced into early retirement by tuberculosis. Not wanting to be idle, Dix volunteered to teach Sunday school at the jail in East Cambridge, Massachusetts, and was outraged at the deplorable conditions that she found. Among the inmates she found a group of mentally ill women, shaking with cold in an unheated room. When she inquired as to why there was no stove to warm the room, she was told that "lunatics" cannot feel heat or cold. Dix was outraged and determined to take action to alleviate such suffering. She began by visiting every jail and poorhouse in the state of Massachusetts, found similar conditions in all of them, and, incensed at the situation, wrote a powerful memorial to the U.S. Congress in 1848, in which she stated she had seen

> more than 9000 idiots, epileptics and insane in the United States, destitute of appropriate care and protection . . . bound with galling chains, bowed beneath fetters and heavy iron balls attached to drag chains, lacerated with ropes, scourged with rods and terrified beneath storms of execration and cruel blows; now subject to jibes and scorn and torturing tricks; now abandoned to the most outrageous violations. (Zillboorg & Henry, 1941, pp. 583–584)

Dix then asked the legislature for funds for an institution specifically designed to treat people with mental illness. Shocked by the facts that Dix had presented to them, Congress acquiesced. Between 1841 and 1881, Dix traveled thousands of miles alone state to state, publicizing the terrible conditions she found. Always observing the rules of feminine propriety, she rarely spoke publicly, but she was a persuasive lobbyist behind the scenes. During this time, Dix helped to establish 32 new mental hospitals in New Jersey, Pennsylvania, Indiana, Illinois, Kentucky, Missouri, Tennessee, Mississippi, Louisiana, North Carolina,

---

Zillboorg, G. & Henry, G.W. (1941). A history of medical psychology. N.Y.: Norton.

and Maryland. She also helped establish a government hospital, later named St. Elizabeth's, in Washington, D.C. Where new institutions were not needed, Dix was active in reorganizing, enlarging, and improving the staffing of existing hospitals. Her efforts played a significant role in the emergence of the mental hygiene movement, and in 1901, a resolution passed by the U.S. Congress declared that Dorothea Dix is "among the noblest examples of humanity in all history" (Karnosh & Tucker, 1945, p. 18).

Some critics (see, e.g., Bockhoven, 1972) have argued that Dix's work undermined the principles of moral treatment by situating institutions far from patients' families and community. However, one of the basic principles of moral treatment at that time was to provide the patient with an environment that was deliberately separate from the community that the patient was unable to cope with, to provide a haven or asylum. The belief at that time was that insanity is usually caused by life circumstances and stresses (Shore, 1989) and, therefore, the hospital institution would provide protection and care, which is the basic meaning of the word "asylum." There is no question that Dorothea Dix's contributions vastly improved the conditions and care for individuals with mental illness who, prior to her endeavors, were forced to exist in cruel and inhumane conditions (Viney & Bartsch, 1984). Even our clients today know her name:

> In 1979, I was working for San Joaquin County Mental Health Services in Stockton, California, and our offices at that time were located on the grounds of Stockton State Hospital (SSH)—billed as the oldest state hospital west of the Mississippi. One day a middle-aged client I knew well, who had schizophrenia, came to our clinic for a refill of medication. He was always very quiet and withdrawn and I was able to engage him in short conversations only on occasion. Just as I was about to escort him to the crisis doctor's office to get his prescription, he looked up at me and said he wanted to go and see the picture of Dorothea Dix in the SSH library. We walked silently to the library and went in. The library was old and dimly lit except for a ceiling light that shone on Dix's portrait almost like a spotlight. My client looked at the portrait for several minutes and then said, "I'm ready to go now." On the way back to the clinic, I asked him why he wanted to see Dix's picture, and he said with astonishment at my question, "Why, she built all the mental hospitals—she helped us mentally ill—I wanted to see her picture again." and then he fell silent for the rest of the walk. (Newhill, 1995)

The Demise of Moral Treatment, the Beginning of Moral Management, and the Rise of the Mental Hygiene Movement

By end of the nineteenth century, the state mental hospital was an established institution, often out in the country and away from public view. Many resembled small towns, others resembled fortresses, and most seemed alien and apart from the rest of society. Nobody, except the patients and staff, knew what went on behind the walls and locked doors of the asylum. In fact, hospital psychiatrists were called "alienists." However, most of the asylums, in the early days after Dorothea Dix's efforts, tried hard to adhere to the principles of the new humanitarianism that Dix advocated for. The general term for this new humanitarianism was "moral management."

In the practice of moral management, less physical restraint was employed in treatment and there was the increasing practice of more positive therapeutic activities, such as engaging patients in learning skills for farming, cooking, and carpentry. This so-called occupational therapy, however, soon became free labor that the hospital came to depend

---

Newhill, C.E. (1995). A mental health casebook. Unpublished manuscript.

upon. As the hospitals became larger and larger, they resembled factories more than havens for therapeutic care and, just like the outside world, there were bosses and workers, upper and lower classes, patients with nothing, and patients with privileges (Mondale & Patton, 1990).

Moral management was amazingly effective for some people, even though there were no antipsychotic drugs at that time. However, it was nearly abandoned by latter part of the nineteenth century due to a number of factors shaped by the forces and changes in society at that time. First was the emergence of racial, class, and ethnic prejudice within the hospital in the aftermath of more and more immigrants being admitted to the hospital along with soldiers, freed former slaves, and individuals of lower socioeconomic classes (Mondale & Patton, 1990). Many new immigrants who were hospitalized were unable to explain their troubles because staff were not bilingual and little provision was made to provide interpreters; thus, such individuals often languished for years with nobody caring to determine why they were in the hospital and whether they even needed to be there, much less what might help them. Here is an example:

> In the early 1960s, there was a patient, Ms. A., who had been a resident in a state mental hospital in an eastern state for over 20 years. Nobody could remember the circumstances of her hospitalization and very little information could be found in the hospital records. The patient appeared to be white, but she could not speak English and nobody knew what her ethnicity was. Over the years, she became quite withdrawn, the staff eventually paid little attention to her, and she received no visitors. One day, a new patient, Mr. B., was admitted to the hospital. Mr. B. had attended the local university and had done some traveling in Scandinavia earlier in his life. He told the staff that he had tried to engage Ms. A. in conversation and from what she said, he suspected she spoke Finnish, adding that he had a professor who was born in Finland and perhaps he could help. The hospital social worker took action, contacted the professor and asked him if he would be willing to come to the hospital. The professor, in fact, had a son who was a patient at the hospital, and he visited his son every week, so he said he would be happy to meet with Ms. A. When he arrived, he was escorted to the day room where Ms. A. was, and greeted her in the Finnish language. Ms. A. fell to her knees, and said "Oh, thank you, thank you" in Finnish. They had a long and animated conversation and with the professor's interpretations, the staff determined that Ms. A was completely sane, did not need to be in the hospital, and had been forced into the hospital originally by relatives who wanted her money. Although she had, tragically, lost over 20 years of her life, the hospital social worker helped her with the process of discharge and the start of a new life. (Newhill, 1995)

The second factor that negatively impacted the quality of state hospital care in the late nineteenth century was the failure of asylum leaders to train their own replacements to provide a good continuum of leadership and oversight. Under the second and third generations of leadership, the original mission of the asylum became distorted.

Third, the large state mental hospitals encountered the problems shared by other large public institutions at that time, such as prisons and dependent children's homes, which included issues such as the expansion and overextension of the facilities to the point where they became unmanageable (bigger is not necessarily better). This was compounded by inadequate resources, poorly trained staff, inadequate and cumbersome staffing systems, and the increasing admission of impoverished individuals or paupers who could not assist in paying for care (Shore, 1989). Finally, it had become impossible to create a therapeutic

---

Newhill, C.E. (1995). A mental health casebook. Unpublished manuscript.

atmosphere in such a large, impersonal, crowded setting. As David J. Rothman, Ph.D., Professor of Social Medicine and History at Columbia University, put it:

> Whoever came up with the idea that collecting all the mad together and putting them in one building and putting them through a particular regimen would be a curative intervention? That seems a like very odd and very strange idea. Could you at the same time carry out a treatment regime, and hold people against their will—at the same time hold troublesome people that the community was, in many ways, glad to be rid of against their will? Could you at the same time cure and lock up? Could one institution, if you will, do both good and do guard duty? (quoted from Mondale & Patton, 1990)

One of the problems with the asylum at that time was that nobody, except for the patients and staff, really knew what was going on inside the walls and behind the locked doors. Asylum life was invisible to the public. However, beginning in the mid- to late 1800s, there was a rise of consumer activism in the form of shocking first-person accounts of asylum life written by former patients. Such accounts included appalling descriptions of mistreatment of patients by staff, including forced ice water baths and other unpleasant "treatments" and various forms of physical abuse. For example, Mrs. Elizabeth P. W. Packard wrote several lurid exposés of her three years as a patient in the Jacksonville State Insane Asylum in Illinois (Packard, 1868). Mrs. Packard claimed that she had been forced into the hospital by her minister husband against her will even though she was sane, "because she had defied him by publicly expressing her liberal religious beliefs" (Levison, 2003, p. 1). Following her release, through her books and lectures and successful legislative lobbying efforts, Elizabeth Packard successfully worked to educate the public about the plight of mentally ill patients, particularly women, who were confined to asylums, and worked to ensure married women's property and child custody rights (Levison, 2003).

These accounts must also include a recognition of the difficulties the often poorly trained and frequently exhausted staff faced that were inherent in working in a large mental hospital in the nineteenth century, as described by noted historian of mental health policy and medicine Gerald N. Grob, Ph.D.:

> To work in a mental hospital [in the nineteenth century] was a very difficult job. The hours were extraordinarily long. There was no such thing as vacations. The pay was low, and the attendants were dealing with patients who behaved in bizarre and frightening ways. You had patients who smeared feces on the wall, who urinated on the floor, who refused to wear clothes and who sometimes behaved in a threatening and violent manner. Consequently, you found the staff, who spent 60 hours a week with these patients, responding in kind. (quoted from Mondale & Patton, 1990)

In 1908, Clifford Beers (1876–1943), who had been hospitalized for three years in a mental institution for the treatment of depression and paranoia, wrote a book entitled *A Mind That Found Itself* (1913), which reported Beers's experiences as a patient. During his hospitalization, Beers claimed that he both witnessed and directly experienced numerous incidents of serious mistreatment at the hands of staff and multiple dehumanizing experiences. Beers's book had a tremendous impact on the public's perception of asylum treatment as well as a significant impact on the psychiatric community, including

---

Mondale, S. & Patton, S. (Producers) & Mondale, S. (Director) (1990). Asylum: A history of the mental institution in America. [Motion picture documentary], Distributed by Direct Cinema Limited.

psychiatrist Adolf Meyer (1866–1950), who wrote a favorable review of Beers's book in the literary magazine *North American Review*. Adolf Meyer contributed many innovative ideas that were relevant to and inclusive of early approaches to social casework. He was the first psychiatrist to advocate a biopsychosocial approach to understanding mental illness and those who suffer from it, and he emphasized that it is important to collect a detailed case history, paying particular attention to the social and environmental factors relevant to the patient's situation. His work served to extend the early approaches developed by Philippe Pinel.

With the support of Adolf Meyer and psychiatrist William James, Beers founded the mental hygiene movement that led to the National Committee for Mental Hygiene in New York in 1909, the Connecticut Society for Mental Hygiene in 1908, and the National Committee for Mental Hygiene in 1909, the group that eventually organized the National Association for Mental Health in 1950. The National Institute of Mental Health was created in 1949, which still sponsors the bulk of funding for research on mental health in the United States (Grob, 1994; Shore, 1989).

What exactly did the mental hygiene movement stand for? It was Adolf Meyer who suggested the term "mental hygiene" to Clifford Beers as a name for the new movement to promote mental health, prevent mental illness, improve the quality of care for individuals with mental illness, and ensure that accurate information about mental illness be provided to the public. Meyer believed that such a movement could "show our people better ways of healthy living, prevention of trouble, and efficient handling of what is not prevented."[1] Beers, however, believed that the most important goal for the movement would be to improve the lives of and treatment received by hospitalized patients. Beers and Meyer also had some differences in their ideas about how to successfully move the mental hygiene movement forward. Meyer believed that the movement would benefit from professional leadership, while Beers believed that professional leadership should be equally balanced with input from lay leaders like himself, and was concerned that, otherwise, consumer views might be ignored or dismissed by the professionals. In the end, Beers's view prevailed, and the mental hygiene movement along with the activities of the National Committee for Mental Hygiene were the first mechanisms for propelling forward the consumer voice in mental health care (Grob, 1983, 1994). The mental hygiene movement led to significant reforms in institutional care, the movement toward community mental health care, and the establishment of child guidance clinics to provide mental health care to children away from the juvenile justice system (Shore, 1989).

Critics of the mental hygiene movement (Viney & Bartsch, 1984) have claimed that the movement's adherents argued that mental illness was caused by brain pathology, not socio-environmental factors, which provided the final blow that ended the era of moral treatment. Because at that time no effective psychotropic medications or other biologic treatments were available to treat the purported brain pathology, the mental hygiene movement led to asylum staff giving up on treatment and resorting to simply providing custodial care until appropriate biologically based cures could be found, even though this condemned many severely mentally ill people to lives of helplessness and dependency. Educating the public about mental illness—another goal of the mental hygiene movement—was also slower than hoped for. However, the movement did propel forward some technological advances, with a major accomplishment being the discovery of organic factors underlying general paresis from syphilis (which accounted for a significant proportion of hospitalized patients in the nineteenth century because of the manifestation of severe psychiatric symptoms) and its treatment via malaria injections. Today, syphilis is treated with penicillin. Despite

[1]Beers to Meyer, October 27, December 22, 23, 31. Meyer to Beers, December 19, 22, 1908, American Foundation for Mental Hygiene Papers.

the emphasis on biological causation, scientific investigation into psychological factors underlying mental illness was also progressing at the turn of the century, with Sigmund Freud as a major figure in these developments. There was also an increasing recognition of the role of environmental and sociocultural factors in the development of abnormal behavior, and it is here that social workers played a prominent role.

Assess your comprehension of *the development of more humane treatment for individuals with mental illness and the establishment of treatment asylums* by completing this quiz.

MOVING INTO THE TWENTIETH CENTURY AND CONTEMPORARY VIEWS ABOUT MENTAL ILLNESS/ABNORMAL BEHAVIOR

The Theory of Degeneration and Efforts to Classify Forms of Severe Mental Illness

By the start of the twentieth century, several types of mental illness had been officially classified along with the development of various theories of causation and ideas about course and outcome. Two French psychiatrists, Bénédict Augustin Morel (1809–1873) and Valentin Magnan (1836–1916), developed the *theory of degeneration*, which argued that many mental illnesses, from psychosis to what would later be termed neurotic conditions, are originally caused by inherited factors and repeated transmission from generation to generation causes such factors to evolve into diseases. The onset of the disease is then triggered by external stressors such as alcoholism or infections (Colp, 2005). Many prominent psychiatrists embraced the theory of degeneration, including German psychiatrist Richard von Krafft-Ebing (1840–1902), who wrote *Psychopathia Sexualis* in 1892, which described various unusual forms of sexual expression including "perversions" or paraphilias. Krafft-Ebing argued that such perversions were the result of mental degeneration. Others proposed that the theory of degeneration explained criminal behavior and that criminals can be identified on the basis of physiognomy, which describes an individual's personality and predilections based on their physical appearance, particularly the person's face (Van Wyhe, 2004).

While these efforts to explain the organic basis of mental disorder and other forms of abnormal behavior continued, German psychiatrist Emil Kraepelin (1856–1926) and Swiss psychiatrist Eugen Bleuler (1857–1939) advanced the understanding and classification of *functional* psychoses, that is, those psychotic conditions without a presumed organic cause. Kraepelin studied the symptoms and behavior of thousands of psychotic patients and concluded that psychotic illnesses could be classified into two groups: (1) manic-depressive psychosis, which he believed had a good prognosis and patients could recover; and (2) dementia praecox, a psychotic illness that evidenced a slow downhill course to dementia. Kraepelin conceptualized dementia praecox as having three subtypes, the nomenclature of which we still incorporate in the descriptions of subtypes for schizophrenia today. Kraepelin's three subtypes were *hebephrenia*, *catatonia*, and *paranoia* (Kraepelin, 1902). Although Kraepelin modified his model later to acknowledge that some individuals with dementia praecox do, in fact, recover, his distinction between manic depression (which we now classify as a mood disorder although psychotic symptoms can occur) and dementia praecox (which we now call schizophrenia) was a breakthrough in classification.

It was Eugen Bleuler who coined the term "schizophrenia" and argued that the course of illness for individuals with schizophrenia did not always evolve into a dementia state, that is, a slow, deteriorating downhill course (Bleuler, 1911). He also introduced the terms *autism* and *ambivalence*, and claimed these were two common features of schizophrenia, and he was the first to describe schizoid personality. Efforts to distinguish other forms of psychosis resulted in the identification of Wernicke-Korsakoff syndrome, caused by chronic alcoholism, by Karl Wernicke and Sergei Korsakoff; Alzheimer's disease by German neuropathologist Alois Alzheimer; and general paresis, a psychotic illness caused by late-stage syphilis, by French physician Antoine Bayle. Bayle first argued for the organic basis of general paresis in 1826, but it wasn't until the turn of the next century that his assertion was accepted as correct (Colp, 2005).

While Kraepelin, Bleuler, and others were struggling to understand, describe, and treat those patients who were the most ill and who occupied the most beds in state mental hospitals, other mental health professionals were inspired by the work of Sigmund Freud and his followers and the attraction of leaving the asylum and working in lucrative private practices with less ill patients.

Contributions of Sigmund Freud and the Concept of "Neurosis"

The less ill patients that the new breed of private practitioners were eager to treat predominantly presented clusters of symptoms that, by the late nineteenth century, were classified as *neuroses*. At that time, a neurosis was defined as a psychiatric illness "that was caused by changes in brain function in which no organic lesion could be found and, unlike a psychosis, was not inherited" (Colp, 2005, p. 4017).

The two most commonly diagnosed neurotic disorders were *neurasthenia* and *hysteria*. Neurasthenia was a syndrome that consisted of a collection of symptoms that span both anxiety disorders and mood disorders plus symptoms of physical and mental exhaustion. "Hysteria" is a syndrome that has been described for centuries and usually applied to explain psychological distress in women. In general, hysteria refers to a condition in which the individual has physical symptoms that cannot be explained by medical illness. Hippocrates believed that hysteria was caused by the uterus wandering to various parts of the body; centuries later such symptoms were often explained by the effects of trauma. In the late nineteenth century, the treatment of choice for hysteria was hypnosis, and French psychiatrist Jean-Martin Charcot (1825–1893) employed hypnosis in an effort to treat female patients hospitalized at the Salpêtrière hospital, where Philippe Pinel had practiced decades earlier. Charcot claimed that hypnosis could *produce* symptoms of hysteria rather than curing them; others saw hypnosis as a cure. In the midst of this controversy, Sigmund Freud—who had studied with Charcot—began to examine the existence of subtypes of illness in neurotic patients, eventually identifying three subtypes: "anxieties," "obsessions," and "phobias." At first, Freud tried to treat such patients with hypnosis, but as the limitations of hypnosis became evident to him, Freud began to talk to his patients and try two new strategies: free association and the interpretation of dreams. These strategies then evolved into the treatment called *psychoanalysis* or what he often referred to as "the talking cure." Freud discovered that the symptoms of many of his patients seemed to originate in illicit sexual encounters in childhood. These experiences, many of which we would classify today as sexual abuse, led to Freud's *seduction theory*. Victorian society, however, was shocked when Freud revealed his theory, and people could not accept the idea of adults actually sexually abusing children. Out of fear of ostracism socially and professionally, Freud changed the theory to say that what his patients had reported to him was only fantasy, not actual life experiences (Sulloway, 1979; Gay, 1988).

One can identify four major ideological trends of the nineteenth century that can be found in Freud's work. These include (1) Victorian morality, (2) the primacy of science and the scientific method, (3) Rousseau's vision of society, and (4) Darwin's vision of human evolution (Corsini & Marsella, 1983). These four ideological trends combined to form a view of human behavior that placed the biological drives of sex and aggression at the center of human nature and motivation. According to Freud, psychopathology occurs because society, with its demands for appropriate social conduct and civility, artificially imposes restrictions on human beings' "true nature" (Freud, 1930).

As originally conceptualized and constructed by Freud, psychoanalytic theory is deterministic; that is, he believed that events that occur in childhood control—or determine—later events in adulthood, and this assumption underlies all of his conceptualizations. For example, Freud saw the infant as having drives that are directed toward certain goals, most notably attaining oral gratification. Therefore, a baby is comforted by nursing at the mother's breast or at a bottle, and many infants suck their fingers and explore objects by putting them in their mouth. If the individual does not obtain adequate oral gratification as an infant, he or she will continually seek such gratification as an adult, for example, being vulnerable to orally oriented addictions such as cigarettes or alcohol.

Another predominant theme in psychoanalysis is the systematic exploration of the basis of what appears to be irrational behavior and the influence of the unconscious in all spheres of life. Psychoanalysis and psychodynamic treatment is predicated on the belief that unexamined unconscious processes impede human functioning and freedom, and that insight into these processes allows individuals, families, communities, and organizations to develop mature and equitable selves. One of the goals of Freud's work, based on one of his core beliefs, was to demonstrate or prove that all experiences, thoughts, feelings, fantasies, and dreams make sense. Nothing is really random, including jokes or slips of the tongue.

There are four core models or derivatives of psychodynamic theory, each with its own theory and therapeutic interventions. These four include ego psychology, drive theory, object relations theory, and self-psychology theory, with feminism, cultural competence, and postmodernism adding theoretical dimensions to these four (Danto, 2008). The extent to which psychoanalysis and psychodynamic treatment are evidence-based practices will be addressed later.

Many of Freud's theories have been discredited due to lack of supporting evidence, for example, his theories about women's sexuality and the origin of homosexuality. However, there is no question that Freud's work has had a significant impact on Western culture and language, on how we view mental illness and mental life, and on how we approach working with people. One of Freud's greatest contributions is that he reanimated the idea that we can help a troubled person by talking to him or her, developing a therapeutic alliance (transference), and facilitating the individual's insight into his or her troubles by examining the individual's life experiences. He also believed that most human beings live lives that are conflicted, but the nature of the conflict and its origin is often hidden from us in our unconscious mind because conscious acknowledgment is too painful to bear without support from others. Like the early social workers of the same era, Freud also believed that change was facilitated by the *relationship* between the patient/client and practitioner. Freud was wrong about a lot of things, but he was thoughtful, self-reflective, imaginative, and curious, and he opened up a new window to perceiving and understanding mental illness (Adler, 2006).

Meanwhile, however, the asylums were continuing to fill up with more and more patients, most of whom suffered from severe and persistent mental illnesses such as schizophrenia, major mood disorders, organic mental disorders, and severe alcoholism. By 1940, public asylums cared for over 400,000 patients (Grob, 1994). During this time, hospital stays were lengthy, often spanning decades. Advances in psychotropic drug treatment and most of the effective psychosocial treatments for individuals with severe mental illness were yet to be developed, and the treatments available were largely ineffective and harsh. Fortunately, five events occurred in succession that propelled some positive change forward. The first event was World War II.

World War II

World War II (1939–1945) was a pivotal point in the evolution of social work and psychiatry. Prior to that time, mental health practitioners generally believed that psychiatrically ill people were simply constitutionally different from other people. As the war progressed, however, transient behavioral difficulties and reactions to the trauma of combat increased dramatically in many soldiers who were considered to be "normal" before enlistment. These problems raised concern largely because they threatened to interfere with the optimal performance of the armed forces. In response to this development, mental health workers were called upon to quickly confront and effectively intervene with distressed military troops. Through this work, it was discovered that many of these acute disturbances in troops had both psychological and psychophysiological components, and thus, treatment had to consider both. The eventual result was a substantial revision in the understanding and classification of mental disorders that allowed for consideration of unusual *environmental factors* as influences on both behavior and mental status. Furthermore, it was discovered, via clinical observation and research, that so-called "normal people" could restabilize in such situations as long as they had appropriate intervention along with removal of the precipitating stressor. The primary target population for this intervention was soldiers evidencing an acute stress reaction following exposure to combat. In World War I, a psychological reaction to combat was called "shell shock," in World War II the term was changed to "combat fatigue," and this was replaced with the term "post-traumatic stress disorder" beginning during the Vietnam War era. In addition, World War II also brought clinicians in contact with civilian victims of trauma including survivors of prisoner of war camps, survivors of Nazi concentration camps, and survivors and families affected by the atomic bombing of Japan (Kinzie, 1989).

At the same time, a radically different approach to *where* treatment is provided was developing as well. This new approach advocated for the development of alternatives to the traditional solution of sending troubled people to the state hospital. This shift was precipitated by military combat requirements during war combined with the creative ingenuity of a new breed of psychiatric practitioners. These modern practitioners advocated (1) treating soldiers close to their home base and (2) intervening quickly to minimize psychiatric morbidity and prevent removal of soldiers from their combat unit, which could undermine the strength of the combat unit group. What began as a necessity of wartime introduced the advantages of secondary prevention, that is, intervening quickly to prevent emotional problems from setting in, which is a cornerstone of crisis theory and crisis intervention practice. These new approaches were deemed so successful that they led to establishing new diagnostic classifications with a major focus on environmental events. The *DSM-I* (APA, 1952) introduced the diagnoses of "gross stress reaction" and "adult situational reaction"; these were then combined and renamed "transient situational disturbance" in *DSM-II* (APA, 1968); and then, beginning with *DSM-III* (APA, 1980) to the present time, the category of "adjustment disorders" was introduced, and certain stress reactions, such as post-traumatic stress disorder, were categorized as anxiety disorders.

This new trend of providing immediate intervention and consideration of environmental factors corresponded with the beginning of the shift of the locus of inpatient treatment from large asylums to community-based treatment units in general hospitals, and opened the door for more outpatient treatment. This then led to the development of methods of intervention that included treating not just the individual, but also couples, families, and groups, and here social casework was at the forefront in recognizing that the environment may be positively altered to reduce the noxious influence of the presumed stressor. This strategy is often referred to as "environmental manipulation."

The second influential event that contributed to propelling positive change forward in developing innovative outpatient care in the aftermath of trauma was the Cocoanut Grove nightclub fire in 1942.

The Cocoanut Grove Nightclub Fire

On November 28, 1942, a fire broke out in the trendy Cocoanut Grove nightclub in Boston, Massachusetts, leading to the deaths of 492 people (Schorow, 2005). It remains the deadliest nightclub fire in U.S. history, and its tragic aftermath shocked a nation already accustomed to loss of life via the war. This terrible fire led, however, to two positive results. First, it led to a reform of fire codes and safety standards across the country. Second, through the work of psychiatrist Erich Lindemann with the families who lost loved ones in the fire, a new understanding of the process of grief and trauma emerged that had implications for how and where mental health treatment should be provided. Lindemann wrote about his experiences treating victims of the fire and family members who had lost loved ones in a seminal paper entitled "Symptomatology and management of acute grief," which was originally presented during the Centenary Meeting of the American Psychiatric Association in May 1944. The paper was then published in the September 1944 issue of the *American Journal of Psychiatry* (Lindemann, 1944).

Employing a detailed analysis of the treatment he provided to the fire victims, Lindemann concluded that in eight to ten sessions "in which the psychiatrist shares the grief work [with the patient], and with a period of four to six weeks, it was ordinarily possible to settle an uncomplicated and undistorted grief reaction. . . . Morbid grief reactions represent distortions of normal grief. The conditions mentioned here were transformed into 'normal reactions' and then found their resolution." (Lindemann, 1944, p. 144). Lindemann's work suggested that if immediate short-term crisis intervention is provided to an individual following a traumatic loss, their grief is more likely to be resolved and less likely to lead to more serious psychopathology. Furthermore, such treatment can be provided in the community and not require hospitalization (Slaikeu, 1984). Lindemann's findings extended the knowledge generated from work with soldiers suffering from combat fatigue by recognizing how providing immediate help and moving the locus of psychiatric treatment from remote state hospitals to community-based services can be advantageous in terms of treatment outcomes for civilians.

The Snake Pit

The third event that served to move forward improvements in the treatment of individuals with mental illness occurred in 1946 when Mary Jane Ward published an influential book entitled *The Snake Pit* (Ward, 1946), which was based on her personal experiences during the three years she spent as a patient at Rockland State Hospital in Orangeburg, New York. The novel is a harrowing tale about a woman in a large, crowded state mental hospital where "therapy" for schizophrenia included being wrapped in ice-cold sheets, soaked in extremely hot baths, and subjected to electric and insulin shock treatments. Her few moments of humane care are provided by the psychiatrist she calls Dr. Kik. Ward's book was made into a film, released in 1948, and both the book and film were lauded as one of the most honest and sympathetic portrayals of life in a mental institution in the twentieth century. The film in particular raised the awareness of the general public about the plight of severely mentally ill patients in institutions, with this awareness further reinforced by the publication of Albert Deutsch's journalistic exposé *The Shame of the States* that same year, which powerfully reviewed the deplorable conditions in most state mental hospitals (Deutsch, 1948).

Because the film begins by portraying the main character, Virginia, as a normal wife and mother, and the story explores incidents in her childhood that may have contributed to causing her breakdown, the story served to convey the message that mental illness can happen to anyone and in anyone's family, and thus engendered the public's empathy and concern for the welfare of individuals with mental illness. The film has been criticized, however, for the implication that accepting a subservient role as a wife and mother was part of her "cure" (Fishbein, 1979).

Ms. Ward's actual psychoanalyst, Dr. Gerard Chrzanowski (1913–2000), who was humanistic and progressive in his approach to treatment of individuals with severe mental illness, considered the film important in elevating public concern for the mentally ill. Dr. Militades Zaphiropoulos, who worked at Rockland State Hospital in Orangeburg,

New York, when Dr. Chrzanowski was treating Ms. Ward, said his colleague was one of the first in the United States to use psychoanalysis to treat patients with schizophrenia even though Freud himself had concluded that psychoanalysis was ineffective for treating schizophrenia. But Dr. Chrzanowski disagreed and used a derivative of Freudian analysis called *interpersonal analysis*. "He was not fond of the restraints and that people were treated with hot tubs and cold pack sheets," Dr. Zaphiropoulos recalled. Ms. Ward suffered a second breakdown in 1957, and a third in 1969. She died in 1981.

Establishment of the National Institute of Mental Health

The fourth important event in advancing the treatment of serious mental illness was the establishment of the National Institute of Mental Health (NIMH) in 1946 to provide support for the development of research initiatives and training programs for mental health professionals and programs. More than any other single individual, Robert H. Felix played a key role in creating the NIMH (Grob, 1994) and leading the organization for the next decade and a half. He also framed mental illness as a public health problem equal to any other public health concern and designed the NIMH "to help the individual by helping the community; to make mental health a part of the community's total health program, to the end that all individuals will have greater assurance of an emotionally and physically healthy and satisfying life for themselves and their families" (Felix, 1949, p. 402). No longer was mental health separated from physical health, and no longer was mental illness something that should be dealt with in isolation. Mental health was now, Dr. Felix declared, a *community* issue.

Assess your comprehension of *our more contemporary views about mental illness as we have moved through the first half of the twentieth century* by completing this quiz.

Finally, also in 1946, the Hill-Burton Act was passed, which contributed funding for the development of community mental health hospitals. This development laid the groundwork for the eventual passage of the Community Mental Health Services Act in 1963.

CONCLUSION

It is now 1950, and in this chapter we have traveled over two thousand years. This journey has not been a steady progression in terms of the societal conditions and treatment for people with mental illness. Rather the history is better characterized as jumpy, with steps forward, steps backward, periods of great progression, and periods of stagnation.

By 1950, the state mental hospital was an established institution, often out in the country and out of sight of anyone who didn't live or work there. Many resembled fortresses and seemed, to the public, as alien, frightening places. Educating the public about mental illness was slow; however, via the mental hygiene movement, some technological advances were occurring. A major accomplishment was the discovery of organic factors underlying general paresis from syphilis and the development of its treatment via malaria injections (although today, it is treated with penicillin). Despite the emphasis on biological causation, scientific investigation into psychological factors associated with mental illness was progressing too, much inspired by Freud and his followers. There was also increasing recognition of the role of environmental and sociocultural factors in abnormal behavior, and it is here that social workers had a prominent role. In the next chapter, we will examine the extraordinary history from 1950 to the present time and the context of practice in mental health services settings today.

Assess your application and analysis of this chapter's contents by completing the *Chapter Review*.

Chapter 2

1950s to the Present-The Community Mental Health Services Act, Deinstitutionalization, Evidence-Based Practice, and Current Status of Public Mental Health Services

The Rise and Evolution of the Family Movement, Consumer Movement, and the Recovery Model

It is now 1950. Our ideas about mental illness, what causes it and how it might be effectively treated, have changed considerably. Americans have finally realized that mental illness can strike anyone and affects more families than previously recognized. The realities of asylum life have begun to enter public consciousness, and many are troubled by what is being revealed. Mental health professionals, civil libertarian–minded lawyers, some community and government leaders, and the lay public begin to ask themselves whether a better method for treating mental illness, particular severe mental illness, could and should be developed. The key question in this regard is how such a goal could be accomplished. Evidence is mounting that some mental illnesses probably have a biological basis, but so far little progress has been made in the development of biologically based treatments. Until such treatments are developed, it is difficult to envision a good alternative to the asylum. Then, in the mid-1950s, more detail begins to emerge about additional aspects of the devastating impact that living in a total institution, like a state hospital, can have on a person.

THE EFFECTS OF INSTITUTIONALIZATION

Up until this time, there was little understanding of the mentally ill consumer perspective aside from what had been revealed by a handful of individuals, such as Elizabeth Packard, Clifford Beers, and Mary Jane Ward, who had written exposés about their personal experiences being hospitalized in a state mental hospital. Sociologist Erving Goffman, however, was interested in a slightly different aspect, and wanted to "learn more about the social world of the hospital inmate, as this world is subjectively experienced by him" (Goffman, 1961, p. ix).

Beginning in 1955, utilizing the sociological research method called participant observation, Goffman conducted a year of fieldwork at St. Elizabeth's Hospital in Washington, D.C., the government hospital for treatment of people with mental illness. At the time of Goffman's work, St. Elizabeth's housed over seven thousand patients. Goffman spent his days in the company of the patients, not the staff, and observed their day-to-day life, immersing himself in their "social world." As Goffman observed in his 1961 book *Asylums*, which reported his findings from this work:

> It was then and still is my belief that any group of persons—prisoners, primitives, pilots or patients—develop a life of their own that becomes meaningful, reasonable, and normal once you get close to it, and that a good way to learn about any of these worlds is to submit oneself in the company of the members to the daily round of petty contingencies to which they are subject. (Goffman, 1961, p. x)

Goffman found, as a result of his yearlong observations, that a mental hospital, like a prison, is a "total institution." A total institution is defined as a place of 24-hour residence in which daily life is regimented and predetermined and controlled by forces that the resident or inmate has little choice about. Furthermore, the individual lives with "like-situated" individuals and is cut off from contact with the larger society by the institution. Prisons serve as a clear example, but mental hospitals—in terms of how they are structured—are quite prison-like except that the residents have broken no laws (Goffman, 1961). Rather, they are there because society has established civil statutes that result in involuntary residence at the institution, or the individual has chosen to enter the institution for help for a condition that society has deemed to be an illness, abnormal, or deviant. Treatment provided in a total institution, however, tends to be regimented and impersonal. Such impersonal treatment over time strips people of all sense of identity or dignity and can result in behavioral and psychological changes that are a separate phenomenon from any mental illness they may have. Sociologist Russell Barton, in 1966, coined the term "institutional neurosis" to describe this by-product of long-term hospitalization that is different from symptoms of mental illness. Barton (1966) defined institutional neurosis as the following:

> [Institutional neurosis] is a disease characterized by apathy, lack of initiative, loss of interest, especially in things of an impersonal nature, submissiveness, apparent inability to make plans for the future, lack of individuality, and sometimes a characteristic posture or gait. . . . Schizophrenia, depression, mental subnormality or organic dementia may predispose [individuals] to withdrawal and apathy, but isolating a patient and forcing him to lead a dependent regimented life will produce apathy and dependence in its own right. (Barton, 1966, pp. 5, 62)

What this suggests is that being subjected to long-term hospitalization can, in and of itself, produce impairment, something we call an *iatrogenic condition*. An iatrogenic condition is a disease, impairment, or disability unintentionally caused by the impact of a diagnosis, treatment provided, or the setting in which the treatment is delivered, such as a psychiatric hospital (Barton (1966) argued that institutional neurosis is an iatrogenic *disease* and as such could and should be treated. Barton then describes a series of steps that

---

Goffman, E. (1961). Asylums: Essays on the social situation of mental patients and other inmates. Garden City, N.Y.: Anchor.

Barton, R. (1966). Institutional neurosis (with a forward by Noel Gordon Harris). Bristol, UK: John Wright & Sons, LTD.

could be taken to change an institution's practices to treat and prevent institutional neurosis. These steps included:

- Actively making efforts to reestablish the patient's contacts with the outside world;
- Providing patients with daily activities including occupational activities, recreation, and social events, 14 hours a day, seven days a week;
- Taking supportive and constructive actions to change the negative attitudes many medical and nursing staff hold toward patients;
- Encouraging and enabling the patient to have friends and personal possessions and participate in personal events;
- Reducing the use of drugs as much as possible;
- Providing "a homely, friendly, permissive ward atmosphere" (p. 53); and
- Helping the patient to be aware of options for him or her outside the confines of the hospital, such as housing, work, and finding friendship. (pp. 28–61)

Thus, Barton's view was that institutional neurosis is not an inevitable consequence of long-term hospitalization and there is much that can be done to prevent and treat it. As the reader can see, his recommendations are akin to modern efforts to develop and maintain high-quality inpatient care, partial hospitalization care, and care provided in long-term structured residences. Whether it is the 1950s or the 2000s, the basic needs and wants of human beings have not changed very much, and mentally ill individuals want and need the same things we all do including respect, friendship, personal space, recreation, a comfortable place to live, and meaningful work. In many ways Barton's recommendations mirrored the early efforts of moral treatment, and like those previous efforts, his were not very successful in changing most mental institutions of the time.

Goffman's (1961) work reported not just negative attitudes by staff toward patients, but he also observed significant maltreatment of patients by staff and by other patients. Rather than places where help was provided, Goffman argued that many state hospitals had evolved into little more than human warehouses, not far removed from the conditions in the poorhouses observed by Dorothea Dix a century before. Moving forward to change the primary locus of mental health treatment from the state hospital to the community was facilitated by such reports, along with a number of other developments, all of which converged into the process called *deinstitutionalization*.

MOVING FROM THE ASYLUM TO THE COMMUNITY

The term "deinstitutionalization" in mental health policy refers to the shift in the principal locus of treatment from the large remote state hospitals to services provided in the community, and then closing part or all of those large state institutions. Deinstitutionalization may be thought of as comprising three things: a philosophy, a process, and an ideology (Sands, 2001). It began to unfold in the 1950s parallel to the development and subsequent widespread use of the first effective psychotropic drugs to treat psychosis and depression, converged with the community mental health movement of the 1960s along with the passage of federal Medicaid and Medicare (Torrey, 1997a), and evolved through the next four decades to the point that the vast majority of state mental hospitals were permanently closed. The policy affected those mentally ill people who were hospitalized, but the policy also slowly *eliminated* the option of state hospital care as part of the continuum of care for all individuals with mental illness.

Who the Patients Were and How the Numbers Dropped

Although many types of institutions were affected by the policy of deinstitutionalization, the institutions most affected were the state mental hospitals. Deinstitutionalization of the state mental hospitals, however, varied from state to state in terms of how rapidly it progressed and the steepness of the census reduction, although three quarters of the national reduction of state hospital beds came upon the heels of the expansion of welfare programs in the middle 1960s (Mechanic & Rochefort, 1990). The magnitude of the process of deinstitutionalization of individuals with severe mental illness has been described as one of the most significant—and largest—social experiments in U.S. history (Torrey, 1997b; Torrey, 2008). Evidence supporting this statement is clearly seen if one simply looks at the numbers. In 1955, there were approximately 559,000 individuals residing in our nation's state mental hospitals. By 1994, this number had dropped to 71,619 (SAMHSA, 1994). The number of hospitals also decreased significantly, from 310 in 1970 to 222 in 2002 (SAMHSA, 2004). Segal (2008) points out, however, that the *number* of hospital admissions for psychiatric care has actually *increased* over the decades of deinstitutionalization due to a revolving door pattern in which individuals are hospitalized for shorter periods but more frequently than in the past—one of the many unanticipated consequences of the policy of deinstitutionalization.

Most of those who were deinstitutionalized from the nation's state mental hospitals had severe mental illnesses and/or brain disorders. The majority, estimated at between 50 and 60 percent, had schizophrenia, and the remainder were diagnosed with manic-depressive illness, major depression, and various organic brain syndromes, such as dementia, conditions produced by strokes, and traumatic brain injuries. Other patients had pervasive developmental disabilities such as autism, mental retardation, and brain dysfunction as a result of alcoholism or drug addiction (Torrey, 1997b). One of the significant events that affected the ability to move individuals from the asylum to less restrictive settings was the development and dissemination of effective psychotropic medications for many of the disorders that necessitated hospitalization.

Factors That Converged to Propel Deinstitutionalization Forward

The role of the development of psychotropic medications

It is indeed true that deinstitutionalization was, in part, facilitated by the development of more effective medications for treating some of the conditions that made hospitalization necessary. Beginning in 1952, two French psychiatrists reported that a new drug—chlorpromazine—significantly tranquilized behavior and reduced psychotic thinking in hospitalized patients with schizophrenia (Colp, 2005). Then in 1957, Swiss psychiatrist Roland Kuhn and American psychiatrist Nathan Kline reported that two newly developed drugs were found effective in the treatment of moderate to severe depression. One of the drugs was the tricyclic antidepressant imipramine (Tofranil), and the other was a monoamine oxidase inhibitor (MAOI). It was soon discovered, however, that eating certain foods could result in a hypertensive crisis in an individual taking an MAOI, and thus, the tricyclic antidepressant was determined to be the preferable first course of drug treatment for depression. Following these developments, in the early 1960s, the first benzodiazepine compounds, chlordiazepoxide (Librium) and diazepam (Valium), were developed and proved to be effective in treating nonpsychotic anxiety. Later, the potential for addiction to these benzodiazepines was revealed. Lithium was developed by the Australian psychiatrist John Cade for the treatment of mania in 1949; however, lithium was not approved by the U.S. Food and Drug Administration until 1970. These medications were the first to be effective in controlling many of the symptoms that made hospitalization necessary, but this alone would not have resulted in deinstitutionalization (Colp, 2005). Other key factors included the passage of the Community Mental Health Services Act and the rise of civil libertarian ideology coupled with a desire to save money.

The Community Mental Health Centers Act

In 1952, the World Health Organization's (WHO) Committee on Mental Health recommended that countries consider moving away from the asylum model and, instead, pursue developing community-based psychiatric hospitals that would include outpatient treatment, rehabilitation services, research, and community education. By the mid-1950s, the U.S. federal and state governments were concerned about the increasing cost of state hospital care and were inspired by the recommendations of the WHO. In response to this, Congress passed and President Dwight D. Eisenhower signed the Mental Health Study Act in 1955, which authorized a national study of the state of mental health treatment in the United States and established the Joint Commission on Mental Illness and Mental Health (Colp, 2005). The joint commission produced a report in 1961 entitled "Action for Mental Health," which provided the foundation for President John F. Kennedy's plan for new community-based programs for mental health and mental retardation. In 1963, President Kennedy delivered an address to the 88th Congress that recommended a "bold new approach" for caring for individuals with mental illness:

> [I am proposing] a national mental health program to assist in the inauguration of a wholly new emphasis and approach to care for the mentally ill. . . . Central to a new mental health program is comprehensive community care. . . . If we launch a broad new mental health program now, it will be possible within a decade or two to reduce the number of patients now under custodial care by 50 percent or more. . . . This approach is designed in large measure, to use Federal resources to stimulate state, local, and private action. When carried out, reliance on the cold mercy of custodial isolation will be supplanted by the open warmth of community concern and capability. Emphasis on prevention, treatment, and rehabilitation will be substituted for a desultory interest in confining patients in an institution to wither away. (Kennedy, 1963, pp. 3–5)

President Kennedy's address to Congress was the first one in U.S. history to focus squarely on mental health issues. In response, Congress quickly passed the Mental Retardation Facilities and Community Mental Health Centers Construction Act (P.L. 88–164), issuing in a new era in mental health treatment. Responsibility for monitoring the development of the new community mental health centers (CMHC) was given to the National Institute of Mental Health.

The new CMHCs were constructed for defined catchment areas serving 75,000 to 200,000 people each and were required to provide five core services: inpatient care, outpatient care, day treatment/partial hospitalization, psychiatric emergency services, and consultation/education services. Subsequent amendments to the act in 1975 expanded these five core services to twelve, including services for children, aging services, substance abuse services, screening before admission to state hospitals (which usually becomes an additional component to the psychiatric emergency service), follow-up care for patients discharged from institutions (which evolved into case management services), and transitional housing (Colp, 2005). If a CMHC did not provide at least the original five core services, it risked losing federal funding, as illustrated by the following example from the author's practice:

> Following completion of my undergraduate degree in sociology, I embarked on the process of looking for a job. I saw an ad in my hometown paper for an "emergency coordinator" for the local community mental health center. I had some experience as a community organizer so I called and scheduled an interview. When I asked about what the job entailed, the interviewer put it to me bluntly. Their CMHC had never had a psychiatric emergency service, even though it is one of the five core services required for federal funding of a CMHC. Instead, when a psychiatric emergency occurred, the individual in crisis was simply transported by the police to the local state mental hospital for evaluation. Recently, a federal audit concluded that what they were doing was not acceptable and if they did not develop a community-based

---

Kennedy, J. F. (1963). Special message to the Congress on mental illness and mental retardation. Public Papers of the Presidents of the United States: John F. Kennedy, 1963. Washington, DC: GPO.

psychiatric emergency service within the next six months, they would lose federal funding. The interviewer told me: "You're free to figure it out however you want to, but we need a service up and running as soon as possible." With a bit of trepidation, I took the job and within two months we had a 24-hour psychiatric emergency service up and running. My approach was to recruit community volunteers with at least a bachelor's degree in psychology or social work along with graduate students in psychology (there was no social work department offering the MSW degree at our local university), which managed to cover the shifts. We only had a part-time psychiatrist to provide backup because this was a predominantly rural area with few resources, but we managed, and what we offered was better than a trip to the state hospital in police custody.

Civil libertarian ideology and a desire to save money

Although the development of effective psychotropic medications and the passage of the Community Mental Health Centers Act played a role in facilitating deinstitutionalization, David Rothman (2002) argues that the most important component in pushing this paradigm shift forward was the developing civil libertarian ideology that emerged soon after. Central to this ideology was the importance of acknowledging and upholding the rights of oppressed and marginalized populations including people of color, poor people, women, people with developmental disabilities, and people with mental illness. Civil libertarian demands that mentally ill people should be provided with more choices and freedom was appealing to liberals, while conservatives warmed to the idea that deinstitutionalization would save money by slashing mental health budgets and closing down the state hospitals (Torrey, 1997a, 1997b). Thus, deinstitutionalization held appeal across the political spectrum.

Deinstitutionalization also encompassed a philosophy about the appropriate use of hospitals, recommending that psychiatric hospitals still be utilized but only as a last resort. Avoiding hospitalization became a priority, long-term custodial care was no longer acceptable as a primary purpose and role for the hospital, and consequently hospitalizations became brief and often in a local facility with clients then released to community care. I recall clearly when, during an interview I had for a psychiatric emergency room clinical social work position in the late 1970s, the director of the service said to me: "Your primary job is to keep people out of the hospital. Do whatever you have to do—but don't hospitalize unless there is absolutely no choice about it."

Civil libertarian advocates based their "demonization" of the state mental hospital largely on the work of Goffman (1961) and Barton (1966), and their conclusion that many of the symptoms of abnormal behavior amongst hospitalized patients was due to institutionalization, not mental illness. Although aspects of institutional neurosis or institutionalization can occur with long-term hospitalization, abundant research over the past two decades has clearly shown that disorders such as schizophrenia and bipolar disorder are physical disorders of the brain, although with psychological manifestations (Eack, 2012; Roberts & Tamminga, 2005; Thase, 2005). Furthermore, most individuals with the most severe and persistent mental illnesses require medication in order to manage their symptoms, benefit from psychosocial treatment, and achieve recovery, as defined currently. Individuals with serious mental illness also characteristically experience relapses, and restabilization often depends upon access to hospitalization. Thus, deinstitutionalization rested on some false assumptions, but appealed politically to both liberal and conservative ideologies and, thus, was propelled forward.

Colp, R. (2005). History of psychiatry. In: Sadock, B.J. & Sadock, V.A. (Eds.). Kaplan & Sadock=s Comprehensive textbook of psychiatry, 8th edition, Volume II. Philadelphia, PA: Lippincott Williams & Wilkins (pp. 4013-4047)

The Consumer Movement and the Consumer/Survivor Movement

Another potent force behind deinstitutionalization was the development of the consumer movement, beginning in the mid-1960s. The roots of the consumer/survivor movement go back to the turn-of-the-century writings of Elizabeth Packard, Clifford Beers, and Mary Jane Ward (see Chapter 1), who documented their personal—mostly adverse—experiences as patients in the asylum, with Beers and Packard inspired toward subsequent efforts to change policies affecting the insane. The next milestone leading to the consumer movement was the development of psychosocial rehabilitation and the clubhouse model.

Psychosocial rehabilitation for individuals with mental illness emerged in the late 1940s, when a group of ex-patients, who had been discharged from Pilgrim State Hospital, began to meet together in New York City to help each other survive in the city and satisfy their needs for acceptance and emotional support. The group called themselves WANA (We Are Not Alone) (National Mental Health Consumers' Self-Help Clearinghouse [NMHCSHC], n.d.). WANA emphasized self-help, mutual interdependence, and reliance on strengths. Eventually, the group obtained permission to meet in an empty storefront building, and they established the first psychosocial rehabilitation clubhouse program, which they named "Fountain House," in 1948. This "clubhouse model" has served as a prototype for developing hundreds of similar programs during the 1960s to the present time.

What was unique about the Fountain House clubhouse model? First, instead of calling themselves "patients," participants referred to themselves as "members," and they formed groups and teams to accomplish tasks, plan activities, solve problems, and develop their own social support network. In doing this, the quality of their lives improved. Second, a primary emphasis was on the importance of positive relationships with others. Thus began the development of collective peer self-help (see www.fountainhouse.org).

In the 1960s, the civil rights movement provided the context for former mental patients living in the community to begin to "organize groups with the common goals of fighting for patients' rights and against forced treatment, eradicating stigma, ending economic and social discrimination, and creating peer-run services as an alternative to the traditional mental health system" (NMHCSHC, n.d.). The basic premise was that, unlike the traditional medical model, self-help can assist people to improve their lives through mutual support. Some of these groups, however, became radicalized in terms of desiring to reject all forms of psychiatric treatment.

Satel and Redding (2005) make a clear distinction between the "consumer movement," which has been positive through "empowering patients, increasing patients' involvement in their own health care . . ., reducing the perceived shame of mental illness, and lobbying efforts to achieve parity for mental health care" (p. 645), and the "consumer/survivor movement," which has a general "anti-psychiatry" stance, argues that psychiatry "makes" people sick and, some have argued, has exerted efforts to undermine the ability of psychiatrists to provide optimal psychiatric care via its sociopolitical influence on mental health legislation and policy.

Essentially, the consumer/survivor movement sees mentally ill individuals as an oppressed class of social dissidents, and psychiatrists and other mental health professionals as agents of social control. Some psychiatrists and sociologists supported this stance, for example, psychiatrist Ronald D. Laing (1960), who argued that psychosis is a rational adaptation to an insane world. Thomas Szasz, whose writings lent considerable support to the consumer/survivor movement, argued in *The Myth of Mental Illness* (1961) that it is incorrect to claim that a mental illness, such as schizophrenia, is a disease, because no clear biological proof is there. One has to keep in mind, however, that his book was written in 1961, long before we had the biologically based evidence that we do today that schizophrenia and many other severe mental illnesses have a clear biological basis. In a famous quote, Szasz states: "If you talk to God, you are praying; if God talks to you, you have schizophrenia. If the dead talk to you, you are a spiritualist; if you talk to the dead, you are a schizophrenic." (Szasz, 1974, p. 113). Other scholars who have questioned the validity of mental illness and if psychiatry is a true science or a pseudoscience include Michel Foucault (1965), Herbert Marcuse (Healy, 2004; Marcuse, 1964), and Andrew Weil (1972). All of these individuals argue, essentially, that one's personal reality is separate from any definition of what is normal from the authority of organized psychiatry (Rissmiller & Rissmiller, 2006). Finally, the Church of Scientology has lent considerable support to the efforts of the antipsychiatry and consumer/survivor movement for decades (see, e.g., Hubbard, 1969). Rissmiller and Rissmiller (2006) conclude that:

> Organized psychiatry has found it difficult to have a constructive dialogue with the evolving radical consumerist movement. Consumerist groups are viewed as extremist, having little scientific foundation and no defined leadership. . . . Psychiatry continues to fight antipsychiatry disinformation on the use of involuntary commitment, electroconvulsive therapy, stimulants and antidepressants among children, and neuroleptics among adults. Conversely, radical consumerists remain disinclined to soften their antipsychiatry stance toward a territorial and biologically oriented profession that, in their view, has profited from patients it neglected and abused . . . they will undoubtedly continue to play an assertive role in the delivery of mental health services worldwide. (p. 866)

Today, the vast majority of consumer groups emphasize the importance of combining self-help and mutual support with psychiatric treatment. "Recovery" does not mean denial of mental illness and rejection of all forms of formal psychiatric treatment; rather, it means acceptance of one's illness and receptivity to treatment guided by consumer choice (Barber, 2012). In other words, most of today's consumer groups encourage members to be as informed as possible about the mental health system, be informed about psychosocial and pharmacological treatments available, and to demand a "voice" in treatment decisions and the determination of life goals. Consumers also want a "seat at the table" with regard to mental health policy making and input in the protocols of psychiatric treatment research studies. These efforts have generally been supported by the social work profession because of our core belief in the importance of self-determination, empowerment, and collaboration.

The advent of managed care, however, presents an ongoing challenge to the consumer self-help/advocacy movement. Many peer-run services depend on funding from state, federal, and local agencies and, like other types of service agencies, are being required to make changes with regard to credentialing and accountability that may force such groups to function like more traditional service providers, which risks abandoning their more relaxed consumer-driven missions.

The Values Underlying Deinstitutionalization

As noted before, deinstitutionalization moved rapidly forward during 1960s and 1970s, which was a time of heightened social consciousness and advocacy for the rights of marginalized populations. Certain practices, such as involuntary commitment, custodial care without treatment, and coercive forms of intervention, began to be challenged in the courts on constitutional grounds. The patients' rights movement (now consumer/survivor movement) gained a more influential voice, and a series of judicial decisions supported many of these identified rights, such as the right of hospitalized patients to receive treatment, the right to refuse treatment except under clearly defined circumstances, the right to be

---

Szasz, T.S. (1974). The second sin. Garden City, N.Y.: Anchor.

Rissmiller, D.J. & Rissmiller, J.H. (2006). Evolution of the antipsychiatry movement into mental health consumerism. Psychiatric Services, 57, 863–866.

paid for labor provided while hospitalized, and the right to live in the least restrictive environment. With the establishment of limits on the power of institutions to restrict clients' rights, admitting and retaining clients in the hospital became more difficult.

As an ideology, deinstitutionalization was associated with certain specific values that drove the parameters of the policy (Mechanic, 2008). The first key value is that institutionalization is undesirable, that is, hospitals are necessary evils to be used as last resort only. A second key value is that independence is extremely important and persons with mental illness deserve to live as independently as possible and be allowed to assume responsibility for themselves and set self-directed goals that will facilitate their adaptation to community life. Finally, the third key value is that clients have a right to treatment but also have a right to have freedom of movement and to be provided with the supports necessary to facilitate and uphold the *principles of normalization and integration*.

Normalization and integration mean that clients should be helped to adapt to community life as seamlessly as possible so their "patient status" is not apparent. This means that their membership in the larger community is fostered, and they have the opportunity to enter fully into the fabric of community life (Rosenheck, 2012; Wolfensberger & Nirje 1972). Importantly, such integration is not a privilege—rather, it is their *right* as a citizen and human being. Normalization and integration does *not* mean trying to make individuals with disabilities "normal" and forcing them to conform to society's norms. It also does not support "dumping" people into the community without appropriate supports and treatments for their disabilities. Finally, normalization does not provide a justification for eliminating necessary services and supports for clients and families (Perrin & Nirje, 1985). What it *does* mean is that individuals with mental illness should be able to use public facilities; be welcomed by churches, synagogues, and temples; be able to go shopping in stores; be able to use the library and public swimming pool and so forth without discrimination. The following is an example of how fostering the dual principles of normalization and integration can be a challenge and often requires the actions of an advocate—in this case, a social worker.

The Case of John

I had a client, whom I will refer to as "John," who was released from one of the state hospitals in California after having been a patient for over 20 years. John had schizophrenia and his level of psychosocial functioning was quite low, to the extent that he was unable to live independently. As a result, he lived in a board and care home[1] in a rural area of central California and attended a psychosocial rehabilitation program during the day. Because of his illness, John had been unable to complete high school, but he was extremely bright and loved to read. During his years at the state hospital, he spent much of his time in the hospital's library, which was well stocked with John's favorite kinds of reading, that is, books on history, science, and medicine. Soon after he moved to his board and care home, he asked the care home operator if she could take him to the local library.

The local library turned out to be two boxcars that had been hooked together and then furnished with a couple tables, chairs, and as many books as could be crammed into the small space. The librarian was an elderly woman who had been the only librarian for the place since it opened over 30 years ago, thus, it was Her Library. The board and care operator, Yvette, dropped John off at the library and then came back to pick him up a couple hours later. When Yvette entered the library, she was met by the librarian, who said, "I'm sorry, but this man cannot return to the library." Yvette asked why, and the librarian responded by saying that she

[1]The terms used for sheltered care for individuals with mental illness varies. In California, "board and care home" is used, "personal care home" is used in Pennsylvania, many states use the term "group home," all under the umbrella of supervised group residential care in which in-house therapeutic programming may or may not be provided.

thought John was "strange" and "might *do something.*" Yvette escorted John to the car and then told him he couldn't return to the library. "But what did I do wrong? Why am I in trouble?" John asked. Yvette couldn't answer, because she knew he hadn't done anything wrong, but she also knew that John looked strange. He shaved his head, rocked back and forth, talked softly to himself at times, and wore mismatched clothes. She didn't know what to do.

John, however, knew exactly what to do. On the wall of the board and care home was a sign entitled "Client Rights Advocate" with an address and phone number. He called the advocate, and the advocate called me. I went out to the board and care home and met with John, and then suggested that we both go over to the library and meet with the librarian. The ensuing conversation went something like this:

Christina: Hello, my name is Christina Newhill, and I am a social worker. I would like to introduce John—John and I work together.

Librarian (warily): Oh, um, hello—my name is Mrs. Smith.

John: Hi . . . (John begins to rock back and forth so I put a hand on his arm and he stops)

Christina: Mrs. Smith, could we sit down and talk for a few minutes? All sit down at one of the tiny tables.

Christina: Mrs. Smith, you've got a really nice library here. It's great that a little town like this has a library. John was telling me how much he enjoyed being here yesterday.

John: Yup.

Mrs. Smith: Hmmm . . .

Christina: You know, John is a big reader—he loves to read and, you know, whenever he is in a new place, the first thing he wants to know is where the local library is.

Mrs. Smith: Really?

Christina: Oh, yes! John—tell Mrs. Smith what you like to read.

John: Well, uh, I like to read lots of stuff. I like the encyclopedia and I like to look stuff up and I like science magazines and stuff having to do with history—I like that too—and I like to read the Bible sometimes but I do that in my room. And I like to just sit in the library, around all the books, and I always find interesting stuff to read.

Mrs. Smith (brightening up): Why, that's great. We have a complete encyclopedia here and, well, we don't have much money to spend for magazines and journals but we do get *Scientific American* magazine.

John: Yeah . . . I was looking at it yesterday and there was this article . . . (goes on to describe it). The next 10 minutes are spent with John and Mrs. Smith having an animated conversation about what John likes to read.

Christina: Mrs. Smith, would it be possible for John to visit the library again sometime?

Mrs. Smith: Well, John sounds like a real reader and I always love to have people here who like to read and, well, he seems like a nice fellow. . . . Sure, John, you can come to the library anytime. Here, let's go and get you your own library card so you can check out books.

John: Oh—thank you—but I thought you didn't want me to come here anymore.

Mrs. Smith: Oh no . . . I . . . well, I don't know . . . I didn't know what a reader you are—no, there's no problem . . . you're welcome here anytime. . . . Let's go get your card.

The outcome of this was that John and Mrs. Smith became friends around their mutual love of books and reading and, in time, Mrs. Smith became a natural social support for John, and during the rare times when John wasn't doing well, she would call me and alert the mental health center. John was happy about the outcome because he now had a "home" away from the board and care home and mental health services, where he was around everyday people and accepted as a library patron, just like everybody else. This is an example of how one can put the principles of normalization and integration into action. One of the keys to helping individuals with severe mental illness make it successfully in the community is the development of natural social supports, and this will be addressed later in more detail in Chapter 9, which addresses case management. The "point person" to facilitate this happening may be a family member but, in lieu of that, it is often *you*—your client's social worker—who can advocate on his or her behalf and make a big difference in the client's day-to-day life.

Assess your comprehension of *the forces that led to the policy of deinstitutionalization* by completing this quiz.

THE RESULTS OF DEINSTITUTIONALIZATION: A FAILED POLICY BASED ON GOOD INTENTIONS

Evaluating the successes and failures of the policy of deinstitutionalization is complicated. There is no question that thousands of mentally ill patients benefitted from the policy by being able to leave the state hospital and successfully make the transition from the hospital to receiving services in the community and, over time, developing a life with quality and meaning. These successful individuals generally possessed certain common characteristics. Those who were able to make the transition to community living typically had involved and supportive family members, were less severely ill, had resided in the state hospital for a shorter period of time, were less likely to use illicit drugs or alcohol, were better responders to treatment with regard to both medication response and response to psychosocial treatment, often had insight into their illnesses and, finally, they had the capacity to develop daily living skills, work skills, and skills for coping with stress. These are the successes. However, there were also many other individuals who did not make the transition easily or successfully, experienced suffering in the community equal to or worse than what they may have experienced in the hospital, and who encountered many of the unanticipated consequences of deinstitutionalization including poor adherence and response to treatment, repeated rehospitalizations, homelessness, poverty, being victimized by others, abuse of drugs and/or alcohol, poor physical health, and involvement in the criminal justice system.

Finally, there were many individuals who eventually made the transition, but it was a continuous struggle along the way. Deinstitutionalization was not an easy process for many patients. One of the things that can happen when a patient has been institutionalized for a long period of time is that, as his or her discharge date approaches, he or she may experience feelings of anxiety and fear about leaving the hospital, resistance toward being discharged, and even a reemergence of their psychiatric symptoms as hospital discharge approaches. Here is an example of what can occur.

> From 1976 to 1978, I worked for an agency in upstate New York that provided transitional supported housing for individuals being deinstitutionalized from Auburn State Hospital. I was a "state hospital transition liaison" and my job was to facilitate the process of moving long-term patients from the hospital to sheltered care in the community. Some of the patients had resided at Auburn for decades. The transition from the regimented total institution community of the state hospital to the open

community was very difficult for many of these individuals, particularly for those who were elderly. Many were literally terrified of leaving the only home they had known as adults and, for some, the only home since adolescence.

To help a person make the transition in a way that reduced these fears, I would begin by visiting him or her in the hospital well before discharge, so they could get to know me and begin to feel comfortable and trust me. Then I would take a very careful inventory of their needs and wants from a range of perspectives, soliciting input from the hospital social worker, the psychiatrist, the patient's family (if they had one—many did not), and the patient him or herself. Many patients/consumers wanted a lot of structure in their new home in the community, recognizing that it would take a while to feel comfortable with freedom and, as their social worker, it was important for me to respect that. After they had made the move to the transitional residence, I would continue to visit them for about a month until their new outpatient social worker could develop a relationship with them. Supporting client self-determination and facilitating the development of empowerment was an extremely important process but a very slow one. However, when fear turned to joy as a former patient—now client—would make a decision on his or her own and feel empowered by doing that, it was wonderful to behold. Some folks did not make it in the community on the first try, and had to go back to the hospital temporarily. But, eventually, most of my clients settled in and slowly began to construct their new lives in the community—a community, however, that was not always welcoming to them.

The Ideal versus the Reality

Ideally, deinstitutionalization should have involved two processes: first, the avoidance of long-term hospitalization, but also the concurrent development of high-quality community-based mental health services as alternatives to hospitalization (Bachrach, 1976). In most cases, however, the money did not follow the patients to support the development of such services. Instead, most states siphoned the money saved by deinstitutionalization into the general state coffers, and instead of building community services and supports, the money was used to build highways and reduce taxes (Grob, 1994). The result is that many communities did not and have not developed these services and, as a consequence, hundreds of discharged patients have been dumped on our streets and in our parks "dying with their rights on" (Treffert, 1973). Treffert (1973) argues that it is important for individuals with mental illness to have the freedoms all citizens enjoy in the community; however, at the same time, such individuals should be provided with protection. In other words, one has the right to make choices, but one must also retain the right to be protected and even rescued from harmful choices. For example, on October 29, 2007, in Pittsburgh, Pennsylvania, Anthony Fallert, a former state hospital consumer who had schizophrenia, walked away from a community mental health program and jumped or fell from a high bridge into the Monongahela River and drowned (Fahy, 2007). No one was there to rescue him.

The continued presence of seriously mentally ill individuals amongst our homeless populations today is clear evidence of continued community indifference and an inadequate mental health service system (Schutt & Goldfinger, 2011). The assumption held by advocates of deinstitutionalization was that communities would welcome mentally ill individuals and that, magically, they would be prepared to care for them and provide the supports necessary to do so. This was not the case, in large part because the resources necessary to make that happen were not provided or were provided in a scaled-down manner. Many communities were not welcoming, and patients—if they were fortunate enough to have housing—ended up being forced to live in single room occupancy (SRO) hotels, flophouses, and mental patient housing ghettos—the polar opposites of the principles of normalization and integration (Feuer, 2009; Segal & Baumohl, 1980). Example:

Review an *example* from the Author's experience.

Another result of the failed policy of deinstitutionalization is the revolving door syndrome (Segal, 2008). The main problem here is that brief hospitalization does not afford enough time for recovery for many clients, much less stabilization on medication. Advocates for deinstitutionalization assumed that mentally ill individuals would voluntarily seek and accept treatment, would see the need for treatment, and would willingly take their medications. The reality is that some clients don't follow up with aftercare including taking medication that could control their symptoms and, thus, are frequently rehospitalized. Part of this is due to the fact that some mentally ill individuals do not believe they are ill and lack insight into their difficulties and therefore do not perceive that treatment is necessary (Amador, 2000). In addition, many of the psychotropic medications prescribed for the most serious mental illnesses are hard to tolerate due to side effects and the need for lifestyle changes, and this includes the newer atypical antipsychotic and mood-stabilizing medications. Unless a client's doctor, case manager, and/or social worker is skilled in implementing strategies to improve adherence, some clients stop taking their medication, relapse, and end up back in the hospital, in jail, or on the streets (Winerip, 1999).

Read more about *Public Mental Health Social Workers* today.

So—what is the final verdict on the success of deinstitutionalization?

Good Intentions but Ultimately a Failed Policy

Many mental health policy scholars have noted that deinstitutionalization arose from the best of intentions. However, one must bear in mind the old adage attributed to Saint Bernard of Clairvaux (1091–1153): "Hell is full of good intentions or desires." The bottom line? After almost 40 years of programmatic experience, Mechanic and Rochefort (1990) and others have concluded that deinstitutionalization—although instituted with many good intentions—is "one of the era's most stunning public policy failures" (p. 302). Critics of deinstitutionalization emphasize that the core of this failure was "the incomplete development and inadequate performance of the supportive services that were meant to accompany patient discharge and patient diversion activities" (Mechanic & Rochefort, 1990, p. 302). To put it bluntly, the United States tried to do deinstitutionalization and community mental health care "on the cheap" and we got what we paid for, and the ensuing price for this has been considerable suffering on the part of mentally ill individuals, their families, and the professional and paraprofessional staff who have tried their best to care for clients and help support families but without adequate resources to draw upon (Interlandi, 2012). Other contributing factors that have undermined efforts to correct the deficiencies of the policy of deinstitutionalization include the following (Mechanic, 2008; Segal, 2008):

- The new financing protocol introduced by the passage of Medicaid and Title XIX of the Social Security Act in 1965 that enabled the placement of mentally ill individuals in nursing homes at a much lower cost than state hospital placement, which did not facilitate the transition to the community and often was an inappropriate, even harmful placement alternative (Johnson, 2009).
- Diverting mental health monies to support efforts to address alcoholism and drug abuse in the late 1960s and early 1970s.
- Efforts by the Nixon administration to dismantle the Alcohol, Drug Abuse, and Mental Health Administration (ADAMHA) programs associated with Presidents Kennedy and Johnson; by 1977, this resulted in funding only 650 of the originally proposed 1,500 community mental health centers.

- Failure to develop a universal health care system that would provide protection to individuals with mental illness.
- Failure of many CMHCs to adequately serve individuals with the most serious mental illnesses.
- Failure of the Reagan administration to implement President Carter's Mental Health Systems Act, which was passed one month before Carter left office. Instead, the Reagan administration began its New Federalism initiative, which returned federal mental health monies along with monies for other social service programs back to the states as "block grants." Funds were cut, and many programs serving the mentally ill were closed. Mental health program decision making moved to the state and local arena, and significant disparities evolved across states in terms of quality and quantity of services.
- Escalating health care costs that led to the implementation of various forms of managed care. The impact of managed care is complex and will be discussed throughout the course of this book. Some of the impact has been positive; other aspects have been less positive.

In summary, during the past three decades after the start of deinstitutionalization there have been steps forward but then steps backward in the efforts to develop a comprehensive system of community mental health care for individuals with serious mental illness. Where do things stand today as we move into the second decade of the twenty-first century? According to the National Alliance on Mental Illness, the picture remains bleak (Aron, Honberg, Duckworth, et al., 2009).

Re-criminalizing People with Mental Illness

In the 1800s, Dorothea Dix was shocked at the conditions suffered by mentally ill inmates living in poorhouses, workhouses, and jails. As reviewed in Chapter 1, Dix conducted a tireless campaign to build therapeutic asylums to house and treat individuals with mental illness and stop their inappropriate incarceration in jails and prisons. In yet another unanticipated consequence of deinstitutionalization, however, we have come full circle and are once again confining mentally ill people in jails and prisons (Committee on Psychiatry and the Community, 2009; Hawthorne, Folsom, Sommerfeld, et al., 2012; Steadman, Osher, Robbins, et al., 2009; Torrey, Stieber, Ezekiel, et al., 1992). Many of these individuals have histories of psychiatric hospitalization, including state hospital care, along with repeated failed attempts to live in the community. Our jails and prisons have become the new asylums, not by intent or choice, but by default (Torrey, 1997a). Today, the Los Angeles County Jail, with 3,400 mentally ill inmates, operates as the nation's largest mental hospital, with New York's Riker's Island Jail following close behind with 3,000 mentally ill prisoners (Butterfield, 1998; Satel, 2003). In fact, in 2007, an estimated 2,161,705 people with severe mental illness were incarcerated in jails or prisons in the United States (Steadman, et al., 2009).

In one of the first studies to examine the extent to which individuals with mental illness are being "criminalized," Teplin (1984) found that for similar offenses, individuals with mental illness had a significantly greater chance of being arrested than non–mentally ill individuals. In a 2003 report by Human Rights Watch, investigators reported that between two and three hundred thousand individuals incarcerated in prison in the United States suffer from mental illness, including the most serious mental illnesses (Human Rights Watch, 2003), with the numbers even higher if mental illnesses such as severe personality disorders are included. The National Alliance on Mental Illness reports that the number of jail and prison inmates who are dually diagnosed with both mental illness and substance abuse disorders is well over 50 percent (www.nami.org). Recently, Steadman et al. (2009) reported in a study of the prevalence rates for serious mental illness in jails that 14.3 percent of male inmates and 31 percent of female inmates suffer from serious mental illness.

In essence, our jails and prisons house three times more mentally ill people than do our psychiatric hospitals (Satel, 2003).

There are many factors underlying the increasing criminalization of individuals with mental illness. These factors include the effects of deinstitutionalization and state hospital closings combined with more rigid criteria for civil commitment; the inadequate planning, funding, and resources for community care and support for individuals with mental illness; the difficulties faced by mentally ill offenders in accessing mental health treatment; and the attitudes held by police officers and society as a whole (Lamb & Weinberger, 1998). In addition, for many who end up incarcerated, their mental illness is compounded by a high incidence of abuse of drugs and alcohol, a factor not anticipated by the early advocates for deinstitutionalization. Finally, the tougher sentencing laws that were instituted beginning in the 1980s led to a precipitous increase in the prison population, which has also served to increase the number of mentally ill inmates (Torrey, 1997a). Many of these influential factors, however, can be modified with sufficient effort and commitment to doing so (Hawthorne et al., 2012).

Incarcerating individuals with mental illness is both expensive and inhumane. For example, it costs $40,000 per year to provide minimal care for a mentally ill person housed in a Florida jail and up to $60,000 per year for incarceration in a state prison in Florida (Wickham, 1999). In contrast, a mentally ill individual could receive intensive community mental health treatment for only $20,000 a year in most states (Wickham, 1999). Imprisonment is a stressful circumstance for most people, but particularly so for those with mental illness. Part of this is because inmates with mental illness are more likely to be segregated into solitary confinement, the isolation of which can exacerbate their symptoms (Editorial, 2012; Goode, 2012; Satel, 2003). "If you're mentally ill when you go into segregation, you're going to become worse invariably," says Fred Cohen, prison mental health consultant for the Ohio Department of Corrections. "If you're not mentally ill, the risk of becoming mentally ill is very high from isolation. Some people dispute that, but in my experience, the people who are just so unsocialized and so psychologically fragile to begin with are deprived of any kind of social support, any kind of psychological stimulus. And they just fall apart." (Frontline, 2005).

Mental Health Courts

Fortunately, pressure from the criminal justice system, politicians, and advocacy groups led to a new development—the mental health court. On July 27, 2000, Congress passed and President Clinton signed into law the "America's Law Enforcement and Mental Health Project Act" (S. 1865), which provided grants to communities for the development of mental health courts. Two years later a study by the Judge David L. Bazelon Center for Mental Health Law found only 20 specialized mental health courts nationwide (Judge David L. Bazelon Center for Mental Health Law, 2003); however, by the mid-2000s, all but a handful of states had instituted mental health courts, particularly in heavily populated urban areas.

The main goal of the mental health court is to prevent individuals with mental illness from being incarcerated in jail or prison for minor crimes and, instead, to divert them to a community mental health treatment program for services (Sarteschi, 2009; Sarteschi, Vaughn, & Kim, 2011). Some courts also provide monitoring and oversight of defendants' follow-through with prescribed treatment and can impose criminal sanctions for nonadherence. Mental health courts, however, only address the needs of individuals who have been accused of nonviolent offenses including misdemeanors, misdemeanor probation violations, felonies involving property damage, and nonviolent felonies, and do not serve

---

The New Asylums (2005)

individuals involved in violent offenses. Clients are typically eligible for mental health court if they have an Axis I mental illness, except for substance abuse only, and can have an Axis II disorder only if they also meet criteria for an Axis I disorder. Individuals with only a substance abuse problem can be diverted to a drug court.

How effective are mental health courts? The research on the effectiveness of mental health courts in reducing recidivism and improving access and adherence to treatment is quite promising so far and, for many, such improvements are maintained even after the individual is no longer under the court's supervision (McNiel & Binder, 2007). Advocacy organizations, such as Mental Health America (MHA), however, caution that we must be careful to avoid the misuse of mental health courts. In "Position Statement 53: Mental Health Courts," MHA argues that although the goal of mental health courts is to reduce the criminalization of the mentally ill, they could have the opposite effect if they do not appropriately manage the needs of individuals whose offenses are the product of their lifestyle, for example, being homeless and living in the streets. Also, mental health courts are not a substitute for efforts to improve access to mental health services, train police officers in crisis intervention, and employ non–criminal justice alternatives to improving treatment adherence for individuals with mental illness, or for further efforts to change the federal regulations for the use of Medicaid and Medicare money that prevent the large-scale provision of certain evidence-based treatments, such as assertive community treatment (Satel, 2003). Individuals with mental illness who are involved in mental health courts or other aspects of the criminal justice system present particular challenges to clinicians, and this will be addressed in Chapter 5.

THE CONCEPT OF RECOVERY AND THE EMPHASIS ON EVIDENCE-BASED PRACTICE

What Is "Recovery"?

Beginning in the 1990s the voices of clients/consumers, family members, and some providers began to challenge some of the old assumptions and stereotypes about mental illness and the lives of those who live with mental illness. These voices, some speaking from personal experience and others from observation, argued that being diagnosed with a mental illness—even a serious mental illness—is not a death sentence in terms of hopes for one's future. Instead, many people who have mental illness also have fulfilling lives and can achieve many of the goals that most of us hold for ourselves, such as friendships, romantic partnerships, meaningful work, enjoyable recreational pursuits, and independent living. Many people, in other words, can achieve "recovery." These voices soon coalesced into a recovery movement that, over time, succeeded in having a significant impact on mental health systems of care around the world at all levels "by challenging mental health providers, administrators, policy makers, funders, workers, and the people who experience mental health problems and their families to look at how negative or limiting assumptions are driving approaches to services, to funding, to treatment, to policies, and ultimately to the course of everyday lives" (Pennsylvania Office of Mental Health and Substance Abuse Services, 2005).

Assess your comprehension of *the impact and results of deinstitutionalization on clients, families, and the community* by completing this quiz.

"Recovery" should not be equated with "cure," although many individuals with mental illness do experience what might be termed a cure, in that their symptoms, with or without treatment, recede and they do not have any subsequent episodes of illness. For example, about a third of individuals who experience an episode of psychotic illness that looks like schizophrenia have only one episode, get well, and never get sick again. Today, we no longer call such an illness schizophrenia; rather, the diagnosis is schizophreniform disorder. Someone who has schizophreniform disorder recovers in the complete sense of the word in that they remain well and symptom free. For most people with serious mental illness, however, recovery means achieving a fulfilling life while living with and managing symptoms that may wax and wane over time (Barber, 2012).

But how is "recovery" defined exactly? Here is an example: In November 2004, the Pennsylvania Recovery Workgroup developed a definition of recovery that was subsequently endorsed by the Pennsylvania Office of Mental Health Substance Abuse Services (POMHSAS) as the definition to be used to guide transformation of the state's mental health system. This definition is very similar to the general definitions of recovery used by other states in the United States and other countries as well (see, e.g., O'Hagan, 2001). Embracing recovery is not just an American phenomenon, it is a worldwide paradigm shift:

> Recovery is [defined as] a self-determined and holistic journey that people undertake to heal and grow. Recovery is facilitated by relationships and environments that provide hope, empowerment, choices and opportunities that promote people reaching their full potential as individuals and community members. (POMHSAS, 2005, p. 7).

In all areas of mental health care, it is critical to hear and respect the voices of those who are the recipients of service efforts, particularly consumers and family members. Recovery is a personal journey, and that journey differs for each individual, although common threads cut across individual experiences and across a range of types of experience (Windell, Norman, & Malla, 2012). For example, recovery can be embraced when the consumer is engaging in services voluntarily, but recovery-oriented care can also be embraced when treatment is not voluntary (Geller, 2012). The following quotes from the National Alliance on Mental Illness website (www.nami.org) illustrate what recovery means for individual consumers as expressed in their own words (retrieved March 18, 2009):

> Recovery does NOT mean I will be rid of my mental illness. It means I can learn how to manage my symptoms better and better all the time. I will still have occasional set-backs, but my mental health is in the process of recovery.
>
> Recovery means managing illness to maintain stability. A person in recovery has found a sense of accomplishment. They are contributing to society making lemonade from the mental illness lemon they were given.

How to go about incorporating the recovery perspective and proactively using it to guide the strategies used in our practice as social workers will be an ongoing theme throughout the book. This short introduction is provided here to help the reader to better understand the framework used by the National Alliance on Mental Illness in developing their recommendations for improving the mental health system today and in the future that is described below.

Another important educational and practice paradigm that has had a strong influence on managed care dictates and on the practice approaches used today is what is called evidence-based practice (EBP) or evidence-based treatment. Let's take an introductory look at how EBP is defined, what we mean by "evidence," some of the limits inherent in EBP, and the basic steps a practitioner takes in choosing one intervention from among alternatives, that is, choosing the best approach for a particular client or client group.

What Is "Evidence-Based Practice" or "Evidence-Based Treatment"?

One of the major shifts in mental and behavioral health care is the emphasis on providing treatments that are "evidence-based." What does this mean? Jenson and Howard (2008) state that evidence-based practice is a paradigm that can be used to help practitioners and agencies choose and implement interventions for clients that are effective. Effectiveness is

---

POMHSA, 2004, p. 7
National Alliance on Mental Illness (www.nami.org)

demonstrated by the presence of some form of evidence—usually statistical data—that has demonstrated that this particular treatment, delivered in a specific way to a particular type of client, is effective in producing some kind of change, usually a decrease in symptoms or amelioration of a problem targeted by the treatment.

Evidence-based practice began in the early 1990s in the field of medicine as an effort to bridge the gap between research and practice and to encourage physicians to consider research findings in their clinical decision making. Another purpose was to control health care costs by encouraging or requiring provision of the treatment with the most solid evidence supporting effectiveness. Medical consumers are also much better educated about their illnesses and available treatments via the influence of the Internet and direct-to-consumer advertising by pharmaceutical companies and other product entities than in the past. As a result, consumers often demand certain treatments, and physicians must be well informed about the evidence with regard to effectiveness so they can discuss the choices that are right for their consumer-patient (Gambrill, 2006). These developments have had a direct impact on social work practice (Gambrill, 2012).

There is a range of definitions of what constitutes "evidence-based practice," and one of the well-known and accepted definitions states that EBP is "the integration of best research evidence with clinical expertise and [client] values" (Sackett, Straus, Richardson, et al., 2000, p. 1). In an earlier more comprehensive definition by Sackett, Rosenberg, Gray, Haynes, and Richardson (1996), evidence-based medicine is defined as "the conscientious, explicit, and judicious use of current best evidence in making decisions about the care of individual patients. The practice of evidence-based medicine means integrating individual clinical expertise with the best available external clinical evidence from systematic research" (p. 2). Thus, the proper application of EBP combines what research findings can tell us coupled with clinical judgment and expertise, and neither one alone is sufficient—this is a very important point. Furthermore, Sackett et al. (1996) emphasize that evidence-based medicine is not "cookbook medicine" and requires a systematic series of steps before a decision to use a particular treatment is made by the practitioner.

One of the major areas of controversy, however, is the debate over what constitutes acceptable or adequate "evidence." Does the evidence have to evolve from a controlled clinical trial, or do single subject design results count as evidence? Some social workers argue that consumers' self-reports about the effectiveness of treatments constitute valid evidence. How does a practitioner then evaluate the evidence offered in the support of the efficacy of a particular treatment? What limits are there in determining whether the evidence presented can predict treatment outcomes for *this* particular client? Some of the concerns about how to interpret various sources of evidence include the following:

- **Research findings may not be applicable to the clients we see in everyday practice settings.**

Although randomized clinical trial (RCT) research controls for a range of variables that might confound findings, thus enabling the researchers to conclude with more confidence that improvements in a consumer's symptoms of mental illness are due to the intervention being tested, that also limits how generalizable the findings are to the consumers we actually treat in public mental health services. For example, the researcher may exclude research participants who use alcohol or drugs, who take psychotropic medications, who have more than one diagnosis of mental illness, or who are above or below a certain age range. In the past, women were routinely excluded from most medical and psychiatric research, until it was recognized that findings that apply to men may not generalize to women. All of us who see clients today in public mental health services know that the majority use substances, are on medications, and have multiple complex problems that warrant more than one diagnosis. An intervention might have evidence for effectiveness for the individuals included in the clinical trial, but those individuals may represent but a small proportion of the consumers we see in day-to-day practice. How confident, then, can we be in using that intervention for our substance-abusing, antisocial, multiple-medication-using client?

- **Some of the evidence reported is mixed.**

Sometimes a particular intervention is effective in relieving only some of the individual's symptoms or problems, but not others. For example, the evidence-based treatment for borderline personality disorder called "dialectical behavioral therapy" shows good evidence of its effectiveness in reducing parasuicidal behaviors and use of inpatient care but has limited effectiveness in ameliorating some of the other common symptoms of borderline personality disorder. If consumers and practitioners don't understand this, they may have unrealistic expectations for what the intervention can and cannot do.

- **The treatment has not been tested for efficacy across diverse groups.**

A particular intervention may produce strong evidence for effectiveness in white middle-class female consumers, for example, but that doesn't mean it will be equally effective for other groups. One cannot assume, for example, that the effectiveness will be the same for men, African-Americans, Latinos, Asian-Americans, low-income consumers, or gay and lesbian consumers. Thus, the practitioner must ask whether the intervention has been shown to be effective for groups of which their particular client is a member. Perhaps the intervention is equally effective but that cannot be known until it is tested (Aisenberg, 2008).

- **It can be problematic to deliver an intervention developed in a resource-rich research environment in a resource-poor community environment.**

Many treatments are effective when the resources are there to provide the treatment fully in all its components for as long as necessary to produce the desired outcome. For example, let's say a treatment to improve social cognition in schizophrenia has shown excellent results in that the participants are significantly more likely, after treatment, to be employed, live independently, and have rewarding social relationships. The treatment was delivered via 2-hour, three times a week sessions over the course of a full year. A community-based agency wants to use the treatment, but can only afford to offer it for 1 hour, once a week for 3 months. One cannot be confident that a similar outcome will occur, because the treatment has been diluted significantly in terms of intensity and length of time it is offered (Hohmann & Shear, 2002).

These are just a few of the issues that we must wrestle with as we try to implement evidence-based practice in community-based settings. These issues will be revisited throughout the book. Some of the well-established evidence-based treatments available for the treatment of serious mental illness include the following: assertive community treatment, family psychoeducation, interpersonal psychotherapy, dialectical behavior therapy, cognitive-behavioral therapy, cognitive-enhancement therapy, supportive employment, solution-focused brief therapy, integrated treatment for co-occurring disorders, and a wide range of psychotropic medications. In the chapters addressing specific serious mental illnesses, all of these treatments will be addressed along with how to deliver the effective components of the treatments (to the extent that we know what they are) in community-based settings that are not necessarily "resource rich."

Fortunately, there are some decision-making tools that can help practitioners to "select, deliver, and evaluate individual and social interventions aimed at preventing or ameliorating client problems and social conditions" (Jenson & Howard, 2008, p. 158). Sackett et al. (2000) suggest five essential steps for employing evidence-based practice in one's clinical practice with clients.

Step 1 *Converting Practice Information Needs into Answerable Questions*

Answerable questions help the practitioner gather information with regard to the client population, type of intervention, and the desired outcomes. This helps to individualize the evidence-based practice approach to the client who will actually receive the treatment. For example, let's say a practitioner is working with several African-American clients with borderline personality disorder. These clients have experienced repeated hospitalizations because of depression and parasuicidal behavior. The practitioner is skilled in providing both dialectical behavior therapy (DBT) and brief psychodynamic psychotherapy (BPP). The question, then, is:

> *What is the evidence with regard to whether DBT or BPP is more effective in reducing symptoms of depression and repeated parasuicidal behavior in African-American clients with borderline personality disorder?*

Step 2 *Locating Evidence to Answer Questions*

Here the practitioner looks for evidence to answer their question from Step 1. So, the practitioner would look for studies comparing the two treatments, DBT and BPP, see if the researchers report evidence on the effectiveness of each treatment on symptoms of depression and parasuicidal behavior and, finally, check and be sure that African-American subjects were included in the studies. The Internet and search engines like Google Scholar can be helpful and quick, but books and, particularly, peer-reviewed journal articles are good traditional sources. Peer-reviewed journal articles provide some assurance that the study meets standards of scientific rigor. Many such articles are accessible via the Internet; however, more recent ones often require payment of a fee in order to read more than just the abstract.

Step 3 *Appraising the Evidence*

Here the practitioner evaluates the quality of the evidence and the methodology that produced it. The old standard is that randomized controlled clinical trials produce the most reliable evidence but, as noted above, their findings may not be generalizable to the population of clients the practitioner plans to treat. Meta-analyses, correlational studies, single-subject studies, quasi-experimental studies, and experimental studies are also good sources to evaluate. Many, however, have argued that research training in BSW and MSW schools of social work is inadequate to the task of preparing most practitioners to evaluate published research evidence (Thyer, 2004). If that is the case, then it is incumbent upon the practitioner to seek consultation from a colleague who has the requisite training.

Step 4 *Applying the Evidence in Practice*

Here the practitioner chooses the intervention with the most solid evidence of effectiveness to use in his or her treatment of the client. Sometimes, however, practitioners run into the kinds of barriers outlined in the previous section, and then have to weigh the advantages and disadvantages to offering the treatment under less than ideal circumstances. Sometimes something is better than nothing, other times not offering the treatment exactly as it was developed undermines any confidence in predicting what the outcomes may be. These are issues we will revisit as we talk about the established EBPs for the various mental illnesses discussed in subsequent chapters.

Step 5 *Evaluating the Process*

Having the knowledge and skills for evaluating one's own practice is a basic practice expectation today. Good intentions and being helpful are not enough for the current requirements for accountability by funders, government entities, and third-party payers. Direct practice social workers are commonly involved in evaluating the outcomes of their work with individuals, families, and small groups. Other social workers may be involved in efforts to evaluate the outcomes of whole programs of service. These efforts are important because they provide data to help us determine what works for whom. Even if a particular treatment has an established evidence base, most such treatments need additional studies done to expand the knowledge base with regard to how the treatment works. Social workers are often in a prime position to evaluate an EBP's effectiveness with populations that may not be included in clinical trials, such as low-income clients, clients of color, and clients with multiple complex challenges. Thus, evaluating the process of providing an EBP gives us data about how well the treatment works with the client population it treated and has the potential to extend the knowledge base further, which can inform future efforts to provide the treatment. Back to the hypothetical example given in Step 1:

After reviewing the peer-reviewed literature by using Google Scholar on the Internet, the practitioner concludes that, so far, research suggests that DBT and BPP are equally effective in reducing symptoms of depression and parasuicidal behavior in borderline personality disorder (see, e.g., Clarkin, Levy, Lenzenweger, & Kernberg, 2007). However, none of the studies compared the effectiveness with Whites and African-Americans and, in fact, the practitioner could find no studies with a significant proportion of African-American subjects. The practitioner had heard from a couple individual African-American clients who received DBT elsewhere that it had been helpful for them. After consulting with her supervisor, the practitioner decides to do a short trial of DBT skills groups with her African-American clients for 6 months, carefully evaluating at pre-determined intervals whether any changes in the target symptomatology occurs. It turns out that DBT significantly reduces both the depressive symptoms and the parasuicidal behavior for the clients treated. This finding is extremely important because it suggests that DBT, even when offered for a shorter time than that developed by the clinical trial, is effective with a new population of clients, that is, African-Americans with borderline personality in terms of two important target areas: depression and self-harming behavior. In collaboration with a social work professor at the local university, the practitioner disseminates this knowledge by writing a brief narrative report, which is published in a social work research journal.

Gibbs (2003) provides a concise summary of the process of evidence-based practice for practitioners as follows: "Placing the client's benefits first, evidence-based practitioners adopt a process of lifelong learning that involves continually posing specific questions of direct and practical importance to clients, searching effectively for the current best evidence to each question, and taking appropriate action guided by evidence" (p. 6). One way to obtain such lifelong learning is for social work practitioners to set a priority on learning about evidence-based practices when fulfilling continuing education requirements for one's practice license renewal. These continuing education units (CEUs) have to be earned anyway if one is to remain in active practice, and thus, it is a good avenue for busy practitioners to learn about EBP without undue burden.

Now that the reader has a basic understanding of recovery and evidence-based practice, we will turn to examining the current status of public mental health services.

THE STATUS OF PUBLIC MENTAL HEALTH SERVICES TODAY

NAMI: The National Alliance on Mental Illness

The National Alliance on Mental Illness (NAMI) (formerly the National Alliance for the Mentally Ill) is the largest grassroots advocacy group in the United States for individuals with mental illness and their families, and has multiple affiliates in every state in the nation and many worldwide. NAMI was founded in 1979 by a small group of parents, most of whom had adult children with schizophrenia, who felt that families' voices were not being heard by providers and policy makers, yet families were being asked to take on more responsibility in caring for their ill loved ones in the wake of deinstitutionalization. With determination and hard work, the NAMI organization was born, and its strength and influence has become greater over the decades. NAMI provides support to families and individuals affected by mental illness, education to families and communities about mental illness, and is involved in multiple advocacy efforts on behalf of families and consumers. NAMI members are also actively involved in raising awareness about mental illness, fighting stigma, and engaging in ongoing efforts to evaluate the services provided to families and consumers. NAMI is an invaluable resource for social workers working with families of loved ones with serious mental illness, and NAMI members view social workers as the key mental health professionals providing the link between families and provider systems (Handler, 2006).

Assess your comprehension of *the concept of "recovery" and what is meant by "evidence-based practice* by completing this quiz.

Grading the States 2009: NAMI's Report on the State of America's Mental Health System

In 2006, NAMI produced its first national report reviewing, state by state, the status of public mental health services in the United States. NAMI's second report, *Grading the States 2009*, lists which states have improved their grades, fallen, or remained stagnant and provides narrative descriptions of the status of public mental health services for each state. Today, our economy is continuing to struggle, cuts in many state budgets are adversely affecting mental health services and, once again, the issue of health care reform is on the national agenda. The 2009 report is introduced with a powerfully worded letter from Michael J. Fitzpatrick, who is a social worker and the executive director of NAMI. The letter begins as follows:

> Mental illness causes more disability than any other class of illness in the nation. One in four Americans experience mental illness at some point in their lives; twice

> as many of us live with schizophrenia than live with HIV/AIDS. Yet in 2003, the presidential New Freedom Commission on Mental Health found that the service system responsible for helping those with mental illnesses was fragmented and "in shambles". In America today, the people who must rely on this system are actually being oppressed by it, and many years of bad policy decisions have left emergency rooms, the criminal justice system, and families to shoulder the burden of responding to people in crisis. (Fitzpatrick, 2009, p. vii)

It is clear that in 2012, our national mental health care system is fragile, fragmented, inadequate and in crisis. Hope arose with the release of the President's New Freedom Commission on Mental Health report in 2003, which promised to transform mental health care in America (New Freedom Commission on Mental Health, 2003). That promise, however, has not been fulfilled, with the average state grade, according to the NAMI report, at a "D." It isn't a problem of not knowing what works to help people with serious mental illness. We have an array of evidence-based treatments—both psychosocial and pharmacological—that work. But we are falling short of getting these effective treatments, particularly the psychosocial treatments, to the consumers and families that need them (Steinberg, 2012). "We know what works to save lives and help people recover. In the face of crisis, America needs to move forward, not retreat. We cannot leave our most vulnerable citizens behind" (Aron, Honberg, Duckworth, et al., 2009, p. ix).

A Vision for Improving Community Mental Health Care

In every crisis, however, lies opportunity, and the *Grading the States 2009* report makes a number of specific, achievable recommendations based on information and data garnered from state mental health agencies, academic researchers, health care associations, and federal agencies (Aron, Honberg, Duckworth, et al., 2009). To further inform the recommendations, NAMI conducted a nationwide web-based survey that resulted in over 13,000 responses from consumers and family members. Following a review of all this data, NAMI identified what it calls "pillars" that should collectively form the framework producing a high-quality public mental health system of care. To achieve the goal of transforming our current system, these 10 pillars, or characteristics, must be in place. Such a transformed system would be

- Comprehensive
- Integrated
- Adequately funded
- Focused on wellness and recovery
- Safe and respectful
- Accessible
- Culturally competent
- Consumer-centered and consumer and family driven
- Well staffed and trained
- Transparent and accountable

These 10 pillars are very similar to the basic principles of community mental health care proposed as an underlying framework for the Community Mental Health Centers Construction Act in 1963 (Sands, 1991), although they deconstruct some of the broader

---

Fitzpatrick, M.J. (2009). Letter from NAMI Executive Director. In: Aron, L., Honberg, R., Duckworth, K., et al. Grading the states 2009: A report on America=s health care system for adults with serious mental illness. Arlington, VA: National Alliance on Mental Illness. (pp. vii–viii).

principles into more specific components. It is important to recognize that these pillars also incorporate many aspects of the traditional principles of clinical practice that social work has always embraced, such as the focus on recovery as it is defined today, client self-determination, respect for the consumer's inherent worth and dignity, cultural competence, transparency, and services that are consumer and family driven and emphasize collaboration (Hepworth, Rooney, Rooney, et al., 2009). These are not new approaches for social workers, although they represent a new perspective for many others who are involved in administering and providing services to consumers and families, and for the system as a whole.

Read How the States are Faring on Four Basic Components of Mental Health Care.

Policy Recommendations for Positively Transforming the U.S. Public Mental Health System

NAMI argues that in order to transform our nation's mental health system and make the New Freedom Commission's vision a reality, "the federal government, governors, and state legislators must take action in five key areas" (Aron, Honberg, Duckworth, et al., 2009, p. xi). These areas are as follows (pp. xi–xii of Executive Summary section in the report):

1. *Increase Public Funding for Mental Health Care Services* The first policy recommendation is to increase public funding for mental health care services. There are a number of avenues for accomplishing this, including creative reallocation of resources, encouraging the establishment of dedicated trusts, and instituting modest tax increases. A good example of a creative, non-burdensome tax increase is California's Proposition 63, known as the Mental Health Services Act (MHSA), passed in November 2004. Proposition 63 authorized funding of the MHSA by imposing an additional 1 percent tax on individual, but not corporate, taxable income in excess of 1 million dollars. By increasing the taxes of only high-income individuals, the voter-approved MHSA initiative obtained the necessary funding to develop, through an extensive stakeholder process, a comprehensive approach to expanding and transforming community-based mental health services and supports for California residents. Programs that have been enhanced or developed thanks to Proposition 63 funds have enabled more consumers to get the help they need and avoid homelessness, hospitalization, or other negative outcomes (Bhavnani, 2009).

   Bambauer (2005) states that Proposition 63 was successful for three reasons. First, the tax increase would be paid by less than 0.1 percent of the California population and people generally support health-related expenditures as long as they don't have to be the ones to pay for them. Second, the groups that supported Proposition 63 (e.g., nurses, teachers, and police officers) were well funded and viewed as trustworthy by the general public. And, finally, the public was unconvinced by the arguments posed by the opponents of Proposition 63.
2. *Improve Data Collection, Outcomes Measurement, and Accountability* The second policy recommendation suggested by the NAMI report for positively transforming the U.S. public mental health system is to improve data collection, outcomes measurement, and accountability. As noted previously, mental health data collection in the United States is fragmented, uneven, and uncoordinated. In order to truly transform mental health care nationally, the federal government must reestablish mental health data collection as a priority and develop standardized data collection

procedures that are applied consistently across all the states. Evidence-based practices outcomes must be tracked, particularly as EBPs are translated to community-based services, and utilization of high-cost services should be monitored, such as tracking wait times in psychiatric emergency rooms.

3. *Integrate Mental and Physical Health Care* The third policy recommendation suggested by the NAMI report for positively transforming the U.S. public mental health system is to integrate mental and physical health care. Examples of steps that could facilitate this goal include expanding successful pilot programs that integrate physical and mental health care, house primary care services and mental health services in the same clinic building, increase private and public insurance coverage for preventive care, and increase incentives to encourage the use of health and wellness programs. *Learn about a study utilizing consumer focus groups.*

4. *Promote Recovery and Respect* The fourth policy recommendation suggested by the NAMI report for positively transforming the U.S. public mental health system is to enhance and improve efforts to promote recovery and respect for consumers and families. To promote recovery and respect for consumers, public mental health services must support the development of consumer-driven services as much as possible. Such efforts include employing peer specialists and funding peer-run services and peer-education programs. This also means instituting linguistically competent services, an essential component of culturally competent services. Additional recommendations voiced by the NAMI report include investing resources in reducing violations of client and family rights, increasing supportive and competitive employment opportunities for consumers, and providing a full range of housing options to meet clients' individual needs from fully supported housing to independent living. The final policy recommendation suggested by the NAMI report for positively transforming the U.S. public mental health system is to increase services for those individuals with serious mental illness who are most at risk.

5. *Increase Services for People with Serious Mental Illnesses Who Are Most at Risk* In an ideal world, all people who suffer from psychological and emotional problems should receive treatment to help alleviate their distress. Unfortunately, the real world does not offer unlimited health and mental health care resources to meet everyone's needs. As a result, we must set priorities for how our increasingly scarce resources should be allocated. Repeatedly, public mental health initiatives have set a priority on serving those individuals suffering from the most severe and persistent of mental disorders. However, repeatedly, this goal has not been achieved. We cannot continue to repeat this failure. The NAMI report suggests a number of steps to enhance the probability that our nation can succeed in serving those individuals with the most severe and disabling mental disorders who are most at risk.

In summary, NAMI's *Grading the States 2009* report on the state of America's mental health system is an urgent call for action."We need to rise above existing inadequacy. We need to save lives and help people to recover. Transformation of the mental health care system will take time. It will occur incrementally. We can measure its progress, but progress will only occur if we make it happen" (Aron, Honberg, Duckworth, et al., 2009, p. xii).

Assess your comprehension of *the status of public mental health services today* by completing this quiz.

THE STATUS OF PSYCHIATRIC SOCIAL WORK FROM THE 1950S TO THE PRESENT TIME

The Social Work Profession Begins to Evolve

Where was the profession of social work at the time that Erving Goffman was doing his fieldwork and the country began to see that alternatives to the asylum must be explored? By 1950, the profession of social work was well established and those social workers who worked with individuals with mental illness were called "psychiatric social workers." Psychiatric social work began at Massachusetts General Hospital in 1907 when social workers were hired to work with mentally ill patients, but it wasn't until 1914 that a social services department was established at the Boston Psychopathic Hospital and the title "psychiatric social worker" was used for the first time.

Social workers, however, were stunned and dismayed when, in an address to the National Conference on Social Welfare, educator Abraham Flexner concluded that social work did not qualify as a profession (Flexner, 1915). The impact of this was significant and long lasting. Flexner acknowledged that social work exhibited some traits associated with the professions; for example, he said that social work was intellectual, derived its knowledge from science and learning, had a professional self-consciousness, and was altruistic. However, he concluded that because social work lacked an "educationally communicable technique" and was overly broad in areas of responsibility, it could not be considered a profession. Social workers immediately and consciously set out to remedy these identified deficiencies by emphasizing professionalization based on social casework with individuals, families, and small groups, eschewing the former focus on public welfare and labor reform.

Mary Richmond's book *Social Diagnosis*, published in 1917, was viewed as a seminal work in establishing an educationally communicable technique for social work (Richmond, 1917), and in 1926 the American Association of Psychiatric Social Workers (AAPSW) was founded, as social work was increasingly comprised of social caseworkers and clinically oriented practitioners. Some social workers, however, were not clinicians, and so in 1928 the Milford Conference convened to discuss whether social work should be a unified profession with knowledge and skills cutting across practice specialties or should be simply an umbrella for several different technical specialties. The conference concluded that social work can and should be unified via *eight generic aspects of casework.*

Soon thereafter, textbooks designed to teach the knowledge, values, and skills for social casework emerged (see, e.g., Coyle, 1930; Robinson & Taft, 1930) and social workers established roles for themselves helping people with mental illness in the asylums and in the community. By 1950, social work was considered one of the key professions, along with psychiatry, psychology, and nursing, providing important therapeutic services to individuals with mental illness.

The Role of Clinical Social Workers in Public Mental Health Services

Clinically trained social workers are the primary providers of public mental health services today overall, and the main providers of services to individuals with severe and persistent mental illness and their families (Eack & Newhill, 2008). In resource poor areas, social workers are often the only professional providers of such services (O'Neill, 1999) and, thus, are critically important in serving those clients who are the most vulnerable and disadvantaged. For many of our severely mentally ill (SMI) clients, struggling with the consequences of living in poverty is one of their greatest challenges (Saraceno & Barbui, 1997).

How do the numbers stack up? The latest edition of *Mental Health: United States*, published in 2006 by the Substance Abuse and Mental Health Services Administration (SAMHSA) indicates that social workers constitute the largest group of mental health care providers in the United States (Center for Mental Health Services [CMHS], 2006). As of 2004, NASW reported that, amongst their members, there are over 103,000 clinically trained social workers in the country as compared to only 25,000 psychiatrists, 85,000 psychologists, and 9,000 psychiatric nurses. Given that only about half of clinical social workers are members of NASW (O'Neill, 1999), the actual total estimate would be around 206,000—more than the combined totals of the other three allied mental health disciplines.

A 2003 NASW membership survey (Smith, 2003) also showed that mental health is the leading field of social work practice, with half (50%) of currently employed social workers reporting that their primary, secondary, or tertiary practice area was in mental health. Thirty-seven percent reported that their primary practice area was mental health, three times higher than any other area of practice identified by the respondents. The prominent role of social workers has even been noticed by the media. In 1985, an article in the *New York Times* reported a quiet but definitive revolution in psychotherapy, stating that social workers outnumber psychiatrists two to one in terms of who is providing psychotherapeutic services (Coleman, 1985). Today, based on the SAMHSA and estimated NASW data, social workers outnumber psychiatrists eight to one.

How Social Workers Are Alike and Different from Psychiatrists, Psychologists, and Nurses

It is important to recognize that the four allied mental health disciplines—psychiatry, psychology, clinical social work, and psychiatric nursing—are both alike and different in important ways that shape and inform their respective approaches to practice with individuals with severe mental illness and their families. This is an issue that is often confusing to clients and their families and, thus, it is important that all mental health practitioners are able to explain to service recipients "who does what and how," that is, what type of professional one should seek out for what kind of problem and, equally important, what kind of help one can expect to receive.

Social workers are, indeed, similar to psychologists, psychiatrists, and nurses in several ways. First, across all the disciplines, there is the use of the face-to-face relationship as the primary vehicle to promote awareness, change, and growth and improve psychosocial functioning for individuals, families, and groups. This face-to-face relationship includes working with people via a range of mechanisms for interaction including in-person contacts, contact via the telephone, home visits, Internet communication, and snail-mail letters. One of the strengths that social workers possess is the ability to be flexible and resourceful in meeting clients' needs. *Read an example from the author's practice.*

In addition to sharing the use of the face-to-face relationship, all four disciplines share a body of knowledge about theories of human behavior along with evidence based intervention approaches and techniques. Finally, practitioners across the four mental health disciplines are capable of making client assessments and providing treatment

Clinical social workers are different, however, from the allied disciplines in three important ways. The hallmark of the social work perspective is viewing individuals within the context of their environment, and their work in mental health is multidimensional, combining psychological, social, and practical elements (NASW, 2009). Unlike psychiatrists and psychologists, social workers have traditionally viewed clients and their problems in relation to multiple contexts in which problems occur, and they pursue interventions that focus on clients' community and political environments as well as intra- and interpersonal domains. This perspective is rooted in the origins of the profession in that social work "was established to address a panoply of social concerns associated with industrial growth and turmoil, poverty, child welfare, family relations, malnutrition and health care, infant mortality, waves of new immigrants and internal migration and other maladies associated with terrible slums in rapidly expanding cities and urban areas" (Hopps & Lowe, 2008, p. 144). Although psychiatry, psychology, and nursing have recently developed subspecialties that address practice in the community and with families (CMHS, 2006; Shore, 1989), many professionals within these disciplines still deliver treatment to mentally ill individuals separate from the family and community, and may not see the importance of doing so. *Review an example from the author's practice.*

Another difference is that social workers place a strong emphasis on identifying and supporting clients' strengths along with promoting connections between clients and the strengths present in the client's family and community that support optimal psychosocial functioning. Of course, social workers identify the problems and challenges that lead clients to seek help, but this is balanced with an active recognition of strengths and resources. For example, the *Diagnostic and Statistical Manual of Mental Disorders*, which is the "diagnostic bible" produced by the American Psychiatric Association, is often criticized by social workers because of its heavy emphasis on identifying pathology to the exclusion of identifying strengths (Corcoran & Walsh, 2008). In addition, where institutional and interpersonal barriers interfere with clients' needs, social workers act to eliminate these obstacles and create new resources that address the identified needs. Example:

> Joan was a social worker for a child and family service agency in a rural area of Mississippi. One day, a young woman came to the clinic asking for help. She had been battered by her husband and was afraid to return home. Joan's small town did not have a battered women's shelter or any formal services for abused women. However, Joan did not tell the client that no services were available. Instead, she told her that, although their town did not have a shelter, she would find the client a safe place for the night and pull together whatever resources she could to help her. In addition, Joan took action to mobilize some of the local charitable organizations in the town with the goal of securing funding to build a battered women's shelter. When needed resources do not exist, social workers take action to develop new resources to meet clients' needs.

Finally, social work is unique because the profession has always emphasized the importance of serving oppressed, at-risk, and vulnerable populations as part of its central mission. In spite of criticisms from some that we have abandoned our mission to serve the disadvantaged (Specht & Courtney, 1994), more recent research by Newhill and Korr (2004) shows that in the area of the care and treatment of individuals with severe mental illness, "social workers have not abandoned their mission, but continue to forge ahead despite sometimes overwhelming systemic obstacles," adding, "our results make us proud of our profession and its continued commitment to serving members of society who are most in need," specifically, those with severe and persistent mental illness (p. 304).

Read *The Varied Roles of Social Workers in Community Mental Health Services.*

The Importance of Empowerment and Advocacy

There are two important aspects of social work practice that are particularly relevant to working with severely mentally ill clients that must be highlighted. These two aspects are *empowerment* and *advocacy*. In general, both empowerment and advocacy are concerned with the management of power to meet clients' needs. As Leadbetter (2002) notes:

> Empowerment and advocacy are both concerned with a shift of power or emphasis towards meeting the needs and rights of people who otherwise would be marginalised or oppressed. Beyond this generalisation, the concepts of empowerment and advocacy are not simple and as such are almost impossible to define. Where the term 'empowerment' is used it often covers a whole range of activities from consulting with service users to involvement in service planning. (Leadbetter, 2002, p. 201)

The notion of empowerment as central to the mission of social work is recognized worldwide. The International Association of Schools of Social Work (IASSW) and the International Federation of Social Workers developed a definition of "social work," which was jointly agreed upon June 27, 2001, at a meeting of the two organizations in Denmark. The IASSW definition emphasizes the importance of change through problem solving and the promotion of empowerment to enhance people's self-efficacy and well-being with the overall goal of social justice (IASSW, 2001).

First, let's consider how empowerment can be defined. We talk about empowerment all the time in social work, often with the assumption of a shared definition but, sometimes, without being explicit about that definition. Payne (2005) defines empowerment as the following:

> Empowerment seeks to help clients to gain power of decision and action over their own lives by reducing the effect of social or personal blocks to exercising existing power, increasing capacity and self-confidence to use power and transferring power from the group and individuals. (p. 295)

More simply, empowerment may be defined as enhanced feelings of competence resulting from self-directed activity on the part of clients. Why is this important?

There is an old Chinese proverb that says "Give a man a fish and you feed him for a day. Teach a man to fish and you feed him for a lifetime." This sums up the basic rationale for the importance of empowerment. Unless you intend to take all of your clients home with you and take care of them for the rest of their—and your—lives, you have a responsibility to facilitate your clients' ability to become empowered. When people are empowered, they achieve what Albert Bandura (1997) calls "self-efficacy," that is, the client holds the belief that they are capable of accomplishing a particular task or reaching a goal.

The second aspect of the therapeutic process particularly relevant to working with individuals with severe mental illness is a commitment to *advocacy*. Everybody needs an advocate at some point in his or her life. Most people can call upon their *natural advocates*, that is, their friends, family members, church members, or neighbors. This, however, requires that one have a sufficient, resilient social support network. In the absence of that and to keep a client's natural support system from burning out, you as your client's social

---

Leadbetter, M. (2002) >>Empowerment and Advocacy== in Adams, R., Dominelli, L. and Payne, M. (eds) Social Work: Themes, Issues and Critical Debates, Basingstoke, Palgrave in association with the Open University.

Payne, M. (2005) Modern Social Work Theory (3rd ed.). Chicago, Ill.: Lyceum.

worker may take on the role of advocate. Commitment to advocacy involves a range of activities, including

- Working on behalf of clients
- Linking clients with resources
- Monitoring clients' treatment plans
- Mediating solutions to problems
- Reducing institutional barriers

The basic principle for being a good advocate who promotes empowerment is that you aim to *facilitate* clients reaching their goals and resources on their own, and are directive only if facilitation is not sufficient. In other words, you support and teach the client how to learn to be his or her own advocate with his or her own voice as much as possible, but you step in to do that for the client only if and when the client is unable to do so. For example, let's consider that a social worker is working with a client who has bipolar disorder. When the client is stable, he is able to advocate on his own behalf for what he needs effectively. However, during periods of illness, he cannot effectively advocate for himself, and so you may step in to do that on his behalf. Here is where tools such as an advance directive can maintain self-advocacy during times of illness. This will be discussed in the next chapter.

CONCLUSION

Since 1950, there have been monumental changes in how individuals with serious mental illness are treated and cared for in the United States. Our ideas about mental illness, what causes it and how it might be effectively treated, have changed considerably, and most realize that mental illness can strike anyone and affects more families than previously recognized. As the realities of asylum life began to enter public consciousness, many were troubled by what was revealed, particularly by evidence that living in a total institution can not only cause an individual to become institutionalized but also can produce a syndrome called institutional neurosis. The combination of the development of newer effective psychotropic medications and developing civil libertarian ideology, coupled with the desire to save money, led to the idea that perhaps treatment for people with mental illness ought to be provided in the community, where people would have more freedom of choice and the deleterious effects of long-term hospitalization could be avoided. Thus, deinstitutionalization emerged and the Community Mental Health Services Act was passed.

There is no question that deinstitutionalization arose from the best of intentions, however, many unintended consequences, such as the revolving door syndrome, emerged, and we began to realize that although long-term hospitalization is not desirable, brief hospitalization may not afford enough time for recovery for many clients, much less stabilization on medication. Decades after its beginning, most mental health policy analysts have concluded that deinstitutionalization has, overall, been one of our most stunning public policy failures, even though it proved successful for countless individual clients.

Many new, more effective, evidence-based interventions for the treatment of mental illness have been developed that have benefitted many consumers and families, although full access to these treatments remains a challenge. Consumers and families, through grassroots efforts, have developed strong advocacy organizations, and this has contributed to a paradigm shift in how we perceive people who live with mental illness and how we perceive their families. This paradigm shift is called *recovery* or the recovery perspective, that is, the idea that all individuals who live with mental illness have the capacity to live fulfilling lives, provided they have the right supports and resources. This has served to combat stigma to some extent. Families are no longer blamed for causing their loved one's illness and are seen as valuable partners in treatment. These changes, however, have not occurred evenly across all areas of the country and the old stereotypes and ways of providing services stubbornly persist, but change continues to occur for the better, and social workers have played a prominent role in instituting and supporting these changes. In the next chapter, we will look at some of the legal and ethical issues that currently exist that must be considered when delivering services to our clients.

Assess your application and analysis of this chapter's contents by completing the *Chapter Review*.

Chapter 3

Legal and Ethical Issues Relevant to Practice with Individuals with Serious Mental Illness and Their Families

INTRODUCTION

The Case of Jack and Bob

Jack is a community mental health agency social worker who rotates with other social workers in the role of "officer of the day" (OD) for crisis situations. One day, when Jack is OD, several individuals come to the agency to complain about one of their neighbors, a young man named Bob who is well known to Jack and the mental health center and has been treated for years off and on for chronic undifferentiated schizophrenia. Bob is an only child, and after his parents passed away he inherited their home, located in an upscale neighborhood of the city. Things went well for a while, the neighbors report, but one day Bob began hanging empty milk cartons from the branches of the trees in his front yard. He also tied brightly colored bows on the trees along with other odd and unusual ornaments. Then, Bob began piling old junk and garbage in his front yard, and the neighbors complain the whole thing is an eyesore, it smells bad, and "you just don't do that kind of thing in our neighborhood." To top things off, Bob has been seen sitting on his fence and talking to himself, and the neighbors state that they are "just sure he is going to do something." They demand that "somebody pick him up" and hospitalize him. In response to the neighbors' concerns, Jack makes a home visit to see Bob. Bob is the same as he always has been, although he seems a little more anxious and admits to hearing voices. He denies any suicidal or homicidal thoughts, is eating and sleeping well, and claims he is taking his medication. Jack concludes that Bob does not qualify for involuntary civil commitment. When the neighbors are informed of this, they threaten to make sure Jack is fired from his job. Agency policy is to provide clients with the least restrictive alternatives but to keep community relations positive as well.

What should Jack do? Should Jack "stretch" the civil commitment criteria and hospitalize Bob anyway, and thus pacify the neighbors—and perhaps Bob would improve a little? Or should Jack interpret the civil commitment criteria strictly, support and respect Bob's right to live as he pleases, and tell the neighbors they'll just have to live with the situation? What are the ethical principles involved? What solution would be in Bob's best interest? How does Jack resolve such complicated issues?

This chapter will address the legal and ethical issues that clinical social workers and other mental health professionals commonly face when practicing in community mental/behavioral health settings with clients with serious mental illness. The case of Jack and Bob, above, involves complicated ethical and legal dilemmas that need to be resolved. This case is based on an actual real-life case from the author's practice, although identifying information has been disguised. Towards the end of the chapter, we will revisit the case of Jack and Bob and address how the issues were actually resolved and what alternatives were considered by the social worker. Before addressing the specific legal and ethical issues, however, it is important to have a good understanding of the basic principles of practice in community mental health settings, because the various ethical and legal issues relate to and often challenge these basic principles.

BASIC PRINCIPLES OF COMMUNITY MENTAL/ BEHAVIORAL HEALTH PRACTICE

The 1961 Joint Commission on Mental Health report "Action for Mental Health," which provided the foundation for President John F. Kennedy's plan for new community-based programs for mental health and mental retardation, was based on certain guiding principles that provided a framework for the 1963 CMHC Act. Although much has changed in the way community mental health services are provided, these basic principles are still in place today and are reflected in the recommendations made in NAMI's recent *Grading the States 2009* report, discussed in Chapter 2.

Langsley (1985) states that there are six basic principles of how good community mental health services should be delivered. These principles are based on Gerald Caplan's (1964) model of "preventive psychiatry" in which the responsibility of community mental health services is to meet the needs of the total community population, provide comprehensive services, ensure continuity of care, have active participation of consumers, linkage to other health and service sectors, and provide good accessibility (Langsley, 1985). The six principles are as follows:

1. Community mental/behavioral health services should be *accessible* to those who seek treatment;
2. Community mental/behavioral health services delivered to local service units or catchment areas must be *accountable* to the entire community;
3. Community mental/behavioral health services should be *comprehensive*;
4. Community mental/behavioral health services must *ensure continuity of care*;
5. Community mental/behavioral health treatment providers should be composed of a *multidisciplinary team*; and
6. Community mental/behavioral health care services must *emphasize prevention.*

What do these principles mean in terms of implementation? Let's review each of them.

Community Mental/Behavioral Health Services Should Be Accessible to Those Who Seek Treatment

The first principle is that community mental/behavioral health services should be accessible to those who seek treatment. Accessibility takes a variety of forms. First is location. To be accessible, services must be located in a place that is convenient for those who need services. Thus, the service facilities must be near where people reside and where they work, not off in a remote area. The facilities must be located near reliable sources of public transportation since many of the clients we serve, particularly those who are most at risk and disadvantaged, rely on public transportation. Another aspect of accessibility is the facility's hours of service. Services must be available in the evening and on weekends, not just during the day. Many of our clients have jobs that do not allow them to take time off for personal business and, if they do, they lose wages.

Another aspect of accessibility is how easy it is for someone to find out information about the agency, that is, what services are provided, and the agency's address and phone number. For example, a mental health agency should be listed in the phone book under "mental health" and the name of the agency should reflect what the agency does. Some agencies sport euphemistic names that are meaningless to the lay public or the name is along the lines of "County X services for Title Y," again, meaningless to the lay public. My colleagues and I would wryly joke that it seemed as if some agencies didn't *want* people to find them, fearing that the demand might be overwhelming if everyone needing services actually showed up asking for services (Langsley, 1985).

Another aspect of accessibility is affordability. The cost of services must be made affordable, on a sliding scale, or subsidized so all people in need can access and receive the services without financial hardship. Finally, services provided should match the needs of the populations served, that is, services must be culturally competent and culturally relevant, and flexibly tailored to meet individual needs. Language translators, including individuals trained in sign language, should be available when needed. Finally, services should be accessible to those with disabilities and, overall, clients must feel comfortable, welcome and encouraged to use the services (Langsley, 1985; Sands, 1991).

At this juncture some introductory comments should be made about the key findings from an important groundbreaking comprehensive report on the mental health status of racial and ethnic minorities in the United States by former surgeon general David Satcher, M.D. (U.S. Department of Health and Human Services [DHHS], 1999a, 1999b). What this report concludes speaks volumes about the problem of unequal access to mental health services in America today. Although the report was released over a decade ago, the problems identified are, at best, only partially resolved and continue to persist in many areas of the country today. We will be returning to various aspects of this report throughout the book, but the key findings are summarized below.

Mental Health: Culture, Race, and Ethnicity

In 1999, former surgeon general David Satcher released an unprecedented comprehensive report entitled *Mental Health: Culture, Race, and Ethnicity*. In it, Dr. Satcher reports that members of minority groups in the United States suffer a disproportionate burden of mental illness because they often have less access to services than other Americans; receive lower quality care, often from services that are fragmented, costly, and inadequate; and are less likely to seek help when they are in distress, in part because of the considerable stigma attached to mental illness in many cultures. The report concluded that a large gap remains between the need for services and the services actually provided (Ault-Brutus, 2012; DHHS, 1999a).

Although mental illness does not discriminate on the basis of race and ethnicity, racial and ethnic minorities are overrepresented among those who are the most vulnerable and in need of mental health care, including those who are poor, homeless, institutionalized, incarcerated, and survivors of trauma (DHHS, 1999a). Left untreated, mental illness exacts a heavy toll not only on the ill individual, but also his or her family, community, and society as a whole. Unfortunately, most individuals with a diagnosable mental illness, regardless of race or ethnicity, do not receive appropriate treatment, with minority individuals least likely to access such treatment (DHHS, 1999a; Newhill & Harris, 2007). When it comes to mental health and access to mental health care, race, culture, and ethnicity matter (Ault-Brutus, 2012; Newhill, 1990).

Dr. Satcher offers a number of recommendations in his vision for the future to solve the persistent gap between the need for services and the services actually provided (DHHS, 1999b). These courses of action include the following (DHHS, 1999b):

- **Continue to build the science base today** for improving existing treatments and developing new effective interventions.
- **Overcome stigma,** which is powerful and pervasive, to reduce the burden of mental illness by dispelling myths, providing accurate knowledge, and encouraging help-seeking by those in need.
- **Improve public awareness of effective treatments** so people can be informed about the choices they have amongst the range of effective treatments. Treatments generally fall within several broad categories—psychotherapy, medication therapy, and rehabilitation—with multiple alternatives within each category.
- **Ensure the supply of mental health services and providers** across all areas of the nation.
- **Ensure delivery of state-of-the-art treatments** developed and refined by research studies to community settings to more effectively bridge the gap between research and practice.
- **Tailor treatment to age, gender, race, and culture,** which is the essence of what we call culturally competent practice. (DHHS, 1999b).
- **Facilitate entry into treatment** by improving access at both the private and public levels via multiple "portals of entry" from services where clients in need of mental health services are often first identified, such as primary health care settings, schools, and child welfare services.
- **Reduce financial barriers to treatment** via establishing and maintaining parity between mental health coverage and other health coverage in insurance plans, subsidized services, sliding scales, and basic national health care reform.

All of these actions will improve access to care for all Americans, including those who are most vulnerable and disadvantaged. Although we have made progress in some areas, there is much left to be accomplished.

Community Mental/Behavioral Health Services Delivered to Local Service Units or Catchment Areas Must Be Accountable to the Entire Community

The key to community accountability is ensuring that the voices of all stakeholders are heard and every constituent group has a "place at the table" for input on developing mental health policies and how and what services are delivered. For example, agency boards should be made up of local citizens who have a broad sense of the needs of the community, clients/consumers who receive services and family members of consumers who receive services, as well as representatives of the agency.

Community accountability also means ensuring that services are commensurate with changing community needs via conducting regular needs assessments (Langley, 1985).

For example, a community may at one time have been a "young community" and, thus, their community mental health center provided a wide array of children's mental health services. However, let's imagine that the primary source of employment disappears, the young families move away, and the community begins to age. A needs assessment might reveal that the need for children's mental health services has significantly diminished and, instead, there is a growing need for aging services and mental health services for older adults. The service providers must change if they are to meet the community's changing needs.

Community accountability also means meeting the needs of those community members who are the most vulnerable and at risk for having their mental health needs unmet. Such members might include members of culturally different groups, undocumented immigrant workers, and individuals who are poor, incarcerated, homeless, and economically disadvantaged.

Community Mental/Behavioral Health Services Should Be Comprehensive

The third principle of community mental health practice is that community mental/behavioral health services should be comprehensive. As noted in Chapter 2, the Community Mental Health Services Act mandated that every community mental health center must provide, at a minimum, five core services: (1) inpatient care, (2) outpatient care, (3) community care/day treatment/partial hospitalization care, (4) psychiatric emergency services, and (5) research and education. In addition, it mandated that there should be a range of alternatives within each core service area. ***Read an example from the author's experience.***

Community Mental/Behavioral Health Services Must Ensure Continuity of Care

The fourth principle of community mental health practice is that community mental/behavioral health care services must ensure continuity of care. The concept and importance of assuring continuity of care in planning services has been emphasized in medicine and nursing since the 1940s (Rosenthal & Miller, 1979; Straub & Parker, 1966), and its importance in assuring good client outcomes is rarely questioned. To wit, Becker, Drachman, and Kirscht (1974), in an article on pediatric outpatient services, state that "the need to provide 'continuity of care' is a basic public health and medical care tenet, a fundamental of comprehensive health services and a sine qua non to what is currently viewed as good medical care" (p. 1062). But how do we define the concept of "continuity of care"? What is it, exactly?

Bachrach (1981), in a conceptual analysis of continuity of care for "chronic mental patients," says that "continuity of care may be best understood as a process involving the orderly, uninterrupted movement of patients among the diverse elements of the service delivery system" (p. 1449). When deconstructed, the concept of continuity of care has four essential dimensions:

1. A *temporal dimension*, in terms of continuity of care being longitudinal in nature;
2. An *individual dimension*, in that "the care is planned with and for the patient and his [or her] family" (Straub & Parker, 1966, p. 217);

3. A *cross-sectional dimension*, meaning that "at any point in the course of a patient's treatment he [or she] may receive a variety of services related to his [or her] many needs," that is, continuity of care must be comprehensive (Bachrach, 1981, p. 1450);
4. Finally, continuity of care has a *flexibility dimension*, meaning that care moves forward at a pace commensurate with what the client can and wants to do. In other words, care that is flexible "relieves the patient of pressures that may be placed on him [or her] always to exhibit 'progress' or to move 'forward' along a continuum" (Bachrach, p. 1450).

Thus, continuity of care is longitudinal, cross-sectional, flexible, and client and family centered. This is very compatible with today's notion of recovery. Although all of us who have worked with individuals with serious mental illness know that continuity of care is essential to clients doing well and achieving recovery, the research data has yet to prove this conclusively. Adair, McDougall, Beckie, et al., (2003), in a meta-analysis of journal articles on the topic of continuity of care published 1990–2002, concluded that there is little existing empirical evidence *proving* that continuity of care leads to positive client outcomes, *however*, this "may be primarily attributable to the underdevelopment of measures . . . measurement of continuity of care must become more sophisticated before key questions about the association of continuity of care with outcomes can be examined and before the effectiveness of interventions designed to improve continuity of care can be rigorously evaluated" (p. 1351).

Meanwhile, social workers who work with this population know all too well what happens to clients with serious mental illness when continuity of care is not present. They often "fall through the cracks," meaning that lack of continuity, coordination of services, and follow-up often results in clients relapsing from their illnesses, ending up on the streets or in jail, using substances again, or experiencing other adverse outcomes. Supporting and maintaining continuity of care is usually accomplished through developing positive cooperative relationships amongst providers and consistent liaisons across service entities, which is an ongoing task usually shouldered by social workers and case managers.

Treatment Providers Should Constitute a Multidisciplinary Team

This fifth principle of community mental health practice recognizes that clients have multiple needs and wants that can only be met collectively by a team of individuals representing a range of disciplines. Such a team also facilitates the multidimensional bio-psycho-social-spiritual-cultural approach to working with clients and families and contributes to a holistic understanding of each client and family. Such a team draws from a wide range of professionals including clinical social workers, psychiatrists, psychologists, psychiatric nurses, psychiatric technicians, case managers, recreation therapists, psychosocial rehabilitation workers, residential treatment staff, music therapists, art therapists, and nutritionists, all of whom can participate in the client's care. In addition, the client/consumer and family would participate as members of the treatment team as well. Not every consumer requires each discipline represented, it depends on each individual's needs and wants. Consumer participation means that consumers should be able to make informed choices in what treatments are provided and, with the consumer's agreement, family members may also participate in treatment planning meetings and in the development of advance directives about care (advance directives are discussed in more detail below). The evidence-based treatment modality that embraces this principle the fullest is the Program for Assertive Community Treatment (PACT), in which a team of mental health professionals from a range of disciplines provides the treatment. PACT will be discussed in detail in Chapter 9.

Community Mental/Behavioral Health Care Services Must Emphasize Prevention

The sixth and final principle of community mental health practice is that community mental/behavioral health care services must emphasize prevention. Ways of implementing this principle include case finding, crisis intervention and psychiatric emergency services, education, rehabilitation, and psychotherapeutic interventions. As an example, "case finding" is an approach to prevention that is well established in the fields of medicine and public health, and may be defined as "the act of locating individuals with a disease" (Mosby's Medical Dictionary, 2009). The idea behind case finding is that rather than waiting for a sick individual to seek help and then reacting to that, the case finder goes out into the community to proactively *locate* individuals who are ill, preferably at the early stages of the illness, or who are at risk for becoming ill.

In social work, this concept extends to individuals suffering from other kinds of social problems or who are at risk for developing such problems. The hope, with case finding, is that such proactive efforts can serve to "catch" difficulties early on when they are easier to solve or treat, thus *preventing* more serious problems or pathology from setting in. This is the primary argument for the provision of crisis intervention: Addressing people's crises early and quickly may serve to prevent the onset of more serious problems later (Slaikeu, 1984).

Good examples of the use of case finding can be found in many homeless outreach programs. There are many outreach programs in the United States to serve individuals who are homeless and living in the streets. Street life, in general, is not good for one's health, physically, mentally, or spiritually. People who are homeless and living in the streets are likely to be victimized by others; become depressed and malnourished; get involved with taking illicit drugs and using alcohol; engage in behaviors placing them at risk for contracting a range of diseases including HIV, sexually transmitted diseases, hepatitis; and such folks are at risk for ending up involved in the criminal justice system for a variety of legal infractions that may actually simply represent their efforts to survive.

Assess your comprehension of *the six basic principles of community mental/behavioral health practice* by completing this quiz.

THE IMPORTANCE OF PREVENTION IN COMMUNITY/ BEHAVIORAL MENTAL HEALTH SOCIAL WORK

The community mental health principle emphasizing the importance of prevention draws heavily from the public health model "and in its most simplistic form emanates from the infectious disease [model] where an accurate understanding of etiology permits the total avoidance of disease" (Langsley, 1985, p. 1885). Preventing a disease with a single etiological agent, for example, the mycobacterium that causes tuberculosis, is straightforward. Most mental illnesses, however, are caused or brought to bear by the interaction of several actual or hypothesized etiological agents from genetics, biology and environment. The primary prevention of mental illness, therefore, is more complicated and difficult. As a result, we often engage in preventive efforts at the secondary or tertiary levels. Community mental health incorporated the public health model of prevention, which consists of three levels of prevention.

Primary Prevention

The first level of prevention is *primary prevention*. Primary prevention involves efforts to eliminate a particular illness before it occurs and thereby reduce the incidence (i.e., rate of new cases) of the illness. Vaccinations against infectious diseases are the clearest example from the field of medicine. In mental health–related social work practice, mounting effective primary prevention efforts is more challenging. Most primary prevention efforts in mental health have involved attempts to identify populations at high risk for a particular disorder and then providing education or other preventive interventions in the hopes of warding off the onset of the target illness. For example, early screening and in-home supports to new mothers may be used to prevent the incidence of new cases of postpartum depression, or identify women who might develop postpartum depression and provide them with supportive services to ward off its onset. The effectiveness of primary prevention is difficult to assess, though, because if it works, nothing happens. On the other hand, if nothing happens, perhaps nothing would have happened anyway even if the preventive efforts had not been made. Most prevention in mental health occurs at the secondary and tertiary levels.

Secondary Prevention

Secondary prevention involves efforts to reduce the *duration* of mental disorders that do occur. The goal of secondary prevention "is to shorten the course of the illness by early identification and rapid intervention" (Langsley, 1985, p. 1886). Thus, secondary prevention reduces the prevalence of active illness, but not the incidence rate of illness. A good example of early secondary prevention efforts was the provision of crisis intervention help to soldiers during World War II to decrease the duration of symptoms of combat fatigue, which enabled affected soldiers to return more quickly to the battlefield (see Chapter 1). Another example is maintenance treatment of recurrent major depression with antidepressant medication plus cognitive-behavioral psychotherapy. The individual has depression, but the medication and psychotherapy reduces the duration of the depressive episode and, if the person stays on a maintenance dose of medication and completes the course of psychotherapy, reduces the frequency of relapse. Finally, we have tertiary prevention.

Tertiary Prevention

The goal of tertiary prevention is to reduce the degree of impairment that results from the individual's mental illness. For example, let's say an individual has schizophrenia, which is a serious mental illness that often is lifelong in duration. Schizophrenia can vary in course of illness and degree of impairment but, if left untreated, most individuals with schizophrenia suffer considerable psychosocial disability. Treating an individual who has schizophrenia with a combination of antipsychotic medication, at as low a dose as possible, in combination with the new evidence-based psychosocial treatment called "cognitive-enhancement therapy (CET)" (Eack et al., 2012; Hogarty & Flesher, 1999) won't cure the individual's illness, but will reduce the impairment the illness causes. Studies have shown that individuals treated with medication and CET are significantly more likely to achieve success with competitive employment and enjoy satisfying social relationships than those only receiving treatment as usual, i.e., medication and supportive psychosocial therapy (Hogarty, Greenwald, & Eack, 2006). This is an example of tertiary prevention. Tertiary prevention reduces the level of impairment that an existing illness inflicts.

These three kinds of prevention, along with their goals and methods, are directly related to the six community mental health practice principles just discussed. Unfortunately, in recent years these principles and associated prevention efforts have not been adhered to in ideal form. Critics have argued that many mental health centers have become less comprehensive and more specialized, the range of services are not equal across communities, for example, services are generally more sparse and less accessible in rural areas versus urban areas and particularly sparse in both poor rural and poor urban areas. Services may not be uniformly accessible to all populations in need, accountability is being questioned, and a common complaint of consumers is that the needs of those with good insurance have priority over those who are poorly insured, uninsured, or indigent (Aron, Honberg, Duckworth, et al., 2009). Very often, it is clinical social workers who are called upon to fill in the gaps and advocate for services on behalf of consumers and families. What we can and cannot do to remedy these gaps is guided, facilitated, and sometimes limited by the ethical principles and legal mandates we must abide by. The next section of the chapter addresses this.

VALUES AND ETHICS

Introduction

Values and ethics are integral to social work practice. Our profession is driven by such values as the inherent worth and dignity of the client, the importance of social justice and client rights, and the values of self-determination, integrity, and competence in practice. Frederic G. Reamer (2006) notes that social work values play a key role in:

- Defining the mission of the social work profession;
- Guiding the nature of the relationships social workers have with their clients, colleagues, and society as a whole;
- Underpinning the interventions that social workers utilize in their practice activities; and
- Guiding the steps that social workers take when facing and resolving ethical dilemmas. (Reamer, 2006, p. 13)

Although close in meaning, values must be distinguished from ethics. Let's look at a couple of definitions. Charles S. Levy, who wrote the first comprehensive text on social work ethics, defines "values" as *preferences* with respect to which persons, groups, or societies feel an "affective regard," that is, an emotional connection to the value (Levy, 1976). For example, an individual may place a high value on the attribute of honesty. Honesty, as a value, is seen as positive, and dishonesty—its opposite—is viewed negatively. To this particular person, honesty is very important in a relationship with another person, and honest relationships are associated with positive feelings. The individual likes other people who are honest in their dealings with others and dislikes people who are dishonest.

"Ethics," though also involving affectively charged preferences, connotes a partiality toward certain *actions* or behaviors. Thus, values represent verbally or behaviorally expressed preferences, while ethics represents verbally or behaviorally expressed preferences about action and behavior (Levy, 1979). The person who values honesty, for example, also looks at how honest another person's behavior is. In their mind, honesty is not just a value but should also drive how a person behaves. Part of behaving honestly is behaving ethically. So the honest person tells the truth and is transparent and forthcoming about his or her actions.

Read *Professional versus Personal Values and Ethics.*

The National Association of Social Workers (NASW) Code of Ethics

The social work profession's ethics, values, principles, and standards are outlined in the NASW Code of Ethics. The Code of Ethics serves to guide the professional conduct of social work practitioners across professional functions, settings, and client populations, and ***serves six purposes*** (NASW, 1996). Thus, the code provides both guidance and protection for the social worker, client, agency and general public. Based on this code, one can identify certain values that drive the ethical guidelines. Those values central to the social work profession, providing the underlying framework of the NASW Code of Ethics, are called the "core values" of social work. These values have been essentially the same throughout the history of the profession; however, how they have been worded and which components have been emphasized has varied according to the ebbs and flows of the politics of the profession and changing societal conditions that have affected the practice of social work.

These core values derive from the overall purpose or mission of social work. The Council on Social Work Education (CSWE), which is the accrediting body for professional social work education programs on the bachelor's and master's levels, defines the purpose and mission of social work as the following:

> The purpose of the social work profession is to promote human and community well-being. Guided by a person and environment construct, a global perspective, respect for human diversity, and knowledge based on scientific inquiry, social work's purpose is actualized through its quest for social and economic justice, the prevention of conditions that limit human rights, the elimination of poverty, and the enhancement of the quality of life for all persons. (CSWE, 2008, p. 1)

Embedded in this purpose, then, are the core values. In the 2008 CSWE Educational Policy and Accreditation Standards, in Educational Policy section 1.1, "Values," CSWE defines the core values of social work as being "service, social justice, the dignity and worth of the person, the importance of human relationships, integrity, competence, human rights, and scientific inquiry are among the core values of social work. These values underpin the explicit and implicit curriculum and frame the profession's commitment to respect for all people and the quest for social and economic justice [and reflect the NASW Code of Ethics]" (CSWE, 2008, p. 1).

Articulating the Core Values

How do social work practitioners apply what CSWE says to day-to-day practice? The NASW Code of Ethics (NASW, 1996) provides the answer to this question by first describing the core values of social work that underlie and guide social work practice. I always tell my students that they should "tattoo" these core values onto their brains so they can call upon them at any time. These core values are the following:

- Service
- Social justice
- Dignity and worth of the person
- Importance of human relationships
- Integrity
- Competence

Now, how do the social work core values connect with the social work ethical principles? The NASW Code of Ethics provides a helpful mapping of the core values to the ethical principles, including a description of the practice behaviors associated with both the value and the principle. The following table provides a grid that maps the values with the ethical principles and then provides an illustrative example of practice behavior in the field of community mental health that relates to the particular value and ethical principle.

Assess your comprehension of *social work values and ethical principles* by completing this quiz.

Reprinted with permission of the Council on Social Work Education

How the Social Work Core Values Connect with Social Work Ethical Principles

Core Value	*Ethical Principle*	*Practice Behavior Example*
1. Service	1. Social workers' primary goal is to help people in need and to address social problems.	A social worker donates two hours of time each week to provide pro bono counseling to mentally ill clients living at the battered women's shelter.
2. Social justice	2. Social workers challenge social injustice.	A social worker participates in a demonstration at the state capitol to protest a 30% cut in the state's mental health budget, which would cut services to homeless mentally ill clients.
3. Dignity and worth of the person	3. Social workers respect the dignity and worth of the person.	A social worker always takes a collaborative approach with the treatment team, consumer, and family when treatment plans are reviewed and changed.
4. Importance of human relationships	4. Social workers recognize the central importance of human relationships.	A social worker works hard to facilitate the development of natural social supports for seriously mentally ill clients to enhance their quality of life.
5. Integrity	5. Social workers behave in a trustworthy manner.	When a client signs a confidentiality waiver, the social worker tells the client exactly what information will and will not be shared.
6. Competence	6. Social workers practice within their areas of competence and develop and enhance their professional expertise.	Because of changes in immigration patterns in the community, the social worker is seeing more mentally ill clients from Southeast Asia. The social worker immediately seeks training in cultural competence for working effectively with Southeast Asian clients.

LEGAL ISSUES AND SOCIAL WORK PRACTICE: INVOLUNTARY CIVIL COMMITMENT

Social work practice in community mental health is guided not only by our professional code of ethics and our core values, but also by state and federal court decisions, laws, regulations, and public policies. These may or may not coincide with social work's ethics and values. In this part of the chapter, we will discuss the convergence and divergence between laws and regulations and social work ethics and values, illustrate these topics via some case examples, and go over some of the major concerns in the area of legal and ethical issues that social work practitioners need to be aware of as they prepare for practice. Although court decisions in states other than where you practice may not apply directly to you, such cases may be cited as precedents, and thus it is incumbent upon all practitioners to stay up to date on what is happening nationwide in the area of legal and ethical issues. Case law from the state where you work along with Supreme Court decisions do affect you directly. Let's begin by discussing involuntary civil commitment.

Involuntary Civil Commitment

Katie

Katie is a 29-year-old divorced white female who came to the crisis clinic after taking, she claims, 40 tablets of 7.5 mg. Tranxene. Katie has been escalating over the past week, i.e., coming to the crisis clinic several times a day, alternating between threatening suicide and stating she is in control and won't harm herself, and becoming more regressed and acting out against herself. Two days ago she cut herself superficially on the side of her torso and, later, on her arm.

Today, Katie called the crisis clinic stating she was definitely going to kill herself—either overdose or "blow my head off with a gun"—and then she hung up. Later she came to the clinic and, upon evaluation, Katie's voice is slurred, and she is drowsy and staggering. I believe she requires inpatient care at this time and the inpatient staff are directed to, immediately upon admission, send her to the county general hospital for medical treatment of the overingestion of Tranxene. The client is deemed a danger to herself at this time. (Newhill, 1995)

At the time I hospitalized Katie, I had known her for about three years. She has recurrent thoughts of taking her life secondary to chronic depression and an ongoing inability to handle stressful life situations. She has a long history of repeated brief hospitalizations, repetitive self-harming behavior, and mild acting-out behavior toward others, and has generally impaired functioning in interpersonal, school, and occupational spheres. In terms of her strengths, Katie is very bright and has completed two years of college. When stable, she is likeable and has the capacity to be quite competent in her day-to-day responsibilities. However, although she has several years of work experience, she has been "let go" from about half of her jobs because she is unreliable about showing up for work during times when her symptoms increase. Thus, she presents with a complex network of strengths and problem areas. Katie has been diagnosed with bipolar II disorder and borderline personality disorder. At the time of admission, her Global Assessment of Functioning was rated at 15. The decision to hospitalize Katie was based on my clinical judgment that she posed an imminent danger to herself at the time she was evaluated.

Overview of the Evolution of Civil Commitment Laws

In all 50 states in the United States, clients may be involuntarily committed to psychiatric hospitals through specific civil procedures. The states have assumed authority to do this via two historic roles: (1) through the state's role as "parent," or *parens patriae*, in which the state is in a benevolent role acting in the best interest of the client, and (2) through the role of a *police power* to protect the public from danger that a client may pose to that public. Here, the state's focus is on the best interest of the community (Stavis, 1995).

In the course of acting on these powers, however, certain abuses have occurred, for example, situations in which clients have been hospitalized without due process. In such cases the states have deprived clients of their civil rights. In an attempt to remedy such abuses, certain court cases, beginning in the 1970s, contributed toward limiting the state's authority to commit without procedural safeguards. *O'Connor v. Donaldson* (1975) was one of the key landmark decisions in mental health law that served to affirm client rights and force states to change their civil commitment statutes from a simple "need for treatment" standard to what has been called the "dangerousness standard" (Newhill, 1989).

In the case involved, Kenneth Donaldson had been confined to Florida State Hospital for 15 years because of "need for treatment" involving, essentially, custodial care because Mr. Donaldson consistently refused any and all therapeutic interventions. Donaldson sued

Newhill, C.E. (1995). A mental health casebook. Unpublished manuscript.

the hospital, claiming that the confinement violated his constitutional rights. Donaldson won his case in the U.S. District Court, won the appeals, and in 1975 the victory was reaffirmed by the Supreme Court. In *O'Connor v. Donaldson*, the United States Supreme Court ruled that states could no longer confine individuals to a mental institution without treatment unless they were dangerous and/or incapable of caring for themselves, referred to as "grave disability." In lieu of such conditions, citizens deserved freedom. The Supreme Court said the case raised "a single, relatively simple, but nonetheless important question concerning every man's constitutional right to liberty." ***Read a key paragraph.***

In other cases, however, clients have not been hospitalized and have harmed themselves or others as a result. ***Review is an example of how such a tragedy can occur.***

The Lanterman-Petris-Short Act

The Lanterman-Petris-Short Act (LPS Act) established the criteria for involuntary civil commitment to a mental health institution in the state of California and set the precedent for modern mental health commitment criteria and procedures in the United States. It was co-authored by California State Assemblyman Frank Lanterman (R) and California State Senators Nicholas C. Petris (D) and Alan Short (D), signed into law in 1967 by Governor Ronald Reagan, and went into full effect on July 1, 1972 (the full document of the LPS act can be found at www.leginfo.ca.gov). It cited seven articles of intent:

- To end the inappropriate, indefinite, and involuntary commitment of mentally disordered persons, people with developmental disabilities, and persons impaired by chronic alcoholism, and to eliminate legal disabilities;
- To provide prompt evaluation and treatment of persons with serious mental disorders or impaired by chronic alcoholism;
- To guarantee and protect public safety;
- To safeguard individual client rights through judicial review;
- To provide individualized treatment, supervision, and placement services by a conservatorship program for gravely disabled persons;
- To encourage the full use of all existing agencies, professional personnel, and public funds to accomplish these objectives and to prevent duplication of services and unnecessary expenditures; and
- To protect mentally disordered persons and developmentally disabled persons from criminal acts.

The LPS Act is important because it set the precedent for civil commitment criteria across the nation and shifted mental health law from the "need for treatment" threshold to the "dangerousness standard," a standard that attempts to balance client rights with public protection.

The Three General Criteria of the "Dangerousness Standard"

Although the details of civil commitment statutes vary somewhat across states, most recognize three general criteria that apply to the client as follows:

- First, mental illness must be present as demonstrated by a diagnosis of mental disorder.
- Second, the individual must be judged to be a danger to themselves or others, with the usual evidence being the presence of suicidal or homicidal threats or acts (some states include destruction of property); but regardless of the behavior, the dangerousness must be related to the mental illness. Violent behavior does not always indicate mental illness is present—that is, "bad is not necessarily mad."
- The third criterion is whether the client has an inability to provide for basic necessities, that is, food, clothing, and shelter, the lack of which is usually termed "grave disability."

Each state provides for several levels of commitment, from short-term emergency commitment, which are most commonly limited to 72 hours, to longer-term commitments. However, to assure due process, court hearings of different formats are required before instituting a new commitment period.

Read *Pennsylvania's different commitment statutes.*

Every state has a mental health act that has been approved by that state's legislature and which outlines the various legal procedures in the area of mental health law. The Treatment Advocacy Center website (www.treatmentadvocacycenter.org) provides a regularly updated breakdown of civil commitment statutes state by state. For example, in Pennsylvania, the Pennsylvania Mental Health Act of 1976 provided for emergency civil commitment on grounds of "clear and present danger to self or others"—the notion of "grave disability," however, is not specifically included, although many states, such as California, include grave disability along with danger to self or others. ***Review the Pennsylvania Mental Health Act definition of "clear and present danger" and an example of a client situation that would* not *meet this requirement.***

The Dangerousness Must Be the Result of Mental Disorder

An individual may engage in violent or dangerous behavior, but unless the dangerousness is the result of a mental disorder, civil commitment is not appropriate. The purpose of hospitalization is not to treat dangerousness, per se, but to treat the mental illness. The assumption is that once the symptoms of mental illness are treated, the dangerousness will abate. However, that, of course, assumes that the mental disorder is directly related to the dangerousness. Here is an example of a client situation in which the dangerousness *is* the result of the individual's mental illness:

> Tyrone has been diagnosed with paranoid schizophrenia, and as long as he adheres to taking his prescribed medication, he functions quite well, lives independently, and holds a part-time job. One day Tyrone decides that he does not want to put up with the side effects of his medication anymore, and stops taking it. Several days later, he begins to hear critical threatening voices, telling him that he has committed a horrible crime (not actually true) and that the police have him under surveillance. As a result, Tyrone becomes very paranoid and anxious. One day he decides to go out for coffee, becomes frightened of the crowd in the coffee shop, and begins to shout, telling everyone to "leave me alone." A police officer notices the commotion, enters the shop, and tries to talk to Tyrone. Seeing the police officer, Tyrone is convinced his life is in danger and he assaults the officer. Recognizing that Tyrone is mentally ill, the police officer handcuffs him and then transports Tyrone to the psychiatric emergency room where he is hospitalized involuntarily as a danger to others.

In this case, Tyrone's assaultive behavior is directly caused by the symptoms of his mental illness, the exacerbation of which resulted in paranoid delusions about the police. His delusion that the police were watching him resulted in his being terrified when approached by a police officer. His assault on the officer was, given his mental illness, an act of self-defense. Fortunately for Tyrone, the police officer had been trained in crisis intervention and, rather than sending Tyrone to jail, the police officer appropriately transported him to the psychiatric emergency room. In contrast to the case of Tyrone, the following is a case in which the individual's dangerous behavior is *not* a result of his mental illness:

> Luis has been diagnosed with paranoid schizophrenia, and as long as he adheres to taking his prescribed medication, he functions quite well. When he was a teenager, Luis began running with a bad crowd and getting into trouble with the law, mostly burglarizing homes to get money for drugs. One day Luis and his best friend decide

to rob a jewelry store so they can get money to buy some cocaine. The two men, however, are intercepted by the police in the middle of the robbery, guns are drawn, and Luis shoots one of the police officers in the leg. More officers arrive on the scene, Luis and his friend are arrested, and both are taken to jail.

In this case, Luis decides to commit a robbery to get money to buy drugs. The violence that occurs is not directly related to his mental illness, therefore Luis is appropriately taken to jail. However, he does have a mental illness and, therefore, it will be critically important that Luis receive appropriate mental health care while he remains in jail and that his mental illness be considered when decisions arc made about what happens next for him.

The Criterion of "Grave Disability"

All states include the criteria of danger to self and danger to others in their emergency involuntary civil commitment criteria. Some states also include the criterion of grave disability to provide emergency protection for individuals who present what might be called a "passive threat" to their own well-being but are not actively suicidal or a danger to others. Grave disability also covers individuals who are grossly psychotic or manic and are unable to exercise good judgment in providing self-care. How is grave disability defined in the law? As an example, the LPS Act defines "grave disability" as:

> A condition in which a person, as a result of a mental disorder (or impairment by chronic alcoholism), is unable to provide for his (or her) basic personal needs for food, clothing or shelter. Lanterman-Petris-Short Act (LPS Act) (California Welfare & Institutions Code section 5008(h)(l)(A),(2))

The court also noted that the definition of grave disability is "sufficiently precise to exclude unusual or nonconformist lifestyles," and that "it requires a causal link between a specifically defined and diagnosed mental disorder and an inability to care of one's basic personal needs . . ." and must be based on the person's current condition at the time of evaluation. There is a catch in the grave disability criterion, which is that evidence of third-party assistance must be considered as part of the evaluation, which means that "a person is not gravely disabled

Arthur and His Father

One day, when I was working for a psychiatric emergency service, a middle-aged father came to the service asking to speak with a social worker. I remember how he sat slumped in the chair, looking like a man who was carrying the burdens of the world on his shoulders. He told me that he had a son named Arthur, 26 years old, who was probably seriously mentally ill. His son has never been willing to get any treatment and, as the father described him, my thought was that he probably had schizophrenia. Arthur lived alone in a shack located in a far corner of the father's asparagus farm. The shack had no running water and no electricity. Arthur had no source of income and, according to his father, could not take care of himself. For months, the father had carried food and water to Arthur, did his laundry, and tried to clean the shack when Arthur would allow him to do so. Arthur has never hurt himself or been violent toward others, but the father was hoping that we could hospitalize him as gravely disabled. I went out to visit Arthur and then sat down with his father. I told him that, under the law, I could not hospitalize Arthur because I had no evidence, currently, that he is unable to care for his basic needs. The only way we could get such evidence would be for the father to withdraw his support and see what happens. The father could not bring himself to do that.

California Welfare & Institutions Code section 5008(h)(l)(A),(2)

within the meaning of the LPS Act if he or she is capable of safely surviving in freedom with the help of willing and responsible family members, friends or third parties" (Pone, 2009). This requirement can result in heartbreaking cases, as the following situation illustrates:

This was a very sad situation. Arthur's mother had left the family because she could not handle what was happening in the family any longer. I tried to provide Arthur's father with support and I assisted him in trying to coax Arthur to come in to the clinic, but Arthur continued to firmly refuse treatment. It is very difficult for loving parents to do something like withdrawing support from an ill child, including an adult child, but the way the law is set up, that is the position that families are in if the ill loved one persistently refuses to consider voluntary help and is not imminently dangerous to self or others.

In sum, a finding of grave disability requires that a person must (1) currently (2) be unable to provide for their basic necessities (food, clothing, and shelter) (3) due to a mental disorder and (4) the failure to provide for basic necessities will result in harm to the individual. In making such a decision, the clinician must consider whether third-party assistance in meeting basic needs is available or not (Pone, 2009).

Documenting Dangerousness in a Civil Commitment Petition

When hospitalizing a client involuntarily on an emergency basis, the petitioner—who may be a social worker, a police officer, or other designee—must complete a petition form for the state where the hospitalization occurs. The information provided must be clear, succinct, and complete in terms of covering all of the state's requirements for emergency civil commitment. This includes documentation of dangerousness (and/or grave disability, if

During the time I was a clinical social worker with the psychiatric emergency service, there was a client, "Fred," whom we saw regularly every 1–2 months. Sometimes Fred would stop by just to talk with us if we weren't busy, other times he came in to get an injection of medication if he missed his appointment, and sometimes he came to see us because a crisis was going on. Fred was a 42-year-old single man who was first diagnosed with paranoid schizophrenia at the age of 21. He lived with his mother, and their relationship was very tempestuous. Fred was a large man, weighing over 400 pounds and, because of his weight, he had to take very high doses of Prolixin Decanoate to control his symptoms. When Fred and his mother got into fights, which were frequent, the stress would often exacerbate his symptoms and sometimes throw him into a crisis so severe that he had to be hospitalized. On one of these occasions, I was the one who evaluated Fred and had to hospitalize him. Below is the actual text of what I wrote (with identifying information altered) on the civil commitment form, including the directions for the write-up per California civil commitment law:

The circumstances under which said person's condition was called to my attention as follows:

This is a 42- year- old white male, who has been seen at the outpatient clinic at county mental health for years. Recently, he has not been doing well—has been seen in the psychiatric emergency service both during the day and at night several times over the past 2–3 weeks because of complaints about smelling foul odors and he fears that he will lose control and kill his mother. The client has been treated with tremendous doses of Prolixin and Mellaril but has continued to manage only marginally.

The following information has been established: (Please state with sufficient detail information to warrant the belief that the person for whom evaluation and treatment is sought is, in fact, a danger to others, danger to self, or gravely disabled.)

A stay at our Transitional Care facility was attempted, but when he arrived, the client would not get out of the car, stating there were foul odors in the air that would contaminate him. Tonight he states that he cannot control himself any longer from killing his mother. Upon evaluation, he is calm and fairly appropriate except when talking about his mother, whereupon he becomes agitated. He states that he cannot stand living with his mother but also cannot stay away and thus the only solution is to kill her, plus he feels that she is influencing the increase in foul odors. He states that he must be in the hospital for control, which I concur.

☐ A danger to himself ☑ A danger to others ☐ Gravely disabled

the state's statute includes that), the presence of mental disorder, and evidence that the dangerousness is related to the mental disorder. Let's look at a real-life case example.

As can be seen by the write-up, I first describe the recent history of what has been going on with Fred and, later, the attempt to meet his needs via a less restrictive alternative, that is, our transitional care facility. This facility provided fully supervised short-term (up to three weeks) care for individuals at risk for hospitalization and, for many clients, provided sufficient intensive care to avoid hospitalization and return to the community. This, however, did not work for Fred.

Then I indicate clearly the nature of the dangerousness to others, that is, that Fred states he cannot control himself any longer and will kill his mother. Clients' self-perception of their ability to control or not control their behavior is very important information as part of assessment. The vast majority of clients we see do not want to harm other people and are often quite forthcoming in being honest about their perception of their level of control and what they need for adequate protection. Of course, there are exceptions to this, but it is always important to ask clients about their perception of their level of control. In this case, Fred clearly stated that he needs to be in the hospital in order to control his urges to kill his mother.

Emphasizing Rights, Sometimes, over Needs

It is important to remember that today's commitment policies emphasize rights over needs, which makes it illegal to impose treatment without informed consent and due process except in emergency situations. And, even then, it is expected that the clinician provide advisement to the extent that he or she can. For example, in the upper right-hand corner of the State of California's application for 72-hour civil commitment detention for evaluation and treatment, there is a detainment advisement that reads as follows:

> My name is ____________. I am a (Peace officer, etc.) with (Name of Agency.) You are not under criminal arrest, but I am taking you for examination by mental health professionals at (Name of Facility). You will be told your rights by the mental health staff.
>
> *If taken into custody at his or her residence, the person shall also be told the following information in substantially the following form:*
>
> You may bring a few personal items with you, which I will have to approve. You can make a phone call and/or leave a note to tell your friends and/or family where you have been taken.

Because a premium is placed on client rights, unnecessary hospitalization has been reduced, but clients can "fall through the cracks." An example would be a decompensating homeless individual who is not dangerous enough to be committed but refuses to accept the mental health care he or she needs. Social workers can face difficult ethical/legal dilemmas when working with clients who are homeless, mentally ill, behaving in ways that upset the community, but who refuse voluntary treatment. Such clients may not be acutely suicidal/homicidal, that is, not making direct threats to harm self or others, but are clearly using poor judgment, caring for themselves only marginally, and are vulnerable to the dangers of living on the streets. Further, such clients may not adhere to aftercare and housing plans, and this increases the risk that such individuals may eventually end up in the criminal justice system, our so-called "new asylums" (Erickson & Erickson, 2008; PBS, 2009).

The Role of Social Workers in Emergency Civil Commitment Procedures

How does the issue of civil commitment relate to our work as social workers? Social workers employed in community mental/behavioral health care services often participate in involuntary commitment procedures. Typically, the social worker may do the initial screening to determine if hospitalization is clinically warranted, if the client is willing to be admitted to the hospital and, if not, whether the client meets the criteria for involuntary hospitalization. In most cases, the psychiatrist may do the actual admission, although not always. In our crisis service, the crisis team members, who were social workers or registered nurses, did the actual admission from start to finish, and then, once the client was admitted to the hospital, the inpatient psychiatrist would review and sign off on the admission. The role of the social worker in such procedures is usually strongly influenced by the culture of the clinic or hospital, that is, whether the culture is hierarchical or egalitarian. In hierarchical cultures, the social worker may only advise the doctor and the doctor (who is at the top of the hierarchy) makes all the admission decisions. In an egalitarian culture, such as our clinic, all professional staff collaborated as equal peers in most clinical decision making except for writing prescriptions for medication and administering medication.

An Ethical Dilemma

Now, let's revisit the topic of ethics and values. Which social work value runs *counter* to involuntary civil commitment? Keep in mind that involuntary civil commitment can be a coercive procedure that involves temporarily suspending certain client rights and temporarily taking away certain client freedoms. As such, it runs counter to the social work value of *affirming client self-determination* and begs the following questions:

- How do we reconcile an ethical dilemma between a legal/agency work responsibility mandate and a social work value that is incorporated in our code of ethics?
- Is there a way of maintaining some aspects of self-determination in the face of this type of loss of freedom?

Appropriately resolving ethical dilemmas is an ongoing professional responsibility in the practice of social work. Although they may be legally appropriate, many of the actions we must take as social workers present ethical quandaries that must be resolved in a way that facilitates the best outcome for our client while maintaining ethical standards in practice (Loewenberg & Dolgoff, 1988).

Self-determination versus Paternalism

Our first task is to clearly define what is meant by "self-determination" in social work. Felix Biestek (1957) points out that as part of the process of social casework, clients' need and right to freedom must be recognized by the social worker, however, such recognition must be tempered by the requirements of civil and moral law, the social worker's role and agency function, and the ability of the client to make positive and constructive decisions. Biestek (1957) defines self-determination clearly and also acknowledges its limits in the real world of practice. Your role as a social worker is to allow your client maximum control over his or her destiny but, when there are limits, it means safeguarding your client's rights and interests. This is in contrast to paternalism, which essentially says, "I know what is best for you." Although there are times when paternalism is justified, generally it tends to be counterproductive, because it discourages open communication, undermines opportunities for clients to gain strength from working through their problems themselves and, finally, paternalism can foster dependency, as Goffman (1961) and Barton (1966) showed clearly (see Chapter 2).

So, under what circumstances is paternalism justified, such as imposing hospitalization on a client involuntarily? Or, phrased another way, what are the limits of self-determination? There are three main conditions under which most ethics and legal scholars have argued paternalism is justified:

- When the client is considered mentally incompetent or lacking in rationality to the extent of being unable to comprehend the results of decision making on their behalf;
- When the consequences of an act are far-reaching and are irreversible; and, finally,
- When temporary interference with liberty insures future freedom and autonomy.

The first condition for which paternalism can be justified is when the client is considered mentally incompetent or lacking in rationality to the extent of being unable to comprehend the results of decision making on his or her behalf (Callahan, 1994; Kapp, 1988). This condition is the basis for the criterion of grave disability, is part of the statutes governing the granting of conservatorship, and is part of the criteria determining whether someone accused of a crime is incompetent to stand trial. Determining the threshold above which paternalism is justified, however, can be difficult, and client rights must be protected. So, for example, how does one differentiate incompetence from eccentricity? An individual's behavior may be judged as being outside of the norm for society, but that doesn't necessarily mean the individual is incompetent.

How does one differentiate grave disability from an unusual lifestyle? In the case of Arthur and his father, above, the social worker had to support Arthur living the way he did *unless* removal of third-party support revealed that Arthur's mental illness rendered him incapable of caring for his basic needs.

Another condition in which paternalism can be justified is when the consequences of an act are far-reaching and are potentially irreversible, such as a suicide attempt (Gambrill, 2006). In such cases, the social worker is "interfering with an individual's freedom for his or her own good" (Reamer, 1983, p. 254). The civil commitment criterion of danger to self is supported by this argument, and most statutes attempt to balance this with supporting client rights by limiting such judgments to those representing imminent danger. But, how imminent is imminent? Thirty days? Sixty days? At any point in the future? What evidence and how much evidence should be required? What about the "right to commit suicide" in the face of a terminal illness with chronic pain and suffering (Szasz, 2002)?

Finally, paternalism can be justified under situations in which temporary interference with liberty insures future freedom and autonomy. So, for example, hospitalizing someone involuntarily so they get treatment for their mental illness may enable them, once they are well, to be more capable of working, developing relationships with other people, living independently, and achieving other recovery goals. But, how temporary is temporary? Also, temporary can become permanent, such as long-term hospitalization or a nursing home placement. How do we define the limits to "interference with liberty"? What are the parameters?

Resolution

Committing a client involuntarily to a psychiatric hospital temporarily interferes with the client's freedom and self-determination. However, no values are absolute and immune from the effects of competing values and legal and ethical mandates. Those who support involuntary civil commitment argue that such a paternalistic act is justified because the commitment criteria incorporate the conditions that justify paternalism as outlined above. One of the ethical assessment tools that can help guide social work practitioners in resolving such ethical dilemmas in their real day-to-day practice is a rank ordering of ethical principles in which certain principles take precedence over others. An example of such a tool is the Ethical Principles Screen, developed by social work educators Ralph Dolgoff, Frank Loewenberg, and Donna Harrington (2009), which provides a rank ordering or prioritization of seven ethical principles from the most important to the least important.

The top rung of the screen, which is the ethical obligation that supersedes all others, is *protection of life* (p. 66), that is, the basic survival needs of the client and others in society. This protection of human life supersedes Rung 3, which is *autonomy and freedom* (p. 66), that is, self-determination. If an individual's behavior, in relation to his or her mental illness, poses a danger to self or others, then taking action to ensure that individual's safety and the safety of others is justified. If the risk to human life is imminent, then hospitalization is justified, even if it is against the person's will.

> A person does not have the right to decide to harm himself or herself or anyone else on the grounds that the right to make such a decision is her or his autonomous right. When a person is about to make such a decision, the social worker is obligated to intervene. (Lowenberg & Dolgoff, 1988, pp. 121–122)

In less imminent circumstances, the means for protecting human life might include various health and social services, food, clothing, shelter, money, and so forth, depending on what is appropriate for the situation (Lowenberg & Dolgoff, 1988).

It is still, however, important for the social worker to foster and support self-determination to the greatest extent possible. Involuntary hospitalization does not eliminate all means of exercising self-determination, and it is very important that social workers support clients' civil rights, advocate on their behalf, and actively identify areas where self-determination can be affirmed. How does this play out in practice? Below is a dialogue between a social worker and a client that illustrates a range of ways that self-determination can be supported even though the client is facing involuntary hospitalization:

Fostering Self-Determination in Hospitalization

The client, Eliana, is a 30-year-old single woman who had recently immigrated from Guatemala and was seen by the social worker in the county general hospital after she was medically stabilized following an overdose of acetaminophen (Tylenol) and lorazepam (Ativan). Eliana overdosed after her fiancé broke off their engagement, and she tells the social worker that she is sorry she didn't die and still intends to kill herself. She is very depressed, her family is not very supportive and have told her that they are ashamed because what she did is sinful, and Eliana feels very much alone and quite hopeless about her life. After assessing the situation thoroughly,

---

Loewenberg, F. & Dolgoff, R. (1988). Ethical decisions for social work practice (3rd ed.). Itasca, Ill.: F.E. Peacock.

the social worker concludes that Eliana must be hospitalized involuntarily on an emergency basis because she is still an imminent danger to herself. The social worker is visiting Eliana in her hospital room prior to the transfer to the psychiatric inpatient unit. After establishing some initial rapport and beginning trust, the social worker begins to evaluate whether Eliana should be hospitalized:

Social worker (SW): Eliana, it sounds as though things have been very difficult for you lately and, from what you are telling me, you seem to be feeling quite hopeless and sad about your life.

Eliana: Of course I am—my life is over. What is left for me? I can't stand the pain anymore. I just want to die.

SW: I understand. What has happened must be very painful for you . . . (pause) . . . I am very concerned about how sad you are feeling, and you must have felt quite desperate to have taken all those pills. That worries me.

Eliana: How could you understand? You don't know what I've been going through.

SW: I don't know everything you are going through, but from what you are telling me, I sense you are feeling angry and helpless and you don't know where to turn. I would like to help you, and even though you've had a terrible loss with the breakup with your fiancé, and you feel like your life is over, we can help you with your sadness and help you feel better so we can work together to figure out some solutions to your troubles. Right now, though, I am worried about your safety. You made a serious attempt to take your life and are telling me that you still want to die. Because of that, I think the best option to protect you while you are receiving help is to arrange for you to go into the hospital for a few days.

Eliana: I don't WANT to go to the hospital. Santa Maria—what are you people trying to do to me?!

SW: Being told to do something you don't want to do is hard, but we want to help you and make sure you are safe.

Eliana: So I have no say in anything anymore.

SW: In some ways, but you still have some choices. You will need to be admitted to the hospital, but you do have a say in what happens there, what kind of treatment you get, who visits you, and the goals you choose to work on while you are in the hospital.

Eliana: Huh? Hmmm. . . . What do you mean?

SW: You have the right to tell the inpatient doctor and social worker about what medications you do and do not want, what kind of treatments have and have not worked for you, and you have the right to have a collaborative partnership with the treatment team as you plan the goals for your recovery. The treatment team will bring their expertise in treatment to the table and you will bring your expertise on you and your life, needs, and wants to the discussion. It's not a one-way street.

Eliana: Well . . . okay . . . if I have some choices once I get there, I feel better about the whole thing. I'm willing to go to the hospital, but let me make it clear, if it were up to me I wouldn't go, but . . . maybe it won't be so bad.

SW: Good. I know it is tough to have to go into the hospital, but I believe you will get the help that you need right now. Let me tell you a little more about what will happen next.

In this scenario, the social worker made the decision to hospitalize the client, Eliana, on the basis of danger to self because of her recent suicide attempt by overdose, lack of good social support, her feelings of hopelessness, and her continued desire to die. The social worker was honest and straightforward in explaining the basis of her decision to the client. The social worker was cognizant of the fact that she was temporarily taking away Eliana's self-determination by making the decision to hospitalize her, but she also informed the client about the choices and freedoms she still retained and that the treatment while she was an inpatient would be a collaborative process. The social worker also continually empathized with the client's feelings.

Appropriately resolving ethical dilemmas is an ongoing professional responsibility in the practice of social work. Although they may be therapeutically appropriate, some of the actions we must take as social workers present ethical quandaries that must be resolved in a way that facilitates the best outcome for our client while maintaining ethical standards in practice. Self-determination remains a central, honored, and important value for social work, and a value that we must continue to uphold (Murdach, 2011).

The Process of Positively Facilitating Hospitalization

When hospitalizing someone involuntarily, it is very important to be honest, direct, and informative with regard to what is going to happen during the hospitalization process itself and providing the client with an overview of what he or she can expect once getting there. Although we may, over the course of our careers, hospitalize many clients, it is important to not let such repetition make us cavalier or callous about what such a procedure means from the client's and family's perspective. Hospitalization, particularly the first hospitalization a client has, is a very significant experience. It is important that the experience be as positive, supportive, and therapeutic as possible, because it will have a lasting impact on the client's view of services and getting help in general. There are many things that we can do to make an enforced hospitalization more humane (Green, 1997).

First: Take time to talk to the client. Empathically explain who you are, what your role is, why you are meeting with the client, what is happening, and exactly why you are making the decisions you are making. Solicit the client's input and empathize with and validate his or her feelings about what is happening.

Second: Communicate respect and support the client's inherent worth and dignity in both your verbal and nonverbal communication.

Third: Always remember that even if a client is actively psychotic, there is a place within the person that is not psychotic, that understands and will remember the kindness and respect you give them and your support for their rights and worth as a human being. I had many clients come back to the crisis clinic to see me after they had been discharged from a hospitalization I had facilitated, and they would say something along the lines of the following to me:

> I just want to thank you for talking to me when I was hospitalized. I know I was "crazy" and you probably didn't think I understood what you were saying, but I did, and what you said made me feel safe and made me feel like I was worth something as a person.

Fourth: Always talk with and support any family members or friends who are with the client. These friends and family members have probably been through a very difficult experience. They may have been desperately trying to help and care for the ill person for a long time before the situation reached a crisis point and they had to go to the emergency room or call the police for help. They are probably feeling scared, guilty, frustrated, exhausted, and completely overwhelmed. Your support and willingness to provide information about what is happening with their loved one is extremely important and can provide significant comfort to them in this time of crisis. As a psychiatrist colleague once commented to me: "Many families that I see at the time a loved one is hospitalized look like they have just emerged from a train wreck. They are in crisis, and we must understand that and respond accordingly."

Read *Proposed Changes in Civil Commitment Laws.*

Involuntary Outpatient Treatment/Commitment

Involuntary outpatient treatment (IOT), also referred to as involuntary outpatient commitment (IOC), is a growing practice in community mental/behavioral health care as an approach to force non-adherent consumers to adhere to prescribed psychosocial and pharmacological treatment via a statutory and/or court-derived mandate (Geller, 2006). With this procedure, a client is involuntarily committed to a community treatment center instead of the hospital, with community tenure contingent upon compliance with treatment, usually medication and/or other prescribed aftercare. Some argue that without mechanisms such as outpatient commitment, ill individuals would deteriorate, end up on the street, and—for some—end up in jail or prison, particularly if they use drugs or alcohol. Thus the intent is to improve consumers' quality of life and reduce the use of inpatient care (Geller, 2006). In other cases, however, consumers want treatment—even hospitalization—but are refused that treatment, or the treatment isn't available. Thus, the problem is not just one of consumers rejecting or being non-adherent to treatment; sometimes, treatment is desired but the resources are not adequate or providers refuse provision of the treatment that the consumer specifically wants—such as hospitalization or a particular form of treatment.

Geller (2001) observes that the topic of involuntary outpatient commitment "is a contemporary lightning-rod issue in American psychiatry," with heated arguments about its strengths and limitations as a tool for ensuring treatment adherence for individuals with serious mental illness. Involuntary supervision of individuals with mental illness is actually not a new concept or approach. In the early decades of the last century, during the heyday of the asylum, patients were routinely put on "visit status" or "parole" from the state hospital and their ability to remain in the community and avoid readmission was contingent on their compliance with community-based treatment. Paternalism and the effect of coercion was not questioned until much later when client civil rights became a priority in mental health policy and service provision (Geller, 2001).

Kendra's Law

New York State has been one of the more aggressive states in moving forward court-ordered assisted outpatient treatment (AOT) in response to the tragic death of Kendra Webdale, a young woman who, in January 1999, was pushed to her death in front of a New York City subway train by Andrew Goldstein, a man with a documented history of serious mental illness. On August 9, 1999, then-governor George Pataki signed Kendra's Law (Chapter 408 of the Laws of 1999), which created a statutory framework to ensure that individuals with mental illness with a history of repeated hospitalization and/or violent behavior participate in community-based treatment (Kendra's Law, 1999). The irony, however, is that the death of Kendra Webdale was not solely the result of Andrew Goldstein refusing to comply with treatment or mental health staff not being fully aware of his propensity for violence (Winerip, 1999). Not long before Goldstein pushed Webdale to her death, he asked for hospitalization but was turned down. Furthermore, when he was hospitalized, he was not provided with adequate follow-up after discharge. Social workers who worked with Goldstein knew that he should not be living on his own, but every placement they could find could not or would not take him in. This was due in large part to draconian cuts in services, long waiting lists for housing and intensive case management and, of course, shuttering of New York State's state hospitals.

Fortunately, the state and governor were shamed into ensuring that Kendra's Law established mechanisms for identifying high-risk individuals and ensuring that local mental health systems give priority to such individuals in providing the case management and other services necessary to ensure their and others' safety. The New York State Office of Mental Health's final report on the status of Kendra's Law and assisted outpatient treatment (2005) concludes that the long-term impact of AOT for recipients has generally been positive, including (pp. 17–20):

- A reduction of the incidence of hospitalization, homelessness, arrest, and incarceration;
- A reduction in days of hospitalization when hospitalization occurs; and
- Sustained improvements in overall functioning and reductions in harmful behavior while enrolled in AOT.

Equally important, the recipients of AOT reported that, overall, the program had been a beneficial means to achieve recovery. About half of the recipients reported feeling angry or embarrassed by being court-ordered to AOT, however, "62% of AOT recipients also reported that, all things considered, being court-ordered into treatment has been a good thing for them" (NYOMH, 2005, p. 20) and helped them stay well, gain control over their lives, and adhere to prescribed treatment.

Concerns and Cautions about Mandated Outpatient Treatment

Americans tend to seek "simple silver bullets" as solutions for complex social problems and, like so many other solutions, involuntary outpatient commitment has some strengths but is no silver bullet or panacea for the problem of treatment non-adherence. It is not a remedy for an inadequately financed, resource-poor mental health system. It also "should not be embraced as a means to address headline-grabbing random acts of violence" committed by individuals with mental illness (Gilman, 2012). It also is not a solution for forcing provider-determined treatment on a consumer who wants treatment but treatment of a different kind or form. Many consumers want treatment but cannot get what they prefer. Thus, many questions are left to be answered, including the following, posed by Geller (2001, p. 265):

- If outpatient commitment commits both patients and providers to treatment, whose commitment has the more robust effect on outcome?
- Given practical and ethical considerations, can a truly randomized, valid study of outpatient commitment be done?
- Where are the studies of the purported harm of outpatient commitment?
- Where is research on competency-based rather than dangerousness-based outpatient commitment?

The RAND Study of the Effectiveness of Involuntary Outpatient Treatment

In 2001, the RAND Law and Health Initiative conducted a study led by Susan Ridgely to examine the effectiveness of involuntary outpatient treatment (Ridgely, Borum, & Petrila, 2001). They examined all the existing studies on the effectiveness of involuntary outpatient treatment and interviewed stakeholders in eight states about their experiences with it. Their findings were a "mixed bag" of positive and negative perceptions and experiences, leading the research team to conclude the following: First, although most of the stakeholders thought IOT was an effective legal tool in managing consumers who were non-adherent to treatment, they were skeptical about how practical such laws are because of the shortage of services. In other words, one can mandate that a client receive services, but if the services aren't available, the mandate is moot. To work, IOT must be reciprocal in that both the consumer and the provider must be "committed" to providing/receiving treatment.

Second, IOT is usually used as part of the discharge plan when consumers are released from inpatient care but, overall, is not used very frequently. In particular, consumers who might benefit the most—dually diagnosed individuals with both mental health and substance abuse problems—are, for the most part, not the ones who are targeted most. Third, there are significant regional differences in the "culture" of the local community and services providers, which can affect whether IOT is used and how effective it can be. For example, in rural areas where resources are scarce, IOT isn't very practical. Finally, some states are looking at alternative ways of leveraging compliance, for example, employing mental health courts modeled after drug courts (Watson, Hanrahan, Luchins, & Lurigio, 2001). Another mechanism to facilitate adherence to treatment that takes a collaborative, rather than a coercive, approach is the use of psychiatric advance directives.

Assess your comprehension of *the dangerousness standard and the criteria and process of involuntary civil commitment* by completing this quiz.

OTHER LEGAL ISSUES AND SOCIAL WORK PRACTICE

Psychiatric Advance Directives

Psychiatric advance directives (PAD) are legal documents that tell others what an individual's treatment preferences or service needs are. They are, essentially, directions for others to follow that are made in advance of an illness or injury and can exist in either the physical health or the mental health context (Appelbaum, 2004; Backlar, McFarland, Swanson, & Mahler, 2001). Over the past 30 years, we have increasingly recognized the value and expertise "brought to the table" by the person receiving services, and that the individual service recipient should have voice and choice in determining the treatment he or she receives. In addition, we must recognize that family members are often the ones who will be providing care before, during, and after a crisis and, therefore, they must also be allowed to appropriately participate in crafting the advance directive plan. A PAD is especially important for individuals with serious mental illnesses in which the severity of symptoms during episodes of illness may render the individual incapable of making decisions on their own behalf (Joshi, 2003).

Types of Psychiatric Advance Directives

There are two basic types of advance directives. The first is the *instruction directive* or *advance instructions (AI)*, which is a written document that specifies what services or treatments the individual does or does not want. These instructions can guide others when the individual is experiencing a period of illness and/or is in crisis and unable to make decisions on his or her own behalf. The specific aspects of treatment that may be addressed in the instruction directive include the following (National Mental Health Association [NMHA], n.d., p. 3):

- Preferences with regard to treatment facilities or agencies;
- Preferences with regard to experimental studies and drug or other treatment trials;
- Alternatives to hospitalization that have been helpful;
- Activities that the individual consumer finds helpful and comforting during times of crisis;

- Specific individuals who should be contacted when the client is in crisis;
- Activities that should be avoided during times of crisis because they increase stress for the individual or make the symptoms worsen;
- Medications (and their dosages) that are and are not acceptable to the consumer;
- Effective alternatives to restraint and seclusion for ensuring safety;
- Other acceptable interventions during a time of crisis that the consumer has found helpful, for example, electroconvulsive treatment (ECT); and
- Other interventions that the individual consumer *does not* want, for example, ECT.

Although the laws vary somewhat from state to state, as long as what the client specifies does not contradict established standards of treatment, the advance directive should be followed. Organizations that can provide assistance and access to advance directives forms include the National Alliance on Mental Illness (www.nami.org) and Mental Health America (formerly the National Mental Health Association; their website address is www.nmha.org).

The second type of advance directive is the *agent-driven directive* or *health care power of attorney (HCPA)*. This is a document that specifies a particular individual to act as a surrogate decision maker in situations in which the client's right to make his or her own decisions has been suspended, for example, the court has judged that the client is incompetent. This type of advance directive is also referred to as a *durable power of attorney*, a *proxy*, or an *attorney-in-fact* (NMHA, n.d.).

Benefits of Psychiatric Advance Directives

Psychiatric advance directives offer several important benefits for the client, provider, and family. Correctly implemented and executed, they can:

- Promote individual autonomy and empowerment in the recovery from mental illness and help consumers take a more active role in their care;
- Enhance communication between individuals and their families, other caretakers, mental and health care providers, and other professionals;
- Help protect individuals from being subjected to ineffective, unwanted, or possibly harmful treatments or actions; and
- Help in preventing crises and the resulting use of involuntary treatment or safety interventions such as restraint or seclusion.

Psychiatric advance directives offer an opportunity for mental health consumers and family members to express their preferences for treatment and services during psychiatric crises. Three questions emerge, however:

1. How effective are psychiatric advance directives in achieving the purported benefits?
2. To what extent are psychiatric advance directives actually being used in practice?
3. What are the limits or cautions in using psychiatric advance directives?

The next section will address each of these questions.

Effectiveness, use in Practice, and the Limits of Psychiatric Advance Directives

Existing empirical studies have, overall, supported the effectiveness of psychiatric advance directives in helping consumers and families to prepare for future crises and ensure that preferred treatments are provided (O'Connell & Stein, 2005; Srebnik, Russo, Sage, Peto, & Zick, 2003). For example, Amering, Stastny, and Hopper (2005) found that clients with severe mental illness reported that developing a PAD provided them with a sense of empowerment and security. However, Backlar, McFarland, Swanson, and Mahler (2001) found that many consumers were concerned about the lack of education about PADs on the part of providers and encountered providers who refused to honor existing PADs. This suggests that, although PADs can be effective and helpful to all involved, they are infrequently used and may not be honored (Swanson, Swartz, Ferron, Elbogen, & Van Dorn, 2006). Let's examine some of the reasons why social workers, in particular, are underutilizing psychiatric advance directives.

Using data from an exploratory survey (N=193), Scheyett, Kim, Swanson, Swartz, et al., (2008) investigated social workers' familiarity with psychiatric advance directives to understand possible reasons for the underutilization. Survey respondents were drawn from the membership roster of the North Carolina chapter of NASW, and were selected if they reported that they had provided services to adults diagnosed with serious mental illness (defined by the survey as individuals with "schizophrenia, schizoaffective disorder, bipolar disorder, major depression" (p. 231) over the course of the past year. The authors found that the majority of the social workers were "not at all familiar" or only a "little" familiar with psychiatric advance directives, with only 15 percent being "very familiar" (p. 232). In addition, very few reported any experience with PADs in their practice, and many had inaccurate knowledge about PADs. Thus, the underutilization of PADs with clients was largely due to lack of experience and lack of knowledge or inaccurate knowledge. The authors recommend that "PAD content should be included in practice courses addressing services to adults with mental illnesses, and should include both an understanding of what PADs are and how they can support client autonomy, as well as skill building in the process of engaging in partnership with clients to prepare a PAD within the context of a therapeutic alliance" (p. 234). Beyond providing advance instructions, the process of developing a PAD fosters client empowerment and enhances the alliance among the consumer, providers, and caretakers, thus, it is a tool that social workers should learn about and use in their practice as much as possible.

Limits in using psychiatric advance directives include the following. First, the preferred hospitals or other provider facilities may not always be available. Second, the doctor treating the person during a crisis may not prescribe the drugs the patient wants because they are not appropriate or not covered by insurance (Fahy, 2005). And, finally, providers do not have to comply with the instructions if they go against good medical practice or are unethical. However, if the provider cannot comply with the PAD instructions, they should inform the consumer or personal representative and try to resolve the differences or arrange for a transfer to another provider. A PAD should be part of the individual's medical record. Important roles for social workers include assisting consumers in the development of the PAD, making sure that all participating parties have a copy of it, and helping to overcome obstacles to fulfilling the PAD. One unanticipated use of the PAD is as a mechanism for consumers to refuse psychiatric treatment. Example:

> [A] lawsuit arose over a patient's right to use an advance directive to refuse mental health treatment. The case involved Nancy Hargrave, a Vermont woman with schizophrenia who was administered psychiatric medication even though she had stipulated in an advance directive that she opposed such treatment. She alleged that the treatment violated her rights under the Americans with Disabilities Act. A federal court agreed, and the decision was upheld on appeal. (Fahy, 2005, p. C-2)

One of the important components in any psychiatric advance directive is articulation of the client's preferred choices of treatment. In most cases, consumers prefer those choices that maximize the therapeutic benefit while minimizing restrictiveness and loss of choice and freedoms. This brings us to the topic of the "least restrictive alternative."

The "Least Restrictive Alternative" (LRA)

Origin of the Least Restrictive Alternative (LRA)

The notion of "least restrictive alternative" evolved from the legal term "least drastic alternative," as used in a series of court cases (*Shelton v. Tucker*, 1960; *Lake v. Cameron*, 1966; *Covington v. Harris*, 1969; *Wyatt v. Stickney*, 1971; *Lessard v. Schmidt*, 1972) that laid out the obligation of mental health and mental retardation treatment services to provide treatment meeting therapeutic goals in a manner that maximizes freedom and independence (Miller, 1982). All of these court cases involved lawsuits against state hospitals or state schools serving individuals with mental retardation, with such institutions viewed as the most restrictive amongst alternatives for care (Miller, 1982). Miller (1982) comments that this view was most directly communicated in the famous patients' rights lawsuit, *Wyatt v. Stickney*, when the plaintiff's attorney claimed that the motivation for the lawsuit was to "make it too expensive to run large mental institutions and encourage the development of noninstitutional alternatives," thus facilitating the process of deinstitutionalization (Schwarz, 1974, p. 461).

In 1977, as deinstitutionalization was rapidly moving forward, President Jimmy Carter convened the President's Commission on Mental Health, chaired by First Lady Rosalynn Carter, to focus on developing new policies to address the significant deficiencies in the mental health system (Grob, 2005). One of the basic principles of deinstitutionalization was to provide clients with community services and residences that were less restrictive than that provided by the state mental hospital. The commission viewed the "least restrictive alternative" as a basic right and defined it as

> [that which] maintains the greatest degree of freedom, self-determination, autonomy, dignity and integrity of body, mind and spirit for the individual while he or she participates in treatment or receives services. (President's Commission on Mental Health, 1978)

The President's Commission on Mental Health faced numerous challenges. "Bureaucratic rivalries within and between governments; tensions and rivalries within the mental health professions; identity and interest group politics; the difficulties of distinguishing the respective etiological roles of such elements as poverty, racism, stigmatization, and unemployment; and an illusory faith in prevention all influenced the commission's deliberations and subsequent enactment of the short-lived Mental Health Systems Act" (Grob, 2005, p. 425). The commission eventually formulated the National Plan for the Chronically Mentally Ill, but the system of care and treatment for persons with serious mental illnesses presented in the plan was never realized because after Carter left office, the incoming president, Ronald Reagan, refused to act on the commission's recommendations.

What the LRA Means in Social Work Practice

What is important to understand is that the notion of a "least restrictive alternative" provided a conceptual underpinning for the deinstitutionalization movement (Miller, 1988) and was a reaction to recognizing the process of dehumanization and degradation that occurs in "total institutions." We began to recognize that regimented impersonal treatment strips people of all sense of identity or dignity. To restore dignity to those affected by institutionalization and to avoid the risk of institutionalization to those not yet affected required a shift in the locus of care from institutionalizing individuals with mental illness to offering treatment in the least restrictive manner.

To foster the use of the least restrictive alternative (LRA) in practice, it is important to realize that LRA applies both to the treatment environment as well as the modes of treatment used. For example, therapies that affect physical functioning are more intrusive than those that do not (Sands, 2001). Thus, treatment with medication is more intrusive than talk therapy; aversive treatment is more coercive than systematic desensitization;

and physical restraint is more intrusive than verbally persuading a client to do something (Sands, 2001).

In addition, within each modality are differing levels of restrictiveness. When considering treatment with medication, the least restrictive alternative is the medication that has the fewest negative side effects yet fulfills treatment goals. The mode of administration of a medication is significant too. A long-acting injectable medication is more restrictive than a daily oral medication. Why? Because once that injectable medication is in the person's body, it remains there for a certain length of time, usually two weeks, regardless of whether the person might change his or her mind about wanting the medication during that period. In contrast, each time a consumer takes an oral medication, he or she is making a choice: "Do I want to take this medication or don't I?" and thus there is choice every time a dose is taken, not just every two weeks.

Although long-acting injectable medication may be a convenience for staff, it carries side effects additional to those associated with the oral version of the same medication. Most injectable psychotropic medications are suspended in peanut or sesame oil. Oil is thick, and so a thick needle must be used, and the medication is then forced deep into the person's muscle. Such injections can be painful. Then, after the injection, oil often leaks out and stains the person's clothing. Some consumers also develop a painful lump at the injection site. We may not think of all these aspects of taking injectable medications, but these aspects can be very significant for consumers with regard to comfort, both physical and psychological. I vividly recall incidents in which consumers who received an injection of medication would leave the nurse's office with a large oil stain on the back of their pants and other consumers would laugh at them as they walked through the waiting room. If a consumer can be medication adherent with oral medications, he or she should be allowed to exercise that choice. However, for some consumers an injectable medication is the wisest choice, and there are strategies clinicians can use to avoid or mitigate some of the problems associated with injections. Social workers have a responsibility to be knowledgeable about medication and, thus, this will be addressed in great detail in Chapter 7.

It is also important to recognize that community care is not always the least restrictive amongst alternatives. A particular placement's restrictiveness depends on many variables including the type of setting, the size of the facility, the location of the facility, and the personalities and philosophies of operators, caretakers, or providers. Example:

> Dorothy, 56 years old, had spent many years at Napa State Hospital, located in the beautiful Napa Valley area of California. Dorothy had a developmental disability and, thus, stayed at Napa longer than those individuals with other mental illnesses who had been deinstitutionalized much earlier. Dorothy was very happy to leave the hospital and start a new life in the community. However, her first placement was very disappointing to her. The board and care home where she was placed was way out in the country in the San Joaquin Valley, which is the agricultural center of California. There was no public transportation from the home to the nearest town and very little programming was provided in the home. Once a week, the care home operator took Dorothy and the other residents into town, but there was no individual freedom. Everyone was instructed to stay together as a group, the care home operator dictated where they went and residents had little to no input and choice. The care home operator was very rigid, inflexible, and controlling with the residents and regularly punished them for any transgressions, usually by withholding outings. Dorothy was miserable and told her social worker that she had more freedom at the state hospital than in her current placement. Fortunately the social worker was able to find another placement for Dorothy in town with a care home operator who struck a good balance between appropriate supervision and individual freedom. Dorothy was able to enjoy community life, was able to access more therapeutic programs, was nearer to her family, and was much happier.

Social workers are in a key position to put the LRA standard into practice because we are trained to view clients within the context of their environment and we understand the complexities of social systems. In other words, we take a holistic approach to working with clients and families and are inclusive in considering the myriad of factors that affect whether interventions or placements are more or less restrictive. In determining what constitutes the least restrictive alternative, the social worker must balance considering which environment provides the greatest amount of appropriate freedom versus restrictiveness with what environment is most therapeutic for the client. The main objective is to try to achieve a *balance* between supporting the client's freedom and right to self-determination and fulfilling therapeutic goals. To achieve this objective, there are three things that you should strive to do as you work with clients.

First, you must know your client's needs, strengths, and challenges, and clearly know and understand *their* perceptions and attitudes about increased freedom. If you ask clients directly about this, some will say that they are comfortable and ready for a lot of freedom and choice, while others want some freedom but also want support and structure in their living situation and programming. For many clients, the move toward increased freedom is a very gradual process, particularly if they have left a highly structured institution such as a state hospital or prison. An important rule of thumb is to not make assumptions about what your client wants before asking them and discussing the range of options available.

Second, know your community's resources and make sure that you stay current on the status of the various services you refer your clients to. The unfortunate reality is that many nonprofit client services are dependent on "soft money," that is, money obtained via grants from foundations and state and federal funding entities. As a result, they may open and close like clams. A particular service may be great, but when the funding runs out, the service must close unless an alternative funding source is found. You don't want to send your client to an empty storefront. Another issue is that eligibility criteria change, meaning that providers may change who they serve and what services they provide. Also, agencies—particularly small ones—may change their address or phone number. Such services may be operating on a shoestring and when the rent goes up, they have to move to stay solvent. When I was in practice, I kept a notebook and updated it on a regular basis in terms of such changes, going through many bottles of "white out" over the course of a year! Today's technologies provide much more efficient ways to keep track of changes in service providers. A personal digital assistant (PDA) is much more convenient than a paper-and-pencil notebook.

Finally, you should foster the principle of the LRA by proactively helping clients progress from more restrictiveness to less restrictiveness. Sometimes, however, a placement or treatment program fails because the social worker or other mental health professional pushed the client toward independence too quickly or too soon. In such cases, the social worker and client must reassess the treatment plan and make appropriate modifications. Concerns about encouraging less restrictive alternatives may come from a variety of sources including family members, colleagues, the client him or herself—and even political interference in the form of community pressure to keep clients' freedom of movement restricted. It is important to listen to any stakeholders and thoughtfully consider their concerns. For example, family members—who have had a lifetime of experience with your client—may express strong reservations about increased freedom. It is important to ask the family for details about that. The family may have had experiences in which increased freedom has led to negative outcomes. For example, they may tell you that, in their experience, increased freedom has often led to their loved one using drugs and alcohol again. That is important information to consider as you collaboratively develop the client's overall treatment plan. Additional strategies for fostering the LRA will be discussed in Chapter 9, which addresses case management.

Confidentiality and the Duty to Warn

Confidentiality

The next important topic to address in the area of legal and ethical issues is confidentiality and privileged communication. Confidentiality is an important social work value and is an ethical principle specified in the NASW Code of Ethics. Why is safeguarding confidentiality so important in practice with individuals with serious mental illness?

The first reason is that confidentiality protects clients from the effects of society's continuing and pervasive negative attitudes toward mental illness and those who suffer from it. In spite of anti-stigma efforts, stigma remains alive and well in our society and worldwide (Baum, 2000; Green, 2009). Second, safeguarding confidentiality is critical to maintaining the strength and viability of therapeutic alliance between the client and the clinician and/or treatment team. Confidentiality implies the mental health professional will protect his or her client's interests so that the client feels safe to share feelings openly.

Confidentiality is not the same as privileged communication. Privileged communication means that information shared in confidence between client and social worker is protected from inquiry by the court. Instances in which privileged communication is set aside include when a client signs a waiver or when the clinician is mandated to break confidentiality because of suspected child abuse or elder abuse, involuntary commitment, and the management of behavior dangerous to self or others, for example, if a social worker requires assistance by the police to assure safety during a home visit to a suicidal client, he or she can provide the police with details necessary about the client situation to enable them to prepare, such as informing them that the client has a lethal weapon.

It used to be that only California granted privileged communication to licensed social workers. However, a Supreme Court decision in June 1996 changed all this when it ruled that there is a psychotherapist–patient privilege in federal courts and that psychotherapists—including licensed social workers—cannot be compelled to disclose client records in federal judicial proceedings ***(Jaffee v. Redmond, 1996)***.

The Duty to Warn

In 1976, in the landmark case of *Tarasoff v. The Regents of the University of California*, the California Supreme Court laid out the obligation of psychotherapists to warn third parties of possible harm that their clients might cause to other people. Gradually over the years, and usually in reaction to a specific act of violence committed by an individual under mental health care, courts and legislatures in other states began to examine the issues raised by the *Tarasoff* ruling, and by the mid-1980s, the "duty to warn" became law across much of the United States and an important component of clinical training and practice (Herbert & Young, 2002). The following is a summary of the original *Tarasoff* case:

> Prosenjit Poddar, a graduate student who was receiving psychotherapy at the University of California Student Health Service in Berkeley, told his therapist that he intended to kill Tatiana Tarasoff, a female student who had indicated that she was not romantically interested in him, although he was interested in her. The therapist responded by (a) getting Poddar to promise that he would not act on his homicidal thoughts; and (b) informing the campus police in order to initiate an involuntary commitment. The police investigated the matter and were assured by Poddar that nothing would happen and he would not harm Tarasoff. At the time all of this was happening, Tatiana Tarasoff was on vacation and out of the country. When she returned, however, Poddar went to her apartment, and killed her. Tarasoff's family sued the therapist, the campus police and the University of California stating that Tatiana should have been warned she was in danger. (*Tarasoff v. The Regents of the University of California*, 1974)

Tarasoff v The Regents of the University of California, 551 P.2d 334 (Cal. 1974/1976)

An initial 1974 ruling by the California Supreme Court concluded that the therapist and police could be liable for failing to warn Tarasoff. In the aftermath of the 1974 Tarasoff ruling, mental health professionals voiced a number of concerns regarding the impact of the duty to warn mandate on clinical practice, which remain issues of concern today (Newhill, 2003; Appelbaum, 1985; Beigler, 1984; Cocozza & Steadman, 1978; Gordon, 1977; Huber, Roth, Appelbaum, & Ore, 1982; Kozol, 1982; Meyers, 1984; Shah, 1978; Steadman, 1980, 1982; Wise, 1978). These include the following:

- The duty to warn is incompatible with sustaining an effective therapeutic relationship and would deter clients who could benefit from treatment from seeking treatment;
- The duty to warn would deter therapists from treating dangerous patients;
- The duty to warn is a serious breach of confidentiality and forces a shift from the clinician's alliance with the welfare of the client to an alliance with the welfare of the public;
- The duty to warn will inappropriately increase the number of civil commitments;
- Considering the general inaccuracy of clinician predictions of dangerousness, the duty to warn would only produce more false positives (i.e., predicting a client will be violent when, in fact, the client is not violent) since the evidence supports the conclusion that therapists tend to over-predict rather than under-predict dangerousness; and
- The duty to warn will result in reluctance on the part of both therapists and patients to probe the topic of violence in treatment, thus eliminating an opportunity to intervene and potentially reduce the probability of violence occurring.

These concerns were taken seriously by the California Supreme Court and, on appeal, a subsequent 1976 decision (*Tarasoff II*) ruled that "when a therapist determines, or pursuant to the standards of his profession should determine, that his patient presents a serious danger of violence to another, he incurs an obligation to use reasonable care to protect the intended victim against such danger" (*Tarasoff*, 1976, p. 34). "Reasonable care" was defined as warning the victim directly, warning others who could warn the victim, or notifying the police. Paul Appelbaum (1985) developed a three-stage model that, if followed, would constitute reasonable care:

Stage 1: The clinician should conduct a thorough violence risk assessment by gathering all relevant data and then evaluating the client's level of risk based on the data. This assessment should be documented thoroughly, and consultation with colleagues is an important component.

Stage 2: If the conclusion is that the client poses a threat of violence toward others, the clinician then decides upon a course of action designed to reduce the probability of harm. Such action could include any of the following: (1) hospitalization; (2) intensifying treatment via increasing the number of clinic visits, changing the dosage of medication, and so forth; (3) taking steps to increase treatment compliance; (4) involving family or other community supports in reducing risk by, for example, preventing access to weapons; (5) consulting with colleagues to coordinate the plan of action; (6) issuing a warning to the intended victim or, in the absence of an identified victim, notifying the police; and (7) continuing to gather risk assessment data.

Stage 3: Implement the plan developed in Stage 2, and follow up by monitoring the outcome of each step.

Areas of Confusion with Regard to the *Tarasoff* Mandate

There are three issues that continue to plague an adequate understanding of the *Tarasoff* ruling and its associated mandates (Herbert & Young, 2002). The first area of confusion relates to the change in language from the 1974 ruling to the 1976 ruling. In 1974, the court ruled that clinicians have a "duty to warn," and the 1976 ruling replaced that phrase with "duty to protect." However, legal scholars have generally concluded that the former phrase "duty to warn" continues to be the more accurate description of what courts across the nation have expected clinicians to do (Herbert & Young, 2002). This is why most current *Tarasoff* state statutes—including Alabama, California, Connecticut, the District of Columbia, Florida, Idaho, Illinois, Kansas, Louisiana, Minnesota, Mississippi, Montana, Nebraska, New York, Oregon, Pennsylvania, Rhode Island, Texas, Utah, Washington, and West Virginia—describe the duty exclusively in terms of a warning, making no mention of a duty to protect or any other obligation, including civil commitment. Warning alone always fulfills the mandated duty. Herbert and Young (2002) state that "if anything, *Tarasoff* thus weakens the case for a duty to protect by providing a potential defense (if a warning was given) against a suit for negligent non-commitment" (p. 275).

The second area of confusion is the incorrect belief that the *Tarasoff* ruling was an action in response to the clinician not "protecting" the victim, Tatiana Tarasoff. In fact, the clinician had done everything *except* for warning Tarasoff or warning her family. The problem was not one of protection; it was the failure to warn the victim or her family that she was in potential danger.

Finally, the courts have generally ruled in the direction of viewing the issuing of a warning as the most direct and adequate method of alerting a potential victim of potential harm. Means of protection, such as referring a client to treatment or monitoring medication, has been shown to not impress juries when looking at therapist liability (see, e.g., *Sherrill v. Wilson*, 1983), but a warning is clear and direct, discharges the clinician's duty, and shifts the responsibility to the potential victim.

How the States Differ in the Duty to Warn

Kagle and Kopels (1994) provide an excellent review of the status of the *Tarasoff* ruling two decades later and discuss how the statutes reflecting *Tarasoff* have varied across the states. In all cases, the statutes require actions involving a breach of confidentiality by warning a third party of potential harm, but there are some differences in what clinicians can or must do to fulfill the mandate. In the state of Kentucky, for example, clinicians are required to use reasonable efforts to warn the victim along with notifying the police (Kentucky Revised Statutes Annotated, 1988). In Indiana, clinicians can choose amongst several methods of discharging their duty including warning the victim directly, civilly committing the client, reporting the threat to someone else who can warn the potential victim, notifying the police, and taking steps to prevent harm from taking place until the police can intervene. Review a specific example: *Evolution of the Pennsylvania Statute.*

Dilemmas for Clinicians

The duty to warn mandate poses a couple of dilemmas for clinical social workers and other mental health professionals. First, the duty to warn requires that the social worker breach confidentiality, which can jeopardize the therapeutic relationship with the client. A second dilemma is that the duty to warn calls for a difficult clinical judgment, that is, whether the potential danger constitutes a compelling enough reason for a warning to be issued, thus forcing clinicians into predicting violent behavior, which, as noted above, tends to be inaccurate (Newhill, 1989).

To address these dilemmas, Reamer (2003, pp. 38–39) offers four general guidelines to help social workers balance the safeguarding of client confidentiality with the duty to warn mandate of their state. First, the social worker must have evidence that his or her client may potentially harm a third party. Such evidence could include a verbal threat of harm made by the client in the presence of the social worker, a written threat in a letter indicating the client may harm the third party, and so forth. Second, the social worker should have evidence that the potential harm is foreseeable, meaning that the harm is expected and easy to foretell. An example of such evidence would be a history of the client actually harming the person who is currently being threatened. This was the case with Gad Joseph and Theresa Hausler (see above). Third, the social worker should have evidence that the violent act is imminent, that is, the social worker predicts—on the basis of a good risk assessment—that there is a likelihood the act of violence will occur in the near future. Finally, the social worker must be able to identify the probable victim. This means that the client mentions the person by name or refers to the person in a way that clearly identifies him or her, for example, "my wife," "my boss," etc. If these four guidelines are met, Reamer (2003) argues, then the breach of confidentiality that the duty to warn requires is justified.

Now, how does one apply such guidelines in an actual practice situation? How does one fulfill the duty to warn without permanently rupturing the therapeutic alliance? How does the social worker look out for the client's best interests and consider the welfare of a third party? To answer these questions, let's revisit the situation of my former client Fred, described earlier in this chapter, who was hospitalized involuntarily as a danger to others because he feared he might lose control and kill his mother. In this situation, because of the threats toward his mother, I determined that I must issue a warning to his mother. Although I had hospitalized Fred, I did not believe this absolved me of the duty, because the conflict between Fred and his mother was ongoing and I was concerned that even after his discharge, her life might be in danger. Furthermore, at that time in California, civil commitment alone was not considered sufficient to fully discharge the duty to warn.

When issuing a warning to a third party of possible harm from a client, it is important that the social worker be honest and forthcoming with the client involved. Although there may be clinicians that disagree with me on this, I always tell the client honestly that I am going to issue a warning and then describe the basis for it. Two points are important to emphasize in this regard. First, it is important for the client to know that this is a legal mandate, an obligation that I must fulfill. It is not arbitrary or personal; it is not done with malicious intent; it is simply a mandated duty. Second, it is important to empathically tell the client that the goal of the warning is to protect both the client's well-being and that of the third party. The following is an approximation of the conversation that I had with Fred during the admission process:

Christina: Fred, as you know, I am concerned about your safety and your mom's safety, and that is why I am arranging for your admission to the hospital. From what you have told me, it sounds like this is something that you want to do too.

Fred: Yeah . . . I really don't have any choice. I don't really want to have to be in the hospital, but if I don't go in, I'm afraid I'll kill my mom.

Christina: I know. Things have been pretty rough for you recently. But in the hospital you'll be safe, your mom'll be safe, and we can help you to get better . . . to feel better and back in control.

Fred: Yeah.

Christina: Fred, there is something I need to talk with you about before John [the admissions nurse] comes down to take you to your room. When a client makes a threat to harm someone else—like when you said you wanted to kill your mother because she was causing you to smell the bad odors—one of the things I have to do legally is to contact your mom and tell her about the threat. It's a legal duty that we social workers don't have any choice about. And I know this is kind of hard for you. Do you understand what I'm saying?

Fred: Oh, shit, man—I was afraid of this. Oh, man . . . do you have to? She'll get really mad at me.

Christina: Fred, I know you love your mom—that's why you came to the hospital. You don't want to hurt her but you're not feeling good right now and you don't want to lose control. . . . It took a lot of courage for you to come down here and tell us honestly what was going on, and I bet your mom is going to understand that. You're kind of between a rock and a hard place right now. You don't want to hurt your mom but you can't stay in control right now—the important thing is that you came in and asked for help. That's a really good thing.

Fred: I guess so—I guess it was good I didn't go ahead and hurt her. I really love my mom, it's just that sometimes I can't stand her.

Christina: I understand, Fred. It's a tough situation. Once you start to feel better, I think it would be a good idea for you and Bill [the inpatient social worker] and your mom to meet and talk about things. Perhaps you could try living somewhere else for a while, instead of with your mom, and see how that goes.

Fred: I guess so. . . . I like Bill . . . he's helped me before. Okay, well . . . I guess you have to make that call. Can I go on into the unit and get some dinner? I'm kind of hungry.

Christina: Sure—I'll call John to come and get you. Fred, I'm really glad you came in today, and when you get out of the hospital, please stop by and see me—let me know how you're doing—okay?

Fred: Okay—thanks.

Now that the client—Fred—has been informed that I am going to call his mother and tell her about the threat, the next step is making the call. When contacting the person who is the potential victim, it is critical that support and counseling be provided in tandem with the actual warning. For example, discussing with the potential victim what kinds of steps he or she can take to ensure safety and offering support, counseling, or other clinical assistance. Below is an approximation of my conversation with Fred's mother, "Mrs. Smith":

Mrs. Smith: Hello?

Christina: Hello, Mrs. Smith. This is Christina Newhill—I'm a clinical social worker with the crisis team here at county mental health. We met a couple weeks ago when I came out to see your son, Fred, and we talked for a while—do you remember me?

Mrs. Smith: Oh, yes, I remember—I really appreciated you coming out here. I just don't know what to do with Fred sometimes. Is he okay? Are you calling about him?

Christina: Yes, I am. Mrs. Smith, Fred came in today and he's not doing very well. As you know we have tried increasing his medicine and tried to encourage him to come in to transitional care for a stay, but he didn't want to do that. Today, he came in and told me he was feeling a lot worse. Have you seen him today at all?

Mrs. Smith: Yes—he was really cranky this morning . . . wouldn't eat anything . . . didn't matter what I said—he'd fly off the handle. When he gets like that, I don't know what to do with him. You know, he threatened to hit me yesterday—I told him to just leave if that's how he felt. I don't know if he's taking his other medicine—what is it now? I can't recall the name of it. I know he's getting his shots, that's good, but that other medicine—I don't think he's taking it.

Christina: I know you've been really trying to help him—it's got to be pretty hard for you sometimes.

Mrs. Smith: Well, it is . . . but he's my son, you know.

Christina: I know. Mrs. Smith, the reason I called was to tell you about something that Fred said when he came into the hospital. . . .

Mrs. Smith: He said he was going to kill me, right?

Christina: Yes, that's what he said and, legally, I have to inform you that he did, indeed, make a threat to kill you. But, Mrs. Smith, the good thing is that Fred came in and asked to go into the hospital. He was afraid he would lose control and rather than letting that happen, he came in for help.

Mrs. Smith: Oh, he won't do anything—he makes these threats but I don't think he'd actually hurt me.

Christina: Quite frankly, Mrs. Smith, I am concerned about your safety. I know that you love your son very much, and you have been so kind to him, supporting him and letting him live with you. But I would take his threat seriously. I think it would be a good idea to meet with Bill, the hospital social worker, and consider the possibility of having Fred live somewhere else for a while.

Mrs. Smith: Well, okay, but that's been tried before—he always comes back.

Christina: Let's see what the options are. I want to be sure that both you and Fred are safe.

The outcome of the situation was that Bill, Fred, and Fred's mom agreed to a plan that involved Fred moving into a supervised apartment. Things went well for about a month, but then Fred insisted on going back to live with his mother. Years after I left the agency, I heard from a former colleague that Fred had, tragically, killed his mother. He was deemed incompetent to stand trial and remains hospitalized indefinitely at a maximum-security forensic facility.

The remaining topics that I want to address in this chapter on legal and ethical issues are the subjects of client rights and privacy, HIPAA, and diagnostic labeling.

Overview of HIPAA

The acronym "HIPAA" stands for the Health Insurance Portability and Accountability Act of 1996, which was passed by Congress to establish standardization and greater efficiency in the health care industry along with establishing privacy standards for the electronic transmission of consumers' health information. Those impacted by HIPAA include health care providers who transmit patient health information electronically, health insurance plans, and health care clearinghouses. (U.S. Department of Health and

Human Services [DHHS], 2009). There is a lot of confusion about what HIPAA requires and does not require and, thus, it is important for social workers to understand its basic parameters in order to practice ethically and within legal boundaries. One of the best resources for HIPAA information for social workers is the NASW website, although only active NASW members can access the HIPAA information. The website address for NASW is www.socialworkers.org. Another useful website for general HIPAA information is the Centers for Medicare and Medicaid Services website at http://www.cms.gov. There are four basic parts to HIPAA: (1) electronic transaction and code set standards requirements; (2) privacy requirements; (3) security requirements; and (4) national identifier requirements (DHHS, 2009). The electronic transaction and code set standards requirements standardized the way in which health care information is transmitted electronically. The goal is to establish a common language that all health care providers use and understand that facilitates accurate interpretation of health care information across settings. An example of a standardized transaction would be an inquiry about eligibility and the response to the inquiry.

The privacy requirements of HIPAA set limits on the release of identifiable patient/consumer health care information without the patient's knowledge and informed consent. HIPAA argues that health care information is particularly sensitive and personal and, thus, special protections must be in place to ensure privacy. This is the component of HIPAA that most affects the day-to-day practice of social workers.

Read more about the *HIPPA Privacy Requirements.*

The security requirements in HIPAA address the administrative, technical, and physical safeguards to prevent unauthorized access to consumer/patient information. Finally, the national identifier requirements mandate that employers, health plans, and health care providers have standard national numbers (selected and issued by the Internal Revenue Service) that identify them on standard transactions.

Working with Families: What HIPAA does not Prohibit

One of the major frustrations of family members of those with serious mental illness is the unwillingness of providers treating ill loved ones to talk with families and hear their concerns. Such providers often cite HIPAA or confidentiality in general as the reason for refusing to talk with families. The requirements of HIPAA and confidentiality *do not prohibit* treatment providers from meeting with family members and *listening to their concerns.* HIPAA and confidentiality requirements do not prohibit *receiving* information from others. They only set rules for the *disclosure* of protected health information. It is very important that we are supportive and receptive to what family members have to say and listen to their concerns.

In addition, it is important to talk with consumers about how limited disclosure of certain information might be helpful for them in enabling their family or other caretakers to understand their illness and treatment and to support their recovery. This is particularly critical if the family is in the role of primary caretaker. One approach that works well is to have the initial family meetings include participation of the consumer. Then the consumer can decide what to reveal or not reveal and, because he or she is present for the discussion, everything is up front and transparent, and the consumer won't feel that things are being said behind his or her back. Once trust and collaborative relationships amongst the family, consumer, and social worker (or other provider) have been established, then the consumer can decide, with the social worker's input, how and what to disclose in the consent form. There is a difference between disclosing information so everyone centrally involved can talk about the individual's treatment and recovery in a collaborative manner versus "poking noses" into the consumer's private business or handing over their clinical record.

Often, all that is needed to facilitate a collaborative partnership amongst provider, family, and consumer is very limited disclosure of information.

Clients' Rights to Their Health Information

All health care recipients have a right to access their medical records and request a copy of the record, although they may be responsible for the costs incurred. It is not unusual for errors to appear in a medical record, and consumers have the right to request corrections of such errors when identified. Access to psychotherapy notes is more complicated, and they are generally excluded from the right to access with the exception of information on the consumer's medication and medication monitoring, the status of their psychosocial functioning, their treatment plan and progress in it, and their diagnosis and symptoms. Clients can also expect that communication with providers via letters, telephone, and email should be kept private and confidential.

Diagnoses and the Right to Know

Clients have a right to know what illness they are being treated for, what that means, and what they can expect for their future. In other words, in today's world of mental health care, the consumer has a right to know his or her diagnosis. Furthermore, such knowledge plays an important role in the consumer's recovery, because it helps the individual gain insight and understanding of his or her symptoms and treatment, and informs the goals and choices the client makes for his or her life.

If the social worker encounters an agency stance that diagnostic information should not be provided to clients, there are a couple steps that can be taken. First, it is very appropriate to bring up for discussion in a regular team or staff meeting the issue of talking to clients about their diagnosis and illness. Out of that discussion can emerge a policy to address this. A second step that can be very effective is to bring in a speaker from a consumer advocacy group to talk with staff about how diagnostic and illness-related information can be helpful for clients in their recovery. This may serve to open up discussion and raise staff awareness.

Making a psychiatric diagnosis serves three main functions. First, a diagnosis provides a succinct and standardized means of communicating a large amount of information about a client's illness, incorporating biological, psychological, and social perspectives (Blashfield & Draguns, 1976). Second, a diagnosis can serve to guide appropriate treatment and avoid initiating treatment based on isolated symptoms alone (Fauman, 2002). For example, just because a client is experiencing psychotic symptoms doesn't mean it is appropriate to treat the symptoms with antipsychotic medication. Finally, a diagnosis documents medical necessity or need for continued care, which is often required by third-party payers, such as insurance companies, or for certain legal procedures, such as involuntary civil commitment. These functions or purposes of a diagnosis make clinical sense and enable providers to provide treatment. However, from an ethical perspective, it must also be recognized that psychiatric diagnoses are *labels* and, as such, carry the risk of being misapplied or misused.

Diagnoses and Labeling

Properly applied, a psychiatric diagnosis should serve as a shorthand summary designed to communicate both a description and appreciation of the client's clinical presentation. This is its proper use in medicine and social work. However, there are three main issues of concern with regard to diagnoses as labels that remain unresolved but should be always kept in mind by clinical social workers in our work with clients and their families.

Labels should Classify Defined Disorders, not People

The first issue is the contention that labels should classify defined disorders, not people; however, they often end up classifying people. The latest edition of the *Diagnostic and Statistical Manual of Mental Disorders* (APA, 2013) recognizes this, and it avoids using expressions such as "a schizophrenic" or "an alcoholic" and emphasizes that classifications of mental disorders do not classify people—rather, they classify disorders that people have. However, if one hangs around psychiatric inpatient units long enough, one will see that a person quickly becomes defined by a disorder, and the person him or herself becomes lost. Example:

> One day, when I was working as a clinical social worker on a locked inpatient unit, I was sitting in the nursing station writing up my notes. The phone rang and a staff member answered the phone, spoke briefly, rolled his eyes, and then slammed the phone down. He looked at the rest of us and sighed, "Oh great—just what we need—another borderline. . . ." Interpretation: A client with borderline personality disorder was being transported to the unit for admission. Before this unfortunate client even entered the unit, everybody hated him. As yet, nobody knew anything else about the client coming in, but the attitude was, essentially, that it didn't matter. The client "was borderline," and that's all that the staff needed to know.

This is an example of how psychiatric labels can serve as a conduit for stigma—sometimes profound stigma (Corrigan, 2007). Rather than placing the person first before the reference to a disability, for example, "a person with schizophrenia," the individual is equated with the diagnosis, for example, "a schizophrenic" or "a borderline." Diagnoses describe disorders—not people—but sometimes that distinction is lost in everyday practice (Williams, 2008).

Once the Label is Applied, it will Close off Further Inquiry

A second issue with regard to labeling is the concern that once the label is applied, it will close off further inquiry. It can be argued, however, that closing off further inquiry is less a problem of the diagnostic label than an issue of poor practice skills. Competent diagnostic formulations and bio-psycho-social-spiritual assessments should address more than the diagnostic label and serve to open up inquiry, rather than closing it off. For example, let's assume the social worker is doing an intake evaluation on a client who has been treated for depression. The client's diagnosis is only the beginning of knowing who that client is and what kind of help he or she needs. Immediate questions for further inquiry might include:

- What, if anything, precipitated the onset of the client's depression?
- How long has the client been depressed, and how intense are the symptoms?
- How well is the client able to function interpersonally, occupationally, and in other ways?
- How does the client perceive his or her depression and life in general? What is his or her perspective?
- Does the client have family and friends to rely on?
- What kind of help does the client want? What are his or her goals for that help?

Identifying a client's diagnosis is just the beginning. Furthermore, any diagnosis is always a "working diagnosis" that requires regular reassessment for the possibility of change. Sometimes a diagnosis is incorrect, or the person recovers and the diagnosis no longer applies, or the person may develop another illness or an additional illness, or our knowledge about the particular illness changes and requires diagnostic reassessment.

Sometimes such reassessment is not done, however, and a particular diagnosis follows the person for years even though it may not be correct, and this can result in inappropriate treatment. Example:

> "Robert" is 63 years old and is currently diagnosed with pervasive developmental disorder, sometimes referred to as "atypical autism." For years, however, Robert was incorrectly diagnosed and inappropriately treated. Here is how that happened.
>
> In 1956, at age 11, Robert was hospitalized and given the diagnosis of "childhood schizophrenia" per the *DSM-I*. Back then we knew very little about autism, and many children diagnosed with childhood schizophrenia in those days would have been diagnosed with autism today. Childhood schizophrenia *can* occur but is extremely rare. As Robert grew up, his diagnosis remained the same, and when he was admitted to the state hospital at age 18, his diagnosis was simply changed to "schizophrenia." However, Robert had never experienced any psychotic symptoms or negative symptoms of schizophrenia; rather, he exhibited many—although not all—of the symptoms of autism. Because of his diagnostic label, Robert was submitted to heavy doses of traditional antipsychotic drugs—Thorazine, Stelazine, Mellaril—which never helped him and only served to "dope" him up. Finally, in the 1980s, Robert was deinstitutionalized, placed in a board and care home, and prescribed partial hospitalization treatment. Robert was able to convince the community mental health psychiatrist to not give him any medication, but the programs at the community mental health center weren't helpful to him and the staff was continually frustrated by his persistent behavioral problems and grossly inappropriate social interactions. Finally, in the mid-1990s, a young psychologist was hired at the program and after observing Robert for a while, she approached the center's director and told him that she didn't think Robert had schizophrenia. Instead, she said, he probably has some form of autism. With her persistence, Robert was thoroughly reevaluated, and the conclusion was that he had autism, not schizophrenia, and should be treated by the developmental disabilities system, not the mental health system. Today, Robert is doing very well. He attends a daily behavioral program, works part-time in a sheltered workshop, lives in a small group home, and is treated by caring staff who understand his pervasive developmental disability and who set appropriate, feasible goals for him. After a lifetime of being inappropriately diagnosed and treated, Robert is finally receiving the help he needs.

Effect of the Label on an Individual's Behavior and View of Self

The third and final issue with regard to labeling is how a label of mental illness can affect an individual's behavior and view of self. Originating in sociology and criminology, labeling theory focuses on the tendency groups with power and status have to negatively label minority groups, especially those seen as deviant from established social norms. Labeling theory is concerned with how an individual's self-identity and behavior may be determined or influenced by the terms used to describe or classify him or her, and is associated with the concepts of a self-fulfilling prophecy and the process of stereotyping. The concern is that once an individual is labeled, he or she may accept that defined identity and play out the expectations of that role. For example, a person with a substance abuse problem might say to himself: "I'm a substance abuser, therefore everyone expects me to take drugs, so I might as well get high." This certainly reflects the pejorative and stigmatizing effects of psychiatric labels, and suggests such labels can result in devastating harm to the individual's sense of self, morale, and/or self-esteem. A label of mental disorder can also cause other people to perceive the individual in a biased way, for example, as "dangerous" because he or she is labeled mentally ill.

Critics of labeling theory argue that labeling theory does not meet the standards of a scientific theory because it is too ambiguous and inexplicit (Gibbs, 1972) and is ideologically biased (Davis, 1972), however, the basic notion that a label of mental illness can affect the individual's view of him or herself certainly has face validity (Scheff, 1975).

Social work has also embraced aspects of labeling theory, particularly with regard to the labeling of vulnerable and oppressed groups, such as those that participate in behaviors that might be labeled as deviant, including people with mental illness. Social workers' primary concern is that such labels lead to stigma and affect individuals' willingness to seek help (Corrigan, 2007). Social workers are also concerned with using labels, such as psychiatric diagnoses, on the basis that they are merely "labels" and the negative consequences outweigh the positive consequences. In sum, the labeling issue remains an ongoing debate, but one that has some very valid concerns that we must remain sensitive to in our work with clients. Properly applied, a diagnostic label can guide treatment. However, at the same time, diagnostic labels—like other labels—have the potential to harm a client in three ways: (1) by equating the client with the diagnosis, (2) by following the individual without question or reassessment as they move through the system, and (3) by its influence in shaping the individual's identity and sense of self.

Assess your comprehension of *psychiatric advance directives, the least restrictive alternative, confidentiality, the duty to warn, and HIPAA* by completing this quiz.

RESOLUTION OF THE CASE OF JACK AND BOB

At the beginning of this chapter, a case vignette was presented that illustrated a number of legal and ethical issues. By now, presumably, the reader has a good understanding of some of the important legal and ethical issues that practicing social workers must wrestle with and is ready to tackle the questions posed by the vignette. Below is a description of how the situation with Jack and Bob was actually resolved in real life, a decision that took into consideration many of the issues addressed in the chapter.

Discussion of the Case of Jack and Bob

Jack goes back to the agency and discusses Bob's situation with a trusted co-worker. After sorting through all the issues with his co-worker, Jack decides that he is not going to let the neighbors bully him into taking an action that is not justified, namely hospitalizing Bob against his will when he is not an imminent danger to himself or others, nor is he gravely disabled. It simply would not be ethical to hospitalize him, because Jack could not provide legal justification without falsifying the evidence. Bob does have the right to live in his house as he pleases, and without a threat to his survival, Bob has the right to independence, freedom, and self-determination. However, as Jack mulls over his recent conversation with Bob, he recalls that Bob seemed kind of sad and lonely. "Hmmm," Jack thinks, "maybe that's why he's been sitting on the fence . . . maybe he is trying to reach out to people . . . maybe this is the key to the solution for the problem." With his hopes up, Jack makes another home visit to Bob. The following conversation ensues.

Bob: Oh, hi, Jack—hey, you came back really quick this time.

Jack: Hi, Bob. It's good to see you. Do you mind if I come in?

Bob: Sure, sure—come on in. Uh, the place is kind of a mess . . .

Jack: No problem. You know, Bob, I've been thinking about the situation going on here with you and the neighbors and so on, and I just wanted to talk with you a little more.

Bob: So, can I get you a cup of coffee? I think I have some coffee around here somewhere. (begins to rummage in the kitchen) Gee, I guess I'm out, um, I've got water, though—can I get you a glass of water?

Jack: Sure, that'd be great. Thanks.

Bob: Lemme find a clean cup. (rummages around some more) Okay—this looks pretty clean. (rubs the glass on the sleeve of his dirty shirt)

Jack: How about using some soap? That would help clean it better.

Bob: Okay—good idea!

Bob gives Jack the water, shoves newspapers and boxes off the couch so Jack can sit down, and they begin to talk.

Jack: So, Bob, tell me honestly—how are things going for you? Do you like living out here?

Bob: Sort of . . . I like having my own place, but the people around here aren't very friendly, though. They kind of give me dirty looks.

Jack: Hmmm . . . is that why you were sitting on the fence? To try to meet people?

Bob: Well, my mom said that she used to sit on the porch and the neighbors would come over to talk, and since my porch is covered with junk, I figured I'd sit on the fence. But it didn't work out so well.

Jack: Porch sitting generally works out better than fence sitting, in my experience.

Bob (sadly): Yeah.

Jack: I get the sense that you may be a little lonely?

Bob: Well, yeah, sort of . . .

Jack: You have friends at the socialization center, don't you? When I stopped by there a while back you were playing air hockey with Ramon.

Bob: Yeah, I have some friends there—at least I think they're my friends.

Jack: You're not sure about that?

Bob: Ramon and Tyrone came out to visit once, but they wouldn't come back even though it's just one bus ride here from Pershing Avenue.

Jack: Why haven't they come back?

Bob: They said my house was a pigsty and it stunk and they didn't want to visit anymore.

Jack: That had to be kind of disappointing for you. Would you like to have more visitors, Bob?

Bob: Well, sure I would.

Jack: What do you think might help that to happen for you?

Bob: I could clean the place up, I guess—it *is* kind of a mess—but I don't know where to start—there's my stuff and all my mom and dad's stuff. Could you help me?

Jack: Let's see what I can do. I can help some and I'll see if I can get some help from some of the peer case managers. I bet if you cleaned up your place, you'd get your friends to come visit and you'd probably enjoy your house more too. One more thing—I'd get rid of the bows and ornaments on the trees—I know you like them but I think trees might look better with just leaves.

Bob: Okay.

What Jack succeeded in doing was, essentially, reframing the situation so that Bob saw cleaning up his house and yard as a means for achieving a goal *he* wanted, which was to get some visitors so he wouldn't feel so lonely.

In the course of their conversation, Bob also admitted to Jack that he was forgetting to take his medicine—with all the mess in the bathroom, he couldn't find his pills and the disarray made him more cognitively disorganized than usual. Once the place was cleaned up, Bob was treated in a friendlier manner by the neighbors, he made friends with the neighbors next door, and he once again adhered to taking his medication, which controlled his auditory hallucinations. All this was done without any ethical or legal compromises.

Assess your application and analysis of this chapter's contents by completing the *Chapter Review*.

Chapter 4

Overcoming Barriers to Treating Clients with Serious Mental Illness and Developing and Maintaining a Therapeutic Alliance

INTRODUCTION

This chapter will address the principles of engagement when working with clients with severe mental illness and their families and the barriers that can impede the development of a therapeutic alliance both with clients and with their families. Such barriers include the impact of stigma, lack of or poorly developed insight, negative clinician attitudes, biases and stereotypes, cultural factors, and the nature of long-term illness. Most social workers are well aware of what might be called the structural barriers to working with clients with serious mental illness, such as lack of resources, the fragmented structure of the mental health system, lack of or inadequate insurance coverage, cost of services, and lack of transportation. However, the main focus of this chapter is on the kinds of barriers that may not immediately come to mind when considering the general topic of barriers to engagement and treatment.

When we consider the idea of working with clients with severe and persistent mental illness, or what used to be called "chronic mental illness," and their families, the first task that we have to address in preparing for such work is examining our *own* feelings about these types of disorders and, by extension, those who live with the illnesses. Not how we *should* feel; not how our field instructors, professors, supervisors, and colleagues have told us we should feel; but, rather, how we honestly feel emotionally about working with such individuals and the attitudes we hold about the illnesses that they have (Eack, Newhill, & Watson, 2012; Eack, Bahorik, Newhill, et al., 2012). Part of this is sometimes referred to as countertransference, but it goes beyond just the reactions to an individual client and involves our reactions to the illness itself, which may be severe, long term, and chronic in course.

Why is this so important? It is important because the feelings and attitudes we hold toward our clients are real and will directly or indirectly affect our ability to work effectively with them. Even if we know certain feelings—negative ones in particular—are problematic, rather than engaging in self-reflection and working through the feelings to constructive resolution, we may "stuff the feelings down" into the inner recesses of our psyche because honestly confronting our feelings is too threatening. Unfortunately, this doesn't work very well, because the feelings don't disappear, rather, they will sit and fester and will emerge eventually and possibly destructively. Many decades ago, some schools of clinical social work strongly encouraged or even required social work students to go through psychotherapy as part of the preparation for work as a clinician. That is rarely the case anymore, but the rationale behind it is still valid: one must develop the capacity for self-reflection and self-understanding as part of becoming a competent clinician, and that involves examining the good parts of ourselves and the parts that may be problematic—the parts that are judgmental and may hold biases and negative attitudes toward certain aspects of clients and the problems that they and their families bring to us.

What we have to remember is that we, as social workers, are not immune to the stereotypes, biases, and continuing social stigma that surrounds society's attitudes toward people with serious mental illness and their families. Although we are taught that mental illness should not be seen differently than any other kind of illness—for example, diabetes or cancer—the reality is that diabetes or cancer do not carry the same kind of stigma (Anonymous, 2007). "People diagnosed with a mental illness inhabit a different space in public perception from those hospitalised for physical conditions such as cancer or heart disease" (Shaw, 1998, p. 1050).

STIGMA

Bachrach (1988) identifies three criteria that define serious and persistent mental illness, or what used to be termed "chronic" mental illness—diagnosis, duration, and disability. Many serious mental illnesses, such as schizophrenia, bipolar disorder, depression, and borderline personality disorder, are both severe in terms of symptoms and level of disability, and they are persistent, meaning that they are long-term conditions requiring ongoing care and management.

Up until recently, the term "chronic mental illness" was used as an umbrella term to include such conditions, but since language can drive perception, consumers and families began to argue that the term "chronic" should be abandoned because it served to exacerbate stigma by communicating hopelessness about recovery. Instead, terms such as "serious mental illness" and "severe and persistent mental illness" are preferable because such terms communicate the fact that such illnesses are major disorders but do not assume the level of disability or the outcome, thus conveying hope.

For a variety of reasons, which will be discussed below, long-term conditions are particularly vulnerable to becoming stigmatized. However, no longer are individuals with serious long-term mental illness locked away in asylums, invisible to the larger society. Instead, they are now living with us, in our communities and in our neighborhoods, even right next door. Gill Green observes that "we are witnessing a realignment of social relationships—the old order in which the sick and disabled are disempowered and marginalized is being replaced by a world characterized by their increasing confidence and a reassertion of their essential personhood" (Green, 2009, p. 1). This realignment, however, is threatening to many in society who do not understand disabilities such as mental illness and, instead, fear it and want to distance themselves from those who live with such illnesses. In the midst of such fear rises the ugly head of stigma and the prejudice and discrimination that it fuels.

Falk (2001) states that mental illness is the "ultimate stigma." Stigma may be defined as a "mark of shame" (Hinshaw, 2007) or disgrace and "denotes the possession of a trait that marks one out as different from others and is negatively regarded" (Green, 2009, p. 3). Stigma is so powerful that it can eclipse a person's identity so that he or she is treated only as a member of the stigmatized group, such as "the mentally ill." We have developed a range of disparaging terms for such members, for example, "nutcase" or "lunatic." In fact, only recently was the word "lunatic" stricken from federal law (Ap. 2012).

Mental illness is one of the few illnesses that is still accompanied by considerable stigma. We lump individuals with psychiatric disabilities into a group we call "the mentally ill"; we do not refer to individuals living with cancer as "the cancers." Other conditions that, across many societies, carry stigma almost as great as that associated with mental illness include being HIV positive or having acquired immune deficiency syndrome (AIDS), having a sexually transmitted disease (STD), and—particularly in Western society—being morbidly obese (Puhl & Brownell, 2001).

Why is stigma as associated with certain conditions so persistent and intractable? Phelan, Link, & Dovidio (2008) argue that one reason is that stigma and the prejudice associated with it serves three functions for society as a whole. First, stigma keeps people down, thus serving the function of exploitation and domination. Second, stigma enforces social norms by keeping people in their place and, finally, it serves the function of disease avoidance by keeping the "diseased" or disabled person away from the so-called normal people. In some societies, stigma also serves as a moral reproach, inflicting the "scarlet letter" on those who are members of the stigmatized group, and "blames the victim" for their condition (Ryan, 1976). This is seen particularly clearly when examining the history of HIV and AIDS and how various societies and cultures have handled those who are HIV positive or who develop AIDS. The only way to reduce stigma is to confront and ameliorate these functions. So, for example, research has shown that having personal contact with an individual with a stigmatized condition serves to reduce prejudice and discrimination. Rather than being kept away from each other, the persons are brought together, which facilitates connection and understanding (Eack & Newhill, 2008a; Corrigan, Edwards, Green, et al., 2001) and through that process, they recognize their common humanity (LeCroy & Holschuh, 2012). Thus, efforts to help consumers with psychiatric disabilities live successfully in the community and increase their natural social supports may serve to reduce stigma.

How is stigma experienced by those who are the targets of it? One of my former clients put it this way:

> Stigma is something I have lived with for decades, ever since my first episode of illness. My extended family is very much involved with their own lives and I really don't think I will ever be able to discuss personal things with them in a loving caring way. I'm more of an emotional liability to them than anything else. . . . They are ashamed of me because of my mental illness, although they don't really know anything about my illness, only how it affects their lives. I haven't really been a part of theirs for so long, due to my illness, that I think it is moot at this point whether it would be possible to establish a link with them. There is this emptiness I feel, like I am just an acquaintance and will be more so as time progresses. . . . It is hard to find friends who continue to be a friend after they find out I'm mentally ill. I am getting older and as time slips by, I feel that I am getting lonelier with fewer avenues of true friendship.

In this client's statement, all three functions of stigma are embedded. The stigma she lives with keeps her isolated and marginalized, limits her social relationships, and keeps her estranged from her family members.

Defining and Understanding the Components of Stigma

There are three basic components of stigma. First is *stereotype*, which is a negative belief about a particular group of people that extends to individuals who are deemed members of the stereotyped group. Stigma is "an attribute that links a person to an undesirable stereotype, leading other people to reduce the bearer from a whole and usual person to a tainted, discounted one" (Goffman, 1963, p. 11). For example, there is a pervasive stereotype that individuals with mental illness are dangerous, therefore—to confirm the stereotype—Jane Doe, who has mental illness, is assumed to be a dangerous person (Theriot & Lodato, 2012).

The second component of stigma is *prejudice*, which is agreement with the negative belief and/or negative emotional reaction to the group. For example, prejudice is usually a big part of the not-in-my-backyard (NIMBY) phenomenon in which a community will express profoundly negative feelings about allowing certain groups to live in their neighborhood, for example, people who are disabled, poor, or members of certain racial, ethnic, or cultural groups, although research has shown that such negative attitudes may dissipate over time once ongoing personal contact occurs (Zippay & Lee, 2008).

The third component of stigma is *discrimination*, which is the behavior in response to the prejudice. The following is a hypothetical example of what can happen. Imagine that a community does not want a halfway house serving adults with mental illness to be built in their neighborhood because of the stereotyped belief that all mentally ill individuals are dangerous. Spurred by this belief, the community holds a rally protesting the plans for the new halfway house. Let's say the local government's plan prevails and the house is built. Discrimination may then occur, with community members shunning the mentally ill individuals living in the house and—worst-case scenario—in the middle of the night an arsonist sets fire to the house and it burns to the ground.

The Two Forms of Stigma

Stigma can take two main forms—public stigma and private stigma. Public stigma involves how others stereotype and exhibit prejudice and discrimination toward the particular group or person, while private or self-stigma occurs when an individual internalizes the negative stereotype and views him or herself as being "less than," unworthy, or abnormal. The stigma of mental illness is real, it is painful, and it can be damaging to the lives of people living with mental illness and to their families (Wahl, 1999). Stigma not only affects the afflicted person, it also affects those who love them.

Social worker Robert Bjorkland, who was diagnosed with bipolar disorder as an adolescent, discusses in a personal account essay how the psychiatric diagnostic label itself can promote and sustain stigma (Bjorkland, 1996; Corrigan, 2007). For some individuals, the only way to "shake off" the label is to deny they have the illness, but eventually that can lead to destructive consequences. Bjorkland states ". . . self stigma fueled my denial [of having mental illness] and contributed to my sense of urgency to stay off the medication. With my savings depleted, ostracized by my friends, and fired from my job, I became depressed and nearly successful at suicide" (p. 1329). Fortunately for Bjorkland, these negative experiences eventually led to insight and helped him to break through the denial of his illness and face and fight against the painful stigma, both self-stigma and public stigma. Eventually, this led to Bjorkland finishing his MSW degree and amassing the courage to be open about his mental illness and use his experiences to inform his strengths-based approach to empathically helping his clients. Similar personal accounts are included in Chapters 12 and 13 in this book.

The Effects of Stigma

As noted, stigma is painful for those who are stigmatized because of a disability, and the effects can be profound. Stigma discourages people from getting help; it keeps people from getting good jobs and advancing in the workplace; it leads to fear and mistrust, particularly in relation to fear of violence; it results in prejudice and discrimination; and, finally, stigma results in inadequate insurance coverage and inadequate resources for social services and treatment.

Stigma Discourages People from Getting Help

One of the most problematic effects of stigma is that stigma discourages people from getting help (Townsend, Gearing, & Polyanskaya, 2012). The Substance Abuse and Mental Health Services Administration reports in *Mental Health, United States: 2010* (SAMHSA, 2010) that in 2009, approximately 11 million adults (4.8%) had a serious mental illness, more than a quarter of these adults had a co-occurring substance use disorder and, although more than one in eight adults received some type of mental health treatment in the past year, 40 percent reported not receiving any treatment. In 2007, more than 34,000 deaths in the United States were due to suicide (SAMHSA, 2010). Overall, the vast majority of individuals with mental illness do not get the help they need (Pratt, 2012). This is of great concern, because today in the United States mental illness is the second leading cause of disability and premature mortality (U.S. DHHS, 1999, p. ix). Early intervention with appropriate services can be the best way to prevent a mental illness from developing and, if it develops, can prevent it from getting worse and evolving into a long-term disability. However, many people don't seek such services because they don't want to be labeled as "mentally ill" and suffer the consequences of that. As an African-American consumer commented:

> In the Black community, stigma comes from what others think of you and that affects what you think of yourself. Publicly, mentally ill people are viewed negatively by the Black community and, if the person is a man, he's labeled as "just another angry black man," while a woman is labeled as "crazy" or "evil". Black consumers have a double stigma—once, for being black and, second, for being mentally ill. When you're mentally ill, you feel "less than", not as good as other folks. You don't want that so you don't get help—you're afraid of what others will think of you, how they'd react, knowing you had to get mental health help, maybe seeing you walk into the clinic. (Newhill & Harris, 2007)

This consumer added that one thing that would help to reduce stigma would be to develop "one-stop shopping like Walmart" in which all services—medical, social, dental, and mental health—would be located in the same clinic building. If a person was seen going into the clinic, nobody would know for sure what service he or she was seeking.

Stigma Keeps People from Getting Good Jobs and Advancing in the Workplace

Another effect of stigma is that it keeps people from achieving competitive employment and advancing their careers. Some employers are reluctant to hire people who have mental illness, assuming that a mentally ill employee is not as good or as reliable as a non–mentally ill employee. Thanks to the Americans with Disabilities Act (ADA)—signed into law by President George H. W. Bush on July 26, 1990, and later amended with changes effective January 1, 2009—such discrimination is illegal, but it still happens. As a former bank manager, now a nursing student, stated:

> I used to work as a manager at a bank and did really well for many years. I have borderline personality disorder and post-traumatic stress disorder but I've been through therapy and decided to be open with my co-workers about my disorders. Everybody seemed supportive, but I was regularly passed over for promotion. I accepted that, didn't think too much about it. But on the anniversary of my trauma a couple years ago, I began to have flashbacks so I checked myself into the hospital for a week. When I came back to work, I found out I was let go. My employer said they had to replace me because they had too much work to do and couldn't wait until I came back. I was only out for a week and my employer health insurance covered it! It's like they give you coverage for mental health care, but you better not use it or you get punished. That's when I decided to leave the banking business and go into nursing. I guess I could have sued them, but I wanted to just move on and, anyways, I'm happier in nursing than I ever was in banking.

Newhill, C.E. & Harris, D. (2007b). African-American Consumer Project Field Notes. Unpublished manuscript.

Stigma Leads to Fear and Mistrust, Particularly in Relation to Fear of Violence

Another aspect of stigma toward people with mental illness is that the public stubbornly holds the belief that people with mental illness are dangerous (Eisenberg, 2005). This belief produces fear, mistrust, and feelings of social distance toward individuals with mental illness. The reality, however, is that seriously mentally ill people are much more likely to be the victims of violence rather than the perpetrators of violence (Teplin, McClelland, Abram, & Weiner, 2005). Lack of confidence that mental disorders are valid treatable health conditions (U.S. DHHS, 1999) along with blaming the victim—that is, blaming the person with mental illness for their condition—helps the public justify the ongoing neglect and maltreatment of those with mental illness and serves to perpetuate the stigma (Eisenberg, 2005). The reality is that if one controls for the effects of substance abuse, the vast majority of people who have mental illnesses are no more violent than anyone else living in their neighborhoods (Steadman, Mulvey, Monahan, et al., 1998). Those incidents that do occur, however, are often given heavy media coverage.

The average American gleans most of their information about mental illness from television, and the average television viewer sees people with mental illness portrayed in programs each week. These portrayals are rarely positive, with most showing the mentally ill character as violent and unpredictable (Owen, 2012). In a content analysis of prime-time network television programs, Diefenbach (1997) found that mentally ill individuals were commonly featured in violent crime programs and were nearly 10 times more violent than the general population of television characters. Furthermore, the mentally ill characters "were judged to have a negative impact on society and a negative quality of life" (p. 289). Other media, such as newspapers, are not much better. For example, in a content analysis of over 800 news stories that mentioned mental illness or mental health that were published over the past 10 years in the state of Washington, nearly one third of them used negative or derogatory terms to refer to individuals with mental health issues such as "looney, psycho, scumbag, whacked out, ticking time bomb, mentally defective and bonkers" (Schwarz, 2009). Headlines identifying perpetrators of heinous crimes as having histories of mental illness are commonplace. What one rarely sees is the opposite, for example, "John Doe, who has a history of mental illness, was just elected president of the school board." When mental illness is mentioned in the popular media, it is almost always related to news features about crime, violence, or another negative context.

Stigma Results in Prejudice and Discrimination

The inaccurate and exaggerated media portrayals of people with mental illness increase stigma and "lead people to avoid socializing, employing or working with, or renting to or living near persons who have a mental disorder, especially a severe disorder like schizophrenia" (U.S. DHHS, 1999, p. viii). This can result in another major effect of stigma, which is prejudice and discrimination. Examples of how this manifests include efforts to prevent people who have mental illnesses from living in certain neighborhoods or participating in certain parts of community life.

Stigma Results in Inadequate Insurance Coverage

Finally, stigma plays a role in a long history of inadequate insurance coverage for mental health and substance use disorders because it deters the public from wanting to pay for social services and mental health treatment (Smith, Damschroder, Kim, & Ubel, 2012; U.S. DHHS, 1999). If mental illness is the person's own fault, then why should people without mental illness have to pay for treatment? Many insurance plans do not cover mental health services to the same degree as other illnesses and, when mental illnesses are covered, coverage may be limited, inappropriate, or inadequate. For example, a consumer I interviewed commented:

> I have lived with schizophrenia for 27 years. As long as I take my medication, I do okay. But I have three medications. Two of them are generic and I can afford them most of the time, but the third is brand name and sometimes I can't get my prescription filled because I don't have enough money. It's hard because I have to have all three to stay well.

Progress in insurance parity, however, has finally occurred. After years of efforts by congressional representatives and consumer and family advocacy groups, hope for genuine parity in insurance coverage arose with the passage of the *Paul Wellstone and Pete Domenici Mental Health Parity and Addiction Equity Act of 2008* (MHPAEA), which was signed into law on October 3, 2008. MHPAEA intends to assure parity between coverage for mental health/substance use disorders (MH/SUD) and medical/surgical benefits in insurance plans that offer coverage for both benefits. Concerns remain, however, with regard to how the act will be interpreted and implemented. To truly achieve parity, the act must be implemented so that all aspects of medical management (utilization review, preauthorization, preferred provider network criteria, use of fee schedules, use of evidence-based review criteria, reviews for experimental vs. nonexperimental) are regulated, and are not more restrictive for MH/SUD services as compared to medical/surgical services. What the outcome will be remains to be seen, however, passage of the MHPAEA represents a significant step in the right direction.

Impact of Culture on the Experience of Stigma

Although stigma toward mental illness and people living with mental illness is a global phenomenon (Pintard, D'Sa, & Sciascia, 2012), the nature of stigma varies across different cultures. Throughout history, as noted in Chapter 1, explanations for the causes of mental illness have often been—with some exceptions—confounded with beliefs about the supernatural, and such beliefs are still sustained in many cultures today. For example, in Morocco, people believe that mental illness can be caused by evil sorcery and one can "catch" the illness by stepping on sorcery or accidentally drinking it down (Shepherd, n.d.). Shepard (n.d.) notes that blaming an evil spirit or a bit of sorcery may breed fear of mental illness and those afflicted, however, it also can reduce some aspects of stigma because it suggests the individual is blameless, unlike Western society, where the victim of mental illness may be blamed for their plight. In general, however, mental illness is highly stigmatized across countries and cultures, and the stigma often affects not only the individual with the illness, but also the individual's family, resulting in family shame and dishonor.

For example, Asian-Americans are often very reluctant to seek mental health services even though they are affected by many of the same mental health and social problems as other Americans (Busko, 2007). Furthermore, those who do use mental health services often terminate early and, therefore, do not receive the full benefit of treatment. Part of this stems from some unique cultural dimensions of stigma. Asian-Americans constitute a group consisting of very diverse cultures and ethnicities, but one element that cuts across all groups is the stigmatization of mental illness and the strong cultural value of honoring one's family—"saving face," avoiding shame and dishonor, and solving problems within the family unit rather than seeking help from outsiders, including mental health professionals. "There's a stigma associated with personal problems, and Asians also hold beliefs that associate health with the environment, and they equate the physical with the emotional and spiritual" (Chang, 2007).

Other barriers faced by Asian-Americans that undermine seeking care for mental health problems include lack of access, cost, the shortage of mental health professionals who speak the individual's language and are competent in understanding the individual's culture and ethnic background, and lack of knowledge about mental illness and the services available to treat it (Busko, 2007). What happens as a result is that many Asian-Americans suffer in silence and never get the help they need, or the individual or family delays seeking care until a crisis occurs, and then their entrance into care may be highly stressful and traumatic. Example:

> The first time I met Duong, he was brought into the emergency room by the police in handcuffs, his shirt spattered with blood. He was accompanied by his distraught family who, through an interpreter, told me what had happened. The family had recently moved to our town from Vietnam, and the adjustment had been difficult, particularly for 16-year-old Duong. He was struggling in school, largely because he was not yet fluent in English. Duong is smaller than most American boys his age and had been bullied by some of the boys in school, and all this resulted in Duong becoming depressed, which was experienced largely in somatic terms, that is, headaches, stomachaches, and fatigue. Not understanding depression, his father told him to snap out of it. When he couldn't, his parents told him he was bringing dishonor upon the family. This triggered suicidal feelings, and tonight Duong cut his arms with a knife. I asked the police to remove the handcuffs, obtained medical treatment for Duong's wounds, and then sat down with Duong and his family to talk about what depression is and how we could be of help to them.

The process of immigration to a host country that is dramatically different culturally than one's home country can be very stressful and even psychologically damaging (Williams & Berry, 1991). Like Duong, many new immigrants struggle with depression and anxiety as they move through the process of acculturation (Ly & Peterson, 1993), and stigma plus lack of information about mental/health care resources prevents them from seeking help. Although a devastating crisis had occurred, the visit to the emergency room facilitated the process of getting help for Duong and, ultimately, this proved to be very beneficial to him and to his family.

Here is another example of the intersection of culture and stigma. In India and Pakistan, mental illness is also highly stigmatized, but the nature of the stigma and the cultural factors that sustain it are rooted in a patriarchal family and a collective community system. For example, it is considered highly inappropriate for men to express emotions, and doing so is a sign of weakness. As a result Indian and Pakistani men often hide problems to avoid the stigma (Bender, 2001). Women are allowed to express emotions but are strongly discouraged from seeking professional help, and the belief in keeping problems within the family and solutions within the family is strongly held (Bender, 2001). Because it is highly stigmatized, having a history of mental illness in a person's family can hurt their opportunities to marry and affects the social status of the family in the community. As a result, mentally ill individuals are generally hidden away from others' sight at home, and the burden of care falls disproportionately on the women in the family (Juvva, 2007). These are just a few examples of how mental illness carries considerable stigma across cultures, although the finer nuances of that stigma and how people cope with it is shaped by specific cultural norms.

Combating Stigma

What can clinical social workers and other mental health professionals do to combat and reduce stigma? Sartorius (1998), former president of the World Psychiatric Association, identifies several steps that all of us can take that can help in reducing stigma suffered by those with schizophrenia, steps that are fully applicable to other serious mental illnesses. First, he says, we must examine our own attitudes toward working with individuals with serious mental illness and "try to increase our tolerance and capacity to deal with [the illness]" (p. 1058). Examining our attitudes and increasing our acceptance are facilitated by "trying to continue updating our knowledge . . . with results of research and listening to what patients and their families have to say about stigma and its consequences" (p. 1058). Second, we must be proactive and assertive advocates on behalf of clients with serious mental illness and their families in efforts to uphold clients' and families' rights, which may require stepping out of the clinician role and stepping into the realm of politics.

Third, although knowledge about psychopathology and clinical symptoms is important, we must shift our research, teaching, and practice priorities to include emphasizing ways in which clients can achieve a satisfying quality of life, regardless of where they are in the course of their illness. This step is at the center of the notion of "recovery." Sally Satel (2009) argues, however, that there is a danger in the attempt to combat stigma by the claim—by some—that if a client achieves recovery from mental illness, he or she is no different from anybody else. Satel believes that this "soothing fiction" may serve to undermine the importance of treatment. If individuals receive treatment so that their most dramatic symptoms are under control, they may superficially "look like" anyone else, but that does not mean that they are "cured" and do not need continued treatment as part of their recovery.

Fourth, we all must be vigilant for signs of discrimination and proliferation of stigma toward individuals with mental illness along with taking appropriate action when evidence of discrimination and stigma occurs. There are three approaches to combating stigma: protest, education, and personal contact (Corrigan & Gelb, 2006). NAMI StigmaBusters, which takes a protest plus education approach, is an organized global network of grassroots advocates who are committed to fighting inaccurate and hurtful representations of mental illness in the media. NAMI StigmaBusters also make efforts to educate the public about the realities of living with mental illness and the challenges faced by consumers and families. Other major anti-stigma efforts include the World Psychiatric Association's anti-stigma "Open the Doors" educational campaign across 20 countries (Warner, 2005) and SAMHSA's Resource Center to Promote Acceptance, Dignity and Social Inclusion Associated with Mental Health (ADS Center) (see promoteacceptance..samhsa.gov). Finally, "In Our Own Voice," developed by mental health consumers in collaboration with NAMI, takes a personal contact approach by presenting programs in which two trained consumer speakers share their personal stories of living with mental illness and achieving recovery (In Our Own Voice, 2009).

Targets for Anti-Stigma Efforts

What types of situations or products are the targets of such anti-stigma efforts? One of the more egregious examples of the exploitation of the stigma of mental illness for commercial interests was the production of the "Crazy for You" teddy bear for Valentine's Day in 2005 by the Vermont Teddy Bear Company, which is one of the largest producers of Internet and mail-order teddy bears. The "Crazy for You" bear was dressed in a strait jacket with a red heart embroidered on the front of the jacket. A tag, labeled "Commitment Papers" was attached to the bear with the message "Can't eat, can't sleep, my heart's racing. Diagnosis—crazy for you." The National Alliance on Mental Illness immediately protested the sale of the bear and asked that it be pulled from the company's shelves. Jerry Goessel, executive director of the Vermont chapter of NAMI, called the bear "a tasteless use of marketing that stigmatizes persons with mental illness. A straitjacket is not a symbol that we want to associate with sales of a teddy bear for loved ones over Valentine's Day, and the use of commitment papers, legal documents committing an individual to involuntary treatment, is not something to be taken casually" (Associated Press, 2005). The Vermont Teddy Bear Company, although expressing regret that its bear may have been perceived negatively, refused to pull it from sales until after February 14.

Another example of how anti-stigma advocacy groups such as StigmaBusters have succeeded in eradicating stigma-enhancing products was their action to successfully halt the continued broadcast of an ABC drama series entitled *Wonderland* in 2000 after just two episodes aired. The stories in *Wonderland* were about daily life in a mental hospital from the perspectives of both the doctors and patients, but the show was strongly criticized by mental health advocacy groups for its incorporation of depictions of suicide and violent behavior toward others in the storylines and its graphic portrayals of psychosis and other severe symptoms of mental illness. But are such anti-stigma programs and actions effective in changing people's attitudes toward individuals with mental illness?

Effectiveness of Anti-Stigma Programs

Only a few studies have attempted to examine the effectiveness of anti-stigma efforts (Corrigan & Gelb, 2006), and these have found that such efforts do lead to more positive and less stigma-inducing news stories (Stuart, 2003), reduction in negative attitudes toward individuals with mental illness (Vaughn & Hansen, 2004), and more positive feelings about the treatment of mental illness, specifically depression (Vaughn & Hansen, 2004). Corrigan and Gelb (2006), however, caution that more research must be conducted to examine the penetration (i.e., the proportion of the target audience that is exposed to the effort), outcome, process, and exportability (i.e., how easily the program can be used by advocacy groups). Satel (2009) also cautions that appeals for compassion and providing education may change people's behavior to some degree, but aren't necessarily effective in changing people's basic attitudes. She argues that a more effective approach lies in providing effective treatment to enable individuals with mental illness to achieve recovery and be able to demonstrate success in their lives. This, she says, "sets in motion a self reinforcing momentum: the more that treatment is observed to work, the more it is encouraged. . . . No matter how sympathetic the public may be, attitudes about people with mental illness will inevitably rest upon how much or how little their symptoms set them apart" from others (Satel, 2009, p. A-22), a position also endorsed by psychiatrist E. Fuller Torrey (1997).

A recent meta-analysis of outcome studies of anti-stigma efforts suggests that both education and personal contact have positive effects on reducing stigma for individuals with mental illness. Education, however, was most effective for adolescents, while personal contact was more effective in reducing stigma for adults (Corrigan, Morris, Michaels, et al., 2012). Anti-stigma public service announcements, however, seem to have limited positive effects (Corrigan, 2012).

A final approach to reducing stigma involves efforts to note how certain abilities, for example, artistic and creative abilities, are linked with certain mental illnesses and how individuals with mental illness can achieve greatness with their talents. Some consumer and family support groups, with the goal of inspiring hope, list names of famous people who have suffered from (or who are believed to have suffered from) various mental illnesses yet made wonderful contributions to society via their creative work. It is believed, for example, that Ludwig van Beethoven, Vincent van Gogh, Virginia Woolf, and Ernest Hemingway all suffered from mood disorders. Many current celebrities, such as Carrie Fisher (Fisher, 2008) and Patty Duke (Duke & Hochman, 1992), have written and talked openly about their struggles with mental illness. Such connections do help to lessen stigma, show people they are not alone, prove that it is possible to be successful despite mental illness and, just as Betty Ford raised awareness via her experiences with alcoholism (Ford, 2003), celebrity revelations about mental illness can have a positive impact on public awareness.

Although it is well established that societal stigma remains an ongoing obstacle to people seeking care for mental illness and can have a devastating impact on individuals' lives and self-esteem, the challenges presented by societal stigma are compounded further by the nature of the attitudes of mental health professionals about mental illness and those who suffer from it. The sad truth is that the individuals that people with mental illness turn to for help may themselves harbor negative attitudes about the very illnesses they are trained to treat.

This brings us to a critically important question: How do we, as social workers, know if we ourselves hold stereotypes about people with mental illness? Remember, we may be educated about mental illness, its symptoms, and treatment and understand the problem of stigma, but that doesn't mean we are immune to internalizing the negative stereotypes so prevalent in our society (Covarrubias & Han, 2011; Minkoff, 1987). How do we approach such a self-examination and confront the stereotypes we may carry within us so such stereotypes do not negatively affect our work with clients? Before looking at what the research reveals about the nature of negative attitudes held by mental health professionals toward individuals with serious mental illness, we must first look within ourselves.

Assess your comprehension of *the definition of the components of stigma and how stigma affects the lives of individuals with mental illness* by completing this quiz.

A VALUES CLARIFICATION EXERCISE ADDRESSING STIGMA AND BIAS

As the author of this book, I cannot tell you what you should or should not feel or believe or value, and even if I did, it wouldn't work. Most of us have already had our parents tell us what is right and wrong, what are acceptable or unacceptable attitudes about various aspects of life. Instead, what does work for examining our own attitudes and biases as we prepare for our work as social workers is to engage in a process called *values clarification* (Simon, Howe, & Kirschenbaum, 1995). Values clarification does just what the term implies. It doesn't *tell* you what to think or value or believe, rather, it helps you identify and clarify your values and beliefs, both positive and negative ones. Furthermore, in doing this, it helps an individual identify his or her own particular areas of vulnerability in terms of values conflicts or biases and, in the case of social work, how that fits with the principles of our Code of Ethics. The underlying theoretical approach for values clarification was originally formulated by Raths, Harmin, and Simon (1966), who based their work on the writings of education reformer John Dewey (1859–1952).

The goal of values clarification is not to place your preferences against a particular moral standard, but to begin working toward developing *values awareness.* Values awareness means that one becomes conscious of what one's values are, how they drive the choices and preferences we make, and how such personal values may adhere to, or conflict with, our professional values and responsibilities as social workers.

The best way to begin approaching the achievement of values awareness is through participating in a values clarification exercise. Simon, Howe, and Kirschenbaum (1995) offer a wide range of values clarification exercises for general use in teaching, all of which guide the process of values awareness. Of these exercises, the exercise that is most easily adapted for the purpose of examining stereotypes and biases about individuals with severe mental illness is an exercise called "Rank Order" (Simon, Howe, & Kirschenbaum, 1995, p. 42–68). Based on the Simon, Howe, and Kirschenbaum model, an original Rank Order exercise, developed for this book, is provided at the end of this chapter. What this exercise does is to address the task of choosing between competing alternatives and, in that process, recognizing value preferences and setting priorities, which is a process we engage in continually in our work as social workers. Many times in our work, there is no ideal solution to a difficult client problem, rather, we must sometimes choose the "least of the evils" amongst several less than ideal options.

If the exercise is done in a small group with other social workers or social work students, you will have the experience of discussing your choices with others and publicly explaining the basis of your choices—which, again, is something we are challenged to do in everyday practice. Finally, the outcome of the exercise may suggest possible conflicts you may have between personal values and professional ethics along with identifying hidden biases or negative attitudes that must be addressed as part of your professional work.

Now that you have had an opportunity to move toward your own values awareness via values clarification (assuming you have done the exercise!), let's look at what research on the resistance of mental health professionals to working with individuals with serious mental illness reveals and what the implications are for professional practice.

RESISTANCE OF MENTAL HEALTH PROFESSIONALS TO WORKING WITH INDIVIDUALS WITH SERIOUS MENTAL ILLNESS

Over 30 years ago the American Psychiatric Association Task Force on the Chronic Mental Patient concluded that most clinicians do not want to work with individuals with severe and persistent mental illness, stating that "among professionals such as ourselves, and among paraprofessionals, there are prevailing attitudes that working with these patients is unrewarding and dull, that outcome is hopeless—[and] that prestige is not available for working in programs directed toward these [chronically mentally ill] patients" (Meyerson, 1978, p. 130). Unfortunately, in spite of better knowledge about mental illness, improvements in treatment, and anti-stigma efforts, the current research shows that such negative attitudes are still common today (Sharfstein, 2012; Eack & Newhill, 2008b; Markham, 2003). As Minkoff (1987) pointed out many years ago, the negative attitudes and continued resistance of many mental health professionals toward working with individuals with serious mental illness contributes significantly to the difficulty of providing such consumers with good quality care regardless of other problems related to the system or setting.

Although there is no question that there are other obstacles to quality care such as the limits imposed by managed care, bankrupt state budgets, the continued fragmentation of the mental health system, and poor coordination with other key service components such as child welfare and criminal justice, "problems in each of these areas are magnified significantly by the caregivers' own negative attitudes" (Minkoff, 1987, p. 3). How does this follow? Because underlying resistance to working with severely mentally ill clients results in a lack of assertive committed efforts on the part of mental health professionals to overcome these other barriers (Minkoff, 1987). No solution to overcoming barriers to caring for mentally ill clients will work until we systematically address the significant resistance of professionals themselves to working with this population and, although this is best accomplished during the early years of professional training, it is never too late to address this issue. The backdrop for the formation of the attitudes of mental health professionals toward individuals with serious and persistent mental illness, however, is composed of the prevalent attitudes held by the general public toward individuals with mental illness, and this has been studied extensively over the past four decades (Corrigan, 2012).

Societal Attitudes toward Individuals with Mental Illness

In 1974, sociologist Judith Rabkin conducted a comprehensive review of studies over the previous three decades examining public attitudes toward individuals with mental illness. Her rationale for the importance of such a meta-analysis is summarized in the following quote:

> Knowledge of [the public's] attitudes is not only germane to those concerned with the origins and maintenance of disturbed behavior, but critically important to workers involved in primary prevention programs, early intervention, and community treatment of psychiatric patients. . . . In short, it is becoming generally recognized that mental patients, and those who deal with them, exist in the larger framework of society and that it is imperative, in both planning and carrying out treatment programs, to be aware of the attitudes toward mental illness and treatment that prevail in this larger framework. (Rabkin, 1974, p. 9)

Rabkin's review revealed that people with mental illness are excluded and rejected by society at large to a significant extent, and that most members of the general public exhibit evidence of social distance when considering individuals with mental illness. The term *social distance* refers to the extent to which distinct social groups are willing to participate in social contact with each other. The Bogardus Social Distance Scale (Bogardus, 1926), for example, was developed to empirically measure people's willingness to have contact with different social groups such as different racial groups or different ethnic groups. Sociologists who study social distance claim that, across studies, the public consistently identifies four specific groups to be especially unacceptable. These four groups are (1) "ex-convicts," that is, individuals with histories of incarceration in jail or prison, (2) "addicts," that is, individuals with alcohol or drug addiction problems, (3) people with mental retardation or other developmental disabilities, and (4) people with mental illness. Mentally ill individuals were identified as the most unacceptable group out of the four (Tringo, 1970). More recent studies, unfortunately, show that such attitudes have not changed much and individuals with mental illness are still viewed in highly negative ways by the general public (Martin, Pescosolido, & Tuch, 2000; Phelan, Link, Stueve, & Pescosolido, 2000). To what extent have these societal attitudes affected those who provide services to individuals with mental illness? What does the research on professional attitudes tell us?

Studies of Mental Health Professionals' Attitudes toward Individuals with Serious Mental Illness

Although public attitudes toward individuals with mental illness have been extensively examined, there have been fewer studies on professionals' attitudes. But those studies that are available are pretty discouraging with the following overall findings (Cohen, 1990; Hromco, Lyons, & Nikkei, 1995; Markham, 2003; Mirabi, Weinman, Magnetti, & Keppler, 1985; Eack & Newhill, 2008b; Schwartz, Krieger, & Sorenson, 1981; Talbott, 1978):

- Most studies report that clinicians demonstrate attitudes no different from those of the general public, displaying much evidence of social distance and rejection toward clients with severe and persistent (a.k.a. chronic) mental illness.
- Staff burnout and job dissatisfaction are directly related to working with more severely ill clients, particularly those with schizophrenia and borderline personality disorder, and the higher the proportion of such clients in a worker's caseload, the higher the level of reported burnout.

Rabkin, J. (1974). Public attitudes toward mental illness: A review of the literature. Schizophrenia Bulletin, 1(10), 9–33.

- Most clinicians report that chronically/severely mentally ill clients are not a preferred population to treat.
- Most clinicians believe their colleagues prefer to avoid clients with severe mental illness.
- Most clinicians believe there are little to no satisfying professional rewards in treating this population.

Such alarming findings indicate the problem of professional resistance is substantial. As I reviewed these studies several years ago, I began to wonder if social workers would have equally negative attitudes as those reported in the literature with other professional groups, since none of the studies had looked specifically at professional social workers with regard to their feelings and attitudes about working with seriously mentally ill consumers. My hopeful hypothesis was that they would not, given our profession's commitment to working with those most disadvantaged coupled with our emphasis on the importance of identifying client strengths. Studies of social work students had shown positive findings in terms of commitment to working with severely mentally ill clients (Shera & Delva-Tauiliili,1996; Werrbach & DePoy, 1993a; Werrbach & DePoy, 1993b), but the extent to which this holds after graduation, once one is actually out in the field, was unknown.

Attitudes of Direct Practice MSW Social Workers toward Individuals with SMI

To answer this question, Newhill and Korr (2004) conducted a national random survey of 2,000 NASW members (response rate = 60%; N=1,200) in post-master's practice in mental health to investigate their experiences with and attitudes about working with individuals with severe and persistent mental illness (SPMI). Contrary to the literature that claims social workers have abandoned their mission to serve vulnerable populations (Specht & Courtney, 1994), Newhill and Korr (2004) found that the majority of the social work respondents were currently practicing with this population and reported that they found their work rewarding. The initial analysis of the data suggested that social workers experience frustration and obstacles in their practice with individuals with SPMI, but these were related to systemic problems, not client-related ones. This made sense, since studies of community mental health center (CMHC) staff have reported similar findings, that is, that system issues, such as large caseloads and the burden of paperwork, are some of the key frustrations of community mental health professionals, and that these frustrations can lead to burnout and staff retention problems (Acker, 1999; Acker, 2004; Mason, Olmos-Gallo, Bacon, McQuilken, Henley, & Fisher, 2004).

A second set of more sophisticated analyses on the same data set used by Newhill and Korr, however, revealed somewhat different findings (Eack & Newhill, 2008b). Results from a series of structural equation analyses suggested that social workers' attitudes toward working with individuals with SPMI are actually primarily influenced by their frustrations related to *client behaviors and treatment issues*, rather than frustrations with system-related issues. Some of these client-related frustrations, leading to negative attitudes, included the following:

- When clients are too demanding and violate personal boundaries via manipulative intrusive behavior;
- Frustrations related to the disruptive behavior of clients with personality disorders, who are perceived to not benefit much from treatment and don't take responsibility for their behavior;
- Frustrations related to clients who repeatedly abuse substances;

- Frustrations related to the nature of chronic illness, for example, slow progress, "when nothing seems to work," dealing with chronicity of illness, and feelings like there is "no end," no resolution, no cure;
- Feeling frustrated when clients decompensate, fail treatment, leave treatment prematurely, are no-shows for appointments, or are difficult to engage in treatment;
- Feeling frustrated when clients do not adhere to prescribed treatment, for example, clients who go off their medications over and over, and then need repeated hospitalization;
- Working with clients who are violent and worrying about personal safety; and
- Frustrations related to negative family issues, for example, high levels of family conflict, difficulties in engaging families as treatment partners, or unrealistic family expectations, such as the wish for an immediate cure for the ill person.

Harboring negative attitudes or feelings toward one's clients can have significant adverse effects on clinicians and clients. For example, negative attitudes held by professional caregivers working with individuals with schizophrenia are positively related to increases in the clients' levels of symptomatology (Heresco-Levy, Ermilov, Giltsinsky, Lichtenstein, & Blander, 1999; Moore and Kuipers, 1992; Snyder, Wallace, Moe, et al., 1995). A 2001 longitudinal study (Barrowclough et al., 2001) found that in an inpatient hospital setting, the more that clinicians held negative attitudes towards their clients with SPMI, the more likely the clients were to have behavioral problems, such as incidents of aggression, during their inpatient stay. Other studies have indicated that treatment environments characterized by a highly critical and negative atmosphere are also associated with poorer outcomes for individuals with SPMI (Ball, Moore, & Kuipers, 1992; Snyder, Wallace, Moe, & Liberman, 1994). Thus, not addressing negative attitudes and professional resistance to working with individuals with serious mental illness can have significant repercussions for the clients we serve (Eack & Newhill, 2008b). The big question is: Where do these negative feelings and attitudes really come from? Is it just a reflection of society's attitudes, or is something else going on as well?

Origin of Negative Feelings and Attitudes

Minkoff (1987) suggests that the literature on the topic of mental health professionals' attitudes reveals that resistance toward working with clients with severe and persistent (a.k.a. chronic) mental illness is related to three things. First is the avoidance of people with chronic illnesses—both mental and medical—by society at large. Long-term illness makes many people feel uncomfortable and, as a result, they avoid individuals who suffer from such illnesses. As a client living with cancer commented to the author:

> When you're in the hospital for a long time—for any reason—cancer, mental illness, whatever—you find out who your real friends are. Some people visit, but it is the rare person who continues to visit you until you get well or are discharged to go home again. Most people stop visiting after a few days. I have one friend, in fact, who says hospitals give her "the creeps."

In fact, individuals who suffer from chronic illnesses, such as lupus, fibromyalgia, or arthritis, are often advised not to reveal their illness to employers to avoid discrimination (Nakazawa, 2009).

Second, negative feelings and attitudes stem from the avoidance of chronically ill patients by the medical profession in general. And, finally, avoidance of people with severe and persistent illnesses is related to the failure of professional clinical training programs to provide support and adequate appropriate training in caring for clients with serious long-term illnesses and lack of training in how to manage a client's illness over a lengthy period of time which is, essentially, training in case management. Lack of such training results in the provider not understanding the realities of long-term illness and, thus, experiencing frustration when the client does not show rapid progress. Clients with severe and persistent mental illness "do not reward our efforts by getting 'better' within an easily observable period of time, or, if they improve, they backslide, and we can begin to feel much as they do about the hopelessness of their situation" (Mirabi, Weinman, Magnetti, & Keppler, 1985, p. 405). If we intend to fully embrace the new recovery movement, we must first address and learn how to overcome our own negative attitudes. Education and training can cause people to believe they should regard mental illness as just another illness, but doesn't serve to actually change people's underlying attitudes that mental illness is somehow more unacceptable and abhorrent than other illnesses (Elinson & Padella, 1967; Minkoff, 1987). There is another crucial issue, too, that relates to findings from studies of physician attitudes toward their patients involving the *ideal norm* versus the *reality norm* for practice.

Attitudes of Physicians toward Individuals with Chronic Illness

The ideal norm of the medical profession is that doctors should not prefer one type of patient over another and should treat all patients equally and with respect. The reality, however, is that most physicians prefer those patients who respond well to treatment (Merton, 1957). When a patient responds well to the physician's efforts and, ideally, gets well, that provides a positive feedback loop to the doctor that he or she is competent and skilled (Nuland, 2009). "Doctors and psychotherapists generally don't like it when their patients don't get better. But the fact is that lots of patients elude our clinical skill and therapeutic cleverness. That's often when the trouble starts" (Friedman, 2008, p. B-4). This problem is particularly acute with chronic illnesses that are not well understood, such as chronic fatigue syndrome or fibromyalgia, and some mental illnesses, such as personality disorders. There are even some types of patients that doctors admit to disliking intensely, and these are typically characterized by certain personality types, such as the so-called help-rejecting complainer, the malingerer, the clinging dependent type, and the patient that will not listen to the doctor's recommendations (Crane, 2009; Springer, 1992).

These issues are salient when considering severe, particularly persistent, mental illness. With many severe and persistent mental illnesses, there are no clear, immediate, dependable cures. Although we have made considerable progress, there is still a lot we don't know about many of these illnesses. For example, we have some theories about the causes of autism but, as yet, no definite specific cause has been established. As a result, many clinicians—doctors, nurses, social workers—and many families respond to such clients with frustration and feelings of helplessness. Added to this is the fact that professional education tends to be diagnosis-oriented, not management-oriented, that is, teaching students how to follow a client or patient over the long-term course of a chronic illness. Lack of case management training and orientation—and valuing that kind of practice—is partly responsible for negative attitudes toward chronic illness, including chronic mental illness (Minkoff, 1987).

Professional social work education is not immune to this. Social work education tends to focus on problem solving, solution-focused treatment, brief treatment, and case resolution, rather than how to manage a client's illness over the course of her or his lifetime. Some social workers and social work students "look down on" case management practice and see it as not worthy of professional attention and training. Finally, all of this is compounded by the clinician's affective reactions, particularly the negative affective reactions that can emerge.

The importance of identifying, addressing, and "overcoming affective [or emotional] barriers to working with the chronic mentally ill cannot be overstated" (Minkoff,

1987, p. 7), regardless of the type of treatment employed. Crucial to this is developing the ability to make an empathic connection with the client, which can be very difficult when the client is severely ill and symptomatic. But, "regardless of how the clinician conceptualizes treatment, making empathic connection with the chronic patient is crucial to the success of any therapeutic intervention" (Minkoff & Stern, 1985, p. 863), and that includes both psychosocial treatment and treatment with medication. It is amazing how a little empathy can work wonders in facilitating medication adherence.

Although we have made remarkable advances in psychosocial treatment technologies and newer, better-targeted psychotropic medications, the basic skills of effective communication, establishing rapport, and use of empathy are absolutely the keystones to successful treatment. If the clinician does not possess such skills and value their use, the rest of the treatment efforts will be undermined. During a focus group study on the perceptions of African-American consumers with severe mental illness about racial disparities in mental health care (Newhill & Harris, 2007), a consumer made the following comment:

> I, myself, have not encountered racism at the mental health clinic. But what I do encounter is professionals just not seeming to care. No empathy—no bedside manner. It's like they're thinking, "oh, here's another mental patient," but not caring to get to know me, who I am, and making a connection with me as another human being. I know they all have paperwork to deal with and I know it's just a job for them maybe, but that's what gets in my way—not racism—it's lack of empathy.

Assess your comprehension of *the origin of negative attitudes by society and health care professionals toward individuals with chronic health and mental health illnesses* by completing this quiz.

AFFECTIVE OBSTACLES THAT CHALLENGE MENTAL HEALTH PROFESSIONALS IN THEIR WORK WITH CLIENTS WITH SERIOUS MENTAL ILLNESS

People choose the kind of work they do or don't do for many reasons. Most people who love their work feel that way because they get positive rewards from doing the work. I frequently ask my students, as they are preparing for graduation, what specific areas of social work they plan to pursue. A couple years ago, in response to my query, one of my soon-to-graduate students indicated that she wanted to do outpatient psychotherapy but definitely did not want to work with people with schizophrenia. When I asked why she didn't want to work with individuals with schizophrenia, she replied:

> Well, one of my field placements was in a partial hospitalization program, and I was just really uncomfortable the whole time. I mean—and I know this sounds terrible and I shouldn't feel this way—but I just couldn't connect with the consumers with schizophrenia. Some of them didn't take baths very often, and I just didn't like being around them. I never knew what to say or how to connect.

What this student encountered and was not able to overcome were the affective or emotional barriers that can get in the way of working effectively with individuals with serious mental illness and experiencing the work as rewarding. Psychiatrist Kenneth Minkoff (1987) identifies several affective or emotion-laden obstacles that pose challenges to clinicians when working with individuals with severe and persistent (a.k.a. chronic) mental illness. These obstacles consist of a complex mix of attitudes, feelings, stresses, and paradoxes that all challenge the clinician in his or her efforts to provide effective treatment not just for the illness but for the whole person who has the illness (Lamb, 1982; Stern & Minkoff, 1985; White & Bennett, 1981).

For many clinicians, facing the devastation, stigma, and despair of the experience of severe mental illness, especially psychosis, can be overwhelming and makes developing an empathic connection with the client difficult. Part of this is the struggle of getting past the severe symptomatology to connect with the person behind the symptoms. As noted previously, it is critical to remind oneself that there is a *person* who has worth and dignity behind the paranoia, the mania, and/or the psychosis; and that person is probably feeling frightened and needs your help. For some clinicians, this challenge feels like an impossible task. Even when the empathic connection is made, the clinician, together with the client, must learn how to contend with the client's daily struggles to cope and live with their mental illness. Sometimes the challenge of living with a long-term severe mental illness is too much for the client to bear. Five to ten percent of individuals with schizophrenia, for example, eventually take their own lives through suicide (Newhill, 1993). Knowing that you have a serious mental illness and that your life may be forever changed is hard to deal with.

Sometimes the challenge is too much for the clinician to bear (Minkoff & Stern, 1985). So, how do many clinicians cope when this happens? Many clinicians cope by intellectually and emotionally distancing themselves, which adversely affects their ability to provide effective treatment both to their clients and to their clients' families. Some clinicians completely distance themselves by leaving the clinic or agency and seeking work in areas where they feel more comfortable. But this can be avoided. The first step toward avoiding the recourse of distancing oneself and, instead, developing a more constructive response, is to clearly understand the complex variety of attitudes, feelings, and stresses that constitute the affective barriers that are at the heart of the discomfort and then learn how to overcome them. These complex feelings, attitudes, stresses, and paradoxes can be organized into four categories, as follows (Minkoff, 1987, pp. 7–10):

- Feelings of hopelessness and despair
- Feelings of helplessness and inadequacy
- Feelings of dislike or disgust
- Feelings of discomfort

Let's address each one and discuss how clinicians can learn to manage and overcome the barriers to provide good services to individuals with severe mental illness. First, we have the barrier of feelings of hopelessness and despair.

Feelings of Hopelessness and Despair

Feelings of hopelessness and despair usually involve three issues that many clinicians have great difficulty with. These issues are:

- Confronting the issue of incurability while preserving hope for recovery;
- Learning to work with clients and their families on adaptation to and management of the client's illness; and
- Adjusting to different expectations for success.

Many of us were trained in our professional education programs to engage our clients in problem solving, planned change, and solution-focused treatment and, in today's world of managed care, to solve these problems in six to eight sessions of some form of evidence-based treatment. This time crunch breeds an "intense need to be actively changing and improving people" (Nielsen, Stein, Talbott, Lamb, et al., 1981, p. 772). Severe and persistent mental illness "challenges our wish to cure and our sense of competence and control" because rapid change is often unrealistic (Group for the Advancement of Psychiatry, 1986, p. 63; Steinberg, 2012). For many clinicians, such a situation is threatening and shakes their confidence.

Recognizing a poor or guarded prognosis means acknowledging our own helplessness and the therapeutic limitations of our knowledge and skills. To satisfy our own need for success, many of us want evidence of therapeutic improvement, and we may end up blaming the client when he or she doesn't improve. Richard Friedman (2008) relates a story involving a colleague who had been working with a severely depressed client for three years but without much improvement in his symptoms. The colleague asked Friedman if he would try working with the client, cautioning, "I think he has an unconscious desire to remain sick." Eventually, the client did overcome his depression and, looking back on it, Friedman commented that "chronically ill, treatment-resistant patients can challenge the confidence of therapists themselves, who may be reluctant to question their treatment; it's easier—and less painful—to view the patient as intentionally or unconsciously resistant" (Friedman, 2008, p. D-4).

A more appropriate reaction, therefore, and one that is the most difficult challenge of all, is to acknowledge the times when the client feels despair or frustration, bear it with him or her, and then put the client's move toward recovery into a hopeful but realistic perspective. It is critical to communicate to clients during these times that they have not failed and to point out all the ways they have shown strengths and success. For example, the client may still be depressed, but may have achieved insight into the causes of his or her depression, have sought help and, although he or she is still depressed, the depression is beginning to lift. It is important to reassure clients that you will not abandon them and will stick with them through thick and thin and that having well periods along with ill periods is part of the reality of having a long-term illness. As social workers, we must learn to modify the intense need to actively change and improve people quickly, and resist the expectation of achieving a lot of progress in a short period of time. As H. Richard Lamb comments:

> Mental health professionals must accept the slow pace at which most long-term patients progress. We are not surprised when intensive psychotherapy with persons who possess character ego strength takes years to achieve character change. Yet we are frequently dismayed when the long-term severely disabled [who don't possess such strength] take years to progress in social and vocational rehabilitation (Lamb, 1979, p. 396).

Directly related to this is the critically important issue of learning how to set appropriate goals and how to adjust our ideas about what constitutes therapeutic improvement. Clinicians can have great difficulty with this because "successful outcome" and "therapeutic improvement" are often traditionally measured by so-called normative standards, in other words, standards that individuals without severe mental illness are able to achieve, sometimes quickly and easily. Thus a successful outcome is viewed as including absence of symptoms, full competitive employment, avoidance of relapse, fully independent living, and full social interaction (Strauss & Carpenter, 1977). Such goals may take a while to achieve or even be unrealistic for most severely and persistently ill clients. Recovery should not be equated with "cure."

What happens, then, is that as clinicians repeatedly experience clients not being able to meet such unrealistic goals, they begin to avoid working with severely ill clients rather than recognizing that the basic problem is setting unrealistic and inappropriate goals. To resolve this difficulty, clinicians must learn to develop *individualized outcome criteria* and develop *attainable treatment goals* based on the client's own history and baseline via a *life-course perspective* of the client's mental illness (Minkoff & Stern, 1985). That is, the social worker must assess the client not just cross-sectionally (how the client is doing right now at this point in time), but also assess the client from a longitudinal perspective as well (how they have functioned over time). This is extremely important. "Failure to learn this new value system for measuring therapeutic success with [severely and persistently mentally ill

---

Lamb, H.R. (1979). Staff burnout in work with long-term patients. Hospital and Community Psychiatry, 30, 396–398.

clients] results in the continued perception that [they] are impossible to treat and should be avoided," transferred to another clinician, or only provided with medication (Minkoff, 1987, p. 8).

Today, the "best-case scenario" for recovery is sometimes used as the "normative standard," and although some clients may achieve that, some clients cannot, or cannot in a short period of time. Unfortunately, the paradigm shift that recovery represents has not been accompanied by a cure for serious mental illness or medications with no side effects. Recovery does provide the opportunity for consumers to achieve quality of life, make informed choices about their goals, and learn how to live with and manage their illness successfully, but it does not always ameliorate the significant long-term disability that accompanies severe and persistent mental illness for many of the clients we serve. Let's look at a case example to illustrate what I mean by this.

The Case of Mark

As an adult, Mark was diagnosed as having schizophrenia, disorganized type, chronic, with autistic features, a diagnosis that did not carry a good prognosis in terms of Mark's ability to work, live independently, and develop meaningful social relationships. Mark had had emotional problems from the time he was a toddler and showed many of the classic symptoms of autism. His mother reported that he preferred solitary play that was often stereotyped; for example, he would spend hours pouring water back and forth from one container to another. When Mark's mother would take him to the park, hoping he would play with other children, Mark would turn his back to the other children and play by himself.

Mark entered elementary school in the mid-1950s, long before the Americans with Disabilities Act and before much was known about autism, and soon the school officials informed Mark's parents that his behavior was too problematic and they could not allow him to continue in school. Mark was subsequently hospitalized for two years at a highly regarded child and adolescent inpatient service with, conveniently, an elementary school across the street. During the day, the children from the psychiatric hospital would leave the hospital to go to school and then return to the hospital after school. Because the school was so accustomed to having mentally ill children in the classroom, Mark's behavior did not cause significant problems. His teachers were skilled in managing behavior problems and the other children accepted Mark and, for the first time, he had some peer friends. Mark's diagnosis at that time was childhood schizophrenia.

After Mark was discharged from the child and adolescent psychiatric hospital, his behavior deteriorated and worsened to the point that his family could not manage him and he was hospitalized for the first time in a state hospital. Multiple hospitalizations followed, with the longest one for 16 years. During his state hospital years, Mark was given the diagnosis of schizophrenia and given high doses of traditional antipsychotic medications, such as chlorpromazine. Mark, however, regularly "cheeked" his medication and was regularly punished by the staff for doing so. Such punishment usually involved increasing his prescribed dose of medication.

Finally, in the early 1980s, Mark was deinstitutionalized and placed in a transitional care facility in a large urban area. From that point on he had a series of case managers, therapists, and psychiatrists and suffered repeated treatment failures. The reason this happened was that Mark had a number of unique characteristics. In addition to his serious mental illness, Mark was extremely bright intellectually, and he had what could best be described as an obsessive-compulsive personality style. He organized things in his room, would take notes during therapy sessions, and asked numerous questions. This behavior impressed his clinicians and led them to view him, superficially, as more capable than he actually was. As a result, therapists and case managers would always plunge in immediately and set unrealistically high goals. Mark would inevitably fail at meeting their expectations, the failure would be seen as deliberate and willful on his part (rather than a consequence of his inability to meet the goals), and the therapists would get angry and then reject Mark, also known as "transferring the case." Poor Mark had over 10 case managers and therapists over the course of four years, with the same thing happening each time.

Finally, however, Mark was assigned to a case manager, Edward, who was able to work well with him, and Mark was able to make positive progress and feel good about his achievements. What was different this time?

Here were the keys to Edward and Mark's success. First, before Edward even met with Mark, he thoroughly familiarized himself with Mark's extensive case record, even going back to microfilmed records from his early days on the child and adolescent unit. Edward sketched out a time line that summarized how Mark had functioned over time during various periods of his life. This gave Edward a longitudinal perspective of Mark's life and psychosocial functioning over time. Second, Edward spent time getting to know Mark before any goals were set. Edward was creative with how they spent their appointment times. For example, rather than just meeting in his office, Edward played air hockey with Mark at the socialization center, took him for a walk in the park while they talked, and took him out for coffee. Mark felt listened to, felt that Edward empathized with the frustrations and failures that Mark had experienced, and they developed a trusting rapport. This gave Edward the cross-sectional perspective in terms of how Mark was functioning at this point in time, who he was as a person, and his personal needs and wants.

Third, Edward took a *collaborative* approach to negotiating goals with Mark and ensured that the goals were designed to be flexible and attainable. For example, one goal Mark wanted to achieve was to attend partial hospitalization three times a week. To make the goal flexible with a greater probability of success, Edward built in a clause that if the three times a week schedule was too much for Mark to handle, they would cut back to twice a week but not terminate Mark from the program (which is what had happened in the past). Fourth, Edward regularly elicited Mark's feedback about how things were going and what Mark wanted for his life. For example, previous therapists had pushed Mark into independent living quickly, which he could not handle. When Edward asked Mark what kind of living situation he wanted, Mark said he would like to live independently eventually but for now he wanted to stay in sheltered care. Mark knew what he needed and what he could handle, and Edward respected that.

Finally, Edward kept regular contact with Mark but avoided being too intrusive or demanding. Remembering Mark's autistic features, Edward became aware that his best conversations with Mark often occurred over the phone rather than face to face, so they alternated between phone and face-to-face meetings. In essence, Edward developed a *collaborative partnership* with Mark, he let Mark help set the parameters of that partnership, and he set realistic goals that slowly, step by step, moved Mark successfully forward in his recovery at a pace he would manage. Mark and Edward were also fortunate that the agency allowed them to approach Mark's recovery in this manner. Sometimes staff are subjected to intense pressure from agency administrators to move consumers quickly forward in their rehabilitation efforts, and that pressure serves to propel treatment failure if the consumer cannot handle the expectations. "Staff must have a realistic view of long-term patients and the wide variations in their needs and potential. And staff must not be subjected to administrative pressure to accomplish the impossible" (Lamb, 1979, p. 398).

Now that we have addressed the issue of hopelessness and despair and the steps a clinician and client can take to move toward hope and recovery, the next affective barrier is feelings of helplessness and inadequacy.

Feelings of Helplessness and Inadequacy

Studies have shown that risk of burnout is significant in social work and other helping professions (see, e.g., Kim, Ji, & Kao, 2011; Savava, 2012). Burnout is highly associated with persistent feelings of helplessness and frustration, which are common feelings clinicians experience when treating seriously mentally ill clients. Further, clinicians often report that their professional training did not prepare them to work with this population and, in fact, the skills they had tended to result in treatment failure. The result was that clinicians assumed they would fail no matter what they did with the client and, thus, they resisted learning skills that could help overcome feelings of helplessness. The assumption was that severely mentally ill clients can't be helped, and it then becomes a self-fulfilling prophecy and a vicious circle. Paradoxically, the more invested the clinician is with the client's progress, the more helpless and inadequate the clinician feels when the client doesn't do well (Minkoff & Stern, 1985). Thus, the key to overcoming feelings of helplessness and inadequacy is obtaining good training in the treatment of serious mental illness.

Feelings of Dislike or Disgust

The third affective barrier is feelings of dislike or disgust toward severely and persistently mentally ill clients. As previously noted, mental health professionals are not immune to feelings of repugnance toward mentally ill people shared by society at large. In fact, many clinicians prefer the so-called YAVIS client, that is, young, attractive, verbal, intelligent, and successful (Schofield, 1986). In contrast, clients with severe mental illness may be unkempt, uncooperative, bizarre, psychotic, and smell bad. This is the "big elephant in the room" that clinicians are often reluctant to acknowledge, but the elephant is there and must be dealt with honestly.

Another problem that clinicians often complain about is distaste for the passivity and dependency of many severely ill clients, with complaints of feeling emotionally drained from working with such clients over time. H. Richard Lamb (1979) notes that some mental health professionals share "the basic moral disapproval in our society of dependency, of a passive, inactive life style, and of accepting public support instead of working" (p. 398). Such disapproval may be covert, but it pervades all strata of our society (Krugman, 2012). Lamb adds that "perhaps no other factor is so likely to lead both to staff resentment and to unrealistic expectations and, ultimately, to staff burnout" (Lamb, 1979, p. 398).

This situation stems from the ancient debate in the United States and in social work relating to the "worthy" versus "unworthy" poor (Shaw, 2007; Trattner, 2007). Americans don't like people who are viewed as chronically on the public dole and so, as a society, Americans keep the safety net as thin as possible, although this waxes and wanes, depending on the political atmosphere (Stiglitz, 2012). Yet, such a lifestyle is necessary for many severely mentally ill clients to reduce stress and avoid exacerbation of symptoms, which is the only way to enable them to maintain tenure in the community and avoid hospitalization.

This leads to a dilemma for the clinician: If the clinician provides necessary caretaking, he or she feels guilty of fostering dependency, of being an enabler (in the parlance of the addictions field). But if the clinician pushes for independence the client can't manage, it can precipitate relapse, and then the client is blamed and rejected for not improving. It's a no-win situation for everyone involved. What the clinician must do is achieve a balance between providing the supports the client needs to maintain wellness and facilitating and encouraging the client's move toward more self-sufficiency in recovery. Furthermore, the clinician must help the client learn skills that will enable him or her to achieve success in living, working, and developing and maintaining social relationships in the community.

How does this play out in actual clinical practice? Let's look at a case example.

The Case of Joe, the Client Who Rarely Bathes

Joe is 42 years old, resides with his elderly mother, and has been living with schizophrenia since his first episode at age 19. With the help of antipsychotic medication, Joe rarely experiences the positive symptoms of schizophrenia, such as hallucinations, delusions, or formal thought disorder, but he struggles with severe negative symptoms including alogia or poverty of speech that involves a kind of "emptiness" in the ability to organize one's thoughts and express them; affective blunting, which is an inability to express one's emotions well; avolition or lack of motivation; and anhedonia, in which Joe lacks the capacity to feel pleasure or enjoyment in activities that normally would be enjoyable and pleasurable.

Since the onset of his illness, Joe has had an ongoing problem with poor hygiene and, in the past, would go for a month or more between baths. Joe's poor hygiene was not inconsequential, and it interfered with his ability to make and keep friends—and some of his peers were pretty blunt about it, for example, "Joe—you stink—go away!" At times his body odor was so pungent that I could not tolerate meeting with him in my office, and so, instead, we often sat outside on a bench to talk. I realized I was getting disgusted with Joe's not bathing and decided I had to take it up with him. I liked Joe and we worked well together, and I didn't want to do the cowardly thing and just refer him to someone else.

Tomorrow, Joe has an appointment and, knowing he tends to miss his appointments because he gets disorganized, I give him a call on the phone.

Joe: Hello.

SW: Hello, Joe. This is Christina, your social worker. How are you doing today?

Joe: I'm good. So why are you calling me?

SW: Well, tomorrow you have an appointment with me and so I thought I'd call and just give you a reminder—our appointment is at 10 a.m. tomorrow morning.

Joe: Yeah.

SW: Joe, tomorrow morning before you come to see me, I would like you to take a bath. Remember how we talked about the importance of bathing regularly?

Joe: Yeah. I can remember that.

SW: Great—then I'll look forward to seeing you tomorrow.

Joe comes to his appointment on time, but he smells as bad as ever. It turns out that he did, indeed, take a bath, but he put his dirty clothes back on instead of new clean clothes. I realize that Joe needs help in understanding each step of the bathing process, knowledge that most of us just take for granted. If one thinks about it, however, bathing actually involves a number of separate and integrated steps. The following week, prior to Joe's next appointment, I decide that I need to give Joe another reminder call.

Joe: Hello.

SW: Hi, Joe. It's Christina, your social worker. How are you today?

Joe: Um—I'm good, I guess. I suppose you want me to take a bath again.

SW: Yes—and I thought it would be helpful for you and I to walk through the steps one by one. Last week you did a really good job with the bathing part, but you forgot a couple things, and I know it's hard to remember everything. Do you remember what you forgot to do?

Joe: I just went into the water and forgot to use soap.

SW: Right—good job remembering—and what else did you forget to do?

Joe: I forgot to put clean clothes on . . . but the dirty clothes weren't that dirty and I figured I could get another day out of them, you know.

SW: I understand what you're saying but, to smell clean after your bath, you always want to put on completely clean clothes that haven't been worn since they came out of the wash.

Joe: Okay.

SW: And before you put your clean clothes on, what do you need to do?

Joe: Use a deodorant. But that's expensive.

SW: Joe, I'll make sure you have money to buy deodorant—don't worry about that.

Joe: Okay.

SW: Okay—so let's just run through it so I'm sure you know what to do. Tell me step by step what you're going to do.

Joe: Okay, well, first I take my dirty clothes off, then I run the water, get into the shower, use soap, rinse the soap off, dry off, use deodorant, put on clean clothes, and . . . that's it, I think.

SW: Excellent job! I have an idea for you—why don't you write each of the steps down on a piece of paper so you won't forget, and take that piece of paper into the bathroom with you when you take your bath so you can refer to it. Does that sound like a good idea to you?

Joe: Yeah—that'd help me remember.

SW: Okay, then—I'll look forward to seeing you tomorrow.

Joe: Okay . . . bye.

Poor hygiene is part of the symptom picture for many seriously ill clients with schizophrenia, major depression, and other conditions, such as autism. What is important to remember is that poor hygiene is part of the illness, it is not deliberate or willful behavior on the part of the client. Empathically "feeding back" to your client how poor hygiene is not pleasant for others gently helps the client to begin to understand what attracts and repels other people and how basic self-care skills, such as bathing, play an important part in making and keeping friends. You like Joe; you don't like bad body odor. Many clients with severe mental illness are very isolated and lonely. Taking a bath represents a major accomplishment that can potentially lead to developing more peer and natural social supports and can be achieved with a combination of communicating directly and concretely, along with providing support, acceptance, and empathy.

At this point, we have discussed three of the affective barriers in working with seriously mentally ill clients. The fourth and final issue is feelings of discomfort.

Feelings of Discomfort

Recall the statement made by the soon-to-graduate social work student who didn't want to work with individuals with schizophrenia because she felt uncomfortable and didn't want to be around such clients. Where do such feelings of discomfort come from? Part of the discomfort for many clinicians stems from the fact that work with severely mentally ill clients is often more demanding than work with clients who are less ill, requiring more active efforts and case management (Lamb, 1982), a "multiaxial psychosocial approach" (Minkoff & Stern, 1985, p. 861) in which a variety of resources are involved in the consumer's treatment, individualized treatment strategies (Minkoff & Stern, 1985; Nielsen, Stein, Talbott, et al., 1981), family psychoeducation and other involvement with families (Hatfield & Lefley,

1987; Lefley, 2009), and a willingness to embrace role flexibility and variability over time commensurate with the individual consumer's changing needs.

White and Bennett (1981) comment that clinicians "must learn how to adapt their therapeutic stance to fit the needs of the individual [consumer] rather than take the same stance with all [consumers] regardless of diagnosis" (p. 341). Although many social workers may embrace the challenges inherent in individualizing treatment to fit the client's needs, others may react by "feeling exposed and uncomfortable with this new therapeutic posture" (White & Bennett, 1981, p. 341). For example, when working with consumers with severe and persistent mental illness, a home visit may sometimes be indicated. Home visits are a very different type of contact from the traditional 50-minute office-based psychotherapy session and can be extremely valuable in a variety of ways. First, a home visit can provide the social worker with a better understanding of the consumer's living environment, which can reveal areas of strength and areas where there are problems. The nature and quality of a consumer's community environment is a powerful influence on the consumer's ability to stay well. Second, a home visit can have a positive impact on the development of the client–clinician therapeutic alliance and is a concrete demonstration of the social worker's concern and desire to help. Finally, for clients who have poor insight into their illness, are paranoid and fearful about getting treatment, or whose families are hesitant about getting help, the home visit can serve as a means for bridging these barriers and coaxing the consumer and family into care. Example:

> I was on call for the crisis service one day, when a woman called me with concerns about her neighbor. The caller stated that her neighbor, a young woman, had barricaded herself in her apartment, had not been seen in weeks, and would not answer the door.
>
> "She's a real sweet girl, but the last time I saw her, she seemed really scared—I don't know of what, though," stated the caller.
>
> The caller gave me the young woman's name, and I checked and saw that we had never seen her before. I drove out to her apartment and knocked on the door, but there was no answer. I knocked again, stating who I was and why I was there and, although nobody came to the door, I could hear someone moving around. Before I left, I said the following.
>
> "Ms. X., I know you don't know me, but your neighbor, Mrs. B., and I are concerned about you and want to make sure you're okay, that you have food and water, and we just want to talk with you a little bit. I'm going to come back tomorrow, and maybe you'll feel up to talking with me then. I'm going to slide my business card under the door, and you are welcome to call me, too, if you would prefer. Bye for now."
>
> The next day, the young woman called me and we talked on the phone. She was then willing to let me come out and talk with her, and eventually I was able to coax her to come in to the clinic. She had had her first psychotic break, was terrified of what she was experiencing, and didn't know where to turn. The concern of her neighbor, coupled with a home visit that attempted to connect with her in a nonintrusive, nonthreatening way, succeeded in enabling her to receive the treatment she needed. She responded very well to a combination of antipsychotic medication and psychosocial treatment and was able to continue to live on her own, work, and go to school as she had done before her illness began.

For some clinicians, however, engaging in this kind of proactive, community-based social work is uncomfortable, and such clinicians may prefer to see clients in their offices rather than somewhere in the community. That may be fine for the less ill client, but for clients with serious mental illness, social workers must be willing to engage in activities outside of the office, often in the community, meeting the client where they are. As Mary Richmond stressed decades ago, it is important to give the client "a fair and patient hearing" on their own terms in order to establish a "sympathetic and mutual understanding" (Richmond, 1917, p. 114) or, as Howard Goldstein phrased it, "[start] where the client is" (Goldstein, 1983, p. 267). Starting where the client is may mean meeting the client on his or her own turf and in the way that is most comfortable for the client.

Suggestions for How Practitioners Can Overcome Affective Barriers

The solutions for overcoming affective barriers to working with individuals with serious mental illness and their families all fall under the broad umbrella of provision of appropriate and adequate training in the treatment of serious mental illness that addresses knowledge, skills, and values/attitudes coupled with good clinical supervision. Eack and Newhill (2008b) comment that because many social workers get frustrated when working with SPMI clients and such frustrations can have a marked impact on the development of negative attitudes and affective barriers, "it is important that adequate agency structures be established to anticipate and productively address such frustrations" (p. 425).

> One of the most important areas in this regard is the role of clinical supervision. Clinical supervisors are in an ideal position to address not only the practical issues related to their supervisees' clinical work with clients, such as treatment strategies and resource mobilization, but can also play a role in acknowledging and discussing how to handle the frustrations their supervisees experience in the process of working with their clients. Indeed, guidelines for clinical supervision indicate the importance of attending to burnout and frustrations with clients (Kadushin, 1992), however, our clinical observations suggest that such issues may not be discussed constructively in clinical supervision when working with SPMI clients. Formally attending to these issues as a regular aspect of supervision could produce substantial improvements in staff retention, as many social workers have already sought out informal methods of debriefing with their colleagues and find this quite helpful in reducing their frustrations (see, e.g., Acker, 2004). (Eack & Newhill, p. 425)

In addition, social workers must learn how to take care of themselves and set appropriate limits and boundaries in their work to avoid burnout.

So far, this chapter has addressed stigma; public attitudes toward individuals with mental illness; doctors and mental health professionals' attitudes toward individuals with severe and persistent (chronic) illness, including mental illness; and the affective barriers that can get in the way of clinicians engaging and working effectively with individuals with serious mental illness. There are two more important issues, however, that have yet to be addressed. First is one of the most challenging aspects of serious mental illness, which is when a consumer is not aware of having a mental illness or denies having one, something that is often referred to as lack of insight. A lack of awareness or insight into the fact that one is ill can be a significant barrier to seeking and accepting treatment along with developing a positive partnership with treatment professionals and family members for one's recovery. The second issue to be discussed—which takes into account all of the aforementioned barriers—is how to develop a positive therapeutic alliance with someone who has a serious mental illness and the therapeutic tools that can facilitate achievement of a positive working alliance.

Assess your comprehension of *the affective obstacles that challenge mental health professionals in their work with clients with serious mental illness* by completing this quiz.

Eack, S.M. & Newhill, C.E. (2008b). What influences social workers= attitudes toward working with clients with severe mental illness? Families in Society: The Journal of Contemporary Social Services, 89, 418–427.

I AM NOT MENTALLY ILL AND I DON'T NEED HELP FROM YOU OR ANYBODY ELSE

> Since her first episode of illness, Jamie had ten hospitalizations over the course of two years, all of them involuntary. Jamie had her first psychotic break at the age of 17 and was first hospitalized at that time. Jamie was angry about being in the hospital and did not want to take medication, telling the inpatient social worker: "I am not mentally ill—don't you understand me? My parents made me come here just because I was smoking weed. I won't smoke anymore, okay? I don't want your medicine and I don't want treatment."
>
> During each hospitalization, Jamie's psychiatrist and social worker tried to help her understand her illness, schizophrenia, and help her understand the importance of taking medication to stay well. Her family participated in family sessions with the social worker, emphasizing psychoeducation, but Jamie continued to refuse medication or any form of psychosocial treatment, stating, "I am not the problem here!"
>
> Before the onset of her illness, Jamie was a stunningly beautiful young woman who was an excellent student academically and had a bright future ahead of her. But, over the course of several years, with only intermittent treatment, Jamie's symptoms became more chronic and unremitting in nature, and her psychosocial functioning significantly deteriorated. Finally, her family turned to the courts and obtained an order of conservatorship that forced Jamie to accept outpatient treatment, including medication. Jamie was incensed at the court's action, borrowed money from a friend, and took a bus to San Francisco. The last time her parents heard from her, she was living in the streets and prostituting herself to obtain money for drugs.

Here is a consumer with a loving and supportive family who tried their best to work with the treatment team to help her. She also had a team of concerned mental health professionals who tried to help her. Yet she ended up on the streets, addicted to illicit drugs and engaged in prostitution. What went wrong? The most stubborn barrier between this client and her recovery was what is often referred to as "lack of insight." Jamie was unable to see and accept that she had a serious mental illness. Because of this, she was unwilling or unable to see the need for treatment, which resulted in a refusal to accept treatment. What, exactly, is "lack of insight"? Where does it come from? Why do some clients have insight while others do not? How can we, as social workers, help our clients to develop helpful insight into their illnesses and other problems they may have?

What Lack of Insight or Lack of Illness Awareness Is and Where It Comes From

The inability to perceive and acknowledge that one has a serious mental illness when, in reality, one does have an illness is not denial, in the sense that one knows one is ill but refuses to admit to it. Lack of insight in serious mental illness involves the individual truly not believing that they are ill. One thing that can be helpful in understanding the perspective of the individual who lacks insight into one's illness is to imagine that someone takes you to a doctor and the doctor tells you that you have cancer. You know that you *don't* have cancer, yet this doctor is telling you this—out of the blue—and then tells you to undergo chemotherapy. Knowing you don't have cancer, you refuse the chemotherapy treatment. That is just common sense. This is how the consumer with schizophrenia responds when someone urges him or her to take an antipsychotic if the individual does not have illness awareness. The person thinks, "I don't have schizophrenia. Why should I take an antipsychotic medicine for something I don't have? That wouldn't be good judgment . . . in fact, it might hurt me, poison me." Those of us who work with individuals with serious mental illness who evidence poor insight hear this kind of reasoning all the time (Amador, 2000, 2011).

Many clients with schizophrenia, schizoaffective disorder, delusional disorder, other psychotic disorders, and bipolar disorder suffer from poor insight, which functions as a formidable barrier to getting the treatment they need. In fact, one study (Amador, Strauss, Yale, et al., 1993), using a novel multidimensional scale measuring mentally ill respondents' insight into having a mental illness and their awareness of signs and symptoms, showed that nearly 60 percent of the individuals with schizophrenia or schizoaffective disorder were unaware of being ill.

Because it is so common, the *DSM-5*, released in 2013, identifies poor insight as an associated feature supporting the diagnosis of schizophrenia, stating that

> Some individuals with psychosis may lack insight or awareness of their disorder (i.e., anosognosia). This lack of "insight" includes unawareness of symptoms of schizophrenia and may be present throughout the entire course of the illness. Unawareness of illness is typically a symptom of schizophrenia itself rather than a coping strategy. It is comparable to the lack of awareness of neurological deficits following brain damage, termed anosognosia. This symptom is the most common predictor of non-adherence to treatment, and it predicts higher relapse rates, increased number of involuntary treatments, poorer psychosocial functioning, aggression, and poorer course of illness (APA, 2013, p. 101).

Thus, the problem of poor insight has significant negative consequences for the consumer. Poor insight also adversely affects those who care about the ill individual. Family members and friends can become extremely stressed, frustrated, angry, and overwhelmed as they try to "get through" to the ill individual, to make the person see that he or she is ill and needs treatment.

Clinicians can experience the same frustrations if they do not understand lack of insight and how to address it. Rarely, however, do attempts at reality testing or arguments to that effect lead to improved insight, because it isn't that the person is being stubborn or resistant—the person truly does not believe that he or she is ill, and this belief is rooted in a neurocognitive deficit specifically linked to executive (or frontal lobe) dysfunction and abnormalities over which the individual does not have voluntary control (Amador & David, 1998). As a result, even psychoeducation (discussed in Chapters 6 and 10) may have a limited impact. However, the good news is that there is an approach that has been shown to be effective in terms of facilitating insight and adherence to treatment.

An Approach to Overcoming the Barrier of Lack of Insight and Facilitating Illness Awareness

Xavier Amador, a psychologist who has a brother with schizophrenia, has extensively studied and researched the problem of lack of insight in serious mental illness (see, for example, Amador & Shiva, 2001; Dell'Osso, Pini, Cassano, et al., 2002; Pini, Cassano, Dell'Osso & Amador, 2001; Pini, Dell'Osso, Amador, et al., 2003). He argues that what clinicians and families need to do is to adopt a new paradigm for how they interact and engage with the ill person. The problem of lack of insight is a problem that is frequently further exacerbated by the way we often provide treatment.

The traditional approach to dealing with someone who is psychotic or manic is to assess the person, diagnose the person, and deliver treatment—usually medication, although sometimes psychosocial treatment is also recommended. If the person refuses the treatment, then the person is evaluated for involuntary care, and if he or she meets criteria, a civil commitment is drawn up. This is the traditional medical model, in which those who are trained as experts in psychiatry, psychology, nursing, or social work decide what the ill person needs and, essentially, tell him or her what to do; and if the individual doesn't comply, they impose consequences, usually involving forcing treatment against the person's will. Amador (2000) argues that what needs to happen, instead, is to employ a very different approach to treatment engagement, an approach that fits well with the practice traditions of social work. The acronym for his approach is "LEAP," which stands for *Listen*, *Empathize*, *Agree*, and *Partnership*, with an overarching emphasis on collaboration.

LEAP is an approach that utilizes many of the elements of motivational enhancement therapy (MET). Here is how each element plays a role.

Step One: Listen

When I started out as a young social worker, I wanted to solve problems . . . I wanted to help people . . . I wanted to see change occur . . . and I was sure that I had lots of knowledge and skills garnered from all my hard work in my MSW program to achieve those goals and I was ready to change the world. But then I learned an important lesson. Many times, I discovered, the most helpful thing I could do was to not engage in active problem solving but, instead, to be quiet and simply listen—really listen. It is harder than it sounds. When somebody starts telling us about a problem or just what is going on in his or her life, most of us are tempted to jump in and push for a solution. The sad reality, however, is that many people come to us because they have nobody who is willing to listen—not give advice but to simply listen. Thoughtful, reflective listening coupled with the next component—empathy—can be the most helpful thing you can do for your client, and if you listen well and empathize, often the client figures out solutions to the problems and, by doing that, achieves a sense of empowerment and competence.

"Effective listening is really a skill that needs to be cultivated" (Amador, 2000, p. 56). It takes practice, especially because the way people communicate today via various technological mechanisms—Twitter, texting, email, and so forth—does not serve to cultivate good listening skills (Hafner, 2009). It takes practice to be a good listener. A good listener does not make assumptions about what the other person thinks or feels, rather, he or she inquires about the individual's hopes, dreams, expectations, wants, and needs. In the case of an individual with a mental illness, it is important to ask about what the person is experiencing: What does "having a mental illness" mean to him or her? What are the person's perceptions about taking medication? This information is critical to developing a collaborative treatment agreement. Amador (2007) comments that "when you are doing [reflective listening] right, you're asking a lot of questions. You sound like a journalist conducting an interview" (p. 52). Example:

> In this scenario, the client, Amy, has been brought to the psychiatric emergency service by her family. Amy was discharged from the inpatient unit three weeks ago, stopped taking her medication a week after discharge, and is now hearing voices again. The family is frustrated because Amy refuses to restart her medication. The following dialogue is an approximation of what occurred between me (the psychiatric emergency room social worker) and Amy.

I invite Amy to come into the interviewing room and we both sit down.

SW: Amy, my name is Christina Newhill, and I am a social worker here at the psychiatric emergency service. Could you tell me a little about what brought you here today?

Amy: My parents brought me. And I don't want to be here.

SW: Okay—could you tell me what happened today that resulted in your parents bringing you in to the crisis service?

Amy: They said if I don't take my medicine, they're going to kick me out. I don't know why I am told to take medicine—I am not sick—I am not the problem here.

SW: That must be hard for you.

Amy: Yeah. How would you feel if someone told you to take medicine you don't think you need?

SW: I hear you. Let me ask you this—when you took the medicine in the hospital, how did it make you feel?

Amy: It made me feel like crap. I hated taking it.

SW: That must be awful, to feel like crap. Amy, what do you want for yourself?

Amy: (suspiciously) What do you mean?

SW: I mean, in an ideal world, what things would you like to have for yourself that would make you feel good?

Amy: I want my own place. I want a job. I want my parents to get off my back. I want out of here.

SW: It sounds like you have some good goals for yourself. You'd like to be on your own and self-sufficient. Is anything getting in the way of working on and achieving those goals?

Amy: I keep trying but nothing seems to work . . . I don't know why. If my parents would just let me make my own decisions about my life, I'd be fine. But they hover over me: "Did you take your medicine? Did you take your medicine?" I hate it. I'm not a little kid—I'm 18 years old, for cripes sake.

SW: Amy, it sounds like you want to be allowed to make some decisions for yourself. It may feel like your parents are hovering, but my guess is that they love you and want what they think is best for you, like most parents do. I understand that you don't want to take a medication that makes you feel crummy, but the good news is that there are lots of different medications. If the one you were on makes you feel like crap, we can discuss with the doctor, together, what other options there might be. You're the expert on yourself and your input is important. . . .

In this example, the client, Amy, is brought to the crisis service by her family because she has stopped taking her medication—a very common scenario. Rather than immediately focusing on the topic of medication, I make a point of asking Amy what she wants for herself, and Amy identifies some goals (which may not be realistic at this point, but that is okay) for which I then provide validation. This leads to Amy opening up a little about her relationship with her parents, and then I share with her that if she doesn't like the medication she is on, there are other options to try and, importantly, I make the point that Amy's input is valued.

Step Two: Empathize

Listening well and listening reflectively usually leads naturally to empathizing with the other person's situation (Amador, 2007). But what is empathy, exactly? Empathy involves the accurate perception of and the ability to clearly communicate about another person's inner feelings and emotional state at the moment—that is, their immediate feeling state. The intended result is that empathy nurtures and sustains the relationship and creates a nonthreatening, supportive atmosphere.

Empathy also fosters the development of a reciprocal attachment and commitment to the helping process and involves three levels of perception. First is the ability to perceive a client's immediate surface feelings—what is right out front in the communication. Second is the ability to perceive a client's underlying deeper feelings and emotions. The third level of perception is the ability to perceive not only verbal but nonverbal messages via the client's body language, facial expression, tone of voice, and gestures. This process of perception also involves "being with" the client and entering the world experience of that person, which is not the same as being emotionally affected in the same way—that is the difference between empathy and sympathy (Hepworth, Rooney, Rooney, et al., 2010).

Sympathy connotes "I would feel and do the same as you have in the same situation," while empathy involves understanding the other person's feelings without taking that person's position and, thus, retaining one's separateness and objectivity. Being objective does not mean that you "hide" behind a cold distant professional shield—rather, you are warm and genuine as part of the empathic stance.

Developing Rapport

The appropriate employment of empathy is the keystone to developing a rapport with a client who does not believe he or she is ill. Empathy helps in gaining the client's trust and fostering open communication. Developing rapport successfully with a client is based on certain practitioner values and attitudes, including assuming a nonjudgmental attitude (which is not the same as being nonjudgmental) and approaching the client with acceptance of who the client is as a human being. This doesn't imply blanket condoning or agreement with the client's views or behaviors. What it does mean is accepting the client as a person and demonstrating respect for the client's worth and dignity. The following is an example of beginning to establish rapport via the use of empathy:

> In this scenario, an inpatient social worker is meeting with a client named Bianca who was admitted to the psychiatric inpatient unit the night before after the police brought her to the emergency room. The police apprehended Bianca because she was directing traffic at an intersection and causing a disturbance downtown. The emergency room social worker noted that Bianca was manic and has a documented history of bipolar disorder, subsequently arranging for involuntary commitment on the basis of danger to self. In the morning, the inpatient social worker makes a visit to Bianca's room. As Bianca paces back and forth in her room, the social worker begins the initial interview with her.

SW: Bianca, could you tell me what happened last night before you were admitted to the hospital?

Bianca: Just get me out of here!! I have important things to do that you would never understand!

SW: I'd like to try to understand. Bianca, do you think you can sit down here with me so we can talk a little bit?

Bianca: Okay, okay. (sits down but her knee bounces up and down)

SW: It sounds like things have been, and still are, pretty stressful—how are you feeling right now?

Bianca: I don't want to be in the hospital. . . . My life's a mess! (bursts into tears)

SW: From what the nurses told me, it sounds like you've been through a lot. You're safe now, and we want to help you. When a person has manic symptoms, it can be hard to put one's thoughts together and do the things you need to do. Are you feeling pretty overwhelmed right now?

Bianca: (sniffs) Sort of. I don't know what to do.

SW: It's hard to figure out what to do when your thoughts are moving so fast. Let me help you take a break—I'll get you some breakfast and when you're feeling a little better, we can sort things out together. You deserve some rest first.

Bianca: Okay. I want to lie down now.

SW: I'll get you some breakfast—try to eat something if you can—you can rest for a while and then I'll come back later so we can talk.

In this scenario, the social worker empathizes with the client's feelings and does not push his or her own agenda to talk about what has been going on. The offer of food and rest is another way that empathy can be expressed and, through this, communicates to the client that she will be cared for and helped. After allowing the client space, the social worker will return and see how the client is doing and whether she is up to talking more. Empathy is a very critical component to successfully connecting with clients and families, yet many clinicians fail to employ it. Why? A social work student, who worked as a case manager, once said to me, "I don't have time for empathy! It's not billable!" My response to him was: "Employing empathy actually saves you time and increases your billable hours because, if you use empathy, you are more likely to establish a strong therapeutic alliance as a result and engage your client successfully in treatment. Plus, you save all the time you would otherwise spend in arguing or engaging in other destructive communications with your client." He thought about it and eventually agreed it made sense.

Step Three: Agree

Now that you have listened to your client's perspective and concerns and have established some rapport via the strategic use of empathy, you are now ready to move to the third step in the LEAP approach. In the third step of LEAP, you attempt to identify areas of agreement that both you and the client endorse. "When you share common goals, you can work together instead of being at odds" (Amador, 2007, p. 88). Working together helps to cement the therapeutic alliance so the client can perceive you as an ally, not as an adversary. Once you identify some common goals, then naturally move to Step Four, which is partnership.

Step Four: Partner

When you partner with a client, you establish a collaborative approach. When you collaborate with another person, you work with one another and cooperate on a shared goal. Collaboration is the best approach for supporting a client's recovery, and it facilitates empowerment. Let's return to Bianca's situation to illustrate the steps of "agree" and "partner":

> It is the fourth day of Bianca's hospitalization following a manic episode, and she is doing well but verbally fights with the nurse each time he brings mood-stabilizing medication to her, which is lithium. Although it seems that she is taking the medication, the whole process is fraught with conflict. Today, Bianca comes for her regular meeting with the social worker, this time in the social worker's office on the unit.

SW: Hello, Bianca. Please come in and have a seat. You're looking good today—more rested, perhaps?

Bianca: Yes, I'm sleeping better . . . but . . . I just want to get out of here.

SW: I'm sure you do, and we want to get you well and out of here, too. How are you feeling on the lithium?

Bianca: I hate it. It just doesn't make me feel good. I'm an artist—I write and paint. With the lithium, it's like all my creativity just drains away. I feel like I'm looking through gauze—all the colors of life are gone.

SW: Hmmm . . . that doesn't sound pleasant at all. I imagine you must feel pretty frustrated. . . .

Bianca: I am, but I don't have any choice about it.

SW: Well, actually, you do have some choices. Lithium doesn't work best for everyone, and the good news is that there are other medications that don't have lithium's side effects that can help stabilize your mood but not sap your creativity and perceptions. At our last meeting, you told me that one of your top goals is to stay out of the hospital.

Bianca: Yes—I definitely don't want to come back here.

SW: And what are some of the tools you can use to stay out of the hospital?

Bianca: Doing my social rhythm therapy.

SW: Right—and we also talked about the importance of taking the right medication to keep your moods steady.

Bianca: But I don't want to take lithium.

SW: Okay, let's put lithium aside. What if there was a medication that kept your moods stable but didn't have the side effects of lithium? One such medication is called divalproex sodium or Depakote—for lots of folks, the side effects of Depakote are a lot easier to tolerate.

Bianca: Gee, I don't know . . .

SW: Let's look at it this way. You and I have a couple of common goals here—to work on keeping you out of the hospital and supporting your creative work.

Bianca: Right. Yeah. Those are my goals.

SW: And when your moods get too high or low, things begin to get out of control and you end up in the hospital.

Bianca: Yeah, unfortunately . . .

SW: Two things can help you achieve those goals.

Bianca: Social rhythm therapy and, I guess, (sighs) the damn medicine. What if the—what did you call it? Depakote? What if it doesn't work?

SW: The best way to find out is to try. How about if you and I both meet with the doctor, and you can tell him what your goals are, what you didn't like about lithium, and then talk about the pros and cons of Depakote?

Bianca: You'll go with me?

SW: Sure—we're partners in this.

Bianca: (brightens) Okay.

In the first dialogue with Bianca, the social worker used empathy and reflective listening to begin to establish rapport. As Bianca is more stabilized, she and the social worker began to talk about goals, agreeing on two—staying out of the hospital and supporting Bianca's creative work. The means for achieving the goals was adhering to two treatments—social rhythm therapy and medication. Bianca did not like taking lithium, and the social worker listened to Bianca's explanation as to why lithium was problematic for her, then suggested an alternative medication. Emphasizing a collaborative stance, they discuss the alternative medication, Depakote, and the social worker offers to meet with Bianca and the doctor, which represents a concrete action in support of their collaborative partnership.

Assess your comprehension *of what lack of insight is, where it comes from, and how one can work with a client to facilitate illness awareness* by completing this quiz.

Rather than engaging in fruitless arguing and failed attempts at persuasion, the LEAP approach emphasizes good basic clinical social work skills and can be very effective in helping to overcome the barrier of poor insight and lack of illness awareness. Nowhere in the illustrative dialogues does the social worker try to convince the client that she is mentally ill; rather, the focus is on what needs to happen in order for the client to reach her self-identified goals. Along the way—hopefully—insight may evolve, which can serve to strengthen their mutual efforts.

CONCLUSION

This chapter addressed strategies for overcoming barriers to treatment when working with clients with serious mental illness and how to maintain the development of a therapeutic alliance both with clients and with their families. Such barriers include the impact of stigma; lack of or poorly developed insight; negative clinician attitudes, biases, and stereotypes; cultural factors; and the nature of living with and managing a long-term illness. Affective barriers, in particular, such as feelings of hopelessness and despair, feelings of helplessness and inadequacy, feelings of dislike or disgust, and feelings of discomfort, can impact the development of burnout, staff turnover, and job dissatisfaction.

Along with access to good clinical supervision, there are many steps that social workers can take as individuals to overcome these barriers and ultimately lead to better outcomes for clients. These include learning how to confront the issue of incurability while preserving hope for recovery, learning how to work with clients on adaptation to and management of severe and persistent illness, and learning and adjusting to different expectations for success. Strategies such as the LEAP approach to overcoming lack of illness insight can also be very helpful in the process of engagement and goal setting. When social workers learn how to overcome barriers to treatment, they will then be in the best position to truly ally themselves with their client and the client's family and be a partner in the client's and family's journey of recovery.

RANK ORDER VALUES CLARIFICATION EXERCISE

Answer each of the following questions. For each question, think about what attitudes and values your answer reflects.

1. Which of the following conditions would you *least* want to have? Why?
   _____ cancer
   _____ mild mental retardation
   _____ schizophrenia
2. Which would you *least* like to be? Why?
   _____ very poor
   _____ paraplegic
   _____ manic-depressive
3. You decide to adopt a "hard to place" child. Three children are available. Which child would you choose? Why?
   _____ a child with cerebral palsy
   _____ a child with moderate mental retardation
   _____ a mildly autistic child

4. You have been looking for a social work position for three months, and there are only two available choices. One is to work as a social worker in a maximum-security prison. The other is to work at a state hospital with profoundly retarded adults. Which job would you choose? Why is that choice preferable to the other choice?
5. You and your partner have recently bought a home. You both work and you have two small children—a 6-month-old baby boy and a 3-year-old girl. The city announces that they are building a halfway house for dually diagnosed consumers next door to your home. How would you feel about that? Would you move?
6. You are walking down the main street in your community. As you walk, you pass three people begging for money. One person wears a sign that says, "I am unemployed, please give me money for food," the next person's sign says, "I am alcoholic, please give me money for food," and the third person's sign says, "I am mentally ill, please give me money for food." Which person is most deserving of a handout? Would you give any of the people money? Why or why not?

Assess your application and *analysis of this chapter's contents* by completing the *Chapter Review.*

Chapter 5

Working with Legally and Socially Involuntary Clients

INTRODUCTION

Imagine that you are a social worker employed by a public mental/behavioral health clinic. Your first appointment of the day is with a new client, DeShawn, who is an 18-year-old African-American man on probation for motor vehicle theft and reckless driving. His probation officer has sent him for counseling because of concerns about the client's inability to control his temper, thus counseling has been made a condition of probation. Failure to comply with this condition will result in jail time. In addition, during his brief stint in jail, the client was diagnosed as having bipolar disorder and chemical dependency (marijuana and alcohol), although this has not been confirmed by anyone outside the jail behavioral health services.

You review the client's paperwork for a second time, and then call him from the waiting room, inviting him to come into your office and sit down. You introduce yourself by name, and add that you are a clinical social worker in the intake and assessment sector of the clinic. Immediately, the client interrupts you, folds his arms across his chest, and says sullenly, "Look, man, I don't need no social worker. I've got to find me a job and a place to crash—the courts have messed me over enough already. I don't have nothing to talk about."

What is going on? Why is the client so angry, even hostile, toward you when the two of you have just met? You're not sure what to say or what to do next. You decide the best way to respond to this client is to convince him that you are not the enemy and, instead, want to help him, so you respond as follows:

SW: DeShawn, I would like to help you with what is going on.

Client: Can you get me a job and a place to crash?

SW: Well, no . . . at least not right away . . . but we can work on that.

Client: Uh huh . . . right . . . can I go now?

SW: Wait a minute. Your probation officer says you need counseling or you'll go to jail. Do you want me to set you up with counseling?

Client: I told you already, I got nothing to talk about.

SW: It sounds like you've got some problems with your temper.

Client: Look, I'm outta here. I'm sure you're a nice person and all, but there's nothing you've got that I want. See ya.

SW: Wait—are you taking your medication?

The client walks out of the office and you're left with the feeling that you failed. What could you have done differently that would have more successfully engaged DeShawn and connected him with the treatment he needs? What you didn't fully appreciate is that DeShawn is in the position of being an *involuntary client*. He doesn't want to be there and have to talk with you, and resents being forced to do something he didn't choose to do. His situation is very different from a client who chooses to seek treatment or services.

This chapter addresses working with involuntary, resistant, and/or hard-to-reach clients, clients like DeShawn. Rooney (1988) defines an involuntary client as "a client who does not seek help from a social worker and who receives treatment due to pressure by legal authorities or fear of consequences for failure to participate" (p. 131).

One of the realities of public mental health social work practice today is that many clients don't seek services on their own volition; instead, they may be referred by the courts, probation or parole officers, child welfare personnel, or some other entity that requires the clients to obtain services even though the clients do not want the services and may not see that they have a problem. In other cases, someone in the client's life—perhaps family members, employers, or friends—may insist that he or she seek help, usually to change some kind of behavior the referral source doesn't like. In both types of situations, the clients are under external pressure and are usually facing some kind of negative consequence if they don't comply. The clients are, essentially, between a rock and a hard place. Either they do what they don't want to do or they will be punished. This is the essence of being an involuntary client.

Lack of Motivation and Unwillingness to Change

One of the common complaints of practitioners who work with involuntary clients is that they "lack motivation" and are "unwilling to change" (Miller & Rollnick, 2002). Decades ago, social workers often referred to such clients as the "hard-to-reach client," that is, "that individual who cannot utilize our services because he refuses . . . to fit into our neat ideas about how a client should act, what kind of problems he should have, and how he should conduct himself in our relationship with him" (Lindenberg, 1958, p. 23).

One of the central issues in engaging and working with involuntary clients is understanding the nature of human motivation, that is, what motivates people to change their behavior and what strategies social workers can use to enhance motivation when it doesn't seem to be present. There are a number of conceptual models for understanding motivation, including the conflict ambivalence model, the health beliefs model, the decisional balance model, self-perception theory, self-regulation theory, and reactance theory. One of the most widely incorporated models for practice and research, which has been the basis for a number of motivational enhancement intervention approaches, is the transtheoretical model of change, initially conceptualized by psychologists James Prochaska and Carlo DiClemente (Prochaska & DiClemente, 1983), which pulls together and integrates some of the key constructs from these other theories.

THE TRANSTHEORETICAL MODEL OF HOW PEOPLE CHANGE

The transtheoretical model (TTM) is a conceptual framework that focuses on how people decide to make changes in problematic behaviors, with such changes involving not only the behavior, but also changes in the emotions and cognitions that are associated with the behavior. The TTM has provided a useful heuristic structure for the development of interventions addressing the amelioration or reduction of a wide range of problematic behaviors, including smoking, alcohol abuse, obesity, unsafe sex practices, drug abuse, medication non-adherence, and stress-related problems. The TTM states that people go through certain *stages of change* as they move from not recognizing that a certain behavior is a problem to intending to take action to change their behavior to taking action and then maintaining the changes that occur. Understanding these stages and respecting where the client is in the process is critical for successful engagement and building of trust and rapport, especially for an involuntary client. Three important things to remember are that:

- Ambivalence is normal, albeit a key obstacle to change;
- Making change is a process, and clients need time and support to move through that process; and
- Arguments supporting change must come from the client, not the practitioner.

The transtheoretical model posits that people go through *five specific stages* as they move toward changing a problem behavior. Looking at change as a *process*, rather than as an event, more aptly represents how people actually change. For example, quitting smoking or stopping drinking alcohol involves a series of decisions and modifications in emotions, cognitions, and behavior until the person reaches the point of changing the behavior, in this case, not using the substance. This contrasts with the notion of someone deciding, "I'm going to quit drinking," and then immediately ceasing substance use now and forever more. People rarely do that or do it successfully largely because embedded in such decisions are normal feelings of ambivalence. People are more likely to move toward change in stages, resolving the ambivalent feelings along the way, bit by bit. Determining where the client is in this process of change and where the ambivalence lies are key variables in successfully engaging the client. Example:

Ms. DUI

In this scenario, the client is a 30-year-old White female who has been ordered to substance abuse treatment because of a DUI (driving under the influence) conviction. This is her first interview with the social worker. This client demonstrates some passive resistance and a lot of ambivalence.

SW: So I understand that you're here because the court ordered you to treatment?

Client: Yeah. Did you get the paperwork they were supposed to send over?

SW: Yes, I did. Could you tell me a little about what you want to do about all this?

Client: I honestly don't know what I want to do about it. I know I could've killed someone driving drunk and I don't want to take that chance again, but then again . . . I don't want to stop drinking, really. I like to drink. (shrugs her shoulders)

SW: Okay. Tell me a little about why you like to drink. What are some of the positive things about drinking?

Client: Well . . . drinking helps me relax. . . . It is the one thing I do just for me that isn't good for me, you know. It's like I'm doing something that makes me feel good just to feel good.

SW: Okay . . . anything else?

Client: Um . . . I like the taste . . . I like how it feels . . . mostly it helps me deal with stress. I work full time, I've got three kids, issues with aging parents—it's like when I drink, I can deal better with all that. But . . . I don't want another DUI.

SW: It sounds like you enjoy drinking but, on the other hand, you don't want another DUI.

Client: I don't know if this will make sense to you, but it's like I don't want to give up drinking, but I don't want to drink if I'm going to get in trouble. I don't know what to do.

SW: I hear you. What you're saying makes total sense. . . .

In the dialogue above, the client is quite direct about her ambivalence about stopping drinking. She doesn't want to risk harmful consequences of drinking, but drinking has many positive attributes for her and she also doesn't want to give up those good parts about drinking. This is an example of ambivalence. Working through the ambivalence and supporting clients in developing their own reasons for change is the practitioner's role. Most clients move through several stages of change and may seek or be referred for help anywhere along the continuum. The five stages of change per the TTM are as follows (Prochaska, DiClemente, & Norcross, 1992):

- Precontemplation
- Contemplation
- Preparation
- Action
- Maintenance

The Five Stages of Change

The first stage of change is called *precontemplation.* In this stage, the individual has not decided to take action about a particular problematic behavior, and may be uninformed or underinformed about the consequences of the behavior. Sometimes the person has taken steps to change but the steps haven't worked, and the person has given up trying, or become hopeless about his or her ability to change. Some individuals may deny or minimize the reality that their behavior is a problem and may refuse to talk about it or become angry if others push them to change or talk about their problem behavior. The social worker's role at this stage is to provide information and feedback in order to raise the client's awareness and increase his or her perception about the harmful consequences of continuing the problem behavior. Clients who present for treatment at this stage are often there because of pressure from others, for example, spouse, employer, or the court system, not because they see there is a problem. Change may be demonstrated but only as long as the pressure is on and, once it is off, they go back to their old habits (Prochaska, DiClemente, & Norcross, 1992).

The second stage of change is called *contemplation.* Contemplation is the stage in which the individual recognizes that there is a problem and is considering initiating change over the course of the next 4–6 months. The person is, however, still quite ambivalent about change and unsure if change can be successful. Individuals at this stage are very aware of the risks and benefits of change and acutely cognizant of the pros and cons of change, which can keep the person "stuck" at this stage for a while. The terms "chronic contemplation" or "behavioral procrastination" are often used to describe the situation of being "stuck" in the contemplation stage. The social worker can help the person resolve the ambivalence by talking through the reasons for changing and the risks of not changing. The practitioner can assess and help support and strengthen the individual's level of self-efficacy to enhance hope that change is possible and can be successful. If the individual and practitioner are successful in resolving the ambivalence, the person is ready to take on the role of being a client, and may then be ready to move forward to the preparation stage.

The third stage of change is *preparation.* At this point, the client is ready to take action in the immediate future, that is, the next 1–4 weeks. The individual has begun preparing for action, such as finding out the meeting times for a support group, consulting with a social worker or other counselor, and planning a schedule for change. Such individuals may have already made a few changes in their behavior, but the problem has not been resolved as yet. The social worker's role at this stage is to help match the client with an acceptable, appropriate, and effective strategy or program for changing the problem. The client, however, has to decide what is right for him or her and should not be pushed in a particular direction, although the social worker can help the client weigh up the pros and cons of various alternatives.

The fourth stage is *action*. Here the client takes overt behavioral, cognitive, and emotional steps to change the problem behavior and has made considerable commitment of time and energy. If the individual has a serious mental illness, for example, this stage is central to moving toward recovery. The individual acknowledges he or she has an illness and demonstrates actions central to effective management of the illness, such as adhering to prescribed treatment, including medication, and actively participating in ancillary therapeutic support activities. For the involuntary client, this is the stage in which the client moves from being "involuntary" to "voluntary," that is, fully taking on the role of client and collaborating with the practitioner to achieve success. The action stage is also the stage where vigilance against relapse is critical.

Maintenance is the fifth stage, in which the client is working to maintain gains and prevent relapse. He or she is more confident that recovery/change can be maintained, and self-efficacy is more evident. For individuals with severe and persistent mental illness, the maintenance stage is equated with recovery and is lifelong in duration. The social worker's role in the maintenance stage is to collaborate with the client and the client's family in identifying and using strategies to prevent the return of old patterns of behavior and habits and maintain the gains achieved.

Some clinicians add a sixth stage to the TTM—*relapse*—however, others argue that relapse, or "recycling," is not really a stage but, rather, requires a return to the action or maintenance stage to recoup the previous gains. What is important for the clinician to remember is that relapse is normal, and normalizing relapse for the client by presenting relapse as simply part of the process of recovery is important. Relapse does not mean the client has failed. No matter what stage the client is in, that stage is normal.

Many clinicians and researchers endorse the TTM as a valid model of how people change, although others (see, e.g., West, 2005) argue that the TTM is a flawed model and the idea that people always move through distinct stages as they change a behavior has not been adequately validated. Regardless, the model is useful in acknowledging that clients vary significantly in their motivation, insight, and willingness to change and part of the challenge in engaging involuntary clients lies in the fact that, for many such clients, changing their behavior is not something they want to do or see as reasonable. Respecting that can help the clinician to start where the client is at and partner with the client by allowing him or her to determine where he or she wants to go. Sometimes, however, a client will not budge, and the clinician needs another set of strategies to assist in moving change forward, particularly when not changing a behavior places the client at risk for significant negative consequences.

Assess your comprehension of *the five stages of change in the transtheoretical model of how people change* by completing this quiz.

APPLICATION OF REACTANCE THEORY FOR UNDERSTANDING THE BEHAVIOR OF INVOLUNTARY CLIENTS

When a client is involuntary and under pressure to comply with requirements he or she disagrees with because such compliance means loss of choices, self-determination, and freedom, it is normal for the client to resist the pressure. The term "resistant" is a common term that clinicians use when faced with a client in such a situation. Clinicians often use the word "resistance" to describe the behavior of involuntary clients. The problem is that labeling the client as "resistant" can influence the practitioner's perception of the client in a negative way. For example, it can cause practitioners to blame clients, and it can create a self-fulfilling prophecy of failure. A "self-fulfilling prophecy" is an assumption or prediction that directly or indirectly causes itself to become true by means of feedback influenced by the prediction that occurs between the belief and behavior. Sociologist Robert K. Merton (1968) originally coined the term "self-fulfilling prophecy," and formalized its definition and structure as follows:

> The self-fulfilling prophecy is, in the beginning, a false definition of the situation evoking a new behavior which [then] makes the original false conception come true. This specious validity of the self-fulfilling prophecy perpetuates a reign of error, for the prophet will cite the actual course of events as proof that he was right from the very beginning. (p. 477)

Thus, if a social worker believes treatment will fail with a particular client, the social worker will treat the client differently than if the social worker believes treatment will be a success and thus influence the actual treatment outcome. In turn, clients are exquisitely sensitive to how they are perceived by their clinician and will pick up on whether the clinician holds hope for them or views them as a potential treatment failure. How can one avoid creating such a situation?

Rooney (1988, 1992, 2009) states that, rather than viewing the involuntary client as "resistant," the social worker should pose the question "resistant to what?"—that is, what is the client pushing back against? Rooney argues that a better lens for understanding the cognitions, emotions, and behaviors of involuntary clients is *reactance theory*. Reactance theory, originally developed by psychologist Jack Brehm (1972, 1976), posits that "reactance," defined as an aversive emotional reaction, occurs in response to the imposition of demands or regulations that impinge on freedom and autonomy. Reactance theory is a more strengths-based theory for explaining the reactions and behavior of involuntary clients and, furthermore, helps in predicting how people respond or react to the loss of valued freedoms (Brehm, 1972). Loss of freedom is the essence of being involuntary, and recognizing this can help the clinician be more understanding and empathic toward what the client is feeling and why the client may be uncooperative and unwilling to be adherent with what he or she has been required to do (Brehm & Brehm, 1981).

Predictable Reactions to Loss of a Valued Freedom

According to reactance theory, a person who faces the loss of a valued freedom can be expected to react in one of five ways (Rooney, 1988; Wicklund, 1974):

1. Seek to restore his or her freedom despite the consequences; *or*
2. Show hostility or aggression toward the threatening source, even when such efforts are unlikely to remove the threat; *or*
3. Find a loophole or technically comply with regulations while violating other norms that were not expressly prohibited; *or*
4. Attempt to incite others to perform a forbidden behavior; *or*
5. Become increasingly attracted to prohibited behaviors.

A good example of normal reactance is what can happen when parents insist their teenage daughter stop seeing her boyfriend because they believe he is a bad influence. The daughter may realize the boyfriend is a jerk and may even have been thinking of breaking up with him, but her parents' actions result in her deciding to continue to see him "because they aren't going to tell me what to do." Her "reactance" involves hostility toward her parents' attempts to control her along with their demands serving to reverse her feelings and increase her attraction to the oafish boyfriend.

Assess your comprehension of *clients' predictable reactions to loss of valued freedoms and strategies practitioners can use to reduce reactance* by completing this quiz.

How strong the client's reactance response is depends on two things: (1) how important the particular lost freedom is to the client, and (2) the proportion of freedoms that are threatened. Reactance theory doesn't view the above responses as pathological; rather, such reactions are considered to be normal and the job of the clinician is to figure out what the client is reacting to and "roll with the resistance," thereby reducing the tension and moving toward engagement.

STRATEGIES TO REDUCE REACTANCE

Sharon Brehm (1976) suggests a number of strategies that clinicians can employ to help reduce reactance and support client self-determination. First, when communicating with the client, social workers should avoid giving directions or orders to the client; rather, communication should focus on increasing the client's choices in making decisions, using language such as: "Only you can determine what is best for you in your situation. Why don't you think things over and then decide what direction you want to take."

Second, when making decisions, explore all sides to the situation, and avoid one-sided communication. One-sided communication tends to make people feel cornered, serving to increase their resistance. For example, use language such as "Well, there are many different possibilities for fulfilling the court's requirement that you seek treatment. We offer residential treatment, outpatient treatment, individual treatment, group treatment. Different types work more or less better for different individuals. There are many choices available to you, and we can discuss the pros and cons of each." Clients also may be more willing to try out new options if the clinician presents an option in a matter-of-fact way and doesn't overemphasize or "make a big deal" out of it.

Finally, the client's reactance is likely to be less if the client is given the message that he or she only needs to change certain specific behaviors, while other behaviors can be maintained without change. This avoids giving the client the impression that he or she has to change everything about who he or she is and serves to validate the client as a person, that is, "You're not a bad person, there is just this particular behavior that is a problem." These recommendations support the stance that the clinician and the client are partners in moving toward the goal of eventually restoring the client's freedom.

In summary, emphasizing that the client has choices, developing an intervention contract that has the goal of restoring freedom, pointing out where clients do not have to change, emphasizing client strengths, and focusing on specific circumscribed changes rather than global changes are all compatible with the social work core value of supporting client self-determination. Achieving this is often most effectively done by using bargaining and negotiating as the core strategy, collaboratively setting goals that are feasible and support client strengths, and increasing the client's choices (Murdach, 1980; Raynor, 1978). Further, the more clients know about what is expected of them, what their role is, and what the clinician's role is in the process, the more likely reactance will be reduced and the client will engage in the process of treatment (Videka-Sherman, 1985).

Preparing for the First Meeting with an Involuntary Client

There are two types of involuntary clients: the legally involuntary client, who is under legal mandate to participate in treatment, and the socially involuntary client, who is under social pressure to participate in treatment (Rooney, 1988). Because both types of clients have not yet taken on the client role, the social worker must employ strategies designed to socialize the individual into the client role during the initial rapport development and engagement stage of work, when roles are clarified and problems identified. Research has clearly shown that the most important factor in achieving success in the initial sessions of treatment is whether client and practitioner goals and communication are congruent. Here we address the social work practice factor called content relevance, defined as the extent to which the content of the practitioner's responses "is perceived by clients as relevant to their substantive concerns" (Hepworth, et al., 2010, p. 129). The presence of this is essential to satisfaction and continuance in treatment. In fact, whether a client is voluntary or involuntary may be less important than the quality of the interaction between the client and the practitioner.

Before meeting with an involuntary client, the practitioner has *three tasks* to address in preparation for the first interview (Rooney, 1988; 1992). These tasks all draw from reactance principles. If the client is legally involuntary, that is, the client has been ordered to treatment by a legal entity and lack of compliance will result in some kind of legal consequence, the first task for the social worker is to clearly identify the nonnegotiable requirements that have been imposed on the client. With nonnegotiable requirements, the client must comply with legal requirements and the social worker must enforce them.

Social workers who work for substance abuse services or public mental health services are often in this position. For example, a client may be brought in by the police for an evaluation following a commotion in the community, or be seen as part of an outpatient commitment order, or be court-ordered to substance abuse treatment. In such cases, the social worker must be clear about what the nonnegotiable parameters are and, equally important, where there is room for freedom of choice, including behaviors and lifestyle choices that do not have to change and, thus, can be maintained. For example, the legal requirements may specify that a social worker must monitor a client's compliance with a court order but, at the same time, the social worker can be flexible with the client regarding how often, when, and where they meet. It is important to remember, however, that mandated legal problems constitute only one area to focus on. Like with any other client, the social worker can still address specific problem areas the client identifies and chooses to work on, and addressing these client-identified issues are often key to enhancing client motivation to participate fully in treatment.

For the second task, involving both legally and socially involuntary clients, the social worker should identify areas where there are negotiable options and areas of free choice. Less reactance will occur if options are available. The task for the social worker is to help the client distinguish between the nonnegotiable requirements and the negotiable aspects of those requirements. For example, a client on an outpatient commitment may be mandated to get outpatient treatment, but the specifics of what that treatment consists of are negotiable. The client may be able to choose amongst a number of options for psychotropic medication, and may be able to choose whether he or she wants group treatment or individual treatment.

As noted above, some involuntary clients are not under legal mandate but, instead, are under social pressure to obtain treatment, and are "socially involuntary clients" (Rooney, 1988). An example of this would be demands from a spouse who gives the message "either you get help or I'm taking the kids, going to my parents to live, and filing for divorce." In such cases, since the choice not to participate is *legally* available, the clinician's strategy is to clarify, collaboratively with the client, the personal advantages and disadvantages of continuing treatment voluntarily. Utilizing reactance principles, the clinician would present all sides to the situation, emphasizing where the client has choices, and sort out the pros and cons of different decisions. Example:

> Mr. A. is a high-powered lawyer with bipolar II disorder, whose wife has told him that she is tired of his erratic moods, his refusal to be adherent with taking his prescribed mood-stabilizing medication, and his self-centered behavior and has issued him an ultimatum: "Get help or I'm leaving you." Mr. A. is angry about the situation but follows through with an appointment with a clinical social worker at a private mental health counseling facility. Empathizing with Mr. A.'s feelings about what has happened, the social worker collaboratively discusses with Mr. A. the advantages and disadvantages of getting treatment:

Advantages of getting treatment:

- My wife won't leave me and my family will stay intact.
- My moods will be more stable and I won't have as many conflicts at work.
- My marital happiness might improve.
- Maybe I'll get to know who I am more—not sure if I want to go down that road, though.

Disadvantages of getting treatment:

- I'll lose my hypomanic moods, and when I'm hypomanic, I get more work done and make more money—I feel on top of the world.
- My wife will have me by the testicles—I don't like being told what to do.
- Treatment takes time—I don't have that kind of time.
- I don't like touchy-feely stuff, like talking about my feelings because it makes me uncomfortable.

The important last step to take before meeting with an involuntary client is monitoring one's own feelings, that is, the social worker must reflect on how he or she feels about the basis or reasons for the client's involuntary status, meaning their alleged offense or problem behavior. Involuntary clients are often accused or convicted of offenses that are contrary to the social worker's personal and professional values or beliefs. Some clients have engaged in behavior that has hurt other people, and they may or may not express any remorse or guilt about what they have done. Social workers must reflect on and monitor their feelings, or those feelings will adversely affect their ability to provide the client with the help he or she needs. If the client gets the right help, that help may ultimately prevent further harm to others in the future. In addition, if the social worker does not appropriately monitor his or her feelings, the legal requirements may get mixed up with what the clinician personally believes should be done, for example, feeling that the client should be punished more than what is required. What can help to keep this under control is to be careful to restrict the nonnegotiable expectations to the specific mandated requirements and/or to the targeted problem behaviors only. For example, let's say the social worker is working with a client with schizophrenia who was convicted of sexual abuse of a child. The social worker *can* require that the client attend a child sex abuse treatment and prevention group, adhere to taking prescribed antipsychotic medication, and control his or her behavior, including staying away from children and places where children congregate. The social worker *cannot*, however, expect that the client be monitored 24 hours a day or check in with the clinic more often than required.

Having completed the three preparation tasks, the social worker is now ready to interview and work with the client. Setting up the treatment process with the involuntary client involves two major phases of engagement (Murdach, 1980; Rooney, 1992; Simons, 1982): (1) socialization of the client in the initial session, and (2) contracting strategies.

THE TWO PHASES OF ENGAGEMENT WITH INVOLUNTARY CLIENTS

Socialization of the Client in the Initial Session

There are four tasks the social worker and client have to address in the initial session, which constitutes the first phase of engagement with the involuntary client (Rooney, 1988; Simons, 1982):

- Explaining the cause of contact, including nonnegotiable requirements and options;
- Anticipating the client's reaction to involuntary involvement;
- Expressing appropriate empathy; and
- Providing appropriate confrontation on nonnegotiable conditions of contact.

Explaining the Cause of Contact

The legally involuntary client has not sought contact and, may not really know why he or she is being mandated to see the social worker and, thus, is entitled to an explanation. The client may have been told to "get help" without much more detail, may recall the judge or probation officer telling him or her to make an appointment at the local mental health clinic, but may not truly understand the basis for the mandate, why he or she is here having to see you, and who you are and how you can help.

For example, consider the situation in which a client is brought in to the emergency room by the police for an evaluation for civil commitment. In this kind of situation, the social worker should first introduce him or herself, make sure the client understands where he or she is (i.e., in an emergency room of a hospital), ask, "Do you know why the police brought you here?" and then listen to the client's understanding of why he or she is there and his or her version of what happened up to the point of the current evaluation. Then the social worker can explain objectively and nonjudgmentally the social worker's understanding of the precipitants for the contact, for example, the input that other people have had regarding the circumstances (police, family members, and/or others), so that both perspectives can be brought together. It is important that descriptions of the client's behavior are concrete, objective and specific.

At this juncture, then, the nonnegotiable requirements should be identified and distinguished from negotiable ones. In the example of evaluating someone for civil commitment in the emergency room, the nonnegotiable requirement is that the social worker must make an evaluation; what is negotiable can be determined based on findings of the evaluation. For example, if the client doesn't meet criteria for involuntary hospitalization, negotiable options could include voluntary hospitalization, transitional or respite care, medication, follow-up outpatient care that is appropriate and acceptable to the client, and finally, as a last resort, the client can just be discharged to go home. Of course, for some clients, there is no "home" other than the streets, and in such cases it is incumbent upon the social worker to identify and connect the client with resources so he or she has a safe place for obtaining food and safe shelter. For all the options, the social worker should weigh the advantages and disadvantages and pros and cons with the client.

If the client must be hospitalized against his or her will, there are still some negotiable choices. Every involuntary situation has "wiggle room" for choices, and it is the social worker's responsibility to identify what these choices are for the client. For example, if the client refuses to go to the hospital, the social worker can say the following to the client:

> I understand that you don't want to go to the hospital, and I appreciate your feelings about that. It is hard to be forced to do something you don't agree with. However, you do have some choices here that you need to weigh up. As we discussed, the

> nonnegotiable is that you must be hospitalized for your own safety and the safety of others. You have choice, though, in how that process unfolds for you. You can choose to control your behavior and let me walk with you over to the unit peacefully, or you can choose to have me call four inpatient staff to come and escort you. It is your choice how you want to do this.

This emphasizes that, although being hospitalized is not a choice, the manner in which the hospitalization process is carried out includes some choices for the client.

Anticipating the Client's Reaction to Involuntary Involvement

After clarifying the cause of contact, no matter how well it is explained, one can anticipate that the client will have a reaction to the involuntary contact as the client realizes that he or she has lost freedom. Predictable client reactions include the following (Sagarin, 1975; Saltmarsh, 1976):

- Anger at imposed services
- Denial of wrong or harm
- Viewing him or herself as a victim
- Blaming others as unworthy and deserving of harm
- Hostility toward you—the social worker—as an agent of social control
- Passive deception
- Deception

All of these responses are reactance reactions to perceived loss of freedom. To reduce this reactance, the social worker should respond by engaging in the third socialization task, which is expressing appropriate empathy toward the client's thoughts and feelings, while remaining firm about the nonnegotiable requirements in the client's situation.

Expressing Appropriate Empathy

Sometimes, the client's reactance responses can be so strong and so emotionally negative that the client has difficulty in "hearing" what the social worker is saying, including hearing what choices he or she has. This can serve as a real barrier to client and practitioner collaboration in developing a treatment contract; thus, these negative feelings must be recognized, empathized with, and discussed. The expression of empathy should focus on communicating your understanding of what it is like to be forced to do something against your will. Empathy on the part of the practitioner can be facilitated by the practitioner recalling times when he or she was in a similar position, for example, having to do an unpleasant chore or assignment without choice (Seabury, Seabury, & Garvin, 2011). Then the practitioner can say to the client something along the lines of:

> I imagine you are feeling pretty frustrated and angry about having to do something you didn't choose to do and having to be here and talk with me because someone else is forcing you to do that. That's a tough position to be in. I imagine you'd like to be almost anywhere else but here with me right now.

Strategic use of empathy can be a powerful tool for engaging an angry, reactive client. Empathy is essentially the emotional and cognitive reactions that an individual has to the observed experiences of another person (Davis, 1983). Carl Rogers (1961) defined empathy as "accurate understanding of the [patient's] world as seen from the inside. To sense the [patient's] private world as if it were your own, but without losing the 'as if' quality—this is empathy" (p. 284). Empathy, then, is the social worker's "ability to perceive and communicate, accurately and with sensitivity, the feelings of the client and the meaning of those feelings" as the client shares and describes his or her situation and concerns (Fischer, 1973,

p. 329). Ultimately, empathy is the means by which the practitioner and client become emotionally significant to each other, thus fostering a reciprocal attachment and a mutual commitment to the helping process. The reality is that many involuntary clients, because of their problem behavior, haven't received much empathy from others. It is important to remember that one can empathize with a client's feelings without condoning the client's behavior.

The last socialization task to prepare the client to address developing a mutual treatment contract is the use of appropriate confrontation with regard to the nonnegotiable requirements.

Providing Appropriate Confrontation on Nonnegotiable Conditions of Contact

As noted above, accepting the person and affirming his or her worth and dignity does not mean condoning the problem behavior the person has engaged in. Via the appropriate use of confrontation techniques, the social worker can respond empathically to the client's feelings about it being involuntary, while remaining firm about limits, requirements, and the nonnegotiable aspects of the client's situation.

Hepworth and Larsen (1990) suggest that confrontation is most likely to succeed if it comes from a helper that the client respects and if the behaviors targeted by the confrontation are very specific and defined, including clearly defined consequences. An effective strategy for using confrontation is to begin by empathizing with the client's feelings about the situation and then adding the confrontation. Empathy serves as the "lubricating oil" to make the confrontation go more smoothly and with less risk of inciting more reactance. Using the conjunction "and" instead of "but" most effectively joins the expression of empathy with the confrontation, because it suggests the two can coexist and don't contradict each other (Saunders, 1982). Example:

> I understand your hurt and anger when your wife insults you and taunts your manhood, and responding by hitting her only escalates the situation and, most recently, resulted in your ending up in jail and, now, here with me. Another option you can choose when your wife insults you is to walk out the door and cool down.

This example is worded to validate the feelings of hurt and anger and, furthermore, such feelings can coexist with a nonviolent response—not only a violent one. The message to the client is: "You can both be angry *and* avoid hitting your wife."

Assess your comprehension of *the tasks involved in the initial session of the socialization/ engagement process with involuntary clients* by completing this quiz.

The first phase of engaging the involuntary client has now been completed. The cause of contact, including nonnegotiable requirements and options, has been explained and the client's reactance has been responded to with empathy and appropriate confrontation. The next phase of engaging the client and setting up the process of treatment is developing a contracting strategy.

Strategies for Developing a Working Intervention Contract in the Initial Session(s)

The term *contracting* can be defined as the technique used for exploring an agreement between the practitioner and the client about the goals for the work together, the methods to be used in the work, and the roles of the participants in this working relationship, that is, the client, the practitioner, and possibly other people, such as the client's family (Hepworth et al., 2010; Maluccio & Marlow, 1974). The process of formulating a contract protects the client's individuality and maximizes his or her opportunities for self-determination by providing the client with opportunities for meaningful choices about the situation, which is critically important for the involuntary client.

Ideally, the first phase of the engagement or socialization process prepares the way for a real contract in which the involuntary client identifies goals to pursue. Exploring the client's view of his or her situation and any problems the client identifies is an important initial step in identifying goals. Based on that, the practitioner can explore several strategies for negotiating the goals further and formulating a beginning contract (Rooney, 2009).

Exploring the Client's View of His or Her Problems

Once the social worker has explained his or her understanding of the reason for contact, the involuntary client typically presents his or her own view of the problems and their cause—which may be very different from the practitioner's view—or may deny there is a problem at all. There are several strategies that can address such differences and move toward mutually identifying a focus for the contract (Rooney, 1988, 1992, 2009). These strategies may be put in an order of descending desirability, that is, if the first strategy doesn't work, move on to the second strategy, then the third and, finally, the fourth strategy is the strategy-of-last-resort. The basis for this ordering will become clear as each strategy and its advantages and disadvantages are discussed below. These four contracting strategies identify both the nonnegotiable and negotiable requirements, support self-determination as much as possible, and highlight the ultimate goal of restoring the client's freedom, thus reducing reactance responses (S. Brehm, 1976). The first strategy, and the most desirable one, is the *agreeable mandate strategy* (Rooney, 1988).

Agreeable Mandate Strategy

For legally involuntary clients, there is always some kind of nonnegotiable mandate imposed by the court that must be enforced by the practitioner or agency where the client is referred. The social worker should first assess what the mandated concern is and, then, whether the client sees that there is a problem to be addressed. *If* he or she expresses a problem, the social worker then examines whether the problem the client has identified is similar to the court's mandated concerns. For example, let's consider a male client referred to the local community mental health center for treatment because he was convicted of engaging in the sexual abuse of a child. The social worker would assess the following:

- Is the client concerned about his urges to molest children?
- Is there guilt or remorse about the abusive behavior?
- Does the client want to learn how to control his behavior and avoid abusing another child in the future?

If the client answers "yes" to each of these questions, the treatment goals can be framed to easily encompass both the client's concerns and the court-mandated concerns, that is, the client wants to learn how to stop engaging in abusive behavior and the court wants the same outcome.

An alternative situation is when the client may agree with the concerns of the mandate but may disagree with the referral source on the *cause* of the problem. For example, in the above case, the referral source (court) claims that the cause of the client's sexual abuse of children lies within the psychopathology of the client, that is, he meets criteria for the *DSM-IV-TR* paraphilia called pedophilia. The client, however, claims that the cause of his abusive behavior is that children act seductive and, thus, he can't keep himself from abusing them. In essence, the client admits to being a pedophile but blames the victim. The social worker can reframe the situation by suggesting that the client's goal will be learning how to handle his *perception* that children are seductive along with learning to control his behavioral response to that perception. This re-frames the cause as client's perception rather than fact and, furthermore, the responsibility for managing this is solely the client's, not the child's.

Another variant of the agreeable mandate strategy is when the involuntary client finds his or her own reasons for complying with the required mandate. Example:

> Mary, a 34-year-old mother of two young children, was first diagnosed with bipolar I disorder five years ago. Since that time, she has been hospitalized 10 times, each time because medication nonadherence led to relapse of her illness. Mary's bipolar illness is severe, and her psychiatrist had difficulty finding a combination of medication that worked well to control her symptoms. A combination of lithium, Depakote, and olanzapine works best for Mary. However, although Mary would adhere to the medication regime for a short time, she always eventually stops taking it, stating to her family, "I feel fine—why do I need to keep taking meds?" Frustrated, the psychiatrist placed Mary on an outpatient commitment following her last hospitalization. Today is her first visit to the outpatient clinic, as mandated by the commitment.

SW: Hello, Mary. My name is Sue Brown, and I am a clinical social worker here in the outpatient department. I understand that you were recently in the hospital and today is your first appointment since discharge. I imagine it was hard for you, having to go back to the hospital. Since you were released, how have things been going so far?

Mary: Okay, I guess. . . . I suppose you know I have to be here. . . . I have no choice in the matter.

SW: Yes, I understand you were placed on what is called an outpatient commitment. Do you know what that means?

Mary: Yeah, it means I have to be here whether I like it or not.

SW: True, however, the main goal is to ensure that you will get and adhere to the treatment that has been shown to keep you well. What are your thoughts about what might be helpful for you?

Mary: I want to see my kids. When I went into the hospital, my mother took the kids and she said I can't be alone with them unless I take my medication.

SW: It must be painful to not be able to see your children. I know one part of the outpatient commitment is that you are required to take your medication. How do you feel about taking medication?

Mary: I don't like meds—they slow me down, my hands shake, and I get fat—I hate that. Look, I was feeling so good before—I thought I could get by without my medicine.

SW: I know—these medications are tough to be on. Have you talked with your doctor about the side effects and whether some adjustments could be made so you could be more comfortable?

Mary: No . . . I guess I could do that. I don't like being committed, though.

SW: It's hard to be told to do something you don't want to do, like take medicine you don't want to take. On the other hand, it sounds like you really want to be with your children. Maybe talking with the doctor to see if any changes could be made to reduce the side effects and then staying on the medications prescribed, even when you are feeling well, would result in your being able to be with your children more. What do you think?

Mary: (brightening) Yeah . . . I want to see my kids. Okay, I'll talk with the doctor. I don't like taking meds, but if it means I can see my kids, I'm guess I'll have to do it.

In this scenario, the client, Mary, found her own reasons to comply with the mandate of the outpatient commitment. The commitment goal was for Mary to adhere to taking her medication so she would stay well and avoid hospitalization. Mary doesn't like being on a commitment and doesn't want to take medication but is willing to do so if that means she can see her children. In addition, the social worker's suggestion that Mary consult with her doctor gave Mary hope that perhaps a medication reevaluation could result in changes that would work better for her. The result was that the client complied with the mandate, but the reason was so that she could see her children.

The main advantage of the agreeable mandate strategy is that it enables the involuntary client to find positive reasons for doing what is required, hence, the client complies more willingly. Once an agreeable mandate has been established, the client and practitioner can then proceed to elaborate a formal semivoluntary or voluntary contract. However, if an agreeable mandate isn't possible because the problem cannot be reframed or the client's concerns don't fit the mandate, the next strategy to consider is the *"quid pro quo" or "let's make a deal" strategy* (Murdach, 1980).

The "Quid Pro Quo" or the "Let's Make a Deal" Strategy

If an agreeable mandate cannot be identified, it is easy for the client and practitioner to fall into a trap of partisan conflict rather than cooperation and, thus, it is important to employ strategies designed to address power imbalances (Murdach, 1980). The two approaches that can achieve this are bargaining and negotiation. Bargaining is "a process through which mutual expectations are redefined and costs and rewards allocated by each party" (Murdach, 1980, p. 459), and moves through several phases that include: (1) "discovering the bargainable," that is, determining where the wiggle room is for agreement and disagreement; (2) "finding areas of agreement" that are new; (3) "critical bargaining," where compromises and decisions are negotiated; and, finally, (4) "public presentation of results" in which an agreement is achieved and noted through some official means (Mitchell, 1973, pp. 588–590).

Bargaining and negotiation can be integrated into a strategy that can work when the client expresses a problem or concern that is not related to the mandate but which the client is motivated to get help with and resolve. The social worker can then propose to "make a deal" with the client using a "quid pro quo" approach as an inducement for the client to cooperate in the mandate. That is, the social worker agrees to help the involuntary client with his or her self-identified personal problems or concerns as long as the client is willing to work on the mandated concern.

An example would be a client with borderline personality disorder who wants to live with her sister instead of in the subacute facility where she has been staying. However, the client has not been compliant with attending her prescribed dialectical behavioral therapy (DBT) group, and the sister has been hesitant to allow the client to live with her if she isn't in treatment because of a history of repetitive parasuicidal behavior that occurs when she is not in regular treatment. This client is in a "socially involuntary" position—she wants to live with her sister, but the sister won't let her live with her unless the client complies with treatment. Here the client talks about her situation with her social worker:

Client: I don't want to go to DBT. I work full-time and it is too much hassle to get over to the clinic after work to go to group.

SW: It sounds like you would like to be able to stay with your sister, though, instead of continuing to live at the subacute facility. Am I correct in this?

Client: Yeah, but she won't let me stay with her unless I'm going to DBT regularly, and DBT sucks—it doesn't help.

SW: I've known you for quite a while now, and one thing I've noticed is that during the times you have gone to DBT regularly, your moods have been more stable and you haven't engaged in any self-harming behavior. Maybe it's a coincidence, but I'm wondering if DBT is helping in some way to keep your emotions and behavior more regulated. What do you think?

Client: Maybe . . . I don't know.

SW: I'll tell you what. If you'll agree to return to DBT and stick with it for at least the next three months, I'm willing to give your sister a call and "go to bat" for you about your staying with her.

Client: You'd do that for me?!

SW: Sure—but only on the condition that you'll go to your DBT group and meet with me once a week as well. Is that a deal?

Client: It's a deal. Thanks—thanks so much.

Granted, the "let's make a deal" strategy is less positive than the agreeable mandate strategy because it acknowledges up front that the involuntary client finds little to no value in complying with the mandate for its own sake; for example, as the above client stated eloquently, "DBT sucks." However, the advantage of this strategy is that it does create a positive incentive for adhering to the mandate because it offers a benefit in exchange that the client wants. Hopefully, as the client participates in the mandated treatment, he or she will begin to see value in the treatment for its own sake, not just because it enables the additional desired benefit.

An important caution, however, is that the quid pro quo exchange must be negotiated ethically, around offering an additional benefit, not by withholding rights. For example, a board and care operator telling a client with schizophrenia that if he doesn't clean up his room she won't let him attend partial hospitalization isn't an ethical deal. Clients have a right to treatment, and so this kind of a "deal" is unethical because it involves withholding a right rather than providing additional benefits. Also, the inducement or benefit offered should be relatively small, so clients will more readily attribute any positive change to themselves and adherence to the mandate, not solely because of the benefits provided by the inducement (Simons, 1985).

If a "deal" is successfully negotiated, the client and practitioner can then go on to develop a semivoluntary contract and, eventually, a voluntary working contract for treatment. However, if the "deal" doesn't work or the client indicates there is nothing he or she wants from the social worker or from any available services, the social worker moves on to the third strategy, which is called the *get rid of the mandate* strategy.

Get Rid of the Mandate Strategy

Some involuntary clients disagree with the concerns of the legal mandate or social pressure and, furthermore, deny they have any problems or concerns that they need help with, that is, "my only problem is having to be here with you" (Rooney, 1988). Under these circumstances, what can the practitioner offer that might serve to motivate and engage the client? Seabury, Seabury, and Garvin (2011) argue that in certain respects, "there is no such thing as an involuntary client" (p. 170). What they mean by that is we as social workers often label a person as an involuntary client or unmotivated client when he or she doesn't want our services, not recognizing that all clients have motivation, but the motivation may not be directed toward where we think it should be. In the case of clients who are refusing to comply with the mandate and saying they have no problems other than being forced to see you, motivation lies in getting rid of the "monkey on their back," that is, the mandate and, by extension, you. It is this source of motivation that can be tapped.

One approach that can tap into this motivation is to suggest that having to continually see you and having the legal mandate hanging over his or her head is a problem in itself. Therefore, the goal you offer to the client is to work together to get rid of the mandate and restore the client's freedom. The client may accept contracting around a problem, even if he or she sees it as invalid, if doing so gives the option to end the contract early. Example:

Jack

Jack has been diagnosed with narcissistic personality disorder and has severe marital problems that have led to his wife insisting he get treatment or she will file for divorce. She complains that he is self-centered and controlling. Jack disagrees with his wife's complaints about him and doesn't think he has any problems that warrant services of any kind. He is angry and resentful over his wife's demands but doesn't want a divorce.

Jack: Look, I am not the problem here! You know, my wife wants a big house, a nice car, and all that, and where does she think that stuff comes from? It doesn't fall out of the sky, I can tell you that! I bust my butt every damn day at my job to make the money to give her the lifestyle she wants, and this is the thanks I get? Telling me I'm self-centered and need help? Who the hell does she think she is, anyway?!

SW: I bet it makes you pretty angry to be told to get help when you're trying to work hard to support your family.

Jack: You bet it does. (crosses his arms defiantly) Look, this is wasting my valuable time.

SW: Okay—let me see if I have this straight. . . . Your wife has told you to quote-unquote "get help" or she is filing for divorce?

Jack: Yeah.

SW: And the only reason you're here is because of your wife's demand.

Jack: You got that right.

SW: Well, what do you want to do about the situation, Jack?

Jack: I want her to get off my damn back.

SW: Do you want to get a divorce?

Jack: Hell, no—I love my kids and she sure as heck isn't going to take them from me.

SW: Are there any concerns that perhaps I could help you with?

Jack: Nope.

SW: Sounds like you're between a rock and a hard place. Your wife is telling you to get counseling or she's filing for divorce. You don't want a divorce because you love your kids and want to be with them. You work hard trying to provide for your family and now this happens. And it sounds like the only reason you're here is because of what your wife is demanding—you don't think you have a problem.

Jack: You got that right.

SW: I know this is a tough place to be at. How about if you go along with what your wife wants for a couple weeks or so—you know, just to humor her. You come in and see me three to four times, and that'll take care of it and get your wife off your back. We'll talk about whatever *you* want to talk about and then you'll be done with it.

Jack: (snorts derisively) It's a waste of time, but okay. I guess I can do that.

In this example, as is common with individuals with a personality disorder, Jack does not see that he has a problem; he externalizes blame for his difficulties and shows a number of reactance responses including anger at the imposed services, denial of wrong or harm, viewing himself as a victim, and blaming others. He doesn't want help but is motivated to avoid a divorce and get rid of the socially involuntary mandate of his wife's demands. What the social worker does is to empathize with Jack's feelings about the situation without condoning his behavior, highlight the bind he is in, and then negotiate the frequency and number of contacts to just a few, which gives Jack choice. As long as Jack is willing to meet with the social worker three to four times, the mandate can end relatively early. This strategy creates a motivation that the client does not initially perceive and, because it is designed to restore freedom rather than restrict freedom, it can reduce reactance. The hope is that, in the course of those agreed-upon sessions, the client will find the counseling with the social worker (framed as consultation with an expert to help Jack save face) useful, and eventually he may "buy into" some aspects of the counseling and stick with it. Even if that isn't the case, he will have had the experience of talking with someone who empathizes with his feelings, is "in his corner" in trying to support him in resolving the problems he is facing, and that will result in at least a positive therapeutic experience, leaving the door open in case Jack decides to seek further help in the future.

If the client accepts the "get rid of the mandate" strategy, the social worker can then formulate an initial semivoluntary contract and move forward. If, however, no agreement is reached and even getting rid of the mandate is too symbolic of agreeing to lose freedom, the next step is for the social worker to point out the self-defeating consequences of that choice, via the final—last resort—strategy option, which is the *self-defeating consequences strategy.*

Self-Defeating Consequences Strategy

For some clients, even contracting to get rid of the mandate early is unacceptable, because it is viewed as acquiescing to a situation that involves giving up freedom. The client thinks, "I'll be darned if I'll agree to cooperate—just try and make me." When this happens, the practitioner needs to point out the self-defeating consequences of such a decision: that by not participating the client is giving up self-determination and the opportunity to have his or her voice and views heard.

For example, consider a client brought in by police for an evaluation for hospitalization who refuses to talk to the evaluating clinician. The clinician can respond to the refusal by saying the following:

> Mr. X, I have to make a psychiatric evaluation whether you agree to talk to me or not. If you refuse to talk to me, I will have to base my decision on what the police and your family have told me, and they're telling me enough to warrant an involuntary hospitalization as a danger to yourself and others. If you refuse to talk to me, you are giving up the power you have to exercise *your* choice to present *your* side of things. Is this what you want to do?

Here you are presenting the client a real paradox: by refusing the option to participate, the legally involuntary client is giving up power to control his or her own destiny and is placing critical decision-making power in your hands. This strategy usually works if the client is *able* to participate and is not, for example, involuntarily mute or catatonic or so grossly psychotic they cannot communicate. If the client responds by agreeing to participate, the social worker can begin with the agreeable mandate strategy and move forward until an agreement is negotiated.

In summary, intervention strategies guided by reactance theory provide proactive options for clients and practitioners designed to increase self-determination and increase adherence with mandated goals.

Assess your comprehension of *the four basic strategies for developing a working intervention contract in the initial session(s) with an involuntary client* by completing this quiz.

MOTIVATIONAL INTERVIEWING

The strategies described so far are reflected in the engagement/intervention approach called "motivational interviewing" (www.motivationalinterviewing.org). Motivational interviewing (MI), a solidly evidence-based intervention, was initially developed as a strategy to engage problem drinkers (Miller, Sovereign, & Krege, 1988), and since then has been successfully applied to a range of concerns including anxiety, depression, post-traumatic stress disorder, suicidal behavior, obsessive-compulsive disorder, eating disorders, gambling problems, medication adherence, and problems associated with having a mental illness and chemical dependency (Arkowitz, Westra, Miller, & Rollick, 2007; Lundahl, Kunz, Brownell, et al., 2010). It is an approach to engaging and working with difficult clients, particularly those who are ambivalent, resistant, or involuntary, that embraces a set of principles, targeted techniques, and a philosophy about how people change to resolve ambivalence. The principles and strategies of MI are also incorporated in a time-limited intervention called motivational enhancement therapy, which was developed to treat alcohol abuse and alcoholism by exploring and enhancing client motivation for change (Miller, 2000).

Motivational interviewing is a client-centered approach (Rogers, 1961) emphasizing self-determination, choices, and collaboration that fits well with social work's traditional approach to working with people. It recognizes that clients are more willing and able to change a problem behavior if the practitioner creates a supportive environment, explores what the client wants and why the client wants it now, establishes trust, draws the client into a collaborative partnership, and focuses on the goals the client has self-identified. This is in contrast to pushing a client to change. Rather than "installing" change, the practitioner aims to "draw out" change.

Motivational interviewing draws from the transtheoretical model of how people change, recognizing that change is not linear, rather, change is a process that may be circular in nature. Miller & Rollnick (1991, 2002) believe that client-centered empathic collaboration that supports client self-efficacy is the spirit of motivational interviewing, and its broad principles include the following (Miller & Rollnick, 1991, 2002):

- Express empathy (this is the cornerstone to engagement and establishing rapport);
- Develop discrepancy (when people become aware of a discrepancy between what they want and what they are doing, they are more likely to make efforts to self-regulate and move toward change);
- Roll with resistance (the practitioner tries to avoid arguments, acting like an expert, or misusing power); and
- Support self-efficacy (defined as an individual's beliefs about his or her ability to produce results and exercise influence over events in his or her life, which affects motivation and behavior [Bandura, 1994]).

In addition, motivational interviewing emphasizes utilizing specific skill methods throughout the MI process and "woven together, they begin to form the fabric of motivational interviewing" (Miller & Rollnick, 2002, p. 65). These methods are summarized by the acronym OARS (open questions, affirm, reflecting, and summarizing) as follows:

- Ask **Open** questions to encourage the client to express his or her perspective and views on problems and what the client wants in his or her life.
- Directly **Affirm** and support the client and respect and validate the client's inherent worth and dignity as a human being.

- Listen **R**eflectively. Here the practitioner is quiet and listens to what the client has to say. Reflections are declarative statements with a period, not a question mark, at the end, which repeat, rephrase, paraphrase, or reflect emotions in the client's messages to confirm the practitioner's understanding of what the client is trying to convey. Reflections avoid common obstacles to thoughtful listening, such as giving advice, sympathizing, or changing the subject.
- **S**ummarizing and linking together the points conveyed by the client's messages.

Using OARS helps the practitioner avoid a number of counseling "traps" that can derail effective collaboration (Miller & Rollnick, 2002). These traps include the question–answer trap, the confrontation–denial trap, the labeling trap, the premature focus trap, the blaming trap, and the expert trap. MI is very systematic and concrete, and MI training is composed of many sets of guidelines and strategies, often organized into groupings with acronyms that are easy for a beginning practitioner to remember and incorporate. For example, another acronym describing the elements of providing client feedback is FRAMES:

F– **Feedback:** Where the practitioner provides feedback about his or her perception of the risk the problem behaviors pose for the client.
R– **Responsibility:** The belief that only the client holds responsibility for his or her behavior and its outcomes.
A– **Advice:** If brief and not demanding, well-timed advice can enhance motivation for change.
M–**Menu of Options:** Identifying where the client has choices and freedom, including the range of approaches that can be used to address the client's problems.
E– **Empathy:** Always a central element in maintaining rapport and accurate understanding.
S– **Self-Efficacy:** The belief in one's ability to effectively learn a new skill and complete a task.

In summary, motivational interviewing is a client-centered, focused approach for engaging and eliciting motivation to change behavior by exploring and resolving client ambivalence about change. It recognizes that change is a process in stages and clients may appear for help at varying points in that continuum. Many involuntary clients may be at the stage where they do not think they have a problem at all, much less that they need to change. However, by being nonjudgmental, empathic, and nonadversarial, the MI approach is often effective in engaging clients who might not be amenable to treatment using traditional intervention approaches. MI has also been shown to be effective as a strategy used throughout the therapeutic process, and posits that engagement is an ongoing part of treatment, not just something that is accomplished at the beginning.

Now, let's revisit the situation with the client DeShawn, presented at the beginning of the chapter, and, applying the principles and strategies discussed above, illustrate how the interaction between DeShawn and the social worker could be modified to achieve a better engagement outcome.

Revisiting DeShawn

DeShawn: Look, man, I don't need no social worker. I've got to find me a job and a place to crash—the courts have messed me over enough already. I don't have nothing to talk about.

SW: It sounds like you've been through the wringer and are pretty upset about what you've been through. Can you tell me a little about how the courts have messed you over?

DeShawn: Okay, look, I had too much to drink one night, and I wouldn't have driven but my buddy passed out and so I had to take the wheel. What do you know but the old black-and-white pulls me over, gives me a Breathalyzer, and arrests me. I try to explain I had no choice, but the dude wouldn't listen. Then I get into court and the judge throws the book at me and puts me in jail. Then, when I want a sleeping pill 'cause I'm jazzed up, you know, they tell me I have to see a shrink. So they send me to this so-called shrink, who looks to be a hundred years old, and he tells me I'm bipolar and have a drinking problem! Sheesh.

SW: Wow—you have been through a lot. Is this the first time that someone has told you that you have bipolar disorder?

DeShawn: Nah. That's not news.

SW: Have you ever received any treatment for bipolar?

DeShawn: (suspiciously) Why do you want to know?

SW: Well, you seem to suggest this isn't news, and I want to be able to help you the best way I can, so if I can get an honest picture of what is going on with you, I'll be able to help you better, whether it's finding a job or getting the court off your back.

DeShawn: Yeah, well, okay. So, like, when I was sixteen, I ended up in the hospital. They said I was bipolar then and put me on medication that I didn't like. Then I found out that drinking helped me more than the meds, so I started drinking, you know.

SW: I understand what you're saying.

DeShawn: You do? Yeah, well, so I guess things are kind of messed up now.

SW: It sounds like things *are* kind of messed up and must be pretty overwhelming for you.

DeShawn: Yeah. I don't want to keep going on like this, you know, screwing up my life.

SW: You know, maybe it would be helpful for you and me to work together to figure out what is going on and what could be helpful in dealing with the court thing. We could also look toward what you want to do in terms of getting work, finding a place to stay, and just getting things back together again.

DeShawn: Yeah? How, exactly?

SW: A good place to start would be for you and me to meet a couple times and do what we call a psychosocial assessment. All that means is that you and I will talk about your life and how things are going and what your goals are for yourself. I'll ask you some questions and you try to answer honestly, and it will be like trying to put the pieces of a puzzle together to get a picture of what your situation is, and then I can give you some feedback about where we might go from here and you can decide what you want to do. This will also fulfill what the court and probation officer want you to do and take care of that issue. What do you think?

DeShawn: Okay, that's cool, I guess—I'm willing to give it a try.

In this dialogue, the social worker and DeShawn have developed a tentative initial treatment agreement utilizing the agreeable mandate strategy. Instead of leaving the social worker's office in anger, as depicted in the first version of the dialogue, the social worker engaged DeShawn with empathy and skillful interviewing utilizing the principles of MI.

The result was that DeShawn agreed to give counseling a try, which may prove to be helpful with his self-identified concerns as well as fulfilling the requirements of the legal mandate. The outcome of the interview between the social worker and DeShawn as depicted in the second version of the dialogue proved to be more positive and constructive than the outcome depicted in the first interview at the beginning of this chapter.

CONCLUSION

This chapter has addressed social work practice with involuntary, resistant, and/or hard-to-reach clients, defined as clients who do not seek help by their own choice. Such clients present unique challenges for the social worker, and this chapter has introduced a number of strategies for engaging involuntary clients, guided by reactance theory and the principles of bargaining and negotiation. Understanding motivation, how to identify where it lies, and how to tap it are key to achieving successful work with such clients. Most involuntary clients can be engaged through use of these strategies and, even if they aren't, the social worker will have provided the client with a positive empowering therapeutic experience that may pave the way for the client to seek help in the future. A client may refuse help one time, but the next time they are facing problems, they will remember the acceptance, the empathy, and the efforts at partnership from the previous contact, and this may prompt them to seek help on their own this time. That is success.

WORKING WITH INVOLUNTARY CLIENTS ROLE-PLAY EXERCISE

Below are four client situations in which the clients are legally involuntary, socially involuntary, resistant, or a combination thereof. Students should be divided into pairs—one student plays the role of the client, the other plays the role of the practitioner.

Using the principles of reactance theory, the "practitioner" should interview the "client" and try to accomplish the following goals:

1. First, establish initial contact and rapport and, then, explain the cause of contact.
2. Identify nonnegotiable requirements for legally involuntary clients; identify advantages and disadvantages to seeking contact for socially involuntary clients.
3. Identify negotiable options and free choices for both legally and socially involuntary clients.
4. Monitor your own feelings.
5. Express appropriate empathy.
6. Provide appropriate confrontation.
7. Establish a tentative intervention plan.

Client Situation #1

The client is a Hispanic male, age 36, who had been ordered to counseling by the court because he was convicted of a second DUI. Failure to comply will result in jail time. He looks angry, slouches in his chair, and glares at the social worker.

"I don't know why I have to talk to you. So I had a couple of beers one night. So what? I don't have a drinking problem—I can stop anytime I want to. My only problem is having to see you."

Client Situation #2

The client is an African-American female, age 45, who was told to get counseling by her husband after she admitted to him that she had an affair with her boss. The husband told her that if she doesn't "get her head straight," he is going to file for divorce and demand custody of their two children, ages 6 and 8.

"My husband told me to come here. I had an affair with my boss, okay? It just happened. It's over. I don't see why I have to see a counselor."

Client Situation #3

The client is a White female, age 21, ordered to counseling by the court and CYS after she left her two children, aged 5 months and 6 years, home alone for two days. The court claims she was out copping dope with her boyfriend; she also has a history of bipolar disorder. To get her children back, she must comply with treatment. She sits sullenly in the chair and digs out a crumpled yellow paper from her purse and throws it at the social worker.

"Here's the damn court paper. Do what you have to do and let me get out of here."

Client Situation #4

The client is a Japanese-American male, age 21, seen in the jail infirmary after trying to hang himself in his cell. The jail has requested that you evaluate the man for a possible 302 commitment. He was jailed on a charge of assault with a deadly weapon and has been diagnosed with antisocial personality.

"You don't give a shit about me—it's just your job. You think I should live? Well, just give me one good reason. Don't have one, huh? (turns face toward wall) Just leave me alone."

Assess your application and analysis of this chapter's contents by completing the *Chapter Review*.

Chapter 6

Social Work Practice with Clients with Severe Mental Illness from Diverse Client Groups

Hyung Jik Lee, Yoo Jung Kim, and Christina Newhill

INTRODUCTION

America's ethnic, racial, and cultural diversity is an enduring strength that has enriched our country immeasurably (Newhill & Harris, 2008). Such strength depends upon maintaining a healthy society by supporting the health and well-being of all Americans. A fundamental part of health, of course, is mental health, which underpins the development of social and communication skills, learning, resilience, self-esteem, and the ability to participate fully in the community (U.S. DHHS, 2001b, p. 11).

Over a decade ago, in a groundbreaking comprehensive report on the mental health status of racial and ethnic minorities in the United States, former surgeon general David Satcher, M.D., reported that individuals who are members of minority groups in the United States suffer a disproportionate burden of mental illness because they often have less access to services than other Americans; receive lower-quality care, often from services that are fragmented, costly, and inadequate; and are less likely to seek help when they are in distress, in part because of the considerable stigma attached to mental illness in many cultures. The report concluded that there is a large gap between the need for services and the services actually provided and received (U.S. DHHS, 2001a).

Although mental illness does not discriminate on the basis of race and ethnicity, racial and ethnic minorities are overrepresented among those who are the most vulnerable and in need of mental health care, including those who are poor, homeless, institutionalized, incarcerated, and survivors of trauma (U.S. DHHS, 2001a). Left untreated, mental illness exacts a heavy toll not only on the ill individual, but also his or her family, community, and society as a whole. Unfortunately, most individuals with a diagnosable mental illness, regardless of race or ethnicity, do not receive appropriate treatment, with racial and ethnic minority individuals least likely to receive such treatment (U.S. DHHS, 2001a). When it comes to mental health, race and ethnicity matter (Newhill, 1990). While science has made unprecedented strides in developing effective psychosocial and pharmacological treatments for many serious mental illnesses in the past three decades, not all Americans enjoy equal access to those treatments (U.S. DHHS, 2001b). What can be done? Dr. Satcher's report offers a number of recommendations, including more research in the area of minority mental health, improvement in provider cultural competence, increased efforts to address the needs of minorities in shaping the delivery of services, public education about mental health issues in minority communities, integrating mental health services with general medical care, and, finally, insurance coverage for mental illness comparable to that for physical illness. These recommendations depend upon agreement in all sectors of society that a commitment to promote mental health for all Americans is fundamental to a healthy society.

Watch the video *Building Self-Awareness*. Why and how is building self-awareness important in achieving cultural competence and bridging cultural differences for establishing trust and rapport with a culturally different client?

This chapter will address several diverse groups for whom social workers often provide behavioral health services, and highlights important differences in history and culture, and how behavioral health services should be modified and delivered to ensure cultural relevance, sensitivity, and competence. Achieving cultural competence and establishing trust and rapport with clients who are culturally different from the clinician can be challenging, and the first step is self-awareness of differences and a genuine desire and interest in learning about the client's culture, country of origin, and that culture's values and worldviews.

WORKING WITH ASIAN-AMERICANS AND PACIFIC ISLANDERS WITH SERIOUS MENTAL ILLNESS

Asian-Americans and Pacific Islanders (AAPIs) are one of the most diverse and fastest-growing populations in the United States (Kim-Ju, Maeda, & Maffini, 2009). The estimated number of U.S. residents in 2010 who claimed to be "Asian alone" or "Asian in combination with one or more other races" was approximately 17.3 million, showing a rapid increase from 10 million in 2000, and taking up about 5.6 percent of the total U.S. population. At the same time, the number of U.S. residents who identified themselves as "Native Hawaiians and Other Pacific Islanders" or "Native Hawaiians and Other Pacific Islanders in combination with one or more other races" totaled 1.2 million (0.4% of the U.S. population), having increased since 2000 (U.S. Census Bureau, 2012d). The growth rates of Asian-Americans and Pacific Islanders were 43.3 percent and 35.4 percent, respectively, significantly higher than the national U.S. population growth rate of 9.7 percent. It is projected that, by 2030, there will be approximately 25 million Asian-Americans and Pacific Islanders (AAPIs) in the United States, with almost half of them native-born (Ong & Scott, 2008).

Demographic Background Information: Diversity within Asian-Americans and Pacific Islanders

Most studies of clients from diverse groups do not make a distinction between Asians and Native Hawaiians and other Pacific Islanders (Paniagua, 2005). However, historically and culturally Asians and Pacific Islanders do not have much in common. We should also notice that, even after drawing a line between Asian-Americans and Pacific Islanders, there is still a great diversity within each group. As a matter of fact, the U.S. Census Bureau has specified 25 Asian-American and 23 Pacific Islander subgroups since 2000 (Ghosh, 2010). Interest has grown in recent years in disaggregating AAPIs into specific racial/ethnic subgroups, both because of the rapidly growing subgroup populations and because of rising awareness of the significant differences across subgroups regarding economic status, immigration history, and risk of specific health-related problems (Wong, Palaniappan, & Lauderdale, 2010). Levels of mental health service need and corresponding rates of service use also may vary across different AAPI subgroups (Akutsu & Chu, 2006; Kinzie et al., 1989). Therefore, it is not adequate to provisionally assume AAPIs are a homogenous and integrated group for which provision of universal services would be appropriate.

Within Asian-Americans, Chinese-Americans are the largest Asian subgroup, followed by Filipinos, Asian Indians, Vietnamese, Koreans, and Japanese. In the Pacific Islanders group, Native Hawaiians are the largest subgroup followed by Samoans, Guam/Chamorros, Tongans, and Fijians. These estimates represent the number of people who identified themselves as a particular subgroup in the most recent U.S. census estimate (U.S. Census Bureau, 2012d).

History of Asians in America

The histories of the various Asian ethnic/cultural subgroups are, in many ways, substantively complex and varied from other "immigrant" or "racial minority" experiences in America. In fact, AAPI groups have simultaneously experienced what most ethnic and racial groups in America experience, with the added dimension of being seen as "perpetual foreigners" in their own land (Lee et al., 2009; Wu, 2003). Historically, this unique set of conditions has led at times to exclusion from immigration, denial of landownership and naturalization rights (a right given to all European immigrants), segregation in public schools, exclusion from certain areas of employment and housing, being victimized by physical violence, and even exclusion from health care services.

Let's begin with the history of Asians in America. The history of Asian immigration to the United States can be divided into four sections: early immigration, the 1965 Immigration Act, Southeast Asian immigration, and recent immigration. The actual contributions of AAPIs to the continental United States date back to the 1840s when the discovery of gold in California initiated immigration from China to make up for the shortage of slaves from Africa. These early Chinese immigrants were mostly indentured in the mining and railroad industries. Later, Japanese immigrants crossed over the Pacific to work on the Hawaiian sugar plantations, and many settled in California. Between 1848 and 1924, hundreds of thousands of immigrants from China, Japan, the Philippines, Korea, and India journeyed to the United States to seek a better life and escape political and economic turmoil in their home countries. At first, America welcomed this cheap source of labor, but as anti-Asian sentiment spread, Asian groups faced restrictions on their immigration to the United States. Many of the early Asian immigrants lived in "bachelor societies," because U.S. immigration policies at that time did not allow Asian women to immigrate to the United States since the primary purpose of Asian immigration was to provide a source of cheap physical labor for American industries. It was not until after World War II that significant numbers of Asian women were allowed to enter the United States.

The political climate of the Cold War years, combined with the civil rights movement and specialized labor needs, led to the passage of the 1965 Immigration Act, which abolished the system of "national origins" that had been used to severely restrict the numbers of immigrants from Asia. Instead, this act implemented a system based on preferences that favored family reunification and immigrants with professional skills. After World War II, the United States was partly trying to attract immigrants with scientific and technical knowledge who could help to win the cold war. At the same time, the United States was facing a shortage of health care workers. During this period, educated professionals in Asia realized that they would not be able to find commensurate work in their home countries because of economic conditions, and thus emigration offered an attractive alternative. Many of the immigrants also came from allies of the United States, such as the Philippines and Korea, where American culture was familiar and attractive. Thus, compared to the earlier waves of Asian immigrants, those coming into the United States in the 1960s and 1970s were generally from more educated, middle-class, and urbanized backgrounds and were coming as family units with the intention to settle permanently rather than being sojourners (Fong, 2002). Although it was not the intention of the legislators, the 1965 Immigration

Act resulted in a large-scale immigration wave of Asians into the United States. This has shaped Asian-American communities today. The status of Asian immigrants remained contingent on the fluctuating demands of the U.S. economy, and consequently, immigration opportunities were restricted again.

By the late 1970s, the numbers of East Asian professionals immigrating to the United States had declined; in contrast, during this same period, large numbers of Southeast Asian refugees began to enter the United States. Many of these people from Vietnam, Cambodia, and Laos had not intended to immigrate to the United States. Rather, they were refugees forced to leave countries devastated by wars in which the United States played a major role. The U.S. government had become enmeshed in the politics of Southeast Asia beginning in the 1950s in an effort to combat communism. After Saigon fell in 1975, high-ranking Vietnamese military and government personnel, most with close ties to the U.S. military, and many Amerasian children were evacuated and brought to resettle in the United States (Huer, Saenz, & Doan, 2001).

Read more about *Southeast Asian refugees.*

Cultural Variables Important to Consider in Treatment of the AAPI Client

Prejudice, Racism, and Discrimination

Throughout their history, AAPIs living in the United States have experienced prejudice, racism, and discrimination (Sue & Sue, 2003; Yamamoto, 1986). In the early stage of Asian immigration, Chinese, Japanese, Filipinos, and Koreans started to work in gold mines, railroad construction sites, and sugar cane fields. Even doing the hardest, dirtiest, and most dangerous jobs, Asian immigrants were only paid 60 percent of what European immigrant workers got paid. When the labor of Asian immigrants was no longer needed, anti-Asian sentiment was rampant as the Whites began to see them as an economic threat (Le, 2012). Many people considered the Asian immigrant men, who served as a source of cheap labor during that period, as "sneaky, sinister, and inscrutable," and laws prohibited them from owning American land or bringing their wives with them (Paniagua, 2005). Even the diligence of Asian-Americans built up a negative image that they were misers. Pacific Islanders have dealt with prejudice as well. Social workers dealing with AAPIs need to be aware of the history of racism and discrimination that Asians and Pacific immigrants have experienced in the United States and try to avoid any kind of verbal or nonverbal behaviors that such clients might interpret as signs of prejudice.

Watch the video *"Asian American."* How are Asian-Americans viewed in the United States that is different from how other diverse groups are viewed?

Another kind of prejudice AAPIs deal with is the "model minority myth" (Lee et al., 2009). This myth is not only limited to the thoughts that Asian-Americans have greater achievements economically and academically but also that they are more "mentally healthy" and have a lower incidence of mental disorders. We will see later that this is not true. Social workers should be careful not to underdiagnose their Asian clients based on this myth.

The prejudice does not come only from the outside of the community. AAPI have prejudice toward mental illnesses and sometimes misunderstand them as "craziness." Although they accept physical diseases as natural phenomenon, mental diseases are considered to be unnatural and unusual. The cultural tendency toward self-control makes AAPI individuals view mental health problems as a sign of weakness, resulting from a lack of discipline or willpower. Many AAPI people believe good mental health could be achieved by avoiding morbid thoughts and that getting help with this "weakness" reflects poorly on character. Such prejudice also hinders AAPI people from seeking professional help.

The Nature of the AAPI Family Structure and Communication Styles

Familism

As is true for all the other racial/ethnic groups discussed in this chapter, AAPIs tend to place great emphasis on the importance of family relationships (Sue & Sue, 2003). Asians' lives are based on families and the Asian identity is thoroughly familistic, putting the family in front of the individual (Ying & Han, 2007). The kind of individualism associated with European American society is not appreciated in this culture. Like Hispanics and African-Americans, AAPIs also place great emphasis on the extended family (grandparents, uncles, and aunts). This cultural familism seems to be strengthened within the immigration process where the immigrants of this group came to the United States having little source of support and having to deal with various challenges, including discrimination.

In addition, among AAPI people, each family member's role is clear and unchanging; unlike in African-American families, "role flexibility" within the AAPI family is not rewarded (Paniagua, 2005). As in Hispanic families, the father is the dominant figure, and his authority is paramount. In many cases, when the father is absent, the head of the family responsibility moves from father to son, elder brother to younger brother, rather than to the mother or wife. Many Asian-Americans, especially the sons, tend to live together with their parents even after they marry, because taking care of old parents is valued. When a family member has medical or mental health issues, the family members usually take full responsibility in caring for him or her, and prefer having the ill person within the family home rather than putting him or her in an institution (Fuligni, Tseng, & Lam, 1999). Social workers working with AAPI clients and families should recognize and appreciate the importance of the family to the clients as well as the importance of the sick individual to the family.

Forms of Communication

One of the central issues related to communicating with AAPIs is language. For the immigrant generation, fluency in English may not be sufficient enough to describe their symptoms accurately. According to the 2000 U.S census, approximately 22 percent of AAPIs who have lived in the United States for over 5 years and use their native language at home report that they speak English "not well" or "not at all" (U.S. Census Bureau, 2003a). The American Community Survey from 2006 to 2008 indicated that about half of AAPIs over the age of 5 reported themselves as "less than very well speaking English" (U.S. Census Bureau, 2012a). Social workers working with AAPI clients should be aware of this issue and may consider having interpreters under the permission of the clients, as it has been found to be effective (Flores, 2006; Jacobs, Shepard, Suaya, & Stone, 2004).

Another issue that is important to recognize is related to the communication mechanism itself. AAPIs have different patterns of communication from other racial/ethnic groups. They may use an indirect communication style rather than directly expressing themselves. Instead of mentioning a sensitive issue directly, they may "beat around the bush." Sometimes silence is a sign of respect and politeness (Paniagua, 2005). In addition, AAPI culture does not require active response from the listener during conversation. The listener's lack of nodding or continuous short replies is not an indicator for loss of interest or distraction. Some AAPI individuals feel uncomfortable making eye contact with the practitioner, especially when the practitioner is far older or of a different gender. This should not be considered as rude. Social workers with AAPI clients should understand the different communication style and realize what the true meanings are.

Suppression of Problems Outside the Family

In general, AAPIs do not encourage family members to reveal information about family problems to people outside the family (Sue & Sue, 2003). All problems, including medical and mental health issues, are to be shared only within the family. AAPI families use shame and guilt as mechanisms to enforce norms within the family (Dana, 1993). These mechanisms play a crucial and powerful role in preventing AAPI clients from reporting or admitting their problems in public, that is, to anyone outside the family including health care professionals such as social workers (Paniagua, 2005).

AAPIs get a strong sense of shame and guilt when they think that they have lost the trust and support of other family members by not behaving as expected within and outside the family. This sense of shame and guilt may lead to considerable anxiety and depression around the fear that family support may be withdrawn (Chua, 2011; Newhill, 1993). As a result, an important guideline for social workers working with AAPI clients is to explore with them this sense of shame and guilt in order to understand how difficult it is for these clients to talk about their problems to someone outside of the family. In contrast to African-American or Hispanic clients, who tend to respond more quickly to questions posed by the practitioner at the beginning of an interview, AAPI clients may not express their emotional problems as soon as the practitioner asks what their problems are.

Confucianism, Patriarchy, and the Role of Children and Wives in Asian-American Families

Instead of having a religion in common, Confucianism permeates the daily life and consciousness of Asians. Confucianism, as applied to the Asian-American family system and social life, demands children's one-sided absolute obedience to and respect for parents and other adult members (Min, 1988). Confucianism emphasizes a clear role differentiation and specific behavior expectations between the husband and wife, parents and children, and the elder and the youth. This principle helped establish a rigid form of patriarchy and hierarchy in Asian cultures. Traditionally, in Asian families, the husband was the decision maker and exercised authority over his wife and children. The wife, as well as the children, was expected to follow the decisions made by her husband. This strong cultural expectation may explain why Asian women and children appear less autonomous and assertive, and more conforming, dependent, inhibited, and obedient to authority as compared to the women and children in other ethnic groups (Ho, 1992; Sue & Sue, 2003). Social workers working with Asian-Americans should know and understand that such behavior is culturally appropriate and normal for their families. Instead of expecting independent decision making in Asian children or women, the social worker may need to talk more with the husband (father) and establish a positive relationship. Example:

Christeta

Christeta, an 18-year-old Filipina teenager, was seen in the intensive care unit following an overdose of Tylenol in response to family stresses. Christeta tells the social worker that she is depressed because her parents, especially her father, are too controlling and expect her to obey them, while her American friends are given "lots of freedom." Christeta sees the situation as largely a "cultural clash" between trying to abide by the traditional cultural expectations held by her parents and the American values "like freedom and being able to do what you want" enjoyed by her high school friends, along with normal adolescent separation/individuation. After being released from the hospital, Christeta followed up and saw the social worker four times for counseling in the walk-in clinic but didn't want to be referred to outpatient treatment, because then her parents would know about it—since outpatient

> treatment is billable—and would disapprove "because you're not supposed to talk about problems to anyone outside the family." At the end of the four sessions, Christeta was feeling much better. She denied any suicidal feelings and indicated that she can hold on until she goes off to college in the fall, where she will naturally have more independence.

As mentioned before, Asian-Americans and Pacific Islanders are diverse and cannot be categorized into a homogeneous group. In addition, there may be a significant difference between overseas-born immigrant AAPIs, such as Christeta's parents, and America-born AAPIs, like Christeta herself. Nevertheless, AAPIs have some cultural characteristics in common that are distinctive from other ethnic groups, and social workers dealing with AAPIs with severe mental illness and their families should be aware of these to provide effective treatments.

Mental Health Conditions in the Asian-American and Pacific Islander Populations

Mental Disorders in AAPIs

There is a lack of adequate formal epidemiological data about the mental health status of AAPIs. For a long time, a significant controversy has surrounded the assessment of mental disorders in Asian-Americans and Pacific Islanders. Two opposing hypotheses have been advanced in predictions about the prevalence of psychiatric problems among AAPIs. The first suggests that rates will be low, because AAPIs are seen as an extremely well-adjusted group, as exemplified in the "model minority" stereotype (Leong & Lau, 2001; Sue & Morishima, 1982). The second suggests that rates of mental illness will be high due to the stress associated with immigration and acculturation (see Chapter 11 for further discussion of this issue). Ironically, various domestic and international studies have provided partial evidence for both hypotheses.

Clinical impressions support that AAPIs share many of the mental illnesses of other racial/ethnic groups and have rates similar to Caucasians (Chu & Sue, 2011). Although historically, conduct disorders, delinquent behavior, and substance abuse problems were considered to be rare among Asian youngsters, there is currently a tendency for problems in these areas to increase. Alcohol-related problems are generally low for most AAPIs (Substance Abuse and Mental Health Services Administration, 2000; Wong, Klingle, & Price, 2004). Clinicians' and scholars' reports indicate a prevalence of post-traumatic stress disorders (see the case of Mr. C in Chapter 11), with depression very high among Southeast Asian refugees (Kinzie et al., 1990). There are some culture-related specific syndromes related to AAPIs, but the prevalence of mental illness in total seems not to be significantly different from other ethnic groups (Chu & Sue, 2011). For accurate comparison, there need to be more empirical studies on investigating the prevalence of mental illness among AAPIs. Before this, we need to focus on preparing the right culturally valid diagnostic tools that can accurately capture the mental illness conditions of AAPIs. The current *DSM-IV-TR* may fit well to the European Americans (Whites) while it may not fit as well for other ethnic groups (Novins et al., 1997). The upcoming *DSM-5* is expected to incorporate more cultural competency than the past and current versions (Garcia & Petrovich, 2011).

Treatment Strategies for Optimal Treatment Outcomes

Many investigations conducted in the United States have pointed out that in contrast to the majority group of Whites, AAPIs tend to underutilize the existing mental health system regardless of region, age, gender, and education (Abe-Kim et al., 2007; Kearney,

Draper, & Barón, 2005; U.S. DHHS, 2001a). The National Latino and Asian American Study (NLAAS) showed that only 8.6 percent of Asian-Americans, compared to 17.9 percent of the general population, sought official assistance for their mental health issues (Chu & Sue, 2011). Other studies also supported that Asian-Americans were least likely to use mental health services (Eisenberg, Golberstein, & Gollust, 2007; Garland et al., 2005; Matsuoka, Breaux, & Ryujin, 1997). AAPIs prefer to deal with mental health issues with the support of family or friends instead of seeking help from mental health services (Chu & Sue, 2011). Even when they seek professional help, AAPIs tend not to adhere to the services. It is reported that one third to half of Asian-Americans drop out of treatment after initial contact with mental health professionals, and premature treatment termination is common (Akutsu & Chu, 2006; Leong & Lau, 2001; Sue & Zane, 1987). The stigma attached to mental illness, problems of language, and unfamiliarity with the mental health system are among the major reasons contributing to the underutilization of mental health services (Sue & Sue, 2003). There are a number of recommended treatment modalities helpful in working with Asian-American and Pacific Islander clients that can improve treatment adherence. These include using medication, behavioral approaches, and family therapy, and avoidance of "talk therapies" and group therapies (Lee, 2000).

Many AAPI clients prefer and expect to receive medication as a part of mental health treatment. Many believe that talking or acting will not help improve the mental health problems. Social workers should note that, for genetic and environmental reasons, the dosage requirements and side effect profiles may be different for AAPI clients. If medication is used with AAPIs, the overall recommendation is to keep doses low, as AAPIs have been shown to have a tendency to respond therapeutically at much lower doses than non-Asians (Chung, 2002; Iwamasa, Hsia, & Hinton, 2006; Lin & Cheung, 1999; Zhou, Koshakji, Silberstein, Wilkinson, & Wood, 1989). In addition, AAPIs tend to expect the medications to relieve all the symptoms in the short term (Du & Lu, 1997). When they perceive that the medication is not working immediately or some symptoms are not treated, they may lose trust in the services. Social workers should not only know about adequate doses and side effects of the medications, but also should fully explain what the medications do or do not do, and how long the client should be taking them.

Behavioral therapies are recommended for AAPI clients because these approaches are concrete and directive. AAPIs tend to prefer a structured situation and practical, immediate solution to the problem. Also, behavioral approaches do not emphasize the exploration of internal conflicts, which can tend to enhance feelings of shame that an AAPI client may experience as a result of reporting his or her problems to the practitioners. AAPI individuals have lower tolerance for ambiguity (Leong, 1986), so practitioners should make themselves clear and accurate during the sessions.

The use of family therapy is recommended for AAPI clients for two reasons (Berg & Jaya, 1993). First, family support is a strength for AAPI clients. As AAPI families have strong connectedness and share time and space together in a great amount, family members can help at home as well as in the sessions. Second, because withholding information among family members is considered foreign, the AAPI clients generally expect that their family members will be actively involved in their assessment and treatment. The AAPI clients expect social workers to share all information regarding treatment issues with the family members, rather than only with the client (Berg & Jaya, 1993).

The use of talk therapy is not recommended with AAPI clients, who generally prefer therapies that are more active and direct (Bae & Kung, 2000). In other words, the AAPI clients want the therapy to deal with the targeted problems directly and immediately (Gaw, 1993). AAPI clients "expect tangible evidence of intervention, not abstract discussion" (Tsui & Schultz, 1985). For this reason, AAPI clients find therapies that involve self-exploration and psychodynamic interpretations of symptoms ineffective and tend to stop coming to the sessions.

Because of the tendency among AAPIs to avoid sharing their problems with people outside their immediate families, group therapies are also generally not recommended for AAPI clients, particularly in cases involving sensitive issues. However, group therapy might be appropriate for an AAPI client if the client has no support system, such as relatives or close friends, available and needs an alternative support system quickly.

Guidelines for Social Workers Working with AAPI Clients

The following are some basic guidelines for social workers who work with AAPI clients with serious mental illnesses and their families.

Display Expertise and Authority

AAPI clients sometimes question the practitioner's expertise when the practitioner is not able to display expertise and authority. In addition, they tend to consider practitioners as authority figures (Paniagua, 2005). To ensure that an AAPI client will return for therapy, the practitioner should demonstrate both expertise and authority during the sessions, which helps in establishing trust. Displaying diplomas and licenses will be the basic way to give official confidence. The practitioner may mention prior experiences with other clients who had similar problems to the present client's. It is necessary for the social worker to express confidence in what he or she suggests, assuring the clients that the solution to the problem is possible (Paniagua, 2005).

For AAPI clients, it may be better for the social worker to determine what the clients should do instead of discussing it. In this case, of course, the practitioner should have enough information about the client to make appropriate, accurate, and effective suggestions.

Maintain Formality and Conversational Distance

In general, AAPI clients tend to feel that their role in therapy is to be passive, respectful, and obedient in the presence of the authority, the practitioner. As a result, they expect formalism in the practitioner–client relationship. The practitioner should avoid making jokes during the early sessions (Paniagua, 2005). This may be somewhat different from the description of how we train clinicians in the West to be warm, empathic, and welcoming with smiles. Even though the practitioner should provide a comfortable atmosphere, he or she should not violate the guideline of using formalism.

In most of the AAPI cultures, the physical distance between participants in conversation is determined by the nature of the relationship. The social worker should allow the client to define the relationship and the distance accordingly (Paniagua, 2005). Physical contacts should be considered carefully, especially for clients of the opposite sex. In some Asian cultures, offering a handshake by a woman to a man is considered to be inappropriate.

Check Whether the Client Fully Understands

AAPI clients may think asking questions are violating the authority of the practitioner and tend not to ask any about the therapy even though they haven't fully understood. The practitioner should check and make sure that the clients are aware of what they are getting and what they need to do. Especially for those whose English is not fluent, preparing a note on a paper or index card would be very helpful.

Understand the Concept of Time

The concept of time among AAPI people, just as with Hispanics, is different from the punctuality among Whites. The practitioner should understand that the Asian-American can be constantly late for the sessions. Practitioners should ask the clients to abide by the appointment time, but also should be flexible with the treatment hours.

Consider the First Session as the Most Important Step

As mentioned previously, many AAPI people believe that mental illness brings shame and humiliation to the entire family. As a result, by the time AAPI clients have come to the practitioner, they may have dealt with the mental problems by themselves for a long time, and the condition of their mental illness has a high chance of being chronic and severe (Sue & Morishima, 1982). In addition, without any source of proper support, the AAPI client may have adapted negative coping skills such as avoiding interactions with friends, drinking alcohol, or smoking. These all add up to worsen the problematic symptoms. Thus, the practitioner should consider the first session with an AAPI client as a potential crisis point (Paniagua, 2005) and try to immediately but accurately explore the severity of the problems.

However, considering that the client is an AAPI doesn't mean everything should be done in a rush. Rushing may block clients from coming to the next session. AAPI individuals do not easily reveal problems to anyone outside of the family, which may bring shame to the family. The practitioner should be patient and should wait until the clients are ready to discuss their problems. Before this, practitioners should gather information as much as they can from objective indicators.

Start with General Questions

The practitioner should avoid asking questions about specific and sensitive issues (e.g., "How is your sexual relationship with your wife?") until the rapport between the client and the practitioner is built up. Instead, the practitioner should ask more general questions (e.g., "How is the relationship between you and your wife?"). By emphasizing general questions in the early sessions, the practitioner can enhance the practitioner–client relationship and prepare the way for asking the client about more intimate matters in the following sessions (Paniagua, 2005).

If Possible, Seek Alternatives to Hospitalization

Even though hospitalization may be considered as a potential option to most effectively deal with the AAPI client's mental health problems, practitioners should avoid mentioning it during the early sessions unless it is an emergency situation. This may scare off the AAPI clients. Instead of perceiving it as the best given method, many AAPI clients consider psychiatric hospitalization to be the worst and the last resort. They sometimes get discouraged and end up abandoning any type of treatment. AAPI clients strongly prefer alternative solutions such as outpatient treatments or medication at home (Paniagua, 2005). The practitioner dealing with AAPI clients may sometimes fall into ethical and legal dilemma situations where hospitalization is required and the clients and their families refuse. If hospitalization is the only or best solution to improve the mental illness, the practitioner should follow certain guidelines (Fujii, Fukushima, & Yamamoto, 1993; Kinzie & Leung, 1993).

Firstly, the practitioner must consult with the client's family members, who must approve the hospitalization. Most of the time, the key persons are the head of the household—the father or first son. In addition, the practitioner must provide the client and the family with detailed information of the hospitalization such as the expected period of stay, treatment modality, and sometimes the cost. The practitioner should inform the client's family members about the hospital visiting hours and policies. During the entire period of hospitalization, the diagnosis should be kept secret from the client. Only the family members should share this information, as AAPIs tend to believe that the client may lose hope and the symptoms get worse when the client gets to know. Rather, the practitioner and family members should constantly give hope to the client that he or she will get better.

As AAPI clients or their families may not agree to hospitalization, it is suitable for the practitioner to determine the availability of alternative care services. The practitioner might consider discussing with the clients and their families the possibility that the clients could receive outpatient treatment from home or be cared for at home with some professional assistance. It would be desirable to provide a list of the local community mental health service agencies especially devoted to treating AAPIs (Paniagua, 2005).

However, such preference for alternative services over hospitalization may be changing for AAPI families. The sizes of the AAPI families are getting smaller, and there are not many sources of support within the family. As a consequence, AAPI clients and their families may be left with no choice other than inpatient care.

Understand the Expression of Mental Problems in Somatic Terms

AAPI clients tend to express their emotional problems in somatic terms (Sue & Sue, 2003). Under the culture, which embraces the theory of mind–body holism, AAPI clients often experience great difficulty distinguishing between psychological and physical ailments. Moreover, AAPI clients feel more comfortable talking about physical disturbance than psychiatric symptoms. Different styles of symptom expression and a tendency toward somatization can make it much more difficult to recognize and treat mental illness in Asian-Americans using traditional Western diagnostic strategies. First, the practitioner should always acknowledge the somatic complaints of the AAPI client. When an AAPI reports only the somatic symptoms, the practitioner should ask about the emotional symptoms in detail, informing that having them may be the cause for their somatic disturbances and it is nothing to be ashamed of.

Assess your comprehension of ***the strategies that can be used to achieve cultural sensitivity and optimal treatment outcomes when working with AAPI clients*** **by completing this quiz.**

WORKING WITH AFRICAN-AMERICANS WITH SERIOUS MENTAL ILLNESS

Introduction

When considering clinical work with African-Americans and their families, it is important to recognize that, in contrast to other minority groups in the United States, African-Americans are the only group whose history in this country includes centuries of enslavement. The legacy of slavery has had an enduring impact on African-Americans' perceptions of and trust in the majority culture, including the health and mental health care systems. It also underlies the persistence of institutionalized racism and discrimination, intractable economic and educational obstacles, and cultural views about health, mental illness, and mental health treatment within the African-American community (Norris, 1999). Although evidence suggests that African-Americans do not necessarily have negative ideas about mental health services (Newhill & Harris, 2008), stigma, cost, and lack of information about available treatment may compromise actual treatment seeking (Thompson & Bazile, 2004). Controlling for socioeconomic status, rates of mental illness in African-Americans are comparable to those of Whites (Tseng, 2003), with the exception of a slightly higher rate of dementia in older African-American adults, which may relate to the higher rates of hypertension in African-Americans, and higher rates of certain phobias (U.S. DHHS, 2001a). However, the quality of treatment received is not equal between African-Americans and the majority culture in the United States.

Although African-Americans are a heterogeneous group (Black, 1996), and poverty describes life for only one-quarter of them, African-Americans are more likely than Whites to live in severe poverty for longer periods of time (O'Hare, 1996; U.S. Census Bureau, 1999).

In general, poverty is associated with poorer mental health and greater disparities in mental health service access and use (Chow, Jaffee, & Snowden, 2003), and being poor places one at risk for becoming homeless, incarcerated, or institutionalized (Eaton & Muntaner, 1999; Rank, 2004).

Considerable strides have been made in advancing civil rights over the past four decades, and many African-Americans have achieved gains in education, income, political influence, and other indices of social well-being. Nevertheless, inequities in health care, economic opportunity, and social justice persist (U.S. DHHS, 2001a; Proctor & Davis, 1994). Thus, despite progress, racial disparities still exist, particularly for the most vulnerable African-Americans.

Demographics

Although Hispanics are considered to be the largest ethnic minority group, African-Americans constitute the largest racial minority group in the United States (U.S. Census Bureau, 2011a). The number of U.S. residents who claimed to be "African American" or "African American in combination with one or more other races" was approximately 42.0 million, about 13.6 percent of the total U.S. population. However, this figure is considered to be lower than the actual number, because many African-Americans who are homeless or incarcerated are hard to reach through the census. In fact, more African-American men are now incarcerated or under the watch of the criminal justice system than the number who were enslaved in 1850 (Alexander, 2012). In spite of being the second largest racial group in the United States, the Black alone population grew slower than most other major racial groups since 2000, exhibiting the smallest percentage growth (12.3%; 34,658,190 to 38,929,319) outside of the White alone population. However, the African-American population is increasing in diversity as greater numbers of immigrants arrive from Africa and the Caribbean.

Terminology and Diversity within Black America

Collective terms for particular racial or ethnic groups provide a name and a status for the group in our society (Sigelman, Tuch, & Martin, 2005). For Americans of African descent, the terminology has undergone many changes over the centuries. In the past, some assumed that African-Americans as a group represented cultural, social, and economic homogeneity, presuming similar values, attitudes, and experiences, and sharing a collective perception of themselves as a social unit. Overall, African-Americans were assumed to have a qualitatively different culture and dissimilar life experiences as compared to the European Americans (Smith & Moore, 2000). However, we now recognize that the term "African-American" is very broad, and there is a great deal of intraracial cultural diversity within this group.

Some argue that the term "African-American" should only be applied to the descendants of the West Africans who were brought to America during the slavery period (Dickerson, 2004). However, others contend that "African-American" should be viewed as more diverse and include, for example, Spanish-speaking Blacks, American Indian Blacks, West Indian Blacks, and Haitian Blacks, as well as recent immigrants from Africa (J. Lee, 1999). Practitioners should be cautioned about making assumptions about people from some of these subgroups, because the vast majority of research on African-Americans is based on those whose ancestors experienced the American version of slavery, the legacy of which has continued for generations.

Read about the *History of Slavery* for more infirmation.

In this chapter the term *African-American* is used in the broader context referring to Americans with African ancestral origins (from the whole African continent and the Caribbean islands) who refer to themselves as African-Americans. This is basically because people of this group prefer this term and because the U.S. Census Bureau classifies this group as Black and African-American.

History of African-Americans in America [1]

The ancestors of most African-Americans were brought to North America as slaves. The first African-American people were brought to Jamestown, Virginia, in 1619, a year before the Pilgrims arrived on the Mayflower. As the European settlers died from harsh conditions, more and more Africans were brought to work as laborers. By 1860, 3.8 million slaves accounted for one third of the total population of the southern states. However, not all African-Americans in America were slaves. By 1830, there were 319,000 free Blacks in the United States, and over 11 percent of the total African-American population in 1860 was free. The majority of these African-Americans living in poverty started to organize in order to help strengthen the African-American community and fight against slavery.

In 1863, during the Civil War, President Abraham Lincoln issued the Emancipation Proclamation, freeing slaves in the southern states at war against the North. The Thirteenth, Fourteenth, and Fifteenth amendments to the U.S. Constitution were ratified between 1865 and 1870. They outlawed slavery, granted African-Americans full citizenship, and extended to Black men the right to vote. Women, as a whole, did not achieve suffrage in the United States until 1920.

After the Civil War, southern African-American men began to vote. African-Americans were elected to the U.S. Congress, held local public office, established schools, and built towns and businesses. Seeking to return African-Americans to their subordinate status under slavery, however, White supremacists enacted new laws (represented by the Jim Crow Laws enacted between 1876 and 1965) enforcing segregation and suppressing the right to vote. White paramilitary violence against African-Americans intensified. After its founding in 1867, the Ku Klux Klan became a power in the South and beyond. The Klan employed lynching, cross burnings, and other forms of terrorism, violence, and intimidation.

In 1905, W. E. B. DuBois and 28 other prominent African-American men produced a manifesto calling for an end to racial discrimination, full civil liberties for African-Americans, and recognition of human brotherhood. In 1909, a group of concerned Whites joined them to create the National Association for the Advancement of Colored People (NAACP). During the first half of the twentieth century, over 5 million African-Americans moved from the southern U.S. states to northern cities, in hopes of finding better jobs and greater equality. In the 1930s, the concentration of Blacks in urban areas led to the cultural movement known as the Harlem Renaissance. In the army, all-Black units such as the Tuskegee Airmen and U.S. 761st Tank Battalion proved their valor and value in combat, leading to desegregation of all U.S. armed forces by order of President Harry S. Truman in July of 1948.

In 1954 the Supreme Court ruled against segregated schools in the case of *Brown v. Board of Education of Topeka*. This decision led to the dismantling of legal segregation in all areas of southern life, from schools to restaurants to public restrooms. In 1955 Martin Luther King Jr. led the bus boycott that ended segregated busing in Montgomery and 9 years later was given the Nobel Peace Prize. He was a co-organizer and keynote speaker at the 1963 March on Washington, which brought more than 200,000 marchers to the grounds of the Lincoln Memorial.

The "Mississippi Freedom Summer" of 1964 brought thousands of idealistic youth, Black and White, to the state to run "freedom schools," teaching basic literacy, history, and civics to prospective Black voters. The murder of a young African-American freedom rider, James Chaney, together with two of his White friends, Andrew Goodman and Michael Schwerner, created national outrage and brought about the passage of the Voting Rights Act of 1965. The act struck down barriers to Black enfranchisement and was the capstone

[1]The History of African-Americans in America section is mostly drawn from the personal blog of philosopher Christopher Sunami (http://kitoba.com/pedia/Black+History.html) and the Wikipedia article African-American history (http://en.wikipedia.org/wiki/African-American_history#African_origins) under the terms of the GNU Free Document License.

to more than a decade of major civil rights legislation, including the Civil Rights Act of 1964 banning discrimination in public accommodations, employment, and labor unions.

By this time, however, African-Americans who questioned the effectiveness of nonviolent protest had gained a greater voice. More militant Black leaders, such as Malcolm X of the Nation of Islam and Eldridge Cleaver of the Black Panther Party, called for Blacks to defend themselves, using violence if necessary. "Black Pride" and "Black Power" became watchwords in the 1970s, and Black politicians began to gain mainstream acceptance in the 1980s, culminating in the 1984 and 1988 presidential campaigns by the Reverend Jesse Jackson. Although the 1990s were largely a period of racial optimism and increasing social integration, the nation's underlying racial tensions were revealed by events such as the beating of Rodney King, the trial of O. J. Simpson, and the shooting of Amadou Diallo. Even today African-Americans in America still face many challenges, such as a high rate of incarceration, disproportionate poverty, and the widespread failure of quietly resegregated inner-city schools.

Socioeconomic Status

The 2010 U.S. census reports that more than half of African-Americans (55.0%; 23.1 million) live in the South, 18.1 percent live in the Midwest, 17.1 percent live in the Northeast, and 9.8 percent live in the West. The South (20.2%) was the only region in which the percentage of African-Americans was higher than the national percentage (13.6%). The top five states where African-Americans are most populous include New York, Florida, Texas, Georgia, and California (in order). In Washington, D.C., more than 50 percent of residents are African-American (U.S. Census Bureau, 2011b).

Although most African-Americans do not live in poverty, social research studies on African-American have focused mainly on poor African-Americans, and have implied that they are a homogeneous group (Day-Vines, Patton, & Baytops, 2003). However, as a group, African-Americans are relatively poorer than other ethnic minority groups. According to the report from US Census Bureau (2012b), the median annual income of the African-American households in 2011 was $32,229 as compared to $50,054 for the total population. They had the lowest median income among all the major racial/ethnic groups, and roughly half of the highest Asian American groups' ($65,129). In terms of the poverty rate, about quarter (27.6%) of African-Americans were estimated to live under the poverty line while the national poverty rate was 15.0%. The poverty rate of the African-Americans was the highest among all the ethnic groups, even twice as much higher than the Whites (12.8%).

The poverty of the African-Americans leads to not having or having deficient Health Insurance coverage. 40.3% of African Americans were covered by Government health insurance (28.6% Medicaid and 12.0% Medicare) compared to the 32.2% of the general population. In addition, while the 15.7% of the total population in the United States were without Health Insurance coverage in 2011, 19.1% of the African-Americans lacked Health Insurance coverage. This means that more than 8 million African-Americans will be at risk when they encounter mental health problems.

Cultural Variables Important to Consider in the Treatment of African-American Clients

Racial Labels

Even though the expression of outright racism and discrimination has greatly reduced since the 1960s, discrimination against racial/ethnic minorities is still pervasive in more subtle, chronic, and institutionalized forms (Pascoe & Smart Richman, 2009). Racial labeling has been one of the greatest concerns African-Americans have in terms of racism and discrimination (Smith, 1992). African-Americans have been influenced by exposure to racism and prejudice in the society, and they sometimes are sensitive to how they are referred to. If the practitioner is from a different racial/ethnic background from the African-American client, he or she should ask the client's preference and use the term the client prefers. Another reason for asking directly is that if, for example, the client has emigrated from another country, he or she may wish to be referenced according to the country of his or her heritage, for example, Nigerian American, Kenyan American, or Caribbean Black. There are African-Americans who are also Latinos that prefer to be called Latino or Hispanic.

Familism and Role Flexibility

Like other racial/ethnic minority groups, African-Americans put a great amount of value on their families and family relationships. However, there is a difference in that their concept of family is not limited within blood ties. Many African-Americans have a large range of "extended family," including close friends, clergy, and others in the neighborhood who provide social support along with relatives such as grandparents, aunts, and uncles (Boyd-Franklin, 2006). This wide concept of family comes from various sources. First is the transmission of the traditional African view that child care is the responsibility of the entire community, that is, the old African proverb "it takes a village to raise a child" (Boyd-Franklin, 2006; Cowen-Fletcher, 1999). The second reason may be because many African-American families were not able to maintain the traditional two-parent family structure during the period of slavery and, later, because of the high divorce/separation rate and the high incarceration rate for African-American men. African-Americans above the age of 15 have the highest rate of "never married" (men 41.6% and women 39.7%) and the lowest rate for "now married with the spouse within the household" (men 34.2% and women 27.5%) among all the racial/ethnic groups. African-Americans also had the highest rate reporting marital status as "separated, divorced and widowed" in 2000 (U.S. Census Bureau, 2003b). In addition, as noted earlier, African-American men have the highest incarceration rate among all the racial/ethnic groups (Alexander, 2012). About 4,347 African-Americans per 100,000 are in state/federal prisons or local jails as compared to only 678 Whites (U.S. Department of Justice, 2011).

The practitioner with African-American clients should not assume that all the family members are present when conducting a family psychosocial assessment. It may be a person outside of the family who plays an important role in the life of the African-American client. Therefore, it is recommended that the practitioner utilize a genogram emphasizing the extended family tree or an eco-map rather than simply identifying the biological family tree to get accurate information about the client's extended family ties.

Another important issue in African-American families is the presence of "role flexibility." Many African-American families have a family structure that is different from other racial/ethnic minority families in that it is not necessarily the father who is the head of the household (Boyd-Franklin, 2006). African-American families are more matriarchal, mainly because of the absence of the father in the family due often to the fact that usually the children live with their mothers after the parents' divorce (Martin & Bumpass, 1989) and men have higher incarceration rates. Therefore the mother sometimes has to play the role of both mother and father and thus functions as the head of the family (Paniagua, 2005). Because single mothers with children usually have to work outside the home to support the family, older children sometimes act as parents or caretakers for their younger siblings. In addition, grandparents, aunts, uncles, cousins, or other relatives can carry out the parental role. Sometimes it is a person outside of the family, for example, clergy or a godparent, who may play the most important parenting role for an African-American child. The practitioner should be aware of this role flexibility and should explore who is the head of the family and who is considered part of the family during the early sessions.

Spirituality and Religious Beliefs

Black churches in America are recognized as the most influential and dominant institutions in the African-American community (Lincoln & Mamiya, 1990). A survey reported that more than 80 percent (75.7% Protestant of various denominations and 6.5% Catholic) of

African-Americans attend church regularly (Religionlink, 2007). Research has shown that African-Americans have stronger religious beliefs, attend services more frequently, and engage in religious activities more often than do Whites across all generations (Chatters, Taylor, Bullard, & Jackson, 2009; Gallup & Lindsay, 1999; Krause & Chatters, 2005).

For many African-Americans, the church is a primary source of guidance, inspiration, and healing. Research has shown that religion and spirituality play an important role in African-American health and well-being (Chapman & Steger, 2010). African-Americans who attend church often rely upon religion and religious guidance when having personal problems, including mental health issues, and tend to utilize religious coping methods (Chatters, Taylor, Jackson, & Lincoln, 2008). As a result, multiple aspects of religiousness such as attending church and participating in church activities can have a very positive effect on psychological outcomes, such as lower levels of distress, depression, and anxiety, and a higher level of life satisfaction (Chatters, et al., 2008; Ellison, Musick, & Henderson, 2008). Church attendance has also been a protective factor against suicidal thoughts and behaviors among African-Americans and Caribbean Blacks (Lincoln, Taylor, Chatters, & Joe, 2012). It has also been argued that the reason why African-Americans have lower rates of many anxiety disorders than Whites is because they are more active in church participation (Breslau et al., 2006).

The relationship between religious beliefs and mental health for African-Americans can be explained in several ways. First, spirituality has a positive impact on engaging in specific behaviors affecting health, such as not using drugs, alcohol, and tobacco, which contributes to a healthy lifestyle. Secondly, African-American churches have been a strong resource for support to African-American communities as a whole. In particular, the churches have provided social and human capital for community organizing and social service institutions. In addition, churches can provide financial and material assistance and various programs for children, families, and the elderly (Pinn, 2002). The church clergy have played a great role in helping members with mental health problems. They give African-American parishioners with mental health problems comfort and positive hope, encouraging them to seek professional help when needed, and to stay in treatment (Neighbors, Musick, & Williams, 1998; Taylor, Ellison, Chatters, Levin, & Lincoln, 2000; Weaver, Flannelly, Flannelly, & Oppenheimer, 2003).

The practitioner working with an African-American client should be aware of the client's and family's level of spiritual involvement, primarily by allowing the family members to talk about it. It is helpful to incorporate their religious beliefs into the formal therapy that is provided. Having the African-American spiritual connection involved, such as talking with the clergy, is also a good idea. However, the practitioner should not prematurely assume or conclude that all African-American clients have a high level of spirituality (Brennan, 2011).

Folk Beliefs

Although Western biomedicine is the most dominantly accepted form of health care in the United States, many African-American clients, especially those recently arrived from the Caribbean countries and Africa, believe that folk medicine can be effective in the treatment of their mental health problems (Baker & Lightfoot, 1993; Gurung, 2012). These folk medicine remedies are passed down from their countries of origin, but also are reinforced because of a long history of oppression and poverty. Being excluded from even rudimentary medical care, African-Americans needed to develop their own healing traditions and methods using easily accessible herbs, foodstuffs, and other natural resources (Barnett et al., 2003).

Although there is diversity by age groups, geographic distribution, and socioeconomic levels, the general folk belief that African-Americans hold about mental illness is that causes can be either physical or spiritual. When African-Americans think it is the case of the former, the recommended remedies for treatment include using herbs, teas, or other natural resources (Paniagua, 2005).

If a mental illness or mental health problem is perceived to be caused by spiritual factors, it is usually viewed in two ways. The first view is that the mental illness is caused by "God's will" or as "punishment for sins" (Welch, 2003). In this case, the afflicted individual will usually turn to their religion, pray to God, or ask God "to take care of everything" as means to cope with the problem (Welch, 2003, p. 13). If, however, the cause of the mental illness or problem is attributed to evil influences such as sorcery or a curse, the person may look for help from a psychic or spiritual healer to win over or overcome the evil influence. Voodou healers or Houngan among Haitians and other West Indian Blacks is an example (Welch, 2003). Voodou is a type of religion originally from one of the world's oldest religions that existed in Africa since the beginning of human civilization.

Although such spiritual or shamanistic treatments may seem to be unscientific and ineffectual, they have meaning to the individual believer and should not be ignored or ridiculed (Gurung, 2012). If the practitioner responds with skepticism or disrespect for the client's beliefs, this can undermine trust and, ultimately, undermine rapport and the therapeutic alliance, leading to less than optimal treatment outcomes. When such beliefs or proposing the use of such medical or health-related information is revealed, practitioners should accept it and place it in its proper cultural context, making efforts to integrate the client's beliefs into the treatment plan (Welch, 2003).

Healthy Cultural Paranoia

The African-American history of slavery was continued to the history of racism. The cultural mistrust—in other words, cultural paranoia—is a sense of apprehension, suspiciousness, or distrust that African-Americans have for people with different cultural values, especially Whites, because of the historical and contemporary experiences of racism and oppression (Whaley & Hall, 2009). The consequences negatively affect the African-Americans' access to mental health services, particularly when the practitioner is not from the same racial/ethnic group. When a practitioner perceives that an African-American client does not trust him or her, it must be understood that the mistrust may not be only within the context of the client–practitioner relationship but within the historical context. Therefore, instead of asking for an explanation for the mistrust, the practitioner should be patient and wait until the African-American client understands that the personal relationship with the practitioner really matters.

Language

The language between the client and practitioner is very important in mental health services in the matter of "conveying the message accurately." While Asian-Americans and Pacific Islanders or Latinos/Hispanics may have issues with English language proficiency, African-Americans' issue is related rather to the different style. Many African-Americans use a different style of English (Black English, African-American Vernacular English, or street talk) from the Standard English. Practitioners of other cultures may have trouble understanding accurately when African-American clients use unfamiliar words, syntax, and phonology (Wilkinson & Spurlock, 1986). One of the differences in the language that practitioners may not understand is the hidden meaning in the words the African-Americans use. For instance, many African-Americans use the verb *be* to internally express "continuous action or infrequently occurring activity" (Smitherman, 1995, p. 7). The African-Americans' "My head be sick" means that his or her headache has existed for a while, but "My head sick" means the headache currently exists. Another thing is using double negatives, such as "I ain't going nowhere" or "He doesn't know nothing."

Street talk, used mostly by African-American teenagers and young adults, typically includes many slang terms. The slang terms may be shortened words such as *gansta* (for gangster) or *hang* (for hang out with). They may also be words that derive from characteristics, such as *Benjamins* (for $100 bills) or *bling* (for flashy jewelry). There are words such as *hog* (car) or *holla* (get in touch with someone) where the original meaning changed into something different.

Practitioners who cannot understand the language of the African-American client should not feel embarrassed to ask questions to clarify what he or she means. This will help with enhancing efficient communication and assessing the problem accurately. There are also dictionaries that practitioners can refer to, however, it is better to ask the clients directly because the slang terms may be used differently in different communities. A corollary to this guideline is that the African-American client must understand that the practitioner is not questioning the correctness of Black English or the particular word. The client must understand, both verbally and nonverbally, that the main goal of such questions or inquiries is to facilitate verbal communication between the practitioner and the client, which is critical for understanding the client's main concerns (Paniagua, 2005).

Mental Disorders and Conditions in African-American Clients

Epidemiological research has shown that African-Americans have lower lifetime rates of several psychiatric disorders including depression, generalized anxiety, social phobia, panic disorder, substance use disorder, and impulse control disorders compared to European Americans (Breslau et al., 2005, 2006). This may lead to a conclusion that African-Americans have less of a need for mental health services. However, such research has also shown that, although having lower risk of having a psychiatric disorder in their lifetime, African-Americans who become ill tend to have disorders that are more persistent in course (Breslau et al., 2005).

Mental Health Service Utilization

Various studies report that African-Americans, in general, are less likely to seek mental health services than are Whites (Barksdale & Molock, 2009; Conner et al., 2010; U.S. DHHS, 2001a; Diala et al., 2000; Harris, Edlund, & Larson, 2005; Kales et al., 2000; Merikangas et al., 2011; Neighbors et al., 2008). The National Survey of American Life (NSAL, 2001–2003) reported that older African-Americans make fewer outpatient visits for most mental health issues except for substance use disorders (Kales et al., 2000). The National Institute on Alcohol Abuse and Alcoholism (NIAAA) sponsored epidemiologic survey reported that African-Americans were less likely to get treatment for mood and anxiety disorders than their White counterparts (Keyes et al., 2008). From the results of various studies, we are able to see that the overwhelming majority of African-Americans in need of mental health services are not receiving adequate treatments (Cooper-Patrick et al., 1999; Merikangas, et al., 2011; Williams et al., 2007).

One major reason that can explain this is lack of health insurance. As mentioned previously, one-fourth of African Americans are uninsured (U.S. Census Bureau, 2012b). Another barrier to seeking treatments may be the African-Americans' attitude toward mental illness. Seeking treatment in the African-American community is discouraged by the highly negative stigma associated with mental illness (Barksdale & Molock, 2009). African-Americans expressed the fear of stigma that makes them avoid formal mental health treatments where they may negatively be labeled as "angry" for men and "crazy" or "evil" for women (Newhill & Harris, 2008). In addition, the long history of discrimination and oppression formed a deep mistrust in the mental health professions. People in the minority group, when they do seek care, are likely to find health care offered by professionals that look like them. However, only 2 percent of psychiatrists, 2 percent of psychologists, and 4 percent of social workers self-identified themselves as African-Americans (Holzer, Goldsmith, & Ciarlo, 1998). The place where the African-Americans live can also affect the availability of mental health services. As shown above, a relatively high proportion of African-Americans live in the rural

South, where there are fewer available services. Furthermore, African-Americans in urban areas are often concentrated in poor communities with less medical resources. In such areas sometimes services are not available, as the practitioners will not accept Medicaid or offer services to high-need clients (U.S. DHHS, 2001).

Treatment Strategies to Guide Practitioners for Optimal Treatment Outcomes

There are a number of recommended strategies and modalities for optimal mental health treatment when working with African-American clients. These include (1) discussion of racial differences; (2) including the religious or spiritual advisors in the assessment and treatment process; (3) defining the role of those accompanying the client; (4) using a present-time focus approach; (5) handling family secrets with care; (6) emphasizing strengths and empowerment rather than deficits and pathology; and (7) avoiding making causal explanations for problems prematurely.

We have discussed both here, and later in Chapter 11, how many African-Americans may hold feelings of cultural mistrust or healthy cultural paranoia due to the long history of racism and discrimination by the dominant White majority in the United States. African-American clients referred to a White American practitioner might view the practitioner as "different" and think that he or she will not be able to understand the client's problem because of the racial differences. To minimize the mistrust, the practitioner should first acknowledge the racial difference and ask how the client thinks or feels about this issue during the early sessions if possible. Bringing such an issue to the surface may first let the client feel safe that he or she will not be (at least openly) discriminated against during the sessions. It will also make the practitioner appear more comfortable and sensitive to the clients' expectation and beliefs (Baker, 1988). The clients may think of the practitioner as an individual, not a person of a different race/ethnicity, and think they can discuss anything, even sensitive issues. However, the practitioner should not expect the client to lower his or her guard as soon as the issue is discussed. The history of racism has existed for a long time, and the mistrust against the people of other groups will not easily diminish. The practitioner should remain patient and focus on the client's problem that is the purpose of the treatment. It will make the clients more suspicious or anxious about the racial issue if the practitioner continuously brings it up.

As discussed previously, including the religious or spiritual advisors in the assessment and treatment process can be helpful. The church's various programs in the community can provide material support, and the members of the church can provide psychological support as well. Furthermore, religious beliefs have been found to be very important in the lives of African-Americans. Among African-Americans the church plays an additional role as an influence in terms of the selection of how one seeks help. Thus, a practical guideline is to assess whether the client is a member of a particular church and check the availability of economic and emotional supports from the particular church. The practitioner may inform the client that he or she may bring church members to subsequent meetings to help with the assessment and treatment of the client's concerns.

With African-American clients who are new in the community, it is important to explore whether the clients have already found a church that they consider as "my church." In case they haven't, the practitioner can make the treatment be more effective by introducing churches in the community that can provide resources to the clients. Therefore, it would be good for the practitioner to be familiar with the churches available in the particular community. Boyd-Franklin (2006) pointed out that including church into the therapy may be very effective in treating African-Americans (e.g., the clergy encouraging clients to remain in the therapy or to follow the practitioner's recommendations). In addition, this type of assistance may also help in narrowing the emotional gap between the client and the practitioner.

Many African-Americans expect the practitioner to allow them to bring people they see as important to the treatment sessions. Those members can be biological family members or relatives (father, aunt, cousin, etc.) or nonrelatives (friends, godfather, church members, etc.). Practitioners should not rush and make assumptions about these relationships. During the first session, the practitioner should ask and clarify the role of each person. Some of the people may play a crucial role in the treatment while some may be of only a little help. The practitioner needs to determine who is important and should be included as a partner in the treatment.

Using a present-day approach can be helpful in starting where the client is. During the sessions, an African-American will discuss the core or most essential problem he or she feels should be considered first at present. The client would expect the practitioner to provide an immediate intervention focusing on the core problems from the first session. What the client puts as additional problems can be handled in later sessions (Baker, 1988).

Unlike Asian-Americans and Pacific Islanders, African-Americans are generally less concerned about keeping family secrets strictly within the boundary of the family, and they will be eventually revealed to the practitioner (Boyd-Franklin, 2006). The secrets could be related to drug use or other crime records of a family member, fatherhood issues (the marriage experience of the mother), or reasons for adoption. Some of the secrets may be shared by several members while kept secret from others (e.g., the mother might have told the children that their incarcerated father has gone far away to work). Practitioners should be sensitive in handling such family secrets. When the practitioner senses a secret within the family or family member, he or she should stop asking for more information. When handling documents that carry sensitive issues (e.g., divorce, adoption), the practitioner should use extra caution when mentioning those during the session.

The basic guideline in the identification of suspected family secrets includes three elements: listen carefully to what the client says, attend to the amount of silence when the client is questioned about an issue that appears to be sensitive, and do not ask questions that may imply negative judgments or criticism.

Emphasizing strengths and empowerment instead of focusing on deficits and pathology will be more helpful and therapeutic when working with African-American clients and their families. In therapies during the 1960s, there was an assumption that, because of the skin color, the client comes from a disorganized, unstable, or psychologically unhealthy family. For example, the assumption that a stable, organized, and psychologically healthy family "must consist of two parents" suggests that any family lacking this attribute is inherently pathological (Boyd-Franklin, 2006). Because this attribute is not shared by many African-American families (many of which are headed by single mothers), the conclusion could be that these families are unstable, disorganized, and psychologically unhealthy. This is not only untrue, but also does not take into consideration the roles of other factors that can lead to positive family functioning in African-American families with a single parent. For example, the role of extended family members, role flexibility within family, strong religious orientation, and strong emphasis on education are strengths of African-American families that the practitioner should emphasize.

When the mother of an African-American client reports being a single mother, it is important for the practitioner to further explore the definition of "extended family" in the mind of the client and the family. The stepfather, for instance, may play an essential role in the therapy, or at least in family functioning during the sessions. This role, however, may not be revealed by the mother unless the practitioner explores the impact of extended family. It is also important to explore the strengths and resources present in the African-American client's family, and try to emphasize them within the therapy.

Finally, it is helpful to avoid causal explanations of problems prematurely, particularly in the first sessions. Like Asian-Americans and Pacific Islanders, African-Americans prefer therapies that immediately tackle the problem directly instead of dealing with the causes of the problems. African-American clients generally believe that emotional problems are caused by environmental factors. Linking the mental health problem with a certain family member's behavior, for example, will put guilt within the family, and the chances are high that the treatment will not be effective. The best approach would be to avoid explanation regarding the origin of the problem during the first session. Instead the practitioner should provide suggestions regarding the solution to their mental problems (Baker, 1988).

Assess your comprehension *of the strategies, informed by cultural variables, that can be used to achieve optimal treatment outcomes when working with African-American clients* **by completing this quiz.**

AMERICAN INDIANS AND ALASKA NATIVES WITH SEVERE MENTAL ILLNESS

"American Indian or Alaska Natives" refers to the group having origins in any of the original peoples of North and South America including Central America (U.S. Census Bureau, 2011a). They were self-governing people who resided within the present U.S. territory long before Western Europeans came to the continent and Russians to the land that is now Alaska. This includes people who identified themselves as "American Indian or Alaska Native" or reported their enrolled or principal tribe, for example, Navajo, Blackfeet, or Cherokee (American Indian) (Beals, Novins, Whitesell, et al., 2005) or Alaskan Athabascan, Aleut, or Eskimo (Alaska Native).

Approximately 5.2 million residents claimed to be "American Indian or Alaska Native" or "American Indian or Alaska Native in combination with one or more additional races," representing 1.7 percent of the total U.S. population in 2010 (U.S. Census Bureau, 2011a). They are the second smallest racial group in America when Native Hawaiian and other Pacific Islanders are separated from Asian-Americans. The number of U.S. residents self-reporting that they are American Indian and Alaska Native in combination with one or more additional races is nearly the same as the people who indicated American Indian and Alaska Native alone (2.3 million and 2.9 million respectively), indicating the widespread incidence of interracial marriage. Among those who reported specifically whether they are American Indians or Alaska Natives, Alaska Natives comprised only about 4.5 percent (U.S. Census Bureau, 2012c). An 18 percent growth in the American Indian and Alaska Native alone population occurred between 2000 and 2010, even though its proportion within the total population was maintained at 0.9 percent. This increase is predicted to be coming not only from the increased birthrate but also better data collection in capturing people of this group within the U.S. census (U.S. DHHS, 2001a).

Despite the fact they constitute a small proportion of the population, American Indians and Alaska Natives have a distinctive place in American history and American life. While other minority racial/ethnic groups were newcomers to America, brought by force (African-Americans) or seeking opportunity, American Indians and Alaska Natives were already living in America, but lost their lands to the White European colonists, and had to struggle to survive.

Demographics of the American Indian and Alaska Native Peoples

American Indians and Alaska Natives constitute a relatively young group. The median age of this population in 2000 was about 28.5 years, compared to the national median of 35.4 years. Approximately 33 percent of the American Indian and Alaska Native population was under age 18, compared with 26 percent of the total population. In addition, American Indians and Alaska Natives are very family oriented: 73 percent of their households were family households, compared with 68 percent of all U.S. households. Another difference from other ethnic/racial groups is that a significant proportion of households are maintained by women with no husbands (U.S. Census Bureau, 2006b). American Indians and Alaska Natives also have lower educational attainment compared to the general population. Only 11.5 percent of this group obtains at least a bachelor's degree and 29.1 percent have less than a high school education, compared to 24.4 percent bachelor's degree achievement and 19.6 percent less than high school education completion in the total U.S. population (U.S. Census Bureau, 2006b).

Diversity within American Indians and Alaska Natives

Even though the U.S. census categorizes American Indians and Alaska Natives into one group, they are two distinct populations (U.S. Census Bureau, 2006b). They have totally different historical and cultural backgrounds. Even within each group there is a great level of diversity. There are over 565 American Indian tribes that are federally recognized as sovereign entities, 100 state-recognized tribes, plus additional groups that are unrecognized (Fletcher, 2010; Heinrich, Corbine, & Thomas, 1990; Office of Minority Health, 2012). In 2000, the Cherokee tribe, with more than 300,000 members, was the largest recognized tribe (U.S. Census Bureau, 2006b), and the smallest tribe may have only 1 remaining survivor (W. M. L. Lee, 1999). Each tribe has its own unique language, individual customs, and beliefs. There are estimated to be 200–220 distinct languages spoken by this population (Campbell, 2000). The Alaska Native people are also a diverse group that includes Eskimo, Aleut, Athabascan, Tsimpshian, Haida, Tlingit, and other groups (Norton & Manson, 1996; U.S. Census Bureau, 2006b). Despite such diversity of the American Indians and Alaska Natives, much of what is written about this group is based on broad generalization, primarily from specific North American Indian tribes (Deyhle & Swisher, 1997). There is research evidence that the degree of cultural variation between subgroups (tribes) can be greater than that between other populations and American Indians and Alaska Natives (Walters & Simoni, 2009).

Terminology Related to American Indians and Alaska Natives

There are multiple terms that have been used for American Indians and Alaska Natives. "Native Americans" became one of the most popular; however, this term is intended to apply only to tribes residing in the continental United States (Dayer-Berenson, 2011; Paniagua, 2005). As a result, it excludes Alaska Natives (e.g., Eskimos, Aleuts) or indigenous peoples from Central/South America and Canada (e.g., Canadian and Mexican Indians) that have come to live in America (Flemming, 1990). In addition, "Native American" is sometimes used in a broad context including Native Hawaiians, whom the U.S. census categorizes into Pacific Islanders. "Indigenous people," "First Nation People," "Amerindian," "Indian," "Original Indian," "North American Aboriginal People," "Natives," and "Native People" are also used to refer to this group (W. M. L. Lee, 1999; Waldram, 2004; Yellow Horse Brave Heart & Chase, 2005). In this chapter, however, we will use the terms American Indians and Alaska Natives (AIAN), just as in the U.S. census.

When referring to the ethnicity of an American Indian and Alaska Native client, it is generally best to use the name of the person's tribe, because many of these clients strongly identify themselves as a tribe member (Shore & Manson, 2009). When the tribal affiliation is not known, American Indian and Alaska Native is the most preferred term by the members of this group. However, some people object to using the term "Indian" because it comes from Columbus's misunderstanding that he had reached India. Practitioners should also avoid using discriminatory terms such as savage, noble warrior, and squaw. Asking the AIAN client how he or she wishes to be identified is the best approach.

History of the American Indians and Alaska Natives

The origin of American Indians and Alaska Natives is still debated in the context of the historical settlement of the Americas. While some scholars argue that the ancestors of the AIAN originated in the Americans, it is mostly accepted that the very first people known to live in the North American continent were those from northeastern Eurasia who crossed the Bering Strait when Siberia and Alaska were connected during the Ice Age more than 12,000 years ago. The Paleo-Americans diversified into many groups as they spread throughout the continent. Some stayed in the Alaska area while many others headed south and settled down where now it is the territory of Canada, the United States, and Mexico. The migration kept on for a long time, and the groups became tribes with distinct cultures. However, American Indians and Alaska Natives do share the same historical root.

Walker and LaDue (1986) suggest that practitioners who want to assess and treat American Indian clients should be familiar with certain critical events experienced by the groups across four time intervals. These periods are the Pre-contact period (prior to 1492); the Manifest Destiny period, (1492–1890); the Assimilation period (1890–1970); and the Indian Self-Determination period (1970 to present). Five key stages were also suggested for the AIAN history: the removal stage, the reservation period, the reorganization period, the termination period, and the self-determination period (Marbley, 2011). Whatever the distinction should be, the stages can be a framework for understanding the emergence of mental health issues in American Indians and their response to mental health services. We will follow the five stages in this chapter.

Many people have studied American Indian history focusing on their relationship with the European settlers. However, it is important to bear in mind the lives of the American Indians before the European settlers arrived. American Indians had lived throughout the North American continent for thousands of years. It is estimated that 20 to 40 million American Indians had lived throughout the North American continent for thousands of years before the settlement of Europeans. Since then, American Indians have developed many of their distinct cultural rules, roles, values, and beliefs that still exist today (Paniagua, 2005).

The American Indians' encounter with the Europeans before the seventeenth century was a disaster in terms of exposure to infectious diseases such as smallpox, syphilis, malaria, pneumonia, cholera, and typhoid fever, which led to massive deaths of 75%–90% of the population at the period (Diamond, 1999). The authority of the traditional medicine men was diminished as they were powerless in curing the diseases (Walker & LaDue, 1986), and their traditional treatment style was questioned. In addition, the deaths of elders and tribal leaders made it hard to transmit their traditional beliefs and lifestyle to the next generation.

The removal stage (1600s to 1840s) was characterized by migration and the forceful removal of American Indians from the lands newly owned by the European settlers—with and without policies, and with and without treaties. The main purpose of the relocation policy of the U.S. government was to drive the American Indian tribes out to the west of Mississippi River. Racism and discrimination were tactically used. The saying, "The only good Indian is a dead Indian" (Mieder, 1993) was made up during this period. Many American Indians tried to assimilate to and adopt the European ways to survive. In other words, the American Indians lost their lands or were forced to abandon their lifestyles and traditions. Given such history, practitioners may understand why many American Indian clients do not trust European American mental health professionals (Paniagua, 2005).

Next was the reservation period (1860s to 1920s). In 1887, after the bloodiest war between American Indians and European settlers ended, the U.S. government changed its strategies from removal and relocation to civilization by granting the American Indians citizenship, formal education, and allotment of land. The Daws Allotment Act was passed in 1887, and reservation lands were distributed to tribes. However, even though the intention of this legislation was to integrate American Indians into the main society, it turned out to be one more method of pushing the population to the edge. By the early twentieth century, the American Indian population was less than 5 percent of the estimated original population before the Europeans arrived (Thornton, 1987). Even for the American Indian residents in the reservation, it was tough. Their lives in the reservations were considered to be pitiful and shameful. They lived in impoverished conditions, given the poorest quality land, stripped of their natural resources, and excluded from the labor market. Their traditions and cultures were depreciated, and their formerly proud identity of being American Indians was almost destroyed as well.

The third important historical period was the reorganization period (1930s to 1950s). The U.S. Congress realizing the miserable lives of American Indian passed the Indian Reorganization Act in 1934 in order to reform and develop American Indian lands, people, and resources. It was intended to create jobs, schools, and business as well as to serve as a welfare system for the American Indians. It was a measure to increase their self-governance by empowering and simultaneously decreasing federal governmental control.

The termination period (1950s to 1960s) was filled with governmental relocation programs claiming to end American Indians' reliance on the federal government. For American Indians, however, it was an experience of deception. Instead of instilling independence, the government adopted an official policy of 'termination' declaring that the goal was 'to make American Indians in the United States territory subject to the same laws and entitled to the same privileges and responsibilities as the other White citizens. As a result, the tribes were weakened and the American Indian identity diminished.

During the self-determination period (1975 to the present), the federal government began to be more responsive to the American Indian issues. This period has been characterized by an increase of American Indian leaders in federal American Indian programs and the passage of four laws designed to benefit American Indians (Walker & Ladue, 1986): the Indian Self-Determination Act (1975), the Indian Health Care Improvement Act (1976), the Indian Child Welfare Act (1978), and the Indian Religious Freedom Act (1978). These are positive events in the history of American Indians, but even given these events, many American Indians find it very difficult to forget the ill treatment received from the Whites. This causes a tendency to mistrust anyone outside their society who makes promises to them concerning socioeconomic, political, and cultural opportunities outside their own lands.

The history of Alaska Natives is similar to the history of their American Indian counterparts to the south, yet differs in some important ways (Norton, 1996). While the so-called American Indian groups moved southward to what would become Canada, the United States, and Mexico, early Alaskans settled down in what is now Alaska. In the late eighteenth century, Russians started settlements for fur trade and missionary purposes. Just as it happened to American Indians, the Europeans introduced new diseases to the Alaska Natives that killed many of them.

Even though Alaska was considered to be their territory, the Russian government did not have full control of this land, allowing the Spanish and British to continue to settle in Alaska. In 1867, Russia sold Alaska to the United States for $7,200,000 to resolve financial difficulties. This purchase was popularly referred to as "Seward's Folly," "Seward's Icebox," or "Andrew Johnson's Polar Bear Garden" until the later discovery of gold and oil. After the gold mines and oil fields were discovered, many people moved to Alaska and started to work with the Alaska Natives. The Alaska Natives not only decreased in numbers but also began to lose their distinct culture as a result of the assimilation to European American ways.

There is no denying that American Indians and Alaska Natives have not fared well within the American history, mostly by the Whites. Mental health practitioners involved in the assessment and treatment of AIAN clients should be familiar with the history of discrimination and exploitation and its continued impact on the AIAN people. Like other minority groups, they have been treated poorly by such systems and, thus, tend to underutilize mental health services, have higher treatment dropout rates, and are less likely to respond positively to Western style treatments (NAMI, 2003). Especially White practitioners should understand this to gain trust from AIAN clients and establish positive rapport with them (Barcus, 2003).

Where AIAN Peoples Live Today

According to the U.S. census 2010, 41 percent of American Indians and Alaska Natives live in the West. The South (33%) had the second largest population of AIAN, followed by the Midwest (17%) and the Northeast (10%). Over half of the American Indians and Alaska Natives resided in 10 states—California, Oklahoma, Arizona, Texas, New York, New Mexico, Washington, North Carolina, Florida, and Michigan. Alaska, Colorado, Illinois, Minnesota, and Oregon were the only five other states with more than 100,000 AIAN population (U.S. Census Bureau, 2012c). Contrary to the general idea that American Indians and Alaska Natives live in the rural areas where the reservations and trust lands are located, over half of them live in urban or nonreservation areas for better job opportunities. New York and Los Angeles had the largest American Indian and Alaska Native populations (U.S. Census Bureau, 2012a). In the past several decades, American Indians and Alaska Natives have also experienced rapid urbanization due in large part to federal policies of termination and relocation. The relocation has put many of this population at risk for psychosocial problems (Evans-Campbell et al., 2006).

Socioeconomic status

American Indians and Alaska Natives have a lower average socioeconomic status than the average of the total American population. In 2009, the median household income for American Indians and Alaska Natives was $37,398, while the national median household income was $51,190 (www.census.gov). American Indians and Alaska Natives had the second lowest income, following African-Americans, at $34,001 (U.S. Census Bureau, 2008). During the same period, the AIANs had the highest poverty rate at 25.3 percent, far higher than the national poverty rate (13.0%). The poverty rate for the AIAN was the highest among all racial groups in the United States (U.S. Census Bureau, 2008). About 47 percent of American Indians and Alaska Natives reside in areas that are poor, with limited chances for employment or other economic opportunities (Brammer, 2004). In sum, American Indians and Alaska Natives are considered to be the most disadvantaged ethnic/racial group in terms of socioeconomic characteristics, mortality, and life expectancy (Sue & Sue, 2003).

Cultural Variables Important to Consider in the Mental Health Treatment of AIAN Clients

There are several important cultural variables that social workers and other mental health practitioners must be aware of and sensitive to when working with AIAN clients. These include (1) familism or tribalism; (2) spirituality (e.g., pantheism, shamanism, totemism, and animism); (3) sharing and the concept of time; (4) use and forms of nonverbal communication; (5) individualism; (6) attitude toward Western medicine; and (7) how pain and problems are conceptualized.

Like other minority groups (i.e., African-Americans, Asian-Americans, and Hispanics), priority is given to the extended family over the self in the American Indian and Alaska Natives cultures. The tribe is also more important than the individual. Unlike Asian-Americans and Hispanics, the American-Indians and Alaska Natives receive part of their identity and family belonging from their tribe (Brammer, 2004). Individuals who bring great benefit to the tribe are rewarded, with the expectation that all members should place the needs of the tribe above individual needs. Members who leave the tribe for better opportunities often face a threatened sense of identity (Anderson & Ellis, 1995).

Strong family relationships are emphasized, but independence among family members is rewarded at the same time, especially among American Indian children and adolescents. For example, American Indian children are encouraged to make their own decisions and are rarely told directly what to do (Ho, 1992). In most of the American Indian tribes, few rules exist, and even when they do, they are flexible (Richardson, 1999). This cultural value includes the administration of the family and children by parents, relatives, and tribal leaders. During the assessment and treatment of American Indians and Alaska Natives, it is important not to look for the "head" of the family with the authority to make decisions for the entire family. In comparison to Asian-Americans and Hispanics, the father (or older male adults) only administer the family and do not control the family in the sense of being "authoritarian" or "macho" (Paniagua, 2005).

An important cultural value among American Indians and Alaska Natives' perception of familism is the consultation of tribal leaders, the elderly, and the medicine man or woman when marital conflicts emerge. This is particularly important when the husband and the wife are from two different tribes and the main conflict involves the discipline of their children. If the practitioner thinks that such conflicts may be the result of different values, norms, and beliefs between tribes, an elder from either tribe should be consulted to clarify cultural differences between the two tribes and the contribution of such differences in the manifestation of these conflicts.

For traditional American Indians and Native Americans, everything in nature has a spirit: all animals, inanimate objects, the sky, and the earth. Respect and reverence for nature exists in both physical and spiritual ways. Respect may take the form of noninterference, which can be considered as passivity or neglect by people who are not familiar with the AIAN culture. In contrast, disrespect for and overuses of natural resources are believed by many AIAN to lead to imbalance and disharmony in the world and dysfunction in human relationships. Thus, harmony with nature is a very important value in many AIAN cultures.

The AIAN concept of time is intuitive and flexible. There is a strong belief in cause and effect, and a present time orientation, and space is viewed as having no boundaries. Time is not used as a measuring tool (i.e., to measure hours or minutes); rather, it is related to whatever task is being performed. This means that the event or task the AIAN is involved in is what is considered important rather than the clock. This cultural concept of time is the result of the belief that many things are outside of a person's control. Time starts when the group gathers, and an event does not usually begin or end at a designated time. The practitioner should recognize that session appointments may not be strictly kept by AIAN clients. This is not because the client wants to be late or is resistant to therapy, but he or she may have met a friend on the way to the session and stopped to talk about family matters, business, or other issues. Practitioners with AIAN clients should understand this cultural value and avoid forcing punctuality.

Similar to Asian-Americans, nonverbal forms of communication have special meaning for American Indians and Alaska Natives. For example, AIAN believe that listening is more important than talking (Richardson, 1999). They value listening as an important source for learning (Paniagua, 2005). Thus, American Indians and Alaska Natives will communicate feelings and emotions not only through the actual words, but through their body gestures, eyes, and tone of voice (Barcus, 2003). An AIAN client who seems to be quiet and passive during a session with their social worker is actually listening and attending very carefully to the practitioner's verbal remarks. Similarly, when the client is talking, he or she expects the practitioner to listen and deal carefully with both the verbal and nonverbal signs from the client. When the AIAN client perceives that the practitioner is listening, the AIAN client perceives that the practitioner understands the problem and will be able to suggest helpful solutions (Barcus, 2003).

It is important to realize that a nonverbal communication in one culture may not be the same or acceptable in another culture. There are two special forms of nonverbal communication that social workers with AIAN clients should be aware of. While eye contact is a sign of respect and attention to others in many cultures, to American Indians and Alaska Natives, it is a sign of disrespect. As a result, it would make an AIAN client very uncomfortable if he or she is forced to look directly at the eyes of the practitioner (Thompson, Walker, & Silk-Walker, 1993). A strong handshake, in many cultures, is a sign of confidence or friendliness. However, AIAN clients may consider a firm handshake as a sign of aggression. Knowing and understanding such cultural differences will help the practitioner avoid making errors in the assessment of AIAN clients. For example, a practitioner may be careful in diagnosing an AIAN client who avoids eye contact and firm handshake, and generally shows other nonverbal communication style considered as psychomotor retardation associated with depression in Western culture (Johnson et al., 1988).

Similar to Hispanic and Asian-Americans, AIANs reject the traditional sense of individualism leading to competition among family members and between AIANs and other people (Richardson, 1999). AIANs may be seen as "lazy," "unmotivated," and "unproductive" because they do not share the American emphasis on individualism. Among AIANs, the emphasis is on collectivism and the sense of "working together" to achieve common goals among all members in the tribe. At the same time, the qualities of the individual and his or her independence are also stressed. So the practitioner needs to understand the implicit harmony between the individual and tribal values. Psychotherapeutic treatment may be unsuccessful if the AIAN client feels that the practitioner is recommending a procedure or technique that may lead to discord and disharmony among family or tribal members (Sue & Sue, 2003).

For most AIAN clients, medicine and religion are tightly interwoven. As they strongly believe that the cause of mental illness is rooted in the spirit world, they believe that the spirit world must likewise be involved in the treatment and that Western medicine is not sufficient. In addition to this gap between Western medicine and their traditional concept of medicine, the history of mistrust against Whites has made some AIAN clients associate colonialism with the acceptance of Western biomedical treatment (Tseng & Streltzer, 2008). Practitioners should be aware of this fact, put extra effort into working through this barrier, and check carefully whether the AIAN client is adhering to taking prescribed medication.

Another important cultural variable is the AIAN concept of pain and what it signifies. AIANs commonly hold the view that complaining of pain is a sign of weakness. Therefore, they will avoid complaining of pain and hardship directly and explicitly to the practitioner. Instead they may refer to the problem indirectly in general terms, such as "I don't feel so good," or "Something doesn't feel right." If an AIAN client reports being uncomfortable in any context, the social worker should check with the person's family members or whoever accompanied the client to the appointment, as he or she may have shared complaints about the pain or problem to them (Tseng & Streltzer, 2008).

Mental Health Disorders and Conditions of American Indians and Alaska Natives

The history of American Indians and Alaska Natives has been, essentially, a 500-year war. This war has culminated in a loss of lives, culture, and dignity, and in widespread and extreme poverty for the AIAN people. This economic hardship and the environmental stressors associated with the AIAN holocaust have, in turn, led to poor physical and mental health for AIANs. In addition to this holocaust, AIAN service in American wars, such as the Vietnam War, also increased their risk of having mental health disorders such as suicide (and suicidal ideation), clinical depression, PTSD, and drug and alcohol addiction (Marbley, 2011).

Past research among American Indians and Alaska Natives has revealed high rates of mental disorder (Beals, Novins, et al., 2005). The lifetime prevalence of psychiatric disorder among AIANs is 36 percent to 50 percent, with high comorbidity (Walters & Simoni, 2009). Alcohol dependence (9% to 31%) and post-traumatic stress disorder (12% to 23%) are much higher than in other groups (Beals, Manson, et al., 2005; Beals, Novins, et al., 2005).

Mental Health Service Utilization, Access, and Affordability

The principal provider of mental health and substance abuse treatment service specifically targeted for American Indians and Alaska Natives in the United States is the Indian Health Service (IHS), which is administered directly or through tribally contracted or tribally compacted programs. In addition, just like other racial/ethnic groups, AIAN people might also qualify for mental health services through the usual variety of other venues: state and county public health clinics and programs, HMOs, and private or independent providers who accept Medicare/Medicaid or personal insurance reimbursements. Even with these sources for mental health treatment, AIAN people significantly underutilize mental health services for several reasons. First, because many AIAN families contend with poverty and unemployment, a disproportionate number are uninsured or underinsured (Brown, Ojeda, Wyn, & Levan, 2000), and therefore are unable to afford quality mental health services, and only a small percentage (20%) have access to medical care on reservations (via clinics; Marbley, 2011).

Another factor affecting the access and availability of mental health services for AIANs is the infinitesimal number of AIAN psychiatrists in the United States (only 29) and the small number of other mental health professionals available (Marbley, 2011). Also, as noted previously, the historical and sociocultural factors that American Indians have endured over the last 500 years certainly had led to major distrust of European American people and governmental services, including mental health. Nevertheless, mental health is one area in which AIAN groups have taken the lead and have clearly demonstrated self-determination for their people. Although a large number of AIAN people are in dire need of mental health care, Native Americans are exercising self-sufficiency and reaching out for healing within their own communities. As a proud and resilient people, they are rising up, regaining control of their lives and the welfare of their people, and slowly rebuilding the mental health of their own communities (Marbley, 2011).

Recommended Treatment Strategies and Modalities for Optimal Treatment Outcomes with AIAN Clients

First, a practitioner who is not an AIAN should recognize his or her limited understanding of the cultural values, religions, and traditions among AIANs. The practitioner should openly and clearly state this fact, adding that he or she would like the client to alert him or her to any errors or offensive statements he or she might unintentionally make. In addition, it might be good for the practitioner to make statements recognizing AIAN history or people that would make the client feel proud of his or her heritage (Paniagua, 2005).

It is recommended that practitioners avoid pushing the AIAN client to reveal confidential information or personal secrets during early sessions. This is because, in their history, AIANs have heard such kinds of statements many times, and each time they have been deceived (Walker & LaDue, 1986; Richardson, 1999). It would be better for the practitioner to wait until the AIAN client feels sufficient confidence and trust in the practitioner to tell his or her story. The practitioner should also avoid asking questions that are not related to the client's core problem. For example, it may not be appropriate to ask an AIAN client about his or her political opinion on policies or traditions that are related to the AIAN people before the therapeutic alliance and relationship has been strongly established. Most AIANs are likely to consider such questions offensive (Richardson, 1999).

As noted before, listening rather than talking is valued. Many American Indian and Alaska Native clients come to see the practitioner because they want the practitioner to listen to what they have to say about their problem(s); they do not come to the service to listen to the practitioner. Thus, it is important that the practitioner use his or her ears rather than his or her mouth during the sessions with an American Indian and Alaska Native client.

During a session with an AIAN client, it is important to avoid taking too many notes. An AIAN client expects the practitioner to listen, and the practitioner taking notes may appear to such a client as "not listening" and "disrespect." Also, AIANs place a high value on simplicity and flexibility in their social contacts, and if the practitioner takes notes, the client may see the process of the interview as uncomfortable, formal, and too structured (Richardson, 1999). If the practitioner has to take notes, it is important to fully explain to the client why taking notes is necessary, and ask his or her permission to do so first. Then, at the end of the session, the practitioner should summarize the notes for the client to show that he or she was listening while taking notes and understood the client's main concern. If the practitioner senses from nonverbal signals from the client that the client does not want the practitioner to take notes, the practitioner should indicate that not taking notes is an acceptable option.

If psychotropic medication is indicated, the practitioner must provide a full explanation of why medication is recommended, how it works, and what the effects will be. Many American Indian and Alaska Native clients believe that synthetic medication is not good for their health (Thompson et al., 1993). If possible, it is best for the practitioner to avoid making any references concerning the use of medication to treat the client's problem in the early sessions. If medication is an unavoidable part of recommended treatment, the practitioner should fully explain the name of the medications and their impact on the client's body.

Finally, if the AIAN client refuses to answer to certain questions during the early sessions of treatment, the practitioner should be cautious of concluding that this represents resistance. Many AIAN families live in a small community where information is shared easily. It may not be because the client does not trust the practitioner but because the client is afraid that the information might be revealed to others. If the AIAN client had responded well to other questions, then it is more appropriate not to label such response as resistance but to consider that the confidentiality issue has not been resolved.

HISPANIC/LATINO AMERICANS WITH SEVERE MENTAL ILLNESS

Hispanics or Latinos are not a racial group (U.S. Census Bureau, 2011a) but an ethnic grouping of people from Cuba, Mexico, Puerto Rico, Nicaragua, El Salvador, Dominican Republic, Brazil, Guatemala, Costa Rica, Argentina, Colombia, and all the other Spanish-speaking nationalities from South America, Central America, and the Caribbean. As a result, many Hispanic/Latino Americans self-identify with their country of origin (Dayer-Berenson, 2011). Most of them are immigrants to the United States.

Hispanics/Latinos make up the largest minority in the United States and are rapidly growing (U.S. Census Bureau, 2011a). In 2010, approximately 50.5 million residents claimed to be "Hispanic" or "Latino origin," taking up 16.3 percent of the total population. This group has experienced a 43.0 percent increase since 2000, when the Hispanic and Latino origin population stood at 35.3 million, which was 12.5 percent of the total population. Because of high fertility rates and the continued immigration from the Latino origin countries, this growth will continue, and by 2050, the number is expected to increase to 102.6 million—almost a quarter of the U.S. population (U.S. Census Bureau, 2006a). The actual number of Hispanics/Latinos who reside in the United States, however, is expected to be higher because of the undocumented immigrants who are not counted in the official census. According to the U.S. Census Bureau (2006a), most Hispanics/Latinos live in the West (43%) and the South (35%), while 14 percent live in the Northeast, and 9 percent live in the Midwest. California was the state with the largest Hispanic/Latino population, with more than 13 million residents, followed by Texas, Florida, New York, and Illinois (U.S. Census Bureau, 2006a).

Demographics and Terminology

As Hispanic/Latino is not a race, people of Hispanic or Latino origin may be of any race (U.S. Census Bureau, 2011a). According to the most recent U.S. census, more than half of Hispanics/Latinos identified their race as White. The reason why a high portion of people (36.7%) in this group were classified as some other race is because many individuals self-identified their race as "Latino," "Mexican," "Puerto Rican," "Salvadoran," or other national origins or ethnicities. They were all put into the "some other race" category. Much smaller portions of Hispanics identified as other race groups alone: African-American alone (2.5%), AIAN (1.4%), Asian-American alone (0.4%), and Native Hawaiian and other Pacific Islander alone (0.1%).

The Hispanic/Latino population is young relative to other racial/ethnic groups in the United States. In 2000, the median age of the group was 25.8 years, while the national average was about 35 years; 25.7 percent of the total U.S. population was under age 18, but about 35 percent of the Hispanic population was under age 18. Many of the Hispanic/Latino people were not born in America. In 2006, the Hispanic/Latino population who reported to be foreign born was about 40.0 percent, while the national rate was only 12.5 percent (U.S. Census Bureau, 2006a).

Although they share a common language (Spanish), Hispanics/Latinos are a diverse group with many ethnic subgroups. Hispanic or Latino people in the United States come from more than 20 countries, and each country has its own distinct culture, and each subgroup has differing dialects, foods, and traditions determined by the country of origin. A recent study found that the differing histories of relationships between the Hispanic/Latinos' home countries and the United States contributes to the diversity within the group (Guarnaccia et al., 2007). This study also found there is diversity in language preference and use. Hispanics from Cuba prefer speaking Spanish while those from Puerto Rico prefer speaking English in their daily life (Guarnaccia, et al., 2007) . In addition, as most of the people in this ethnic group are recent immigrants or descendants of recent immigrants, there is diversity even within the same Hispanic/Latino subgroup according to the level of acculturation.

Mexican Americans are the largest group of Hispanics/Latinos in the United States. Given the fact that Mexico has been suffering with significant financial problems for a long time and the country shares a common border with the United States, it is expected that

Mexican immigration will continue. Puerto Ricans are the second largest Hispanic/Latino group in the United States. As Puerto Rico was declared a commonwealth of the United States in 1952, Puerto Ricans are officially American citizens, and they can easily move back and forth between mainland America and the island. This fact distinguishes Puerto Ricans from the other Hispanic/Latino subgroups.

The terms *Hispanic* and *Latino* do not have the same meaning. The word *Latin* comes from a tribe in early Italian history called the Latins. The Latins were those who established the Roman Empire. Their language was called Latin as well. As the Roman Empire spread its dominance, the Latin language evolved into several other languages: Italian, Spanish, Portuguese, and French. The term *Hispanic* was developed from Hispania, which the Iberian Peninsula was named by the Romans after they conquered the area that is now Spain and Portugal. In general, the term *Hispanic* refers to individuals of Latin American or Spanish heritage living in the United States; a person may be considered Hispanic if he or she speaks Spanish or is descended from a Spanish-language culture, or he or she has a Spanish surname. *Latino* refers to the people who are from or who are descendants from the Latin American countries.

There is no universally accepted term for describing and defining the people we call Hispanic or Latino (LaVeist, 2005). In 1995, the U.S. Census Bureau conducted a survey to determine which term was preferred by most Americans of Latin American descent. The survey found that the majority (58%) preferred "Hispanics," whereas only 12 percent preferred "Latino." Since 2000, the U.S. government has used the term *Hispanic* in forms to identify people with Spanish heritage. People from Latin America are all Latin, but not all are Hispanic. For example, Brazilians speak Portuguese, which makes them Latin but not Hispanic. To be inclusive, both terms will be used in this book.

History of Hispanics/Latinos in America

To examine the history of Hispanics/Latinos in America, it is necessary to take a glance at the history of Latin American people first. In mid-fifteenth century Europe, the East Roman Empire was collapsed by the Ottoman Turks. Losing the bridgehead for silk and spice trade between Asia and Europe, the European empires started to develop sea routes to get to Asia to avoid collision with the Ottoman Turks. In 1492, an Italian named Cristoforo Colombo (known as Christopher Columbus in the United States) first reached the land that he thought was the eastern part of India. The first sailing trip he made was actually to the Caribbean including Juana (now Cuba) and Hispaniola (now the Dominican Republic and Haiti), which was not yet known to the Europeans.

This discovery was the flare for the European empires' rush to this newly discovered continent. The Spanish dynasty, having the strongest maritime power at that period, was the leader to sail to the American continent in order to expand the empire and gain treasure. The missions soon followed with the goal of winning new religious converts. Colonial administrators began to spread the Spanish culture throughout Central and South America. They destroyed the indigenous civilizations developed in the area and exploited the people for their economic needs. Many natives were killed and exploited by the European conquerors (Diamond, 1999).

The first confirmed landing in North America was in St. Augustine, Florida, in 1515 by Juan Ponce de León. The Spanish conquistador kept moving west, reaching the Appalachian Mountains, the Mississippi River, the Grand Canyon, and finally the Pacific coast. Although the Spanish explorers reached the western part of North America, there was no settlement until the mid-eighteenth century because the empire was focused on the Central American areas. During the last quarter of eighteenth century, the first European settlements were established in California. The Spanish missionaries and troops continued the colonization of southern and central California. As late as 1783, at the end of the American Revolutionary War, Spain held claim to roughly half of today's continental United States, including three of today's most populous states: California, Texas, and Florida. After the Mexican-American War, the Hispanics/Latinos in this area became the first citizens in the United States' newly acquired Southwest Territory.

Many Latin Americans, mostly Mexicans, immigrated to California during the Gold Rush. These new Americans became an important part of the western American society, although they faced animosity and discrimination by Anglo Whites. However, Hispanic Americans managed to retain some measure of political or economic power, and made up a significant percentage of the community. Immigration was also impacted by U.S. policies, such as Manifest Destiny and the Monroe Doctrine. The Spanish-American War that brought Cuba and Puerto Rico under U.S. administration in 1898 and various invasions of the Dominican Republic, Nicaragua, Honduras, and other parts of Central America caused waves of immigration precipitated by war, rebellion, and occupation. This process has continued as recently as the 1980s, when large numbers of Guatemalans, Nicaraguans, and Salvadorans fled to the United States to escape civil wars.

Socioeconomic Status of Hispanics/Latinos

Hispanic/Latinos are, overall, relatively poor. The report from the U.S. Census Bureau (2012b) shows that the median income of the Hispanic/Latino Americans' (of any race) households was $38,624 in 2011. This is higher than the African Americans' income ($32,229), but still far lower than the median income for the total population ($50,054) or for the Asian-Americans ($65,129). Also, the fact that the median income of the entire White population ($52,214) is lower than the income of the Whites who are not Hispanic ($55,412), tells us that the Hispanic/Latino Americans may have an even lower income within a race. The poverty of the Hispanic/Latino population is clearly seen in the poverty rate, i.e., 25.3% of America residents who claimed to be Hispanic/Latino were below the poverty line in 2011 (U.S Census Bureau, 2012b). This means that close to 13.2 million Hispanic/Latinos live in poverty. This rate is very close to African Americans (27.6%) who had the highest poverty rate, and is almost the twice of the national poverty rate (15.0%). In the same period, the poverty rate for the entire White population was 12.8% while the rate for the non-Hispanic Whites was only 9.8%. The fact that Hispanic/Latino Americans account for the majority of the undocumented immigrants (Huntington, 2004) shows us that the actual poverty rate for the Hispanic population may be even higher.

The poverty of the Hispanic/Latino Americans leads to the absence of health insurance coverage, with 30.1% of Hispanic/Latino Americans uninsured in 2011. Approximately 16 million Hispanic/Latino Americans were without any health insurance, and this could be higher when the undocumented immigrants are included. The uninsured rate for the entire White population was 14.9% while the rate for the Whites who are not Hispanic is 11.1%. This high uninsured rate in the Hispanic/Latino population indicates that these people may not seek professional medical help when they encounter mental illness.

Cultural Variables That May Be Important in the Treatment of Hispanic/Latino Americans

Important cultural variables that must be understood when working with and providing mental health services to Hispanic/Latino clients include (1) religious and folk beliefs; (2) *familismo*; (3) *machismo*, *marianismo*, and *respeto*; (4) *personalismo*; (5) *individualismo* (individualism); (6) *fatalismo* (fatalism); and (7) perceptions of skin color.

In terms of *religious and folk beliefs*, Hispanics/Latinos hold religious beliefs that are somewhat similar to those found among African-Americans (Dana, 1993; Ho, 1992). These beliefs are rooted in a fusion of folk culture and Spanish culture (Dayer-Berenson, 2011); both emphasize the important role of religious leaders. The practitioner should realize that religious leaders such as priests or folk healers are key figures in the process of understanding and assisting Hispanic/Latino clients with mental health problems.

The Central and South American influences include folk beliefs derived from certain forms of animism and shamanism. Many people in Central and South America believe that the natural forces of the sun, moon, and sea play important roles in a person's health, thus showing respect to them is key to having a healthy life (Dayer-Berenson, 2011). They also believe that health is based on the balance of the four humors of the body: blood, phlegm, yellow bile, and black bile. Physical and mental illness is believed to occur when these humors are out of balance or the balance is broken. Components of the Hispanic folk beliefs on health care practice include the use of herbs, rituals, ointments, and other various remedies as well as consultation with folk healers known as *curanderos* (Gordon, 1994). Rather than just ignoring such traditions, practitioners working with Hispanic/Latino clients should understand the folk beliefs and practices to improve the treatment delivery and efficacy. Some of the folk remedies, such as drinking herbal tea, can be beneficial (Gordon, 1994). However, the practitioner should be aware of some common misunderstandings that folk beliefs may give, such as "depression is caused by aging, so it can't be helped" or "psychiatric medicines are addictive," and help the clients and their families understand the truth about these issues.

The Spanish religious influence is Christianity, especially Catholicism. In fact, besides sharing the Spanish language, Christianity is the most unifying characteristic of the Hispanic/Latino population, with 93 percent of Hispanic/Latino Americans self-identifying as Christians (Espinosa, Elizondo, & Miranda, 2003), over half as Roman Catholic, and about 40 percent claiming they attend church weekly (Lopez & Minushkin, 2008). Some Hispanics/Latinos may believe that mental problems are caused by evil spirits and so believe that prayers will help in dealing with and curing the problems. Some may rely more on the church or church leaders (priest or ministers) for help with mental health issues, and may seek professional help only after they have exhausted all religious remedies (Dayer-Berenson, 2011). Practitioners should realize that the church can serve as an important resource for support in treating Hispanic/Latino clients. To enhance treatment adherence and effectiveness, practitioners should be familiar with the religious and folk beliefs of Hispanics/Latinos and should know who the religious leaders and folk healers are in their community.

Familismo refers to the importance of maintaining close relationships with extended family members, which is expected and highly valued in the Hispanic/Latino community (Gannotti, Kaplan, Handwerker, & Groce, 2004). Similar to the other racial minority groups, Hispanics/Latinos put family values and family well-being ahead of the individual. Familismo refers to this cultural emphasis on strong family loyalty, closeness, and getting along with and contributing to the well-being of the nuclear family, extended family, and kinship networks (Guilamo-Ramos et al., 2007). It is known that familismo is a protective factor for the mental health of Hispanic/Latino Americans. The strong ties between family members have helped newly immigrated individuals deal with the acculturation stress, confront social discrimination, and therefore adjust in the United States (Zinn, 1994).

Hispanic/Latino Americans often consider the needs of an individual to be a family issue and commonly consult with other family members before important decisions are made. For example, a decision to seek professional help in order to deal with the mental health problems of a family member would usually be discussed within the family, and the family members will expect themselves to be involved in the treatment or at least in the decision-making process. Therefore, practitioners should be aware that any attempt to conduct therapy with a Hispanic/Latino client without the involvement and support of the family is bound to fail (Paniagua, 2005).

The family structure of Hispanic/Latino Americans is different from African-American families. It is rather similar to the Asian-American traditional family structure in terms of not having much role flexibility. Traditionally, the father is the head of the family and the wife plays the role of homemaker and handles child rearing. However, practitioners should realize that the family structure and culture of a Hispanic/Latino family differs by the level of acculturation, that is, how long the family has been in the United States and to what extent American culture has been adopted. In fact, research has conclusively shown that long-term residence in the United States significantly increases rates of mental disorders, particularly substance abuse disorders, in Hispanics/Latinos (U.S. DHHS, 2001).

Another major quality of the Hispanic/Latino culture is "machismo" and "marianismo." Machismo and marianismo refer to the different expectations for men and women in the family and society. Machismo can be seen as a form of masculine ideology while marianismo is its feminine counterpart. The characteristics of machismo, which literally means "manliness" in English, include physical strength, sexual attractiveness, masculinity, aggressiveness, and the ability to consume an excessive amount of alcohol without getting drunk (Comas-Diaz, 1988). Hispanic/Latino tradition sees the ideal man as proud, brave, courageous, devoted, loyal, and an honorable figure, expecting him to be an unquestioned authority figure (Sobralske, 2006). Therefore the men in the family or the society expect respect, which is called "respeto," from women, younger people, and those in lower social positions. "Marianismo," which comes from the name of the "Virgin Mary," is a personal quality in women that is highly expected in the Hispanic/Latino society. The characteristics that make up marianismo are submissiveness, obedience, dependence, timidness, docility, sentimentality, gentleness, and virginity until marriage (Comas-Diaz, 1988). As a result, women are not expected, or even allowed, to have strong opinions, and even if they do, they would not express them directly or actively.

The gender stereotypes in the Hispanic/Latino culture represented by machismo and marianismo are similar to that of the patriarchy or male-oriented values in Asian society. Both consider men as the leaders and decision makers, with women as followers. However, in Asian culture, the men having power is more a matter of having an authority role. Age and relationship, as other aspects of authority, are equally valued. In Asian culture, an old lady of a higher position (mother, grandmother, aunt, elder sister, senior) may have the power of decision making equivalent to a younger man in a lower position. In contrast, machismo in Hispanic/Latino culture is more focused on the man's physical aspects of sexual appeal. Having more physical strength, machoness, and aggressiveness, for instance, are valued as "manliness" in the Hispanic/Latino culture, while Asian culture may not value such qualities or even consider them as violent.

Practitioners who work with Hispanic/Latino families should be aware that usually the father (or husband) makes the decision for the entire family. In understanding the role of machismo, the practitioner might need to present concrete examples that will lead the father (or husband) to understand why many of the elements of machismo are not helping. When a female practitioner is dealing with a male Hispanic/Latino client or the father (husband), she should make sure that her professional opinion is understood and accepted.

While Asian-Americans expect distance in interpersonal relationships, especially in official ones such as the client–practitioner relationship, Hispanics/Latinos value warmth over distance. In a conversation, a Hispanic/Latino may maintain a relatively close distance to the other person, make direct eye contact, and even may attempt frequent physical contact. This, called "personalismo" (personalism), is also expected in their interaction with mental health professionals. They may feel upset when they feel that the practitioner is too objective and they don't perceive warmth within the sessions. Hispanics/Latinos usually expect the practitioner to give them a hug after a handshake and to share personal information in conversation (Paniagua, 2005). If the practitioner is not aware of these expectations, the client may sense a lack of warmth.

Hispanic/Latino clients who seek professional help may select the practitioner not only on the basis of the practitioner's professional credentials but on the basis of the warmth that the practitioner shows during the sessions. They expect the practitioner to share personal information (excluding intimate information) that is not relevant to the session itself, such as hobbies, family background, or favorite foods. Such sharing may enable the Hispanic/Latino client to develop a certain level of trust within the relationship. However, practitioners should be aware that not all Hispanic/Latino clients value personalism to a large degree.

One expression of personalismo that Paniagua (2005) points out that practitioners may not understand is the offering of gifts. This is a way to express their gratitude for the provided service. When the gift offering is repeatedly rejected, the Hispanic/Latino client might perceive a lack of personalismo and probably drop out from the sessions. In the case of gift offerings, the practitioner should explain well to the client and the family and set up an example of from where the gifts are appropriate for him or her to receive. Example:

> José, age 21, suffered from depression and alcohol abuse. José's family tried to help him and prayed for his recovery, but his symptoms only got worse. Finally, the family sought professional help from the local community mental health center. Their social worker, Janine, helped José obtain detox treatment and then a two-week stay at a dual-diagnosis rehabilitation center. A week after he was released and returned home, José's mother, Maria, came to see Janine at the clinic.

Maria: Miss Janine, I want to thank you for your kindness to José and for helping him recover from his sadness and the drink. He is so much better, and may God bless you for all you have done.

SW: Mrs. Lopez, I am very happy that Jose is doing well and am glad we were able to help him.

Maria: (taking a basket out of her tote bag) Here, I have brought you a basket of tomatoes from our garden and some homemade tamales that my mother and I made yesterday evening. I hope that you like them. It isn't much, but I wanted to bring you a gift to show our thanks.

SW: Thank you! Thank you so much—I love tomatoes and nothing is better than homemade tamales.

Maria: (beaming) Let me give you a hug. (hugs) I know you are busy and I will go now, but thank you, again, for everything.

SW: You're welcome. Take care. Please give José my best wishes.

The American ideal of individualism is to achieve success with one's own ability through competition (Sandoval & De La Roza, 1986). At the same time, the concept of individualism stresses what is unique about each member of the community and how this uniqueness leads to cooperation among community members rather than to competition. Among Hispanics, "individualismo" (individualism) means that the effort and ability of everyone accumulates to build up and sustain the community (Paniagua, 2005). This is important for the practitioner to know, because the Hispanic/Latino client may feel that his or her individualism is threatened by treatment involving modifying or changing the client's behavior. In such cases, the practitioner needs to warmly explain to the client that the suggestions are only for treating the mental or "nerve" problems, not for changing the person's "self."

From the mixture of Catholic religion and folk culture beliefs, there is an underlying theme in Hispanic/Latino culture called "fatalismo" (fatalism). Fatalismo refers to a general belief that what's given in life cannot be changed and that life events may not be fully under one's control. It is very common for Latinos/Hispanics to make reference to "*si Dios quiere* (God's will)" or "*el destino* (destiny)". It is cited as a dominant cultural belief that deters Hispanics/Latinos from engaging in various early detection and other health preventive behaviors, such as cancer screening and diabetes/HIV testing and prevention (Abraido-Lanza et al., 2007). When a Hispanic/Latino has a mental health issue, considering it inevitable will hinder the individual from seeking professional help.

When providing services, the practitioner should be mindful of the fatalismo construct. When the client experiences fatalism as a lack of perceived individual control, the practitioner can begin to process with the client strategies for increasing his or her sense of self-efficacy. However, if the client experiences fatalism as evidence of a divine intervention, the practitioner should first explore the client's spiritual beliefs before proceeding with interventions. Otherwise, the practitioner runs the risk of being perceived as oppositional or arrogant, and the client may drop out of the treatment, having hostility toward getting further help.

A final cultural variable prevalent in Hispanic/Latino cultures, as well as many other cultures of color, is *perceptions of skin color*. There is a wide range of racial denominations existing in the Hispanic/Latino community (Montalvo & Codina, 2001). Hispanic/Latinos who have dark skin color are sometimes called *morenos* or *prietos*. Those with olive skin or dark complexions are called *trigueños*. And those with light skin or kinky hair are known as *grifos*, *jabaos*, or *albinos*. People with Indian features are called *indios* (Paniagua, 2005). Generally, in their own countries, Hispanics think of themselves as one community regardless of the tone of their skin. What matters more is the person's position in the society, and if someone experiences discrimination, it comes primarily from low socioeconomic status rather than skin color (Paniagua, 2005).

However, when Hispanics/Latinos enter the United States, they may experience discrimination in which their skin color is an important variable (Telzer & Vazquez Garcia, 2009). They have seen how differently members of varying skin colors are treated in the United States. Some Hispanic/Latino parents prefer their children have lighter skin color because they think it may decrease the discrimination. The preference for lighter skin color may be an indicator for greater acculturation, thus it may be important for the practitioner to bear this issue in mind. Being aware of Hispanics/Latinos not considering skin color in making racial/ethnic classifications, practitioners should also not use such traditional race categorization by skin tones.

Mental Health Conditions and Disorders in Hispanic/Latino Americans

Historical and sociocultural factors suggest that Hispanic/Latino Americans, in aggregate, experience circumstances that are known to be related to poor physical and mental health outcomes (National Research Council, 2006). As noted in the previous sections, they have relatively low socioeconomic status. They earn less and have higher unemployment rates compared to non-Hispanic Whites, and are more likely to work in physically demanding, stressful, and/or low-paying jobs in which exploitation is common, particularly for those who are undocumented (Duncan, Hotz, & Trejo, 2006). Given such conditions, it is reasonable to expect Hispanic/Latino Americans to exhibit poor health, especially relative to non-Hispanic Whites. Nevertheless, studies tell us that Hispanic/Latino Americans on the whole have shown similar or even better health outcomes than non-Hispanic Whites (Gallo, Penedo, Espinosa de los Monteros, & Arguelles, 2009). This trend is referred to as the "Hispanic paradox" (Markides & Coreil, 1986), which still holds even when narrowed to mental health.

The results from the National Comorbidity Survey (NCS) in 2005 and National Comorbidity Survey Replication (NCSR) consistently showed that Hispanic/Latino Americans generally have lower lifetime prevalence rates for all mental disorders than non-Hispanic Whites (Breslau et al., 2005, 2006). For prevalence rates for any psychiatric disorder in the past 12 months, the rate for Hispanics/Latinos was 16 percent while the rate for non-Hispanic Whites was 21 percent (Alegria, Woo, Takeuchi, & Jackson, 2009). Comparing the NCS results with the National Latino and Asian American Study (NLAAS) results, Hispanics/Latinos showed lower lifetime prevalence of any psychiatric disorder (including depressive, anxiety, and substance disorder) than the non-Hispanic Whites (Alegria et al., 2008).

However, differences in the prevalence of psychiatric disorders were also found among the subgroups. Puerto Ricans (37.4%) had the highest lifetime prevalence, higher than the Hispanic/Latino group average (29.7%) and almost similar to the non-Hispanic Whites (43.2%). Cubans (28.2%), Mexicans (29.5%), and other Latino subgroups (27.0%), on the other hand, had far lower rates (Alegria et al., 2008). Puerto Ricans were also shown to be in the highest risk for the past-year psychiatric disorders (Alegria et al., 2007). Another unusual phenomenon in Hispanic/Latino mental health is the so-called "immigrant paradox." Studies have shown that Hispanic/Latino immigrants in the United States report lower rates of mental illness and substance abuse than their U.S.-born counterparts (Grant, Stinson, Dawson, et al., 2004; Grant, Stinson, Hasin, et al., 2004; Vega, Alderete, Kolody, & Aguilar-Gaxiola, 1998; Vega, Kolody, et al., 1998). This is against one's expectation, because immigrants are known to have more stress during the acculturation process.

Mental Health Service Utilization, Access, and Affordability

Even though the prevalence of mental illness in Hispanic/Latino Americans is similar to that in other ethnic/racial groups, they receive fewer mental health services than other groups (Agency for Healthcare Research and Quality, 2005; Kessler et al., 1994). Compared with White individuals, Hispanic/Latino individuals are more likely to underutilize mental health care services, particularly services for children and youth, are less likely to receive guidelines consistent with best practices care, and are more likely to rely on primary care services to cover their mental health care needs. Hispanics/Latinos are also more likely to be exposed to greater delays in receiving needed mental health care, to be in active treatment, and are less satisfied with the quality of mental health care received. Common barriers identified for accessing mental health care among this ethnic group include lack of health insurance, low levels of acculturation, and associated factors of being foreign-born and not speaking English (Perez-Escamilla, 2010).

Among the barriers, lack of English language fluency and/or professionally trained translators is a major issue influencing the mental health care access of the Hispanic/Latino population. DuBard and Gizlice (2008) found that the Spanish-speaking (or preferring) Hispanic/Latino Americans, whose English skills are relatively lower than the English-speaking (or preferring) Hispanic/Latino Americans, are less likely to have insurance (77% vs. 45%), to have a usual doctor (58% vs. 29%), and to have had a medical checkup in the previous year (64% vs. 55%). The worst access was found in the areas where they have experienced relatively high Hispanic/Latino population growth in recent decades (DuBard & Gizlice, 2008). This indicates that, compared to the other states in the West and South where they are used to having a large Hispanic/Latino population, these areas do not have enough Spanish-speaking professionals in the mental health care services to help the Spanish-speaking Hispanics/Latinos. While Hispanics/Latinos accounted for 14 percent of the total population, only 3–5 percent of mental health professionals (physicians, psychiatrists, psychologists, social workers) were Hispanic/Latino around the same time (Miranda,

McGuire, Williams, & Wang, 2008). Illegal or undocumented immigrant status is also a barrier to mental health care access in the Hispanic/Latino group. The situation prevents them from having health insurance, which leads to avoiding professional help even if they have mental health problems.

Recommended Treatment Strategies and Modalities for Optimal Treatment Outcomes with Hispanic/Latino Clients

The importance of understanding culture-based characteristics, such as familismo, machismo, and personalismo, central to traditional Hispanic/Latino culture, has been addressed previously. However, since level of acculturation affects how deeply the Hispanic/Latino client or family values such characteristics, it is important for the practitioner to explore the client's level of acculturation and assimilation. The more time that the client and the family have spent in the United States, the less they may embrace such ideas and values. Therefore, one of the first things the practitioner should do during the early sessions is to conduct an assessment of both internal and external processes of acculturation. This is important in setting up appropriate therapy plans for the client.

As noted earlier, Hispanics/Latinos expect personal contacts and attention (personalismo) in their relationships with others (Paniagua, 2005). *Confianza* (trust and intimacy in a relationship) plays a critical role in interpersonal relations and is an essential component in therapy as well. When the client feels that the practitioner is not being friendly enough, it may lead to a greater chance of drop out. However, the practitioner should be careful to achieve a balance between formalism and personalism. There are reports that confianza and personalism carry the risk of the client becoming reluctant to work with other clinical professionals when he or she is referred (Anez, Paris, Bedregal, Davidson, & Grilo, 2005).

It is important to understand the client's beliefs with regard to health, including mental health. Hispanics/Latinos have a complicated belief system—folk belief combined with Catholic Christianity that may include superstitious beliefs about their mental health problems. The practitioner needs to carefully explore what the client thinks about the problem and what he or she thinks the causes may be. The practitioner should understand and accept whatever the client believes, even though it may not be scientifically or medically correct, unless it may cause immediate and direct harm to the client. The idea the Latino/Hispanic client has is "what he or she believes" not "what he or she knows." Making rash and insensitive responses, such as bluntly telling the client that his or her belief is wrong, may cause mistrust toward the practitioner. On the other hand, understanding the client's belief will help improve the therapeutic relationship between the client and the practitioner (Paniagua, 2005). This will also help the practitioner find a specific way of thinking that may bring about positive changes for the client.

Assess your comprehension of *recommended treatment strategies and modalities for optimal treatment outcomes with Hispanic/Latino clients with mental illness and with American Indian and Alaskan Natives with mental illness* by completing this quiz.

As mentioned before, Hispanic/Latino families consider the father (man of the family) as the key person for making decisions for the family. When a family member has mental health issues, it is generally considered that the father should play a significant role in the therapy. It is a good strategy to interview the father separately and ask for full cooperation and support for treatment. The same goes for when the father of the family is the client. The father will not express his problems and feelings when the other family members are around.

WOMEN WITH SEVERE MENTAL ILLNESS

Mental illnesses can affect women and men differently. Although, overall, men and women experience mental illness at relatively similar rates, some mental disorders occur more frequently in women than men, for example, depression, while others occur more frequently in men than women, for example, substance abuse disorders (Kessler et al., 2005a). Studies have shown that women are twice as likely to be diagnosed with major depression as men and have higher rates of suicide attempts, although men have higher rates of suicide completion (see Chapter 12 for details) (Mazure, Keita, & Blehar, 2002; Rappaport et al., 2005). Women, compared to men, have two to three times higher rates of anxiety disorders, including post-traumatic stress (PTSD), which affects women more than twice as often as men (Kessler et al., 2005b). Ninety percent of all reports of eating disorders, which have the highest mortality rate of all mental illnesses, are represented by women (Birmingham et al., 2005). On the other hand, women are known to suffer less from impulse control disorders and substance abuse disorders.

Even though the prevalence rates are similar in men and women, there may be notable differences in the treatment or course of particular mental disorders. The rates of bipolar disorder are almost the same between men and women (1.40% and 1.30%), but the onset tends to occur later in women, and they are more likely than men to experience a seasonal pattern of the mood disturbance, depressive episodes, mixed mania, or rapid cycling (Arnold, 2003). Women with bipolar disorders are more likely than men to experience comorbidity, particularly thyroid disease, migraine, obesity, and anxiety disorders, whereas men are more likely to experience co-occurrence of substance use disorders (Arnold, 2003). There is a similar pattern in schizophrenia as well. The prevalence rates are similar in men and women (1.00% and 1.26%), but the average onset is later in women. In addition, the severity of the disorder is less in women than that seen with men.

Despite the difference in mental health between men and women, researchers are only now beginning to tease apart the contributions of various biological and psychosocial factors to mental health and mental illness in both women and men (NIMH, 2012). A biological approach has focused on finding biological differences between men and women that may cause different mental health outcomes. For example, research has demonstrated that the female hormones estrogen and progesterone influence brain function and stress response. Studies of reproductive events such as menstruation, pregnancy, postpartum, menopause, and other changes in female hormone levels find that these changes lead to an increase of the occurrence and intensity of symptoms of depression and other mood disorders, such as bipolar disorder and dysthymia (Burt & Rasgon, 2004; Cohen et al., 2003; Schmidt, Haq, & Rubinow, 2004). Investigations of the neural mechanisms underlying the processing of emotionally arousing information also suggest that there may be distinct differences between women and men in the activation of the amygdala, the part of the brain involved in the processing of emotional information (Cahill, Uncapher, Kilpatrick, Alkire, & Turner, 2004). Studies that investigate male and female differences in brain volume or structure or those that look at differences in the brains of individuals with and without mental illness appear to be inconclusive, suggesting that further research is needed to establish a fuller understanding of how biologically based brain differences may help inform future pharmacologic and medical treatment for women (Castellanos et al., 2001).

Environmental factors also play a significant role in the risk and prevalence of certain mental illnesses. Some environmental factors may be the result of bias in reporting or diagnosis; for example, women may be more likely than men to seek treatment or there may be gender differences in rates of diagnosis for particular disorders. In addition, there are important psychosocial factors from women's environments that may influence the risk, diagnosis, course, and treatment of mental illnesses in women. Examples of these may include such factors as differences in the ways girls and boys are raised; expectations about male and female roles in the family, workplace, or larger society; the higher rates of abuse experienced by girls and women; the higher poverty or single parenthood experienced by women compared to men; or differences in the positive or negative ways men and women cope with stress and adversity (NAMI, 2009).

Factors That May Be Important in Understanding the Mental Health of Women

Poverty

The U.S. census (2012b) shows that women have lower income than men. In 2011, median income of men with earnings was $48,202 while the income of women with earnings was $37,118. The Female-to-Male earnings ratio has steadily risen from 60% in 1960 to 77% in 2011, presenting a good sign that the income inequality is decreasing. But still, inequality exists. 16.3% of females were under poverty while 13.6% of males were. Among all types of families, 'female-householder without husband present' families had the highest poverty rate (31.2%) compared to 'married-couple families' (6.2%) or 'male-householder without wife present' families (16.1%). We have learned that poverty not only relates to higher prevalence of mental disorders and negative mental health outcomes, but also has influence on not having health insurance coverage that obstruct the women's mental health service utilization.

Pregnancy and the Postpartum Period

Pregnancy and the postpartum period are widely considered to be periods of increased vulnerability to mental illnesses. Given the numerous physiological and hormonal changes the body undergoes and the stressors involved in pregnancy, anxiety and depression are the most common emotional disturbances during the perinatal period. Reported rates of depression in pregnant women have ranged from 5 percent to almost 30 percent. Anxiety disorders can also be stimulated or compounded by pregnancy. Panic disorder, obsessive-compulsive disorder, and generalized anxiety disorder appear to be as common as depression in women during pregnancy. Untreated mental illness during pregnancy has serious potential risks for the women (and also the fetus). Symptoms may develop and worsen into the postpartum period and further on.

The reason why pregnancy and the postpartum period is important in women's mental health is not only because of the vulnerability but also because of the treatment options and service utilization. A woman who starts to show symptoms for psychiatric disorders during pregnancy or the postpartum period might not seek professional help. A women who was already diagnosed with a severe mental disorder might stop coming to her treatment when she gets pregnant. This is because they think the medication they are receiving might have negative impact on the fetus during pregnancy or the baby when breastfeeding. In fact, it is said that only 5 to 14 percent of women receive treatment for their psychiatric disorder during pregnancy and the postpartum period.

Practitioners who have pregnant or willing-to-be-pregnant clients should be aware of the influence of the medication on the women, fetus, or baby, and conduct a careful risk–benefit analysis of continuing versus ceasing medications, discussing with the psychiatrist. Also, they need to inform the clients that other treatment options might be available.

The Menstrual Cycle

Exacerbation of various mental health conditions at specific phases of the menstrual cycle, particularly during the luteal and menstrual phases, is a common phenomenon

(Case & Reid, 2001). Preexisting mental health disorders with premenstrual exacerbation include anxiety, bipolar, psychotic, and eating disorder (Pinkerton, Guico-Pabia, & Taylor, 2010). Increase of anxiety symptom severity or number of panic attacks and worsening of obsessive-compulsive disorder (OCD) were reported to have a relationship with menstrual cycle. Also, menstrual cycle–related exacerbation of psychotic disorders, including a worsening of psychiatric symptoms and clinical features of schizophrenia, has been reported (Dennerstein, Judd, & Davies, 1983; Hallonquist, Seeman, Lang, & Rector, 1993).

The menstrual cycle appears to trigger the onset of premenstrual dysphonic disorder (PMDD), a mood disorder specific to the luteal phase of the menstrual cycle that affects up to 6 percent of premenopausal women (see Chapter 12) and may also cause depression associated with the transition to menopause (Cohen et al., 2003; Case & Reid, 2001). During the menopausal transition, fluctuating levels of estrogen are thought to result in variable functioning of serotonin, which may contribute in part to depression. However, although up to 50 percent of women may experience depressive symptoms during the menopausal transition, most are not diagnosed with depression (Bromberger, et al., 2001; Cohen et al., 2006; Freeman et al., 2004).

Violence

The National Violence Against Women Survey indicates that there is a high prevalence of abuse in women's lives, both in absolute terms and relative to the rates experienced by men (National Institute of Justice, Centers for Disease Control, 2000). The unique prevalence of trauma, violence, and abuse in women's lives is important in and of itself and because of the close correlation between being a victim of abuse, having a mental illness, and having a substance use disorder.

Having a history of violence, trauma, or abuse is associated with increased risk of depression, PTSD, panic disorder, substance abuse, and serious consideration of suicide (Dube et al., 2005; Gearon, Kaltman, Brown, & Bellack, 2003; Kendler, Kuhn, Vittum, Prescott, & Riley, 2005; Tyler, 2002). Intimate partner violence (IPV) especially contributes to poorer mental health outcomes because violence in the relationship causes continuous stress (Golding, 1999), and strong and prolonged activation of these stresses, in the absence of any buffering relationships, leaves women vulnerable to a range of mental health problems throughout life (Edwards et al., 2003). Among the victims of IPV, some choose substance as a means to cope with the stressful situation. Studies found that 55 to 99 percent of women in substance use treatment report a history of trauma (Battle, Zlotnick, Najavits, Guttierrez, & Winsor, 2003).

Another issue of violence related to women's mental health is that the women clients who have IPV experience may have a distorted image of men and may not trust male professionals. The practitioner should understand such circumstances from the early sessions when the history of violence was assessed.

Cultural Effects and Disparities

As we have kept stressing throughout this chapter, even though we are describing the general and common characteristics of women, it is irrational to overgeneralize and assume women clients will be the same. Individual attitudes and responses to mental illness are highly affected both positively and negatively by one's family and cultural environment. These environments influence the meaning individuals assign to illness, how they make sense of it, what the causes may be, and how much stigma surrounds mental illness. In addition, they affect whether individuals will seek help (and from whom), how supportive their families may be, the pathways they take to obtain mental health services, and how well they may respond to different types of treatments.

Use of "cultural disparities" can place women at greater risk for mental illnesses. Factors such as racism and discrimination have measurable effects on rates of mental illness (Substance Abuse and Mental Health Services Administration, 2000). These effects are coupled with the finding that racial and ethnic minorities are less likely to receive needed services, including mental health services, and more likely to receive low-quality care (U.S. DHHS, 2001a). Therefore we will talk more about the mental health of women from different racial/ethnic groups.

Mental Health Considerations for Asian-American and Pacific Island Women

Depression

Depression is the second leading cause of death among Asian-Americans and Pacific islanders, who have the highest rate of suicide among women between 15 to 24 years of age (NAMI, 2009). Although depression is a common and highly treatable disorder affecting nearly 20 million Americans annually, only 27 percent of Asian-American women seek help or treatment (NAMI, 2009). However, there is a dearth of research focusing on causal or contributing factors of depression among AAPI women. Please review Chapter 12 for an overview of symptoms and diagnostic criteria for depression per the *DSM* conceptualization.

Risk Factors for Depression in AAPI Women

This section will address Korean immigrant women as a specific example. Korean immigrant women experience psychological conflict when they face opposing cultural demands that trigger values conflict, exemplified by Lee (1988) as women being submissive and passive within Eastern culture versus women being equal and assertive within Western culture. This resulting cultural conflict increases Korean immigrant women's psychological vulnerability.

Another risk factor is the typical working status of Korean immigrant women. Due to racial discrimination and language barriers, most Korean immigrant wives are employed in low-paying jobs such as clerical, service, or manual jobs without opportunities for future promotion or benefits within Korean communities (Lee, 2001). Women are typically employed for the family's economic benefit, rather than for personal career interest or economic independence (Min, 1996 as cited in Lee, 2001). These labor force conditions usually result in Korean women adhering to traditional family roles (Lee, 2001). In many cases, Korean women wish to quit their jobs in favor of staying home due to a lack of satisfaction with their low-status occupations but do not have that choice (Lee, 2001).

Another risk factor relates to the gender-role attitudes of women's spouses. Krause (1983) indicates that a significant determinant of the well-being of married women is not gender-role orientation, per se, but the degree of congruency of between marital partners concerning gender roles. Research findings link depression among women with a presence of conflict regarding female role (Krause, 1984; Van Fossen, 1981). In many cases, Korean husbands maintain a male-oriented gender attitude even when their wives are employed full-time outside of the home. Traditional gender role patterns persist among Korean immigrants regardless of the wives' employment. Compared with other groups of Asian immigrant women, traditional family demands have the most powerful influence over Korean immigrant women (Lee, 2001; Stier, 1991). Even in these progressive times, women are expected to assume the responsibility of performing household duties and child care as their top priority, regardless of their occupations.

Multiple burdens and overload and demands also serve risk factors for depression for Korean immigrant women. Without a process of role definition, Korean American women have experienced role expansion: adding a new role as the "breadwinner" without relinquishing the traditional role of homemaker (Lee, 2001). Thus, Korean immigrant women suffer multiple burdens (child care/housework/income source) from changed economic conditions and endure psychological distress due to their conservative native culture and the persistence of rigid traditional gender roles (Kim & Hurh, 1988). Research findings investigate the relationship between role overload and depression (Barnett & Baruch, 1985). Other studies show that women who receive more help from their husbands experience lower levels of depression (Van Fossen, 1981). Kim and Hurh (1985) report that more than 75 percent of housework is performed by working wives. Korean husbands exhibit a lower level of flexibility with household work as compared to men from other immigrant groups or the general population (Lee, 2001). Rhee (1995) found that symptoms of depression among Korean immigrant women are mainly related to their level of domestic and occupational labor. Said differently, multiple roles may be a risk factor for depression among Korean women (as cited in Lee, 2001).

Mental Health Needs among Southeast Asian Refugee Women

Definition of Asylum Seeker, Refugee, and Immigrant

The terms *asylum seeker* and *refugee* can be confusing. Generally speaking, an asylum-seeker is someone who claims he or she is a refugee, but whose legal status has not yet been established. Under the United Nations Convention Relating to the Status of Refugees of 1951, a refugee is defined (in Article 1A) as the following:

> A person who owing to a well-founded fear of being persecuted for reasons of race, religion, nationality, membership of a particular social group, or political opinion, is outside the country of his nationality, and is unable to or, owing to such fear, is unwilling to avail himself of the protection of that country; or who, not having a nationality and being outside the country of his former habitual residence as a result of such events, is unable or, owing to such fear, is unwilling to return to it. (*Convention, supra*, note 27, at Art 1(A)(2), para. 1)

Thus, the United States recognizes persecution "on account of race, religion, nationality, membership of a particular social group, or political opinion," as a prerequisite condition for seeking asylum. Until a request for refuge has been accepted, the person is referred to as an asylum seeker. After the asylum seeker's request is accepted, he or she officially obtains refugee status, which carries certain rights and obligations on the basis of the legislation of the receiving country.

On the other hand, an immigrant is "an alien who has been granted the right by the USCIS (United States Citizenship and Immigration Services) to reside permanently in the United States and to work without restrictions in the United States. Immigrants may also be known as Lawful Permanent Residents (LPRs). All immigrants are eventually issued a "green card" (USCIS Form I-551), which is the evidence of the alien's LPR status" (see www.irs.gov).

Southeast Asian Refugee Women's Psychological Problems

It has been estimated that 75 percent of the total refugee population is composed of women and girls (Van Overhagen, 1990, as cited in Friedman, 1992). With respect to Southeast Asian refugees, an estimated 80 percent of Khmer households along the Thai-Cambodian border are believed to be female-headed (Friedman, 1992).

One of the most serious risks encountered by refugee women is rape and sexual violence (Friedman, 1992). There have been numerous reports and significant levels of international attention devoted to the issues of sexual abuse against refugee women. However, no official studies or actions to address these issues have been undertaken (Friedman, 1992). The risk for rape and sexual violence particularly increases when refugee women cross borders to seek asylum (Friedman, 1992). Approximately 45 percent of the so-called boat people who arrive in Thailand are subject to attacks by pirates (Taft, 1987). During these attacks, women and girls are often subjected to multiple rapes and/or abduction (Friedman, 1992). In most cases, the rapes are brutal, leading to deformation or mutilation of the genitalia (Burton, 1983). In camp, refugee women experience rape and violence by camp authorities and military guards who are supposed to protect them (Friedman, 1992). Therefore, Southeast Asian refugee women are a high-risk group for developing serious psychiatric disorders due to their traumatic pre-migration experiences (Mollica et al., 1987). Major mood disorders and post-traumatic stress disorder (PTSD) are common psychiatric disorders among Southeast Asian refugee women (Mollica et al., 1987).

In Southeastern Asian cultures, virginity is viewed as a "prized possession" for single women and fidelity to one's husband is a virtue strongly emphasized for married women (Ito et al., 1997). In this cultural context, a majority of women who have been sexually assaulted blame themselves for the rape, and few seek help (Ito et al., 1997). The rape experience causes the victim to be overwhelmed by shame and guilt from the loss of their self-respect and family honor (Ito et al., 1997). Many rape victims repress their feelings and, in some cases, commit suicide. "They do not dare to tell their husband because husbands often will leave them if they know their wives have been sexually violated" (Ito et al., 1997, p. 318). The rape victim may also suffer rejection from their family members or, in some extreme cases, are even murdered because they are regarded as destroying their family's honor (Ito et al., 1997). Thus, feelings of isolation resulting from a lack of social support may exacerbate the rape victim's psychological vulnerability.

In addition to sexual trauma, the experience of widowhood and the loss of children place Southeast Asian refugee women at risk for developing serious psychological disorders (Ito et al., 1997). In many cases, refugee women experience all three traumas—rape, widowhood, as well as child loss (Ito et al., 1997). Many of these women have also witnessed the murder of their husband. Refugee women, in general, are more likely to experience spousal loss than men (Ito et al., 1997). It has been reported that refugee women often lose their children through unnatural and horrific circumstances. Many have witnessed their infants being beaten to death against trees (because they were weak or sick), children being torn limb from limb, or children starving to death (Szymusiak, 1986). As with widowed refugee women, these women are at risk from suffering serious depression, anxiety, and PTSD (Ito et al., 1997).

A Culturally Sensitive Intervention Approach for Southeast Asian Refugee Women

Many refugee women have the capability to utilize clinics as a source of support. They display courage, resilience, and strong will in order to overcome their trauma experiences and rebuild their lives (Ito et al., 1997). It has been reported that refugee women benefit from professional treatment. In many cases, refugee women experience symptom reduction and improvement in social functioning to a sufficient degree (Mollica, Lavelle, & Khoun, 1985).

It is important to include traditional intervention approaches in the treatment of traumatized refugee women. New Buddhist rituals and rites for "cleansing" (mock cleansing or purification rituals) of sexually traumatized women would be required (Ito et al., 1997). Such treatments are essential parts of the client's culture, and may be as effective as any Western treatments (Van Boemel & Rozee, 1992). It may be necessary to train Buddhist nuns to provide counseling for rape victims (Ito et al., 1997). Use of herbs or performance of exorcisms may enhance such traditional or ritualistic treatments (Van Boemel & Rozee, 1992). The usual procedure of exorcism, which is generally combined with amulet usage, is "to cut the victim's upper arm or tongue to obtain blood with which to write a special formula designed to frighten the evil spirits away" (Hickey, 1964, p. 80).

Treatment Considerations for Clinicians Working with Southeast Asian Refugee Women

Developing and building trust in the therapeutic relationship is very important when working with Southeast Asian refugee women, perhaps more so than any other aspect of the therapeutic relationship (Kinzie & Fleck, 1987; Van Boemel & Rozee, 1992). During the reign of Pol Pot in Cambodia, neighbors spied on each other and children were informants against their parents (Van Boemel & Rozee, 1992). In this cultural context, initial resistance to a trustful therapeutic relationship is anticipated.The clinician can build trust by letting his or her clients know that the therapist is aware of and respectful toward the client's culture and is also aware of the client's traumatic experiences (Van Boemel & Rozee, 1992). Other recommendations and considerations when working with Southeast Asian refugee women include the following:

1. Trust can be encouraged by the demeanor of the therapist; thus, it is important to speak softly in a respectful manner.
2. A female interpreter is recommended.
3. It is advised that the clinician use Khmer phrases and remove shoes when entering the client's home.
4. Bowing is encouraged when greeting clients.
5. A client should not be confined in a room where she is the only one with the therapist, since this condition resembles interrogation.

In addition to individual approaches, group therapy may provide the solution to the potential problem of the appearance of interrogation, mentioned above (Van Boemel & Rozee, 1992). Nguyen (1982) suggests that "network therapy" can be used to minimize feelings of isolation among refugee women. Network therapy provides clients with the opportunity to meet with one another and contributes to establishing new social support networks. Group therapy can also help to reconstruct a social network for the clients who experienced the demolition or deconstruction of their social networks due to the death or dislocation of significant members of their network (Nguyen, 1982). A group therapy setting could also be beneficial by increasing the client's sense of power within the therapeutic relationship (Van Boemel & Rozee, 1992).

Consideration of power imbalance between the client(s) and therapist is very important to recognize. In Southeast Asian regions, such as Cambodia, the practitioners of the healing arts were regarded as priests, who had powers to dispel the evil spirit and curses that caused sickness (Van Boemel & Rozee, 1992). The sick individual was not included in making any decisions regarding his or her own illness (Van Boemel & Rozee, 1992). This belief may increase the power differential between the client and therapist within the therapeutic relationship (Van Boemel & Rozee, 1992). Moreover, language and educational differences between the therapist and client may increase the power imbalance (Van Boemel & Rozee, 1992). In many cases, the clients have little formal education and may speak rudimentarily in their native language (Van Boemel & Rozee, 1992). Thus, the clients may regard the well-educated therapist as an expert (as well as a priest), and therefore, they may view the therapist as more knowledgeable about the client's needs than the client herself (Van Boemel & Rozee, 1992). The therapist must consider this power differential or imbalance and continue to reassure the client that the therapist is a facilitator for the client's growth, and that "the client is to set her own goals" (Van Boemel & Rozee, 1992, p. 254).

Assess your comprehension of *factors that may be important in understanding the mental health needs of women, including refugee women,* by completing this quiz.

Community-based education programs should be developed in order to educate both male and female refugees regarding "preventive medicine, primary health care, family planning, support groups, acceptance of both male and female sharing roles within the household, sanitation, and infant and child care" (Ito et al., 1997, p. 321). Active outreach programs for isolated women and bilingual/bicultural staff personnel would be necessary to implement such programs effectively (Ito et al., 1997).

CONCLUSION

This chapter has addressed social work practice with individuals with mental illness across a range of diverse client groups. Embedded throughout the chapter is the argument that treatment effectiveness is maximized if services are provided within the most relevant and meaningful cultural, gender-sensitive, and age-appropriate context for the people being served. Broadly defined, *culture* is a common heritage or set of beliefs, norms, and values that a group of people share. People who are placed, either by census categories or by identifying themselves, into the same racial or ethnic group are often assumed to share the same culture; however, as noted in the chapter, not all members who are grouped together will share the same culture, and there is great diversity within cultures, within ethnicities, and within racially defined groups. Some people may identify with a given racial or ethnic culture to varying degrees, while others may identify with multiple cultures, including those associated with their religion, profession, sexual orientation, region, or disability status (SAMHSA, 2009).

Immigration is a potentially stressful process, and some immigrants are also refugees fleeing traumatic experiences in their own countries and at high risk for mental and emotional problems. Immigrants from different parts of the world arrive in the United States with their own culture but gradually begin to adapt and develop new, hybrid cultures that allow them to function in the dominant culture while maintaining their cultural heritage to one degree or another (SAMHSA, 2009). This process is called *acculturation*, and even groups that have been in the United States for many generations may share beliefs and practices that maintain influences from multiple cultures. Many immigrants are in the position of bridging two or more cultures, for example, their birth heritage culture and the culture of the new host country. This can be challenging and can cause value conflicts within the individual, the family, and the community.

Being a culturally competent clinician is not something that is attained through a workshop or two and then, forever more, one is culturally competent. Instead, cultural competence in social work practice is an ongoing process of continual learning and experience. This is because culture is dynamic. It changes continually and is influenced both by people's beliefs and by the changing demands of their environment. This complexity necessitates an individualized approach to understanding culture and cultural identity in the context of mental health services. It is important to remember that every single person has a culture(s) and every client and family has their own culture(s).

Culture influences many aspects of mental/behavioral health care and services, beginning with whether people think care is even needed. Culture influences the concerns that people bring to the clinical setting and how they describe them, the language they use to express those concerns, and the coping styles they use to try to resolve their problems and concerns. As the chapter discussed, culture affects family structure, living arrangements, and the degree of support that people receive and expect in time of difficulties. Culture also influences patterns of help-seeking, whether people start with a primary care doctor, a mental health program, or a minister, spiritual advisor, or community elder or try to keep problems within the family unit. Finally, culture affects whether people attach a stigma to mental health problems and the nature of such stigma, and how much trust they are able to place in the hands of providers (SAMHSA, 2009). Culture is also not just an issue that is relevant to our clients, rather, it also applies to providers, administrators, agencies, and how health care is provided in our society as a whole.

For decades, mental health and substance use treatment services neglected to recognize the growing diversity around them (U.S. DHHS, 2001b). Often, people from non-majority cultures found programs off-putting, hard to access, and with little relevance to their concerns. They avoided getting care, stopped looking for care, or—if they managed to find care—they dropped out, resulting in significant racial/ethnic/cultural disparities in mental health care and mental health status (U.S. DHHS, 2001b). Disparities were most apparent for racial and ethnic minority groups, including African-Americans, American Indians and Alaska Natives, Asian-Americans, Hispanic Americans, Native Hawaiians and other Pacific Islanders—groups that have been discussed in this chapter. This situation has changed rapidly for the better, but much more needs to be done to ensure that all Americans receive the behavioral health care they need and deserve.

The following can assist social workers and other clinicians in obtaining resources to support cultural competence in practice:

1 *National Leadership Council on African American Behavioral Health*
6904 Tulane Drive
Austin, TX 78723-2823
Phone: (512) 929-0142
Fax: (512) 471-9600
http://www.nlcouncil.org

2 *National Latino Behavioral Health Association*
P.O. Box 387
506 Welch, Unit B
Berthoud, CO 80513
Phone: (970) 532-7210
Fax: (970) 532-7209
http://www.nlbha.org

3 *First Nations Behavioral Health Confederacy*
Phone: (406) 732-4240 Montana
Phone: (505) 275-3801 Albuquerque, NM
pauletterunningwolf@hotmail.com

4 *National Asian American Pacific Islander Mental Health Association*
1215 19th Street, Suite A
Denver, CO 80202
Phone: (303) 298-7910
Fax: (303) 298-8081
http://www.naapimha.org

5 *National Alliance on Mental Illness (NAMI)*
Colonial Place Three
2107 Wilson Boulevard, Suite 300
Arlington, VA 22201-3042
Phone: (800) 950-NAMI (6264)
Fax: (703) 524-9094
TTY: (703) 516-7227
http://www.nami.org

6 *National Institute of Mental Health (NIMH)*
Office of Communications
6001 Executive Boulevard, Room 8184, MSC 9663
Bethesda, MD 20892-9663
Phone: (866) 615-NIMH (6464)
Fax: (301) 443-4279
TTY: (301) 443-8431
http://www.nimh.nih.gov

7 *Center for Mental Health Services*
Substance Abuse and Mental Health Services Administration
SAMHSA's Health Information Network
Rockville, MD
Phone: 1-877-SAMHSA-7 (1-877-726-4727) (English and Español) http://www.samhsa.gov/shin

Assess your application and analysis of this chapter's contents by completing the *Chapter Review*.

8 *Mental Health America*
2001 North Beauregard Street, 6th Floor
Alexandria, VA 22311
Phone: (800) 969-6642

Chapter 7

Understanding and Working with the Families of Individuals with Serious Mental Illness

The Case of Joe

Imagine that you are a clinician in the walk-in services unit of your local public behavioral health clinic. When not working in the walk-in clinic, you work as a clinical case manager with a caseload of 20 clients to follow. Clinical case management involves typical case management activities but you also provide individual psychosocial treatment to your clients and their families. You work in the walk-in clinic every Wednesday, and in this capacity your job is to see people who request mental/behavioral health services without an appointment. You triage these clients, sorting out which ones require emergency intervention, and then coordinating or directly providing what is needed for the client(s). As a walk-in services clinician, you have the authority to set up referrals to any of the available resources in your community, and you have a psychiatrist to back you up for medication or to underwrite any inpatient admission decisions you make.

At 9 a.m. a middle-aged couple walks into the clinic and asks to talk to someone about their son, Joe. This is what they tell you: Joe is 23, lives at home, and is supported by SSI (Supplemental Security Income). Although the parents describe him as "always a little odd—you know, he always marched to a different drummer" since childhood, he did well in school—particularly in science—and won a scholarship to the local state university. During his freshman year, however, he began to have serious problems. His grades slipped, and he became more and more reclusive and gradually stopped talking to anyone. His roommate alerted the resident advisor in his dorm and eventually, after much difficulty, Joe was hospitalized at the university medical center's psychiatric inpatient unit. At that time he was given the diagnosis of schizophreniform disorder and was discharged on low doses of antipsychotic medication (olanzapine). Since then Joe has been unable to return to school, although he tried to work (once as a cashier, once as a grocery store bagger) but was fired from each job within a month because he was slow and "wouldn't stick to the work."

Joe's parents have tried to help him, but say nothing they do is working. He just sits at home, watching TV reality shows, smoking cigarettes and drinking coffee. Joe's mother says that she tries to get him out of the house and encourages him to read, walk the dog, or just do *something* but he just sits. Recently, however, he has been having periods of agitation, has made vague references to "being watched" and has insisted that his mother keep the drapes closed at all times. He won't eat his mother's cooking and has been subsisting on Oscar Meyer bologna and English muffins "because they're wrapped." This morning Joe refused to drink any tap water or drinks made with tap water because he believes his mother is putting a substance into the water system that will make him impotent. Joe's parents don't know what to do.

You ask the parents if they can bring Joe to the clinic. They say they'll try. Finally, six hours later, they appear with Joe. You look out your office window and see them coming—Joe is walking slowly about 20 paces behind them. Joe agrees to see you in your office, comes in, and sits down. The first thing you notice is that he smells very bad. His shirt is dirty and misbuttoned. He hasn't had a shave in a while and his fingers are stained, probably from nicotine. He looks at you with no expression on his face but is willing to sit down when you ask him to.

Questions to think about:

- What would you say to Joe as you begin your interview? What strategies might you use to establish rapport with him?
- What are the most important issues you would address with Joe at this first meeting?
- What issues would you address with Joe's parents? What feelings would you guess that his parents are experiencing that you should be sensitive to?
- How would you go about determining the first goals of treatment for Joe and his family?
- Explain how and why psychoeducation, Johnson's eight-stage healing process, and NAMI could be helpful to Joe and his parents.
- What strengths do you perceive in Joe?
- What strengths do you perceive in Joe's family?

Social workers and other clinicians who work in public mental health services see clients like Joe and his parents frequently, since these days, in the wake of deinstitutionalization, budget cuts, and for-profit managed care, it is families who provide the bulk of daily caretaking for most individuals with serious mental illness. Read through and think about the questions listed above that address the case of Joe and his parents and ponder what the answers might be. These questions will be revisited at the end of this chapter, which focuses on how practitioners can understand, empathize with, and help families like Joe's parents cope with and help a loved one living with serious mental illness.

MENTAL ILLNESS BRINGS FAMILIES TO CRISIS

Similar to alcoholism, mental illness often disables the entire family. Social workers know how challenging it can be to work with someone who is actively psychotic, manic, or profoundly depressed. Coping with hallucinations, delusions, disorganized thinking, and intense mood swings is very hard for mental health professionals to deal with but, for families, what makes it doubly hard is that the person is someone the family members love. In the United States alone, one in four families has a loved one living with mental illness (American Mental Health Fund, 1987), with 1 in 100 Americans having schizophrenia and 5 in 100 having a mood disorder (SAMHSA, 2010). Furthermore, the effects of mental illness are not limited to those directly afflicted. Mental illness brings families to crisis, too (Solomon, 2012; Warner, 2011).

Serious mental illness, especially when left untreated, interferes with one's relationships with other people because it can profoundly affect an individual's interpersonal and communication skills. For example, the social cognitive deficits associated with schizophrenia can make it hard for a person to make and keep friends, obtain and keep a job, and interact with others on a daily basis (Torrey, 2006). Mental illness also affects an individual's ability to handle stress effectively and can negatively affect one's thought processes and emotional patterns. Individuals who have a mood disorder, for example, are often highly sensitive to stress and change, and relatively minor events can throw the person into an emotional tailspin (Rosen & Amador, 1996; Frank, 2005).

Initially, however, such effects are often not recognized as mental illness, and thus, the situation for the client and family may worsen because the illness remains unrecognized, undiagnosed, and untreated (Johnson, 1988, 2007). The ill person or the person's family may respond by denying the seriousness of the symptoms that emerge. In addition, even if the family does recognize that the loved one needs help, certain symptoms, such as paranoia, can interfere with the person being receptive to getting help or allowing the family to seek help.

Family denial may set in and bring on a stalemate, effectively preventing anyone from taking action. As Sigmund Freud pointed out almost a century ago (Freud, 1914), denial is a simple, but powerful, defense. Denial enables troubling feelings, emotions, impulses, and wishes to be disavowed and actively pushed out of consciousness. Denial operates like a "psychological callus" buffering against the hurt underneath. The role of collective denial for a family trying to cope with mental illness is that denial can enable the family to avoid pain—the pain of blaming themselves for the situation and the pain of facing potential social stigma toward the ill person or themselves, for example, "If you have a crazy brother, you must be crazy too," or "Schizophrenia is caused by bad mothers." Denial can work in the short run but doesn't work well in the long run. The primary problem with denial is that it doesn't really make problems disappear, it simply keeps people from recognizing, dealing with, and solving problems. Problems that don't disappear also usually get worse over time, which makes solving them more difficult. Example:

> Tim is an 18-year-old African-American man brought to the emergency room by the police and his grandmother after he was found walking down the highway in his bathrobe with his arm outstretched. For the past year, Tim has been living with his grandmother, and it has been an increasingly difficult situation for her. Just over a year ago, Tim was kicked out of his mother's house for smoking marijuana, and everyone in the neighborhood attributed his increasingly odd behavior to drug use. Over the past three months, Tim has been taking 12 baths a day (most during the night), sleeping a little during the day and staying up all night. Tim's grandmother has Type II diabetes and high blood pressure and is living on a fixed income. The water bill, because of all the baths, has increased so much that the grandmother cannot pay it and the water company is threatening to shut off her water. Her blood pressure has skyrocketed, due to the stress over dealing with Tim, and she had no idea that he was showing symptoms of mental illness, stating to the emergency room social worker: "We don't have crazy folks in our family—I can't believe this is happening." Psychiatric treatment was finally provided to Tim only after things had reached a crisis point, and the police had to be called for help.

Seeking help or being forced into getting help, as was the case with Tim and his grandmother, can be frightening, embarrassing, and threatening for a family. For the well family members, it may force an admission that mental illness is now a part of their family and, by extension, implies something might be "wrong" with them too. In many cultures, as discussed in the Chapter 6, having a mentally ill family member stigmatizes the entire family. In addition, when denial plays a role, the problems may go unaddressed for some time, allowing the problems to escalate and worsen and, then, when help is finally accessed, it is usually the result of a crisis and, thus, the first contact the family has with the mental health system is one of high stress and may involve the police, emergency room personnel, and the like. Thus, rather than having an initial therapeutic experience, the family has a stressful, and even adversarial, experience.

Fortunately, today, there is less of a focus on "who is to blame" for a loved one's mental illness; rather, mental illness is understood more as an affliction that affects the whole family and the focus is on solutions that will benefit all of the members of the family, both the well members and the ill member. Family members are increasingly viewed less as a cause of mental illness than as "hidden victims" (Johnson, 1988, 2007) who must be partners with the ill person and the treatment team on the journey toward recovery. This view helps demystify mental illness and helps families to talk openly about it and how it affects them.

PARALLELS BETWEEN MENTAL ILLNESS AND ALCOHOLISM AND OTHER ADDICTION FOR FAMILIES

The way mental illness affects families is very similar to the way alcoholism and other addictions affect a family. For example, some of the common characteristics of a mentally ill or an addicted person include unpredictable erratic behavior, withdrawal, suspicion of others, and disordered thoughts. Parallel family responses include powerful feelings of frustration, confusion, anger, secrecy, and hopelessness; "covering up" for the ill person's disruptive or illegal behavior; and denial of the illness and its effects. Kenneth Minkoff (Mental Illness Education Project, 2000) identifies 12 specific parallels common to both alcoholism/addiction and mental illness. These parallels include the following:

- Both mental illness and addiction are physiological diseases with strong genetic/hereditary components;
- Both mental illness and addiction are physical/mental/spiritual diseases which result in pervasive (global) effects on the person and his or her family;
- If left untreated, the course of both illnesses is usually progressive;
- Denial of the disease process and noncompliance with attempts to treat the symptoms/illness are common aspects of both types of disorder;
- Both types of illness can manifest loss of control of behavior, thought, and emotions. Both are often seen by others as a "moral" or "character defect" issue;
- Both diseases affect the whole family as well as all interpersonal systems, including occupational, school, neighborhood, and community;
- Growing powerlessness and unmanageability lead to feelings of guilt, shame, depression, and despair in both the ill person and the family;
- Both are illnesses of vulnerability and isolation; the person affected is exquisitely sensitive to psychosocial stressors;
- Both the primary symptoms of each illness *and* the loss of control in behavior, thought, or emotion can be managed, and recovery can be achieved with appropriate treatment and supports;
- Recovery consists of: (1) stabilization of the acute phase of illness; (2) rehabilitation of body, mind, and spirit; and (3) embarking upon an ongoing program of recovery involving both the ill person and the family, which may be lifelong;
- The risk of relapse in either illness is always high, and if the individual has *both* a mental illness and an addiction, a relapse in one of the illnesses will inevitably trigger a relapse in the other; and
- The only hope for lifelong recovery lies in working the program of treatment/relapse prevention *one day at a time.*

Similar to the family of a person with alcoholism or an addiction to drugs, families of individuals with mental illness must learn how to help themselves even if the ill family member has not been willing to accept treatment (Johnson, 2007). Families must learn how to live with mental illness and not allow their loved one's illness to permeate and disrupt every aspect of family life (NAMI Family-to-Family, 2011). When a loved one is mentally ill, all the emotional, financial, and time resources of the family can be devoted to that one person, with little left over for other family members. As Don Meyer, director of the Sibling Support Project, run by the ARC, an advocacy organization for individuals with intellectual and developmental disabilities, commented, "It's Johnny this, Johnny that, the United States of Johnny. Johnny is the sun in the family's solar system" (Gross, 2004). Example:

> Janna is the 15-year-old sister of Sam, 20 years old, who has schizophrenia. She describes her life to her social worker as follows: "Everything revolves around Sam—his problems, his hallucinations, is he taking his meds, Sam, Sam, Sam. When I'm not in school, I stay in my room and read just to get away from it all. My mom told me the other day that I should thank Sam for making me such a good reader."

The ultimate goal for families with a mentally ill loved one is to achieve a healthy adjustment by learning how to meet the needs of all family members, not just the needs of the ill member. When families achieve this goal, the positive family environment usually benefits the ill member better than when everything revolves around him or her. John, a 40-year-old man with schizophrenia, recalls:

> When I first got sick, which was after my first year in college, my family rallied around me and gave me a lot of support. But over time, it was too much. Everyone was hovering over me, pushing me, checking on me all the time: "Did you take your meds?" "You need to get up and do something," blah, blah, blah. I felt under the gun and guilty, too, because I couldn't get back to normal like my parents wanted me to. I wanted everyone to just back off.

Often it is the family's social worker who is in the best position to understand the family system and family dynamics and how families function and who can, as a result, be most helpful to families in reaching the goal of healthy balance. In addition, social workers can help families connect with advocacy/family support organizations such as the Sibling Leadership Network (www.siblingleadership.org) and the National Alliance on Mental Illness (www.nami.org). NAMI has chapters in every state and in many countries around the world and is a comprehensive grassroots advocacy, education, and support organization addressing mental illness and the needs of families. More information on how NAMI can be a helpful adjunctive resource for social workers working with families of individuals with mental illness is provided later in this chapter. To understand where families who have a mentally ill loved one are coming from and what they need, it is important to be aware of the phases that families go through as they adjust to the crisis of mental illness and take the journey toward healthy balance.

Assess your comprehension of *how mental illness brings families to crisis similarly to alcoholism or addiction* by completing this quiz.

THE FIVE PHASES FAMILIES GO THROUGH WHEN MENTAL ILLNESS EMERGES IN A FAMILY MEMBER

Overview of the Five Phases

One of the best models describing the process that families go through when mental illness emerges in the family was developed by social worker Julie Tallard Johnson (1988, 2007). Johnson's model consists of five phases. The first phase is "Early Warnings," which is when the first early signs of mental illness begin to emerge in a family member. The second phase, "Keeping the Peace," describes the reactions of family members as their loved one's behavior becomes increasingly disturbed, symptoms worsen, and family life becomes increasingly disrupted.

The third phase, "Rude Awakenings," represents the phase when the family can no longer manage the ill person, and is often ushered in by a crisis that forces the family to seek help. It is at this time that the family and ill person may receive the diagnosis of mental illness for the first time. During this phase, families often experience a series of crises, for example, repeated suicide attempts, acts of aggression, or severely disorganized behavior, that seriously interfere with family stability. Crises don't last forever, though, and eventually, after living in crisis, the crisis period passes.

At this point, the family begins to adjust in the fourth phase, which Johnson calls "Just Coping." In the "Just Coping" phase, the family members adopt coping skills that allow them to survive their disrupted, chaotic family life. Unfortunately, some families become "stuck" in this phase and never move beyond it.

With appropriate help, however, many families can move to the fifth and last phase, which is "A Delicate Balance." This phase consists of developing alternative ways to cope with the disabling effects of mental illness and deal with the disruption it brings to family life. In this fifth phase, solutions must be found for everyone in the family—parents, grandparents, children, siblings, spouses—and, hopefully, all family members ultimately find hope and strategies to cope with the challenges they face. Below, each phase is described in more detail and, to clinically illustrate these phases, the progression through the phases for a specific client and her family will be provided.

Phase One: "Early Warnings"

Unlike influenza, which has initial symptoms the general public is well aware of, the average family typically knows very little about mental illness (unless mental illness is already part of their family's history and everyone is openly aware of that), and what the average family does know may be distorted because it is garnered from popular media. Media portrayals of mental illness are usually exaggerated and commonly involve violence and depictions of florid psychosis (see, e.g., multiple episodes from the *Law and Order* franchise). When mental illness first emerges in real life, however, the initial symptoms may be subtle and gradual. As a result, even if the family notices changes in their loved one, they usually attribute it to other more common causes, for example, a developmental stage or a temporary change due to stressful life events. They may reassure themselves by saying things like "He's just a typical moody teen," or "She's just under a lot of stress at work," or "It's my fault he's so angry, I need to be more understanding." These kinds of reactions are understandable, because when normal crises occur, the odds are usually in favor of everything eventually returning to normal. So whether it is an illness, a natural disaster, or a work stressor, the crisis is expected to pass and life to go on.

In this phase, families usually have no idea of what may lie in store for them. Family members may not share their concerns with each other and, instead, "begin to build a protective wall of silence around their confusion and the expectations they hold for one another's behavior" (Johnson, 1988, p. 6). What are some of the early warning signs of mental illness? Some of these "early warning signs" of mental illness include the following (Johnson, 1988; Mental Health America, n.d.):

- Withdrawal from social interaction, including interaction with close friends and family;
- An increasingly sad mood, which may be accompanied by crying, expression of feelings of low self-worth, and gradually increasing poor sleep and appetite;
- Deviation from previous beliefs or routines, such as a religiously indifferent person becoming preoccupied with religion and reading a religious text such as the Bible or Koran;
- Suspicion of others, including accusations that others are attempting to harm him or her;
- Agitated, disruptive, or unpredictable behavior;
- Confused thinking and difficulty in communicating logically;
- Excessive fears, worries, and anxieties; and
- Hypersensitivity in family disputes or difficulties, for example, "flying off the handle" over relatively minor disagreements.

Alone, each of these warning signs may not be significant; however, if several of these early warning signs are present, that may be indicative that a mental illness is evolving. However, most families don't recognize this for what it is and just hope and pray that things get back to normal. Some mental illnesses, for example, schizophrenia or depression, may have a slow insidious onset so that symptoms emerge so gradually that people who see the ill person every day, as immediate family members would, don't notice that things are changing. Sometimes, it is not until someone who has not seen the ill family member for a while visits the family that a "red flag" is raised: "You know, I've noticed that Bernicia seems really different—depressed and withdrawn—have you noticed that?" a visiting relative might say.

As time goes on and the affected person does not get better, family members may begin to panic. They know now that their loved one is different—the ill family member is not the same person he or she used to be—but they don't know why and don't know what to do. In many cultures, the family leader—the father or the elder or the oldest son—is the one responsible for family well-being, and expected by the family to manage family problems. That individual is now under the tremendous stress of being responsible for the family but at a loss over what to do. He or she does not want to add to the burden, and so the problems are not discussed and the silence continues. Other family members look to the family head of the household to handle things and feel confused when that doesn't happen. Then a bigger fear emerges—what happens if the problem doesn't go away? What if there is nothing the family can do? At this point, the family reaches a stalemate.

The Case of Velma: Phase 1

Rufus, a 35-year-old married African-American man, recalls when he first noticed that his wife was "not acting normal." Rufus says, "Velma had just given birth to our third child—a baby daughter we named Shatoya, after her sister. Velma was so happy right after Shatoya was born but then, soon afterwards, I'd come home from work and she'd be crying. Just crying and holding Shatoya. I'd ask her what's wrong and she would just say she knew she was a bad mother and Shatoya would be better off without her. I figured it was just the baby blues, you know . . . but it didn't seem to get better. I called Velma's mother and she came to stay with her and that seemed to help at first but then she'd start over again that she was a bad mother and Shatoya deserved better. I prayed to the Lord for guidance. I should have known it was more than the baby blues, but I guess I thought she'd snap out of it and things would get back to normal like with our other babies."

Some families remain stuck in Phase 1, with some never getting through it and getting the professional help needed and with that, confirmation that their loved one has a mental illness. Most families, however, move on to Phase 2, "Keeping the Peace."

Phase Two: "Keeping the Peace"

As the early warning signs become worse, family relationships become increasingly tense, fragile, and disrupted. Immediate family members may have reached out to other family members for help, but things have not improved. In the example above, Rufus reached out to Velma's mother for help, but the improvement in Velma's emotional state did not last. At this stage, families know something is wrong and it isn't going away, although they still may not identify it as mental illness. If the loved one's changed behavior is strange or bizarre, the family may feel shame and embarrassment, which can get in the way of seeking help. To avoid embarrassment, the family may begin to isolate themselves from others, not going out or inviting friends over. In spite of the changes going on, family members may still not openly talk about what is going on, and "keeping the peace" becomes the primary objective; anything that might disrupt that peace is avoided (Johnson, 1988). Family members begin "walking on eggshells" and accommodating the ill person in any way possible to avoid making the situation worse (Mason & Kreger, 1998). In the absence of openly talking about what is going on, family members may make tacit agreements, unspoken rules to keep the status quo, such as:

"Don't upset Mom, she's just a sensitive person."
"If we don't talk about what's going on, that'll make it go away faster."
"Everything will get under control—just keep your head down."

Meanwhile, the ill family member's early warning signs are evolving into real symptoms of mental illness, including, for some individuals, what Johnson (1988) refers to as "pre-psychotic" symptoms. Such symptoms include increased sleeplessness; absence of routine daily patterns, or daily patterns turned around, for example, up all night, sleeping during the day; increased withdrawal and isolation, increased irritability and, for some, aggressive behavior; suicidal thoughts and/or parasuicidal behavior; moodiness and hypersensitivity to others; and disorganized thoughts and communication. It now becomes increasingly difficult for the family to communicate with the ill loved one, manage their behavior, and care for their needs. The family begins to try more desperate means to help the person and manage the increasingly chaotic family environment. One family, for example, set up a chart and had each family member sign up for "shifts" over each 24-hour period to supervise and manage the ill person and their erratic behavior. Another family put the ill person on a gluten-free diet with all organic food, and insisted the ill person take megadoses of vitamins in hope that would bring the person's "old self" back. The well family members become the caretakers and rescuers of the ill person, and if the ill person is a parent that turns normal family roles upside down and may force children to assume parental roles. Example:

> Seven-year-old Sara brought her mother to the psychiatric emergency service for evaluation. Sara was dressed neatly in a white dress, tights, and black Mary Jane shoes. Her mother, in contrast, was disheveled, disorganized, and grossly psychotic. Upon arrival at the ER, Sara told the receptionist in an eerily adult-like manner: "I would like to request an evaluation of my mother. I can't take care of her anymore." Alone, this young child had been caring for her psychotic mother, who had a long history of schizophrenia, for the past two months. Every day Sara got herself dressed, made breakfast for herself and her mother, went to school, came home, fed her mother, did her homework, cleaned the house, and took care of their two dogs. Sara had become her mother's "parent" and caretaker. How this child managed all of this on her own was remarkable. Equally remarkable, she realized when she had reached her limit and was able to figure out where to seek help and how to get her mother to the hospital by bus. The social worker arranged for hospitalization for Sara's mother and was able to reach family members in a neighboring state to come and take care of Sara while her mother was in the hospital. Shortly thereafter, Sara became very depressed and required psychiatric care herself. At last contact, however, both Sara and her mother were doing well.

Families can remain stuck in this peacekeeping stage for a long time, even years, and families who remain isolated and divided are less likely to reach out for the help that could pull them forward and out of the status quo. When mental health professionals finally see families who have been stuck in this stage for a long time, they may ask themselves, "Why didn't this family seek professional help sooner? How could they continue to live this way?" The answer is that there are many reasons why families do not seek help when symptoms of mental illness emerge in a loved one, even as the symptoms worsen. Some of these reasons are rooted in cultural values and traditions; others are rooted in lack of information, resources, and skills. The impact and power of stigma, however, cuts across many of the reasons that families do not seek help (Anderson, Reiss, & Hogarty, 1986). Below are some of the reasons that pose obstacles to seeking help (Johnson, 1988, p. 9):

- For various reasons, the family has been unable to openly and/or constructively discuss the problems together, which could pave the way to a discussion of the need for help.
- In many cultures, families believe strongly that problems should be kept and resolved within the family, and it is not acceptable to admit to or bring family problems to individuals outside the family system. Sometimes this is due to concern that certain family secrets might also be revealed, such as abuse or addiction within the family, but for many families it stems from cultural values and stigma.
- The family has not identified that the problem they are dealing with is a mental health problem and, thus, seeking psychiatric help has not occurred to them.
- The family realizes that the problem is psychiatric but don't know who to contact to get help, or they do try to get help but are thwarted in their efforts. For example, a family might contact the mental health crisis line only to be told they have to bring the person in to the clinic, but the person refuses to go and the family is afraid to push the issue and finally gives up.
- The ill person continues to deny having a problem or simply refuses to get help. Or the person may be paranoid and accuses the family of conspiring against him or her. Sometimes families are then afraid to push the ill person to get help because of fear that the person might make a suicide attempt or become violent.
- The family fears the impact of stigma and blame if they reach out for help.

The Case of Velma: Phase 2

Velma's mother stayed with the family to help for a couple weeks and, after she left, Velma seemed to be a little better and caring for her baby fairly well. But Rufus noticed when he would get home from work that Velma would be rocking the baby but not interacting with her at all, just staring off into space. Rufus figured Velma was just tired since she was up and down at night nursing. Over the next month, Velma began to have spells of crying and, once again, saying she was not a good mother. Rufus persuaded Velma to meet with their pastor, and the pastor suggested that being a full-time mother might be too much for Velma and perhaps she should go back to work. Rufus didn't tell the pastor about Velma's fears that she wasn't a good mother, and Velma kept quiet about that as well. The church had an infant care center that had an opening for Shatoya, and it was affordable. Velma seemed to brighten a bit at this suggestion, and so the family decided to enroll Shatoya in the infant care center, and Velma decided to go back to work. Now, Rufus thought, things will get back to normal.

Phase Three: "Rude Awakenings"

As the ill person's symptoms eventually worsen, families reach their limits in terms of coping, as illustrated in the example above of 7-year-old Sara. Family members begin to realize that things are not going to spontaneously snap back to normal, and then a crisis occurs that forces the family to get professional help.

The Case of Velma: Phase 3

Things went fairly well for Rufus, Velma, and the children at first. However, when Velma tried to get a car loan from her workplace credit union, the loan request was denied. Velma came home very angry about that and began to tell Rufus that she thought her co-workers were conspiring against her, talking about her, and trying to get her fired. Rufus was stunned. Velma had always done well at work, had friends there, and what she was saying didn't make sense to him. When Rufus questioned Velma's assertions, she became enraged and accused him of having an affair with one of his co-workers. A panic-like feeling began in the pit of Rufus's stomach—something very wrong was going on here, but what? Rufus called the pastor, and the pastor told him to just keep Velma home and pray more for the Lord's guidance. The next day, Rufus convinced Velma to call in sick and just stay home, but all day at work, he felt anxious. Finally, too nervous to concentrate on his work, Rufus left work a couple hours early and went home. He walked into the kitchen and there was Velma, holding Shatoya in her arms and a knife in her hand. Velma's eyes were wild and she screamed that Shatoya had the devil in her and had to die for her soul to be with Jesus. Rufus tackled Velma, wrestled Shatoya out of her arms, ran to the neighbor's, and called the police. The police took Velma to the psychiatric emergency room, where she was hospitalized on the basis of danger to others and grave disability. When Rufus sat down with the admitting psychiatrist, the doctor told him, "Your wife is psychotic—probably has schizophrenia—you're lucky your baby is alive."

As illustrated in the situation of Velma and her family, the third phase, "Rude Awakenings," is often ushered in via a crisis. Threats of violence or harm to self, psychotic symptoms that are acted upon, complete breakdown of the ability to communicate, repeated sleepless nights, or disruption in the community outside the home are typical crises that force the family into accessing professional help. As was the case with Velma and Rufus, families often first reach out to those they know, such as extended family, clergy, friends, or neighbors. When a serious crisis occurs, such resources may help facilitate getting help but, alone, are not sufficient to resolve the crisis.

Then, when the family finally sees a mental health professional—usually in a crisis center or emergency room, sometimes with the company of law enforcement, "the family hears the cold reality of a physician's diagnosis" (Johnson, 1988, p. 11), for example, "Your wife is psychotic—probably has schizophrenia." The diagnosis brings with it a combination of shock, relief, and profound feelings of loss. There is relief in knowing the answer to what the ill person and family have been going through, but the sense of loss usually outweighs the relief. The family is also faced with other potential future losses, including loss of the intact family as some family members escape or withdraw from the situation, loss when the ill person is hospitalized, incarcerated, or placed in sheltered care and, for some families, loss from suicide (Johnson, 1988). As one father recalled:

> Yes, I've been caring for my son for the past 10 years. When he first got sick with schizoaffective disorder, my wife couldn't handle it. After a couple years, she told me she wanted a life and couldn't have the life she wanted with us, so she left. Just like that. She has no contact with our son. It has been painful for me, but, I think, worse for him. He blames himself for the breakup of our marriage. But we're managing—we do pretty well together, him and me, but I do still miss her. I don't blame him, it isn't his fault that he has the illness.

A diagnosis of serious mental illness also often means a serious prognosis, that is, what lies in store for the person's future (Johnson, 1988). Today's mental health professionals know that recovery with serious mental illness is possible and that many people learn to manage their illness effectively and go on to live fulfilling lives. But that isn't what the average layperson knows about mental illness. The average person hears the word "schizophrenia" and sees it as being a life sentence to a hopeless future. A diagnosis of severe mental illness seems so final that family members often lose sight of what possibilities can lie ahead through recovery. A major consequence, if loss is not acknowledged, is that family relationships become strained, the ill member receives increasing focus, and healthy family members are given less attention, which may lead some well family members to want to escape from the situation, particularly if they see no other recourse.

Means of escape for spouses can include desertion, abandonment, or divorce, as illustrated in the case above. Another means of bailing out of the situation can be geographical, such as moving to another town in order to escape. One family, whose adult daughter was finally diagnosed with borderline personality disorder after years of living from crisis to crisis, packed up and moved away, leaving no forwarding address, while the daughter was hospitalized. Other less drastic measures of escape include social withdrawal from the family and what is going on in the family. For example, the younger sister of an adolescent boy with severe autism would escape to the basement in her home, lock the door, and spend her time reading or making animals out of clay while chaos reigned on the floor above her. Other family members may act unaffected by what is going on in the family, essentially "sucking down" feelings of anger, anxiety, and fear. Sometimes family members will choose destructive methods of escape, such as drug or alcohol abuse.

When families realize that their loved one has a mental illness, they often feel a loss that is similar to that felt by families whose family member has died. Except the person hasn't died, they are still here, but they aren't the same, they aren't the "original person" who was healthy and had a future. The "old son" or the "old wife" seems to be gone and replaced by someone the family doesn't know what to do with. The primary distinction between loss brought on by mental illness and loss brought on by death is that mental illness is often not recognized as a significant loss when, in fact, loss may be the central trauma that the family members face (Johnson, 1988). Furthermore, unlike a physical death, the loss continues, and the grieving seems endless.

As psychiatrist Nancy Andreasen, M.D., comments:

> If you lose a child from an illness like leukemia or whatever it's horrible, it's painful, you suffer, but it is over—but in the case of schizophrenia, the pain just goes on and on. Sometimes schizophrenia is described as just mourning without end. (University of Iowa Hospitals and Clinics, 1995)

To ease the pain, and avoid loss having a domino effect, families must be helped to learn how to talk about their feelings of loss openly and honestly, so they can deal with the problems and conflicts they face together. Helping families deal with the central issue of loss so it doesn't negatively impact their future relationships is a strategic goal for intervention efforts. Families must be supported in reaching the point where they are able to accept that the ill loved one may never be as before. This will help the family accept the illness and accept the ill person for what he or she is now. Without this, families can sink into chronic silent grieving that evolves into feelings of hopelessness and failure about themselves, their ill loved one, and everyone's options for the future (Johnson, 2007). To avoid all this, there must be an environment in which mourning is permitted for everyone.

The ill family member also experiences loss: loss because the individual may feel he or she has lost much of their original personality, lost his or her goals, expectations, skills, and relationships, including relationships with family as the illness may interfere with being able to feel emotional attachment and affection. As a middle-aged man with schizophrenia sadly observed:

> My extended family is very much involved with their own lives and I really don't think I'll ever be on a footing again with them where we can discuss personal things in a loving, caring way. I'm more of an emotional liability to them than anything else, they all have their careers and families and I feel I'm just out of the loop. They don't really know anything about my illness, only how it affects their lives, and I haven't really been a part of theirs for so long, due to my illness, that I think it is

> moot at this point whether it would be possible to establish a link with them. There is this emptiness I feel, like I am just an acquaintance and will be more so as time progresses. I don't feel this way with my two close friends now and hope not to fall into a similar situation with them; I am getting older and as time slips by I feel that I am getting lonelier with fewer avenues of true friendship.

In the phase of "Rude Awakenings," some families focus all their energy on finding a "cure" for the ill person, desperately trying to get back the "original person" they have lost. They may "doctor shop" and go from therapist to therapist, program to program, becoming angry when each person they consult with cannot provide the cure they want. Other family members, particularly parents, may immerse themselves in advocacy work, hoping that if the mental health system is improved, that will benefit their loved one. Advocacy is a good thing, but it can keep families from facing and working through the reality of what has happened and achieving a balance for their lives that allows them to provide care for their ill loved one but also have fulfilling lives of their own.

In time, with appropriate support and education, families can reach the stage where the mental illness no longer is the total focus or cause of family problems, rather the issue is how the family responds to the illness. It is in this phase that two critical interventions—family psychoeducation providing therapeutic support and information, along with connection to a support group (described below)—should be provided in order to enhance the likelihood that the family will be able to successfully move forward. This brings us to Phase 4, "Just Coping."

Phase Four: "Just Coping"

Case of Velma: Phase 4

Velma was in the hospital for a week. She was given Risperdal (risperdone), which began to ease the paranoia, and the voices that told her to hurt Shatoya gradually went away. But Velma suffered significant side effects from the risperdone—constipation, dry mouth, fatigue, and stomach distress—so the doctor changed her medication to Abilify (aripiprazole), and that seemed to work better. Although the admitting psychiatrist had diagnosed Velma with schizophrenia, the inpatient doctor diagnosed Velma with postpartum psychosis and probable underlying bipolar disorder, adding that schizophrenia has been shown to be overdiagnosed in African-Americans. Rufus felt some relief because there was a church member he knew who had bipolar disorder and he was doing pretty well. The social worker on the unit spent a lot of time talking with Rufus and, after she was stable, with Velma and referred them to a post-hospitalization psychoeducation group for families with a family member with bipolar disorder and to the local National Alliance on Mental Illness chapter. Before Velma was discharged, Rufus went to a NAMI meeting, but he was the only African-American family member attending. Everyone was very nice, but he wished that the meeting was more diverse. Over coffee after the meeting, he tentatively asked another member if other Black families came to the meetings. The member said no but then suggested that Rufus check out one of their affiliates, the NAMI group called Minority Families of the Mentally Ill. Rufus followed up and found a warm, supportive, and helpful group of families who totally understood what he had gone through and provided him with useful information and guidance. Rufus left the meeting thinking, "Maybe we can deal with this after all."

How the family responds to the "rude awakening" in Phase 3, whether it is hospitalization, incarceration, or other crisis that prompts the first psychiatric evaluation, this response eventually evolves into long-term coping strategies that have a range of characteristics. Some are by necessity or circumstances limited. For example, children or adolescents with mentally ill parents often have limited options (Miller, 1995). As noted previously, some coping strategies are destructive—for example, using drugs or alcohol to deal with the difficulties, or "coping" by engaging in denial, or chronic grieving, or becoming a martyr by completely giving up their own needs to care for the ill loved one. In such cases, the family members also become victims of the mental illness along with the ill member (Johnson, 1988, 2007).

Advocating for better mental health services is another way families may cope. As noted before, advocating for better mental health services is important if services are going to improve and if the persistent stigma associated with mental illness is to be mitigated. Services are poorly financed, poorly delivered, and inadequate overall in many communities, and good advocacy can be a potent force in turning things around for the better. Advocates who are family members can join with consumers and providers for powerful collective efforts, as has been demonstrated time and again with the National Alliance on Mental Illness (formerly the National Alliance for the Mentally Ill). Advocacy can also ease feelings of helplessness by providing purpose, goals, and emotional support for family members. As one mother commented, "When my NAMI group meets, I feel I am surrounded by friends who 'get it'—who really understand what I've been through. We plan community mental health awareness activities and plan political lobbying efforts to improve services and it makes me feel like I am really doing something to create change" (Newhill, 1995).

The danger in families immersing themselves in advocacy activity, however, is that family members may use advocacy as a way of avoiding dealing with the immediate family problems and may also assume "if the system is improved, my son or daughter will get well," which may not happen. When system improvements don't directly help their loved one, the family can become very bitter toward "the system" and this can result in families acting out their anger by antagonizing service providers that could be helpful to their loved one. As one mother of an adult son with pervasive developmental disorder, who was misdiagnosed as having schizophrenia for years, stated:

> To be perfectly honest, after all these years, I hate the mental health system—I do. I started the first mental health association in our community and answered the volunteer information and referral line for years. I edited the newsletter and advocated for better mental health services for over thirty years. None of my efforts paid off in terms of helping my son. I know my efforts helped others but I feel bitter sometimes that all the work I did didn't benefit us personally at all. (Newhill, 1995)

As this mother became more bitter toward the "system," she began to take a more adversarial stance with treatment providers and this led, eventually, to one board and care operator banning her from visiting her son because, claimed the operator, the mother was so confrontational and critical about the home that it upset the other residents (which may or may not have been the case). Nobody, however, ever attempted to engage the mother and help her deal with her feelings, particularly her profound feelings of loss and associated anger about her son's mental illness and the fact that he wasn't going to be "cured."

Families also learn to cope by making future plans for the ill member. Usually this includes assuming siblings will care for the mentally ill person when the parents no longer can; however, too often, the siblings are assigned this responsibility instead of freely choosing it, and siblings are left feeling they have no control over their future. This is particularly difficult if the ill family member has been violent or abusive toward the sibling (Butler, 2006). The inability of some families to talk together honestly about the situation of the ill member can also interfere with families talking honestly about future care without rancor or guilt. The style of caretaking may also be assumed, for example, that care will be continued the way the parents have done it. However, the relationships between parents and children, including adult children, is different from the relationships amongst siblings. As an adult daughter commented:

> My mother asked me to move my older brother—he has schizophrenia—from Arkansas to Vermont because services are better here. That was fine, except now she wants to dictate how and when I visit him, how long a time I spend with him on each visit, and what activities we do. It's like my brother and I aren't allowed to work out our own relationship. It got so bad that I started visiting him on my own without telling her and then telling her about the visits afterward if she asked when I was going to visit. I'd say, "Oh, I just made a visit." That made her pretty mad, but I felt better about it, although I know my behavior was kind of passive-aggressive. But, my brother and I are adults—we should be able to make our own decisions about how we want to connect with each other. It is hard to get that across to our mother, though.

Non-parental family members, particularly siblings and adult children, can view caring for the mentally ill relative as a "should," that is, an expectation acquiesced to by guilt, and often such feelings are viewed as taboo to talk about. Marsh et al. (1993) note that "the mental illness of a family member has a pervasive impact on the lives of siblings and children, transforming their childhood and penetrating all of the crawl spaces of their adult lives" (Marsh, Appleby, Dickens, et al., 1993, p. 27). This impact forms a legacy of mental illness that affects the well siblings and children in numerous ways, including the creation of what is referred to as *subjective burden* and *objective burden*.

Subjective burden refers to the *emotional consequences* of a family member's mental illness on the well child or sibling, such as feelings of anger, resentment, guilt, depression, fear, and anxiety. In contrast to subjective burden, objective burden refers to the *day-to-day reality demands* created by the ill family member's mental illness. Aspects of objective burden in caring for the ill family member include dealing with the person's symptoms, time demands related to handling crises, taking the ill relative to appointments, meeting with the treatment team, dealing with insurance and the mental health system as a whole, and coping with the burden of stigma (Marsh et al., 1993). Dealing with the mental health system, or lack thereof, can be particularly burdensome in terms of producing frustration and taking up time with telephone calls and paperwork. As the sister of a mentally ill brother commented:

> It's the mental health system that drives me crazy. It is so frustrating. They say they want me to be involved in the care of my brother, but they don't return my phone calls and give me the run-around constantly. They pay lip service to wanting families to be part of the treatment team, but the first time I met with his therapist, she refused to talk to me, citing HIPAA. My brother had signed release forms and everything. Finally, both my brother and I met with her and she still wouldn't interact with me in any kind of helpful way even after my brother asked her directly to tell me about his treatment. It makes me want to tear my hair out!

Research reported by Marsh and Dickens (1997) also indicates that the legacy left by living with a sibling or parent with mental illness poses considerable risk in terms of the well child or sibling's development, their education and career choices, their capacity for intimacy and commitment including whether to marry or have children, their future caregiving responsibilities, and the nature of coping patterns and resilience in handling stress.

Via therapeutic support and information, such as that provided by psychoeducation (discussed below), families can, however, learn to realize that there are alternatives, that is, there are ways to care for the ill member that will ease the chaos and disruption in the family and avoid losing sight of the well family members' personal goals. Families, however, are often not prepared for this task, and they need our support and guidance. It is at this phase where provision of family intervention, family education, or psychoeducation is important for the family's and ill loved one's recovery. This brings us to the last phase, "A Delicate Balance."

Phase Five: "A Delicate Balance"

Case of Velma: Phase 5

As Rufus looks back over the past couple of years since Velma was hospitalized, he thinks that, overall, they are doing well as a family. Rufus has continued to attend the bimonthly Minority Families of the Mentally Ill support group meetings, and Velma attends a support group meeting at the community mental health center for individuals living with bipolar disorder. Velma is also involved in social rhythm therapy treatment and takes Depakote and Abilify to control her symptoms and keep her moods stable. Shatoya is a lively healthy preschooler and the light of both of their lives, along with their other two children. At first, after Velma was released from the hospital, Rufus watched her every move, monitored her medication and, he ruefully recalls, hovered over her. Finally, one day, Velma told him to step back and allow her to take control of managing her illness. Realizing that Velma was actually doing a good job already at illness management and her recovery, Rufus allowed Velma space, and this relieved him of the anxiety associated with constant watchfulness. Over time, Rufus and Velma achieved their "delicate balance," caring for each other in a healthy way and allowing each other space to live their own lives as individuals in addition to their lives as a couple and family. With psychoeducation, both understand Velma's illness better, and what is helpful and not helpful in keeping everyone healthy and happy.

"A delicate balance" refers to the balance between providing caretaking for the ill loved one and living one's own life. For families to provide care for a mentally ill loved one is a good thing, but problems occur if that results in having one person shouldering all the burden or results in the family sacrificing their own lives in martyrdom to caretaking. Providing love and care to a family member in need is important, but when the task of caregiving is lifelong, as it often is in the case of serious mental illness, caregivers have to strike a balance by picking their battles and pacing their caregiving so they don't burn out. As a man whose wife has severe recurrent major depression puts it:

> I pace myself. My wife has had six severe episodes of depression over the past 20 years, and the odds are this is a lifetime disorder for her. We love each other and I meet occasionally with her therapist and treatment team, but management of her illness rests primarily with her, her social worker, and her doctor. I make sure that depression doesn't rule our lives and I make sure that I have my own life too. I have several hobbies and activities and if Mary wants to join me, fine, but if she doesn't because her mood is down, I go ahead and play my game of golf on my own.

Families learn that there are choices and many different ways to handle the challenges that mental illness brings to a family. Most importantly, families must learn that caring for themselves in addition to caring for their ill loved one is a good thing and should not bring on guilt. Caregivers who take care of themselves are better caregivers in the long run. To be open to this delicate balance view, most families need support, information, and guidance. In the next section, we discuss several approaches and resources for helping families and how these approaches, strategies, and resources can be incorporated in day-to-day social work practice.

Assess your comprehension of *the five phases families go through when mental illness emerges in a family member* by completing this quiz.

A SOCIAL WORKER'S PERSONAL ACCOUNT OF LIVING WITH A LOVED ONE WITH MENTAL ILLNESS

The following personal account, "Family Fear," is an autobiographical personal account essay written by Dawn Zuckerman, LSW. Both Dawn's mother and her late father have serious mental illness, and in her essay, Dawn describes her life growing up. Her experiences reflect many of the issues this chapter has discussed so far with regard to what families go through when mental illness is part of the family.

Family Fear

Today they are referred to as fragile families; I guess we were just that. Both my parents suffered from a serious mental illness, and though my brother and I were spared from such a diagnosis, the thought of having a family of my own fills me with fear. Dad didn't survive past my toddler years while my brother and I were placed in foster care as the system worked against our family in seamless bureaucratic fashion.

In one battle, the Public Housing Authority wanted proof that my mom had custody of her children before being allowed to move into an apartment unit. Meanwhile, the local children and youth service would not grant my mother custody until she acquired a residence, she won the battle but the war was taking its toll. Mom, a single parent, was afraid of everything: harassment, hunger, hell, and helplessness.

Rules were well established with Mom leading by example. She went every week for her shot; I thought she was so brave. At seven years old, I didn't know why she needed it, but she knew and that was enough. After she stopped, it took a few years for before we noticed signs of her psychosis. In the aftermath of a hell that lasted years, my brother and I were told that my mother and my grandfather disagreed over her choice to take medicine. He thought she was using drugs and so she stopped taking the medicine. Ironically, it was his death that provided part of the stressor for a psychotic relapse.

Children adapt to crisis, and by our teens we were accustomed. At thirteen I embraced my independent streak with pride. School, homework, church, laundry, and grocery buying were all done with care. I fought my brother; he seemed to think mom was crazy. But, she was the only one who cared about what happened to us and I desperately wanted to make her happy. I wanted her to see me as anything but evil. Unfortunately, mom's perseverations were influenced by religiosity so I was condemned before I even tried to win redemption. I was a witch and my brother was the anti-Christ, both of us deserved suspicion and righteous retribution. I remember the events of these years in small flashes of an intense terror. My anchor was unhinged and our family drifted out into an endless sea of delusion.

One day I realized I was angry. Not for beating me, forcing me to participate in repetitious tasks, or kneeling in prayer until my legs went numb. I was angry because she wasn't talking care of herself. Long ago she knew what she needed, why had she forgotten? So after a year of strange behavior, I yelled at her. Screaming about the knowledge she used to have about her illness that she had somehow forgotten. The following day she was in the hospital, having checked herself in as Mrs. Jesus Christ.

Now that the members of my small family of birth are adults, the healing process continues. My brother and I entered the world of social service. My mother endeavors endlessly to make up for things she had no power to control. She completed her autobiography and spoke to a group of people who suffer from serious mental illness about what has helped her cope. I can't put into words how proud I am of how much she keeps giving to others.

In the field of social work, we study the term codependency in class. A child of a parent with a serious mental illness has a life-long attachment that goes beyond this general term. As a child, I became the parent. My mother's paranoia constantly forced her to analyze every word in conversation, every look or gesture given by another. In the end, I wonder if she is ever certain of herself or the fact she is loved. Today we are friends more than mother and daughter. It seems those terms have blurred too much to hold true and the ties of our friendship and combined experiences stronger than biologic connection.

I am still processing the past. I adapted to crisis blindly out of need, only now decades later am I able to reflect. I still haven't been able to put the book my mom has written onto the computer. I didn't realize this underlying pain I felt regarding this chapter in our family history until I was an MSW student taking the class "Models of Intervention". The topic, during one class, was therapeutic interventions for people with schizophrenia. I saw on screen two words, Family Therapy. I cried.

The idea seems so simple, so helpful would it be for the wounded to understand what was really happening to their loved one. I lost a piece of myself that night, while looking at those words larger than life on the screen. I was joining a profession that I partly resented and blamed for my family's situation. If someone had told us or had given us some reasoning behind mom's illness we could have had tools to make the burden easier to bear. But we were very much alone, surrounded by helpers who did not seem to know how to help.

I went to the school social worker but she only wanted to know if I was being abused. I lied. I went to the hospital to visit my mother and was instructed on the rules for children in hospitals. Nothing specific to our situation was offered. Why?

We discovered my mother's diagnosis thanks to a show on PBS. I discovered that I was suffering from panic attacks because of an after school special. Our family was in fear because we were powerless against the symptoms of her illness. Imagine if we had known how to help or if she had known what was wrong?

Family education is essential for the support of those living with a serious mental illness. I may have been a child, but my mom was left alone to explain the intangible to us. To explain something she barely understood herself. Imagine how difficult it would be to tell teenagers you have lost a piece of reality?

My mother is a wonderful person who has lived with illness and been able to work. But her brother, her niece, and her husband lost their lives to mental illness. I can't help but feel they didn't have to die. If we, as professionals, empower a family with the tools to support a member who is sick, we provide that person with the best environment in which to heal.

By Dawn Zuckerman, LSW

As Dawn emphasizes in her essay, family education is essential for empowering and supporting families who have a loved one with serious mental illness. The evidence-based practice called illness management and recovery can be helpful to individuals living with mental illness in terms of learning about their illness and the types of treatment and supports that can assist in maintaining wellness. Its counterpart, family psychoeducation, is the evidence-based practice designed for families. Family psychoeducation provides information and therapeutic support to families, and is essential for enabling families to not only provide appropriate caregiving but to also be able to move forward with their own lives without guilt.

FAMILY PSYCHOEDUCATION

Introduction

When mental illness emerges in a family member, that person and those who love him or her need accurate information to help them understand the illness and its treatment along with peer and therapeutic support to help everyone in the family—both the ill person and the well members—successfully move through the phases described above and reach the goal of a healthy "delicate balance" in their lives. One of the best evidence-based interventions that meets these needs is family psychoeducation (SAMHSA, 2009). There are many models of family psychoeducation, ranging from formal program interventions derived from randomized clinical trials to brief family education courses that have not been tested for efficacy (Lefley, 2009). Many books have been written describing the various models in detail (see, e.g., Anderson, Reiss, & Hogarty, 1986; Colom & Vieta, 2006; Falloon, Boyd, & McGill, 1984; Walsh, 2010), and several research reviews and overviews of psychoeducation have been published in journals (see, e.g., Dickerson & Lehman, 2006; Dixon, McFarlane, Lefley, et al., 2001; Falloon, Held, Coverdale, et al., 1999; Marsh & Lefley, 2003; McFarlane, Dixon, Lukens, & Lucksted, 2003).

For the past 30 years, family psychoeducation has been shown to be effective in delaying relapse and rehospitalization, and enhancing illness management and family stability and quality of life for a wide range of disorders including schizophrenia, bipolar disorder, major depression, and borderline personality disorder (Gunderson & Hoffman, 2005; Lefley, 2009; McFarlane, Dixon, Lukens, & Lucksted, 2003). Family psychoeducation has several intervention components that cut across models. These components include empathic engagement, education, ongoing therapeutic support, providing treatment resources during periods of crisis, social network and social support enhancement, and teaching problem-solving and communication skills (McFarlane et al., 2003).

Although some public mental health programs have incorporated formal programs of family psychoeducation, and some practitioners have incorporated psychoeducation strategies and principles into their day-to-day practice with individual consumers and families, wide application of family psychoeducation in clinical services where clients with serious mental illness receive care has been limited. McFarland et al. (2003) suggest that this limited dissemination probably reflects attitudinal, knowledge, practical, and system-related obstacles. Overcoming these obstacles has been accomplished through collective action and consensus across stakeholders, training clinicians in the models, and providing technical consultation and supervision among patient and family advocacy organizations. By using such steps, family psychoeducation has been successfully implemented in routine clinical settings, but more needs to be done. An example of such stakeholder consensus and dissemination efforts is the Evidence-Based Practices KITs developed by the Substance Abuse and Mental Health Services Administration.

The SAMHSA Evidence-Based Practices KITs

The Evidence-Based Practices KITs were initiated by the Substance Abuse and Mental Health Services Administration in 1998 when the Robert Wood Johnson Foundation convened a panel of researchers, clinicians, administrators, consumers, and family advocates to evaluate the research on interventions for serious mental illness to determine which practices demonstrated positive outcomes across multiple research studies (SAMHSA, 2009). Research shows that simply giving written educational materials about EBPs to practitioners alone does not change practice habits (Torrey, Drake, Dixon, et al., 2001). The KITs, therefore, include materials in various formats for a wide array of stakeholder groups including public mental health authorities, agency administrators and program leaders, evidence-based practice (EBP) practitioners, consumers and family members and other supporters, for example, clergy, friends, neighbors, and employers.

These KITs, formerly called Information Resource Kits, were pilot tested in 2003 and have been refined through ongoing field testing. The valuable input of many organizations, researchers, providers, administrators, policymakers, consumers, and family members give these KITs their strength and vitality. Two philosophical tenets steer the KITs (SAMHSA, 2009). First is the tenet that consumers and families have a right to information about effective treatments and, in areas where EBPs exist, they have a right to access effective services. Second, mental health services should have the goal of helping people achieve their personal recovery goals, develop resilience, and live, work, learn, and participate in the community.

Six EBPs were identified for KIT development. These include: Illness Management and Recovery; Supported Employment; Assertive Community Treatment; Integrated Treatment for Co-Occurring Disorders (substance use and mental illness); Medication Treatment, Evaluation and Management; and Family Psychoeducation. The Family Psychoeducation KIT includes a range of teaching materials in different formats, including PowerPoint slides for presentations, brochures, videos and CD-ROMs, practice workbooks and exercises, and program guidelines. All can be accessed free via SAMHSA's website, www.samhsa.gov.

It is beyond the scope of this chapter to describe in detail all of the various models of family psychoeducation; however, one of the most established and successful models will be addressed in detail. This model was developed by social workers Carol M. Anderson, Ph.D., and Gerard E. Hogarty, MSW, along with psychologist Douglas Reiss, Ph.D., for families of adults with schizophrenia (Anderson, Reiss, & Hogarty, 1986), and is adaptable for use with clients with other serious mental illnesses. This author has been involved in directly providing family psychoeducation using the Anderson-Reiss-Hogarty model, and examples from that work will be provided for illustration (Rotondi, Anderson, Haas, et al., 2010).

Introduction to the Anderson-Reiss-Hogarty Model of Family Psychoeducation

The Anderson-Reiss-Hogarty model of family psychoeducation (hereafter in this section simply referred to as "psychoeducation") is a structured, goal-directed modality that provides both instruction/education and therapeutic emotional support to clients and their families. Psychoeducation pulls together psychotherapeutic techniques from a number of schools of practice, particularly family therapy, to promote psychosocial functioning and coping for clients and their families. This discussion of psychoeducation will use schizophrenia as the illness of focus, but the basic model can be adapted for use with other serious mental illnesses, and many of the recommendations cut across disorders.

History behind Psychoeducation

Psychoeducation for families of individuals with schizophrenia evolved from three sources: (1) research on information-processing deficits associated with schizophrenia, which formed the basis for the "attention-arousal model" of schizophrenia; (2) the body of research on the role of expressed emotion (EE) in elevating risk for relapse in individuals with schizophrenia; and (3) the family advocacy model as embodied by the work of groups such as the National Alliance on Mental Illness.

Like many other serious mental illnesses, biogenetic research clearly supports the assumption that schizophrenia involves brain disease. Genetic studies, neurophysiological findings, and responsiveness to medication all provide substantial supportive evidence (see Chapter 10). Recognition of this biogenetic etiology, however, was a major departure from the past, when psychoanalytic and family communication theories predominated as explanations for why an individual develops schizophrenia. Some of these old and now rejected theories include Fromm-Reichmann's theory of the schizophrenogenic mother who is both overprotective yet rejecting toward her child, arguing that the conflicting juxtaposition of overprotectiveness and rejection caused schizophrenia (Fromm-Reichmann, 1948). The following is an excerpt from an actual 1958 discharge statement on behalf of a 12-year-old boy with a DSM-I diagnosis of "#000-x28: Schizophrenic reaction, childhood type, improved" in which this early causal thinking is reflected:

> This 12-year-old boy was admitted to the Children's Residential Treatment Service on October 13, 1956. Admission for residential treatment had been decided upon because, in the opinion of the individual therapist and social worker of the parents, insufficient progress was being made on an outpatient basis . . . also, the parents were becoming increasingly anxious and uncomfortable in having him at home. Although not overtly rejecting, the parents felt tremendously self-conscious about his behavior in the face of neighborhood and small town opinion. The original chief complaints were withdrawn and inappropriate behavior, lack of social awareness, obsessions and fears, and poor school performance. The mother was very concerned and protective, however during individual treatment sessions, the boy revealed feelings of rejection and lack of protection from his mother.

Another prominent but rejected theory was that schizophrenia was caused by dysfunctional interaction patterns in families, which resulted in therapists not just blaming mothers but blaming the whole family for the development of serious mental illness, especially psychotic disorders such as schizophrenia. This gave birth to concepts such as "marital skew," "marital schism" (Lidz, Fleck, & Cornelison, 1965; Lidz & Lidz, 1949), and the so-called "double-bind" theory (Bateson, Jackson, Haley, & Weakland, 1956). Marital skew refers to a marriage in which one parent significantly dominates the other to the detriment of the family. A marital schism occurs when the parents have conflicting views about child rearing and other family concerns, which causes the marital couple's child to be psychologically torn by divided loyalties and, thus, at risk for developing schizophrenia.

The double-bind theory argues that schizophrenia is caused by the individual being placed in situations with conflicting demands that cannot be met simultaneously, and this failure to fulfill the contradictory demands is punished by, for example, withdrawal of love, support, and protection. All of these theories essentially promoted views of the family as a pathogenic agent to be blamed and then cured. Such views served to create much anguish and guilt in parents—particularly mothers. What is amazing is that such theories persisted in spite of the lack of any systematic empirical support (Ferreira & Winter, 1965; Sharan, 1966). Today, enlightened clinicians view families as resources and partners in helping the schizophrenic family member, not as causes of the illness or as adversaries for treatment.

Current Theoretical Models for Understanding Schizophrenia

There are several theoretical concepts that, combined, form the basis for the development of the psychoeducation model and psychoeducation intervention strategies for schizophrenia and other severe and persistent mental illnesses. These concepts include: (1) the stress-vulnerability-coping-competence model of causality; (2) the stimulus window; (3) the attention-arousal model; and (4) expressed emotion.

(1) The Stress-Vulnerability-Coping-Competence Model of Causality

Current state-of-the-art schizophrenia research advocates the stress-vulnerability-coping-competence model of causality, which is in keeping with both biogenetic findings and a biopsychosocial approach to treatment. The stress-vulnerability-coping-competence model of causality is also one of the theoretical bases for psychoeducation (Cardno, Marshall, Coid, et al., 1999; Nuechterlein & Dawson, 1984; Nuechterlein, Dawson, Ventura, et al., 1994; Yank, Bentley, & Hargrove, 1993). The basic premise is that schizophrenia can result in an individual who has (1) a genetic vulnerability for schizophrenia; (2) a low threshold for tolerating stress; and (3) inadequate coping strategies. For someone with such vulnerabilities, in the face of a socio-environmental stressor, an episode of schizophrenia may result.

(2) The Stimulus Window

A related concept is what is called the "stimulus window," which refers to the level of sensory stimulation an individual can tolerate and the range within which one can function (Williams, 1989). For clients with schizophrenia, this means that although a certain amount of internal and external stimulation is desirable, too much or too little stimulation can result in an exacerbation of symptoms. For example, too little stimulation can lead to regression and an exacerbation of negative symptoms (negative symptoms refer to behaviors that everyone should have, such as energy, emotions, and motivation), while too much stimulation can lead to an exacerbation of activating psychotic symptoms (hallucinations, delusions, disorganized thoughts). Furthermore, the range of stimuli tolerated in an individual's "stimulus window" is biologically based and is not something under the individual's voluntary control. Furthermore, it is very individualized—some individuals are inherently able to handle more stimulation than others are.

(3) The Attention-Arousal Model

A similar model directly relevant to understanding schizophrenia is the "attention-arousal model." The attention-arousal model of schizophrenia pathophysiology posits that individuals with schizophrenia have difficulty in processing and handling information and other forms of stimulation. Like with the stimulus window, these deficits are biologically based and not something the individual can control. What happens is that as the demands for information and stimulation processing increase, the individual becomes more distracted, disorganized, and aroused, particularly if the individual is not taking medication that could serve to "buffer" the arousal. External demands for information processing also serve to increase the internal stimuli, that is, the symptoms of the illness, such as hallucinations, delusions, and disordered thoughts. The result is that the individual with schizophrenia is bombarded externally by demands from the environment and internally by elevated symptoms. Each source of arousal exacerbates the other, leads to increasing distraction, dis-attention, and increasing arousal, and this goes around and around like an ever-intensifying "wheel" (Anderson et al., 1986; Tecce & Cole, 1976). The following steps summarize the process:

- First, the person with schizophrenia has a "core psychological deficit" that is biologically based;
- Second, this deficit affects the ability of the individual to select, sort, filter, and evaluate stimuli;
- This deficit results in a lack of ability to differentiate what stimuli is relevant and what could be screened out, thus, the person attempts to attend to all of the stimuli;
- All of the incoming stimuli demand information processing;
- Attending to all incoming stimuli is overly arousing, which results in diffuse responses and hyperarousal, both internally and externally;
- As these demands increase, the individual becomes increasingly distracted, inattentive, and overly aroused, that is, overwhelmed by the stimuli; and
- Finally, the person with schizophrenia copes with all these demands by responding in dysfunctional ways, for example, experiencing hallucinations, delusions, withdrawal, or aggressive behavior.

The most appropriate and effective intervention for buffering arousal and reducing symptoms involves (1) medication, which can serve to modify and buffer the internal conditions associated with arousal and attention deficits, thus reducing vulnerability, and (2) therapeutic intervention with families, which can reduce excessive external stimulation. Like the assumptions underlying the stimulus window, the attention-arousal model assumes that some stimulation is desirable, but excessive stimulation is not. Thus, low-key nonintrusive social interaction facilitates psychosocial functioning for the ill individual, while intensive and demanding interaction is detrimental to the individual's well-being.

(4) Expressed Emotion

The term "expressed emotion" (EE), refers to the level of critical, hostile, and emotionally overinvolved statements and attitudes that caretakers of an individual with serious mental illness express toward the ill person. Such caretakers may be family members, program staff, or other individuals in the role of providing care for the ill person. High levels of EE have been shown, in multiple studies, to be positively related to risk of relapse (Hooley, 1985; Kuipers, 1979; Kuipers, Sturgeon, Berkowitz, & Ixff, 1983).

The extent to which expressed emotion is high or low has been studied using taped interviews coded according to a structured evaluation called the Camberwell Family Interview (Kottgen, Mollenbauer, Sonnischen, Jurth, & Hand, 1983). Families whose members engage in communications high in expressed emotion are more likely to cause illness relapse in their ill relatives than families whose communication is low in expressed emotion. These findings have held for individuals with schizophrenia, bipolar disorder, borderline personality disorder, and learning and developmental disabilities.

To decrease risk of relapse, then, families can learn to change how they communicate with the ill relative by learning low expressed emotion communication skills. So, for example, a family member who tends to be overly intrusive in the ill relative's decision making learns to step back and encourage client self-determination and autonomy even if the family member "can do it better." It is also important to note that the kind of high emotional stimulation that can exacerbate someone's symptoms does not have to be overtly negative, such as arguing and family disagreements. An event such as a wedding or a large family gathering can also create too much excitement and stimulation for a person with a serious mental illness like schizophrenia.

Assess your comprehension of *the theoretical models underlying the development of psychoeducation for individuals with schizophrenia and their families* by completing this quiz.

The stress-vulnerability-coping-competence model of causality and the attention-arousal model plus the findings on expressed emotion led to the development of the psychoeducation approach. As noted before, there are many models of family psychoeducation and different forms of implementation, but we will focus on one of the most well known, which is the Anderson-Reiss-Hogarty model of family psychoeducation (Anderson, Reiss, & Hogarty, 1986).

The Anderson-Reiss-Hogarty (ARH) Model of Family Psychoeducation

The Anderson-Reiss-Hogarty model of family psychoeducation is client and family centered and fosters adaptation of the client to community life by engaging family in efforts to (1) reduce stress by developing a stable predictable family environment; (2) promote medication compliance to enable symptom control; and (3) ease the family's guilt by providing factual information about the ill relative's mental disorder and its treatment, course, and prognosis.

Development of a stable and predictable family environment is characterized by clear communication, consistent specified boundaries, and minimal criticism, hostility/rejection, and emotional overinvolvement, that is, expressed emotion. The ARH model is task centered, proceeds by small incremental steps consistent with a typical client's rate of recovery after an illness episode, and both family therapy and educational principles frame the techniques and strategies used. The model has four stages: (1) connection; (2) the survival skills workshop; (3) re-entry and application; and (4) maintenance. Each stage is summarized in Table 1 on the following page:

Table 1 Phases of the Treatment Process in the ARH Psychoeducation Model

Phase	Goals	Techniques
Phase I: Connection	* Connect with the family and enlist cooperation with the program * Decrease guilt, emotionality, negative reactions to the illness * Reduce the level of family stress	* Joining with the family * Establishing a treatment contract * Discussing the family's crisis history and feelings about the patient and illness * Empathy * Specific practical suggestions that mobilize concerns into effective coping
Phase II: The Survival Skills Workshop	* Increased understanding of illness and client's needs by family * Continued reduction of family stress * De-isolation and enhancement of social support networks	* Multiple families (for education, support, and discussion) * Concrete data about schizophrenia * Concrete illness and family management suggestions * Teaching communication skills
Phase III: Re-entry and Application	* Promoting client maintenance in the community * Strengthening marital/parental coalition * Increasing family tolerance for low-level dysfunctional behaviors * Promoting the gradual resumption of responsibility by the client	* Reinforcement of boundaries (generational and interpersonal) * Task or "homework" assignments * Low-key problem solving
Phase IV: Maintenance	* Reintegration into normal roles in community systems * Increased effectiveness of general family processes	* Infrequent maintenance sessions * Traditional or exploratory family therapy techniques

Phase I: Connection

Phase I begins during the client's acute hospitalization, that is, the "rude awakening" phase for the family and client. While the client is in the hospital, the social worker meets with the family, explains what the psychoeducation program entails, and begins the process. The goals at this stage are to develop a working alliance (a.k.a., rapport) with the family, actively decrease guilt, and work with the family to reduce stress. Methods for reaching these goals include assuming a nonjudgmental empathic attitude, eliciting and acknowledging the family's feelings and experiences, and establishing the social worker's role as an advocate for the family.

Case Example:

In this example, the 18-year-old client, John, has been hospitalized for the first time after a psychotic break. The parents meet with the social worker on the inpatient unit after visiting their son in his room. They are exhausted and feeling scared, anxious, and overwhelmed.

SW: Mr. and Mrs. Jones, it is very nice to meet you. My name is Valerie Jackson and I am the clinical social worker here on the unit. I met with your son John briefly this morning and he seems to be doing better. I imagine that this has been a very difficult time for you. How are you both doing? *(said with sincere concern and empathy)*

Mr. J: (runs his hand through his hair) Yes, it's . . . it's been really hard. I don't know where to begin . . . John first started acting strange about a month ago. . . . *(Mr. Jones continues and describes John's increasingly reclusive behavior, periods of agitation, sleepless nights, and finally a suicide attempt, in which the paramedics were called along with the police and John was taken to the emergency room and subsequently hospitalized)*

Mrs. J: I don't understand what is happening. The doctor says John is psychotic . . . mentally ill! What did we do wrong? Why didn't we see things were getting out of control? I don't understand how this happened.

SW: You didn't do anything wrong and you are not to blame for John's illness. We need to observe John a little longer to confirm exactly what is going on in terms of his illness, but we do know that it didn't occur because of anything either of you did wrong. It sounds like you are very loving parents and tried your best to help John during this difficult time. You must be feeling scared and overwhelmed right now, which is very normal. *(use of empathy)*

Mr. J: It is?

SW: Yes. What you are feeling is very normal and understandable. My role here with you is to support you, help you understand John's illness, provide you with information about the treatment he will be getting, and be your advocate with the treatment team.

Mrs. J: Oh, that's a relief. We just don't know what we should be doing first with all that has happened. It's good to know we have someone to go to. This is all new to us.

SW: I'm definitely here for you. . . . *(pause)* . . . One of the things we will be doing together is something called "family psychoeducation." Family psychoeducation involves me—and the treatment team—providing you with information about your son's illness and how it is treated, and you can ask me any questions you have as we go along. John will join our meetings once he feels better so he can learn about and understand his illness and how to get well and stay well. Later you will meet with me and other families in the same boat to give each other information and share experiences, and we will all work together on this, and I'll be with you to help every step of the way.

Mr. J: That sounds good. I don't know about the part about meeting with other families—we don't know anyone who has gone through this. . . . It might be kind of embarrassing, you know. . . .

SW: All of the families we'll be getting together with have a loved one who has a mental illness—in most cases their loved one was recently hospitalized, just like with John. Their experiences won't be exactly like yours, but you will all have a lot in common because you're dealing with similar issues. It can be helpful to be with others who understand where you're coming from and share your experiences—they will have walked in your shoes at least to some extent. Families I have worked with before have found meeting with other families very helpful.

Mrs. J: Okay, I guess we have nothing to lose.

Initially, during the connection phase, the social worker meets with the family once or twice per week, and when the ill family member's psychotic symptoms recede, then he or she joins the family sessions. Given that the length of inpatient stays have been drastically curtailed in most settings, the social worker might meet with the family once or twice on consecutive days, and then the ill member joins a third meeting before discharge occurs.

The Issue of Family Guilt

An important topic to address at this juncture is the issue of family guilt, as illustrated in the dialogue above. Many families are well aware of the old parent and family-blaming theories that, although discredited, still affect some clinicians' attitudes towards families and contribute significantly to family guilt. For example, a 1998 survey study by Rubin, Cardenas, Warren, Pike, and Wambach revealed that, although clinicians acknowledge biological causal factors in serious mental illness, "they believe that parental and family culpability are also important causes" (Rubin, Cardenas, Warren, Pike, & Wambach, 1998, p. 420).

As a social work clinician, it is important to be respectful at all times toward families and avoid blaming in any way, shape, or form. It can be helpful to state this directly, as in the example above when the social worker explicitly stated that Joe's illness is not the parents' fault and validated that they are loving parents. In psychoeducation, families are encouraged to openly discuss their experiences in caring for the ill relative and the difficulties they have endured. As part of the process, some families may also talk about their positive and negative experiences with other mental health programs, and respectful empathic listening is important. The social work clinician's role in Phase I includes keeping the family informed of the client's progress, working with the treatment team, and acting as the family's representative or liaison. The family's emotional involvement—including what might be viewed as overinvolvement—is reframed as concern, and the family's feelings of helplessness and being overwhelmed is rechanneled into a commitment to perform tasks that are constructive to their relative's recovery. The conclusion of Phase I is marked by (1) development of a treatment contract that includes negotiating specific, realistic, and attainable goals, and (2) establishing "rules" for family treatment (which begins in Phase III) (Anderson et al., 1986). For example, the contract might state that:

- The family will meet regularly with the clinician for an hour every 2 weeks for X amount of time;
- All family members are allowed time to speak during sessions, and no family member may speak for another family member;
- Loss of control physically or emotionally is not allowed during a family session, and if that happens, the family session will be terminated or a "time out" will be required; and
- Everyone agrees and accepts the reality that progress will take place in small "baby" steps, recognizing that recovery doesn't occur overnight.

This then concludes Phase I.

Phase II: The Survival Skills Workshop

Phase II is the "Survival Skills Workshop," which is an all-day event offered early in the ill relative's treatment, and several families participate in the workshop together. A major component of the survival skills workshop is the communication of factual, up-to-date information about the illness of focus (in this case, schizophrenia) and its treatment. The multifamily format of the workshop promotes sharing and the development of a social support network. As noted before, in the discussion of the five phases families go through as the ill relative becomes ill, by the time an ill relative receives professional treatment, many families have become isolated and alone. The workshop experience shows families that they are not alone, and that other families have had similar experiences and struggles and have survived them.

A survival skills workshop on schizophrenia would provide the following information to the families:

- What schizophrenia is
- The biological genesis of schizophrenia

- The private, inner personal experience of schizophrenia
- The public experience of schizophrenia from the perspective of families and friends
- The course of schizophrenia
- The prognosis associated with the illness of schizophrenia
- Treatment modalities and who provides the treatment
- Medication—the therapeutic effects and side effects and how to cope with them
- The impact of stress on the course of schizophrenia
- Family strategies to reduce stress
- The nature of effective communication in the family
- How to avoid social isolation and develop a good social support network
- Helpful community resources for families and consumers

Families are also introduced to strategies to help modulate stress and promote a stable, predictable family environment to modify stimulation (Anderson, Reiss, & Hogarty, 1986). Examples could include:

1. How to establish realistic expectations for the ill relative that are concrete and specific and not too demanding, which risks overstimulation and a setup for failure. For example, "Joe will dry the dishes each night after dinner."
2. How to temporarily revise or modify expectations for recovery, for example, helping families to understand that for many individuals, recovery from a psychotic episode can take time, just like recovery takes time when someone has a massive heart attack. Recovery may be slow, and at times there may be setbacks and plateaus; thus, modifying expectations can help avoid frustration and dashing unrealistic hope.
3. How to set limits without feeling anxious or guilty in order to reduce overstimulation and avoid burning out family resources. For example, an appropriate limit might be "Joe cannot go into other family members' rooms and intrusively poke through their personal possessions." Limits should also be set simply and clearly, for example, "Going into other family members' rooms and poking through their personal possessions is not acceptable."
4. How to set boundaries through distancing, which helps avoid intense emotional overinvolvement. Strategies for this include avoiding criticism and conflict, developing interests outside the family, and considering the needs of all family members, rather than focusing exclusively on the ill member's needs.
5. Learning how to do "structuring," which means having regular family routines and rules for family life to keep the family environment stable and predictable.
6. How to appropriately use "time outs" when conflicts occur to keep them from escalating and overstimulating the ill relative.

As part of the workshop, families identify behaviors they can tolerate (e.g., wearing mismatched clothes), and behaviors they will not tolerate (e.g., physical abuse). Special attention is given to how to effectively communicate with the ill person. Because individuals with schizophrenia have difficulty processing information, families are taught to keep requests clear, low-key, and simple. In general, families are taught regular basic communication and active listening skills, for example, using "I messages."

To give the reader an idea of how the survival skills workshop is laid out in terms of time frame and content, the following is an actual schedule of a survival skills workshop that the author co-facilitated:

Psychoeducation Survival Skills Workshop

9:00–9:15 Coffee and informal discussion
9:15–9:30 Formal introductions and explanation of the format for the day
9:30–10:30 Schizophrenia: What is it?

History and epidemiology

Treatment and misunderstanding causes
There is often a big difference after families are told what actually causes schizophrenia
Explain the misunderstanding of the disease and that we still do not know a lot now

The personal experience—This is from the consumer's point of view and there are two options:

Option #1: A consumer can talk to the families about what it is like to be psychotic
Option #2: Families can read part of "The Inner World of Madness" by E. Fuller Torrey

The public experience:

What the family first notices, early warning symptoms, etc.
What schizophrenia looks like from the outside

Psychobiology:

Causes—The stress-vulnerability-coping-competence model, stimulus window, attention-arousal model, and the concept of expressed emotion
Can have simple diagrams of synapses and the brain that underscore that schizophrenia is a biologically based illness

10:30–10:45 Coffee break and informal discussion
10:45–12:00 Treatment of schizophrenia
The use of antipsychotic medication
Why medication is needed
How medication works
The impact of medication on illness outcome and recovery
Side effects and how to cope with them and minimize them
Psychosocial treatment—who provides it, what treatments are effective for illness of focus
Effects of psychosocial treatment on the course of the illness
Other treatment and management issues

12:00–1:00 Lunch and informal discussion to facilitate social support

** ***Lunch is very important to the workshop*** **

1:00–3:30 The family and schizophrenia
The needs of the patient (Vulnerable to external and internal stimuli)
The needs of the family (Tendency for families to build life around client)
Family reactions to the illness (Grieving process)
Common problems that patients and families face

What the family can do to help
Revise expectations

Create barriers to overstimulation
Set limits
Selectively ignore certain behaviors
Keep communication simple
Support medication regime
Normalize the family routine
Recognize signals for help
How to use professionals

3:30–4:00 Wrap up
Questions regarding specific problems
Informal interaction

Following completion of the survival skills workshop, the next phase in the psychoeducation process is "Re-Entry and Application."

Phase III: Re-Entry and Application

In Phase III, the primary goals include promoting the client's psychosocial functioning and maintenance in the community, strengthening the marital/parental coalition in the family, increasing the family's tolerance for low-level dysfunctional behaviors, and promoting the gradual resumption of responsibility by the client.

Re-entry begins when the client leaves the hospital and usually lasts around 6 months. In this phase, the social worker schedules family sessions including the client once every 2 to 3 weeks in accordance with the family's and client's needs. Crisis phone calls and emergency sessions are accommodated as needed and used to help the family learn crisis resolution skills. A problem-solving, task-centered approach is primarily used as the main strategy, sessions address current problems, and homework assignments are used for practicing the skills learned in the survival skills workshop. Examples of topics addressed during this phase include:

- Strategies to promote medication adherence;
- The client's regular participation in household activities; and
- Recognizing and addressing early warning signs of relapse (e.g., when to call professionals for help, encouraging self-help) along with identifying sources of behavior changes leading to relapse, which can lead to addressing remedies.

Once the goals of Phase III have been achieved, the family is ready to move to Phase IV, "Maintenance."

Phase IV: Maintenance

The final maintenance phase involves continued treatment or disengagement, and is oriented toward consolidating and maintaining the goals achieved and the resumption of normal living. There are many options for families at this stage. Families may choose to terminate treatment entirely, elect to have periodic maintenance sessions with the clinician, continue to work on previous goals, or develop a new contract in which other problems are addressed. Anderson et al. (1986) emphasize that this phase is optional for families. Overall, family psychoeducation has been proven to be very helpful for both families and consumers in terms of educating everyone about the illness(es), treatments available, and how to promote family stability and wellness. It has also been shown to be helpful across diverse groups of clients and families (see, e.g., Kopelowicz, Zarate, Wallace, et al., 2012).

Assess your comprehension of *the four phases of the Anderson-Reiss-Hogarty model of family psychoeducation* by taking this short quiz.

Another source of continuing independent support is reading books written by mental health professionals, family advocates, and consumers that provide information and support in a way that is user-friendly to families and consumers. Finally, it is important that social workers connect families with self-help and advocacy groups. A list of these is provided at the end of the chapter, and a couple of them are discussed below.

SELF-HELP AND ADVOCACY RESOURCES FOR FAMILIES

Two self-help/advocacy resources will be highlighted here. The first is Julie Tallard Johnson's eight-step self-help healing process (Johnson, 1988, 2007), and the other is the National Alliance on Mental Illness, in particular, its successful Family-to-Family Education Program (www.nami.org).

Julie Tallard Johnson's Eight-Stage Self-Help Healing Process

This chapter began with a discussion of how the emergence of mental illness in a family member brings families to crisis and the five phases that most families go through as they try to cope with the ill member's symptoms and changes in behavior, connect with professional help, and then, hopefully, reach the goal of achieving a "delicate balance," that is, providing care for the ill relative, but also caring for oneself and the well family members. The question now is: How can families continue the healing and maintain the balance in their family life?

As the field of addictions has shown (see, e.g., Emrick, 1987), self-help step-wise programs can be valuable adjuncts to professional help. One model, developed by social worker Julie Tallard Johnson (1988, 2007), is an eight-stage self-help program designed specifically for families and friends of individuals with mental illness. The steps can be worked through consecutively by individual caregivers or families on their own via self-reflection and journaling, or as part of an organized group. Such groups can be initiated and facilitated by a social worker or other mental health professional, or by a family member. Johnson's books provide user-friendly detail on exactly how to put a group together, how to conduct a group, and about the process of going through each of the eight stages. Below, each of the eight steps is identified and briefly reviewed. The reader is encouraged to delve further into the details of the program by consulting Johnson's excellent books.

The first stage of the Eight-Stage Healing Process is *awareness*: "I explore the ways in which the relationship/family has affected my life" (Johnson, 2007, p. 160). In this stage, the individual or family reviews and reflects on their relationship with the ill relative, and relationships with other family members, and inventories how those relationships reciprocally affect and are intertwined with each other. Stage One raises awareness and begins the process of identifying feelings about current and past relationships, and where the strengths and problems are/were, including the evolving one with the ill family member.

The second stage is *validation*: "I identify my feelings about this relationship and share those feelings with others" (Johnson, 2007, p. 164). In this step, the individual or family confronts the presence of denial of the relative's illness along with confronting any denial of feelings about the illness. Such denied and often painful feelings include anger, guilt, fear, sadness, grief, resentment, and embarrassment or shame (Johnson, 2007). To make peace with such feelings, the feelings must be acknowledged and shared with others who can understand and validate them. Example:

> Marie recalls how she could never talk to her mother openly about her feelings toward her brother, who had severe bipolar disorder. If she hinted at any feelings of anger or resentment during her brother's repeated crises, which Marie was often

asked to handle by her family, her mother would accuse her of hating her brother. Later, when Marie finally shared her feelings with a therapist, the therapist told her that she clearly was a loving sister and validated not only the value of her caretaking but that her feelings of anger and resentment were valid and understandable. This enabled Marie to let go of the guilt she felt about her feelings and move toward setting some limits with her family and her brother while still maintaining a positive relationship with him. The relationship with her mother, however, remained ambivalent and rocky.

The third stage is *acceptance*: "I accept that I cannot control any other person's behavior and that I am ultimately responsible only for my own emotional well-being" (Johnson, 2007, p. 165). Many times family members are pulled into feeling responsible for a mentally ill relative's emotional well-being, which is part of the subjective burden discussed earlier in this chapter. This is a heavy burden to bear, is potentially endless, and is ultimately not helpful even to the ill person because it absolves the ill person of taking responsibility for his or her emotions and behavior, which is essential for personal recovery. This issue is often central for families who have a relative with an illness involving unstable moods and emotions, such as bipolar disorder or borderline personality disorder. Johnson (2007) suggests that what can be helpful is for the well members to set good examples for the ill member and model strategies supportive of emotional well-being.

The fourth stage is *challenge*: "I examine my expectations of myself and others and make a commitment to challenge any negative expectations (silent agreements)" (Johnson, 2007, p. 168). Expectations about oneself and one's relationships with others is shaped by one's family. The family (however it is individually defined) is the primary socialization group for most individuals and the primary source for meeting its members' social, economic, educational, emotional, spiritual, and health and mental health care needs. It is also within the family that one's psychosocial and spiritual development is formed and vital roles are learned. Like other systems, family interaction is reciprocal interaction in that all members influence and are influenced by every other member. This reciprocal interaction creates a system governed by a set of implicit rules specifying the roles, power structures, forms of communication, and ways of negotiating and solving problems in the family.

In families with a loved one with mental illness, there may be expectations for family members and beliefs about those expectations that may be silent and implicit, even though everyone knows what they are. For example, a child with a mentally ill parent may be expected by the family to care for that mentally ill parent when the child reaches adulthood, an expectation that holds profound implications for that child's future life. Although providing care for a parent in need can be a positive thing, expecting that the child should sacrifice his or her own life choices for the sake of caretaking has negative implications. Such expectations must be openly examined and discussed within the family and the silent agreements brought out into the open in order for each member to exercise their self-determination with regard to caretaking responsibilities, along with looking at all the alternatives for meeting the ill relative's caretaking needs. For example, if there are multiple siblings in a family with a mentally ill parent, rather than expecting that one sibling will shoulder all the care, the siblings could agree to take turns and share the caretaking. This is easier said than done, however, and it is not unusual for some family members to refuse to help or escape geographically to avoid helping.

The fifth stage is *releasing guilt*: "I recognize mental illness as a disease and release the attitude of blame" (Johnson, 2007, p. 171). This step directly challenges the notion that someone or something is to blame for the loved one's mental illness. Most serious mental illnesses have a biological basis upon which the environment impinges, but mental illness is not caused by the family and the family does not need to feel guilt. Furthermore, this step challenges the assumption of over-responsibility, that is, feeling that one must sacrifice one's own life on the altar of caretaking or else one should feel guilt. Many of the distancing and limit-setting strategies taught in psychoeducation can help relieve guilt and mitigate over-responsibility for family members and, ultimately, this stance is more helpful to the ill loved one than assumption of guilt would be. Family members must learn to accept the reality that they did not cause the illness, they can't control the illness, and they can't cure the illness (Johnson, 2007, p. 174). This can go far in releasing feelings of guilt.

The sixth stage is *forgiveness*: "I forgive myself for any mistakes I have made. I forgive and release those who have harmed me" (Johnson, 2007, p. 175). For the past 20 years, there has been increasing interest in a model of intervention called "forgiveness therapy," which focuses on mitigating feelings of anger, anxiety, and depression resulting from various forms of abuse and trauma (Lin, Mack, Enright, et al., 2004). Research suggests that forgiveness can be positive and focusing on forgiveness in psychotherapy can be helpful in improving self-esteem, feelings of empowerment, and finding positive meaning from negative life experiences (Reed & Enright, 2006). "Forgiveness" does not mean that the threatening and abusive behavior of a mentally ill family member is acceptable. What it means is that the other family members learn to acknowledge mistakes they may have made and harm that others have caused them and, then, how to release the feelings of resentment, anger, old hurts, and painful memories festering within "so that they no longer clutter your mind and weigh down your relationships" (Johnson, 2007, p. 174). Forgiveness can bring emotional freedom.

The seventh stage is *self-esteem*: "I return the focus of my life to myself and appreciate my own worth, despite what may be going on around me" (Johnson, 2007, p. 179). Living with someone with mental illness can be difficult. Years of living from crisis to crisis, years of waiting for the other shoe to drop during periods of stability, and years of failure to "cure" the ill person and return them to the person they used to be can leave family members feeling hopeless and worthless. As social workers, we know the importance of affirming the worth and dignity of every client, but many of our clients don't see the worth and dignity in themselves. Helping family members to reframe self-negating thoughts into self-affirming thoughts is central to this step. Johnson (2007) suggests that the practice of mindfulness via meditation or mindfulness exercises is one approach that can help family members return attention to themselves and their well-being instead of just focusing on the problems of the ill person. Mindfulness can also help in managing stress and achieving the ability to pull back and decrease emotional overinvolvement with the ill person.

The eighth and final stage is *growth*: "I reaffirm my accomplishments and set daily, monthly, and yearly goals" (Johnson, 2007, p. 182). This last step helps family members to take control of their own lives rather than allowing their lives to completely revolve around the ill person. Setting realistic measurable goals can help family members put into action the affirming thoughts developed during the previous step. These goals do not exclude providing care for the ill person, but put that caretaking within the larger context of other life goals. Family members learn that they do not have to sacrifice their own goals for the sake of providing care for the ill person. Here is what can happen if that does not occur:

> Fidel remembers how his mother, although she was a very traditional Puerto Rican woman, always dreamed of finishing high school and then going to community college to become a nurse. But then Fidel's sister, Marisol, developed schizophrenia. Fidel's father told his mother that she must keep Marisol home and take care of her, and it was years before Fidel's father finally acquiesced to getting Marisol some professional help. By then, Fidel's mother had given up her dreams. He recalls sadly how she said one day that "wanting to be a nurse was just a foolish idea. My job is to take care of my family, to take care of Marisol."

Sadly, many family members put their lives on hold, waiting indefinitely for the ill person to be cured before they move on with their own lives. The goal for most individuals with serious mental illness is *recovery*, not cure, and the goal for family members is also recovery in the form of that delicate balance between providing reasonable caregiving but also having their own fulfilling lives.

One of the most important sources of information and support for families with a loved one with mental illness, and for the professionals who work with them, is the National Alliance on Mental Illness. The next section will review what NAMI offers to families and professionals as families move through the stages of recovery and achieving life balance.

The National Alliance on Mental Illness (NAMI) Resources

As noted in Chapter 2, the National Alliance on Mental Illness (NAMI) (formerly the National Alliance for the Mentally Ill), founded in 1979, is the largest grassroots advocacy group in existence today for families and friends of individuals with mental illness. NAMI has multiple affiliates in every state in the United States and in many other countries worldwide. NAMI provides support to families and individuals affected by mental illness, provides education to families and communities about mental illness, and is involved in multiple advocacy efforts on behalf of families and consumers. NAMI is an indispensable resource for social workers because it provides a wide range of programs and services that can supplement professionally delivered family and consumer interventions. NAMI's programs and services include the following:

- The *NAMI Center for Excellence* works to provide NAMI's state chapters and NAMI affiliates with technical assistance, resources, and tools needed to achieve the goals for consumers and families that NAMI has set through their Standards of Excellence.
- *NAMI's state chapters and local NAMI divisions* provide information and support related to local and state-relevant services, support, and opportunities for consumers and families.
- *Consumer Support* provides support and education for individuals living with mental illness to meet their needs around care, treatment, services, mutual support, and consumer rights.
- *Child and Adolescent Action Center* provides help to families with children and adolescents who have mental illness, including assistance in efforts to reform the mental health system serving children and adolescents.
- *NAMI on Campus* is a network of student-led and college-supported groups providing mental health awareness, education, and advocacy specific to the needs of each particular college student community.
- *The NAMI Multicultural Action Center* focuses on system reform to eliminate racial/ethnic/cultural disparities in mental health care for diverse communities and ensure cultural competence in services for all people affected by serious mental illness.
- *The NAMI Legal Center* provides legal consultation and lawyer referrals for issues faced by individuals living with mental illness and their families.
- *The NAMI Veterans Resource Center* provides resources and supports for veterans and active duty military members, as well as their families, friends, and advocates.
- *Missing Persons Support* supplements established law enforcement procedures by providing resources and support for locating missing persons with mental illness.
- *The NAMI Providers' Website* was developed by NAMI specifically for mental health services providers to enable them to assist their clients and families better.

- *NAMI Information Helpline* is staffed by trained volunteers who can provide information, referrals, and support to all stakeholders who have questions about or are affected by serious mental illness. The number is 1-800-950-NAMI.
- *The NAMI Education, Training and Peer Support Center* provides a range of education and training programs and services for consumers, family members, providers, and the general public. These programs and services include Family-to-Family, Peer-to-Peer, NAMI Support Group, and In Our Own Voice.

(Source: www.nami.org, retrieved June 15, 2011)

NAMI's Family-to-Family Education Program (FFEP)

NAMI's Family-to-Family Education Program (FFEP) must be highlighted in its own section because it serves as a central resource for families with a mentally ill relative. The program is a 12-week course taught by trained family members and is designed for family caregivers of individuals with serious mental illness. The course, course materials, and instruction are provided at no cost to class participants and, as of 2011, over 115,000 family members nationwide have graduated from the program.

The course covers (1) up-to-date information about schizophrenia, major depression, bipolar disorder (manic depression), panic disorder, obsessive-compulsive disorder, borderline personality disorder, and co-occurring mental illnesses and addictive disorders; (2) current information about medication and strategies for supporting medication adherence; and (3) information about effective treatments for mental illness and how these treatments work. The course also provides families with a better understanding of the experience of living with mental illness, which can increase empathy and teaches problem-solving, communication, and listening skills. Strategies for handling relapse and crises are taught along with information and skills for reducing caregiver subjective and objective burden. In some respects, the FFEP is like an extended psychoeducation survival skills workshop. Research has shown that the FFEP is helpful to family members by reducing subjective burden, increasing feelings of empowerment, increasing knowledge about serious mental illness and the mental health system, and teaching self-care (Dixon, Lucksted, Stewart, et al., 2004).

List of Additional Resources for Families and Other Caregivers of Individuals with Serious Mental Illness

1. _____ American Health Care Association: www.ahca.org
2. _____ Borderline Personality Disorder Resource Center: www.bpdresourcecenter.org
3. _____ Depressive and Bipolar Support Alliance (DBSA): www.DBSAlliance.org
4. _____ Family Caregiver Alliance: www.caregiver.org
5. _____ Families for Depression Awareness (FDA): www.familyaware.org
6. _____ Mental Health America (formerly known as the National Mental Health Association): www.mentalhealthamerica.net
7. _____ National Alliance for Caregiving: www.caregiving.org
8. _____ National Alliance on Mental Illness Family-to-Family Program: www.nami.org
9. _____ National Education Alliance for Borderline Personality Disorder (NEA-BPD) Family Connections: www.borderlinepersonalitydisorder.com
10. _____ National Institute of Mental Health: www.nimh.nih.gov
11. _____ Well Spouse Association: www.wellspouse.org

(Source: Lefley, 2009)

CONCLUSION

Serious mental illness affects not only the ill person, but can profoundly affect the person's entire family. The presence of mental illness in a family member affects how family members relate to one another, it affects the choices families make about their lives and what activities to engage in and, in sum, pervasively affects every aspect of family life. Families typically go through several phases as they adjust to the loved one's illness, hopefully eventually arriving at a delicate balance between providing caretaking for the ill loved one and living their own lives. Psychoeducation, often provided by social workers, is the key intervention for helping families move toward understanding and balance.

Fortunately, today, there is less of a focus on blaming families for the illness of their loved one; rather, the focus is on solutions that will benefit all of the members of the family, both the well members and the ill member. Family members are increasingly viewed as less a cause of mental illness, than as "hidden victims" who must be partners with the ill person and the treatment team on the journey toward recovery. This view has helped demystify mental illness, and helps families to talk openly about it and how it affects them. Social workers are the key members of the treatment team when it comes to working with families. Social workers are trained in family interventions and often provide these interventions, such as psychoeducation, directly to families as well as functioning as the primary liaison among the family, the consumer, and the other treatment team members.

One of the most important sources of information and support for families with a loved one with mental illness, and for the professionals who work with them, is the National Alliance on Mental Illness. NAMI is an indispensable resource for social workers because it provides a wide range of programs and services that can supplement professionally delivered family and consumer interventions.

SKILL DEVELOPMENT EXERCISES FOR WORKING WITH CONSUMERS AND FAMILIES

Discussion of the "Case of Joe"

At the beginning of the chapter, the "Case of Joe" was presented. Below are responses to the questions listed, and readers can review them and then add more ideas to the responses provided. Following the psychoeducation role-play is another case analysis for further practice.

Questions to consider:

1. What would you say to Joe as you begin your interview? What strategies might you use to establish rapport with him?

Important components of what you would say to Joe include identifying who you are and your role and purpose in meeting with him; strategic use of empathy; clear communication skills; and rapport-building skills

2. What are the most important issues you would address with Joe at this first meeting?
    - His clinical/mental status—he seems to have primarily negative symptoms, and these should be assessed.
    - How does Joe perceive his situation? Does he identify any problems? How does he get along with his parents? Does he think he needs psychiatric care?
    - Does Joe have any thoughts of harming himself or others?
    - Is there any evidence that Joe is using drugs or alcohol?

- Is Joe taking any psychotropic medication? If so, is it helpful and in what way? If not, has he ever taken a medication that has been helpful?
- What does he think his parents' concerns are? Does he agree with the parental concerns?

3. What issues would you address with Joe's parents? What feelings would you guess that his parents are experiencing that you should be sensitive to?
   - What kind of help are the parents looking for? What help have they received in the past, and did they find that help useful?
   - Emphasize directly that they are not the cause of their son's illness.
   - Emphasize that we will all work together collaboratively in a partnership to help Joe.
   - Can Joe continue to live with them and be supported by them?
   - Feelings they may be experiencing, such as fear, loss, guilt, anxiety, frustration, anger, shame.
4. How would you go about determining the first goals of treatment for Joe and his family?
5. Explain how and why psychoeducation, Johnson's eight-stage healing process, and NAMI could be helpful to Joe and his parents.
   - By collaborating with Joe and his parents and the treatment team so that a service plan or treatment plan has input from everyone.
6. What strengths do you perceive in Joe?
   - He's bright and was very high functioning before he became ill for the first time.
   - He's young and hasn't been ill for too long.
   - He has good social support from his parents and a supportive place to live.
   - He was willing to come to the clinic with his parents.
   - There seems to be no evidence of violence toward self or others—he is more withdrawn than aggressive.
   - He has tried to work although it hasn't been successful.
7. What strengths do you perceive in Joe's family?
   - They have been caring for Joe, a task that is both frustrating and difficult.
   - They clearly love Joe and have actively sought help for him.
   - Joe may be difficult, but he is cooperative enough with his parents that they were able to bring him in.
   - The family has been willing to accommodate Joe's symptoms but also has been able to identify when limits must be set and help is needed.

Psychoeducation Role-Play

Family Member Role Description:
Your name is Mary Smith, and you are a 45-year-old married mother of two. Your youngest son, Dave, is 13 years old. Your older son, John, is 18 years old and was hospitalized for the second time in a year on the local mental health inpatient unit. During this hospitalization, the psychiatrist confirmed that John has schizophrenia.

You are very scared. Schizophrenia sounds like a terrible disease. You don't even want to think about the fact that your son is "crazy." You feel it must be your fault. Maybe you didn't love John enough, or perhaps his friends led him down the wrong path. Could he have taken drugs? You don't know what to do and how to behave around John. Everything you say and do seems to upset him more. You know that he'll be discharged soon and have to come home, and you're afraid all the problems will begin again.

John ended up in the hospital this time not long after he stopped taking his medication and withdrew into his room and wouldn't come out. He wouldn't bathe and would be up all night. You're exhausted, and now you have to talk to this social worker. Your husband refused to come to the hospital and says that John is an embarrassment to the whole family. You sit down with the social worker and say the following:

> I'm not sure why I'm meeting with you. I don't know what to say. Dr. Jones said you could help us. Can you?

Social Worker Role Description:

You are the inpatient social worker. This is the second admission for your client, John. Last time, you had hoped he had schizophreniform disorder, but now he is back in the hospital and Dr. Jones has concluded that John has "the big S," as he put it—that is, John has schizophrenia. You have been asked to speak with John's mother. She looks exhausted and frightened. Begin by responding to Mrs. Smith's initial question. Connect empathically with her. Then, at some point in your role-play meeting, address the following with her:

- what schizophrenia is, its causes, and what the course and prognosis can be
- how to interact with John to reduce stimulation and stress
- what treatment will be provided and what her role is in that
- decrease her guilt about "causing" John's illness

Case Analysis: The Case of Sara

You are a clinical social worker in the walk-in services clinic of your local public community mental health center. When not working in the walk-in clinic, you work as an outpatient therapist with a caseload of 25 clients to follow. As a walk-in clinic social worker, you have the authority to set up referrals to any of the available resources in your community, and you have a psychiatrist to back you up for medication or to underwrite any inpatient admission decisions you make.

At 9 a.m. one Wednesday morning a woman, Janice Smith, who looks to be about 30 years old, walks into the clinic and asks to talk to someone about her younger sister, Sara. This is what she tells you: Sara is 24 years old and has been living with Janice for about a year. Before Sara moved in with Janice, Sara lived with their parents. A little over a year ago, both parents were killed in a tragic car accident. Sara had no place to go, so Janice took her in.

Four years ago, when Sara was 20 years old, she had her first episode of major depression. Previously, Sara did well in school—particularly in creative writing and was an English literature major in college. She did very well academically, although, Janice recalls, Sara never had many friends and tended to be shy and keep to herself. Taking a full load of courses was eventually more than Sara could handle without becoming very stressed so, after her sophomore year, she cut back to a part-time basis. Sara was afraid to move off campus, so she continued to live in the dorm. During the fall semester of her sophomore year, however, she began to deteriorate. Her grades slipped, she became even more reclusive and gradually stopped eating and sleeping well. Her resident advisor noticed that Sara was not looking well, that is, not changing her clothes for a week at a time and not bathing. The resident advisor managed to coax Sara to accompany her to the emergency room, and Sara was subsequently hospitalized at the university's medical center psychiatric unit for two weeks. At that time she was given the diagnosis of major depression and was discharged on both an SSRI antidepressant and a low-dose atypical atipsychotic medication (Abilify). Sara has been unable to return to school to finish her degree. While living with their parents, Sara tried to work but side effects from the medication and residual depressive symptoms have kept her from being able to continue jobs for more than a few weeks at a time.

The loss of their parents has been very difficult for both Sara and Janice. Sara begged Janice to take her in, stating that she couldn't support herself and was afraid to live on her own. Janice works full time as an elementary school teacher and, except for their cat, Sara is alone during the day. Janice reports that Sara spends her days sitting on the couch, watching TV soap operas, smoking cigarettes and drinking coffee. Janice says that she tries to get Sara out of the house and encourages her to read, use Janice's computer, go to the gym or just do *something*, but she just sits. Janice says that she knows Sara is depressed but she doesn't know how much longer she can continue to care for her and it just doesn't seem like Sara is making any effort to get better.

You ask Janice where Sara is now, and Janice says that she is outside the clinic sitting on a bench and smoking. You ask Janice to see if Sara is willing to come in and meet with you. Twenty minutes later, Janice brings Sara to your office. Sara sits down and stares at the floor. Janice takes a seat in another chair and looks at you anxiously.

Questions to Discuss and Answer:

1. Write down a verbatim statement of exactly what you would say first as you begin your interview with Sara.
2. What are the most important issues you would address with Sara at this first meeting?
3. What *issues* would you address with Sara's sister Janice? What *feelings* would you guess that Janice is experiencing which you should be sensitive to?
4. Sara probably needs to be evaluated for medication, but in addition to that, what *psychosocial* interventions might be appropriate for Sara, and why?
5. *How* would you approach determining the first goals of treatment for Sara and her sister?
6. What are Sara's strengths and resources?
7. What strengths do you perceive in Sara's family?

Assess your application and analysis of this chapter's contents by completing the *Chapter Review*.

Chapter 8

Social Work Practice and Psychopharmacology for Individuals with Severe Mental Illness

INTRODUCTION

Over the past five decades, the number of clients receiving psychotropic medications as part of their mental health treatment has increased dramatically. The development of newer, more effective medications has resulted in outpatient treatment for clients who previously would have been hospitalized, briefer stays where hospitalization is necessary, and the deinstitutionalization of most individuals who have severe and persistent mental illness.

Although social work practitioners do not prescribe medications, they often play key roles in the range of issues surrounding the pharmacological treatment of their clients. As a practicing social worker, one must be aware of changes in the medications that have been ordered by the client's physician (usually a psychiatrist, although not always), alterations in the client's behavior prior to and following medication changes; and what contingencies enter into the client's adherence to their prescribed medication regime. Other factors that social workers need to explore with their clients include the client's feelings and attitudes about taking medication, what types of side effects may occur, and street drug use, that is, is the client using street drugs and, if so, how do such drugs interact with prescribed medication?

As part of a mental health team, social workers often play a major role in monitoring a client's adherence to his or her treatment plan including the intake of prescribed drugs. Of note, today the term "adherence" is generally preferred over the term "compliance" because adherence implies active collaborative choice in accepting a recommended treatment, while compliance implies a more passive paternalistic approach. Furthermore, because of our commitment to the core professional values of self-determination, social justice, and human dignity, use of an invasive treatment, like medication, is particularly charged for many social work professionals. Thus, social workers must always balance commitment to the client's treatment plan with concern for client rights.

Psychopharmacology Content in Social Work Education

The first systematic effort to encourage the inclusion of psychopharmacology content in social work education came from a collaborative effort between the Council on Social Work Education and the National Institute of Mental Health in the late 1980s. This effort was precipitated by the findings from a national survey of schools of social work that looked at the extent to which psychopharmacology content was provided in the MSW curriculum. What the survey found was that only about half of schools of social work offered any content on psychopharmacology and, with those that did, the majority offered it only to mental health specialization students. The council, however, recognized that "it is doubtful that there is any area of social work practice in which knowledge about psychotropic medications, their purpose, effects, and side effects is not important" (CSWE, 1990, p. vii). Thus, in combination with a curriculum monograph for social work faculty that was published in 1990 (CSWE, 1990), the council also produced and broadcast three psychopharmacology teleconferences. The first, broadcast on April 11, 1991, provided a general introduction to social work practice and psychopharmacology; the second, broadcast on April 2, 1992, focused on adults and multicultural issues; the third, broadcast on April 1, 1993, focused on psychopharmacology issues with older adults.

The Challenge for Social Work Practitioners

Understanding how medications work is a necessity for effective social work practice in today's health care environment. The last 20 years have brought about unprecedented gains in knowledge and application with regard to the brain and its role in mental illness (Dziegielewski & Leon, 2001; Preston & Johnson, 2012). These gains are going to continue, and eventually science will become so sophisticated that medication and our understanding of neurochemical functioning will have an even greater impact on social work practice in mental/behavioral health (Johnson, 1999). The challenge for social work practitioners will be twofold. First, social workers must stay current on their knowledge about medication and neurochemical research findings. Second, social workers must ensure that all clients benefit from these scientific gains regardless of their obstacles to access, such as ability to pay. And, finally, social workers must always bear in mind that medications have both benefits and limitations, and it is critical that we recall the lessons learned from the prior misuse of medication.

It is important to note at this juncture that the best way to learn about medication and its role in relieving the burden of serious mental illness is through working directly with clients, their families, and their doctors. Information learned solely from a book, article, or lecture can be difficult to remember and apply in practice. What brings such information alive and into context is ongoing practice experience with clients taking psychotropic medication and ongoing experience collaborating with the treatment team. Thus, the purpose of this chapter is somewhat modest, and includes giving the reader a sense of the different classes of medication, identifying some basic conventions and concepts about medication, helping to build the reader's vocabulary to enhance an understanding of the information about medication and the ability to communicate with others about medication, and providing a clear sense of the knowledge and skills that social workers utilize in assisting clients in how to take their medications properly to help them get well and stay well. The best way, though, to remember the information in this chapter is to connect it with the experiences of actual clients. In this, as in many other things about clinical work, our clients are often our best teachers. As an example, a few years ago I was interviewing a client for a study on managing and regulating emotions, and the client interviewee made the following comments after the interview (this is an approximate quote):

> I wish there was a program in which those of us who have been in the hospital and who have been on medication could talk to people coming into the hospital while they're there to give them support and help. I know how scary it is to be in the hospital and I know how awful it is to have to take medication, and you think it won't help and the side effects are terrible but it's not your fault and it will help in

> time—you just have to stick it out. The first medication you're given may not work, but that doesn't mean you won't find a medication that will work. And so many times professionals—well, they have no bedside manner. They don't understand what it's like, but I do.

This client's comments suggest how important it is to listen to our clients, learn from them, and respect what they tell us about their treatment experiences. Furthermore, it suggests how peer support and input can be crucial in helping clients understand the use of medication and its role in their recovery.

PSYCHOPHARMACOLOGY PRINCIPLES IN A NUTSHELL

Three or four decades ago, nonmedical mental health professionals were not expected to have knowledge about the medications used to treat the clients they served and, sometimes, were even discouraged from seeking and using such knowledge under the assumption that medication is the doctor's territory only. That stance has changed dramatically and, today, nonmedical mental health professionals, particularly social workers, are expected by other professionals, consumers, and families to have a working knowledge of psychotropic medication. As Diamond (2009) notes, "It is critically important for nonmedical clinicians to know about the medication that their clients are taking as well as to know what medications could be useful that their clients are not yet taking [because] nonmedical therapists often know their clients better than the prescribing physician and therefore may be in the best position to help identify target symptoms that would suggest a specific medication [and] to evaluate how well a medication is working" (p. 1).

A client may only see his or her psychiatrist once every 6 weeks or even only once every 6 months, whereas the client's social worker may be seeing the client weekly or—depending on the type of setting—even more frequently. As a result, social workers are often in a better position than the doctor is in terms of monitoring how well the client is doing on the medication day to day and whether there are any side effects that must be addressed or problems with adherence that must be resolved.

There are many excellent comprehensive articles and books written by social workers on the topic of social work practice and psychopharmacology, and for more in-depth detail beyond this chapter, the reader can refer to those works (see, e.g., Austrian, 2005; Bentley & Walsh, 2005; Bentley & Walsh, 2013; Dziegielewski, 2009; Dziegielewski & Leon, 2001; Wegmann, 2012). There are also a range of books written by medical mental health professionals for nonmedical mental health professional use (see, e.g., Diamond, 2009; Preston & Johnson, 2012) and some written for consumers and families (see, e.g., Preston, O'Neal, & Talaga, 2005a; Weiden, Scheifler, Diamond, & Ross, 1999).

Ronald Diamond, M.D., who began teaching the basics of psychopharmacology to nonphysician staff members (nurses, social workers, psychiatric technicians) in 1974 in California, suggests that it is helpful to begin the study of psychopharmacology by understanding some simple "rules of the game" (Diamond, 2009, p. 1). These nine rules or topics provide a framework for approaching a basic understanding of psychopharmacology and consist of the following (Diamond, 2009, p. 2–6):

- Identification of the four major classes of medications
- Recognizing side effects and other unintended actions of medications
- Understanding drug–drug interactions
- Asking about other medications the client may be taking
- Asking about other medical problems the client may be having

- Issues related to use of medication during pregnancy and breastfeeding
- Asking about allergic reactions to medications
- Keeping the names of medications straight and accurate
- Recognizing that no one knows everything

In terms of the first topic or rule, there are *four major classes of psychotropic medications*. These include antipsychotic medications (including associated side effect medications), antidepressant medications, mood stabilizers, and antianxiety medications (including sleeping pills). These four categories include the vast majority of psychotropic medications prescribed to handle almost all common mental health problems. If the social worker has a good understanding of these classes, he or she will have a command of the foundation knowledge about the most commonly prescribed psychotropic medications. Within each class, then, are a few different *types* of medications, with specific medications within each type. For example, the antipsychotic class includes two main types, the "traditional" or "first generation" antipsychotic medications, and the "atypical" or "second generation" antipsychotic medications. Each type of antipsychotic medication is represented by many different specific medications, each with its own generic name and one or more brand names. So, for example, the atypical or second-generation antipsychotic medications include the medications risperidone (Risperdal), olanzapine (Zyprexa), quetiapine (Seroquel), ziprasidone (Geodon), and aripiprazole (Abilify). Medications of the same type usually are much more similar than different and, therefore, learning about one or two medications in a type within a class can provide a basic understanding of the other medications in that type and class. Medications within a class are more similar than medications across classes.

Next, we have *side effects and other actions of medications*. All medications have side effects of some kind, that is, some action in addition to the specific therapeutic effect that is desired. For example, in addition to having analgesic or anti-pain properties, the common over-the-counter medication aspirin decreases the ability of the blood to form clots. Sometimes the intended therapeutic effect is to decrease the risk of developing a blood clot. An individual at risk for developing a blood clot may be prescribed a daily low-dose (81 mg) aspirin. Other times, the intended therapeutic effect is pain relief, and thus, aspirin taken as a pain reliever has the potential to become life-threatening because of its anticlotting properties if the individual will be undergoing a surgical procedure. Thus, depending on the target of the treatment efforts, some effects are therapeutic, while others are side effects. Because medications can have multiple effects, medication should not be given without a good reason and without an appreciation and understanding of both its therapeutic effects and its side effects (Diamond, 2009).

Next, it is important to *understand drug–drug interactions* and provide the client with information about such interactions (Diamond, 2009). Many medications that are very safe alone can be dangerous when taken in combination with other prescribed, over-the-counter, or recreational/street drugs. For example, the antidepressant class consists of four types—the selective serotonin reuptake inhibitors (SSRIs), the tricyclic antidepressants, the monoamine oxidase inhibitors (MAOIs), and the so-called atypical antidepressants. SSRI antidepressants can interfere with how tricyclic antidepressants are broken down and disposed of by the liver. Giving someone the SSRI Prozac (fluoxetine) while they are taking the tricyclic Tofranil (imipramine) can result in a dangerous buildup of the tricyclic in the individual's liver. Thus, stopping or switching medications from one type to a different type requires careful titration and monitoring by the individual's doctor (Diamond, 2009), and this is a caution that social workers can share with their clients.

Another example of a common drug–drug interaction is when a person being treated with antidepressant medication ingests alcohol. Mixing an antidepressant with alcohol can result in the antidepressant becoming less effective in treating the depression symptoms, because alcohol itself is a central nervous system depressant (Hall-Flavin, 2009). Alcohol can also worsen antidepressant side effects, such as exacerbating sedation. Finally, mixing an MAOI antidepressant with alcohol can result in a dangerous spike in blood pressure, which may result in a stroke. It is very important that the social worker reinforce information the doctor provides the client about such drug–drug interactions, and help him or her understand the importance of not mixing drugs together that carry a risk for adverse consequences for the client's mental or physical health.

The next rule points out the importance of *asking about other medications the client may be taking*. As part of your psychosocial assessment, always ask your client about all of the other medications that the individual is taking, both prescribed and over the counter, including herbal and other alternative supplements, and encourage the client to share this with his or her physician. Many medications used to treat medical conditions can result in psychiatric symptoms. For example, many medications used to control high blood pressure—the beta-blocker Inderal, for example—can cause or exacerbate symptoms of depression. Sometimes, appropriately changing or stopping the medically prescribed drug can alleviate the psychiatric symptoms and prove more effective than adding a psychotropic medication. Often people won't mention herbal remedies or over-the-counter medications, thinking that because they aren't prescription drugs, there won't be a problem, but all of these substances are drugs and have the potential for interaction effects. Example:

> Joan worked as a social worker for an agency that provided services to older adults. One of her clients, who was 82 years old, had to undergo surgery to replace a defective heart valve. The surgery went well, but afterward the client's blood would not clot, and the surgical team had to infuse her with a lot of blood products. This created a fluid buildup in the client's lungs; she went into respiratory failure and eventually had to be put on a ventilator. Then the client developed sepsis and eventually had to be put on life support. The client's family made the difficult decision to withdraw the life support and she died shortly thereafter. After conferring with the family, the surgeon guessed that what had happened was that the client had not stopped taking the herbal supplement ginkgo biloba, which she had taken for years in an effort to improve her memory and combat evolving dementia. Ginkgo biloba can cause bleeding complications and, thus, may have been the root cause of the clotting failure following the surgery. The client's daughter had urged her mother to tell the doctor about her herbal supplement use, but her mother refused, stating, "You know these doctors—he'll just tell me to stop it because they're all against alternative medicine anyway." (Newhill, 1995)

One approach that can be helpful in getting a clear picture of all the medications a client may be taking is to ask the client to get a grocery sack, go to their medicine cabinet and collect all of the medications in the cabinet and dump them into the sack, and then bring the sack to the clinic. With older adults, in particular, who may be on multiple medications and seeing multiple specialist doctors, this strategy can help in fully accounting for every medication that may be used by the client. In my practice, I would suggest that the client bring their bag of medications to my office (or I would make a home visit), ask them to empty everything out on my desk or floor, and then sit down and go through all the contents with the client. It was not unusual in such cases to find the client's prescribed and over-the-counter medicine along with their deceased spouse or partner's medicine, the neighbor's medicine ("It helped me so much—go ahead and give my medicine a try"), expired medicine, multiple prescriptions of the same medicine from different doctors, and so forth. With the client, I would write everything down, sort it all out, and then share the information with the doctor so he or she is fully informed.

The next task is to *ask the client about any medical problems he or she currently has* or has had in the past (Diamond, 2009). We, as social workers, are in the business of "treating the whole person" (Diamond, 2009, p. 4), and it is important to realize the extent to which medical illness and nonpsychiatric medications can affect an individual's mental status and behavior. Psychiatric symptoms can arise due to medical problems and/or from the medications used to treat such problems. For example, it is not unusual for an underactive thyroid, a condition called "hypothyroidism," to cause symptoms of depression. Once the hypothyroidism is treated, if that is the cause, the depressive symptoms usually abate.

One very thorny issue is related to *use of medication during pregnancy and breastfeeding* (Paton, 2008). The bottom line is that we cannot say with absolute certainty that any psychotropic medication is completely safe in pregnancy, because all diffuse across the placenta (Altshuler, Cohen, Szuba, et al., 1996). A review of all articles written in English from 1966 to 1995 (Altshuler, et al., 1996) revealed three types of effects from prenatal exposure to psychotropic medications: (1) teratogenicity, that is, the capability of producing fetal physical malformation, (2) perinatal syndromes involving a wide range of physical and behavioral symptoms, and (3) postnatal behavioral sequelae caused by exposure to the medication prenatally. The data available suggest that first-trimester exposure to low-potency phenothiazine antipsychotics, lithium, certain anticonvulsants such as valproic acid (Depakote) and carbamazepine (Tegretol), and benzodiazepines elevates the risk for congenital anomalies in infants. However, untreated depression, mania, or psychosis can also be highly stressful for both the mother and fetus and, thus, decisions about continuance of medication treatment during pregnancy and the breastfeeding period rest with careful consultation between the woman and her physician (Newham, Thomas, MacRitchie, et al., 2008; Oberlander, Warburton, Misri, et al., 2008; Ramos, St-André, Évelyne, et al., 2008). "Use of psychotropic medications during pregnancy is appropriate in many clinical situations and should include thoughtful weighing of risk of prenatal exposure versus risk of relapse following drug discontinuation" (Altshuler et al., 1996, p. 592). Social workers can be helpful in such situations by encouraging clients who are or may become pregnant to talk with their doctors, and then assisting them with the resources and supports needed to support their decisions.

Next, we have the concern of *allergic reactions to medications* (Diamond, 2009). People can have an allergic reaction to any medication, although some medications are implicated more often than others. It is important to ask your client about any medication allergies before any medication is prescribed and to encourage the client to be sure to fully inform the doctor. Also, once your client is prescribed medication, one of the important aspects of medication monitoring is to watch for allergic reactions. Neuroleptic malignant syndrome (NMS), for example, is essentially an allergic reaction to the traditional antipsychotic drugs and involves a range of symptoms, including muscle rigidity, high fever, autonomic instability, and cognitive changes such as agitation, delirium, and coma, lasting anywhere from 8 hours to 40 days. NMS is a medical emergency and the first order of treatment is to remove the client from any neuroleptic or antipsychotic drugs being taken and aggressively treating the fever with ice packs. Clients may require intensive care or other medical support and treatment until stable (Benzer, 2007). Up until the development of the atypical antipsychotics, clients suffering from a psychotic disorder who developed NMS had limited alternatives for treatment. However, today, clients who develop NMS as a reaction to a traditional antipsychotic can often switch to an atypical or second-generation antipsychotic and achieve successful relief from many of their symptoms.

Next, we have the issue of the various *names used for medications* (Diamond, 2009). Every psychotropic medication has a generic or chemical name plus one or more brand/trade names. To complicate things further, many of these names sound similar or are spelled similarly. For example, consider the following four medications: Klonopin,

Clonidine, Clozapine, and Clomipramine. All sound similar, are spelled somewhat similarly, but are very different medications (Diamond, 2009). Klonopin (clonazepam) is a benzodiazepine often prescribed for sleep inducement, clonidine (Catapres) is an antihypertensive medication used in the treatment of drug withdrawal, clozapine (Clozaril) is the earliest atypical antipsychotic that was developed in 1990, and clomipramine (Anafranil) is an antidepressant that is effective in treating obsessive-compulsive disorder. One can see how many medications that sound alike actually refer to very different drugs, with very different properties and treatment indications. There have been many tragic cases in which pharmacies misunderstood a doctor's order, since many of these similar-sounding medications are also spelled similarly, and people have died as a result (Bavley, 2009). A good all-purpose resource that cross-lists generic and brand names as well as providing good up-to-date information about all drugs available on the market is the *Physician's Desk Reference* (*PDR*) (2009). Another resource that is designed to be more user-friendly for nonmedical mental health professionals is the *PDR Drug Guide for Mental Health Professionals* (2007).

The final "rule"—and a most important one—is that *no one knows everything*! One of the most important goals for clinicians in the area of psychopharmacology, as in other clinical treatment issues, is being able to acknowledge the limits of what you know and how to get help to find out the answers. At some point, everyone calls on someone else for help. A nonmedical clinician may get help from a psychiatrist, and a psychiatrist may seek help from an expert psychopharmacologist (Diamond, 2009). As a social worker, make sure that you have available the consultation resources that you need in your day-to-day practice, whether they are human experts, books, or online resources. If a client or family member asks a question that you cannot answer, be honest and say, "I don't know the answer to that—but I will find out and get back to you."

Assess your comprehension *of the nine principles that provide a framework for approaching knowledge about psychopharmacology* by completing this quiz.

Next to be addressed is understanding how a drug moves through the body, or what is called pharmacokinetics. A basic knowledge of pharmacokinetics is important in order for the social worker to be able to explain to the client and/or family the basics with regard to how medications work and affect the body.

HOW A DRUG MOVES THROUGH THE BODY

Medication Takes Time to Work

Every intervention, including treatments spawned by modern medicine, takes time, and sometimes clients give up on medications or request a change in dose before the medication has had time to stabilize. Understanding how a medication moves through a person's body and understanding how much time a medication requires to take effect is an important part of developing a successful treatment plan. It is similar to what one expects from psychosocial treatment, that is, improvement doesn't happen overnight—it takes time. However, people often expect drugs in particular to be fast—a quick fix, a miracle pill, a silver bullet—and assume that the beneficial effects will happen immediately and, if they don't, that means the drug isn't working. Often the decision to use one medication over another is influenced by how quickly the medication works, or how long or short a period of time it stays in the person's body. The way in which the human body responds to the presence of a drug is called pharmacokinetics. "Knowledge of pharmacokinetics can help social workers understand why some clients respond differently to the same medication than others do and why, when a client stops taking medication, its effects can continue for a while" (Bentley & Walsh, 2001, p. 55). The four bodily processes that explain how a drug moves through the body are (1) absorption, (2) distribution, (3) metabolism, and (4) excretion.

The Four Bodily Processes That Move Medications through the Body

Absorption

Absorption is the process by which a drug enters the bloodstream, which is, most commonly, via the passive diffusion of the drug into the bowel wall. There are several factors that affect the efficient absorption of a particular medication, including the nature of the chemicals and other materials that make up the medication and the action of the enzymes in the liver as they break down the drug (Bentley & Walsh, 2001, 2013). Some drugs, specifically certain antipsychotics, can be administered either orally, via pills or liquid, or intramuscularly. How efficiently an oral medication is absorbed depends on a number of factors, including how concentrated the medication is, how easily it is dissolved into the intestinal cell membranes' fatty tissue, and the action of the gut, that is, how efficiently the client's intestines move to absorb the drug. Intravenous or intramuscular drug administration bypasses the gut and, therefore, absorption is more efficient.

Distribution

Distribution refers to the process by which a drug travels to the targeted site of action once it has entered the individual's bloodstream (Bentley & Walsh, 2001, 2013). Intravenous administration of drugs is the quickest and most direct route for absorption and distribution, however, for reasons that will be discussed later in this chapter, orally ingested medications are usually preferred—although in some cases, an injectable medication may be the best choice for a particular client.

Now, once the medication is in the blood, it may still take some time to cross what is called the "blood-brain barrier" and enter the brain where it can produce a therapeutic effect. The term "blood-brain barrier" refers to characteristics of blood vessels in the brain, through which a drug must pass to enter the neuron sites in the brain. These tiny capillary blood vessels are very tightly packed and, thus, the blood-brain barrier is difficult to penetrate. Medications differ with regard to how rapidly they are able to cross into the brain. Valium, for example, enters the brain more rapidly, while a similar medication like Serax may take somewhat longer. In general, the benzodiazepines, like Valium and Librium, work almost immediately once they are in the brain, which adds to their addictive potential. Basically, how rapidly a drug enters the brain depends on how lipid-soluble the drug is, that is, how easily the substance can pass through the fatty cell membranes of the blood vessels. Two things affect a particular medication's access to the brain. First is the nature of the way blood flows to the targeted area of the brain. A higher blood flow allows greater access. Second is the drug's particular affinity for the neuronal receptors in the targeted area of the brain.

Metabolism and Excretion

Once the drug has been absorbed, crossed the blood-brain barrier, and has been distributed, then the action called metabolism begins. Metabolism refers to the process carried out by the liver in which the drug is broken down into smaller components that are called metabolites. These metabolites are then excreted by the body. The parts of the drug that are not excreted continue on through the brain until they reach the targeted receptors. So, an antipsychotic drug would seek the dopamine receptors in the brain and an antidepressant might seek the serotonin receptors. There are several factors, such as age, that affect the metabolism of a particular drug, and the doctor takes these factors into consideration when he or she determines the appropriate dosage to be given to a particular client. Most psychotropic medications, including all antipsychotic and antidepressant medications, take weeks to work even after a therapeutic level has been achieved, and this pre–full therapeutic effect period can be a difficult one for the client, although support from the doctor and social worker can help the client to "stick it out" until the time when he or she begins to feel genuine relief from symptoms.

Half-Life

Another important concept for social workers, clients, and families to understand is the "half-life" of a drug, that is, the time required for a drug to reach half or 50 percent of its peak level. While the absorption time influences how long it takes for a medication to work, a medication's "half-life" is also an important variable that often has much more impact.

When an individual takes the first dose of a new medication or drug, the serum level (amount of the drug in the blood) goes up as the medication is absorbed and then falls as the medication is broken down and metabolized and eventually excreted. If the person takes a second dose of the medication or drug before all of the previous dose has left the body, the second dose will add to the remaining part of the first dose. Most medications are eliminated slowly enough that the serum level continues to increase over time, even if the client takes the same dose of medication every day. The ups and downs of the serum level eventually stabilize or level off at what is called a steady state serum level. If the person then stops taking the medication, the serum level of the medication will fall over time. The *half-life* refers to how long it will take for half of the medication to leave the person's body. Example: If a medication's half-life is 12 hours, then half of the amount taken will be out of the body at the end of 12 hours; half of that amount, that is, 75 percent of the original dose, will be out after 24 hours; and half of that, that is, 87.5 percent of the original dose, will be out after 36 hours. It takes approximately five half-lives for a medication that is taken regularly to reach steady state. Some medications, such as over-the-counter pain relievers and antianxiety medications such as the benzodiazepines and certain sleep medications—for example, zolpidem (Ambien)—have very short half-lives, which means the body eliminates the drug very quickly. Short half-lives are good because they avoid the "drug hangover" produced by drugs such as barbiturates; however, the short half-life can be a problem, because drugs like Valium or Xanax produce a sense of calm quickly, but the calm feeling wears off quickly, which may prompt the person to take more of the drug than prescribed and raise the risk for addiction.

Understanding the half-life of a medication is important for identifying how long it takes for the medication to take effect, how long it takes for the medication to reach a steady state serum level, and how to design a titration method to stop the medication without ill effects. Such information can be very helpful to clients so they can understand how the medications they are taking work and why it is important to take medications as they are prescribed in terms of dose and timing.

We will now turn to specific classes of psychotropic medications. Because this is a text addressing serious mental illness in adults, and it is beyond the scope of this chapter to address all of the psychotropic medications available, we will examine in detail those classes of medications most commonly prescribed for the most serious mental illnesses: antidepressant medications, antipsychotic medications, and mood stabilizers. Medications used primarily to treat anxiety and/or sleep problems may be prescribed as adjunctive medications, but these are not first-line treatments for serious mental illness. For excellent overviews of these medications, please see Diamond (2009), Bentley and Walsh (2001), and other psychopharmacology texts.

ANTIDEPRESSANT MEDICATIONS

Almost all social workers will encounter individuals who are depressed across medical and psychiatric settings. For adults, the major indications for the use of antidepressant medications include the treatment of depression, panic disorder, agoraphobia, obsessive-compulsive disorder, bulimia, cocaine craving and depression, smoking cessation, and various miscellaneous uses. There are six major classes of antidepressant drugs:

- Selective serotonin reuptake inhibitors (SSRIs)
- Serotonin and norepinephrine reuptake inhibitors (SNRIs)
- Norepinephrine reuptake inhibitors (NRIs)
- Tricyclic antidepressants
- Monoamine oxidase inhibitors (MAOIs)
- Atypical antidepressants

Let's go over benefits, risks, and side effects for each type.

First, we have the *selective serotonin/norepinephrine reuptake blockers.* These drugs block the reuptake of serotonin and/or norepinephrine into nerve cells in the brain. Because they block only the targeted neurotransmitters, there is a reduction in the number of side effects. There are three subtypes within this type of antidepressant:

1. Selective serotonin reuptake inhibitors (SSRIs), which include medications such as fluoxetine (Prozac), sertraline (Zoloft), citalopram (Celexa), and paroxetine (Paxil)
2. Selective serotonin and noradrenergic reuptake blockers, which include medications such as venlafaxine (Effexor) and duloxetine (Cymbalta)
3. Selective noradrenergic reuptake blockers

For many clients, the serotonin or serotonin/norepinephrine blockers are better tolerated in terms of side effects than the older tricyclic antidepressants; however, they are not side effect free. These medications are "activating" rather than sedating, and their side effects include minor weight loss, anxiety and restlessness, nausea, headaches, and sexual dysfunction in men. However, for clients who evidence "reverse vegetative signs" of depression, that is, oversleeping and overeating, these medications can be very effective in relieving symptoms of depression with the side effects also providing some therapeutic benefit. Clients with agitated depression, however, may not like them. As one client described it:

> I think I have always been mildly depressed since adolescence but didn't get any treatment for it for many years—I just suffered. Then I got a job that involved working the swing shift—my body and brain just couldn't take it and I think that schedule was largely responsible for triggering my first episode of major depression. It was awful. I couldn't sleep at all—I mean at all—I went 48 hours without sleeping. I was very agitated and paced constantly. I felt suicidal and I had no appetite. I went to my primary care physician for help and he prescribed Prozac for me. I hated it—I felt like I was going to jump out of my skin—the medication made me even more agitated and my sleep was even worse. My doctor switched me to Tofranil (imipramine) and, finally, I could sleep and focus my mind. I don't like the side effects—especially the dry mouth—but it is better than being depressed. (Newhill, 1995)

In the example above, the client achieved relief from her depression with the medication imipramine, which is one of the *tricyclic* type of antidepressants. The tricyclic antidepressants are the oldest antidepressants and have been around since the 1950s. Their name comes from the three-ring molecular structure of the substance and they include amitriptyline (Elavil), imipramine (Tofranil), nortriptyline (Pamelor), desipramine (Norpramin), clomipramine (Anafranil), and doxepin (Sinequan). Although newer, safer, and better-tolerated antidepressants have been developed, the tricyclic antidepressants are as effective, or even more effective for some clients, in treating depression as the newer medications. Furthermore, they are very inexpensive, have been available in generic form for decades and, therefore, are not particularly lucrative for the pharmaceutical companies. As a result, such companies do not promote the tricyclics and, perhaps partially as a result of this, they are prescribed less often. Tricyclic antidepressants are best indicated for and are very effective in treating agitated depressions, that is, depression characterized by anxiety and agitation with the traditional "vegetative signs" of depression, that is, mild to severe insomnia and loss of appetite. They are also effective in treating panic disorder, agoraphobia, and obsessive-compulsive disorder. Tricyclic antidepressants can cause heart arrhythmia, thus a baseline EKG is recommended. The usual starting dose for imipramine and amitriptyline is 50–75 mg for 2 to 3 days with a gradual increase in dose to 150–300 mg per day. For some of the tricyclics, there is a "therapeutic window," that is, serum levels within a certain range are more effective than levels below or above the window. Typically, it takes 3 weeks to reach full therapeutic effect; however, the side effects kick in right away and many clients find them hard to tolerate. These side effects include minor weight gain, sexual side effects including decreased libido, and sedation, plus a collection of side effects called *anticholinergic side effects.*

All of the tricyclic antidepressants block the action of acetylcholine, one of the many neurotransmitters in the body's autonomic nervous system, which is the involuntary part of the nervous system responsible for basic body regulation. Anticholinergic side effects include dry mouth, blurred vision, constipation, urinary retention, postural hypotension, tachycardia (speeding pulse), and increased sweating. However, there are many self-help measures that social workers can share with clients that can ease the discomfort of these side effects. For example, to help with dry mouth, clients can keep a bottle of water with them (which won't look odd since these days everyone carries bottled water), chew sugarless gum, or suck on sugarless candy or cough drops. Even just tucking a wad of sugarless gum between the gum and cheek, like snuff, can promote an increase in salivation. Mint-flavored sugarless gum is usually more effective in increasing salivation than other flavors. Dry mouth elevates the risk for dental caries, so keeping the mouth moist is important to avoid this. There are also over-the-counter mouth-moistening products, such as Biotene mouthwash, gum gel, and gum, that can help ease dry mouth. Social workers should also encourage clients to eat a high-fiber diet to ease constipation, and avoid over-the-counter cough and cold medications that cause urine retention because this can compound that particular side effect. Tricyclic antidepressants are particularly dangerous in overdose, potentiated by use of alcohol and, thus, doctors usually prescribe only a 1-week supply to clients at risk for suicide. The SSRIs are safer in overdose, which is one of their advantages. It is important to note that in susceptible people, tricyclic antidepressants may trigger a manic episode, and in individuals with schizophrenia, tricyclic antidepressants may make the person more paranoid or disorganized (Diamond, 2009).

The next type of antidepressant is the *monoamine oxidase inhibitors* (MAOIs), which include phenelzine (Nardil) and tranylcypromine (Parnate). "MAOIs block the action of the enzyme that deactivates neurotransmitters with a single amine group; hence their name *mono* (one) amine oxidase inhibitors" (Diamond, 2009, p. 145). These medications may be taken in pill form or administered in a skin patch. The expected benefits are the same as for the tricyclic antidepressants, but these drugs have some unique side effects, including hypertensive crisis if dietary and other substance restrictions are not adhered to. Specifically, the individual must avoid any foods containing tyramine, an amino acid naturally occurring in certain foods including red wine, aged cheese, smoked or pickled fish, chicken liver, chocolate, sausage, certain beers, and beans. MAOIs can also interfere dangerously with other drugs and, as a result of all this, the MAOIs are usually the choice of last resort and are prescribed usually for atypical depressions, such as depression mixed with dysphoric symptoms, anxiety, or agoraphobic symptoms.

The last category of antidepressants is the so-called *atypical antidepressants*, including trazodone (Desyrel), nefazodone (Serzone), mirtazapine (Remeron), bupropion (Wellbutrin), and desvenlafaxine (Pristiq), which is an SNRI. Trazodone is approved by the FDA as an antidepressant, although it is commonly used as a sleep aid. It is an effective medication, inexpensive and, unlike some other sleep aids, is not addictive. Sometimes trazodone is prescribed in combination with an activating SSRI to combat sleep difficulties. It has a short half-life, thus an individual does not wake up with a medication "hangover." In 2010 a trazodone extended-release form (Oleptro) was approved by the FDA with claims that the long-release form reduces side effects (Wegmann, 2012).

Although nefazodone (Serzone) has the advantage of not causing insomnia and anxiety (like the activating SSRIs), it can cause dizziness, drowsiness, and fatigue. It also can cause a rare, but extremely serious, liver dysfunction and is, therefore, prescribed with caution. Mirtazapine (Remeron), another more recent atypical antidepressant, is effective in relieving depression but it can cause people to feel drugged and fatigued and can also cause weight gain and threaten white blood cell count. Bupropion (Wellbutrin) affects the neurotransmitter dopamine, which accounts for some of its unique effects. It is activating, has fewer side effects than many of the other antidepressants, and seems particularly helpful for depressed individuals who complain of fatigue and lethargy (Diamond, 2009). A big advantage is that it does not cause the sexual side effects of many other antidepressant medications and is sometimes given in combination with an SSRI to enhance the therapeutic effectiveness while balancing out the sexual side effects. In combination with a nicotine patch, Wellbutrin and its slow-release form called Zyban are also effective in helping some people to stop or reduce smoking.

One of the newest antidepressants to be approved by the Food and Drug Administration (FDA) is Pristiq (desvenlafaxine), which was approved by the FDA in February of 2008 for the treatment of major depressive disorder in adults. Pristiq works by preventing the reuptake of the neurotransmitters serotonin and norepinephrine in the brain. Pristiq is one of the "activating" antidepressants and has many potential side effects including nausea, dizziness, difficulty sleeping, increased sweating, constipation, fatigue, decreased appetite, anxiety and restlessness, and sexual dysfunction in men. Pristiq may be a good alternative if a client with depression has not achieved relief from their symptoms with other more established medications; however, it is very expensive and will not be available in generic form for some time (Melin, 2009).

In summary, all of the antidepressants have both advantages and disadvantages. All are effective in relieving depression, and the differences lie primarily in the differing side effect profiles of each medication. Since there is no antidepressant without side effects, one must consider two things when considering antidepressant treatment: (1) What is the symptom profile for your particular client? Does the client have an agitated depression or a sedated depression? (2) Which side effect profile can the client tolerate best? The answers to these questions can help guide the choice of medication.

ANTIPSYCHOTIC MEDICATIONS

For most individuals who have a psychotic illness, medication is an essential adjunct to effective psychosocial treatment. There are a number of antipsychotic medications available and they all work, and while they all have sedating and calming effects, their main targeted effect is to reduce psychotic thinking and behavior. Other medications, actually, are safer if sedation is the main goal. The primary differences in the various antipsychotic medications are in the potency, that is, the dosage prescribed to produce therapeutic effects, and in the side effects.

Different antipsychotics vary in their side effects, and some people have more trouble with certain side effects than others. If a side effect is especially problematic, there are several things the doctor can do to help, including prescribing a different medication, changing the dosage level or schedule, or prescribing an additional medication to control the side effects. There are also some lifestyle changes that can be helpful in easing the impact of side effects, and social workers are often the key individuals to help the consumer make such changes.

Just as people vary in their responses to antipsychotic medications and their side effects, they also vary in their speed of improvement. Some symptoms diminish in days, others take weeks or months, and sometimes symptoms persist even when the individual takes their medication reliably, although the quality of the remaining symptoms may change. For example, the individual may continue to hear voices but, with medication, the voices change from threatening and critical to benign or to a kind of background murmuring that is tolerable. For most clients treated with an antipsychotic medication, significant improvement is usually seen by the sixth week of treatment, although this is not true in every case. If someone does not seem to be improving, a different type of medication may be tried. Some people may need to take medication for an extended period of time, or even indefinitely depending on the type of psychotic disorder that they have. There are two basic categories of antipsychotic medication:

- The "traditional" or "first-generation" antipsychotics; and
- The "second-generation" or what are often called "atypical" antipsychotic medications.

Antipsychotic medications are often indicated for the following conditions:

- Psychosis from multiple causes including dementia;
- Schizophrenia, for both acute treatment and maintenance;
- Bipolar disorder, for the acute manic phase;
- Autistic spectrum disorders to treat agitation and self-harming behaviors;
- Borderline personality disorder (at a low dose off-label) to stabilize mood and affect, control transient psychotic symptoms, and manage agitation;
- Psychotic disorder due to a general medical condition, or what used to be called "organic brain syndrome"; and, finally,
- Major depression with psychotic features, or what is sometimes referred to as "delusional depression" and, once the psychotic symptoms have subsided, the antipsychotic can be tapered with the antidepressant continued for maintenance treatment.

Things to Bear in Mind before Starting a Psychotropic Medication

Before starting any medication, there are several things to bear in mind. First, a careful and thorough diagnostic assessment should be conducted and a "best fit" diagnosis should be made. The primary purpose of a psychiatric diagnosis is to guide treatment. An antipsychotic medication should not be prescribed just because a client is upset, agitated, or even psychotic until two conditions have been ruled out. First, the presence of a medical illness or drug intoxication needs to be ruled out. If the psychosis is caused by drug intoxication or medical illness, then the individual needs to be treated for that.

The second type of condition to be ruled out is delirium. The symptoms of delirium include relatively global cognitive impairment, disorientation, and confusion in which the individual has difficulty mobilizing, focusing, shifting, and sustaining their attention.

Individuals with delirium often evidence a wide and changeable range of strong emotions that do not seem related to environmental events. Delirium can occur as a result of either an acute brain condition or a chronic brain condition and has four general causes: (1) brain disease (e.g., an infection or a tumor); (2) a disease or infection in another part of the body that affects the brain (e.g., a metabolic condition); (3) intoxication from drugs or alcohol; and (4) withdrawal from a substance to which an individual is addicted (e.g., alcohol or drugs). The biological mechanisms underlying all cases of delirium are a general derangement of brain metabolism coupled with an imbalance in the neurotransmitters. A person with delirium can be psychotic, that is, evidence vivid hallucinations and delusions, but the underlying cause must be treated if the individual is to recover (Samuels & Neugroschl, 2005).

One of the most dramatic examples of delirium can be seen in the acute brain condition called delirium tremens, or "the DTs." Delirium tremens results from cessation from alcohol following excessive alcohol consumption over a long period of time and occurs in about 5 percent of individuals with alcoholism. Delirium tremens is characterized by tremors, and vivid visual and tactile hallucinations that result in a state of terror (Galanter & Kleber, 2008). Delirium can be confused with psychosis, and if the individual has a delirium then what is causing the delirium should be identified and treated for the individual to recover. Example:

> One night, when I was working for the psychiatric emergency service, I received a call from a police officer at the local jail. The officer asked me to come to evaluate a man who had been brought in because he was agitated and psychotic. When I arrived at the man's cell, he was cowering in a corner, talking rapidly to himself and vigorously scratching his arms. His pupils were dilated and he kept screaming, "Get them off me, get them off me!" He said that huge spiders were crawling under his skin and he had scratched his skin so hard that he was bleeding. I told the officer that I suspected he was in the midst of delirium tremens and asked him to arrange to have the man transported to the nearest hospital emergency room where he could be treated.

After ruling out a medical condition, drug intoxication, and delirium, a medication history should be taken. If a doctor is not immediately available, the social worker can begin by finding out some basic information. For example, has the client taken any psychotropic medications, especially antipsychotic medication, in the past? If so, the social worker can inquire about which medications the client has taken, whether they have been helpful and with what symptoms, and what dosages have been prescribed. If the client is too distressed to remember such information, family members can often be very helpful in providing historical data.

Once the client has been prescribed an antipsychotic medication, it is then important to follow up with how the client is responding to the medication by identifying certain target symptoms and target goals (Diamond, 2009). The target symptoms should be those that are most prominent or most problematic for the client. For example, for one client, the target symptom might be auditory hallucinations, for another, it might be disorganized thinking or social withdrawal, and so forth. Every client is an individual, and even clients sharing the same diagnosis may present with very different constellations of symptoms. Targeting specific symptoms helps determine whether the medication is working, and then the medication can be adjusted according to the target symptoms and side effects. For example, if a client has experienced relief from symptoms but complains of feeling too sedated, the doctor may try reducing the dose with the goal of maintaining the therapeutic effect but reducing the side effect of sedation. Or the doctor might change the dosing schedule by having the client take the medication at night, when sedation can serve a helpful function in terms of inducing sleep, and by the time the client wakes up the most intense sedating effects may have passed.

Another thing to remember with antipsychotic medication is that more is not necessarily better. All that a higher dosage may produce is more side effects without more therapeutic benefit. Research over the past couple of decades has shown that individuals with psychotic illness have often been treated at doses unnecessarily high and that maximum therapeutic benefit is often achieved at much lower dosages than had been routine in the past (Mackay, 1994). Finally, it is important to proactively look for side effects by both observing the client's behavior and asking the client directly whether he or she is experiencing certain side effects rather than waiting for the client to bring the subject up. This is particularly important for side effects that the client may not identify as side effects or for side effects that the client may feel embarrassed about bringing up, such as sexual side effects.

What If the Medication Doesn't Work?

If an adequate trial of a particular antipsychotic medication has been tried, that is, the client has been on the medication long enough and at the right dose, and the medication is not helping, there are certain questions that the client's doctor, social worker, and the client him or herself need to consider (Diamond, 2009). First: Is the diagnosis correct? Sometimes the client's initial diagnosis is made under less than ideal circumstances, for example, in the emergency room in the middle of the night when the client is in crisis. Under such circumstances, it is best to view the diagnosis as a "working diagnosis" with the assumption that it will be revisited regularly until the "best fit" diagnostic assessment is determined. It is not unusual for someone who is actively psychotic to be given the diagnosis of schizophrenia when the person actually has bipolar disorder, and vice versa.

The second question, if the medication is not working, is: Has a medical illness gone unrecognized? Unidentified medical illness in individuals with mental illness is not unusual. Why does this occur? Sometimes it occurs because the client does not seek treatment, has poor access to treatment, or is so tormented by their psychiatric symptoms that the medical symptoms pale in contrast. I have seen psychotic clients who have been walking around on ulcerated feet, suffering broken bones or other injuries, or are ill in other ways but have not sought or received the medical care they need. Sometimes, medical illness goes unrecognized because the client's complaints are discounted or misattributed as part of the mental illness. Example:

> When I worked for the psychiatric emergency service, I periodically saw a client, Jacinto, who had schizophrenia. Jacinto had the persistent delusion that alien forces had removed his internal organs and replaced them with "alien organs." Two or three times a year, he would show up at the county hospital emergency room, asking for a CT scan or X-ray to prove this had occurred. One time, he went to the ER complaining of chest pain. Because he also said he believed the alien organs were causing the pain, his complaints were dismissed as being just part of his mental illness. In fact, he was having a heart attack. Fortunately, one of the new nurses, who had not seen Jacinto before and did not hold assumptions about him, was concerned and insisted that he be checked out. Heart attack was confirmed, and he received the treatment he needed.

Another question to consider if the medication is not working is whether substance abuse is interfering. This needs to be actively explored, since people are often not voluntarily forthcoming about substance use, particularly illicit substance use. Here, again, the input from friends and family members can be helpful in getting a full and accurate picture.

It is also important to investigate whether the person is taking the medication reliably and correctly. This issue will be addressed in more detail later in the chapter. A final question to be considered if the medication is not working is whether the dose has been high enough for a long enough period of time. If not, then appropriate adjustments should be made.

A Note about Cigarette Smoking, Caffeine, and Antipsychotic Medication

One thing one notices with individuals with psychotic disorders and other severe mental illnesses is that such individuals often smoke a lot of cigarettes and drink a lot of coffee, tea, and/or caffeinated sodas. Why is this the case? For some clients, nicotine and caffeine serve to combat the negative symptoms associated with schizophrenia, such as anhedonia (the inability to gain pleasure from experiences most people enjoy), lack of motivation, and lethargy. I worked with a client once who was so desperate for such relief that he ate instant coffee out of the jar with a spoon. For other clients, caffeine and nicotine can temporarily relieve medication side effects such as sedation, although they can make other side effects, such as akathisia (inner motor restlessness), worse.

For some clients, smoking and drinking coffee are mechanisms to enable socializing with other people. Finally, like for people without mental illness, smoking and drinking coffee are pleasurable. It is important to realize, however, that cigarettes increase the activity of the enzymes that break down antipsychotics and many other medications. This means that smokers generally need a higher dose of medication than nonsmokers. It also means that if someone stops smoking, that person's serum level of medication will increase and he or she may develop more medication side effects, thus, the dose may need to be reduced. It is important to always ask clients if they smoke and how much and if they ingest caffeine and how much and in what form. Preston and Johnson (2012) provide a short questionnaire to assess caffeine use across a range of substances that contain caffeine.

Now, let's take a look at the two major categories of antipsychotic medication: (1) the traditional, conventional or first-generation antipsychotic medications, and (2) the atypical or second-generation antipsychotic medications.

The First-Generation or Traditional Antipsychotic Medications

The first-generation, or what are sometimes referred to as the "traditional" or "conventional," antipsychotic medications were the first antipsychotic medications to be developed, beginning with chlorpromazine (Thorazine) in 1953. All of these older antipsychotic medications work by blocking receptor sites in the brain stimulated by the neurotransmitter called dopamine; specifically they block what is called the dopamine 2 (D2) receptor site. Dopamine is found in several different parts of the brain, and this dopamine receptor blockade accounts for many of the side effects of these medications as well as their intended therapeutic actions. All of the traditional antipsychotics work to reduce psychotic thinking, specifically the "positive symptoms" such as hallucinations, delusions, and disorganized thinking, but it takes different amounts of each medication for them to be equally effective, plus the side effects differ (Diamond, 2009).

One might assume that the higher the dose of medication, the more serious the illness, but this is not always true. One difference that drives dosage levels is the potency of the medication, and with antipsychotic medication there are three main types: low-potency first-generation antipsychotics such as chlorpromazine (Thorazine) and thioridazine (Mellaril), intermediate-potency first-generation antipsychotics such as thiothixene (Navane) and perphenazine (Trilafon), and high-potency first-generation antipsychotics such as haloperidol (Haldol) and fluphenazine (Prolixin). So, for example, the average individual treated for psychosis may be prescribed 400–1500 mg of Thorazine (a low-potency antipsychotic) as compared to only 5–10 mg of Haldol (a high-potency antipsychotic). In addition, a doctor will consider several factors when prescribing an antipsychotic medication besides how ill someone is. These factors include the client's age, body weight, gender, race, and past history. If a person took a particular medication before and it worked, and the client is willing to take it again, the doctor is likely to prescribe the same medication. Also, many clients are afraid of switching medications even when told they might be more comfortable or the new medication is more effective because, as one client put it: "The devil you know is better than the devil you don't know."

Different antipsychotics also vary in their side effects, and some people have more trouble with certain side effects than others. One should not assume a particular side effect is problematic for any specific individual consumer; instead, it is critical to ask the consumer directly if they are experiencing side effects and to what extent the side effects are troublesome. Some side effects are desirable. For example, the sedative effect of some antipsychotic medications is useful for clients who have trouble sleeping or who become agitated during the day. Fortunately, antipsychotic medications can usually be taken just once a day, thus, clients can reduce unpleasant daytime side effects, such as feeling drugged, by taking their medications once before bed.

In general, the high- or intermediate-potency first-generation antipsychotics, such as Prolixin, Haldol, and Navane, are both safer and better tolerated by clients than low-potency medications like Thorazine. This is particularly true for paranoid clients who may respond to the more sedating medications by feeling they are losing control, which further frightens them. Finally, when a medication is needed in an emergency, the high-potency antipsychotics have a quicker and greater antipsychotic effect than the low-potency drugs. Both Haldol and Prolixin are available in a slow-onset, long-lasting decanoate injection that takes effect over days or weeks, and in a fast-onset, short-acting HCL, or hydrochloride injection. Haldol is also available in a liquid concentrate that can be mixed with orange or pineapple juice, which many clients prefer in an emergency situation.

Long-acting injections, such as haloperidol (Haldol) decanoate or fluphenazine (Prolixin) decanoate, have advantages and disadvantages. For clients who evidence poor adherence to oral medication, particularly for those who simply have problems remembering to take their pills, an injection can be a good solution. It can also relieve the family of the burden of daily medication monitoring. However, such injections have disadvantages as well. One disadvantage is that such intramuscular medications are typically suspended in oil, usually peanut oil, and some people develop an allergic reaction or irritation to the oil at the site of the injection and painful lumps can develop at the injection site. Specialized bandages, such as the brand Band-Aid Advanced Healing, consist of a cushioning gel pad that relieves pain, has comfortable adhesive that stays in place for multiday use, and is flexible so it conforms to skin for greater comfort. Such bandages also can lessen "oil leakage" after administration of the injection. However, they are very expensive. Injections of antipsychotic medication are messy, can be painful, and are invasive and contrary to client self-determination, because once that shot is administered, the client has no more choice about having medication in his or her system for the length of time that the injectable medication lasts. This is in contrast to the ingestion of oral medication, in which the client has active choice about each daily dose. This is not to say that injectable medications are bad—they are often very helpful for some clients during certain periods of their lives—but as a social worker, it is important to support the client's right to make choices about how to take the medication, and there are many strategies that can improve a consumer's adherence to orally administered medication.

The biggest drawback to the traditional antipsychotic drugs is that they have some very powerful side effects that affect both comfort and adherence. As a social worker, you must be familiar with and be able to recognize these side effects, which will be discussed shortly. Now, about one third of all clients with psychotic disorders, particularly schizophrenia, do not respond well to these traditional antipsychotic drugs. Either the drugs are unable to control their symptoms or they cannot tolerate the side effects. Up until a couple decades ago, the future prospects for recovery for such clients were quite bleak. However, in 1990, the first completely new and pharmacologically novel antipsychotic drug to be developed in years was released to the market, by the name of clozapine (Clozaril), which is now available in generic form. This brings us to the topic of the second-generation, atypical antipsychotic medications.

The Second-Generation or Atypical Antipsychotic Medications

There are now several second-generation or "atypical" antipsychotic medications on the market, two in generic form, and most psychiatrists now recommend these over the older medications as a first-line treatment unless someone is already doing well on one of the traditional medications and wants to stay on it. Switching medications can be tricky and some clients respond well to the older medications and are able to deal with the side effects either because they are not bothered much by the side effects or the side effects are adequately mitigated by use of a side effect medication such as trihexyphenidyl HCL (Artane), benztropine mesylate (Cogentin), or diphenhydramine hydrochloride (Benadryl). Today, when someone starts antipsychotic drug treatment for the first time, one of the second-generation medications is usually the best option, thus these medications are really no longer considered "atypical."

Clozapine was the first of these second-generation medications, and out of the approximately 20,000 clients with schizophrenia in the United States who did not respond well to conventional neuroleptics, more than half evidenced significant improvement on clozapine. In fact, for a few clients, clozapine was truly a "miracle drug":

> In the 1980s, when I was a clinical social worker with the psychiatric emergency service, I frequently saw a client whom I will call "Joe." The best word I can think of to describe Joe was that he was a mess. He was chronically psychotic and none of the existing antipsychotic medications had much of an effect on his symptoms. He was aggressive and exhibited highly inappropriate intrusive behavior, which landed him in jail multiple times. He was non-adherent to any prescribed psychosocial treatment and spent his days and nights roaming the streets looking for drugs. He lost half of his teeth because of repeated fights in which he inevitably suffered the worst outcome. In spite of all these challenges, I liked Joe and wished there was some way we could help him. Years later, after clozapine was introduced, I asked a former colleague about Joe and whether she knew how he was doing. She told me that he was put on clozapine and it completely transformed him: "You would not recognize Joe," she said. Apparently, clozapine eliminated all of his psychotic symptoms, he was then able to participate in social skills treatment, developed insight into his illness, stopped using recreational drugs, and for the first time in his life made some positive friends. A year after he started clozapine treatment, Joe began taking classes at the local community college, earned an associate's degree, and got a job. A year after that, he found a girlfriend, got married, and lives independently with his wife. Clozapine—literally—saved Joe's life. (Newhill, 1995)

Clozapine is not perfect, however, and has certain significant drawbacks. First, it can cause seizures in some clients and, second, a few clients develop a life-threatening blood disorder called agranulocytosis from the drug, thus it requires ongoing biweekly monitoring via blood draws. As a result, clozapine is expensive and, before it was released in generic form, treatment for one consumer could cost approximately $4,000 annually for the drug itself plus $9,000 more for the cost of blood monitoring. Because of the problem with agranulocytosis, efforts have been made to develop alternative second-generation antipsychotics that would possess the positive traits of clozapine but without the dangerous side effects. These medications include the following:

- Risperidone (Risperdal), released in 1994, available in inexpensive generic form, and available as a 2-week injection;
- Olanzapine (Zyprexa) released in 1996
- Quetiapine (Seroquel) released in 1997
- Ziprasidone (Geodon) released in 2000
- Aripiprazole (Abilify) released in 2002
- Paliperidone (Invega), which is similar to risperidone, released in December 2006
- Iloperidone (Fanapt, Fanapta, and Zomaril) released in May 2009
- Saphris (asenapine) approved by the FDA for the treatment of bipolar disorder and schizophrenia in 2009
- Latuda (lurasidone) approved by the FDA in 2010. Latuda, however, provides no novel characteristics beyond the benefits of the older atypicals (Wegmann, 2012)

How Second-Generation Antipsychotic Drugs Work Differently from First-Generation Antipsychotic Drugs

We now know there are at least five different dopamine receptors in the brain. All of the first-generation antipsychotic medications, like Haldol, work by blocking one kind of dopamine receptor, called the D2 receptor. In contrast, the second-generation antipsychotic medications block a range of different dopamine receptors in addition to D2, along with the serotonin receptors. Each of the second-generation antipsychotics has its own pattern of neurotransmitter blockade, thus consumers may differ as individuals with regard to which medication they respond best to or feel most comfortable taking. The main advantage to the second-generation drugs is that they have fewer extrapyramidal (muscle-related) side effects than the older medications. They are also less likely to cause the irreversible side effect called tardive dyskinesia and, overall, are better tolerated by consumers and more likely to not increase negative symptoms. Finally, many people develop what is called a "dysphoric response," or feeling "zombie-like" a few days after starting a first-generation antipsychotic. What clients say is that they just feel terrible, although they may not be able to describe how they feel specifically. Clients on the second-generation medications are far less likely to report this. However, until they are available in generic form, the second-generation medications remain much more expensive than the first-generation medications, and much criticism has been lobbied with regard to the extent to which the pharmaceutical industry controls medical education and influences mental health policy and medication guidelines (Petersen, 2004). For example, in 2004, the state of Texas spent about $3,000 a year, on average, for each consumer taking a second-generation antipsychotic versus only $250 per consumer for the older medications (Petersen, 2004). That is a huge difference in cost.

The Consumer Perspective on Antipsychotic Medications

What is it like to live with having to take antipsychotic medication to stay well? As social workers, it is very important that we listen to our clients and respect and value their input with regard to the experience of taking medications and what works well for them and what does not. In light of this, in 2003 my colleague, Dr. Helen Cahalane, and I were awarded funding to develop a DVD of interviews with consumers about their experiences taking psychotropic medications (Newhill & Cahalane, 2003). Below is an excerpt from an interview I conducted with Melanie, a client with schizophrenia, in which she talks about her experiences taking medication: (C = Christina; M = Melanie)

> Melanie is a 47-year-old single African-American woman who was first diagnosed with paranoid schizophrenia at age 27, which is the classic time of onset of schizophrenia for women. Prior to her illness, Melanie had a successful career in banking, was raising her young daughter and in the process of buying a house. She believes that the stress over problems related to her daughter and the purchase of the house led to her first episode of psychosis. Melanie describes her symptoms at that time as consisting of auditory hallucinations, headaches, paranoia, and "feelings that just weren't normal." Finding a medication that controls her symptoms without debilitating side effects was a long process, but eventually she and her doctor found a medication combination that works and has side effects that are tolerable. These medications include 2 mg of thioxanthene (Navane) at night, 1 mg of benztropine mesylate (Cogentin) to treat the side effects of the Navane, and 20 mg of fluoxetine (Prozac). Like many individuals with schizophrenia, Melanie has both psychotic symptoms and some symptoms of depression. One time Melanie stopped all her medication but her symptoms quickly returned and she realized that taking medication will be lifelong for her. Currently Melanie lives alone independently in an apartment and participates in individual and group therapy at the local mental health clinic. She also attends a medication information and support group, which has been helpful in supporting her adherence with her medication and providing social support. A great source of pleasure in Melanie's life is spending time with her grandchildren.

C: Melanie, could you tell me first a little about what problems you've been getting treatment for, and when your illness began in the early years?

M: My illness began when I was 27. In 1983, I had a nervous breakdown. When I went to [the hospital], they said it was chronic paranoid schizophrenia, and I had psychotic tendencies. They've been giving me medication for it since then.

C: Prior to that period you were working, and everything was fine, and then it just suddenly hit you. Was there any kind of stress going on at that time?

M: Yes, I was working at [name of the bank and the city] and my daughter was acting out then. I was buying a house and things were just messing up. It was just real stressful for me at that time.

C: Since you first got sick, have you had episodes since then that have caused you to go to the hospital?

M: Yes. I stopped taking my medication for about two years. All my old symptoms—hearing voices—and all the sickness came back. I signed myself back into [the hospital] and stayed a few weeks.

C: Could you describe about what kind of symptoms you experienced and what that was like for you?

M: Yes—headaches, hot flashes, hearing voices, paranoid thinking, hallucinating things that weren't there, feelings that just weren't normal. I had trouble dealing with it because I didn't understand it.

C: So it must have been pretty scary.

M: It was, it was.

C: Could you tell me exactly what kind of medications you've been on from the very beginning until now?

M: I've been on Lithium that didn't work. I've been put on some Prolixin shots, Prolixin pills. I've been on Haldol, the one that gives me headaches. I've been on Thorazine that makes me fall and stumble. There's a list, I've been on quite a few of them.

C: What are you on right now?

M: I'm on 20 milligrams of Prozac in the morning, 1 milligram of Cogentin for the side effects, and 2 milligrams of Navane at night—just those three pills.

C: Are those medications helpful to you?

M: Yes, they are.

C: What specific symptoms do they help you with?

M: The voices, hearing the voices that aren't there. I can sleep with my Navane at night. The problem that I have is that when they get a new doctor to come in, a new psychiatrist, and he's saying that I don't need my medications, and they take me off of my dosages. Before 3 weeks are up, I'm real bad, back where I was. All my illness comes back.

C: How often has that happened to you where you're taken off your medicine and then your symptoms come back?

M: It's happened a few times because at [the clinic] they don't keep the same doctor. They keep rotating them and they come in and out. They'll get new jobs, or move, or whatever. It seems like all the doctors that come in feel that I don't need my medication, but I know that I do. So I've been having this problem for a while.

C: Do you experience any side effects from the medications you're on?

M: Yes. The Navane that I'm on makes me smack my mouth. I do it when I'm eating, and I do it all day and all night. It's just a side effect. They're telling me that there's generic drugs now they could put me on—one was going to make me tired, the other one was going to make me nauseated—so I figured, what the hell, I might as well stay on what I'm on. I'm used to this one.

C: How do you cope with the side effects? I know you also mentioned, earlier . . .

M: It's embarrassing if someone mentions it, but I've grown accustomed to it. It's just something that is normal now with my medication. If that's what I need to keep my medication and stay well, then I have to put up with it.

C: So you've learned to live with it.

M: Yes, I have. Taking medication has helped me out, because I remember how sick I was before I started taking it. I went through a period where I thought that I didn't need it. I was in denial, and I thought it was okay not to take it, and I got sick again. So I realize that medication actually helps me, and I appreciate it.

C: What brought you to that realization? What kind of moved you from denial to . . .

M: I was tired of hearing voices. I was tired of the sweats. Going through a period where I'm laughing real loud, then the next minute I'm crying, or I'm talking loud, or I'm acting out. I still do that on my medication, but there's more control. My emotions were just out of hand. I wasn't in control of anything. But this way I have a better chance of dealing with reality and myself and other people.

C: If you were to give advice to another person who is about to start taking the kind of medication that you're on, what would that advice be?

> ***M:*** Have patience, because with me some of the medications didn't work right. The doctors give you medication for your symptoms, but they don't know how it's going to react in your body. Every medication doesn't work. The medications that I'm on now, they work for me. It was trial and error. Some of them didn't work at all. Some made me stumble, some made me fall. Some made me sleep. Thorazine swelled my tongue up and Haldol gave me bad headaches. So I just had to go through the different medications until I found something that I'm on now that's comfortable. . . . I don't want my medications changed. I don't care what new generic drug they put out, it doesn't matter. Leave me on what I'm on, 'cause it works. It works for me.

Melanie has found a combination of medication that works for her. She takes Navane, which is one of the first-generation intermediate-potency antipsychotic medications, and, like most of the traditional antipsychotics, Navane is accompanied by extrapyramidal side effects. Fortunately, the medication Cogentin controls these side effects, so Melanie also takes Cogentin. Finally, like many individuals with schizophrenia, Melanie has symptoms of depression as well as psychotic symptoms, so she takes Prozac to manage her depression. This medication "cocktail" keeps Melanie well. Antipsychotic medications, however, have some powerful side effects that can be uncomfortable and even life-threatening.

Side Effects of Antipsychotic Medications

The side effects of the antipsychotic medications can be divided into three broad categories. The first is extrapyramidal or muscle-related side effects; the second group includes common non-muscle-related side effects that are uncomfortable and can affect subjective quality of life, but are usually temporary or reversible and not life-threatening; and the third group covers those that are fortunately rare, but can be dangerous and even lead to permanent difficulties.

Extrapyramidal Side Effects

Extrapyramidal or muscle-related side effects are common and uncomfortable but not dangerous or life-threatening complications of antipsychotic drug use. However, they can increase the discomfort of many clients and frequently prompt clients to stop or refuse to take medications. These side effects are usually treatable and, with the exception of tardive dyskinesia, all disappear when drugs are discontinued. Tardive dyskinesia, however, has no reliable treatment and may be a permanent disability even after antipsychotic drugs are stopped. The first-generation antipsychotics, particularly the low-potency ones, posed the greatest risk for tardive dyskinesia, but it can occur with the second-generation drugs as well. The extrapyramidal side effects are much less frequent with the second-generation medications. The following are the specific extrapyramidal side effects that may occur (Bentley & Walsh, 2005; Diamond, 2009; Preston, O'Neal, & Talaga, 2005b):

The first of these extrapyramidal side effects is *dystonia*. Dystonias involve dramatic muscular spasms of the throat, neck, eyes, jaws, tongue, back, or whole body. The individual may present with his or her head tilted up or to the side, with slurred speech, or with eyes deviated up or to one side. Dystonias usually occur hours or days after medication is started or after the dosage has been significantly increased. Fortunately, dystonias are easily treated with anticholinergic drugs like Cogentin or Benadryl, but if a client experiences a dystonia and doesn't know what it is or what to do about it, it can be very frightening. Example:

> When I worked for the psychiatric emergency service, there was a client I'll call "John" who was very paranoid and, as a result of his fears, refused to come in to the

clinic for help. I made several home visits in an effort to develop a trusting relationship with him and eventually was successful in convincing him to come in and see the psychiatrist. The psychiatrist prescribed Haldol for him but did not tell John about the possible side effects of the medication because he was concerned that if John was informed about the side effects, he would be less willing to take the medicine. Two days later, John experienced a severe dystonia, which frightened him very much. His family took him to the emergency room, where they gave him a shot of Cogentin, which relieved the dystonia quickly. However, John was very angry, stating that he knew the doctor had deliberately tricked him, and that ended his willingness to accept treatment.

Another extrapyramidal side effect is *pseudoparkinsonism*. Pseudoparkinsonism is characterized by muscular rigidity, a shuffling gait, muscle stiffness, stooped posture, drooling, and a regular coarse tremor that is worse at rest than with activity. It is similar to some of the symptoms seen in Parkinson's disease, but it is not Parkinson's disease, simply a side effect of antipsychotic medication, and usually occurs about 3 weeks after treatment begins. For many years after the introduction of the traditional antipsychotic medications, it was assumed that such symptoms were part of the clinical picture of schizophrenia. It was only later that pseudoparkinsonism was recognized as a side effect of antipsychotic medication. Esteemed schizophrenia researcher Gerard Hogarty, MSW, once relayed a story to the author that illustrates this. Back in the 1970s, a group of Japanese psychiatrists visited the United States to tour the inpatient facility where Jerry conducted his research. After the tour, one of the psychiatrists asked if Jerry was sure he was really treating people with schizophrenia. "Why do you ask?" inquired Jerry. "Because," he replied, "they don't look like people with schizophrenia." "What do people with schizophrenia look like?" Jerry asked. What the psychiatrist described were the symptoms of pseudoparkinsonism—a shuffling gate, tremors, and so forth. Jerry and his research treatment team had successfully reduced or eliminated this side effect by keeping the medication doses down as low as possible while maintaining the therapeutic effect and, thus, the individuals with schizophrenia on his inpatient unit did not evidence the side effect.

Another extrapyramidal side effect is *akathisia*. Akathisia involves muscular discomfort, manifested by motor restlessness. The client is unable to sit down, appears agitated and, when sitting, their knees may bounce up and down. Akathisia can be misinterpreted as symptoms of anxiety by clinicians, although if one asks clients what they are feeling, clients are often very clear that they are not feeling anxious, rather, a client will say something like, "It feels like my motor is running all the time." Akathisia is very uncomfortable and is one of the most common reasons that clients will stop taking their medication. Fortunately, there are several steps that clients or their doctors can take to reduce akathisia, including:

- Avoiding caffeine, which can exacerbate akathisia;
- Reducing the dosage of the antipsychotic medication;
- Adding a beta-blocker, such as propranolol (Inderal);
- Adding an anticholinergic medication, such as benztropine mesylate (Cogentin); and
- Changing the type of medication, in particular, changing from a traditional antipsychotic to an atypical antipsychotic.

A fourth type of extrapyramidal side effect is *akinesia*. Akinesia is the opposite of akathisia and involves reduced motor activity, reduced social interaction, listlessness, low spontaneity, and apathy. It is frequently overlooked because an individual suffering from it isn't disruptive and, in certain settings, such as a crowded inpatient unit, it may not attract attention from staff. Akinesia is also difficult to distinguish from depression or the negative symptoms associated with schizophrenia and, thus, may go unrecognized and even inappropriately treated. Sometimes akinesia can be effectively treated with anticholinergic medication, but sometimes not, in which case it becomes an ongoing clinical problem that is best addressed by trying a different medication, such as an atypical antipsychotic, and/or keeping the antipsychotic dose as low as possible.

Finally, the last side effect, and one of the most critical ones in the category of extrapyramidal side effects, is *tardive dyskinesia.* Tardive dyskinesia is a late treatment side effect that appears after prolonged use of antipsychotic medication. It appears to be related to the *total lifetime dose* of medication rather than the dosage level alone. The symptoms of tardive dyskinesia involve involuntary movements, primarily of the face, tongue, mouth, and neck, but also of the extremities of the body. Characteristic is grimacing and a writhing motion of the tongue, which can be embarrassing for the client and, in its severe form, can interfere with eating and drinking. The most tragic aspect of tardive dyskinesia is that once the syndrome appears full-blown, it is permanent with no known means of reversal. It is estimated to affect 20–30 percent of clients chronically using antipsychotic medications, particularly the low-potency traditional antipsychotics, and it appears more frequently in women, older clients, and clients having a diagnosis other than schizophrenia (Wolf & Mosnaim, 1988). It used to be assumed that the second-generation antipsychotic medications had a lower risk of tardive dyskinesia, but that is now debated (Diamond, 2009).

The best approach to addressing tardive dyskinesia is to prevent it by treating individuals at the lowest possible dose of antipsychotic medication and for the shortest period of time. Tardive dyskinesia can also be successfully halted by early recognition and, if early warning signs are apparent, discontinuation of the antipsychotic medication. Early warning signs include abnormally frequent eye blinking and the beginning of writhing motions of the tongue. If the medication is continued, this can then progress to rhythmic, disfiguring distortion of the mouth or face, and other parts of the body may be involved. For example, the individual may rhythmically rub the pads of the fingers together as if they were rolling a small bit of clay into a ball. There are a number of scales, including the AIMS (Abnormal Involuntary Movement Scale), that allow clinicians to monitor and track early symptoms (Guy, 1976; Munetz & Benjamin, 1988). Some clients only develop a mild form of tardive dyskinesia, and even if they remain on medication, it doesn't progress. Unfortunately, it is impossible to predict who will progress to a severe level and who will not. Although anticholinergic drugs can usually help other kinds of extrapyramidal side effects, such drugs only make tardive dyskinesia worse (Diamond, 2009). The second category of side effects associated with antipsychotic medication is:

Side Effects That Are Uncomfortable but Usually Temporary or Reversible

The first side effect in this category is *toxic side effects.* Toxic side effects affect almost everyone taking an antipsychotic medication to one degree or another and include feeling drowsy or "drugged" and feeling unmotivated or sluggish. How severe the toxic side effects are is usually related to how high the dose of medication is and, thus, can often be controlled by changing doses (usually lowering the dose), taking most or all of the dose at night, or switching to a different medication. Such effects are more pronounced with the low-potency antipsychotics such as chlorpromazine or clozapine than the high-potency antipsychotics. Some clients become partially tolerant to these side effects over time, but others do not. In addition, some clients develop *psychotoxic side effects,* which include feelings of depression, depersonalization, dysphoria, akinesia, confusion, and even somatic delusions. All the toxic side effects are less of a problem with the second-generation antipsychotics.

Next are *autonomic side effects.* Autonomic side effects refer to the effects on what is called the involuntary or vegetative nervous system, which is the part of the nervous system responsible for maintaining basic body processes, such as temperature regulation and blood pressure. This system involves two neurotransmitters, acetylcholine and epinephrine. All of the antipsychotic drugs block the action of acetylcholine to a greater or lesser extent, causing a variety of side effects called anticholinergic side effects. Medications to treat the extrapyramidal side effects also have anticholinergic side effects. Anticholinergic side effects include dry mouth, constipation, and blurred vision (described in more detail in the section on tricyclic antidepressants). Antipsychotic medications also block some of the actions of epinephrine, which causes orthostatic hypotension (a.k.a. postural hypotension), which refers to a sudden lowering of blood pressure secondary to changes in one's body position such as suddenly standing up. Orthostatic hypotension can result in loss of balance, fainting, and falling. For example, I worked with a client on an antipsychotic medication who loved to take her small daughter to the park. One day she went on the swings alongside her daughter and the action of the swing caused her to faint and fall off the swing. It is important to caution clients who experience this side effect about the dangers of swinging on swings and going on amusement park rides. All of these side effects are greater with the low-potency traditional antipsychotics and clozapine.

Antipsychotic medication can also cause *metabolic side effects*, including weight gain, diabetes, and risk of elevated cholesterol. Weight gain is a problem with any antipsychotic medication, but some of the medications cause more weight gain than others and, generally, weight gain is most common with the second-generation medications. Of these, olanzapine (Zyprexa) and clozapine (Clozaril) cause the most weight gain; aripiprazole (Abilify) is the least likely to cause weight gain. Weight gain with antipsychotic medication can be significant, and it is not unusual for consumers—including children—to gain 50 or even 100 pounds. Not all people taking these medications gain weight, but the medications clearly make it more likely. Why this happens is not entirely clear, but a major culprit appears to be increased hunger, especially carbohydrate craving. Weight gain along with lack of physical activity is often directly related to the increased risk of diabetes, although individuals taking second-generation antipsychotics appear at risk for developing diabetes even in the absence of significant weight gain (Diamond, 2009).

The complicated management of diabetes in someone with serious mental illness can be daunting. "The regimen of blood testing, dieting and exercise that controls Type 2 diabetes is often beyond the attentions of the mentally ill. For patients, the task of taming two debilitating illnesses can haunt their lives" (Kleinfield, 2006). The reality is that, today, more individuals with mental illness die from the complications of diabetes and heart disease than they do from suicide or other complications related to their mental illness. One of the major challenges facing community mental health centers today is how to provide or connect consumers with services to help them live healthier lives, including effective management of serious illnesses such as diabetes. Even when a consumer is willing to make difficult lifestyle changes, the supports to do so are often not available. As one consumer told the author:

> I gained a lot of weight on my medication, but I need my medication to survive. I'm a veteran and get money from the VA, and so I used some of it to join Weight Watchers and a gym. I lost all the weight I had gained and I felt better, but then my rent went up, I couldn't afford Weight Watchers and the gym no more, and the weight went right back on. I was really bummed about it.

This example illustrates how consumers may be able and willing to make lifestyle changes but may lack the resources, financial or otherwise, to sustain such changes.

Another side effect of antipsychotic medication is *sexual and endocrine dysfunction*. All the traditional antipsychotic medications and some of the second-generation medications increase prolactin, which can interfere with menstruation in women and cause spontaneous lactation in women and, even, in some men. In addition, both men and women often experience decreased libido when taking antipsychotic medication, and these medications can cause erectile dysfunction problems in men. Mellaril, one of the first-generation medications, can also cause retrograde ejaculation in which erection and ejaculation are normal, but semen is pushed backward into the bladder instead of through the penis.

Antipsychotic medications can also cause various *skin reactions*, including rashes, itching, and swelling of the skin. Such symptoms usually begin 1–5 weeks after beginning treatment, with the low-potency medications as the worst offenders in this regard. These rashes are uncomfortable but usually aren't dangerous and either spontaneously remit or can be easily treated by a dermatologist. Skin reactions, however, are often complicated by the additional side effect of *photosensitivity reactions*. Individuals taking antipsychotic medication often find that their skin becomes very sensitive to sunlight and at high risk for sunburn. Consumers should be urged to wear sunscreen with at least a 15 sun protection factor (SPF) year round, wear hats and sunglasses when out in sunlight, and avoid being outside between the hours of 10 a.m. and 2 p.m., when the sun is the brightest. When I worked in the Central Valley in California where, in the summer, temperatures were commonly well over 100 degrees with bright sun every day, I knew several clients with schizophrenia who shaved their heads, and those who forgot to wear sunscreen every day suffered terrible sunburns on their scalp as a result. The final category of antipsychotic medication side effects is:

Rare but Serious and Potentially Harmful and/or Permanent Side Effects

The first side effect in this category is *blood dyscrasias*. Many clients who are treated with antipsychotic medication experience a partial block on production of certain blood elements, usually white cells and platelets. Such side effects are usually of no clinical significance and within a few days the individual's system is back to normal. Occasionally, however, the white blood cell count continues to decrease slowly, which is a condition called leukopenia. The decrease must be monitored closely, and sometimes switching to a different medication is necessary. If the client's system does not go back to normal and the white cell count and platelets begin to rapidly decrease, then you have a condition called agranulocytosis. Agranulocytosis is particularly common with clozapine but also can occur with other low-potency traditional antipsychotics, like Thorazine and Mellaril. Symptoms include weakness, high fever, chills, and a sore throat. In such cases, all medication must be stopped immediately. Fortunately, high-potency medications, such as risperidone, are less likely to produce a severe blood dyscrasia like agranulocytosis (Diamond, 2009; Mahmood, Silverstone, & Spittle, 1996; Nair & Lippman, 2005).

Other serious but rare side effects are *neuroleptic malignant syndrome*, which was described earlier, and *temperature regulation problems*. All antipsychotic medications can interfere with an individual's normal bodily temperature-regulation mechanisms during periods of hot weather. During the 1995 heat wave in Chicago, for example, a number of people taking antipsychotics died from heat stroke, including several young men who would not normally be considered at risk for fatal heat stroke. Low-potency medications, such as clozapine and chlorpromazine, are most likely to cause this, but anyone on antipsychotic medication is at risk (Rampulla, n.d.). Clients taking these medications should have access to air conditioning and fans and, at the very least, have a cool place to go if their living accommodations are too hot. Many of our clients, however, are poor and don't have air conditioning or good options to get out of the heat. As a social worker, you can help such clients by identifying public air conditioned areas, such as public libraries, where the clients can go for relief, and helping the clients get the resources to purchase a fan for their apartment or bedroom. Clients should also be encouraged to drink plenty of fluids to avoid becoming dehydrated during hot weather and, of course, to wear sunscreen.

Antipsychotic medications can also have *cardiovascular side effects* that can have serious or even fatal consequences (Piepho, 2002). Such medications slightly increase the time it takes for electrical impulses to spread through the heart. They also increase the time required for the heart to "re-polarize," or reset, after the last heartbeat in preparation for the next beat. On occasion, antipsychotic medications will cause a heart arrhythmia, which means the heart beats irregularly, especially when they are combined with other medications that have a similar effect on the heart or when given to people with certain kinds of heart disease.

Antipsychotic medication can also produce *problems with the eye and with vision.* Blurred vision is a common, reversible side effect from all the antipsychotics, especially the low-potency antipsychotics, and is one of the anticholinergic side effects. Such effects can be worsened if the individual takes additional medications with anticholinergic side effects, such as the tricyclic antidepressants and medications used to treat extrapyramidal side effects, such as Cogentin. The blurry vision goes away, however, once the medications are discontinued, and lowering the dosage, if possible, can help.

All of the antipsychotic medications *lower the seizure threshold.* Seizures are rare in people taking these medications but are something to consider, especially with clients who already have difficulty controlling an existing seizure disorder. Some antipsychotics are more likely to cause seizures, such as clozapine, especially in high doses. Seizures are rarely dangerous (unless the person is driving at the time) but can be frightening to both the client and observers.

Assess your comprehension of *antidepressant medications and antipsychotic medications* by completing this quiz.

MOOD-STABILIZING MEDICATIONS

Mood stabilizers are psychotropic medications that are used primarily to treat bipolar disorder. Bipolar disorder (discussed in detail in Chapter 12) is a severe and persistent mental illness, and people with bipolar disorder generally continue treatment with mood stabilizers for years. There are several different medications with mood-stabilizing properties, but the "first line" mood stabilizers are lithium (Eskalith or Lithobid), and valproic acid (Depakote) and carbamazepine (Tegretol), which are two anticonvulsant medications originally developed to control seizures.

Lithium

Lithium carbonate was the first effective mood-stabilizing medication to be developed. It was initially approved in Europe for the treatment of mania in 1949; however, it was not until 1970 that it was approved by the U.S. Food and Drug Administration (FDA). Lithium can be very effective in controlling symptoms of mania and preventing the recurrence of manic and depressive episodes; however, it has some serious side effects that can be difficult for consumers to tolerate and manage. These side effects include feelings of restlessness, dry mouth, bloating or indigestion, acne, sensitivity to cold temperatures, joint or muscle pain, and brittle nails or hair (NIMH, 2009).

Thyroid Function Problems and Lithium

Clients being treated with lithium must be monitored regularly by their doctors and must have their lithium blood levels checked regularly, along with monitoring their kidney and thyroid function. Many individuals with bipolar disorder have abnormal thyroid gland function. Because too much or too little thyroid hormone alone can lead to mood and energy changes, it is important that this be medically evaluated. People with the rapid-cycling subtype are most likely to have low thyroid functioning and may need to take thyroid pills in addition to their psychiatric medications. Also, lithium treatment may cause low thyroid levels in some people, resulting in the need for thyroid supplementation.

Other Mood-Stabilizing Medications

Valproic acid or divalproex sodium (Depakote), one of the anticonvulsant mood stabilizers, was approved by the FDA in 1995 for treating mania and is one of the first-line alternatives to lithium for the treatment of bipolar disorder. The other first-line anticonvulsant mood stabilizer is carbamazepine (Tegretol). Common side effects for these medications include drowsiness, dizziness, headache, diarrhea, constipation, heartburn, mood swings (surprisingly), and symptoms similar to a cold virus (stuffy, runny nose).

A number of other anticonvulsants have been used as mood stabilizers, but the empirical support for their effectiveness is mixed (Diamond, 2009). These include gabapentin (Neurontin), primarily used for treating anxiety and pain; topiramate (Topamax), which has been also used for the treatment of migraine headache, disordered eating, alcohol abuse, and impulse control problems; and oxcarbazepine (Trileptal) (Diamond, 2009; NIMH, 2009). Most recently, the anticonvulsant lamotrigine (Lamictal) received FDA approval for maintenance treatment of bipolar disorder and atypical depression.

For some individuals with bipolar disorder, one of the second-generation antipsychotic medications may be added to the mood stabilizers to target particular treatment needs. These medications include olanzapine (Zyprexa), which, when combined with an antidepressant or mood stabilizer, can help treat symptoms of severe mania and/or psychosis (Tohen, Sanger, McElroy, et al., 1999), aripiprazole (Abilify), quetiapine (Seroquel), risperidone (Risperdal) and ziprasidone (Geodon). Antidepressant medications are also sometimes used, although usually combined with a mood stabilizer to avoid the risk of a person switching to mania or hypomania, or of developing rapid-cycling symptoms (Thase & Sachs, 2000). A recent large-scale NIMH-funded study, however, reported that combining an antidepressant with a mood stabilizer was generally no more effective than treatment with a mood stabilizer alone (Sachs, Nierenberg, Calabrese, et al., 2007).

Now that the reader has a good understanding of antidepressant medications, antipsychotic medications, and mood-stabilizing medications, the next topic is psychopharmacology and special populations.

PSYCHOPHARMACOLOGY AND SPECIAL POPULATIONS

Social work practitioners encounter a wide range of culturally different clients in their practices who present varied mental health problems and concerns and may benefit from psychotropic medication. As a social worker, you must learn about your clients' cultural backgrounds and develop an understanding of how each client's unique value and belief systems shape who the client is, how emotional and psychological problems are experienced and manifested, and how the individual perceives mental health services. The culturally different client's perceptions, fears, and concerns about both psychosocial and medication interventions will influence treatment adherence and, ultimately, determine treatment success. The beliefs that individuals hold about the role of drug therapy in controlling the symptoms of their mental illness and in promoting their health are intimately linked to their beliefs about disease causation, which varies significantly across cultures.

Given that any medications prescribed to a client are based on the client's diagnosis, making sure that you arrive at the correct diagnosis is critical, and this is more likely if you are prepared to view the client's presenting problems within the context of the client's cultural frame of reference. Diagnostic assessment can be especially challenging when clinicians from one ethnic or cultural group evaluate an individual from a different ethnic or cultural group. A clinician who is unfamiliar with the nuances of a client's cultural frame of reference may incorrectly judge as psychopathology those normal variations in behavior, belief, or experience that are particular to the individual's culture (Newhill, 1990).

The Importance of Informal Helping Systems

When working with culturally different clients, it is important to recognize that for many cultures, members rely on informal rather than formal helping systems, which provide nontraditional therapeutic services (Gray, Coates, & Yellow Bird, 2008). These informal natural support systems are extremely important treatment resources that you, as your client's social worker, should incorporate and draw upon. An example of this is the role of the spiritualist for many Hispanic clients (De La Rosa, 1988). The spiritualist listens, encourages ventilation of feelings, and supports and provides empathy while also providing specific rituals and herbal remedies rather than prescribed Western medication to treat the emotional or psychological ills. It is imperative that social work practitioners ask clients directly about other helping systems used to cope with mental health, health, and family problems and find ways to integrate these culturally relevant systems into the client's treatment plan. For example, including a spiritualist or healer in the client's treatment plan may increase trust, which increases the client's adherence with both psychosocial and prescribed drug interventions.

For many African-American clients, the Black church and clergy serve the same role as the spiritualist does for many Hispanic clients. This is reinforced by a significant mistrust of the American health care system among many African-Americans. This mistrust has evolved based on a terrible legacy of health care neglect and exploitation in this country toward African-Americans. One of the most egregious examples of this was the Tuskegee syphilis experiment that took place beginning in 1932 and ending in 1972. It can be said that the "Tuskegee legacy" still profoundly affects how many African-Americans view the formal health care system and how that view impacts their health and well-being. For readers not familiar with the Tuskegee syphilis experiment, the following provides a brief description of what happened.

The Tuskegee Syphilis Experiment

In 1932, the U.S. government recruited 400 poor African-American men living in Macon County, Alabama, and offered them free treatment for "bad blood," which was a euphemism for syphilis, a sexually transmitted disease (Gray, 2002). Treatment for the disease, however, was never provided for the men—even though it was available at that time—and was, in fact, deliberately withheld from those who were infected. Instead, the men became unwitting subjects for a government-sanctioned medical investigation, entitled "The Tuskegee Study of Untreated Syphilis in the Negro Male." The Tuskegee study, which lasted for four decades, had nothing to do with treatment; rather, it was a nontherapeutic experiment to collect data on the long-term effects of syphilis on Black men. What became clear, after the story was broken by reporter Jean Heller in 1972, was that the Public Health Service (PHS) was interested in using Macon County and its Black inhabitants as a laboratory for studying the long-term effects of untreated syphilis, not in treating the individuals suffering from this deadly disease (Heller, 1972).

"The Tuskegee Study symbolizes the gross medical misconduct and blatant disregard for human rights that can take place in the name of science" (TheTalkingDrum, 2009). The study's principal investigators were not mad scientists; they were government physicians who published reports on their work in the leading medical journals. The subjects of this experiment are a clear illustration of how the burden of medical experimentation has historically been borne by those least able to protect themselves, such as those who are poor, incarcerated, prisoners of war, or those who are mentally challenged. The government doctors who participated in the study failed to obtain informed consent from the subjects in a study of a disease with a known risk to human life. Instead, the Public Health Service offered the men incentives—essentially bribes—to participate, including free physical examinations, free rides to and from the clinics, hot meals on examination days, free treatment for minor ailments, and—of particular importance for poor African-Americans in the South—a guarantee that a burial stipend would be paid to their survivors. This burial stipend of $50 represented the only form of burial insurance that many of the men had.

By failing to obtain informed consent and offering incentives for participation, the PHS doctors were performing unethical and immoral experiments on human subjects. By the time reporter Jean Heller wrote her exposé in July 1972, more than one hundred of the infected men had died. Others suffered from serious syphilis-related conditions that may have contributed to their deaths later, even though penicillin, an effective treatment against syphilis, was in widespread use by 1946. On July 23, 1973, Fred Gray, a prominent civil rights lawyer, brought a $1.8 billion class-action civil suit against the Public Health Service (Gray, 2002). Gray demanded $3 million in damages for each living participant and the heirs of the deceased. The case, however, never came to trial and, in December 1974, the government agreed to a $10 million out-of-court settlement. The living participants each received $37,500 in damages, and the heirs of the deceased, $15,000. However, nobody from the PHS ever admitted any wrongdoing, and some, in fact, were angry at the government for failing to defend the study (TheTalkingDrum, 2009). But as one survivor said: "I don't know what they used us for. I ain't never understood the study" (TheTalkingDrum, 2009).

The impact of the Tuskegee study has been profound in causing understandable mistrust of the traditional health care system by African-Americans. This mistrust still plays a role today in terms of lower immunization rates, poorer health status, lower rates of testing for HIV and treatment for AIDS, lower organ donation rates, higher infant mortality rates, and lower use of mental health services among African-Americans (King, 2003; U.S. DHHS, 1999). If the predominantly White health care system was capable of such a heinous act only 30 years ago, why should it be trusted now?

Thus, when working with culturally different clients, particularly those who have suffered from prejudice, discrimination, racism, oppression, and exploitation, developing a trusting relationship is the absolute cornerstone of effective intervention, particularly for something as invasive as treatment with medication. A final point is that social workers should not take a "cookie cutter" approach when working with culturally different clients. Every client is an individual as well as existing within his or her culture; furthermore, there can be vast differences among different subgroups within each particular culture (Newhill, 1990). These differences can be shaped by gender, education, social class, generation, and by level of assimilation and acculturation within the majority society. These are some of the variables that account for distinctive differences across clients who share membership in the same cultural group. At no time has the statement "start where the client is" been more relevant than when addressing culturally sensitive practice.

Medication Treatment with Culturally Different Clients

There is evidence that, on average, more African-Americans and Asians than Whites are slow metabolizers of several medications for psychosis and depression (Lin, Cheung, Smith, & Poland, 1997). This means that with such clients, the doctor must be careful not to prescribe doses of medication that are too high. On the other hand, one has to be cautious about making treatment decisions with regard to medication based solely on generalizations about certain races or ethnicities. For example, one widely held assumption is that Asians metabolize psychotropic medications at slower rates than consumers of other ethnicities and, thus, should be prescribed lower doses. This is not necessarily the case, however, and can result in Asian clients not receiving adequate treatment (Bender, 2004). It is better to determine the appropriate dose of medication based on how the particular individual responds to the medication, rather than relying on ethnic generalizations.

Cultural differences, however, can significantly affect factors related to adherence to taking psychotropic medication. For many Hispanic, Asian and African-American clients, the extended family unit is a strong influence on health care choices, which can strengthen or weaken adherence with both psychosocial and pharmacological interventions. It is critical, therefore, that family members be included in the treatment process and that psychoeducation about the purpose and value of medication be provided to both the client and the client's family.

Another culture-based issue that can be a barrier to accessing outside treatment for many clients is the belief that problems should be handled within the family and that going to strangers, such as medical professionals, is a sign of weakness and disrespect to the family (Sue & Sue, 1999). Furthermore, having to take medication may be viewed as a sign of weakness and vulnerability. As a result, some clients may be dissuaded from taking and staying on prescribed medication. For many African-American clients, there may be concerns that psychotropic medications are addictive (Newhill & Harris, 2007). Because of this, it is important that doctors and social workers specifically explain the purpose and action of medication and help the client see how medication therapy can be integrated into the client's cultural frame of reference.

It is also important to educate clients and families about dosage patterns and estimated time to achieve optimal therapeutic results. Some Hispanic and Asian clients, in particular, may hesitate to question the doctor about the purpose, directions, or side effects of the medications because of traditional deference to medical authority figures (Sue & Sue, 1999). In such a situation, you as your client's social worker can respect the client's cultural beliefs but at the same time take the initiative to provide the information that the client needs to understand the medication and encourage the client to ask questions. Also, the social worker can support the client in asking the doctor questions within the context of emphasizing that such questions do not disrespect the doctor, rather, they help the doctor to help the client better.

In summary, to best provide culturally sensitive services to clients who are taking medications as part of their treatment, social workers should take the following steps:

- First, the social worker needs to become familiar with the culturally different client's ethnic and cultural background. Ask questions and get the appropriate ongoing training to become culturally competent and maintain that competence over time;
- Second, the importance of the values and belief systems of the client should always be considered and addressed in all counseling and medication interventions;
- Third, include the client's family system as a way of increasing understanding and adherence with the medication regime; and
- Finally, the social worker must be aware of mental health diagnoses and how individuals from different ethnicities and cultures may not fit neatly into a Western therapeutic mold and that traditions and beliefs can be misinterpreted.

It is also important to remember that even though a client may belong to a particular cultural group, there is variation within that group as well, and every individual is unique in different ways. Social workers should start all intervention efforts by taking into account "where the client is," always noting and respecting what the client wants and recognizing that any intervention efforts are a reciprocal process in which the client and social worker are in a partnership to develop the goals and objectives for continued and lasting change. The last topic in the area of special populations is medication and women.

Medication and Women

Up until very recently, women have been largely underrepresented in pharmacological research, which limits our ability to understand the effectiveness and risks of medication for women. When thinking about medication treatment and the needs of women, however, there are a few points to keep in mind. First, women, as a whole, are much more likely to take prescription medication than men are and, in fact, consume 70 percent of all psychotropic drugs (Ettorre & Riska, 1995), even though there is little evidence they have a greater need for medications than men do. Some researchers have suggested that medications may be overprescribed for women, and doctors may be more likely to suggest medication to women than to men (Bentley & Walsh, 2005). Part of this may be the fact that men are less likely to acknowledge psychological distress or report that they take psychotropic drugs (Bentley & Walsh, 2005). Finally, women have biological differences that affect response to medication, including a lower ratio of lean body mass to body fat, differences in hormonal levels throughout the lifespan, differences in brain chemical compositions, the effect of oral contraceptives and hormone replacement therapy on drug responses, neurotransmitter differences between genders (e.g., a greater rate of serotonin-binding capacity in women), the fact that women empty stomach contents at a slower rate than men, which affects drug absorption, women and men metabolize medications differently and, finally, women and men have differential experiences and levels of side effects (Bentley & Walsh, 2005; Yonkers & Ellison, 1996).

Assess your comprehension of *medication treatment with racially and culturally diverse clients, women, and other special populations* by completing this quiz.

HOW SOCIAL WORKERS CAN PROMOTE SUCCESSFUL MEDICATION ADHERENCE

Most people with chronic illness—medical or psychiatric—don't take their medication exactly as prescribed by their doctor. This is sometimes addressed as a problem with medication "compliance." However, the word *compliance* implies that the client should comply or follow the prescription of the physician without question. Ideally, the client–doctor relationship is collaborative and, thus, the term *adherence* may be a preferable term to use.

The primary goal for successful medication adherence is to work with the client so that he or she takes the medication in a way that maximizes its effectiveness and minimizes its side effects. This typically means taking medication regularly and in the dosage and timing that the doctor recommends along with doing what is possible to buffer problematic side effects. However, it is common for obstacles to successful adherence to crop up, and one of the roles of the social worker in the area of psychopharmacology is to identify and seek solutions to such obstacles.

Common Obstacles to Medication Adherence

The first step you should take to increase your clients' adherence to their medication regime is to directly explore, examine, and document what conditions are present which might lead to non-adherence. If your client is not taking his or her medication as prescribed, the first thing to do is to simply ask the client in an empathic and matter-of-fact manner why he or she is not taking the medication. Often, the problem is solvable, but (1) the client has not identified the problem specifically, for example, the client just "doesn't feel better," so stops taking the medication; or (2) the client has identified the problem, but doesn't know what to do about it, for example, the medication costs too much; or (3) the client has identified the problem, but feels hesitant to bring it up to you or the doctor, for example, the client is experiencing sexual side effects that he or she feels embarrassed to talk about. How the client responds to your question about why he or she is not taking the medication usually suggests an intervention to solve the problem, examples of which are discussed below.

Another obstacle to adherence is the client's feelings about having to take medication in general. For example, medication may be perceived symbolically as a crutch and serves as a reminder that he or she has a mental illness. This is often particularly acute for those with severe and persistent mental illnesses that seem interminable, like schizophrenia, bipolar disorder, or recurrent major depression.

Another obstacle is that dependence on medication can reinforce feelings of helplessness and hopelessness, interfering with the client's self-esteem and sense of autonomy. Furthermore, having to take medication in order to be able to function well in life contradicts Western—especially American—sociocultural values about the importance of independence, self-sufficiency, and competence and, thus, may induce feelings of shame (Wegmann, 2012). Consumers may feel inside that they should be able to "pull themselves up by their bootstraps" and that their illness is simply a problem requiring effort and willpower to control and, in fact, others in their life may even say things like this to them.

Another obstacle to successful medication adherence is that some clients may have aspects related to their psychiatric difficulties that affect adherence. Medication is invasive, involving chemical changes affecting the individual's brain and body. Clients who are paranoid and who have ideas of reference or influence are particularly vulnerable to struggling with this obstacle and may hold fears that the medication is part of a plot to control, take advantage of, or even poison them. It is absolutely critical that the doctor and social worker be scrupulously honest with paranoid clients, provide matter-of-fact answers to their questions about medication, be up front and honest about side effects they may experience, be empathic about their fears, and allow the clients to control their own care as much as possible by supporting self-determination, empowerment, and collaboration in decision making.

Another obstacle to adherence is when the client is confused about how he or she should take the medication. Taking a medication once a day instead of twice a day may assist in increasing adherence. Liquid medication may be more tolerable for clients who have difficulty chewing or swallowing, some clients find gel caps easier to swallow than tablets, and so forth. One empowering strategy to help clients remember when to take their medication is assisting them in filling out a medication card. With a medication card, the client becomes responsible for monitoring, recording, and updating the medications he or she is taking.

A common area for confusion is in the area of medical abbreviations that specify when and how often the client should take the medication. Sometimes clients are confused about their medication simply because they do not understand the abbreviations used on the medication label. Below are a few of the more common abbreviations that social workers should become familiar with to understand both medication instructions and chart records:

Medical Abbreviations

qd	once a day	**IV**	intravenous
bid	twice a day	**STAT**	right away
tid	three times a day	**i**	one unit or pill
qid	four times a day	**ii**	two units or pills
hs	before bed	**iii**	three units or pills
prn	as needed	**c** or **q**	with
po	by mouth	**s**	without
IM	intramuscular (injection)	**CBC**	complete blood count

Another obstacle to adherence is that clients may have subjective responses to side effects of the medications prescribed for them that can differ from individual to individual. For example, your client may be particularly uncomfortable with anticholinergic side effects (described above) or self-conscious about obvious extrapyramidal symptoms. Weight gain, skin rashes, and sexual side effects may also prompt clients to stop taking medications. Because clients may not bring up these issues spontaneously, it is important that the social worker inquire about whether the client is experiencing problematic side effects, and then working with the client on alternatives to simply stopping the medication (described below).

Overcoming Obstacles to Medication Adherence

You, as your clients' social worker, can help your clients overcome obstacles to medication adherence by encouraging them to talk about their feelings about medication and about their illness and helping them sort out realistic and unrealistic concerns. One can also be helpful by encouraging clients to be assertive and teaching them how to be assertive in requesting medication reevaluation and in how to approach asking their doctor questions. To increase the likelihood that a medication will work well, clients and their families must actively participate in collaborative discussion with the doctor prescribing the medication. They must tell the doctor about the client's past medical history, other medications being taken, anticipated life changes, such as planning to have a baby or going back to work and, after some experience with a medication, whether it is working positively to relieve symptoms and whether it is causing side effects. Remember, the primary responsibility for taking medication resides with your client, and only secondarily with significant others such as family members or care home operator.

One of the most helpful things you, as your clients' social worker, can do is alert your clients to the kinds of questions they should ask their doctor when they are prescribed medication. The following is a list of questions for consumers to raise with their doctors as recommended by the National Institute of Mental Health (2005):

1. _____ What is the name of the medication, and what is it supposed to do?
2. _____ How and when do I take it, and when do I stop taking it?
3. _____ What foods, drinks, other medications, or activities should I avoid while taking the prescribed medication?
4. _____ Should it be taken with food or on an empty stomach?
5. _____ Is it safe to drink alcohol while on this medication?
6. _____ What are the side effects, and what should I do if they occur?
7. _____ Is there any written information available about the medication, such as a patient package insert?

NIMH (2005) recommends to consumers that once they have been taking the medication as prescribed for a short period of time, they should report back to their doctor about how the medication is making them feel, whether they are experiencing any side effects, and share any concerns they have about the medication.

Risk Factors Associated with Partial Medication Adherence

Rather than completely stopping their medications in response to adherence obstacles, some clients continue to take their medication, but take it erratically or only on occasion. There are a number of risk factors for such partial medication adherence, which include the following (Ayuso-Gutierrez & del Rio Vega, 1997; Lacro, Dunn, Dolder, et al., 2002; Weiden, Kozma, Grogg, & Locklear, 2004; Weiden & Zygmunt, 1996):

- The client has problems in thinking (disorganization, cognitive impairment), which lead to forgetting to take his or her medication every day as prescribed;
- The client lacks insight into his or her illness and therefore does not see the need for medication treatment;
- The client has a history of repeated and recent relapse and rehospitalization;
- The client suffers from ideas or beliefs (e.g., paranoia) that might lead to discontinuing the medication, such as thinking the medication is poison; or
- The client uses or abuses recreational/illicit drugs or alcohol, or he or she has a history of such use/abuse.

These risk factors are things you should be alert for when working with your clients and take into consideration as you and the doctor work together with the client to improve her or his adherence.

How Social Workers Can Help Mitigate Risk Factors for Non- or Partial Adherence

As your client's social worker, you can help mitigate risk factors for non-adherence by listening attentively to your client and joining the client in seeking other alternatives to the current medication. Taking this approach recognizes and validates the client's feelings and concerns while at the same time offering alternatives to stopping medication altogether that the client can discuss with his or her doctor.

One alternative is to change the medication dosage. If the dose is too high, the client may be experiencing an elevated level of side effects. We have learned via multiple research studies that lowering the dose of a psychotropic medication can often maintain the therapeutic benefit while reducing the level of side effects. Sometimes the dose is too low, and in such cases the client may be experiencing the side effects but insufficient therapeutic benefit. In such cases, raising the dose may be appropriate. If the client is having problems with extrapyramidal side effects with an antipsychotic medication, introducing an antiparkinsonian medication to combat such side effects can be helpful. Other alternatives include changing the type or class of drug, using a new or adjunctive medication, or trying a clinically appropriate "drug holiday." A "drug holiday" is when the client, under the doctor's supervision, gradually goes off the medication to see if he or she is able to stay well without it. If the client's symptoms return, then the medication can be restarted. Such a decision should be mutually determined by the client and doctor.

Diamond (2009) provides several suggestions that can help increase medication adherence. These include the following:

- Make the medication regime as simple as possible, for example, if possible, reduce the number of pills and number of times pills must be taken.
- With the client, figure out a time to take the medication at the same time that the client performs a routine daily activity, for example, brushing teeth or having breakfast.
- Package the medication in a container that serves to remind the client to take their medication each day. Plastic containers with compartments for each day of the week where medication can be loaded up a week at a time are very helpful.
- Pay attention to side effects, ask about them, and help the client to develop strategies for coping with side effects to maintain comfort.
- Be genuinely and regularly interested in the client's medication along with the other components of his or her treatment.
- Connect the medication in concrete ways to the person's own life goals. If getting a job or one's own apartment is what the client wants most, then making a connection among improvement of symptoms, getting what the client wants, and

medication adherence can be useful. If staying out the hospital is what the person wants most, he or she is going to be more willing to take medication *if* he or she believes that taking the medication will really prevent hospitalization. Conducting a life history analysis in which you and the client identify how stopping medication is connected to adverse events can help spark insight and motivation.

- Arrange for medication to be supervised when necessary. We all want to support client independence and self-determination, but a client who is willing but regularly forgets to take medication can be helped by regular phone calls, by visits from a clinician if mobile outreach services are available, or by reminders from a family member or group living staff person.

Assess your comprehension of *how social workers and other nonmedical mental health professionals can promote successful medication adherence with their clients* by completing this quiz.

Engage in a *Psychopharmacology Case Analysis Role-Play Exercise.*

CONCLUSION

Social work education has a strong tradition of emphasizing the importance of viewing the person within his or her social environment and the impact of contextual issues such as social justice, poverty, and oppression upon individuals and communities. Traditionally, less attention has been directed toward the influence of biological variables that affect a variety of health problems, including mental illness, although that is rapidly changing. The current practice environment requires social work graduates to be proficient in a range of therapeutic modalities, including biological and social interventions, if they expect to be competitively employed in human services. Furthermore, examinations for social work licensure across states now include content on psychotropic medications.

Evidence-based practice research has demonstrated the efficacy of psychotropic medication as a therapeutic intervention for a wide range of mental disorders, including mood disorders, psychotic disorders, disruptive behavior disorders, and anxiety disorders. For severe and persistent mental illnesses, such as schizophrenia and bipolar disorder, medication is an essential adjunct to provision of psychosocial treatment and to good treatment outcomes and recovery. Without appropriate medication, many individuals suffering from such disorders experience symptoms that interfere with their ability to extract any benefit from counseling or other psychotherapeutic treatments and undermine their efforts toward recovery.

Although social workers cannot directly prescribe psychotropic drugs for clients, social workers often play key roles in monitoring both the effectiveness of the medication and the client's adherence to taking the medication properly. In today's managed care environment, the client's physician may only see the client occasionally to dispense a prescription, whereas the client's social worker may see the client much more frequently, and thus is able to observe even subtle changes in the client's symptoms and functioning. Because of this, social workers are in an ideal position to take on the role of encouraging medication adherence, monitoring side effects, and educating and supporting clients and their families about medication. Successful treatment with psychotropic medication depends upon a strong positive partnership among the treatment team, the consumer, and the consumer's family.

Assess your application and analysis of this chapter's contents by completing the *Chapter Review.*

Chapter 9

Case Management

INTRODUCTION

This chapter addresses the intervention modality called *case management*. The reason for including a chapter on case management is because working with individuals with serious and persistent mental illness (SPMI) and their families inevitably includes some form of case management activity regardless of what a social worker's or other clinician's official job title may be (Stoesen, 2008). One's job title may be "clinical social worker" or "outpatient therapist," but along with providing psychotherapy, psychoeducation, or other clinical interventions, you will probably also be referring your client to additional services and may be responsible for coordinating those services and providing follow-up. Working effectively with individuals with SPMI requires a coordinated, multifaceted, holistic approach to treatment and care.

The chapter will begin by reviewing the community support systems model and philosophy, which is the conceptual framework underlying all models of case management. The chapter will then discuss what case managers do in their day-to-day work and the essential knowledge and skills utilized in such work, including an illustrative case scenario involving a severely mentally ill client and her case management service plan. Finally, the chapter will focus on three evidence-based practices that reflect case management principles and are critical components of many clients' case management service plans. These three practices are the Program for Assertive Community Treatment (PACT), supported employment, and permanent supportive housing. PACT is a well-established, comprehensive, evidence-based outreach treatment alternative to traditional case management specifically designed to meet the needs of individuals with SPMI at high risk for decompensation and rehospitalization (Monroe-DeVita, Morse, & Bond, 2012). Supported employment can help individuals with serious mental illness obtain and be successful in competitive employment (Bond, 2004), while permanent supportive housing helps individuals with mental illness choose, obtain, and maintain decent, safe, and affordable housing that is integrated into the natural community (SAMHSA, 2010).

THE COMMUNITY SUPPORT SYSTEM NETWORK

Case management is only one component of the multidimensional "community support system network," a system of community care for individuals with "chronic mental illness" that was first recommended by the National Institute of Mental Health in 1981 and is still the primary conceptual framework underlying all models of case management today. The community support system network was originally an effort to provide a model for replicating in the community what was previously provided in the state hospital for individuals with serious and persistent mental illness (SPMI). In the past, when most individuals with serious mental illness were in institutional care, the institution—in spite of the many negative aspects associated

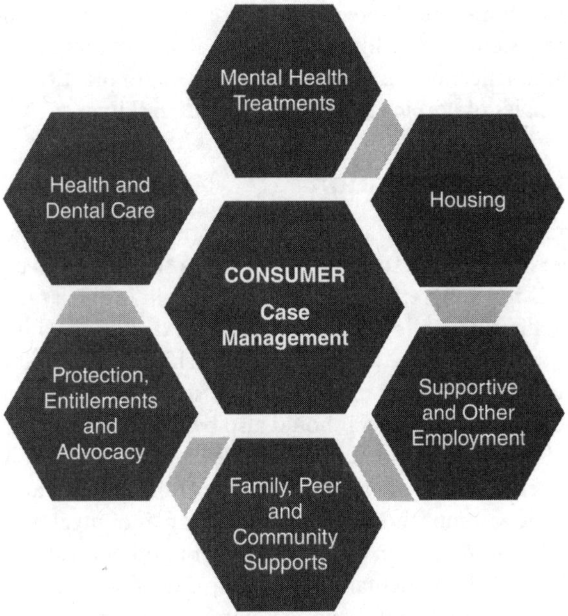

Diagram of the Community Support System Network

Adapted from: Stroul, B.A. (1988). *Community support systems for persons with long-term mental illness: Questions and answers*. Rockville, MD: National Institute of Mental Health.

with it—did provide for all of the patient's needs. Such "total institutions" were intended to provide shelter, food, clothing, structured activities, medical care, therapeutic care, and vocational and psychosocial rehabilitation (Stroul, 1988). Today, however, these diverse needs must be provided in the community for most clients during the majority of their life, and the case manager or resource coordinator is the hub or "traffic cop" responsible for identifying and coordinating all of the services that the client needs.

The philosophy that guides the community support system network is *rehabilitation*, and its principles reflect many of the social work profession's key values: the importance of personal dignity, individualization, self-determination, nondiscrimination, confidentiality, and an overall emphasis on promoting recovery. Let's review what each of these concepts means for case management practice.

Personal dignity refers to the respect communicated to the client by the case manager providing the services. Emphasis is placed on honoring the client's privacy, the client's rights as a citizen, and the client's own self-respect. Although these aspects seem simple and obvious, they are not always promoted in practice (Dillon, 2003). *Self-determination* is the client's right to make informed choices about decisions affecting his or her life. Case managers foster this by actively developing and supporting policies and practices in which clients can establish their own goals, participate in treatment planning meetings, choose their own residences, and maintain the greatest possible control over their lives. All of these factors lie at the heart of today's model of recovery. Social workers, and case managers in particular, promote *individualization* by tailoring services to the unique needs and preferences of each individual client as they change over time. *Nondiscrimination* means that individualized case management services should be provided fairly without prejudice to whoever needs them without regard to a client's race, culture or ethnic group, age, gender, sexual orientation, religious affiliation, disability, or other characteristic. Furthermore, services should be culturally sensitive and culturally relevant. Finally, *confidentiality* means, of course, that case managers must always protect client records and keep confidential information received in the course of professional service activities.

The six principles of community mental health discussed in Chapter 3—accessibility, accountability, comprehensiveness, continuity of care, multidisciplinary service provision, and prevention—are also relevant to case management practice with individuals with severe and persistent mental illness. Additional case management principles associated with deinstitutionalization, and particularly relevant to practice with individuals with SPMI, are the principles of *normalization* and *integration* (Flynn & Nitsch, 1980).

Normalization and Integration

Fulfilling the principles of normalization and integration means that case managers should facilitate consumers' adaptation to community life as seamlessly as possible so that their "consumer status" is not apparent and their membership in the larger community is fostered. Consumers should be allowed, encouraged, and supported in using mainstream community education and recreational facilities, such as the local library or community swimming pool and, furthermore, the community should be willing and able to learn to accept their participation. Consumers should also be able to live—whether independently or in sheltered care—in neighborhoods that include diverse ages, lifestyles, and social strata instead of being relegated to a "ghetto" of consumer housing, as illustrated in Chapter 3. Such an arrangement accomplishes both normalization and integration, because the consumer is living in the community in a similar manner to other residents and participates in community life alongside both mentally ill and non-mentally ill community residents. The most persistent obstacle to achieving this goal in many communities, however, is *NIMBY*, or "not-in-my-backyard" (Zippay & Lee, 2008). Working to overcome this obstacle requires that case managers take on the role of *advocate*, which will be discussed shortly.

Role of Natural Social Supports

One mechanism that can lead to normalization and integration is for case managers to assist in facilitating the development and engagement of *natural support systems* in the lives of their clients. Such natural support systems include friends, neighbors, clergy, barbers and hairdressers, shopkeepers, and other community persons who are connected to the client in a meaningful way. This enhances the client's social support network, relieves the burden on families, and is a crucial resource for providing the client with a line of defense or buffer against stress. Case managers must work collaboratively with the client, family, and other support persons to ensure that any one support person isn't overburdened and to ensure the client's needs can be met across a range of people. Example:

Willie and His Coins

Willie, who has autism and obsessive-compulsive disorder, lives in a group home in a working-class neighborhood primarily composed of modest single-family homes in a small town in central California. Willie spent many years living in the state hospital but has been residing in his current home for over 25 years. Willie has always had an avid interest in learning about and collecting rare coins. His sister gave him a renewable subscription to a coin collector magazine many years ago, and Willie reads each issue cover to cover. Willie is supported by SSI, along with $25 that his sister sends him each month for spending money. He saves as much as he can from the money his sister sends and his P & I (personal and incidental) money in order to purchase more coins. After he buys a coin, he takes it to the bank and puts it in his safety deposit box. Every couple of weeks, Willie visits his safety deposit box, takes out his coins, and the bank employees allow him as much time as he wants to look at his coins in one of the bank's safety deposit box booths.

In Willie's small town there are four shops that sell and trade coins, all of which he can visit by walking to the shop or taking the bus. Over the years, Willie has developed friendships with the men who run the coin shops, and they highly respect his voluminous knowledge about coins and the history of coins. Because Willie is so knowledgeable, the coin shop owners sometimes defer questions that customers have about coins to Willie to answer, and this fills him with great pride. The shopkeepers regularly invite Willie to hang out in their shops, offering him coffee and doughnuts, and have developed a genuine affection for him. One day, one of the coin shop owners noticed that Willie was upset and, concerned, called Willie's case manager. The case manager went out to the shop and Willie revealed that his sister had called the night before to tell him that their mother, who had been seriously ill in the hospital, had died. Over the course of the next week, the coin shopkeepers provided Willie with support and helped him emotionally as he dealt with his grief.

Another important natural support resource for clients is self-help support groups, which can enhance the client's social support network and help empower the client in adapting to the community. As noted, the basic philosophy of community support services is psychosocial rehabilitation, discussed in more detail in the next chapter, and supporting the development of skills for daily living and social skills is often facilitated or directly provided by the client's case manager. Let's look more specifically at what case managers do in their day-to-day work.

CASE MANAGEMENT IN COMMUNITY MENTAL/ BEHAVIORAL HEALTH PRACTICE

What Case Managers Do

To understand what case managers do in their day-to-day work, and who their clients are, let's look at a particular client's case for illustration and then look at this client's individual case management service plan.

The Case of Antonio/Antonia

Antonia Garcia is a 23-year-old Mexican-American transgendered woman who lives with her sister in a small town in the agricultural region of central California. Five years ago, after a suicide attempt secondary to being relentlessly teased and bullied in high school and afterwards in the workplace, Antonia (then using her birth name Antonio and living as a man) told her parents that she felt she was a woman living in a man's body and that she was going to begin exploring the process involved in transitioning from male to female. Antonia's parents, who immigrated to the United States from Mexico 20 years prior, were strong Catholics and socially conservative. Upon hearing this from their only son, Antonia's mother burst into tears, and her father told Antonia that he disowned her. The only family member willing to support Antonia was her older sister Maria. Maria invited Antonia to live with her and helped her find a part-time job in a flower shop. Antonia began living as a woman, but it was very difficult. Young people who knew her as Antonio continued to harass and tease her and, in response to the stress and her increasing social isolation, Antonia began using drugs—marijuana and cocaine. Soon after, she suffered her first psychotic break.

Antonia was hospitalized and given the diagnosis of schizophreniform disorder. During her hospitalization, Antonia experienced considerable hostility from both staff and other consumers on the unit. One staff member complained that "it is impossible to find this person a roommate because of their sexual identity problems," and many made transphobic and homophobic comments intentionally within earshot of Antonia. When Antonia told the unit social worker about what was going on, the social worker immediately took action and held meetings with both staff and consumers to talk about the issue of transphobia and educating participants about gender identity, gender nonconformity, and sexual orientation to help them better understand such issues (see, e.g., IOM, 2011). This seemed to help a little, and by the time Antonia was discharged, her clinical status was stable and her sister welcomed her back into her home. A couple months later, Maria announced she was getting married, and her new husband-to-be was not supportive of the idea of having Antonia live with them. Antonia's job in the flower shop didn't pay enough to live on independently, and Antonia's depressive symptoms began to return. Feeling like she was falling into a hole of despair, Antonia made a suicide attempt. This time, her admitting diagnosis was bipolar II disorder, and she was placed on a mood stabilizer and a second-generation antipsychotic medication. On the third day of hospitalization, Antonia met with the unit social worker, Janice. Antonia says:

> I don't know what to do anymore. Most of my family hates me. I have nowhere to go. I know my sister still loves me, but I can't live with her anymore. I am transgendered, you know, and I want to move to the next step, I know I want to start on hormone therapy and think I will want the surgery eventually, but I have nobody to talk to about this. Sometimes I think I am better off dead, but then I pray to God for his guidance and he tells me to go on living, that I do have something to offer the world. I try to take care of myself, but I know I won't remember to take my meds once I leave the hospital. Please help me—what should I do?

Antonia's situation is quite complex and evidences both strengths and challenges. In terms of strengths, Antonia is intelligent and insightful, she has a loving and supportive sister, she has completed high school and has a good work history including a current part-time job that she likes, and she has realized and accepted that she is a transgendered woman. These are all strengths that can be capitalized on as Antonia moves forward on her journey to recovery. Antonia also faces a number of challenges. Although she has accepted that she is a transgendered woman, she continues to experience prejudice and discrimination due to her gender nonconformity, and has been rejected and estranged from her parents and her sister's husband, which has resulted in having no place to live upon discharge from the hospital. In addition, her part-time job doesn't pay enough for Antonia to support herself independently, she has difficulty managing her psychiatric disorder, for example, remembering to take her medication which is essential for maintaining wellness, and she has had continuing problems with substance use. Finally, she faces a scarcity of medical and other professionals available locally with training in the care of transgendered persons. Given these many challenges, one can conclude that Antonia might benefit from having a case manager, but what do case managers actually do that could be helpful to Antonia?

Defining Case Management and General Case Management Goals

As noted, case management is one of the essential functions of community support programs and is, in fact, the central or pivotal function upon which all the other components are dependent (see diagram above). The term "case management" is a generic term that is not associated with any one discipline or profession, although social workers, because of their orientation and training, are particularly well suited to the case management role (Rose, 1992). Case management services are also used with many different populations, not just clients with mental illness. Some case managers do not have college degrees and are paraprofessionals, while others do have professional degrees in human services and may even have master's degrees. There are also many alternative terms used for "case manager" including "care manager," "resource coordinator," and "care coordinator." Some consumers and families object to the word "case," feeling that it is demeaning, that is, "I'm a person, not a case, and I don't need to be managed." This is a valid point, thus, it can be helpful to tell consumers and families that case managers don't manage people, rather, they help consumers and families manage complex *situations* and coordinate the services needed.

In general, case management may be defined as a process or method for ensuring that clients/consumers are provided with whatever services they need in a coordinated, effective, and efficient manner with the goal of helping the individual achieve positive recovery and quality of life (Summers, 2011). With the case manager as the client's and family's main pivotal relationship, the client is helped collaboratively to use community resources that will facilitate his or her ability to live productively in the community (Rapp & Goscha, 2011).

In community mental health practice, case management goals usually fall into one of two categories. The first category includes goals related to *prevention*, such as preventing or delaying mental illness relapse or decompensation and psychiatric rehospitalization, and preventing harm, such as preventing suicidal behavior and violence toward others. The other category of case management goals involve *recovery goals*, that is, those goals related to rehabilitation, enhancing quality of life, and facilitating promotion of the highest level of psychosocial functioning possible. The parameters of a case manager's role differ depending on the model of case management that is employed; however, across the board, five general functions are standard. These functions are assessment, service planning, linkage, monitoring, and advocacy (Eack, Anderson, & Greeno, 2012; Sands & Gellis, 2012; Summers, 2011).

The Five Functions of Case Management

Assessment

The first step in a case management assessment is developing rapport and trust with the client, leading to the creation of a therapeutic alliance. Once a beginning therapeutic alliance is established, the client will feel safe and comfortable collaborating with the case manager in developing the assessment, which forms the basis for the client's case management service plan. The most critical component to effective case management is *collaboration*, in which the client and case manager work together as partners in the client's recovery journey. If the client's family is involved, the family, too, becomes a partner in the process.

A good case management assessment involves a comprehensive multidimensional evaluation of the consumer's needs based on his or her bio-psycho-social-spiritual history, psychiatric and medical diagnoses, strengths, resources, disabilities, challenges, and barriers to recovery (Summers, 2011). A good case management assessment requires compilation of information from a variety of sources, as well as input from the consumer and his or her family. During the assessment process, the case manager and consumer collaboratively evaluate where the consumer's needs are already met and where there are gaps. Then, on the basis of the assessment, the case manager and consumer develop the consumer's service plan. Collaboration does not always happen, however, and research has shown that consumers and case managers sometimes differ in their perceptions about the consumer's needs (Henwood, Padgett, & Nguyen, 2011), even though consumer preferences are important predictors of achieving successful psychosocial functioning in the community (Greenwood, Schaefer-McDaniel, Winkel, & Tsemberis, 2005). Collaboration is the best approach for both identifying and resolving differences in perceptions about needs and goals.

Service Planning

The service plan is specifically tailored to the individual client/consumer through a collaborative process involving all of the stakeholders. Everyone involved in the client's situation should be figuratively, or better yet, literally, "at the table," providing input. In keeping with the community support system network model and current recovery principles, the consumer should be an active participant in developing the service plan, and the consumer's family should also be a valued participant, particularly if they are providing direct care for the consumer. Ideally, the plan should include representatives from all other service providers included in the plan, such as the personal care/board and care home operator, day treatment/partial hospitalization staff member, psychiatrist, peer counselor, and so forth.

Service plans should include the identified needs, services, goals, means of implementing the goals, and target dates for completion or reassessment. All should be spelled out in behaviorally specific terms. As an illustrative example, below is the service plan developed for Antonia Garcia. First, Antonia's strengths and challenges are spelled out, followed by a grid that clearly delineates Antonia's needs and goals, the plan for implementation of the goals, who the responsible individuals are, and the target dates for each dimension of the plan.

Case Management Service Plan for Antonia Garcia

Strengths: Intelligent and insightful, articulate, attractive, supportive sister, completed high school, has a good work history, and has realized and accepted that she is a transgendered woman.

Challenges and Barriers: Has/continues to experience prejudice and discrimination due to her gender nonconformity; has been rejected and estranged from parents and sister's husband; has no place to live; currently employed only part-time; difficulty managing psychiatric disorder; substance use; and faces a scarcity of medical and other professionals available locally with training in the care of transgendered persons.

Consumer's Needs and Goals	Implementation Plan	Responsible Individual(s)	Target Dates
Psychiatric care plan: Antonia must learn how to adhere to prescribed psychotropic medication and avoid recreational/illicit drug use. Antonia also needs counseling to address issues related to being transgendered, such as gender role exploration and transitioning, the impact of stigma and discrimination on her mental health, internalized transphobia, and body image and management. ***Goal:*** Control psychiatric symptoms, delay/avoid rehospitalization, prevent crisis situations from developing, and maintain wellness as an ongoing goal.	1. Antonia will see Dr. Smith at Acme Community Mental Health Center. Follow-up will be arranged by Dr. Smith, and Antonia will attend appointments independently or be accompanied by her sister, Maria. 2. Antonia will take her medication herself. If she forgets, her Assertive Community Treatment team will remind her. 3. Antonia will avoid recreational/illicit drugs and avoid contact with the individuals from whom she obtained the drugs previously. 4. Antonia will be assigned to Jacinto Menendez, a case manager who specializes in working with LGBT clients with SMI. The case manager will coordinate resources and providers and arrange appointments.	Dr. Smith and Antonia's sister ACT team Antonia, ACT Case manager, Jacinto Menendez	First appointment is 05/05/2011 Ongoing – review monthly Ongoing First appointment is 05/06/2011

Consumer's Needs and Goals	Implementation Plan	Responsible Individual(s)	Target Dates
Housing/shelter: Antonia will live in a mental health transitional living facility until she begins her MtF transition. Then she will move to Rainbow House, which is a permanent supportive housing option that provides safe drug-free housing and is welcoming to LGBT youth, located in a nearby urban area. ***Goal:*** Develop skills in independent living; explore future independent living arrangements.	1. Antonia will be discharged from the hospital to the mental health transitional living facility. 2. Antonia will visit Rainbow House and complete their orientation program. 3. Antonia will move from the transitional facility to Rainbow House.	Antonia and inpatient social worker, Janice Antonia and CM Antonia and sister	05/04/2011 05/30/2011 06/15/2011
Medical health care: Antonia is in good physical health according to her sister and health records. Antonia will make an appointment with Dr. Fisher for an assessment related to the medical aspects of gender transition. If the assessment concurs, Antonia may choose to begin hormone therapy. ***Goal:*** Maintain physical health and explore the process of gender transitioning.	1. Medical care as needed. 2. Make appointment with Dr. Fisher. 3. Case manager will read the *World Professional Association for Transgender Health Standards of Care*, 7th ed., 2011, and use as a resource.	Dr. Y Dr. Fisher Jacinto Menendez, CM	Ongoing as needed 06/01/2011 Ongoing
Economic support: Antonia's only income is from part-time work at the flower shop. Antonia could be eligible for SSI and Medi-Cal, which would provide her with financial support through her transition and until she can secure full-time work. ***Goal:*** Develop long-range financial plan.	1. Antonia will continue her part-time job at the flower shop and look into full-time work. 2. Case manager (Jacinto Menendez) will discuss Antonia's thoughts and feelings about applying for SSI and Medi-Cal.	Antonia and Joe (flower shop manager) Antonia and CM	Ongoing 05/11/2011
Socialization, leisure, and recreation: Antonia spends a lot of time reading and listening to music. She doesn't have many friends and is isolated. She does get together with her sister, but now that Maria is engaged and Antonia is no longer living with her, she doesn't see her as much. Antonia has very little connection to the LGBT community, which is small but growing in her community. ***Goal:*** Antonia will increase social activities to develop a more solid, supportive, and extensive social network in the community.	1. Antonia will join the support group for individuals in early transition at the LGBT Action Center and attend one center-sponsored social activity each month. 2. Antonia will join the Depression and Bipolar Illness Management and Recovery Group at the community mental health center. 3. Antonia will attend Catholic mass with her sister twice a month. 4. Antonia will try attending the local Unitarian-Universalist church, which is a "welcoming congregation" for LGBT individuals. 5. Antonia will try attending the local chapter of PFLAG and get information about PFLAG Transgender Network	Antonia Antonia and CM Jacinto Antonia and sister Maria Antonia Antonia	First meeting 05/09/2011 First meeting 05/11/2011 Begin upon discharge from inpt. Ongoing upon discharge By 06/01/11

(continued)

Consumer's Needs and Goals	Implementation Plan	Responsible Individual(s)	Target Dates
Employment and vocational opportunities: Antonia likes working in the flower shop but would like to obtain full-time employment with better pay. She is interested in a career in floral design and would like to obtain a certificate in floral design, which involves a one-year program of study at the local community college. ***Goal:*** Explore vocational training in floral design.	1. Antonia will meet with a Bureau of Vocational Rehabilitation counselor to get information about vocational options in floral design and other related careers and schedule vocational testing in the next 3 months.	Antonia, CM, and BVR counselor	08/01/2011
Family relationships: With the exception of her sister, Maria, Antonia is estranged from her family. She would like to repair their relationships but doesn't know how. Clearly, her parents are embarrassed and probably feel helpless and confused about the situation. They are uninformed and have no experience with transgendered individuals or individuals with serious mental illness. Maria is very open to learning how to be more helpful to her sister. ***Goal:*** Help Antonia to reconnect with her parents, if possible, and other family members. If successful, Antonia's family can be provided with psychoeducation about being transgender and about bipolar II disorder and receive support from groups such as the Hispanic Families of the Mentally Ill, an affiliate of the National Alliance on Mental Illness and PFLAG.	1. Antonia's sister, Maria, will meet with Dr. Smith, who will provide information about bipolar II disorder and treatment. 2. Jacinto (CM) will meet with Maria and Antonia to discuss how to approach engaging Antonia's parents. 3. Maria will attend a LGBT Friends and Family information session at the LGBT Action Center.	Dr. Smith, Maria Jacinto Maria	05/15/2011 06/01/2011 06/02/2011

Signature of agreement: ______________________
Client (Antonia Garcia) Date

Signature of agreement: ______________________
Case Manager (Jacinto Menendez) Date

As shown above, the case management plan encompasses much more than Antonia's psychiatric needs. It also identifies a wide range of psychosocial and medical needs and who or what services and providers can meet the needs. Target dates are also set, ensuring that monitoring will take place. Typically, the service plan is subject to review in 10 to 15 visits, or after 90 days or sooner if needed.

Linkage

The third function of a case manager is *linkage*. Linkage addresses the role the case manager has for ensuring that the client is linked with the appropriate community support and treatment services. In order to fulfill this function effectively, the case manager must be thoroughly familiar and up-to-date on community resources including what the most current eligibility requirements are and how to apply for and access the resources. When working with individuals with the most serious mental illnesses, simply making a referral is not sufficient, particularly to ancillary services that may not be staffed by people who are well trained in working with individuals with mental illness. Here is an example of what can happen in such a situation.

Marisol

Marisol, who has schizophrenia and lives in the streets when her family is unable to care for her, has a persistent delusion that she was abducted by aliens many years ago and taken to the planet Venus where alien doctors replaced her real internal organs, including her brain, with alien organs in order to track her and control her mind once she was returned to Earth. Marisol has been referred to the Social Security office by her community mental health case manager to apply for Social Security disability. After some difficulty figuring out what bus to take and transfer to, Marisol found the office and approached the receptionist.

Receptionist: (without looking up) May I help you?
Marisol: I need to see someone about getting disability.
Receptionist: What is your name?
Marisol: Marisol Gomez.
Receptionist: What is your address?
Marisol: I can't tell you that.
Receptionist: I cannot help you if you won't give me your address.
Marisol: But ... but I can't ... they'll find me.
Receptionist: I need a street name.
Marisol: Venus.
Receptionist: Is that Venus Avenue or Venus Street?
Marisol: The planet Venus.
Receptionist: I need an address with a zip code.
Marisol: You don't understand.
Receptionist: What I understand is that you're not giving me the information I need.
Marisol: Never mind ... they're trying to take my thoughts. I can't stay here any longer.

At this point, frightened, Marisol leaves and goes back to the encampment under the bridge where she has been living with another homeless woman. It is several months before Marisol goes back to the mental health clinic, this time very psychotic, physically unwell from living on the streets, and still with no source of financial support.

This example illustrates how, when making a referral, detailed steps should be developed by the case manager with the consumer to facilitate access to the services needed and all of the steps involved. In the case above, the client, Marisol, should have been accompanied by someone—the case manager, peer counselor, or a knowledgeable family member—who could have run interference on her behalf and provided the information needed by the receptionist along with explaining to Marisol why such information is needed and assuring her that she is safe.

Another means for facilitating linkage is *modeling* for the client how to do a particular necessary step. For example, the case manager might model how to take the bus including, if needed, going with the client on a "practice" bus trip so the client knows where the bus stop is, how and when to insert the fare money, how to read the map posted on the bus wall, how to pull the cord to indicate that the driver should stop at the next bus stop, and how to keep track of key landmarks in order to know when one's stop is coming up.

Another skill-building form of assistance is *role-playing*. Such role-plays involve helping the client develop and use appropriate social skills including how to ask for services and how to ask for what he or she needs in an assertive and polite manner. Writing a letter of referral emphasizing strengths for the client to present is another mechanism that can help the client to contact the right person at the agency where he or she needs services. Making the referral contact and getting the name of a contact person for the client to ask for can be very helpful. As noted above, mobilizing family members or peer volunteers to provide support by accompanying the client to the agency the client has been referred to can be useful. Peer volunteers, in particular, can be especially helpful to consumers new to the system because they "know the ropes" and can provide empowering tips on navigating the process of seeking services. Arranging for community transportation services is often an essential step and, finally, if necessary, the case manager can escort the client to the service and stay with the client during the process of getting whatever service is needed. The rule of thumb with linkage is to choose facilitation over directive intervention, but if the client isn't ready to be independent yet, then directive hands-on help may be appropriate.

Monitoring

The fourth component of case management is *monitoring*. Here the case manager oversees the client's case to make sure the client is following through with the plan successfully. If some aspect of the service plan is not being implemented, the case manager determines what the obstacles are and how to remedy them. If the client followed through, yet the plan didn't work out, then the case manager and client should work collaboratively on revising the service plan. Many times, obstacles to follow-through are easily resolved once they are identified. Example:

Jermaine

Jermaine, who has schizophrenia, has prominent negative symptoms including social withdrawal, anergia (low energy), anhedonia (inability to feel pleasure), and low motivation. For weeks following his last hospitalization, Jermaine spent his days sitting on his mother's couch, watching TV and smoking. Jermaine lives with his mother, Leota, who recently asked the county's community mental health center to assign a case manager to help Jermaine with getting involved in some kind of daily therapeutic activity. The case manager, Kenji, referred Jermaine to the center's day treatment program, and although Jermaine attended every day for 3 weeks, he abruptly stopped coming. The day treatment center staff called Kenji, who then called Jermaine. Jermaine said he liked day treatment, but his mother, whom he depended upon for transportation to and from the program, got a new job and could no longer drive him to day treatment. After some collaborative problem-solving discussion, Jermaine and Kenji worked out a solution. Jermaine would take the bus to his brother Tyrone's house and then his brother agreed to drop him off at the day treatment center on the way to work, and pick Jermaine up mid-afternoon and take him back to his house. From that point on, Jermaine attended day treatment regularly. With the program's help, he improved his social skills and eventually enrolled in a supported employment program.

In this case, several people were involved in the process of monitoring Jermaine's situation, including his mother, his brother, the day treatment staff, and his case manager. Without all of these individuals doing their part, Jermaine might have "fallen through the cracks" and ended up back on his mother's couch spending his days watching TV and smoking. Monitoring was key to problem-solving the transportation problem and getting Jermaine the services he needed that led to positive steps in his journey toward recovery. Rather than labeling Jermaine's not attending day treatment as "resistance," the day treatment staff and Jermaine's case manager Kenji investigated the basis of his lack of attendance, and the transportation problem was identified and resolved.

Certain changes in the client's presentation or situation can serve as "red flags" for reassessing the client's service plan. Such red flags include an increased use of crisis or emergency services; loss of a stable residence, elevating risk for homelessness; involvement with law enforcement, including arrests and incarceration; change in the client's clinical presentation suggesting return or worsening of psychiatric symptoms, elevating risk for hospitalization; abuse of drugs or alcohol; changes in the client's social support network, especially those involving loss or deterioration of social support; and inability to contact or locate the client.

Advocacy

The fifth, and last, component of case management is *advocacy.* Everybody needs an advocate at one time or another. For most people, advocates come in the form of family members and/or friends who pitch in when there is a problem and help the friend or relative get what he or she needs if the person is unable to be his or her own advocate. When someone is having a problem and must get help from an agency or institution, such as a hospital or other service system, having someone who will "go to bat" on your behalf and be the "squeaky wheel" to get what is needed is critical. For many public mental health clients, however, the advocate they depend on most is their case manager. The reality is that many consumers with serious and persistent mental illness have very small, very fragile social support networks (Holschuh & Segal, 2002). It is not uncommon for a client with SPMI to have only two people they can depend on: a family member (often a parent, sibling, or adult child) and their case manager. Some, unfortunately, have no family and, thus, must rely completely on their therapist, social worker, or case manager.

The role of a client advocate is to act on the client's behalf to assure his or her rights are being protected and that the client is receiving the services to which he or she is entitled. Example:

David and His Stuff

David, who has a long history of serious mental illness (with varying diagnoses over the years), was recently placed in a board and care home several miles from the city where his psychosocial rehabilitation program was located. Recently his home got a new owner/operator who made it clear that she ran "a tight ship." All of his adult life, David has had a habit of scavenging the streets for discarded junk and other odds and ends. One time, he proudly notes, he found a $10 bill on the sidewalk. "It pays to look down," he often says.

Each evening, David spends an hour or so sorting out the stuff he has found that day and then storing what he wants to keep in his dresser and a footlocker on his side of the room he shares with a roommate. When the new care operator inspected David's room one day and saw his collection of stuff, she called it "garbage" and insisted that David get rid of it. David refused, arguing, "It's my stuff. I have a right to keep my stuff." One day, however, when David came home from his psychosocial rehabilitation program, he discovered that the care operator had

(continued)

thrown all his stuff away, claiming that she had warned him to get rid of it and, besides, "It's a fire hazard." She also threatened to punish David by not allowing him to go to his psychosocial rehabilitation program for an entire month.

David, who had been stable symptomatically for many years, was so upset he became quite agitated and began pacing frantically in his room. Fortunately, David had a good relationship with his case manager and so he called her for help. David's case manager, Julie, went out to the home with a patients' rights ombudsman, and the two of them met with David and the care home operator to collaboratively discuss the situation. First, the ombudsman educated the care home operator about David's right to keep his own property, including his "stuff," within limits. Julie and the board and care operator then worked out a compromise plan with David. The plan was that David could fill up his footlocker with stuff but not store stuff in his dresser or closet. When the footlocker was full, he and Julie would go through it, and David would sort out what he wanted to keep permanently and what he was willing to throw away. Then Julie would help David box up the stuff he wanted to keep and mail it off to his parents, who agreed to store it for him in their basement. With the footlocker empty, he could start collecting again. Also, Julie and the ombudsman made it very clear that the board and care operator could not prevent David from going to prescribed services as a form of punishment, because that interferes with his right to treatment.

This case provides a good example of the important work that advocacy entails. Without his case manager and the ombudsman acting as his advocates, David's rights would have been violated and, further, he might have had a psychiatric relapse due to the stress of the situation.

We have now identified five functions that emphasize the varied roles of the mental health case manager. These functions draw heavily upon the basic generalist practice skills that all social workers learn at the BSW and MSW foundation levels: communicating with empathy, authenticity, and genuineness, conducting a multidimensional assessment, negotiating goals and formulating a contract (service plan), conducting careful monitoring and follow-up, and providing advocacy when needed (Hepworth et al., 2010). Adding several clinical practice service functions to the basic five can evolve into what is called advanced case management (Raiff & Shore, 1993), of which a special subtype is termed clinical case management, in which clinical skills are utilized as well as coordinating skills such as problem-solving skills, crisis intervention activities, psychoeducation, developing an empathic supportive relationship, and family intervention work (Kanter, 1989; Surber, 1994; Walsh, 2000). Case management models are also structured according to differences in client needs and ability to function.

Assess your comprehension of *the five key functions of case management* by completing this quiz.

Models and Levels of Case Management

Administrative Case Management

Administrative case management (ACM) is the least intensive model of CM and is appropriate for clients who are relatively high-functioning and independent and who only need occasional assistance in navigating the mental/health care system and obtaining resources (Summers, 2011). Often administrative case management programs are run by a team of ADMs who are assigned a large pool of clients to serve as needed. As a result, if a client needs assistance, whichever ADM happens to be on duty and available responds to the client, and thus, clients end up working with a number of individuals rather than a single case manager.

Resource Coordination

At the next level of intensiveness is *resource coordination (RC)*. Clients assigned to a resource coordinator usually see the same RC over time and the relationship between the client and RC is essential to successful outcomes. Clients assigned to an RC are clients who need more help with navigating the system, more monitoring and follow-up, and more assistance with adherence to their service plan than clients under ACM. However, clients assigned RC should not be at risk for being a danger to themselves or others or at risk of becoming gravely disabled. For such clients, the next level of case management, called intensive case management, is most appropriate.

Intensive Case Management

Intensive case management (ICM) is the most comprehensive and in-depth model of case management. It was originally developed to provide intensive support and monitoring for individuals recently deinstitutionalized from the state hospital who faced considerable challenges in making the transition from a total institution of care to less regimented community care. Today, it is provided to consumers with severe and persistent mental illness, including those with severe personality disorders, forensic involvement, and substance abuse problems, who are at high risk for and heavy users of the most expensive mental health services, that is, emergency rooms, inpatient units, and crisis services. ICM service plans are supposed to be highly individualized and intensive in terms of monitoring and advocacy and geared to the circumstances, needs, resources, and desires of the individual consumer.

ICM is delivered to consumers in the community, and intensive case managers provide assertive outreach to clients, monitor and coordinate assessments and evaluations, and are the central pivotal person in the development of the service plan (with the client's input to the extent possible). ICM is most appropriate for those consumers who have histories of repeated hospitalization, non-adherence to treatment (for a variety of reasons), and who are at risk for becoming a danger to themselves or others or gravely disabled. A client's intensive case manager is an advocate, a friendly and consistent support person and, because of small caseloads (usually 8–10 clients per ICM), able to develop a strong therapeutic relationship with the client. Typical effectiveness outcome criteria for ICM usually include the level of use of the hospital base for the service area—particularly inappropriate use, level of independence in living per client, successful and continued enrollment in vocational programs such as supported employment, and the client's level and perceived quality of social support. For some clients, however, case management delivered intensively by a single provider is not enough to ensure psychiatric and psychosocial stability. For these clients, an intensive multidisciplinary model in which services are delivered by a team of providers is required. This evidence-based practice is called the *Program for Assertive Community Treatment (PACT)*.

PROGRAM FOR ASSERTIVE COMMUNITY TREATMENT (PACT)

What Is PACT?

The Program for Assertive Community Treatment (PACT or, simply, ACT) is an intensive multidisciplinary community mental health service delivery model that provides comprehensive, locally based mental health treatment to people with serious and persistent mental illnesses. Other names used for programs comparable to PACT or ACT include "assertive outreach," "mobile treatment teams," and "continuous treatment teams" (SAMHSA, 2008).

Unlike other community-based case management models, PACT is not a linkage or brokerage case management program that simply connects individuals to various resources and services and monitors their adherence. Instead, PACT provides highly individualized services directly to consumers living independently or semi-independently in the community. PACT recipients receive the kind of multidisciplinary, round-the-clock staffing traditionally provided by a psychiatric inpatient unit, but within the comfort of their own home and community (Phillips, Burns, Edgar, et al., 2001).

To have the competencies and skills to meet a client's multiple treatment, rehabilitation, and support needs, PACT team members are trained in the areas of psychiatry, social work, nursing, addiction treatment, psychosocial rehabilitation, and vocational rehabilitation. The PACT team provides these necessary services 24 hours a day, 7 days a week, 365 days a year.

How PACT Began

The PACT model evolved out of work led by Arnold Marx, M.D., Leonard Stein, M.D., and Mary Ann Test, Ph.D., on an inpatient research unit of Mendota State Hospital, Madison, Wisconsin, in the late 1960s (Stein & Santos, 1998). Noting that the gains made by clients in the hospital were often lost when they moved back into the community, they hypothesized that the hospital's round-the-clock care helped alleviate clients' symptoms and that this ongoing support and treatment was just as important—if not more so—following discharge to maintain wellness. In 1972, the researchers moved hospital-ward treatment staff into the community to test their assumption and, thus, launched PACT (Marx, Test, & Stein, 1973).

The Primary Goals and Practice Principles of PACT

The primary goals of the PACT model are to lessen or eliminate the debilitating symptoms of mental illness that each individual client experiences, minimize or prevent recurrent acute episodes of the illness, meet basic needs and enhance quality of life, improve functioning in adult social and employment roles, enhance an individual's ability to live independently in his or her own community and, finally, lessen the family's caregiving burden. PACT is a service delivery model, not a case management program, and is characterized by a multidisciplinary team approach, in vivo services, a small shared caseload per team, services that are time unlimited (consumers can stay in PACT for the duration of their lifetime), flexible service delivery, a fixed point of responsibility, and crisis management available directly from the team 24 hours a day, 7 days a week.

PACT is designed specifically for consumers with the most challenging and persistent mental/behavioral health problems, and the evidence shows that those programs that adhere most closely to the ACT model, and avoid "watering down" the model or taking shortcuts to save money, are more likely to get the best outcomes (Bond, McGrew, & Fekete, 1995; McGrew & Bond, 1997; McHugo et al., 1999; SAMHSA, 2008; Teague, Bond, & Drake, 1998). Overall, if fidelity is observed, PACT is highly effective in maintaining consumers' community tenure and recovery and avoiding crises and hospitalization (Gold, Meisler, Santos, et al., 2003; Monroe-DeVita, Morse, & Bond, 2012). Below are more details about the unique aspects that characterize PACT.

Rather than working with consumers in an office or hospital, ACT team members work with consumers in their homes, neighborhoods, and other places where their problems and stresses directly arise and where they need support and help with developing problem-solving skills (SAMHSA, 2008). Furthermore, instead of seeing consumers only a few times a month, ACT team members with different types of expertise contact consumers as often as necessary. This is facilitated by the fact that ACT team members do not have individual caseloads, rather, the team shares responsibility for all of the consumers assigned to that team. The model of having a shared caseload provides significant advantages for consumers. For example, because, over time, each consumer gets to know all of the members of their ACT team, if a team member goes on vacation, gets sick, or leaves the program, consumers know the other team members, which promotes continuity of care. This is in contrast to turnover that often occurs in typical case management programs—recall the case of Mark in Chapter 4, who had over 10 case managers and therapists over the course of a 4-year period. Because teamwork is such a central component of the PACT model, efforts are being made to develop measures for examining the role of team processes in ACT performance (Wholey, Zhu, Knoke, Shah, et al., 2012).

How PACT Services Are Provided

Instead of referring consumers to a range of providers and trying to coordinate the services, as is the case with the typical case management program, ACT directly provides consumers with assistance with activities of daily living, housing, family life, employment, benefits and entitlements, money management and managing finances, health care needs, medications, providing integrated treatment for co-occurring disorders (primarily mental illness combined with substance use—see Chapter 14 for more detail), and general counseling (SAMHSA, 2008). PACT specifically targets consumers with severe and persistent mental illness who have significant difficulties in doing the everyday things needed to live independently in the community, such as cooking, cleaning, and paying bills, or who have continuous high-service needs, especially the more expensive services such as emergency and inpatient care. PACT has also been adapted for use with high-risk forensic clients, specifically targeting modifiable risk factors associated with criminal recidivism (Erickson, Lamberti, Weisman, et al., 2009). The model has also been tailored as an effective community intervention for ethnic minority clients with serious mental illness (Chow, Law, & Andermann, 2009).

PACT also has no preset limit on how long consumers receive services. Over time, team members may have less contact with consumers, but still remain available for support if it is needed. Consumers are never discharged from PACT programs because they are "noncompliant" or "treatment resistant." In fact, treatment non-adherence is less of a problem in the PACT model because PACT team members work closely and collaboratively with consumers to develop plans to help them reach their goals and progress is monitored daily. Most PACT programs report that 90 percent or more of consumers have contact with more than one team member each and every week. Such close and careful monitoring is possible because of the team's small, shared caseload.

What Is the Difference between PACT and Traditional Care?

Most individuals with severe mental illnesses who are in treatment are involved in a linkage or brokerage case management program. Under this traditional system of care, the consumer is treated by a group of individual case managers who operate in the context of a case management program and have primary responsibility only for their own caseloads. In contrast, the PACT multidisciplinary staff work as a collaborative team to deliver the majority of the treatment, rehabilitation, and support services required by each client to live in the community. A psychiatrist is a member of, not a consultant to, the team. The consumer is a client of the team, not of an individual staff member. Individuals with the

Comparison between the Program for Assertive Community Treatment (PACT) and a Traditional Community Mental Health Center (CMHC)

	PACT	Traditional CMHC
Treatment Base	In the community	In the clinic
Continuity of Care	Team follows the client through hospital, legal, health, and social services	Therapist or case manager is *less likely* to follow the client through hospital, legal, health, and social services
Staffing Ratio	10 to 1 ratio	30–50 to 1 ratio
Staffing Structure	Multidisciplinary team provides integrated clinical services and case management	Multiple separate providers who function with relative autonomy
Emergency Treatment 24 Hours a Day	Team on call	Emergency room in hospital
Frequency of Contact with Client	Daily if needed	Weekly to monthly or even less
Frequency of Contact with Families	Weekly	Occasional if at all
Responsibility for Medication	Home delivery and administration by team as needed	Client or family
Responsibility for Physical Health	Actively monitored by team	Health care use encouraged
Responsibility for Occupational Rehabilitation	Direct client contact in the occupational rehabilitation setting	Psychosocial programs
Responsibility for Housing	Team has responsibility	Usually client and family

most severe mental illnesses are typically not served well by the traditional outpatient model that directs patients to various services that they then must navigate on their own. In contrast, the PACT team goes to the consumer whenever and wherever needed. The below chart compares PACT with traditional community mental health services across a number of domains.

PACT is effective because of its fidelity to the basic practice principles of community mental health, ensuring continuity of care and improved access to services, and is tailored to the client's individual needs. Multiple studies have shown that for individuals with severe and persistent mental illness, PACT is much more effective than standard community mental health care in avoiding hospitalization, promoting community tenure, maintaining wellness, and achieving recovery (Bond, Drake, Mueser, et al., 2001; Burns & Santos, 1995; Coldwell & Bender, 2007; Herdelin & Scott, 1999; Latimer, 1999).

Assess your comprehension of *the primary goals and practice principles of the Program for Assertive Community Treatment (PACT)* by completing this quiz.

The last interventions to be addressed in this chapter are supported employment and permanent supportive housing. These evidence-based interventions are included in the chapter on case management because they can be helpful to consumers with a range of serious and persistent mental illnesses, and are often components of case management service plans.

SUPPORTED EMPLOYMENT

What Supported Employment Is

Supported employment for individuals with serious and persistent mental illnesses is an evidence-based practice, meaning that its effectiveness has been established across studies that have produced similar positive outcomes (Bond, Becker, et al., 2001). However, like so many evidence-based practices, supported employment does not reach all of those who need it. Two of the main barriers to dissemination of supported employment more widely are perceived financial and organizational barriers.

Part of having a good quality of life in the community for most people, including individuals with serious mental illness, is to have the opportunity to work and earn a living. When people work in a job they feel good about, particularly a job that non-mentally ill people also work in, that enhances a consumer's self-worth and self-efficacy and "reduces disability, boredom, fear, social isolation, discrimination, and stigma" (Becker & Drake, n.d.). Work also provides structure and routine that help people with mental illness maintain stability in their lives. Jobs that involve working with others also enhance natural social support. Supported employment jobs are not sheltered jobs, that is, jobs set aside for people with disabilities, which usually pay less than minimum wage. Instead, supported employment jobs exist in the open competitive labor market, pay at least minimum wage, include both full- and part-time positions, and involve working with people who do not have disabilities.

Sometimes consumers worry about losing important benefits, such as Social Security or Medicaid, if they work. However, supported employment provides employment specialists who, along with the consumer's case manager, can help consumers understand how their benefits are or are not affected by working so the consumer can make informed choices about what they prefer to do in terms of starting or changing jobs. Supported employment works by providing consumer choice, integrated services, competitive jobs, benefits counseling, timely support, continuous supports, and consumer preferences (*What is supportive employment?*, U.S. DHHS, n.d.).

Practice Principles of Supported Employment

There are seven basic practice principles of supported employment. These include the following (*Supported employment*, U.S. DHHS, n.d.):

Practice Principle #1: Eligibility Is Based on Consumer Choice.

Eligibility is simple for supported employment—it is based only on whether a consumer wants to get a job and work. Consumer choice is key, and all consumers who want to work are eligible for supported employment services. Clients are not excluded based on type of mental illness, how severe their symptoms are, whether they use substances, or whether they have recently been hospitalized. The key eligibility criterion is whether or not the consumer wants to work in the competitive job market.

Practice Principle #2: Supported Employment Services Are Integrated with Comprehensive Mental Health Treatment.

Integration of supported employment with treatment services is important and harkens back to the community support system (CSS) network model, described initially in this chapter. That model was the gold standard for the development of community mental health services during the peak of deinstitutionalization, although much of its promise was never realized. The CSS model advocated the integration of all services, clinical and otherwise, into a comprehensive package that would be coordinated by the client's case manager. Like supported employment and other current EBPs, the CSS emphasized consumer choice and self-determination, individualized and flexible services, service integration, and normalized services, which means the consumer would be integrated into the community and work alongside community members who are not disabled. To assure integration, supported employment specialists coordinate services with the other mental health practitioners working with the client, for example, case managers, social workers, therapists, and psychiatrists.

Practice Principle #3: Competitive Employment Is the Goal.

"Normalized employment" refers to jobs in the open competitive labor market that pay at least minimum wage, rather than sheltered employment in which consumers work only with other consumers and, if paid, are often paid below minimum wage. Working with others without disabilities is important for learning job skills and social skills and for developing natural social supports, that is, social supports outside of family and activities associated with treatment services.

Practice Principle #4: Personalized Benefits Counseling Is Important.

The employment specialists help consumers understand the impact of starting or switching jobs on the consumer's benefits, such as Social Security and Medicaid. Most consumers are able to work and continue to receive some benefits through programs such as Ticket to Work (http://ssa.gov/work/aboutticket.html).

Practice Principle #5: Job Search Starts Soon After Consumers Express Interest in Working.

One month after the consumer begins the supported employment program, employment specialists help him or her begin the process of looking for a job with preemployment assessment, training, and counseling kept to a minimum. The first goal is getting a job.

Practice Principle #6: Follow-Along Supports Are Continuous.

Employment specialists engage in continuous regular follow-up contact with consumers and, if appropriate, with the consumer's employer. Like the Program for Assertive Community Treatment and Integrated Treatment for Co-Occurring Disorders (discussed in Chapter 14), consumers are never terminated from supported employment unless they themselves request to leave the program. This is important, because the adjustment to competitive employment can be challenging and eliminating the fear of termination can be very helpful in easing consumers' anxiety about their initial performance and the process of working.

Practice Principle #7: Consumer Preferences Are Important.

Supported employment emphasizes job choice based on clients' individual interests, strengths, and previous work experience and work-related skills. The job search begins by focusing on the kind of work that a consumer prefers to do, because doing work a person wants to do enhances motivation, drive, and commitment. The skilled employment specialist knows it is best to start where the client is.

Effectiveness of Supported Employment

The development of supported employment began with a "place-train model" that was originally designed for individuals with developmental disabilities (Wehman & Moon, 1988). The model was later adapted for psychosocial rehabilitation for individuals with serious mental illness (Corrigan & McCracken, 2005). The idea behind place-train is, rather than waiting until the consumer is trained to place him or her in a job, the program places the person in a job and then provides on-the-job training. A number of studies were conducted to develop the current model of supported employment for individuals with mental illness and by the end of the 1990s the evidence base was well established, although dissemination remains a challenge (Becker & Drake, 2003; Bond, Becker, et al., 2001).

The evidence endorsing supported employment as an effective practice has been based on the results of three quasi experimental studies (Bailey, Ricketts, Becker, et al., 1998; Drake, Becker, Biesanz, et al., 1994; Drake, Becker, Biesanz, et al., 1996) and six randomized controlled trials (Bond, Dietzen, & McGrew, 1995; Chandler, Meisel, Hu, et al., 1997; Drake, McHugo, Bebont, et al., 1999; Drake, McHugo, Becker, et al., 1996; Gervey & Bedell, 1994; McFarlane, Dushay, Deakins, et al., 2000; for reviews of these studies, see Bond, 2004; Bond, Becker et al., 2001). Supported employment has been endorsed by the President's New Freedom Commission on Mental Health (2003), the Surgeon General (1999), the National Alliance on Mental Illness (2001), the National Institute of Mental Health (1999), the Substance Abuse and Mental Health Services Administration (SAMHSA), and many other federal, state, advocacy, and private foundation organizations (Becker & Drake, n.d.).

Supported employment is based on the premise that many if not most people with serious mental illness want to work and, with support, are able to work in jobs in the competitive labor market. Employment programs that follow the evidence-based principles of supported employment have been shown to have better outcomes than other employment programs for consumers including sheltered workshop type programs. Programs must address financial and organizational barriers, though, if they are to be successful. To start a supported employment program, mental health practitioners can obtain the Supportive Employment Evidence-Based Practice Toolkit from SAMHSA (www.samhsa.gov/shin) free of charge. The toolkit includes materials covering how to get started with developing a supported employment program, how to build the program from the ground up, how to train frontline workers to be employment specialists, how to evaluate the quality and effectiveness of your program, brochures that can be duplicated for training and public education, and a set of PowerPoint slides. Additional information about supported employment can be found at www.mentalhealthpractices.org.

Assess your comprehension of the *primary goals, practice principles, and effectiveness of supported employment* by completing this quiz.

PERMANENT SUPPORTIVE HOUSING

Permanent supportive housing (PSH) is an evidence-based practice (EBP) approach for providing voluntary flexible supports to help individuals with mental illness choose, obtain, and maintain decent, safe, and affordable housing that is integrated into the natural community (SAMHSA, 2010). Housing is one of the key dimensions of the community support system network and is always an essential component of a consumer's case management service plan. Across the various models of PSH is embedded the core belief and value that people with psychiatric disabilities have the right to live in a home of their own in the most integrated setting possible without any special rules or service requirements to have the housing, but with access to individualized supports on a voluntary basis (De Beer-Wunderink, Vissor, Sytema, & Wiersma, 2012).

PSH provides flexible wraparound supports sufficient to allow people with significant support needs to be successful living in housing of their choice. Such supports can include case management, assertive community treatment, assistance with daily activities, conflict resolution, and crisis response. Consumer tenants also receive help in becoming fully participating members of the community through assistance with socialization and seeking employment. Permanent supportive housing makes housing affordable to someone receiving disability benefits either through rental assistance or housing development assistance. PSH is a critically important evidence-based practice, because many individuals with serious mental illness are homeless or at risk of becoming homeless during various points in their lives (Allen, 1996; Schutt & Goldfinger, 2011).

The Six Core Components of Permanent Supportive Housing

There are six core components to permanent supportive housing, which include the following: (1) flexible voluntary supports; (2) quality housing; (3) rental assistance; (4) a standard lease; (5) functionally separating housing and supports; and (6) integration. The therapeutic and practical supports offered to consumers are flexible so that consumers can choose which supports best meet their needs. Consumers are also provided with help in obtaining and paying for their housing via rental assistance so they can keep it for as long as they want. Unlike what often happens in many communities, the housing offered is not substandard and/or in a "ghetto" of consumer housing, rather, the housing meets standards for safety and quality established by local, state, and federal laws and regulations and is similar to what is generally available to others at similar income levels in the community. This helps consumers to participate more fully in the regular life of their community. With PSH, consumer tenants typically pay 30 percent of their income toward rent plus basic utilities based on a standard lease. The remainder of the cost, then, is paid through flexible rental assistance that can be used with any housing or through project-based rental assistance linked to a particular housing location. In addition, continued tenancy in the housing is not dependent on the consumer participating in services. Participating in services is separate from the housing arrangement. These six core components are usually used as outcome criteria for assessing the fidelity of any permanent supportive housing program (SAMHSA, 2010).

Consumer Choice and Key Decision-Making Questions

Consumer choice is a core element of permanent supportive housing because settings that meet consumers' identified needs and preferences are more likely to have a successful outcome. Initial basic choices that the consumer must decide on are to look at who else lives in the housing option, what kind of housing it is and, finally, where the housing is located.

There are three main PSH models: the scattered site model, the single site mixed population model, and the housing first model. The scattered site model offers individual units of housing that are dispersed throughout a particular area and may consist of apartments, condominiums, or single-family homes that may be owned or leased. The single site mixed population model offers housing in large buildings or complexes with multiple units that serve many types of tenants including low-income families, people with disabilities, seniors, students, and homeless adults. Single site mixed population models often set aside a certain number of housing options for particular target tenant groups and can be owned by the tenant or "master leased" by a housing agency. Finally, the housing first model is well suited for individuals with co-occurring disorders and other complex situations who have not been well served by traditional housing or residential programs. Housing first approaches allow people to move into permanent housing immediately from shelters, the streets, or institutions and then services are provided, including home-based services such as PACT, for as long as the consumer needs them.

Case managers who refer their clients to a permanent supportive housing program need to address a number of key questions about the various aspects their client needs to consider when choosing the right housing, to ensure that the goal of real consumer choice is met to assure the right "fit." These include:

- Does the consumer want to live alone or with family or friends?
- What location and neighborhood type does the consumer prefer?
- What type and size of housing unit is best?
- What are the maintenance requirements?
- Does the consumer want and/or is the consumer able to take care of maintenance, or does the maintenance need to be provided for the consumer?
- What is the proximity to specific services, resources, and public transportation?

- What is the maximum monthly rent and utilities that the consumer can afford?
- What is the plan for searching for housing, acquiring it, and setting it up (including moving personal things and obtaining furnishings)?
- What help does the consumer need with food shopping and preparation?
- What supports are needed for landlord negotiations?
- What assistance and supports are needed for management of daily living tasks including financial management; credit, references, and security deposits; and arranging for utilities, phone, cable, Internet, and insurance?
- What therapeutic in-home supports are needed, for example, PACT, medication management, medical care?
- How can community integration and development of natural supports be facilitated in partnership with the consumer?

The answers to these questions can help the consumer determine exactly what kind of permanent housing he or she prefers so that identification of housing options can begin.

Maintaining a Recovery Focus

Permanent supportive housing takes a flexible, voluntary recovery focus to the services provided. Although a range of treatment services should be offered, consumers are free to accept or refuse the services and, even if refused, staff are expected to continue to provide support, including risk management and crisis planning, and use flexible engagement strategies. Flexibility and maintaining a recovery focus also means that the type, location, intensity, and frequency of services must adjust to meet consumers' changing needs over time. As noted in Chapter 2, a recovery focus means that the permanent supportive housing program is consumer-centered and directed; holistic, nonlinear, and strengths based; and emphasizes empowerment, respect, responsibility, and hope (Consensus Conference on Mental Health Recovery, 2004).

Effectiveness of Permanent Supportive Housing

Sufficient evidence of the effectiveness of permanent supportive housing exists to deem it to be an "evidence-based practice." Such evidence includes the positive overall impact on consumers' residence stability, more positive outcomes than other types of housing for individuals with mental illness, cost benefits, and fidelity to the core principles (Leff, Chow, Pepin, et al., 2009; SAMHSA, 2010). More specifically, PSH has been shown to reduce emergency room visits, reduce psychiatric inpatient hospitalizations, reduce nursing home admissions, decrease Medicaid costs, reduce days spent in correctional facilities, and reduce the number of alcohol detox admissions and detoxification costs (Andersen & Sherwood, 2000; Culhane, Metraux, & Hadley, 2002; Larimer, Malone, Garner, et al., 2009; Mondello, Gass, McLaughlin, & Shore, 2007; Nogaski, Rynell, Terpstra, Edwards, et al., 2009). In sum, consumers need housing just like everybody else, and the stability and security provided by permanent housing has multiple beneficial effects for consumers in terms of community integration and tenure and psychosocial functioning.

Assess your comprehension of *the six core components, consumer choice and key decision-making questions, and effectiveness of permanent supportive housing* by completing this quiz.

CONCLUSION

This chapter has addressed the important role and functions of case managers for individuals with serious and persistent mental illness. Working with such clients and their families inevitably includes some form of case management activity, whether it is resource coordination, intensive case management, or more clinical forms of case management (Stoesen, 2008). The case of Antonia Garcia illustrates well the complexities that our clients' situations often present for us, illuminating how case management can be the ideal modality for ensuring that all of the client's multifaceted needs are met within a recovery and strengths-oriented perspective (Fukui, Goscha, Rapp, et al., 2012).

The chapter has also reviewed some of the key evidence-based practices that are often employed as part of a case management service plan, including the Program for Assertive Community Treatment, supported employment, and permanent supportive housing. Having a good job in the competitive employment market and a decent permanent place to live can have a major impact on facilitating recovery, sometimes even more effectively than many of the medical model psychiatric treatments offered to clients. Working facilitates recovery by enhancing self-esteem and self-efficacy, and working provides resources to support self-determination and enable independence. As one client put it: "Going to work each day and getting a paycheck is better than a whole bottle of antidepressants!" Of course, for most clients with serious mental illness, medication and psychosocial treatment are essential components to recovery, but only recently have we also recognized the therapeutic power of employment and housing.

Outcome for Antonia Garcia

With her case manager, Jacinto, as the key person to provide support, advocacy, and service coordination, Antonia is now doing well. She has learned strategies to facilitate adherence to taking her medication to maintain wellness and keeping her scheduled appointments with Dr. Smith. At first, the PACT team made regular home visits to help Antonia with her medication regime but, after a month, Antonia was able to manage her medication and appointments independently. She does continue to call on the PACT team for assistance as needed. Jacinto also provided Antonia with emotional support and validation and has helped her connect with and become involved with the LGBT Action Center and PFLAG (Parents, Families and Friends of Lesbians and Gays). Antonia happily told Jacinto that she has become friends with another transgendered woman she met at the LGBT Action Center and they have met for coffee a couple times. Antonia's sister Maria has continued to be an important source of support and resources for Antonia and, although her parents did benefit from psychoeducation about bipolar II disorder and understand the illness and its impact better, they still have been unable to fully accept their daughter's gender nonconformity.

After several consultations with Dr. Fisher, Antonia decided not to pursue medical interventions for transitioning yet, such as hormonal treatment and surgery, until she has experienced at least 2 years living fully as a woman. Finally, Antonia has enrolled in a 1-year floral design program at the local community college, and Joe, her boss at the flower shop, has been able to increase her hours to 30 per week, which entitles her to health care benefits. With the additional income and benefits, Antonia decided to get her own studio apartment, rather than living at Rainbow House. Jacinto referred her to the local permanent supported housing program, which supplemented her rent sufficiently to allow her to secure a nice apartment in a decent neighborhood located not far from her sister's home. All in all, Antonia is doing well, and the key to her progress in recovery has been the relationship she has, and the work she has done, with her case manager.

Assess your application and analysis of this chapter's contents by completing the *Chapter Review*.

Chapter 10

Practice with Individuals with Schizophrenia and Their Families

WHAT IS SCHIZOPHRENIA?

Introduction

Schizophrenia is a term used to describe a complex and pervasive condition that is one of the most persistent and disabling of the serious mental illnesses. It generally begins in early adulthood and, for most individuals with the disorder, it is a lifelong illness requiring some level of treatment and illness management (Dickerson & Lehman, 2006). Schizophrenia may be one disorder as identified by the *DSM-IV-TR*, but research suggests that it may be better described as a set of related disorders, with different causes, courses, and responses to treatment (Blanchard, Horan, & Collins, 2005; Turetsky et al., 2002). Because of the disorder's complexity, few generalizations hold true for all people who meet criteria for schizophrenia.

Schizophrenia is a "pervasive" mental illness, meaning that it affects all spheres of an individual's life. It affects an individual's ability to work, to develop and maintain fulfilling interpersonal relationships, to be able to live independently, to feel pleasure and joy in activities, to express and regulate appropriate emotions, to learn new skills for work or recreation—in short, schizophrenia profoundly affects an individual's life and the lives of those who care for him or her. Unfortunately, we do not yet have a cure for schizophrenia; however, the good news is that we now have an array of psychotropic medications that are effective in treating many of the symptoms associated with schizophrenia along with a number of highly effective psychosocial treatments that can improve psychosocial functioning and enable many individuals with schizophrenia to live successfully in the community and achieve positive recovery.

The symptoms of schizophrenia, such as hallucinations and delusions, can cause individuals with the illness to behave in unusual, inappropriate, and unpredictable ways. Unfortunately, many members of the general public know very little about schizophrenia, and what they do know is often inaccurate and gleaned from sensational media portrayals (Owen, 2012; Marsh & Marks, 2009). This has contributed to prejudice and discrimination toward people with schizophrenia, and the illness carries significant social stigma. For example, one unfortunate stereotype is that people with schizophrenia are violent. Violence does occur with individuals with schizophrenia (Steinberg, 2012), however, research has shown that risk of violence is associated primarily with factors such as untreated psychotic symptoms and/or use of drugs or alcohol (Steadman, Mulvey, Monahan, et al., 1998; Swanson, Swartz, Van Dorn, Elbogen, et al., 2006).

In previous decades, many individuals with schizophrenia were forced to live out their lives in the state hospital, far away from family and community. Today, there are a range of better alternatives to long-term hospitalization which have benefitted many living with the illness; however, these treatments do not reach all who need them, and many individuals with schizophrenia have ended up homeless, living on the streets, or incarcerated in jails or prisons (Lamb & Weinberger, 1998). In addition, too many families who provide care for their loved ones with schizophrenia do not receive the help, support, and services that they need to be able to live healthy happy lives while providing ongoing caregiving.

The Prevalence, Onset of Illness, and Symptoms in Schizophrenia

Prevalence of Schizophrenia

Approximately 1 percent of the population develops schizophrenia during their lives, and this incidence and prevalence cuts across all societies and cultures worldwide (Gottesman, 1991; Tandon, Keshavan, & Nasrallah, 2008). Schizophrenia affects men more frequently than women (1.4:1 male to female ratio; McGrath, 2006) and the age of onset and, to some extent, the course of illness differs across genders. The first psychotic symptoms of schizophrenia are often seen in the teens or early twenties in men, while the first symptoms for women occur generally in the mid-twenties to early thirties. Perhaps because the onset of schizophrenia for many men is during late adolescence, the course of illness for many men tends to be more difficult, with a greater incidence of negative symptoms and associated disability than is the case for women (Haas, Sweeney, Hien, et al., 1991). Because the onset for women is usually later, women tend to have certain advantages that bear well for prognosis and recovery. A later onset means one has left the tumultuous period of adolescence; is more likely to have finished high school and even completed some college; has usually moved out from living with the family of origin and may have an adult partnership, which means more social support; and is more likely to have acquired work skills, which bears well for rehabilitation and recovery.

There are also some important cultural differences with regard to the incidence, prevalence, and course of schizophrenia. Decades ago, sociologists Faris and Dunham (1939) conducted their classic study of the ecology of psychiatric disorder in Chicago, with results showing that the rates of first hospital admission for psychosis, particularly schizophrenia, was highest in the central slum sections of the city and decreased steadily toward the more well-to-do suburban areas. This was later reinforced by Dohrenwend and Dohrenwend (1974) who reported an inverse relationship between overall rates of psychopathology and socioeconomic status. These findings still hold today, with schizophrenia more common among those living in poor urban areas and among those in the low socioeconomic stratum in general (Freeman, 1994; Mortensen, Pedersen, Westergaard, et al., 1999; Saha et al., 2005). There are many theories as to why this is the case. First is the "drift theory," which suggests that the disability exacted by having schizophrenia results in individuals drifting into poverty and, unless they can access appropriate and sufficient treatment and respond well to the treatment, they remain impoverished. Another theory is that the stress associated with living in poverty can trigger both initial episodes and subsequent relapses in individuals at risk for developing schizophrenia (Cohen, 1993).

People with schizophrenia living in developing countries, such as India, generally function better and have smoother courses of illness than individuals with schizophrenia living in developed Western industrialized countries (Hopper et al., 2007; Jablensky, Sartorius, Ernberg, Anker, et al., 1992). Part of this may be the high stress levels in many capitalistic competitive Western countries, particularly those without solid social welfare safety nets, such as the United States. Also, the social Darwinist cultural values inherent in Western capitalism reflect high levels of expressed emotion (see Chapter 7 for detail), which many non-mentally ill individuals can thrive in but isn't a good environment for someone with schizophrenia. Finally, within the United States, research has shown that Latinos and Whites are less likely to develop schizophrenia than are African-Americans (Gara, Vega, Arndt, et al., 2012; Zhang & Snowden, 1999), and Afro-Caribbeans, in particular, evidence elevated rates of schizophrenia, especially among new immigrant populations (Bhugra & Bhui, 2001). At the same time, there is some evidence for overdiagnosis of schizophrenia in African-Americans in the United States (Eack, Bahorik, Newhill, et al., 2012).

Causes of Schizophrenia

We still don't know exactly what causes schizophrenia. Genetic studies, neurophysiological findings, and responsiveness to medication all provide substantial supportive evidence that schizophrenia involves a brain disease of some kind. As noted earlier, the general prevalence of schizophrenia is about 1 percent of the population, however, risk is greater for individuals with a family history of schizophrenia. For example, the risk is about 3–5 percent in second-degree relatives or in half-siblings, 9–12 percent in siblings and dizygotic twins, and 40–50 percent in monozygotic twins of individuals with schizophrenia or in children whose parents both have schizophrenia, all of which suggests a relatively strong genetic basis. However, it is not all due to genes, or the risk would be 100 percent, rather than 40–50 percent, for identical twins. Environment plays a role, too. In fact, research has identified several environmental risk factors for schizophrenia. These risk factors include maternal malnutrition and viral infections during certain periods of fetal development, fetal hypoxia, other birth and obstetric complications such as oxygen deprivation and forceps delivery, winter birth, and maternal use of certain psychoactive drugs (Karlsson, Bachmann, Schro, et al., 2001; Mednick, Machon, Huttunen, & Bonett, 1988).

As noted in Chapter 7, recognition of these genetic and environmental factors is a significant departure from the past when psychoanalytic and family communication theories of causality predominated, all of which generally promoted the view of the family, particularly mothers, as a pathogenic agent to be blamed and then cured. Today, enlightened clinicians take a multidimensional view for understanding schizophrenia and its treatment. A multidimensional and interactional model of schizophrenia is also much more fruitful for guiding the development and application of treatment, both pharmacological and psychosocial. Schizophrenia should be viewed essentially as an enduring bio-psycho-social vulnerability upon which certain stressors may impinge. Thus, a relapse of schizophrenic illness may be precipitated by certain changes in several different arenas that have direct implications for intervention.

Co-morbidity with Other Disorders

Over 90 percent of individuals with schizophrenia meet criteria for another disorder, most commonly mood, anxiety, and substance-related disorders (APA, 2000). Sometimes people have psychotic symptoms that look like schizophrenia, but are actually due to undetected medical disorders or the use of drugs or alcohol. Example:

> Geri is a 30-year-old African-American woman brought to the psychiatric emergency room by the police after personnel from a local fast-food restaurant called saying that Geri was observed sitting in a corner of the restaurant for 5 hours talking to herself and behaving peculiarly. Upon evaluation she was very frightened and agitated, clutching to the social worker's hands in a terrified manner. She was admitted to the inpatient unit with a provisional diagnosis of schizophrenia; however, within a couple days she stabilized and presented as bright and articulate with no evidence of psychosis. The eventual conclusion was that her psychotic symptoms were probably secondary to an exacerbation of lupus.

Because psychotic symptoms can be due to medical problems, a medical history should always be taken and a physical examination and laboratory tests should be done during hospitalization, or even in the emergency room, to rule out other causes of the symptoms before concluding that a person has schizophrenia. Given that the primary purpose of a diagnosis is to guide treatment, an inaccurate diagnosis can result in delivering inappropriate and even harmful treatment. In addition, there are many mental disorders other than schizophrenia that can evidence psychotic symptoms, such as bipolar disorder, severe unipolar depression, and delusional disorder, thus, psychotic symptoms alone do not mean the individual has schizophrenia.

Symptoms of Schizophrenia

Onset of Symptoms

The onset of symptoms of schizophrenia can occur in different patterns. If the onset of severe psychotic symptoms is sudden, the individual may be said to be experiencing acute schizophrenia. The word *psychotic* means out of touch with reality, or unable to separate real from unreal experiences. People who have a sudden onset of symptoms may have been functioning perfectly normally before the onset of illness. It comes on like a bolt out of the blue. As noted in Chapter 7, a sudden onset of symptoms usually creates a crisis, for the affected person and for the family. In such cases, hospitalization may be the only initial alternative. Example:

> Tomas is a 23-year-old Mexican-American man who lives with his parents and two younger sisters. Tomas finished high school successfully and had been working as a house painter and landscaper, hoping to eventually be able to own his own business. One day, Tomas parked his pickup truck on his family's lawn, refused to come into the house, and just sat all day and night in his truck staring at the family's house. When family members tried to talk to him he responded by calling his mother and sisters "whores" because they wore pants. The next morning the family woke up to find Tomas digging a trench around the house and talking about having to hold off the demons of hell. Frightened, the family called the police, who took Tomas to the emergency room for a psychiatric evaluation. The emergency room social worker arranged for a 72-hour hold on the basis of grave disability, and Tomas was diagnosed with schizophreniform disorder during the course of the hospitalization.

Other individuals who develop schizophrenia may experience a slow insidious onset of symptoms, with the psychosis gradually evolving until an acute stage is reached. It is not uncommon for such individuals to be described retrospectively as always having been a little odd, as loners, not having many friends, or having eccentric interests during their premorbid period. Sometimes, prior to the full onset of illness, individuals with a slow insidious onset of symptoms may meet criteria for schizoid personality disorder or schizotypal personality disorder, which are conditions that include many of the nonpsychotic symptoms associated with schizophrenia (see Chapter 13 for more detail on personality disorders).

The Core Symptom of "Thought Disorder"

People with schizophrenia can have any combination of a variety of symptoms, and individuals with different subtypes of schizophrenia can present very differently. However, what is common to all untreated schizophrenia presentations is the core symptom of *thought disorder*, which means that the person is unable to connect his or her thoughts into logical sequences, because the thoughts become disorganized and fragmented. This often leads to great difficulty in connecting and communicating with other people that profoundly affects the individual's ability to develop and maintain interpersonal relationships. Aretha, a 65-year-old woman first diagnosed with schizophrenia in her twenties, commented:

Watch the video *"Psychotic Disorders: Schizophrenia: The Case of Georgina."* How does a client who has schizophrenia describe the experience of the illness in her own words?

> I'm doing okay, I guess, though I don't have much of a life—I live alone in a room at the Brown Hotel. I watch TV, get my coffee at the McDonald's across the street, but I don't talk to no one. I take my medicine but I still hear voices all the time, but the voices keep me company—I don't feel so lonely that way.

The Positive and Negative Symptoms Model

The most common model for categorizing the symptoms of schizophrenia is dividing them into two clusters: *positive symptoms* and *negative symptoms*. An easy way to think of them is that positive symptoms are things that *are* present but *shouldn't be*, such as hallucinations and delusions. Negative symptoms are things that *should be present but aren't*, such as lack of motivation, lack of pleasure (anhedonia), poverty of thought, and lack of appropriate affect and restricted or poorly regulated emotional expression. Medication is often quite effective and helpful in controlling positive symptoms but not very helpful in reducing negative symptoms and even, in some cases, can make negative symptoms worse. Appropriately selected and properly applied psychosocial treatments, such as cognitive therapy, can sometimes help with negative symptoms (Turkington & Morrison, 2012), and it is in this realm where social workers are typically involved. For most individuals with schizophrenia, medication is an essential adjunct to effective psychosocial treatment.

The diagnostic criteria for the schizophrenia spectrum and other psychotic disorders offered in the *DSM-5 (APA, 2013)* encompass five characteristic symptoms:

- Hallucinations (in any of the senses, but primarily auditory and visual)
- Delusions (can be bizarre or non-bizarre)
- Disorganized Thinking (Speech)
- Grossly Disorganized or Abnormal Motor Behavior (including catatonia)
- Negative symptoms (e.g., flat or blunted affect, poverty of speech, difficulty initiating or following through with activities, lack of motivation)

The first four are positive symptoms and the last is the negative symptoms. Cognitive deficit symptoms, which contribute significantly to disability, however, are not explicitly included in the DSM criteria. Cognitive deficit symptoms include problems with attention, problems with working memory, and deficits in executive function. Let's briefly review the various positive and negative symptoms before turning to the psychosocial treatment options for schizophrenia.

Positive Symptoms in Schizophrenia

The positive symptoms of schizophrenia include hallucinations, delusions, disorganized speech, and disorganized and/or grossly inappropriate behavior. A *hallucination* is a perception in one of the senses in the absence of real external stimuli, which occurs when an individual is awake. For example, hearing a voice when nobody else is present would constitute an auditory hallucination. The quality of a hallucinatory perception is vivid and seems very real to the person experiencing it. Hallucinations can occur in any sensory modality; most commonly, hallucinations in schizophrenia are visual, auditory, olfactory, or tactile. Hallucinations can be so intrusive that the individual has difficulty focusing on what is actually going on around him or her. Hallucinations may be unpleasant, pleasant, or benign. For many individuals with schizophrenia during periods of unmedicated active psychosis, their auditory hallucinations involve harsh critical voices that are extremely unpleasant. For example, Lori Schiller, in her 1994 memoir *The Quiet Room*, which describes her battle with schizophrenia, describes "The Voices" as often screaming at her in hoarse harsh tones telling her "you must die, you bitch" (Schiller & Bennett, 1994, p. 21). Other clients describe hearing a chorus of voices carrying on a conversation that is relatively benign. For most individuals with schizophrenia, antipsychotic medication is effective in eliminating auditory hallucinations. For some individuals, however, medication doesn't eliminate hearing voices, but makes a difference in the quality of the voices they hear. Example:

> Jonas has always heard voices, and no medication has ever eliminated them entirely. However, when he takes his antipsychotic medication—olanzapine—the quality of the voices changes and he can tolerate them more. Without medication, the voices shout at Jonas, saying terrible things about him, accusing him of crimes he never committed, commanding him to hurt himself, and screaming obscenities. When on

medication, the voices change to a murmuring background that is not unpleasant and which he is even able to ignore.

Tactile hallucinations can occur with schizophrenia, and usually involve sensations of bugs crawling on or under the skin, or sharp pains that the person may interpret as something attacking them. Visual hallucinations can also occur in schizophrenia, as can olfactory hallucinations in which the person may report smelling foul odors.

In contrast to a hallucination, a *delusion* is defined as a false personal belief based on incorrect inference about external reality, which is firmly sustained in spite of what constitutes incontrovertible and obvious proof that the belief is false (within cultural parameters). Essentially, delusions are abnormalities in inferential thinking (Andreasen, 1994). Delusions may be *bizarre* or they may be *non-bizarre*. A delusion is considered bizarre if the content of the belief could not possibly happen, at least to our current knowledge. For example, a client with paranoid schizophrenia believed that during his first psychiatric hospitalization, nurses had secretly replaced his bone marrow with several hundred small persons. Some of the tiny persons were good and helped to hold his body together, but others were bad and would argue and use electric cattle prods to hurt him (Skodol, 1989). The patient believed that only a special magnetic machine could be effective in getting rid of the bad little persons without harming the good ones. As far as we know, such a situation could not actually happen, thus this delusion would be considered bizarre.

Non-bizarre delusions, typically found in the paranoid subtype of schizophrenia as well as in other psychotic disorders such as delusional disorder and shared psychotic disorder (folie à deux), are beliefs that are realistically possible, even though they are not true for the particular client. For example, the person believes he or she is being sought by organized crime figures, the CIA, the FBI, or—in today's world—Al Qaeda. The most common themes in non-bizarre delusions are persecution, jealousy, grandiosity, somatic fixation (such as being infested with parasites), and erotomanic delusions (believing someone, usually famous, is in love with the individual, which can lead to stalking behavior) (APA, 2000).

Many non-bizarre delusions are systematized, meaning that the belief involves a scheme of actions and concerns that appear logical if the initial premise of the belief, for example, persecution, is taken as factual and correct. In such cases, because the delusion fits together logically, for a while others may not challenge the belief because it seems plausible. The content of such delusions varies enormously according to a number of variables including the client's particular disorder and its etiology, the client's culture, gender, age and ethnic group, and the general social climate and historical context. It can be useful to determine what the content of a client's delusion is, because delusions often have individual meaning, and understanding their content may give clues to the individual's personality and dynamics.

Disorganized speech is another positive symptom that is the most direct expression of the core symptom of thought disorder. The severity can range from speech in which the ideas are clear but somewhat disconnected to what is called "word salad," in which the speech involves a random stream of completely disconnected words, for example, a client might say "door bell clock car mine." Some individuals with schizophrenia make up words that have individual meaning for them. Such a word is called a "neologism." Neologisms are normal with children and are a part of children's literature, such as the work of Lewis Carroll or Shel Silverstein. But in adults, neologisms are usually associated with disorders such as schizophrenia or autism. For example, one of the author's clients went to see his doctor to remove a small cyst on his arm, which he called a "maligamancy."

The fourth, and last, positive symptom is *disorganized behavior*, which involves behavior that is unfocused and doesn't accomplish a basic task adequately or is inappropriate to the situation. For example, a client might pace back and forth in an agitated manner, rock on his heels, and gesture without any particular focus or goal while in a restaurant or church. Other forms of disorganized behavior include inappropriately laughing to oneself, masturbating in public, or not being able to organize one's behavior in steps in order to accomplish basic activities of daily living, such as getting dressed with appropriate clothes. Markedly deteriorating hygiene is a common expression of disorganized behavior. Disorganized behavior can result in clients being socially rejected by others and expelled from community resources, such as churches and libraries, and can be very embarrassing and shame-inducing for families.

Negative Symptoms in Schizophrenia

As noted previously, the negative symptoms found in schizophrenia are so-called deficit symptoms; that is, they involve the lack of important abilities that can profoundly affect psychosocial functioning. Negative symptoms can be defined as the *absence* or reduction of normal mental processes, feelings, or behavior. In fact, it is the negative symptoms and cognitive deficits that contribute most to the psychosocial functioning disability exacted by schizophrenia. People who have these symptoms often feel like they have lost something that is central to what it means to be human and that who they were before the illness struck has somehow disappeared. For families, it can feel like the loved one with schizophrenia is just a shadow of his or her former self. It is as if the "original person" has gone away and been replaced by someone who looks like that person but no longer seems like that person in terms of how he or she interacts and behaves (Andreasen, 1994). As the mother of a 23-year-old son with prominent negative symptoms commented: "It's like the movie *Invasion of the Body Snatchers*. I know this sounds terrible, but it is like my son has been replaced by a pod person—he just isn't the same person he used to be."

There are five primary negative symptoms, the first three of which are included in the current *DSM* criteria for schizophrenia. The first is *alogia* or "poverty of speech," which means that the fluency and productivity of speech, that is, how much is said and the depth of content, is impaired. Alogia probably reflects a slowing down of the individual's thought processes, along with experiencing "blocked thoughts," in which the individual's thought process stops temporarily. This is seen usually during an interview in which questions are posed to the person and the person will not respond immediately and may say later, "What was the question?" People with schizophrenia may explain this phenomenon by saying that someone has stolen their thoughts or the thought just disappeared. Sometimes, thought blocking is due to hallucinations that interrupt the individual's thought process and ability to focus and concentrate.

The second negative symptom is *affective flattening* or *affective blunting*, in which the range and intensity of emotional expression is significantly reduced. This includes facial expression, voice intonation, eye contact, and ability to interpret and respond appropriately to social cues. This symptom can produce a lot of frustration and sadness for families and can be difficult for mental health professionals to deal with as well.

The third negative symptom is *avolition*, which is a reduction in the ability to initiate a behavior and carry it through, that is, engage in goal-directed behavior. Avolition is often mislabeled as laziness or disinterest but, in fact, it is not a willful behavior at all. Avolition can manifest in the person being no longer willing to participate in family activities—in some cases the person won't come out of his or her room and just wants to lie in bed. Mental health providers may become frustrated because the person won't participate in therapeutic activities and thus may inappropriately push the person into activities he or she just cannot manage. Example:

> David, who has schizophrenia, has never experienced many positive symptoms. His main difficulties have been around negative symptoms. David will sit for hours on the porch of his board and care home smoking cigarettes and, although other people are around him, he doesn't make an effort to interact with them and isn't responsive if others attempt to initiate conversations with him. One morning the van came to pick up the clients to go to the day treatment program, and David didn't want to go. Frustrated, his board and care operator began to push him to get up off

> his bed and get into the van, finally threatening to hold back David's P & I (personal and incidental) money for the week if he didn't go. At that point, David yanked the telephone out of the wall and threw it at the operator, yelling, "Just leave me alone!"

Another common, and very painful, negative symptom is *anhedonia*, which is the loss of the ability to experience pleasure or enjoyment from activities that were previously enjoyed by the ill person or are usually enjoyed by people in general. Finally, although some clinicians and researchers call this a cognitive symptom, some clinicians include *attention impairment* as a final negative symptom (Andreasen, 1994). Attention impairment is an impaired ability to focus on tasks or activities. For example, a person may be flipping through a magazine and seem to be reading parts of it, but when asked what he or she is reading, the person says "I don't know." Or the individual is watching TV but can't recall what the storyline is about. It appears like he or she is paying attention but, in fact, is not able to sustain focus. In summary, we have what may be called the five A's of negative symptoms: alogia, affective flattening, avolition, anhedonia, and attention impairment.

Cognitive Symptoms in Schizophrenia

The cognitive symptoms in schizophrenia refer to various difficulties with concentration and memory. These can include aspects often included as part of formal thought disorder, such as disorganized thinking, slowed thinking (sometimes categorized as a negative symptom), difficulty understanding external stimuli, poor concentration, poor memory, difficulty expressing thoughts (sometimes considered part of poverty of thought) and, finally, difficulties in integrating thoughts, feelings, and behavior, which is something people without schizophrenia can usually do automatically.

Although the cognitive symptoms in schizophrenia can be subtle, they are an important explanation for how the illness evolves and the nature of the associated psychosocial impairments. One of the cognitive symptoms in schizophrenia is poor "executive functioning." This means that the individual has difficulty understanding and processing information and using information to make decisions. This can cause individuals to become confused and overwhelmed by stimuli and ambivalent when faced with having to make decisions.

Another cognitive symptom, which is sometimes also classified as a negative symptom, is trouble focusing or paying attention to tasks, whether it is reading a book or participating in an interpersonal conversation. A third cognitive symptom is problems with "working memory," which means the individual has difficulties in using and applying information immediately after learning it. For example, when participating in social skills training, which is described later in the chapter, the individual may learn how to appropriately ask for change but not be able to generalize the skills used in asking for change to other interpersonal interactions. It also explains why "overlearning" and lots of practice are necessary for individuals to learn various types of skills that demand cognitive processing.

Research suggests that the cognitive deficits seen in schizophrenia usually predate the first episode of illness, even extending back to childhood (Cannon, Jones, et al., 1999; Erlenmeyer-Kimling, Rock, et al., 2000; Fish, Marcus, et al., 1992; Fuller et al., 2002; Ott, Roberts, et al., 2002; Torrey, 2002). Furthermore, without targeted treatment, these symptoms persist even after the other symptoms have improved (Hoff & Kremen, 2003; Hughes et al., 2003; Rund et al., 2004). Fortunately, recently developed cognitive remediation therapies (described later in this chapter) have advanced psychosocial treatment of cognitive impairments in schizophrenia and have been shown to dramatically improve clients' functional recovery (Eack, 2012). Not all individuals with schizophrenia have severe cognitive deficits, however. What types of symptoms the person has, across all three spheres of cognitive, negative, and positive symptoms, is in part determined by the subtype of schizophrenia.

Watch the video *"Speaking Out: Larry: Schizophrenia."* How do the symptoms of schizophrenia appear when interviewing a consumer with the illness, and how does a consumer describe his symptoms in the course of an interview?

Subtypes of Schizophrenia

Prior to *DSM-5*, the diagnosis of schizophrenia allowed for the specification of subtypes. What subtype of schizophrenia a particular individual had was determined by the nature of the most predominant psychopathology at the time of evaluation (APA, 2000). In the *DSM-IV-TR*, there were five subtypes of schizophrenia: paranoid, disorganized, catatonic, undifferentiated, and residual. For *DSM-5*, however, the classic subtypes for schizophrenia have been eliminated based on the argument that they have low diagnostic stability, do not exhibit distinctive patterns of treatment response or longitudinal course, and are not heritable. Furthermore, the DSM-5 Work Group argued that, except for the paranoid and undifferentiated subtypes, other subtypes are rarely diagnosed today. Not everyone, however, agrees with this assessment. As most clinicians know, individuals with schizophrenia vary significantly, and the nature and content of symptoms is often relevant with regard to course, prognosis, and outcome.

For example, it is well recognized that individuals with paranoid schizophrenia generally have the best long-term outcome and overall rate of recovery (Fenton & McGlashan, 1991) and have a better prognosis in terms of psychosocial functioning. This is, in large part, due to a later onset of illness for many with paranoid schizophrenia, and because individuals with the paranoid form of schizophrenia typically do not have significant cognitive deficits or pronounced negative symptoms that can undermine recovery (Fenton & McGlashan, 1991). Paranoid schizophrenia is characterized by the presence of hallucinations and delusions that are usually persecutory, jealous, or grandiose in nature. Common themes for paranoid delusions include the person believing others are trying to poison his food, or malicious individuals are trying to hunt her down and kill her, or that others are conspiring to do him harm of some kind, or co-workers are conspiring to get him fired from his job (Mueser & Gingerich, 2006). Individuals with paranoid schizophrenia, therefore, are more likely than those without paranoid symptoms to engage in aggression toward self or others (Kantor, 2004), stemming from the nature of paranoid thinking patterns. Example:

> George has been treated for the past two decades for paranoid schizophrenia. When stable, George works full-time in a research lab and lives independently. When he decompensates, usually as the result of stopping his medication, he complains of smelling bad odors, an olfactory hallucination, which he believes is deliberately caused by his brother, whom he believes is trying to poison him. When this reaches the point where George begins thinking that the only solution is to kill his brother, George shows up at the emergency room asking for hospitalization. This is a significant strength because George is able to ask for help to avoid harming his brother.

In 2006, psychiatrist Wayne S. Fenton, an expert on subtypes of schizophrenia and an advocate of the importance of treatment in preventing violence, was murdered by a young psychotic man he agreed to see at the behest of the young man's parents on a Sunday in his private office (Oransky, 2006). Thomas Insel, M.D., former NIMH director, commented, "He's someone who essentially died in the line of duty doing what he thought was the best thing for this 19-year-old, and he suffered the worst of all outcomes," (Oransky, 2006, p. 1568). Understanding the risks associated with the paranoid form of schizophrenia is critically important in treatment and for clinician safety (Newhill, 2003). Individuals with the paranoid form of schizophrenia often respond quite well to treatment, provided that a trusting relationship with the clinician has been established. How to engage and effectively work with people who are paranoid is addressed in detail in Chapter 11.

In contrast to individuals with the more cognitively intact paranoid form of schizophrenia, individuals whose symptoms are consistent with the disorganized type of schizophrenia evidence disorganized speech and behavior and inappropriate emotional expression and affect. They may dress strangely (e.g., wearing multiple shirts, mismatched clothes), wear garish makeup and accessories, and speak in an incoherent, disorganized manner. The behavioral disorganization seen in such individuals often results in great difficulty in performing activities of daily living, such as maintaining hygiene, dressing, and preparing meals (APA, 2000). As a result, people with the disorganized form of schizophrenia have a poorer prognosis generally and, because of their inability to care for themselves, often require lifelong supervised care. Many people with disorganized schizophrenia are cared for by family, often parents; however, as the parents grow older and have more difficulty providing constant caregiving, the ill son or daughter may require placement in residential sheltered care of some kind. Example:

> Juan lives with his parents, who have worked in the grape-picking business for many years. Juan's first psychotic episode occurred when he was 17 years old, and he has never been able to care for himself since that time. He has had multiple hospitalizations, but after each one he soon stops taking his medication, deteriorates, and must be rehospitalized. He has tried working beside his parents in the vineyards picking grapes, but after a short time of picking, he wanders away and stands in the field, picking his nose and laughing to himself. Eventually, as Juan's parents developed some physical disabilities stemming from their decades of hard labor in the fields, they could no longer care for Juan and were forced to refer him for placement in a board and care home. With the structure provided by the home, Juan functions slightly better and is able to work sweeping floors a couple hours a day.

The catatonic form of schizophrenia was commonly diagnosed in decades past but is more rarely seen today. Catatonia as a symptom is found in a range of mental, physical, and substance use disorders (Daniels, 2009) and features a marked psychomotor disturbance involving stiff or "frozen" behaviors, extreme negativism (i.e., maintenance of a rigid posture that is resistant to attempts to move the person), postures that are often strange and would normally be difficult to maintain, and facial expressions that appear frozen. Catatonic individuals may be mute or exhibit echolalia (repeating words that have been spoken) or echopraxia (repeatedly imitating the movements of another person). Kleinhaus, Harlap, Perrin, et al. (2012), in a recent cohort prospective study of catatonic schizophrenia, concluded that individuals with catatonic schizophrenia show a slightly different profile of risk factors and have a higher risk of completed suicide as compared to those with other forms of schizophrenia, suggesting that catatonic schizophrenia may have its own distinct etiology.

Schizoaffective Disorder

Schizoaffective disorder evidences a combination of the core symptoms of schizophrenia plus symptoms of a mood disorder, either bipolar disorder or depression. Although there has been an ongoing debate over whether schizoaffective disorder is a type of schizophrenia or a type of mood disorder, the general conclusion among most clinicians and researchers is that it is primarily a form of schizophrenia. To diagnose schizoaffective disorder, a person needs to have primary symptoms of schizophrenia (such as delusions, hallucinations, disorganized speech, disorganized behavior) along with a period of time when he or she also has symptoms of depression or a manic episode. Accordingly, there may be two subtypes of schizoaffective disorder: the *depressive subtype*, characterized by depression-type episodes only; and the *bipolar subtype*, characterized by manic episodes with or without depressive symptoms or depressive episodes. Differential diagnosis is difficult with schizoaffective disorder, and individuals with a combination of psychotic and mood symptoms may actually have a mood disorder, a substance use disorder, or a psychotic/mood disorder due to a general medical condition, and thus, such alternatives must be considered before concluding that the person has schizoaffective disorder.

Watch the video *"Josh: Schizoaffective Disorder."* How does a client with schizoaffective disorder describe the array of psychotic and mood symptoms and the struggles to cope with them?

The "Rule of Thirds"

When describing the general diversity in course and outcome with schizophrenia, clinicians and researchers often refer to the "rule of thirds," that is, as an aggregate, there are three general illness courses and outcomes with schizophrenia (Torrey, 2006). About one third of individuals who have an initial psychotic episode that looks like schizophrenia have only one such episode, achieve complete recovery, and never get sick again. Today, we don't even label such a condition "schizophrenia," rather, the individual—if he or she meets criteria—would be given the provisional diagnosis of "schizophreniform disorder." If the individual's psychotic symptoms recur and the person experiences subsequent episodes, however, then the diagnosis would be changed to "schizophrenia." When the author was in practice, and an individual was brought to the hospital in the midst of his or her first psychotic episode, the staff would all hope that the individual had what we called "the little s" (schizophreniform disorder) instead of evolving into having "the big S" (schizophrenia); and about a third of the individuals we saw did, in fact, fully recover with no subsequent episodes.

Some individuals with schizophrenia (the second "third") have many episodes of illness during their lifetime but function reasonably well in between episodes; that is, their psychosocial functioning recovers to normal or close to normal. There are a variety of variables that contribute to this more fortunate course of illness. First, individuals with good recovery in between episodes are often described as being members of the "non-deficit type" of schizophrenia. The non-deficit type evidences primarily positive symptoms, such as hallucinations and delusions, which generally respond well to antipsychotic medications, and show relatively intact cognitive functioning. Such clients are usually less psychosocially impaired, have a better prognosis (McGlashan & Fenton, 1993), and are likely to have the paranoid form of schizophrenia. In addition, such individuals usually don't show many negative symptoms, had good premorbid functioning with a sudden acute initial onset of symptoms, show enough insight into their illness to adhere adequately to prescribed treatment, and are able to maintain good positive social support with family and friends. Example:

> Chin-Hwa is a 28-year-old married Korean man brought by his family to the emergency room. The family was very embarrassed to have to seek professional help, but things had reached the point that they could no longer handle the situation within the family. Chin-Hwa is a successful engineer working for a military research facility. Two months ago he told his wife that he felt his co-workers were conspiring against him. He began missing work and became increasingly paranoid and fearful. He became preoccupied with religion and eventually locked himself and his children in their home and made them go through certain rituals, such as kneeling before the cross for hours. When Chin-Hwa wouldn't let his wife into the house, she went to his parents' home for help. His father insisted that Chin-Hwa open the door, which he did, and then the family brought him to the emergency room. Chin-Hwa was hospitalized and was eventually diagnosed with paranoid schizophrenia. He responded well to medication, was very adherent to the treatment that was recommended by his Korean-American doctor, received much support and care from his family for continuing treatment, and was able to successfully return to work.

The final third of individuals with schizophrenia have what we used to call "chronic schizophrenia." The individual with chronic, that is, continuous or recurring, schizophrenia often does not fully recover normal functioning in between episodes and may even evidence a gradually deteriorating downhill course. That is, with each recurrent episode, the individual's subsequent psychosocial functioning is a bit poorer than following the previous episode. These clients typically require long-term treatment, generally including medication, to control the symptoms, and may always require some level of sheltered care and are unable to ever live completely independently. Some individuals with chronic schizophrenia may never be able to function without assistance of one sort or another and, even with medication, may never be completely symptom free.

Factors That Can Lead to Relapse or Exacerbation of Symptoms

As noted previously, schizophrenia should be viewed essentially as an enduring bio-psycho-social vulnerability upon which certain stressors may impinge. Thus, a relapse of schizophrenic illness may be precipitated by certain changes in several different arenas. For example, a relapse may occur when the individual's underlying biological vulnerability is stressed. An example of a biological stressor would be the abuse of alcohol or street drugs. Although the idea that substance abuse may be a causal factor in schizophrenia is controversial, we do know that, in fact, almost half of individuals with schizophrenia also meet criteria for a substance abuse problem at some point during their lifetime (Buckley, Miller, Lehrer, & Castle, 2009). Also, use of drugs and alcohol is a common trigger for relapse because it taxes the individual's brain, undermines the effectiveness of antipsychotic medication, and is associated with non-adherence to treatment in general. Smoking marijuana, in particular, seems to be associated with an earlier onset of the illness, perhaps serving as a trigger for individuals with a biological diathesis to developing schizophrenia (van Winkel et al., 2011). Example:

> Alan has undifferentiated schizophrenia and a long history of multiple hospitalizations dating back to 1973. Alan's mother also has schizophrenia, and his older brother committed suicide. He has poor insight into his illness and after each hospitalization follows a pattern of being adherent to medication at first, but within a few months he begins to forget to take his medications and starts smoking marijuana and drinking alcohol. The drug use then leads to an exacerbation of his symptoms and bizarre behavior, for example, drinking his own urine mixed with vodka and Coke, and eventually he always requires rehospitalization.

Relapse can also occur when stressful life events or daily pressures and hardships overwhelm the individual's ability to cope (Liberman & Mueser, 1989). Living in a stressful environment with caretakers who are overstimulating, critical, hostile or overinvolved with the client, that is, high in expressed emotion, can trigger a relapse. It is also not uncommon for a first episode of schizophrenia or a subsequent relapse to be triggered by a sudden life change such as leaving home to go to college or entering the military service. Such life events are stressful and place new demands on the individual's coping resources and often require the development of new coping strategies. For an individual with schizophrenia or the biological vulnerability to develop the illness, such stress may be too much to cope with, and an episode of illness is triggered. Example:

> Maura was always a sensitive quiet girl who never had many friends but was close to her family. Maura was very bright and excelled in school, particularly in English literature and writing classes. She won a partial scholarship to an elite private liberal arts college located several hundred miles from home and started her freshman year when she was 18 years old. Although Maura loved her classes, living in the dorm with new people, coping with the stress of living with a roommate who was noisy and messy, and the constant pounding music from other students' rooms proved to be extremely difficult for her to adjust to. Within a couple months, Maura started to hear voices for the first time, began to believe that her hallmates were conspiring against her, and stopped going to her classes. A concerned professor alerted the dorm's resident advisor, who convinced Maura to call her parents and tell them what was happening. Her parents immediately drove to Maura's school, took her home, and then arranged for her to see a psychiatrist, who treated her with antipsychotic medication. After a second psychotic episode a year later, Maura was

diagnosed with paranoid schizophrenia. Her psychiatrist recommended that Maura transfer temporarily to the community college close to home, which would be less stressful and enable her to access the positive social support of her family.

Relapse can also occur when an individual's social or professional support network weakens or diminishes. For example, a client's family member dies, or the client's therapist leaves for another job, or the client has to leave a stable living situation (Liberman & Mueser, 1989). Research has emphasized the importance of positive social support as part of recovery and maintaining wellness in people with schizophrenia (Mueser & Gingerich, 2006), however, research has also shown that individuals with schizophrenia tend to have smaller, less functional, and more fragile social support networks than do nonclinical populations or individuals with other forms of mental illness (Holschuh & Segal, 2002). For example, a client with schizophrenia may have only two key people in her social support network—her case manager and her mother. If her mother dies, that client has lost half of her network of support.

Relapse can also occur when the client loses previously mastered social problem-solving skills (Liberman & Mueser, 1989). This can happen due to disuse or reinforcement of the sick role, which can occur as a result of extended hospitalization or incarceration. It can also be the consequence of, or due to, the impact of negative symptoms.

Thus, how well or symptomatic a particular individual with schizophrenia is at any point in time is determined by two major things: (1) the amount and type of stressors going on in the person's life; and (2) the problem-solving skills, coping skills, social support, and resources available to the individual (Liberman & Mueser, 1989). This suggests what can be called a *bidirectional model of symptom formation* in schizophrenia (Liberman & Mueser, 1989). This means that either (1) too much environmental change, stress, or tension; or (2) a paucity of coping skills and social support can lead to a relapse of illness or exacerbation of symptoms.

What is significant about this bidirectional model is the emphasis given to the active role of the client's coping skills and the importance of the client's social support system, both of which can be targeted by various psychosocial treatments. This emphasis directly suggests both target objectives and target approaches for therapeutic intervention, the overall objective of which is to prevent relapse, maximize psychosocial functioning, and foster recovery (Liberman & Mueser, 1989).

For example, if the goal is to reduce the underlying biological vulnerability, then the treatment of choice would be antipsychotic medication. Medication can buffer internal stimuli, which can help the individual better manage the impact of environmental stresses and life events. Or, if the goal is to reduce the stresses caused by environmental factors, then the treatment of choice would be environmental manipulation, a type of intervention that social workers excel in. For example, hospitalization can be beneficial because a person is removed temporarily from a stressful community situation. Or, staying with a different family member or obtaining a different sheltered care situation can be helpful in reducing stress if the caretaker the client has been living with is overly stimulating. Example:

Jerry, who has the disorganized form of schizophrenia, was placed in a board and care home that had the reputation of being a clean and well-run home. His case manager assumed that the structure of the home would be helpful to Jerry in terms of improving his daily living skills and behavior. However, the board and care home operator was very rigid and demanding, insisting that the clients keep their rooms spic-and-span with everything neatly in its place at all times. Jerry's normal disorganization with his personal things resulted in harsh criticism and punishment from the operator. Jerry became very stressed and anxious and for the first time in years began to hear angry critical voices. He called his case manager, who immediately arranged for his placement in a transitional care facility until placement could be arranged in another home with an organized but more flexible and relaxed atmosphere. With the new living arrangement, Jerry's symptoms stabilized, and hospitalization was avoided.

If the primary goal is to strengthen the client's social support network, then the treatment of choice could include family psychoeducation and group therapies and/or self-help or socialization groups or a peer counselor. Finally, if the goal is to increase the client's resilience to the ups and downs of life, which is an essential component in avoiding relapse, then the treatment of choice would be social and problem-solving skills training or cognitive remediation treatment. All four of these components—reducing biological vulnerability, reducing environmental stress, strengthening social supports, and increasing resilience—both alone and in combination can serve to delay relapse, thus reducing the total lifetime episodes of illness and maximizing recovery.

Assess your comprehension of *the prevalence, onset of illness, and symptoms of schizophrenia* by completing this quiz.

PSYCHOSOCIAL TREATMENT OF SCHIZOPHRENIA

Introduction

Antipsychotic medication can be very effective in reducing the positive symptoms of schizophrenia, that is, hallucinations, delusions, disorganized thinking, and agitation. Although medications alone can serve to delay relapse, medication alone does not permanently prevent relapse, and medication does not teach skills for community living (Hogarty, Anderson, Reiss, et al., 1986). Psychosocial interventions, however, can be very effective in addressing the negative symptoms and cognitive deficits associated with schizophrenia, and it is these symptoms that produce the greatest long-term impairment in psychosocial functioning. To survive in the community, most people with schizophrenia must learn or relearn social and daily living skills via participation in psychosocial treatment. Psychosocial treatment is essential for recovery because these treatments help clients understand their illness and learn how to manage it day to day, help improve difficulties in communication and forming relationships with others, and address the challenges they face in handling self-care and work. The coping and social skills clients learn through psychosocial treatment can help them to learn how to socialize and attend school or work with success. Social workers have been leaders in the development, evaluation, and application of many of the key psychosocial treatments for schizophrenia. These include family psychoeducation (Anderson, Reiss, & Hogarty, 1986), strengths-based case management (Fukui et al., 2012; Rapp, 1998), personal therapy (Hogarty et al., 1997), and cognitive-enhancement therapy (Eack, 2012; Hogarty & Greenwald, 2006), all of which are addressed in this book. When combined with antipsychotic medication, these interventions have helped to lengthen community tenure, prevent psychotic relapse, improve family functioning, and dramatically reduce the disability associated with this condition.

For any psychosocial treatment to be effective and not overstimulating, however, it is important that the client with schizophrenia be stabilized first on antipsychotic medication (see Chapter 8 on psychopharmacology). If the positive symptoms are not under control, the person will have too much difficulty focusing and the stimulation inherent in psychosocial interventions may even serve to exacerbate the positive symptoms (Anderson, Reiss, & Hogarty, 1986). Indeed, a classic study found that providing only psychosocial interventions to individuals with schizophrenia in the absence of medication was worse than only providing placebo medications (Hogarty, Goldberg, Schooler, et al., 1974).

Individuals who regularly participate in psychosocial treatment are also more likely to be adherent to their antipsychotic medication and, thus, have fewer relapses and episodes of hospitalization (Hogarty, Anderson, Reiss, et al., 1986; Hogarty, Goldberg, & Schooler, 1974; Mueser & Gingerich, 2006). This is because the psychosocial practitioner often sees the client more frequently and for greater lengths of time than the client's psychiatrist and, thus, is able to provide and reinforce accurate education about schizophrenia, the symptoms and problems that the client is experiencing or may experience, and the importance of medication as a keystone to recovery. However, not just any psychosocial treatment will do. Empirical data suggests there are specific forms of psychosocial treatment strategies that are especially effective for clients with schizophrenia. These include:

- Psychoeducation and family education
- Illness management and recovery
- Psychosocial rehabilitation
- Supported employment
- Social skills training
- Cognitive-behavioral treatments
- Cognitive remediation therapies
- Personal therapy for schizophrenia
- Self-help and peer support

Psychoeducation and Family Education

Psychoeducation and family education programs have already been addressed in Chapter 7 and, thus, will not be re-addressed in detail here, particularly since schizophrenia was the illness of focus when describing the Anderson, Reiss, and Hogarty (1986) model of psychoeducation in Chapter 7. However, to briefly recap, there are many models of family psychoeducation and family education, and all are designed to help clients and families understand and manage the illness of schizophrenia along with reducing levels of family stress. Family psychoeducation is considered to be an evidence-based practice based on more than 30 randomized clinical trials consistently demonstrating its effectiveness in achieving the targeted goals. Interventions used include empathic engagement, education, therapeutic support, access to clinical resources during times of crisis, social network enhancement, and learning problem-solving and communication skills (McFarlane, Dixon, Lukens, & Lucksted, 2003). Psychoeducation combines education with therapeutic support, while family education programs primarily emphasize the education part and may be peer-taught by family members. Because today, families provide much of the caregiving for individuals with schizophrenia, families must know as much as possible about the illness and be provided with resources and support.

Illness Management and Recovery

The philosophy of illness management and recovery (IMR) is that individuals with schizophrenia, and other serious mental illnesses, can and should be partners in treatment by taking an active role in understanding and managing their illness. The approach is very similar to family psychoeducation, except it is psychoeducation provided directly to the individual living with the illness. IMR programs teach clients/consumers the basic facts about schizophrenia and the various components of effective treatment and how these components work so the client or consumer can make informed decisions about their own treatment and care. Clients learn how to identify early warning signs of relapse and what to do when they occur to avoid relapse. They are also taught coping skills for dealing with persistent symptoms and how to maintain wellness as much as possible (NIMH, 2009).

The strategies employed in IMR are also part of related programs that go by other names, such as wellness management and recovery and symptom self-management (Gingerich & Mueser, 2005; Mueser & MacKain, 2008).

The philosophy and strategies of IMR embrace the National Consensus Statement on Mental Health Recovery (U.S. DHHS, n.d.), which identifies 10 fundamental components of consumer recovery. These are:

- ***Self-Direction:*** consumers can and should make self-directed, informed choices about their path toward their goals for recovery.
- ***Individualized and Person-Centered:*** one size does not fit all. There are many paths to recovery, and each individual's path must incorporate each person's unique strengths, resources, and challenges. Recovery is both a journey and a framework for wellness.
- ***Empowerment:*** consumers have a right to be informed about their illness and all treatments, and have the right to make their own choices and control their own destiny through individual and collective advocacy.
- ***Holistic:*** recovery embraces mind, body, and spirit and requires resources that address all areas of the consumer's life.
- ***Non-linear:*** recovery is not a step-by-step uninterrupted beeline, rather, it is based on continued overall growth that includes setbacks along with progress. A setback does not mean failure.
- ***Strengths-based:*** everyone has strengths to bring to their recovery, including talents, resiliencies, coping skills, and their inherent worth and dignity as a human being.
- ***Peer Support:*** by helping each other, consumers help themselves.
- ***Respect:*** this contributes to empowerment, protecting client rights, and can help to eliminate discrimination and stigma (both private and public).
- ***Responsibility:*** consumers must take personal responsibility for facilitating their own recovery and taking the steps needed to achieve wellness.
- ***Hope:*** defined as the desire for something accompanied by the expectation of obtaining it. Hope is the keystone for the work involved in recovery.

Supported by these 10 components, and strongly informed by the family psychoeducation approach, IMR employs an integrated set of five evidence-based practices in its program (Mueser & MacKain, 2008). These interventions teach people with schizophrenia how to manage their disorder in collaboration with professionals and significant others in order to achieve personal recovery goals. The first practice used is *psychoeducation*, teaching consumers about their illness and its treatment to help them be more informed in their treatment decision making. The second practice is *relapse prevention*, which focuses on identifying one's individual relapse triggers and early warning signs that can lead to relapse, and then learning strategies for delaying relapse. The third practice is *coping skills training*, which teaches consumers skills for dealing with stressful life events and strategies for coping with persistent symptoms. The fourth practice is *behavioral tailoring*, which addresses daily medication enhancement strategies for those consumers who must take psychotropic medication which, with schizophrenia, is almost everyone most of the time. Finally, the practice of *social skills training* is employed to improve interpersonal skills and enhance positive social support, which supports successful illness management.

IMR, like most evidence-based practices, is standardized and manualized and developed for both individual and group formats. Materials are free and available as a SAMHSA EBP Toolkit (store.samhsa.gov). The materials describe the program and how to set it up and all handouts and other materials are provided as part of the kit.

Practice Principles and Process

The underlying practice principles of IMR are: (1) Recovery is determined and defined by the consumer; (2) Education is key to being an informed consumer and a good decision maker; (3) Recovery goals are more likely to be achieved when the consumer, family, and treatment team work together collaboratively; (4) Planning is essential for avoiding relapse and rehospitalization; (5) Consumers have the capacity to learn new skills and strategies for successfully managing their illness, navigating life stresses, and achieving a satisfying quality of life SAMHSA EBP Toolkit (store.samhsa.gov).

IMR can be conducted as individual sessions with consumers or in a group format. The advantage of meeting individually is that the program can be specifically tailored to that individual consumer's unique needs. However, an advantage of meeting as a group is that the group process itself can enhance social support and interpersonal communication skill building, particularly for the social skills training component. Whether it is individual or group, the trained IMR facilitator(s) meet with consumers weekly for 3–10 months. The components of IMR are divided into descriptive handouts that are given to the consumers and then the content of the handouts is discussed during the IMR sessions and the consumers can keep the handouts for reference. Handout topics include SAMHSA EBP Toolkit, (store.samhsa.gov)

- Strategies to maximize recovery
- Practical facts on mental illness
- Understanding the stress-vulnerability-coping-competence model and treatment strategies
- How to build positive social support
- How to effectively use and adhere to your medication regime
- Effects of drug and alcohol use and how to manage issues related to substance use
- Reducing relapses and rehospitalizations
- Skills and strategies for coping with stress
- Managing problems and dealing with persistent symptoms
- Self-advocacy, that is, how to get your needs met in the mental health system

Effectiveness of IMR

How effective is IMR? A review of the studies of illness management programs, broadly defined, concluded that the practice components of IMR significantly improve consumers' knowledge about their illness and adherence to prescribed psychotropic medication, reduce the rate of relapse and rehospitalization, and help in managing persistent symptoms (Mueser, Corrigan, Hilton, et al., 2002). Kim Mueser and colleagues packaged their components into a program that they then named IMR. The IMR intervention itself, so far, has only been examined in one or two studies, although findings from these studies are positive. In sum, the success of IMR reinforces the reality that the more consumers know about their illness and its treatments and the greater their repertoire of skills for managing stress and symptoms, the better they are at achieving recovery and staying well and out of the hospital.

Assess your comprehension of ***the components, practice principles, process, and effectiveness of illness management and recovery (IMR) for individuals with schizophrenia*** **by completing this quiz.**

Psychosocial Rehabilitation

How It Is Defined

Psychosocial or psychiatric rehabilitation is a service that helps clients with serious mental illness to evaluate their strengths, challenges, and needs and set their own goals for recovery. Because the onset of schizophrenia is often in the late teens or early twenties, the prime school and career-building years, and because of the cognitive deficits associated with the illness, most individuals with schizophrenia need some form of rehabilitative training in order to work and move toward independent living. Typically, psychosocial rehabilitation programs provide a range of supports including job counseling, budget and money management counseling, opportunities to learn and practice interpersonal and communication skills and, sometimes, therapeutic interventions such as social cognitive remediation treatments.

There is no universally accepted common definition of psychosocial rehabilitation in the literature, however, Bachrach (1992) offers a very good definition that can be applied across models based on the work of others (see, e.g., Anthony, Cohen, & Cohen, 1983; Rutman, 1987; Watts & Bennett, 1983), particularly that of Cubelli & Havens (1969) and Liberman (1988). Her definition emphasizes that psychosocial rehabilitation involves encouraging clients to define their own goals in their recovery and achieve optimal psychosocial functioning via learning skills and having access to positive environmental supports (Bachrach, 1992).

Founded in 1975, the United States Psychiatric Rehabilitation Association (USPRA: www.uspra.org), which is the professional association for credentialing psychosocial rehabilitation practitioners, defines "psychiatric rehabilitation" as the following (United States Psychiatric Rehabilitation Association, n.d.):

> Psychiatric rehabilitation promotes recovery, full community integration and improved quality of life for persons who have been diagnosed with any mental health condition that seriously impairs their ability to lead meaningful lives. Psychiatric rehabilitation services are collaborative, person-directed and individualized ... [and] ... focus on helping individuals develop skills and access resources needed to increase their capacity to be successful and satisfied in the living, working, learning, and social environments of their choice. (United States Psychiatric Rehabilitation Association, n.d.)

The terms *psychiatric rehabilitation* and *psychosocial rehabilitation* are used interchangeably but for the purpose of this chapter, and in keeping with the nonclinical traditional focus, the term *psychosocial rehabilitation* will be used.

Philosophy of Psychosocial Rehabilitation

The psychosocial rehabilitation philosophy emphasizes common sense and practical needs, with a focus on teaching the essential skills for successful community living in four basic spheres: vocational, social/recreational, residential, and educational. These foci are in recognition that all people, whether they are living with mental illness or not, want many of the same things: going to school or training to learn how to engage in meaningful work, engaging in enjoyable leisure activities, having positive relationships with others, and having a comfortable place to live with or without other people. Most importantly, psychosocial rehabilitation emphasizes an atmosphere of hope and the expectation that all individuals have strengths and the potential for learning personal and instrumental coping skills to attain a level of functioning that will bring them a sense of satisfaction and accomplishment. This is the essence of what today we call "recovery." In many ways, the early psychosocial rehabilitation programs that emerged in the 1940s were way ahead of their time in terms of promoting a philosophy that was, at that time, radically different from how mental illness was viewed and treated.

Models of Psychosocial Rehabilitation

There are several models of psychosocial rehabilitation, including the community lodge, assertive community treatment (addressed in Chapter 9), social learning token economy programs, and the clubhouse model. It is beyond the scope of this section to address all of

---

Defining psychosocial rehabilitation (n.d.) United States Psychiatric Rehabilitation Association (USPRA). Retrieved June 29, 2011 from: www.uspra.org. Reprinted with permission.

the models of psychosocial rehabilitation; however, one exemplar is the Fountain House social club, which started the clubhouse model of psychosocial rehabilitation, and that program and its philosophy and structure will be briefly discussed.

Psychosocial rehabilitation emerged in the late 1940s when a group of ex-state hospital patients began to meet in a storefront social club in New York City in the hopes of getting and providing acceptance and emotional support. From the beginning, the group emphasized self-help, mutual interdependence, and a reliance on one's own and others' strengths. Given that mental health services in the 1940s focused almost exclusively on pathology, the strengths approach of the emerging clubhouse members was novel, courageous, and a radical departure from the status quo.

The members of the fledgling clubhouse named their organization Fountain House to symbolize hope. Since then hundreds of Fountain House clones have been established throughout the United States and worldwide. The International Center for Clubhouse Development (ICCD, www.iccd.org) states that clubhouse members are guaranteed four rights of membership: (1) a right to a place to come, (2) a right to meaningful work, (3) a right to meaningful relationships, and (4) a right to a place to return.

What was unique about the Fountain House model? First, instead of calling themselves "patients," as was the accepted term at that time, clubhouse participants referred to themselves as "members." The members formed groups and teams to accomplish tasks, plan activities, solve problems, and develop their own social support network with the result that the quality of their lives improved (Beard, Propst, & Malamud, 1982). The clubhouse explicitly avoided having any kind of clinical or treatment focus, thus the staff were primarily paraprofessionals trained in vocational rehabilitation. The staff provided support and encouragement, but required that members seek psychiatric treatment elsewhere. Thus, Fountain House had rehabilitative, not clinical, goals.

Fundamental Concepts of Psychosocial Rehabilitation

Based on a review of the literature, Bachrach (1992) identified eight basic interrelated concepts underlying psychosocial rehabilitation that are still applicable today and provide a framework that cuts across the various models. The first concept is psychosocial rehabilitation's primary goal of helping individuals with long-term severe and persistent mental illness achieve recovery to the best of their capacity (Fine, 1980). Second, psychosocial rehabilitation takes an ecological view and focuses rehabilitative efforts on the person within the context of the individual's environment, recognizing that environmental factors are important for the journey to recovery (Liberman & Phipps, 1987). The importance of environmental factors is also central to modern case management. Third, psychosocial rehabilitation emphasizes consumer strengths as a central resource to draw upon for rehabilitation efforts (Saleeby, 2008). Fourth is an emphasis on hope, which is critical for individuals burdened by stigma and loss, as is the case for many individuals with long-term mental illness. Fifth is optimism that all individuals with mental illness have the capacity for reaching vocational goals in the process of rehabilitation. Work provides money, a sense of independence, and empowerment. There is nothing more empowering than money in one's pocket that one has earned and is under one's own control. Work is a "deeply generative and reintegrative force in the life of every human being" and thus must inform all aspects of rehabilitation (Beard, Propst, & Malamud, 1982, p. 67).

A sixth concept is that psychosocial rehabilitation goes beyond just a focus on work, rather, it addresses other important aspects of individuals' lives such as social and recreational needs. Seventh, psychosocial rehabilitation embraces one of the most important components of recovery, which is that consumers themselves can take personal responsibility for facilitating their own rehabilitation and be actively involved in that process. Finally, rehabilitation is a process, not a one-time event, and may unfold across multiple programs and settings. For example, a client may be a participant in an outpatient rehabilitation

Assess your comprehension of *the definition, philosophy, models, and fundamental principles/concepts of psychosocial rehabilitation* by completing this quiz.

program but also receive rehabilitative efforts during times when he or she requires inpatient care. Sometimes, however, programs dubbed "psychosocial rehabilitation" are set up as time-limited ventures in which consumers have only one relatively brief opportunity to participate. Such models may not adequately address the longer-term realities of both serious mental illness and the true process of psychosocial rehabilitation.

Supported Employment

Supported employment for individuals with schizophrenia and other serious mental illnesses is an evidence-based practice, meaning that its effectiveness has been established across studies that have produced similar positive outcomes (Bond, Becker, et al., 2001). However, like so many evidence-based practices, supportive employment does not reach all of those who need it, in spite of the plea in 2003 by the President's New Freedom Commission on Mental Health to "make a life in the community for everyone" (New Freedom Commission on Mental Health, 2003, p. 1). Part of having a good quality of life in the community for most people, including individuals with schizophrenia and other serious mental illnesses, is to have the opportunity to work at a job and earn a living. When people work in a job they feel good about, particularly a job that non-mentally ill people also work in, that enhances a consumer's self-efficacy and "reduces disability, boredom, fear, social isolation, discrimination, and stigma" (Becker & Drake, n.d.). Work also provides structure and routine that help individuals with mental illness maintain stability in their lives. Jobs that involve working with others also enhance natural social support.

Supported employment helps people with schizophrenia find and keep meaningful jobs in the community. Such jobs are not sheltered jobs, that is, jobs set aside for people with disabilities that usually pay less than minimum wage. Instead, supported employment jobs exist in the open labor market, pay at least minimum wage, include both full- and part-time positions, and involve working with people who do not have disabilities. The philosophy is similar to the philosophy of "mainstreaming" in education, where children with disabilities spend all or part of their school day in regular classrooms with children who do not have disabilities.

Sometimes consumers worry about losing important benefits, such as Social Security or Medicaid, if they work. However, supported employment provides employment specialists who help consumers understand how their benefits are or are not affected by working, so the consumers can make informed choices about what they prefer to do in terms of starting or changing jobs. Supportive employment works by providing consumer choice, integrated services, competitive jobs, benefits counseling, timely support, continuous supports, and consumer preferences (*What is supportive employment?*, U.S. DHHS, n.d.). Two of the main barriers to wider dissemination of supportive employment are perceived financial and organizational barriers.

Supported employment is an evidence-based practice that is not limited to the treatment of schizophrenia but, rather, can be helpful for individuals living with a range of serious and persistent mental illnesses. Because supported employment is often a component of a consumer's case management service plan, additional detail about it is provided in Chapter 9, which addresses case management.

Social Skills Training

Social skills training is an intervention originally designed to help individuals with schizophrenia learn the skills necessary to achieve the instrumental and interpersonal goals inherent in day-to-day life in the community (Shepherd, 1978). Instrumental goals are those goals that require skills necessary for community survival and independence, such as how to pay bills or how to use a telephone. Interpersonal goals involve the skills needed to establish, maintain, and deepen supportive and socially rewarding relationships, such as how to say "hello" to another person or how to ask someone for a date (Liberman & Mueser, 1989).

Social skills training is one of the most highly structured systematic forms of group treatment for persons with schizophrenia. Its features include goals that are: (1) concrete and clearly defined; (2) feasible, so that the client can experience success; and (3) measurable, in order to provide feedback about whether the goal was achieved and to what extent it was achieved. Session agendas are usually planned in advance, and the procedures usually follow written guidelines. Many social skills training programs are "manualized," which means that the program follows a standardized written curriculum. In vivo practice and homework assignments are emphasized as the mechanisms for learning and practicing skills.

Because schizophrenia is a pervasive illness and affects all aspects involved in interpersonal communication—affective, cognitive, verbal, and behavioral domains of functioning—it can significantly impair a person's ability to form and maintain positive interpersonal relationships, which is the essence of social quality of life (Mueser & Gingerich, 2006). Schizophrenia affects both the ability to learn and relearn adaptive social behaviors. Social skills training can be helpful in modifying problematic behaviors and learning adaptive behaviors. Example:

> John, who has schizophrenia, continually asked questions in a persistent, intrusive and sometimes irritating way, which would alienate other people. He had a habit of asking strangers inappropriate personal questions, for example, "How old are you?" or "How much do you weigh?" John's inappropriate social interaction had unfortunately progressed to the point that he had no friends and complained that he was lonely.
>
> Social skills training, however, helped John learn that "such questions are personal, and you don't ask personal questions of people you don't know well." The social skills training facilitator worked with John to help him to understand that there are degrees of intimacy in relationships and this guides what you can appropriately ask people or what comments you might make to them. The peer feedback that John received from other clients during the group training sessions reinforced this message, and helped John understand the negative effect his intrusiveness had on how others perceived him.
>
> After a few weeks of training, the staff would overhear John starting to ask something inappropriate, catch himself, and say, "Oops, that's ... too ... personal," and then he would ask an alternative question, "So, how do you like the weather?" At times it was almost comical, as he would paste a big grin on his face in an attempt to seem friendly. What eventually happened, however, is that even though John's initial attempts to practice his social skills were awkward, other people could see that he was trying, and that led to others responding in a positive way, with the eventual outcome that John, at the age of 58, made some friends for the first time in his life.

Social Skills Training Methods

Role-playing is the primary vehicle used to assess both the client's pretreatment social competence and to train targeted behavioral excesses or deficits during treatment (Liberman & Mueser, 1989). John's persistent intrusive questions in the case vignette above would be an example of a behavioral excess. Poor eye contact or being nonresponsive to the social input of others would be examples of behavioral deficits. Which role-play training scenarios are selected is determined by the particular client's individual difficulties along with the types of problem situations that generally apply to the people living with the particular psychiatric condition the client has. For example, most people with schizophrenia have difficulty with interpersonal discourse and, thus, with such clients you almost always address this type of problem in the role-plays. Social skills training is usually done in small groups but can also be delivered on an individual basis.

The social skills training sessions usually vary from around 15 minutes per session to up to 2 hours, depending on the number of clients participating and their level of functioning. Some clients, initially, are unable to tolerate working on social skills for longer than 15–20 minutes because the experience is too stimulating or anxiety arousing. It is important for clients to have a positive experience as they begin the training, so it is best to move gradually in small, more manageable steps and avoid pushing clients to practice beyond the amount of time that is right for them.

Using a group format for the bulk of the social skills training work has a number of advantages for clients with schizophrenia. The group experience provides clients with direct learning experiences plus vicarious learning opportunities via observations of other clients' behavior as they role-play, and the group can provide reinforcement from peers as well as the facilitator. Videotaping role-plays and then playing them back so the client can observe him or herself actually doing a social interaction can be very beneficial, because the client can observe exactly where his or her strengths are and where he or she needs to do more work.

In many psychosocial rehabilitation programs, social skills group training is supplemented with individual training to allow, first, for more focus on individual behavior difficulties and, second, to provide an opportunity for more practice between group sessions to serve as further reinforcement. So, for example, group sessions could be scheduled on Monday and Friday with an individual session in between on Wednesday.

The Process of Social Skills Training

The participants in a social skills training role-play include the targeted client, another client as a respondent, and the social skills trainer/facilitator/therapist. The "treatment package" includes clear focused instructions, modeling (where the trainer models good social skills for the clients to observe), feedback to the participants provided by peers and trainer, and social reinforcement as participants' social skills improve. The modeling and feedback is provided either in vivo (live) or via videotape or, less preferable, audiotape playback.

There are two types of behaviors that social skills training targets. The first type is "process behaviors," which are the various verbal and nonverbal inputs that shape how the content of the interaction is delivered and received. Process behaviors include things like eye contact, voice volume and intonation, response latency (how quickly or slowly the person responds to the other person's input), and affective communications, such as smiles, frowns, inappropriate or appropriate emotional tone. The second type of behaviors targeted is "content behaviors," which are the composition of what is said and the way it is said. Content behaviors include things like empathic responses, assertiveness versus aggressiveness, intrusiveness, compliance, hostile comments, and irrelevant remarks (Liberman & Mueser, 1989). Good social skills are composed of many different elements, elements that most of us combine and use well without thinking about it. In social skills training, however, all these elements must be broken down and, for many clients, relearned, because the illness has caused them to lose skills they had mastered prior to becoming ill.

For example, let's say a client wants to ask another person for change to get a soda out of the vending machine. The trainer first asks the client to demonstrate how he or she would do that. The client says "Gimme change" with poor eye contact, a loud demanding voice, and an aggressive body stance. The trainer inquires what the outcome usually is and the client indicates that often the other person says "no" or just walks away. The trainer then would demonstrate to the client how to ask for change using good social skills, for example, "Hello. Would you be willing to give me change for a dollar so I can get a soda from the vending machine?" with good eye contact, modulated voice, and polite manner. For this situation, the client would work on each problem element, one at a time, and practice, practice, practice. Eventually, the client would be given a homework assignment, which would be to actually approach another person and ask for change. The outcome would then be shared with the group during the next session.

Effectiveness of Social Skills Training

How effective is social skills training? There have been dozens of studies over the past three decades examining the effectiveness of social skills training (SST) for individuals with schizophrenia, although weaknesses in methodology have hampered generalization of some study findings (see meta-analysis studies: Benton & Schroeder, 1990; Pilling et al., 2002). Findings overall are somewhat mixed, with some studies reporting positive findings (Benton & Schroeder, 1990) and others reporting little to no benefit (Pilling et al., 2002).

A number of reviews of nonrandomized controlled trials of social skills training have been published (see, e.g., Corrigan, 1991; Heinssen et al., 2000), which have generally reported positive results. Amongst positive findings, the data has shown that clients with schizophrenia in a treatment setting can be successfully trained to improve social skills in specific situations. Furthermore, moderate generalization of acquired skills to situations similar to the training scenarios can be expected for most clients from the training, provided there is an approbative learning environment. An approbative learning environment is characterized by peer and trainer affirming support, positive feedback, constructive supportive correction, and opportunities for repeated practice. However, studies acknowledge that learning is severely impaired if clients are actively symptomatic with positive symptoms during training, particularly high levels of distractibility. Achieving stability with antipsychotic medication prior to referral to SST is important. In addition, a key limitation of social skills training is difficulty with generalization of the scripted behaviors used in training scenarios to spontaneous and unrehearsed social situation in the client's natural life.

The third major positive finding is that most SST participants report decreases in social anxiety after training, along with increases in self-rated assertiveness (Benton & Schroeder, 1990), which was the case with the client John depicted in the vignette above. Finally, follow-up studies have shown that durability of acquired social skills depends on duration of training, and the key to durability and generalization is practice, practice, practice. Liberman & Mueser (1989) state that overlearning stemming from repeated practice promotes retention, and training must occur three times a week for 3 months straight at a minimum. Ideally, SST training should be provided for 6 months to a year. A 2002 meta-analysis of randomized controlled trials of SST, however, did not show a positive impact for SST on relapse rate, global adjustment, social functioning, quality of life, or treatment compliance (Pilling et al., 2002).

Cognitive-Behavioral Therapy for Schizophrenia

Cognitive-behavioral therapy has been shown to be highly effective in treating both the positive symptoms of schizophrenia (Bustillo, Lauriello, et al., 2001; Pfammatter et al., 2006; Rector & Beck, 2002), and in decreasing the negative symptoms of schizophrenia (Dickerson, 2004; Tarrier, Kinney, et al., 2001; Turkington et al., 2006; Turkington & Morrison, 2012) even in low-functioning clients (Grant, Huh, Perivoliotis, et al., 2012), provided the individual is adherent to prescribed medication (Rector & Beck, 2001). Cognitive-behavioral therapy (CBT) is based on the idea that how we think (cognition), how we feel (emotion and affect), and how we act (behavior) all interact and go together. Specifically, cognitive theory argues that our thoughts influence our feelings and behavior, our feelings influence our behavior and thoughts, and our behavior influences our emotions and thoughts (Beck, 2011).

The objectives of CBT are to identify irrational or maladaptive thoughts, assumptions, and beliefs, because the theory is that such beliefs create debilitating negative emotions. This is done in an effort to reject the distorted cognitions and replace them with more realistic and self-helping alternatives (Beck, 2011). People sometimes think that CBT is a quick fix for problems, but it really isn't. The reality is that CBT is not an overnight process, because even after people have learned to recognize when and where their mental processes go awry, it can take months of concerted effort to change and replace dysfunctional cognitive-affective-behavioral processes or habits with more rational and realistic ones.

For treating schizophrenia, CBT addresses the consumer's symptoms and the distress that the symptoms cause. Initially, CBT techniques focus on symptom management and differentiating real from unreal thoughts, perceptions, and experiences. For example, CBT helps individuals with schizophrenia understand the medication they are taking and how the medication acts to control their symptoms, primarily positive symptoms. It can also help a consumer learn to tell the difference between auditory hallucinations and the voices of people actually speaking. For delusions, sometimes reality testing can help but other times CBT helps the consumer learn how to manage his or her life so the delusion does not interfere with daily activities. Together, the therapist and the consumer work collaboratively to manage symptoms, adhere to medication, and develop coping strategies in order to facilitate recovery. One of the core targets of CBT for psychosis is addressing what is called "jumping to conclusions." Many individuals with schizophrenia, when encountering an ambiguous event, may automatically jump to a conclusion, usually negative, about the event without evaluating the evidence. Jumping to conclusions also occurs commonly with individuals with depression, in which neutral or ambiguous events are interpreted negatively in a personal way.

CBT for psychotic conditions such as schizophrenia has really become the psychosocial treatment of choice for people with treatment-resistant (i.e., antipsychotic-resistant) positive symptoms. In many cases, CBT treatment does not eliminate the positive symptoms, but helps individuals become less distressed by them by helping them evaluate the evidence for their reality, cope with their effects, and challenge egodystonic beliefs. Example:

> Bernice, 35 years old, was diagnosed with paranoid schizophrenia 10 years earlier. Bernice was adherent to her medication, which included 1 cc of fluphenazine decanoate every two weeks and 5 mg of benztropine daily for side effects. Bernice worked as a bookkeeper and lived independently. She was close to her family and active in the local African Methodist Episcopal church. From the time Bernice became ill, she had the persistent unshakeable delusion that the owners of the McDonald's restaurants in town were in a conspiracy to harm her. She believed there was a radioactive shield surrounding every McDonald's restaurant that was specifically designed to harm her by poisoning her blood with radioactivity. She did not believe the radioactivity harmed most other people but only her and a few select family members. She believed this originated from the time she complained that a hamburger she had purchased from McDonald's was poisoned. She attempted to return the hamburger and got into an altercation with the short-order cook, and police were called. The problem with the delusion was that in order to get to her new job, Bernice had to pass a McDonald's restaurant and could not figure out how to avoid it.
>
> As part of her CBT treatment, the therapist and Bernice collaboratively figured out how she could get to work and take care of the other activities of daily life without passing near a McDonald's restaurant, a feat not all that easy. The delusional belief itself was not confronted; rather, the task was how to not allow the belief to interfere with her life. Once Bernice had strategically organized her life to avoid passing by a McDonald's, her anxiety decreased significantly and she told her therapist that her delusion was still there, but it didn't really bother her much anymore.

Cognitive Remediation Therapies for Schizophrenia

As previously noted, the positive symptoms of schizophrenia are often well controlled with reliable administration of antipsychotic medication. However, many individuals with schizophrenia continue to struggle with neurocognitive and social cognitive deficits, which can significantly undermine quality of life by hampering their social, functional, and vocational recovery (Swartz, et al., 2007). *Cognition* refers to the mental processes involved in one's awareness, perception, reasoning, and judgment. *Neurocognition* is defined as the basic cognitive processes involved in supporting thinking and reasoning, which include attention, memory, and executive function abilities. *Social cognition*, on the other hand, refers to the cognitive abilities that support the processing, interpretation, and regulation of socioemotional information (Newman, 2001). Some of the key domains of social cognition that are addressed in cognitive remediation strategies include perspective-taking, theory of mind, emotion perception, emotion regulation, social cue recognition, and causal attributions of social phenomena, all of which are often significantly impaired in schizophrenia. These impairments can profoundly affect the ability to carry on social conversations, respond appropriately to social cues, and develop and maintain positive interpersonal relationships with others.

Fortunately, the past four decades have seen the emergence of cognitive rehabilitation therapies that specifically target deficits in social and non-social cognition. Cognitive remediation therapies involve a variety of methods, such as computer-based or paper-and-pencil rote practice, strategy coaching, and group-based practice approaches. The general focus is to help individuals engage in a "mental workout" to improve information processing and social wisdom. These strategies have shown remarkable success in enhancing consumers' abilities to focus attention, shift attention voluntarily, sustain attention, improve reasoning, increase mental flexibility, and improve social cognition (Krabbendam & Aleman, 2003; McGurk et al., 2007; Wykes, Huddy, Cellard, et al., 2011).

Cognitive-Enhancement Therapy

Cognitive-enhancement therapy (CET) is a performance-based, comprehensive, developmental approach to the rehabilitation of neurocognitive and social cognitive deficits in individuals with schizophrenia (Hogarty & Flesher, 1999a; Hogarty & Flesher, 1999b). Treatment involves a combination of structured group exercises and individual computer-based exercises. CET is designed as a recovery phase intervention, which means that it is appropriate for individuals who are symptomatically stable with regard to positive symptoms, but who continue to have significant psychosocial disability. CET is the culmination of more than 30 years of clinical experience and research by the late Gerard E. Hogarty, who was a social worker, and his colleagues at the University of Pittsburgh (Hogarty & Greenwald, 2006).

There are a number of practice principles and related methods that cut across all cognitive remediation therapies for individuals with schizophrenia, including CET (Eack, 2012). The first is strategic practice techniques. This is similar to the principle of repeated practice and overlearning that is used in social skills training. The therapy participant develops mental strategies, such as mnemonics, to optimize cognitive abilities involved in completing tasks. Drill and practice strategy is just that—repeated practice of cognitive exercises until the performance of the exercise has improved. Other practice principles include the principal of "hierarchy," which means that the participant begins by learning basic cognitive abilities and, once those are mastered, moves on to learning more complex abilities with each successive step building on the previous ones with a total of 16 different cognitive exercises. Initially, the exercises focus on training in attention, and then move on to address memory and then executive function or problem solving. Another practice principle is "cueing," which involves using visual or auditory prompts to support cognitive performance. The principle of "fading" involves the gradual removal of the cues or prompts to increase cognitive mastery and independence. The principle of "adaptive" means that the cognitive exercises are adjusted or adapted for each individual participant so that they are challenging and engaging without being overwhelming and setting the person up for failure. The principle of "anchoring" refers to linking the cognitive exercises to real-world experiences to provide both context and aid in generalization. Finally, CET emphasizes the importance of integration with other treatments and supports that serve to maximize its effectiveness.

CET is unique because it targets both impairments in neurocognition and social cognition. Most other cognitive remediation therapies only target neurocognition. To improve social cognition, CET embeds the computer-based cognitive training in a social context by having the clients work in pairs. Working together, the clients provide each other with peer support and experience in socializing along with enhancing their cognitive abilities. After completing 3 months of training in attention, three to four client pairs team up to form a social cognition group. The group environment enhances the socialization to a more complex level, again employing the principle of hierarchy. This methodology was guided by developmental theories of social cognition (Hogarty & Flesher, 1999a). The group work combines psychoeducation (to help participants understand what social cognition is about), cognitive exercises, and homework assignments.

What CET attempts to do is to increase the individual's mental stamina and the ability to handle stress, increase the individual's ability to process information, and "increase the spontaneous negotiation of unrehearsed social challenges," also known as everyday social conversation (Hogarty & Greenwald, 2006). CET accomplishes this by focusing on enhancing the various components of social cognition, such as perspective taking and social context appraisal, all of which a person without schizophrenia simply does automatically without thinking about it.

How effective is CET? To date, there have been two randomized-controlled trials of the effects of CET in schizophrenia, both of which have documented strong benefits for improved neurocognition, social cognition, and functional outcome (Eack, Greenwald, Hogarty, & Keshavan, 2010; Eack, Greenwald, Hogarty, et al. 2009; Hogarty, Flesher, Ulrich, et al., 2004; Hogarty & Greenwald, 2006). Recent evidence has even shown that when applied as an early intervention strategy for schizophrenia, CET can protect against brain loss and enhance the structural integrity of the brain in individuals with the disorder (Eack, Hogarty, Cho, et al., 2010). Although CET has been proven to be effective, the challenge now is affordable dissemination to community settings and delivering the treatment adequately in more resource-poor environments. Unlike medication, psychosocial treatments don't produce big corporate profits, and thus, the dollar incentives tend to be the reverse; that is, rather than generating immediate profits, psychosocial treatments use resources. The argument that must be successfully mounted is that over the long term, psychosocial treatments like CET are economically advantageous by enabling individuals who would otherwise be highly disabled to have a better chance of living and supporting themselves independently and functioning as productive members of society (Eack, 2012).

Personal Therapy for Schizophrenia

Personal therapy (PT) is a psychosocial treatment intervention developed and tested by social worker Gerard E. Hogarty and his colleagues in the mid-1990s as a novel individually based psychotherapeutic approach for helping people with schizophrenia (Hogarty, 2002; Hogarty, Greenwald, Ulrich, et al., 1997; Hogarty, Kornblith, Greenwald, et al., 1997). Prior to the development of personal therapy, there were four established approaches to the individual psychotherapeutic treatment of schizophrenia, all with both strengths and weaknesses and demonstrating varying levels of success. These approaches include psychodynamic psychotherapy (Gunderson & Mosher, 1975; Katz & Gunderson, 1990; Mueser & Berenbaum,

1990), supportive psychotherapy (Conte & Plutchik, 1986; Kates & Rockland, 1994), various forms of case management (Hornstra, Bruce-Wolfe, Sagduyu, & Riffle, 1993; Ruben, 1992), and behavioral skills training or cognitive problem-solving approaches including social skills training (Benton & Schroeder, 1990; Hogarty, Anderson, Reiss, et al., 1986).

Individual approaches that could be categorized as psychotherapy have been generally viewed as not particularly helpful in treating schizophrenia (Grady, 1998); however, Hogarty believed that helping consumers learn how to manage internal stimuli, including psychotic symptoms and emotion or affect dysregulation, would complement psychosocial treatment efforts to modify external environmental stimuli, such as psychoeducation, to enhance success in delaying relapse (Hogarty, 2002; Hogarty, Kornblith, Greenwald, et al., 1995). Such a treatment would target individuals 2 or 3 years past index episode and help them learn stress management skills (to address external stress and stimuli) and emotion regulation skills (to address internal distress and stimuli). Hogarty named this new treatment "personal therapy." Hogarty recognized that, similar to borderline personality disorder, individuals with schizophrenia often experience emotional upset and affect dysregulation prior to relapse (Hogarty, 2001). Personal therapy helps consumers learn skills for managing emotional upsets and internal distress, and this leads to self-efficacy in illness management. Ultimately, this could have longer-term effects on delaying relapse rather than only attempting to control the external environment, such as stressful life events and issues with family relationships. In many ways, personal therapy takes an empowerment and strengths-based approach, reflecting its founder's social work background, because it teaches consumers how to effectively manage their own distress.

PT takes an individualized approach in terms of treatment intensity and is divided into basic, intermediate, and advanced phases, making it a "disorder-relevant" treatment for persons with schizophrenia (Hogarty, 2002). Personal therapy is based on the stress-vulnerability-coping-competence model of schizophrenia (see Chapter 6), which argues that people with schizophrenia are born with brain abnormalities that make them especially vulnerable to emotional stress. Experiencing overwhelming stress, caused by life events or upsetting interactions with others, can precipitate anxiety and depression, which may then lead to relapse. What the therapist tries to do in personal therapy is to help consumers recognize their particular triggers for stress and learn skills for managing stress and the associated distressing affects, primarily anxiety and depression, to avoid relapse. PT is tailored to each individual consumer's needs and proceeds according to each consumer's own pace.

How effective is personal therapy? The efficacy of PT on late relapse and adjustment was tested in two 3-year trials, one for persons with schizophrenia living with their family members and a second for individuals living alone (Hogarty, Greenwald, Ulrich, Kornblith, et al., 1997; Hogarty, Kornblith, Greenwald, DiBarry, et al., 1997). The study evaluated the effectiveness of personal therapy over a period of 3 years after hospital discharge among 151 patients with schizophrenia or schizoaffective disorder who were randomly assigned to receive either personal therapy or another form of treatment. Each subject was assigned to one of two concurrent trials. One trial included consumers who were living with their family and the other studied consumers who were not living with family. The first set of findings from the study (Hogarty, Kornblith, Greenwald, DiBarry, et al., 1997) showed that although PT had a positive effect for the consumers living with their family, PT increased the rate of illness relapse for individuals living independent of family. This suggested that PT might be best delayed until consumers had solidly achieved symptom and residential stability. The second set of analyses from the study (Hogarty, Greenwald, Ulrich, Kornblith, et al., 1997) looked at the effect of personal therapy on consumers' personal and social adjustment, taking into consideration the effects of relapse. Findings showed that PT had positive effects on social adjustment, but the consumers who received PT continued to experience more symptoms of anxiety than the participants receiving family or supportive therapy. However, for those individuals living with family, PT resulted in better outcomes in overall performance over time than did the other treatments. Although PT outcomes were similar to the outcomes for family and supportive therapy over the short term, PT produced better improvements in social adjustment over the long term, that is, the second and third years after discharge. Hogarty and colleagues concluded that long-term disorder-relevant psychotherapeutic interventions can be effective for individuals with schizophrenia. The reader is encouraged to explore the details of the personal therapy treatment in Professor Hogarty's book *Personal Therapy for Schizophrenia & Related Disorders: A Guide to Individualized Treatment* (2002).

Self-Help and Peer Support Groups for Schizophrenia

Self-help and peer support groups and services for individuals with schizophrenia and their families are becoming more common for a number of reasons. First is the recognition that mutual support from others in similar situations, whether that situation is living with a mental illness or living with a loved one with mental illness, can be invaluable in providing information, tools for recovery, and social support (Leerhsen, Lewis, Pomper, et al., 1990; Marsh & Dickens, 1997). In such groups or services, mental health professionals are usually not regularly involved but, rather, peer members support and provide comfort to each other. Many peer-run self-help services are drop-in centers or socialization centers where peers provide each other with support and recreational and leisure activities are available. For many individuals with schizophrenia, just finding one or two recreational outlets can be invaluable. Example:

> Julie, who has schizophrenia, lives in a board and care home in a rural area in central California. Julie's primary enduring problems relate to severe negative symptoms and problems with social cognition. She has had only one or two friends in her lifetime, and both of those friendships were during her years in the state hospital. She has no recreational activities and spends most of her time smoking, drinking coffee, and watching television. After much persuasive effort, Julie's social worker got her to agree to try attending the socialization center located in a storefront at the nearest small town. The social worker picked Julie up and managed to get a little conversation going on the ride in. For the first half hour, Julie sat on the couch in the socialization center while her social worker greeted other clients and brought Julie some coffee and a doughnut. After Julie had her coffee, the social worker asked her if she'd be willing to play air hockey—just one game. Reluctantly, Julie got up and played with her social worker. For the first time in the 5 years Julie's social worker had known her, Julie broke out in a big smile and said, "This is fun." The social worker then asked one of the consumers to take her place and play with Julie, and for the next half hour Julie and the other consumer played air hockey—the first fun activity Julie had participated in for years.

Second, self-help and peer support groups often evolve into social networks that can provide not only support but also collaboration in advocacy and anti-stigma efforts. A prime example of this, for families, is the National Alliance on Mental Illness (www.nami.org). An example for consumers is the National Mental Health Consumers' Self-Help Clearinghouse (www.mhselfhelp.org).

A third reason that self-help agencies (SHAs), particularly those for consumers, are growing is that local, state, and federal funding agencies for mental health services view SHAs as an inexpensive mechanism for providing services, which is good—however, another piece of the agenda often includes providing a justification for funding cuts (Davidson, O'Connell, Tondora, et al., 2006; Dickerson, 2006). In addition to SHAs and peer support groups, there are also self-help books targeted for individuals and/or families living with schizophrenia, some written by mental health professionals (see, e.g., Miller & Mason, 2011; Mueser & Gingerich, 2006; Torrey, 2006; Temes, 2002) and some written by consumers (Ronen, 2011) or family members (Walsh, 1985).

What has the research told us about the role of self-help groups, their mission, and how helpful they are? Segal, Silverman, and Temkin (1995) examined the characteristics of long-term members of peer-run self-help agencies and found that most of the consumers who sought help from the agencies were homeless and dually diagnosed with mental illness plus substance abuse. The self-help agencies primarily provided the consumers with material resources, such as food or clothing, with the consumers obtaining psychotherapeutic and medical care from community mental health or health care services. Most self-help agencies embrace the philosophy of providing consumers with an environment that supports empowerment and self-determination and avoid focusing on clinical goals, similar to the founding philosophy of the Fountain House psychosocial rehabilitation program described earlier. In a study examining the extent to which consumers perceive that this mission is fulfilled, Segal, Silverman, and Temkin (1997) found, in a national survey of 310 SHA consumers, that although the consumers perceived support for the mission of empowerment, they did not necessarily feel they had equal control over program rules. Furthermore, peer support groups can sometimes be burdensome on the peer mentors and produce stress for them that can be problematic. Example:

> Jim, who has lived with schizophrenia for over 30 years, was doing well and living independently when he decided to volunteer to serve as a peer mentor. At first, Jim felt much personal satisfaction from his work helping other consumers, but over time, it became stressful for him. In particular, Jim felt personally responsible when one of his consumer mentees relapsed and had to be hospitalized. Ultimately, Jim decided that being a peer mentor was just too much to handle.

Self-help groups can be very helpful to their participants, however. For example, in a controlled study of Recovery, Inc., a long-established self-help group for individuals with mental illness, Galanter (1988) found participants reported that involvement in Recovery resulted in a decline in both symptoms and need for psychiatric treatment. In fact, scores on psychological well-being for long-term members of Recovery did not significantly differ from the scores on well-being for the community control subjects. Galanter's (1988) conclusion was that self-help groups like Recovery, Inc. can be effective adjuncts to formal psychiatric treatment. Self-help groups can also provide additional natural support to enable individuals with schizophrenia to maintain community tenure (Snowdon, 1980) and, unlike peer mentoring, are not burdensome to the individual consumer.

Role of Social Workers

There are many ways that social workers can be involved in supporting peer self-help groups and self-help agencies (Kurtz, 1997; Toseland & Hacker, 1982). First, social workers can help by providing material support. Many SHAs operate on shoestring budgets, and social workers can help by assisting in writing small grants for funding support from local foundations and advocating for established agencies to provide things like office supplies and a place to meet. Social workers can also support such groups in the larger community by informing other community agencies about the SHA and providing linkages with other SHAs to share resources. Social workers can also initiate or develop a self-help group. For example, many years ago, when the author was a relatively new assistant professor, two students approached her about helping them to start a support group for students who were friends or family members of individuals with mental illness. She helped the students by

Assess your comprehension of *how social skills training, cognitive remediation therapies, personal therapy, and self-help approaches are helpful for individuals who have schizophrenia* by completing this quiz.

duplicating flyers they could post, obtaining meeting space at the student union, and publicizing the group with an interview in the university's student newspaper. Once the group was "off the ground," she pulled back and let the students move forward on their own. Finally, social workers can serve as consultants for SHAs and groups, by providing information, guidance, expert knowledge, and technical assistance (Toseland & Hacker, 1982, p. 342). In sum, peer and self-help support groups are very helpful natural support adjuncts for traditional mental health services.

CONCLUSION

As this chapter has shown, in a disorder such as schizophrenia, where biological predisposition is a major etiological factor, it is extremely important to combine psychosocial treatment with drug treatment. The activity of drugs can be facilitated or impaired by psychosocial and environmental factors, and such factors have a potent and enduring influence on the client's response to medication. Antipsychotic medications have a primary effect on the positive symptoms of schizophrenia but have less of an effect on psychosocial adjustment. Evidence-based psychosocial treatments designed specifically for the treatment of schizophrenia primarily relieve psychosocial disability, and thus, the optimal treatment of schizophrenia usually involves a combination of medication with psychosocial treatment. Fortunately, today we have a range of highly effective psychosocial treatments for schizophrenia, but dissemination and wider access remain a challenge, particularly for those individuals with schizophrenia who are most vulnerable, that is, the poor, homeless, incarcerated, and/or those with co-morbid conditions. Social workers are the primary providers of psychosocial treatment for individuals with schizophrenia, and thus, we must make every effort to provide treatment well and advocate for access to such treatments for those in need.

Assess your application and analysis of this chapter's contents by completing the *Chapter Review*.

Chapter 11

Practice with Individuals with Paranoid Symptoms and Paranoid Disorders

WHAT IS PARANOIA?

The Case of Ms. A

Ms. A, 65 years old, had been a psychiatric social worker for forty years on the same inpatient unit of a state hospital. She had always been somewhat of a loner, and was considered a bit aloof by her co-workers, but she had performed well in her job at the hospital. Co-workers recalled that she typically arrived early for work and would stay as late as necessary to complete her daily paperwork. Prior to her retirement, however, she had become more moody and the quality of her work had deteriorated somewhat, although not to the degree that her supervisors felt they should take action. Some days, Ms. A would appear irritable, other days she seemed sad and withdrawn. Following her retirement, Ms. A became very reclusive and, approximately three months later, concerned neighbors called the county mental health crisis team to request that someone check on her well-being. The crisis worker went out to her home and found her yard overgrown, her windows boarded up and, when contact was attempted, Ms. A refused to answer her door. The crisis worker returned with the police several hours later, but Ms. A had left the house. Five months later relatives located her, with the help of a private detective, living as a "bag lady" in New York City. Extremely paranoid and malnourished, she was immediately hospitalized locally. While in the hospital, she tried to hang herself with her bed sheet. Her prognosis remained very poor (Newhill, 1989).

As described in this vignette, Ms. A had recently retired from a long-term, stable, structured job where she generally functioned well. Work was the role in which she functioned best, however, according to co-workers, Ms. A took a rather obsessive, rigid approach to her job tasks. When Ms. A retired, depression was precipitated by the loss of this valued role. This was compounded by the fact that Ms. A lacked social supports beyond the relationships with her co-workers, and thus, the major transitional stress of retirement was too much for her to manage without decompensating. Ms. A's work provided the structure she needed to keep her obsessive characteristics mobilized, which protected her from vulnerability to underlying depression. The major stressor of retirement, however, was too much for the obsessive protective structure to cope with in terms of maintaining Ms. A's fragile

From Newhill, C.E., "Paranoid symptomatology in late life," Clinical Gerontologist, 8(4), 13–30.

personality homeostasis. The structure collapsed, she became extremely depressed, which terrified her, and paranoid symptoms emerged as a last-ditch effort to defend against overwhelming despair and the loss of autonomy that would result.

Historical Background of Our Ideas about Paranoia

Literally translated from the Greek language, the word *paranoia* means "a mind beside itself" (Farrell, 2007). Historically, paranoia has referred to a diverse array of conditions and was often used to refer to the presence of any aspects of mental illness characterized by persecutory or jealous delusions. From the time before Hippocrates lived up until the early 1800s, the term *paranoia* was generally synonymous with the concept of "insanity." In 1818, Johann Heinroth reintroduced the term *paranoia* in its more current form and definition. Later, in 1863, German psychiatrist Karl Ludwig Kahlbaum (1828–1899), who was among the first to describe and categorize syndromes of mental illness, used the term *paranoia* to designate a group of disorders that remained essentially stable over time, evidencing significant mistrust and suspiciousness. Psychiatrist Adolf Meyer (1866–1950) was the first to use the term *paranoid personality disorder* (Meyer, 1913), and German psychiatrist Emil Kraepelin (1856–1926), who is generally considered to be the founder of modern scientific psychiatry and psychiatric nosology, described a "pseudo-querulous" type of personality that predisposed individuals to delusional thinking of a paranoid nature (Kraepelin, 1917).

Around the same time, Sigmund Freud (1911/2003), based on his analysis of the jurist Daniel Paul Schreber (Schreber, 1955), who suffered from paranoid schizophrenia, concluded that the core intrapsychic conflict in paranoia was an undesirable homosexual wish. For Schreber, this consciously unacceptable wish was pushed aside via the defense mechanism of denial, and the wish was then transformed via the defense of reaction formation into a belief that a male companion (toward whom Schreber was attracted) hated Schreber. This belief that the man Schreber was attracted to hated him evolved via a third defense mechanism, that of projection. Freud believed that through this process, which was entirely unconscious, Schreber was only consciously aware of feelings of persecution and hatred, which protected his ego from recognizing his homosexual desires, which would result in experiencing unbearable anxiety. Freud's understanding of Victorian morality of that time provided the environmental context for his theory.

Today, however, due to the subsequent lack of any systematic empirical evidence supporting Freud's conjectures beyond the Schreber case, this early analysis of the dynamics of paranoia has been uniformly rejected (Allison, De Oliveira, Roberts, & Weiss, 1988). However, the notion that the defense mechanism of *projection*, that is, displacing one's own unacceptable feelings onto others, is central to all forms of paranoia still has a place in understanding paranoid thinking patterns. Regarding today's nosology, the *DSM-IV-TR* (APA, 2000) identifies four conditions in which paranoia is a prominent feature. These include delusional disorder, which used to be called simply "paranoia"; schizophrenia, paranoid type, that is, the paranoid components of this form of schizophrenia; shared psychotic disorder, which used to be called "folie à deux"; and, finally, paranoid personality disorder.

THE EXPERIENCE OF BEING PARANOID

Feelings of being watched, talked about, lied to, or taken advantage of are universal human experiences (Alper, 2005). In this context, it is not difficult to understand, appreciate, and empathize with some of the symptoms that paranoid individuals experience. The ability to anticipate, perceive, and react to danger in our environment is clearly an adaptive mechanism, and is the first line in assuring our safety in the world. For example, a herd of zebras grazing on a savannah plain must be constantly vigilant and watchful, lest a lioness attack and drag one of the colts back to the pride for dinner (Sapolsky, 2004). Similarly, a young person living in a drug-infested, crime-ridden, impoverished neighborhood must be cautious, hyperalert, and suspicious about his or her surroundings while walking to school each day in order to avoid being victimized by others who have criminal intent (Newhill, 1990). In such scenarios, being too trusting or unaware of one's surroundings can actually be a potentially life-threatening hazard, thus some of the characteristics associated with paranoia may actually be adaptive under such social environmental circumstances (Newhill, 1990).

Trust versus Mistrust

Whether one learns to view the world as a safe or unsafe place may originate in early childhood. Erik Erikson's life cycle model of human development (Erikson, 1950) suggests that basic trust versus mistrust is the first developmental challenge to be met, and negotiating it successfully into the trust realm is essential if further healthy development is to occur. Because an infant's basic needs—food, clothing, shelter, protection, and comfort—must be met by the primary caregiver, usually the parents, the child's basic understanding of his or her world and the way it operates comes from how the parents care for and interact with the child. If the child is provided with secure, warm, and loving care and physical and emotional sustenance, the child develops trust, that is, learns through repeated experience that other people are reliable and the world is safe and secure. If, however, the child is repeatedly neglected or abused, or provided with unpredictable, unreliable, and inconsistent care, the child learns mistrust and begins to see the world as an unreliable, unsafe, and even hostile place. Once this is learned and *introjected* or absorbed into the individual's psyche, it can be very difficult to reverse later in life. At the extreme end, a child's mistrust may evolve into attachment disorder, or it can underlie chronic anxiety or depression, aggressive behavior, or a paranoid adjustment. For some people, the mistrust may be so severe that, over time, it evolves into a persecutory delusion (see Chapter 10 for discussion of delusions). The next section will look briefly at the more global issue of paranoia in our society.

PARANOIA IN OUR SOCIETY

Along with using the term *paranoia* to refer to a group of psychiatric illnesses (see below), the term *paranoid* can also refer to people who would not be diagnosed with a paranoid disorder but, rather, simply function in a suspicious or guarded manner throughout their life. Such individuals have what we might call a "paranoid outlook on life" or a "paranoid style" (Shapiro, 1965). Through this broader lens, paranoid qualities can be found in a variety of sociocultural situations and may include not only those with diagnosable mental illnesses, but also members of nationalist groups, terrorist groups, religious extremists, criminal gangs, and political zealots, populists, and ideologues.

The Paranoid Style in American Politics

During the same month and year that President John F. Kennedy was assassinated, November 1963, Columbia University Pulitzer Prize–winning historian Richard Hofstadter delivered a lecture at Oxford University, which was entitled "The Paranoid Style in American Politics." This lecture was later combined with some of Hofstadter's related essays into a book by the same name (Hofstadter, 1965). In his lecture and subsequent book, Hofstadter argued that a general sense of suspiciousness permeates American political ideologies and underlies some of our more aggressive international and domestic policies. This appears to be still in evidence today. For example, journalist Robert Worth's 2002 essay "A Nation Defined by Its Enemies" argues that throughout U.S. history, American civic and political leaders have repeatedly invoked a warning that sinister conspirators are plotting to undermine and subvert the wondrous exceptional civilization called America, or what Ronald Reagan famously referred to as "this shining city on a hill" (Reagan, 1984). Those who subscribe to this argue that if we are not vigilant against such threats, we will be harmed. Worth goes on to state that peculiar to American political rhetoric is the use of our enemies—whether those enemies are Communists, socialists, fascists, or terrorists—as highly emotional political symbols. The problem that results is that such populist rhetoric only serves to cloud our ability to better understand such enemies, thereby undermining our capacity for defeating or influencing them. It is, in fact, the paranoid style of American politics, a central element of which is the belief in conspiracy theories.

Americans love conspiracy theories as narratives to explain emotion-laden issues or events. Goldberg (2001) defines a conspiracy theory as a belief that cunning calculating forces are working to bend history to their will, for example, by assassinating a president or causing a terrorist attack. How do such theories gain acceptance and power and manage to persist even in the face of evidence that contradicts them? Goldberg (2003) explains that conspiracy theories draw power by tapping into and reinforcing what are viewed as traditional American values and beliefs, including "a sense of mission, Protestant supremacy, concerns about encroachments on liberty, antielitism, maintenance of the racial order, and the sanctity of private property." Since the end of the nineteenth century through today, Christian evangelical fundamentalist beliefs have merged with the American tendency toward conspiracy theories, serving to reinforce such paranoid-tinged theories further with religious faith (Sutton, 2011).

Hofstadter's views about paranoia in American politics have been cited frequently since 2008, primarily in liberal essay and opinion columns, as an intellectually plausible explanation for more recent political developments, such as the evolution of the Tea Party, the celebrity status of Sarah Palin, and claims by right-wing writers, bloggers, and media that President Barack Obama is a socialist with a forged birth certificate who is on course for ruining America and marching it secretly toward communism (Bernstein, 2010). The conservative right-wing response to President Obama's health care reform efforts, for example, have included labeling health care reform as "National Socialist Healthcare" (Krugman, 2009), sometimes coupled with images of Nazi death camps, and warning that health care reform would lead to government-sponsored "death panels" (Frank, 2009). Unfortunately, paranoid thinking patterns in politics also serve to reduce complex social issues to simple ideas that the public finds more palatable and understandable (Carter, 2009). As Paul Krugman noted in 2009, paranoia strikes deep in American politics and American society (Krugman, 2009). To be sure, radical populism is not always tinged by paranoia, nor are Americans always persuaded by it, but it occurs often enough to suggest that paranoid thinking patterns do permeate American political thinking and American society to some degree with surprising frequency throughout our country's post-revolution history.

Everyday Paranoia

Many of the mental mechanisms, interpretations, and distorted perceptions of reality observed in paranoia as an illness are exaggerations of those found in everyday life among persons who are thought of as normal. All of us at times may feel slighted by someone, or feel that our accomplishments go unnoticed and unappreciated, or feel that someone is picking on us, or even blame others for our troubles. The difference, however, is that the normal person is usually able to eventually overlook the tiny slights and setbacks that characterize everyday life. In contrast, the paranoid individual builds up such occurrences into

---

Crichton-Miller, H. (1968). Quoted in: Kolb, L.C. & Noyes, A.P. (Eds.) Modern Clinical Psychiatry (7th ed.). Philadelphia, PA: Saunders (p. 403).

crucial issues and, eventually, formulates these issues into plots and conspiracies against him or her. As the psychiatrist Crichton-Miller (1968) once observed:

> For every fully developed case of paranoia in our mental hospitals there must be hundreds, if not thousands, who suffer from minor degrees of suspicion and mistrust; whose eyes are blighted by this barrier to human harmony; and who poison the springs of social life for the community.

Paranoid thinking patterns can infect whole communities, cultures, and societies and color all aspects of how individual members conduct their daily lives and how such societies are governed and interact with other societies. This can create serious individual, community, and societal problems.

THE PARANOID STYLE

Psychologist David Shapiro (1965, 1994) identifies the paranoid style as one of four basic so-called *neurotic styles* of functioning. A neurotic style may be defined as a generally consistent pattern of emotional/cognitive/behavioral functioning that can be identified and described via certain characteristics that are pervasive, that is, which cut across all spheres of the individual's life. Whether described as a *paranoid style* (Shapiro, 1965, 1994), a *paranoid mode of thinking* (Swanson et al., 1970), a *paranoid outlook on life* (Schwartz, 1963), a *paranoid position* (Klein, 1952), or a *paranoid slant on life* (Sullivan, 1956), the paranoid style of psychosocial functioning is a pattern of adaptation that is utilized to cope with the world and that involves thinking, feeling, and behaving in a way that is pervasive, so that a general paranoid lens develops through which the individual sees the world rather than merely one or two paranoid beliefs or symptoms. Some individuals with a paranoid style of functioning meet criteria for paranoid personality disorder, while others do not meet that threshold but their patterns of thinking and behavior are still clinically significant and affect their ability to function in day-to-day life.

A paranoid style can be recognized by several consistent clinical features that are present in all paranoid disorders from mild to severe, and which can be differentiated from other psychiatric disorders and characterological patterns (Swanson et al., 1970). These basic characteristics are:

- suspiciousness
- projective thinking
- hostility
- centrality
- fear of loss of autonomy
- grandiosity

Shapiro (1994) asserts that in comparison to the other neurotic styles—such as the hysterical, obsessive-compulsive, and impulsive—the paranoid style is intrinsically more psychopathological and, in its extreme forms, can even evolve into psychotic loss of reality. Within the paranoid style, two basic subtypes can be identified: (1) the furtive, constricted, apprehensively suspicious form; and (2) the rigidly arrogant, more aggressively suspicious, megalomaniac form (Shapiro, 1965, 1994). Although these two subtypes present somewhat differently clinically, both employ the same basic paranoid characteristics listed above. A brief discussion of each feature is presented below.

Suspiciousness

"Suspiciousness" describes a mode of thinking and cognition that is usually easy to identify. The suspicious person is intensely alert and attentive but guarded. Rigidity, focused attention that is constantly searching, bias, hyperalertness, and hypersensitivity are also prominent features (Kantor, 2008). Suspicious individuals are always on the alert for danger. It is as if they are always "on duty" and on guard.

Searles (1961) characterizes suspiciousness as the only mode through which the paranoid individual is able to understand the world; he or she constantly searches any new data for "clues" to underlying meanings, filtering such data with extraordinary prejudice and bias. Because suspicious people are extremely hypersensitive and hyperalert, anything unusual or unexpected is threatening. Such individuals may employ fairly accurate, albeit self-referential, perceptions, but their subsequent interpretation and judgment of these perceptions are often distorted, at times reaching the proportion of a loss of reality (Kantor, 2008; Munro, 1999).

In spite of all this, many paranoid people can achieve a limited social adjustment sufficient for living independently because they do recognize many essential facts about the world. For example, the paranoid person may recognize and go along with the necessity of paying his electric bill and at the same time harbor the delusion that the electric company has bugged his apartment and has him under surveillance. This distortion of reality can manifest itself on a continuum from mild suspiciousness to rigid systematized delusions.

Projective Thinking

The consensus of the theoretical literature is that projective thinking is the central dynamic in any paranoid process. Harry Stack Sullivan (1956) observed that the essence of the paranoid dynamics is the transference of blame from self onto others. Freud's (1911) most brilliant contribution to the psychodynamic understanding of paranoia was his development of the concept of projective thinking as the process by which one's impulses, fantasies, or other tensions that are viewed as unacceptable or intolerable in one's self are attributed to others. Swanson et al. (1970), however, point out that for many paranoid individuals, Freud's classic definition of projection is not exactly applicable because what is externalized is not necessarily fantasies or impulses, but can be any uncomfortable tension. Unlike other kinds of reality impairment, such as amnesia or hallucinations, projection does not involve a breakdown in cognition and withdrawal of attention from the external world, rather, it provides an answer or explanation for the paranoia the person is experiencing, which serves to reduce and ease anxiety.

What an individual perceives as an external threat depends on the specific nature of the original internal tension, and the specific nature of the particular individual's defensive concerns, attitudes, and orientation (Shapiro, 1965, 1994). It is not a static process, but involves a continuous dynamic relationship between subject and object. Projection is a process that begins when a discomforting impulse, tension, or emotion threatens the internal rigid psychological balance of the individual resulting in the exacerbation of feelings of vulnerability (Shapiro, 1981). This leads to a defensive mobilization involving an increase in rigidity, activation of suspicious attention, and a contraction of affective experience. This mobilization results in a search for external clues, identifying the enemy and constructing the external threat via the process of projective identification (Waska, 2000).

Just as obsessive people will overcome one worry only to turn to another, the paranoid suspicious individual lives in a continual state of hypervigilance, not so much to avoid threats but, rather, to avoid feeling *vulnerable* to threat (Shapiro, 1965). He or she must stay on top of everything to avoid being vulnerable to victimization.

Hostility

Hostility is not as central to paranoia as projection, but it is a common feeling with paranoid individuals. Defensiveness and antagonism to the outside world, particularly toward those in perceived authority, is intrinsic to the paranoid style. Hostility can create a vicious cycle in that the paranoid individual's angry mistrustful feelings may actually invoke rejection or criticism from others, which only feeds and reinforces his or her hostility further.

The paranoid individual's perception of the world as a hostile place conveniently places blame on others, rather than recognizing that one's own actions may incite hostility or rejection from others. Placing the blame on others protects self-esteem and can even reinforce narcissistic feelings of entitlement and the development of grandiose feelings (Kantor, 2008). Hostility, then, can actually serve an adaptive purpose in that it protects the defensive systems, which protect the paranoid individual from intolerable feelings of emotional discomfort (Sullivan, 1956). Expressions of hostility vary among individuals depending on the degree of vulnerability the person feels. The more vulnerable the client feels, the more hostile and angry he or she is.

Centrality

Schwartz (1963) views the feature of centrality as common to all paranoid illness. Centrality involves situations in which attention and effort is focused on the paranoid individual. Whether the attention stems from projection, ideas of reference, or grandiosity, the person sees him or herself as the focal point. Cameron's (1943/1959) concept of the *paranoid pseudocommunity* also relates to the concept of centrality. The paranoid pseudocommunity is the ever-present "they" who are conspiring, persecuting, and plotting against the person (Munro, 1999). The paranoid individual builds the pseudocommunity around him or herself. The participants in the pseudocommunity all have imagined relationships with the individual, thus making him or her a special central figure. As one client put it:

> They constantly watch me, watch my every move. The only place I feel safe is in my apartment, but I have to constantly check to be sure that, you know, they haven't figured out a way to watch me there. For now, I'm on top of things, but I have to keep changing my identity—that fools them for a while. They know I know their secrets, that's what it is, you know.

Because of their thinking patterns and behavior, the paranoid individual is, in reality, usually quite socially isolated, but desperately wants to be meaningful to some group and therefore creates one which confirms that he or she is worth the attention of others as well as confirming his or her suspicions and distortions of reality (Swanson et al., 1970). It is a challenging task. Even when carried to the extreme of delusions involving ideas of reference, the person is still attempting to retain a feeling of self-worth via the delusional beliefs, to avoid feeling like a "big nobody" (Kantor, 2008, p. 51).

A clear demonstration of the power of the centrality dynamic can be seen in many religious cult figures. For example, Jim Jones, the notorious founder and leader of the People's Temple, has been retrospectively viewed as an extremely paranoid individual. Jones effectively utilized his own belief that he was a superior person with special powers to influence hundreds of people to turn over to him all their worldly goods and follow him to Jonestown, Guyana, ultimately to their deaths. The slavish devotion paid to Jones by his followers fulfilled his great need to be meaningful and powerful and, by believing his rhetoric, they provided ongoing confirmation for his paranoid perceptions of reality (Naipaul, 1982).

Fear of Loss of Autonomy

Fears related to loss of control or autonomy is central to the paranoid style. Such fears can manifest in anything from a refusal to take medication to conflicts with one's boss over job requirements. Paranoid individuals tend to view life as a constant battle, so they often become preoccupied with issues of dominance versus submission, winners versus losers, superior versus inferior, who is up and who is down (Swanson et al., 1970). In response to such concerns, paranoid people must maintain a constant internal state of mobilization, or as Schafer (1954) put it, an "internal police state."

Autonomy has a twofold aspect involving concerns over, first, maintaining independence from external force or authority and, second, maintenance of the ability to direct oneself competently and avoid helplessness or passivity. This is often the key to establishing a treatment alliance when working with a paranoid client. If the clinician can position him or herself persuasively as the client's ally, that is, someone who is invested in the client maintaining control and autonomy, this may serve to lessen the client's fear. The working relationship between the client and clinician then becomes a partnership rather than a battle.

Grandiosity

The paranoid individual who is grandiose often presents as conceited, as if he or she has achieved perfection and is universally admired, similar to the narcissistic individual (Swanson et al., 1970). Manifestations of grandiosity can range from feelings of uniqueness and a condescending attitude to the more extreme expressions seen in many leaders of extremist religious or political groups, such as Jim Jones, described above. Like projection, grandiose ideas and perceptions resist modification in the face of reality. For example, Rokeach (1964), in *The Three Christs of Ypsilanti*, describes three paranoid patients who maintained the belief that each was the real Jesus Christ even though they were all hospitalized on the same psychiatric ward and had ongoing contact with each other.

Generally, it is considered to be a sign of more severe psychopathology when grandiosity develops in someone with a paranoia illness, because such development is usually secondary to the failure of ideas of persecution to provide an adequate defense for underlying feelings of worthlessness and anxiety (Swanson et al., 1970). Salzman (1960), however, takes the opposite point of view, that grandiosity is actually primary and that paranoid illness develops from the realistic rejection by others or from failing to achieve the grandiose claims. Salzman argues that the reaction of others to the paranoid person's grandiosity is usually belittlement and derogation, which then leads to the development of persecutory ideas.

A few comments must be made regarding the paranoid style with regard to behavior. Paranoid behavior is highly focused and defensive. Every move is purposeful, with the pros and cons of actions carefully weighed against the predicted consequences. As the level of intentionality increases, the level of expressive ability and spontaneity of behavior decreases as the person becomes more and more tightly wound and rigid. Needless to say, having a paranoid style of relating to the world is exhausting, because it is as if one is always "on duty."

The entire range of subjective affective experience is severely restricted in paranoid individuals. Such clients rarely laugh or, if they do, it is a caricature of amusement. Even body sensations are restricted, and sensual pleasure becomes mechanical. An internal framework that is constantly in a state of emergency mobilization, rigidly maintained, is simply incompatible with soft and spontaneous affects such as empathy, affection, or love (Salzman, 1960).

This relates to the pervasive overall impairment of interpersonal relations observed in individuals who are severely paranoid. In one study of 2,000 patients with a diagnosis of a paranoid disorder, social maladjustment was significant for the entire sample (Swanson et al., 1970). Not one of the patients reported more than having an "occasional" friend and 48 percent led "frankly isolated lives." Adult sexual adjustment was judged to be uniformly poor and marital disharmony, for those few who were married, was common. Paranoid individuals usually demonstrate an inability to express or accept affection, they are rarely able to trust another person, and interpersonal relationships that do develop are plagued by ongoing suspiciousness, jealousy, irritability, and other traits incompatible with healthy, mutually satisfying relationships. Anhedonia, that is, the inability to experience joy or pleasure, is commonly seen in individuals with a paranoid style or paranoid disorder. Such folks are unable to experience any kind of real pleasure or happiness, and if a pleasurable experience actually develops, they immediately mobilize to shut down such states out of overwhelming feelings of anxiety. Feeling pleasure often involves a momentary loss or softening of control, which is simply too frightening to endure. As the eminent psychoanalyst

Ernest E. Hadley (1894–1954) put it: "Pity the poor paranoid, for he really is persecuted" (cited in Swanson, Bohnert, & Smith, 1970, p. 13).

TYPES OF CLINICAL PARANOID DISORDERS

Delusional Disorder

Classic paranoia, or what is now called "delusional disorder," involves a systematized, encapsulated delusion that, in most cases, is non-bizarre. A delusion is considered to be non-bizarre if the belief is realistically possible albeit untrue for that particular individual, for example, the person believes he or she is being sought by organized crime figures. The most common themes in non-bizarre delusions are persecution, jealousy, grandiosity, erotomania, and somatic fixation. Prior to *DSM-5*, to meet criteria for delusional disorder the individual's delusion had to be classified as non-bizarre. However, *DSM-5* will remove the non-bizarre requirement from the criteria for delusional disorder in order to allow for those rare cases in which an individual has a single encapsulated bizarre delusion. In order to allow continuity with *DSM-IV-TR*, a bizarre/non-bizarre specifier will be added to the criteria for delusional disorder. The current *DSM-IV-TR* criteria specify that the delusion(s) must be present for at least 1 month and that Criterion A for schizophrenia has never been met (APA, 2000).

Unlike in schizophrenia, individuals with delusional disorder do not show marked impairment in psychosocial functioning, outside of issues directly related to the delusion, and their behavior is not obviously odd or bizarre. No major changes are proposed so far for the upcoming *DSM-5* in terms of the overall diagnostic criteria or for the specific criteria for the erotomanic, grandiose, jealous, persecutory, mixed, or unspecified types of delusional disorder. Proposed plans for *DSM-5* also include eliminating the diagnosis of shared psychotic disorder (a.k.a. folie à deux) and incorporating that variation into the diagnosis of delusional disorder via a specifier indicating that the delusions are shared. Below is an example of a client whose presentation is consistent with someone who has delusional disorder, although he was never formally diagnosed:

> John Jackson, 28, came to the emergency room asking to speak to a doctor "privately." At first the triage nurse thought he was a pharmaceutical sales representative because, unlike most of the clientele in this urban ER, Mr. Jackson was well dressed and groomed, and carried a new briefcase. Because the doctor on duty was busy with several admissions, the emergency room social worker asked Mr. Jackson if he would like to speak with her. After staring at her intently for a few moments, he reluctantly agreed. The client sat stiffly in the chair in the interview room, clutching the briefcase, and finally said, "You probably will not believe this, but I am telling you the truth." He then whispered, "I am under surveillance. They think that I am a terrorist, but I am not. Do you see what I am up against?" The client went on to reveal that he had served in the Persian Gulf War and had been discharged honorably from the military but, after discharge, could not find a job and ended up living with his parents. He became convinced that his inability to secure employment was due to a plot hatched by Saddam Hussein's Republican Guard. He firmly believed that Republican Guard representatives had been sent to capture him, take him to Hussein's palace, and execute him. He believed that at this very moment, Guard members were fanning throughout the city looking for him, escalating his fears. When asked for concrete evidence that such a plot existed, the client became indignant, stating that coming to the emergency room was obviously a mistake. He then got up, refused to continue the interview, and left.

Paranoid Personality Disorder

In contrast to delusional disorder, individuals with paranoid personality disorder are hypervigilant, suspicious, guarded, and mistrustful toward the world in general, but fall short of having actual psychotic delusions. In addition, like other personality disorders, their behavior is not encapsulated, that is, the paranoid features are pervasive throughout their interactions with others and are seen across all areas of the individual's life including their interpersonal, occupational, and intrapsychic spheres of experience. The DSM-5 Work Group for Personality and Personality Disorders has recommended that paranoid personality disorder be represented and diagnosed by a combination of core impairments in personality functioning and specific pathological personality traits, rather than listed as a specific categorical type. More detail on paranoid personality disorder and paranoid thinking patterns and how to intervene effectively with such individuals will be discussed later in this chapter.

Paranoid Schizophrenia

As discussed in Chapter 10, *DSM-5* will no longer include subtype specifiers for a diagnosis of schizophrenia. However, as noted in Chapter 10, individuals with the paranoid form of schizophrenia evidence unique characteristics that continue to be relevant to treatment, course, and prognosis. With paranoid schizophrenia, one finds prominent delusions or auditory hallucinations in the context of relative preservation of cognitive functioning and affect. What this means, and this is discussed in more detail in Chapter 10, is that one does not find in the paranoid form of schizophrenia the disorganized thoughts and behavior or the so-called negative symptoms that one finds in other forms of schizophrenia. As a result, individuals with paranoid schizophrenia tend to have a better prognosis in terms of psychosocial functioning, capacity for independent living, and responsiveness to medication. It should be noted that the diagnosis of paranoid personality disorder cannot be made in the presence of schizophrenia, delusional disorder, or other psychotic disorders. The following is the involuntary hospitalization admission note for a client with a long history of paranoid schizophrenia, which presents a good example of the florid presentation of the illness in a crisis situation.

Pedro

Pedro Gonzales is a 24-year-old Mexican-American man who was referred to the mobile psychiatric emergency service by his parents. According to the parents, he had been deteriorating for the past several weeks—more rapidly recently—and was delusional and hearing voices. In the past week he had not slept and was not eating—only drinking a little fluid. He had been preoccupied, rambling, suspicious of neighbors and family. When Pedro was contacted by phone from the clinic, he accused mental health staff of holding his parents hostage and sounded very angry and suspicious. He has not followed up with outpatient treatment since his last hospitalization.

Upon evaluation, he was found standing in the middle of his front yard, holding a copy of *The Watchtower.** In response to the crisis worker's questions, Pedro was vague, preoccupied, and blocking, answering the questions mostly with biblical rhetoric and rambling about demons he had exorcised that morning per God's will. He refused to consider going into the clinic voluntarily, feels there is nothing wrong with him, that he does not need medication or any other treatment. When questioned about his recent behavior and deterioration in his sleep and appetite, he would only reply, "It is God's will." Pedro was involuntarily hospitalized on the basis of grave disability (Newhill, 1995).

* The Watchtower *is a religious magazine published by the Jehovah's Witnesses.*

CAUSES OF PARANOIA: SURVIVAL, THE HUMAN BRAIN, AND PARANOIA

What causes someone to develop paranoia? To answer this question, we have to look at the dynamics of human survival instincts and the role of the human brain. The brain is the major organ of human survival and enables us to think and solve problems. Specifically, the regions of the cerebral cortex are responsible for our ability to use logic, to think in abstractions, to conceive and execute plans, to use reason, and to protect ourselves from the dangers in our environment and from predators. If, however, our cerebral cortex is sufficiently compromised by head trauma, drugs, poisons or other toxic substances, or by a broad range of diseases, we may respond by becoming paranoid, that is, becoming hypervigilant, overly suspicious, and even defensively aggressive.

There are many common medical conditions that can compromise the neurons in the cerebral cortex and can lead to an individual experiencing paranoid symptoms. First are reactions to alcohol (both intoxication and withdrawal) and other substances of abuse such as cocaine or amphetamines. Another cause of paranoid symptoms is side effects from medications used to treat both psychiatric and medical conditions. Some people experience paranoid symptoms during a postoperative surgical state as a consequence of the effects of anesthesia and trauma to the body. In addition, certain central nervous system disorders such as Alzheimer's disease and other forms of dementia, certain brain tumors, seizures, and multiple sclerosis can cause paranoid symptoms. Finally, traumatic brain injuries involving the cerebral cortex can produce personality changes including paranoid symptoms that may last for years.

There is also a range of psychiatric illnesses in which paranoid symptoms are common, including schizophrenia and other psychotic disorders, major mood disorders such as bipolar I disorder and major depressive disorder, agoraphobia, obsessive-compulsive disorder, body dysmorphic disorder, and certain personality disorders. It is important to note, however, that for both neurological and psychiatric conditions, one cannot be certain whether the paranoia results from the direct effects of these conditions on the brain or from the secondary effects of a person feeling vulnerable and endangered by not being able to assess and respond effectively to environmental conditions. Finally, it has long been recognized that paranoia can be induced in almost anyone via severe sensory deprivation. In such circumstances, the individual cannot use his or her senses to monitor the external environment and thus feels exposed and vulnerable.

The next section will examine paranoid personality disorder in more detail and then address how individuals with this disorder present clinically and the barriers to treatment that are unique to individuals with paranoid symptomatology.

PARANOID PERSONALITY DISORDER

People with paranoid personality disorder are pervasively mistrustful and suspicious of the motives of others and interpret other people's behavior as deliberately malevolent. This pattern of pervasive distrust and distorted inferential thinking begins by early adulthood, although it is often seen much earlier and, like other personality disorders, is present in a variety of interpersonal contexts of the individual's life. People with paranoid personality disorder assume that other people will exploit, harm, or deceive them, or that others have already deeply and irreversibly harmed them even if no evidence exists to support this contention. They are preoccupied with unjustified doubts about the loyalty or trustworthiness of their friends and associates, whose actions they minutely scrutinize for evidence of hostile intentions. Any perceived deviation from trustworthiness or loyalty—no matter how minor—serves to support and reinforce their underlying assumptions. Such individuals are so amazed when a friend or associate does show loyalty, that they often cannot trust or believe it and studiously examine minute details of the relationship for evidence that the loyalty is a facade or a disguised means of harming them. For example, Christine, a stockbroker, talks about her struggles maintaining a relationship with one of her co-workers, Whitney. Christine says:

> There are parts of Whitney that I really like. She is smart, funny, quick-thinking. Nobody can tell a story like Whitney—she is great to have a drink with and hash over problems at work. But there is this other part of her that makes me wonder whether we are or will ever truly be friends. Whitney constantly feels that she is being slighted and taken advantage of at work. She will get into these moods where she recites every minute bit of evidence to conclude that others want to bring her down, disrespect her, and even suggests they may be plotting against her. I often find myself walking on eggshells around her, trying to be sure I don't take a wrong step or I'll be accused of disloyalty. It's exhausting. Sometimes I don't think our friendship—if it even is a friendship—is worth it.

People with a paranoid personality are reluctant to confide in or become close to others because they fear that the information they share will be used against them. They often refuse to answer personal questions, saying that the information is "nobody's business" or respond to innocuous questions by becoming defensive ("Why do you want to know that?") or even directly accusatory ("I know why you are asking that—you're going to use it against me.").

Individuals with a paranoid personality read hidden meanings that are demeaning and threatening into other people's remarks or events that are benign. For example, people with paranoid personality disorder may misinterpret an honest mistake on a bill for services as a deliberate attempt to cheat them, or interpret an attempt by a co-worker to make a joke as a pointed snarky remark aimed at them. People with paranoid personalities are notoriously humorless. Even sincere compliments may be interpreted as criticisms or attempts at manipulation.

People with paranoid personality disorder persistently bear grudges and obsessively perseverate about ways others have harmed them, being unwilling to forgive the perceived insults, injuries, or slights that they believe have been directed against them. Individuals with a paranoid personality may be pathologically jealous and, without justification, suspect that their spouse or romantic partner is unfaithful to them. To support their jealous beliefs, they may gather trivial and circumstantial "evidence" and may become very controlling in intimate relationships to avoid being betrayed. Such individuals will constantly question and challenge the whereabouts, actions, intentions, and fidelity of their spouse or partner. Many individuals who perpetrate intimate partner violence have paranoid personalities or paranoid aspects to their personalities.

Because of their quickness to engage in counterattack in response to perceived threats, they are litigious and frequently become involved lawsuits and court battles (Yudofsky, 2005). In essence, people with this type of personality pattern seek to confirm their preconceived negative notions of others by attributing malevolent motivations and intent to them. These attributions, in reality, constitute projections of their own feelings, especially anger and fear. The defense mechanism of projection is, in fact, the central dynamic in their personality style. In response to stress, individuals with paranoid personality disorder may even experience brief psychotic episodes.

Assess your comprehension *of the spectrum of paranoid conditions from the paranoid style to the various types of paranoid disorders including delusional disorder, paranoid schizophrenia, and paranoid personality disorder* **by completing this quiz.**

IMPACT OF RACE, CULTURE, AND ETHNICITY ON THE DEVELOPMENT OF PARANOID SYMPTOMS

Since 1950, the U.S. population has more than doubled, from 152.3 million to 308.7 million circa 2010. In addition, the U.S. population has drastically changed qualitatively over the past 60 years, becoming older and more diverse. In 2000, the proportion of the population identified as White was 81 percent. By 2050, this is projected to decrease to 74 percent. The proportion of Blacks (primarily African-Americans) will slightly increase from 12.7 in 2000 to a projection of 13 percent in 2050, while the proportion of Asians will more than double from 3.8 percent to 7.8 percent. Most dramatic is the increase projected for those who identify as having Hispanic ethnicity. In 2000, Hispanics comprised 12.6 percent of the U.S. population; that is projected to increase to 30.2 percent in the year 2050 (Shrestha & Heisler, 2011). In sum, the United States is becoming less White and European, and more racially, culturally, and ethnically diverse. These changes are due to two main trends: (1) increased immigration of young families who are willing to go through the challenges inherent in emigrating to a new country; and (2) the effect of U.S. immigration policy, which has supported the subsequent immigration of the young families' parents and other family members (Shrestha & Heisler, 2011). Furthermore, in some parts of the United States, such as California, the population is actually shifting from a primarily White to a primarily non-White population.

These demographic changes challenge U.S. policy makers in every arena, including having a significant impact on mental health services. A major issue for many of the recent Hispanic and Asian immigrants is that they are disadvantaged in ways their earlier counterparts were not. For example, many Asians who immigrated in large numbers in the 1970s and 1980s were from war-torn countries in Southeast Asia, such as Vietnam, Laos, and Cambodia. Such individuals often suffer from post-traumatic stress due to war, they face tremendous cultural changes, and they are from poorer and less-educated backgrounds (Eisenbruch, 1991; Kinzie, Boehnlein, Leung, et al., 1990). Many Central American immigrants suffer similar disadvantages, and Hispanic immigrants overall have long been disadvantaged by low levels of education and ethnic discrimination (Valdivieso & Davis, 1988). Low socioeconomic status, the stresses of immigration, and the general disadvantages associated with minority status are significant issues in understanding the mental health needs of these groups. This section of the chapter will address how issues related to race, ethnicity, and culture impact the development of paranoid symptoms and paranoid disorders.

Socioeconomic Status

As noted in Chapter 10, research has consistently demonstrated that as socioeconomic status goes down, rates of mental illness go up (Dohrenwend & Dohrenwend, 1974; Faris & Dunham, 1939; Freeman, 1994; Mortensen, Pedersen, Westergaard, et al., 1999; Saha et al., 2005). It is not uncommon for the expression of paranoid beliefs to be rooted in socioeconomic quality-of-life issues as opposed to solely clinical psychopathology. Paranoid beliefs often serve as adaptive mechanisms to cope with the constant threat and danger inherent in the life experiences of people who live in impoverished, crime-ridden, violent neighborhoods (Mirowsky, 1985; Ross, Mirowsky, & Pribesh, 2001). Many studies have reported that persons of low socioeconomic status are much more likely to be victims of personal crime, for example, purse snatching, assault, robbery, or rape, than those living in more affluent areas (Breslau, Kessler, Chilcoat, et al., 1998; Hindelang et al., 1978; Parisi et al., 1979).

The realistic appraisal and response to the common fears of everyday life by those of lower socioeconomic status may, for some individuals, evolve into the development of paranoid mistrust as an element in their interactions with others (Ross, Mirowsky, & Pribesh, 2001). Mistrust as an adaptive mechanism is often found where opportunities and resources are scarce, protection from social institutions and agencies is weak, and exploitation and victimization are common (Newhill, 1990). In such situations, mistrust and/or the development of paranoia-tinged beliefs can be a rational response toward a harsh, dangerous, and unforgiving world (Mirowsky, 1985; Newhill, 1990).

The Concepts of Healthy Cultural Paranoia, Cultural Mistrust, and Ecosystem Distrust

The concept of healthy cultural paranoia as an adaptive mechanism for coping with a life that is plagued by oppression, prejudice, and discrimination must be differentiated from clinical paranoid psychopathology. The term *culture* may be generally defined as a common heritage or set of beliefs, norms, and values held by a group of people (U.S. DHHS, 2001). More specifically, culture consists of "the categories, plans and rules people use to interpret their world and act purposefully within it . . . the grammar used to construct and interpret behavior. Culture is learned as children grow up in society. . . . Culture is a plan for behavior, not behavior itself." (Spradley & McCurdy, 1974, p. 2).

The term *healthy cultural paranoia* was originally coined to refer to a cultural response style stemming from the racism, discrimination, and oppression experienced by African-Americans and other Blacks in predominantly White American society (Grier & Cobbs, 1968; Ridley, 1984; Terrell & Terrell, 1981; Whaley, 2001). Grier & Cobbs (1968) assert that the Black person's response to an oppressive racist environment must be a self-protective defensive stance in order to avoid the pain that would inevitably occur otherwise. The common result of viewing every White person as a potential enemy and every social system as adversarial, however, is a reluctance on the part of African-Americans to engage in personal self-disclosure, including during interracial clinical or counseling situations, because such disclosure would reveal their inner psychological world and thus expose them to the potential for ridicule, humiliation, and disparagement (Combs, Penn, Cassisi, Michael, et al., 2006; Ridley, 1984; Whaley, 2001).

There continues to be a debate centering on whether the term *cultural mistrust* may be preferable to the term *healthy cultural paranoia* when describing this cultural response to oppression on the part of Blacks/African-Americans, arguing that the term *paranoia* should only be used when referring to mental illness, not cultural responses (Ashby, 1986; Bronstein, 1986). Whaley (2001) suggests that a potential resolution of this debate may rest on taking a dimensional approach for viewing paranoid symptomatology. Cultural mistrust would be on the mild end of the continuum with increasing severity leading, at the other end, to severe forms of paranoid psychopathology (Combs et al., 2006). The advantage of this model is that it makes a clear distinction between cultural, nonclinical, and reality-based mistrust stemming from experiences of oppression and discrimination in normal individuals from the symptoms of paranoia seen in those with mental illness (Ashby, 1986; Bronstein, 1986).

How Cultural Mistrust and Ecosystem Distrust May Be Confused with Paranoid Psychopathology

Although self-protective defensiveness can be an effective strategy on the part of African-Americans and other American Blacks to shield themselves from vulnerability and pain, it may be misperceived by others, especially non-Blacks, as clinically paranoid behavior. Triandis, Feldman, Weldon, and Harvey (1975) label this cultural self-protective defensiveness as *ecosystem distrust*, a syndrome characterized by lack of trust in people, suspicion of the motives of others, a lower degree of certainty about the sequence of events, a sense of individual powerlessness, and a sense that if one is not cautious, trouble may occur.

A close examination of these characteristics reveals a direct correspondence to the classic characteristics of a clinically paranoid style of functioning. *Lack of trust in people* and *suspicion of the motives of others* correspond to paranoid suspiciousness and mistrust. *A lower degree of certainty* and *a sense of individual powerlessness* correspond to the paranoid fear of loss of autonomy; and the *need to be cautious* reflects suspiciousness and corresponds to the paranoid need for constant mobilization against perceived threat. On the surface, therefore, an individual who is experiencing ecosystem distrust can appear to an uninformed outsider to be evidencing paranoid psychopathology. The differential assessment of such a situation must address the person's etiology in several areas including the physical, social, and cultural to determine whether the paranoid behavior is based on an adaptive adjustment, that is, a normal psychological reaction to reality-based racism, or whether there is the presence of psychopathology; and must determine the role that the paranoid beliefs play in the individual's psychological makeup. Effective differential diagnosis between clinical paranoia and cultural paranoia is essential, or the result will be either the minimization of true paranoid illness or mislabeling a normal cultural adaptation as psychopathology.

The following case illustrates how ecosystem/cultural mistrust and clinical paranoid illness can actually coexist in the same individual. In this case, both client and clinician struggled to overcome two major obstacles to establishing a positive therapeutic relationship: mistrust by the Black male client toward the therapist because she was White and female; and the general mistrust by the client toward the therapist as a function of his paranoid psychopathology unrelated to issues of gender and race. Although some trust was eventually established, the client's "double mistrust" forced him to create a safe distance by moving from a face-to-face interaction with the clinician to irregular telephone interactions, which severely limited the therapist's ability to help him.

The Case of Mr. B

Mr. B, a 33-year-old married African-American railroad engineer, walked into the psychiatric emergency service to request "legal advice." Upon evaluation, he was neatly attired, polite but very guarded with the evaluator. He asked to speak with a black male doctor but since none was available, he reluctantly agreed to talk with the triage clinician who was a white female clinical social worker. Initially, he told the clinician that he wanted legal advice to help him pursue a complaint of racial discrimination. He explained that he had come to the conclusion that the management of the railroad company where he worked had a conspiracy of prejudice against him because of his color since all his white colleagues had succeeded over the years in securing promotions while he was continually passed over. The clinician's reaction was that this seemed to be a reasonable perception in light of the facts Mr. B was citing along with the clinician's awareness of the reality of racial prejudice in this country. The clinician asked Mr. B, however, why he had come to a psychiatric emergency service if all he wanted was legal advice. He was visibly uncomfortable with the question and again asked if a black clinician were available. When told that there were no black clinicians employed by emergency service, although he could be referred to someone at another clinical service, he said he would go ahead and talk anyway.

In a very guarded manner, Mr. B stated that he had with him substantial evidence indicating that his wife had been having affairs with several men, both black and white. His suspicions had begun two years ago when he found a business card with a man's name on it in his wife's purse. Immediately he accused her of having an affair, which she denied. Over the ensuing months he continued to collect more "evidence", including shopping lists he claimed proved his wife was meeting her lover at the local grocery store, books of matches "proving" they had been at a motel together, and some blurred photographs of streets and buildings that he claimed were clear evidence but which, when examined by the clinician, showed nothing overt. Mr. B admitted he had reached the point to insist that either his wife must admit to the infidelities or he was going to have to kill her. This was compounded by the fact that the white men he suspected were all work colleagues as well. Remarkably, during all this time he had maintained a good work record and avoided any significant interpersonal conflict with his fellow workers. Mr. B exhibited no schizophrenic or affective symptoms but was clearly very suspicious and angry about both the racial discrimination issue and his wife's suspected infidelity.

The clinician concluded after a thorough diagnostic assessment that Mr. B's complaint of racial discrimination was probably based in reality and should be pursued via legal channels. The complaints about his wife, however, appeared not to be reality based particularly after the clinician called Mr. B's wife to warn her of Mr. B's threats per Tarasoff mandate. During their conversation, Mrs. B adamantly insisted that she was not involved with any men and never had been, stating that she was at her wits end with her husband's threats and accusations. The clinician therefore concluded that Mr. B was experiencing both a functional paranoid reaction, in terms of his suspicions toward his wife, and "healthy cultural paranoia" in terms of his perceptions about his work situation. After referring him to an affirmative action complaint board for the work related problems, the clinician worked with Mr. and Mrs. B. to try to help them resolve their marital conflicts, including his suspicions of her infidelity. This short-term intervention consisted of two sessions at the clinic at which time the clinician was able to convince Mr. B to see the psychiatrist and take some antipsychotic medication. Subsequently, however, he refused to return to the clinic because he didn't like the side effects of the medication although he did contact the clinician time to time by telephone. At last contact, he told her that his homicidal urges had remitted but that he could not give up the suspicions about his wife although he had "learned to live with it" (Newhill, 1990, pp. 178–179).

In this case, the lack of availability of a clinician of the same race and gender as the client may have contributed to the client not following through with more than two face-to-face clinic sessions, but that was only one factor. Another factor was the resistance to intervention characteristic of paranoid clients in general, irrespective of race or gender. In spite of these obstacles, the clinician was able to accurately sort out the difference between the paranoid symptoms that were reality based and those that represented psychopathology. Furthermore, she allowed the client to "pull back" to the distance he needed to continue the contact by telephone instead of face to face without pushing or rejecting him, which had some positive results, that is, his paranoid symptoms eased and his homicidal urges eventually remitted.

The Effect of Culture on Paranoid Psychopathology and Culture-Specific Syndromes

Although the existence of major mental disorders, such as the paranoid disorders, appear to be a universal phenomenon that cuts across societies, cultures, and historical times, there are some syndromes that are culture-specific; furthermore, within diagnostic categories, symptoms may be significantly influenced and shaped by culture. Clinicians encountering clients from other cultures often have difficulty distinguishing culturally acceptable ideas and behavior from psychopathology. A major issue for differential diagnosis is whether the client or patient can distinguish the boundaries of fantasy and reality and whether he

---

From Newhill, C.E., "The role of culture in the development of paranoid symptomatology," American Journal of Orthopsychiatry, 60(2), 176-185. Copyright (c) 1990 John Wiley and Sons, Inc. Reprinted with permission

or she can understand the limits in which culturally meaningful symbols and behavior are meant to operate (Nash, 1983). Even if the thought content is comprehensible and logical, mental illness may be indicated if the cultural beliefs are used in idiosyncratic, exaggerated, distorted, or inappropriate ways within the interpretive context of that particular culture.

Salzman (1960) emphasizes that delusions often represent those areas that reflect the patient's greatest source or lack of esteem, depending on the individual's own culture and value system. For example, in a family that values "good works," the expression of paranoid grandiosity may involve the pursuit of intense religious devotion with delusions revolving around interferences toward fulfilling such goals. If the patient's culture glorifies machismo as a desirable male ideal, paranoid grandiosity may be expressed in terms of success with sexual pursuits and the paranoid delusions will likely contain fears of sexual assault by other men (Chuang & Addington, 1988; Salzman, 1960).

Culture-specific paranoid syndromes

The literature on culture-specific paranoia discusses five distinct syndromes: amok (Saint Martin, 1999; Swanson et al., 1970), whitico psychosis (Cooper, 1933; Nash, 1983), voodoo death (Cannon, 1942; Lester, 2009; Richter, 1957), *ataques de nervios*, a.k.a. Puerto Rican Syndrome (Mehlman, 1961; Ramirez de Arellano et al., 1956; Tolin, Robison, Gaztambide, et al., 2007), and nightmare death in Southeast Asian refugees (Tobin & Friedman, 1983). It is beyond the scope of this chapter to address all these syndromes in detail; therefore only voodoo death will be briefly examined with a case illustration.

Ndetei (1986) reports that evil spirits, witchcraft, voodoo, and magic are common means of imagined injury, particularly within certain African and Caribbean cultures. Voodoo death, also known as psychogenic death and hex death, may be viewed as a cultural construct that is based on the belief that one person can possess the power to inflict mortal harm on another by magic (Lester, 2009; Nash, 1983). What physiological reaction actually causes the death has been a highly debated and speculative question. Cannon (1942), after observing several voodoo deaths in Australia, Haiti, and South America, concluded that a sustained excess of adrenalin produced by fear in the victim causes a fatal state of shock. Richter (1957) theorized that such deaths are caused by vagal overstimulation. Whatever the physical cause is, however, the trigger is a total belief in the power of the magic to kill. Cases of voodoo death are clear demonstrations of how a paranoid mode of reacting can be detrimental rather than adaptive.

The following case from the author's practice describes a man's paranoid reaction following a voodoo death curse within the cultural context of a belief in the power of voodoo to cause human death. His wife joined him in this paranoid reaction to the curse and eventually a shared psychotic disorder developed. A central clinical issue was determining where the cultural construct ended and the psychopathology began.

The Case of Mr. and Mrs. A

Mr. and Mrs. A., a young Jamaican couple who had recently emigrated from their home country to the United States, were brought to the emergency room by the police after Mr. A. was arrested for setting fire to some homemade "dolls" in his yard. The police initially suspected arson as the motive, but after interviewing Mr. and Mrs. A., they determined that psychiatric intervention was necessary. Upon evaluation, both Mr. and Mrs. A. presented as grossly delusional and fearful.

The social worker succeeded in calming them somewhat, and Mrs. A. reported that, six months before, a witchdoctor in Jamaica had placed a voodoo curse on her husband. He had immediately become very sick, confiding to his brother that he felt that his penis was shrinking and his strength was draining out of his body. In spite of his sickness, his wife was able, with family help, to move her husband with her to San Francisco. The family assured them that the magic could not follow them that far, particularly over water. However, although her husband initially felt some relief, he soon became convinced that the witchdoctor's magic had followed them and that he would soon die. He had burned the dolls as effigies in an effort to repel the power of the magic. By now, Mrs. A. was also convinced that she, too, would die via the power of the magic. Both Mr. and Mrs. A. remained so terrified and agitated that both required immediate admission to the local psychiatric inpatient unit. Separated from Mr. A., Mrs. A's psychotic symptoms cleared rapidly. Mr. A., however, remained acutely paranoid. (Newhill, 1990, p. 180)

Death by voodoo curse was an accepted cultural belief in Mr. A's community. The fact that he experienced the curse as a feeling that his penis was shrinking and his strength was draining out of his body was probably unique to his particular psychodynamics. The curse itself did not specify this reaction. Once Mrs. A had stabilized, she told the crisis social worker that Mr. A had always prided himself on his strength and virility as a man. To lose this would be a loss of one of his greatest sources of self-esteem (Newhill, 1990).

This case had an additional facet of being an example of delusional disorder, shared type. The recognition of this was essential in determining that the best initial intervention was separating the two spouses and treating them on different inpatient units. The essential feature of shared psychotic disorder is a delusion—in this case it was related to the voodoo curse—that develops in an individual (Mrs. A) who has a close relationship with another person, referred to as the "inducer" or primary case (Mr. A), who already has a psychotic disorder with prominent delusions (APA, 2000). In most cases of shared psychotic disorder, the person who adopts the beliefs of the ill person is a dependent, suggestible, isolated person who adopts the delusional beliefs when the two are together but readily gives them up upon intervention and separation. Most commonly, the influenced person is the inducer's intimate partner or child. In this case, once Mr. and Mrs. A were separated, Mrs. A stabilized, and she readily told the crisis social worker that she didn't know why she had felt that she was going to die, because the curse had been placed on her husband only and curses do not spread to others, according to her beliefs. Here is the point at which the cultural construct no longer applied, and thus her previous paranoid symptoms were simply a product of being a partner in the shared delusion. A major clue to this was Mrs. A's admission that her former delusion of sharing or being "infected" with the curse was not in accordance with her culture's belief system regarding voodoo and voodoo curses.

In light of the knowledge we have about voodoo death, it can be speculated that if no intervention had occurred and Mr. A's extreme fear of the voodoo curse had escalated, he might have died. At discharge, Mrs. A was completely symptom-free, but Mr. A still retained much suspiciousness and anxiety. Soon after, Mr. and Mrs. A moved away, presumably to again try to escape the curse, and were not heard of again.

Stresses Associated with Immigration and Risk for Developing Paranoid Symptoms

Paranoid psychopathology has been also been associated with the stresses associated with immigration, particularly to a host country that is very different from the home country in terms of culture, race, ethnicity, social structure, and language. Linguistic barriers, problems with acculturation and assimilation, prejudice, and unfulfilled expectations are some of the commonly cited issues that may influence the development of paranoid symptomatology in the new immigrant (Carpenter & Brockington, 1980; Ndetei, 1986; Rack, 1982; Wolfgang, 2001). Another issue, however, that may explain reports of a higher incidence of *perceived* paranoid psychosis in immigrant populations is misdiagnosis by the clinician resulting from

From Newhill, C.E., "The role of culture in the development of paranoid symptomatology," American Journal of Orthopsychiatry, 60(2), 176-185.

cultural misunderstandings and what may be referred to as the cultural relativity of delusions (Eke, 1981). To make a reliable diagnostic judgment on this issue requires a degree of cultural understanding that may not be within the grasp of the evaluating clinician (Editorial, 1980).

Culturally based paranoid attitudes are often representative of adaptive ways of coping as opposed to indicating individual psychopathology. Eke (1981) reports from his work with Nigerian immigrants that the development of paranoid psychosis in new immigrants is more likely to be the result of "ethnic prejudice, social incompatibility, poverty and failure to achieve the desired goals" (p. 226) rather than functional impairment. In addition, misinterpreting an event can result in a paranoid reaction by the immigrant person (Jack et al., 1984).

In general, immigration is a potentially stressful event. The more socially and culturally distant the newly arrived immigrant is from the predominant culture of the new host country, the greater the stress is likely to be. If such a situation is compounded with an inherent vulnerability to paranoid thinking patterns, a paranoid syndrome may develop. The key to providing constructive intervention in such cases is cultural sensitivity and understanding of the immigrant person's culture and the associated precipitating stresses, along with efforts to mobilize culturally relevant supportive community resources.

The next case example is of a Southeast Asian immigrant who suffered from posttraumatic stress disorder secondary to his war experience plus the cultural stresses associated with immigration. These stresses included experiencing prejudice, social isolation, and cultural estrangement and misinterpreting others' actions in a paranoid manner.

The Case of Mr. C

Mr. C, a 30-year-old single Cambodian refugee, came to the psychiatric emergency service on his own asking for help. Upon evaluation, he was polite and cooperative but very constricted and guarded. Although there were no Southeast Asian clinicians available that particular day at the clinic, Mr. C spoke English fluently and the assessment was completed without needing an interpreter. Mr. C told the clinician that he had been feeling "sad" for the past three months and had been experiencing chest pain and headaches. Two days ago he had a thorough physical examination at the county hospital and had been told that there was no organic basis for his complaints. The nurse had then referred him to the community mental health crisis clinic.

Mr. C told the clinician that he had arrived in the U.S. only six months ago, and had a difficult time adjusting to American cultural life. His good command of English was due to his attending a university in England and subsequently living there for two years prior to returning to Cambodia. He made it clear to the clinician that he was *not* Cambodian, but Chinese, and that he felt that he was experiencing some prejudice because of the misconception that he was of Southeast Asian descent. He denied suicidal feelings, did not want to see a doctor but did want to talk about his situation. After seeing Mr. C for several sessions in the emergency clinic, the reasons for his "sadness" became clearer. In the early 1970s Mr. C identified himself as a Communist, but over the course of the Vietnam War his political ideas changed and he abandoned the Communist Party but was confused as to what political ideology to adhere to. Since his arrival in the U.S. he had been impressed with the ideal of democracy although he perceived the reality of democracy as being quite different. However, he had been feeling increasingly fearful that he might be identified as a former Communist and be deported or that he would be found by a Southeast Asian death squad and killed. Mr. C insisted that there were many Communist death squads in the United States whose mission was to hunt down Communist defectors, such as himself, and assassinate them. Mr. C worked as a computer programmer, and had recently come to believe that his co-workers were talking behind his back and accusing him of being a Communist. He felt helpless to do anything about his situation and the prospect of death or deportation continually preoccupied him.

Although the crisis clinic sessions seemed to be constructive in terms of providing support and a forum for Mr. C to share his fears, the clinician did not feel that her help was sufficient for his unique cultural stresses. To address this, she contacted the local Catholic Charities agency that had a Southeast Asian refugee counseling center attached to it. Although the counselors were paraprofessionals, they were able to provide Mr. C with some very helpful assistance and the kind of understanding that can come only from someone who has gone through similar circumstances. Within a few weeks Mr. C reported feeling much better, less fearful and the paranoid complaints about his work colleagues diminished. (Newhill, 1990, p. 181–182)

The fact that Mr. C's psychological stress took the form of paranoid symptoms can be further explained by the following: extreme cultural differences and political ambivalence (as described by Mr. C), the experience of prejudice toward him by Americans, and misinterpreting his colleagues' talking with one another resulting in the paranoid fear that he would be accused of being a Communist. There is also the unanswered question as to what Mr. C's mental functioning was like before he experienced the stresses of war and immigration, that is, whether he manifested any ongoing problems coping with life stress and/or a premorbid susceptibility to psychiatric problems.

Because clinical expertise, clinician sensitivity, and a desire to help were not sufficient to help Mr. C, the clinician employed the services of the refugee counseling center. These counselors, because they were from the same cultural background and had similar life experiences, were able to understand from direct experience why Mr. C reacted as he did to his circumstances and how his culture and past experiences played a role in his emotional and physical distress. They were also able to communicate with him in his native language. Although Mr. C was fluent in English, finer nuances of meaning, expression, and mutual understanding were often lost. Furthermore, because Mr. C *believed* the refugee counselors would understand him better, he was able to open up to them more easily about his fears and problems.

Concluding Comments

When evaluating an individual from a culture different from one's own who is exhibiting paranoid symptomatology of some form, such as believing that he or she is being persecuted, it is important to address several questions first before making assumptions about the presence or absence of psychopathology. Rack (1982, p. 9) suggests clinicians ask a number of questions about the client and his or her situation as part of a culturally competent assessment. First, the clinician should consider whether the client's complaints of persecution might be true. Do others in the client's community behave the way the client is describing? Also, are the client's suspicions explicable within the context of his or her past experiences? If not based in past experiences, is the client perhaps describing something that is a common belief in his or her cultural community? Is what the client is saying simply a figure of speech or a way of expressing anxiety, and not intended to be taken literally?

If the answer to any of these questions is "yes," it suggests that culture is an important variable to take into consideration in both the diagnostic assessment and treatment planning. Treatment strategies and interventions, however, must vary according to the etiological factors underlying the particular paranoid manifestation.

For example, in the case of Mr. and Mrs. A, great fear of voodoo curses was something that was a common belief in their community in Jamaica. In this context, the fear made sense and was understandable. However, Mr. A suffered from both culturally based paranoia and a clinical paranoid illness. The voodoo curse placed on him triggered his psychosis, but a true psychiatric illness compounded the clinical picture. The dynamics with Mrs. A were different. She also believed in voodoo, but the psychotic portion of her reaction was because of her husband's influence on her thinking. Separated from him, she stabilized and her delusion abated. Although Mr. and Mrs. A shared a common culture, their paranoia was compounded by different factors and therefore required different interventions.

With Mr. B, the multiple past experiences he had with oppression and racism provided a context within which his feelings of persecution associated with being passed over for promotion made sense. However, the suspicions about his wife were not reality based even within the context of his community and culture, thereby suggesting the presence of clinical paranoid illness. Again, the two sources of paranoia suggested different tracks of intervention. The complaints of racism were addressed by a referral to a discrimination complaint board. The delusions about his wife, however, were symptomatic of mental illness, which would respond best to medication and psychotherapy (individual and couples therapy).

Mr. C's fear of death squads and accusations that he was a Communist made sense, given his past traumatic experiences. Although the paranoid feelings about his co-workers had reached delusional proportions, the clinician did not think that referral for medication or hospitalization was necessary. In this case, the client was able to mobilize his strengths and coping abilities and utilize the psychotherapy interventions of the clinician and the social supports of the refugee counseling center to recover.

Assess your comprehension of the *impact of race, culture, ethnicity, and the stresses of immigration on the development of paranoid symptomatology* by completing this quiz.

PARANOID SYMPTOMATOLOGY IN OLDER ADULTS

Significance of the Problem

Issues related to the mental and emotional well-being of older adults is of particular concern for society today due to an increasing awareness that the U.S. population, like many other developed countries around the world, is growing older and, as noted previously, more racially and ethnically diverse. In 2009, 39.6 million people, or one out of every eight Americans, were 65 years of age or older. By 2030, this is projected to more than double to 72.1 million older persons, or 19 percent of the total U.S. population (U.S. DHHS, 2011). The proportion of older adults who are members of racial and ethnic minority groups is also increasing, from 16.3 percent of the over-65 population in 2000, to a projected increase of 23.6 percent in 2020.

Single-status older women, many of whom are widowed or divorced, will constitute the majority of older adults, with older women currently outnumbering older men at 22.7 million older women to 16.8 million older men (U.S. DHHS, 2011). Older men enjoy certain advantages as compared to older women in that they are much more likely to be married, and have higher median incomes, $25,877 annually as compared to only $15,282 for women. The majority of all older adults cite Social Security as one of their primary forms of financial support, and thus, some of the proposed changes to this highly successful social insurance program concern many Americans, particularly those at or nearing retirement age.

Health issues impacting older persons, especially older women, are of significant concern, particularly the mental health well-being of this group and the mental disorders most likely to occur within this population. Paranoid illnesses are second only to mood disorders, specifically depression, in the frequency of occurrence among older adults (Fisher, Ziess, & Carstensen, 2001).

Prevalence, Etiology, and Risk Factors Associated with Paranoid Symptomatology in Older Adults

Incidence and prevalence

We know very little about the true incidence and prevalence rates of paranoia in older adults, and the rates reported in the literature probably underestimate its occurrence. For example, based on the DSM-III classification, Varner and Gaitz (1982) estimated that

2 percent of elderly outpatients and 4.6 percent of elderly inpatients evidence clinically significant paranoid symptomatology. A general population study of 997 elderly people living in the community reported that 40 (4%) of the individuals studied had generalized persecutory ideation (Christenson & Blazer, 1984). This persecutory ideation was typically associated with impairments in physical health, especially sensory deficits and cognitive impairment, and loss of social and economic resources.

Similar to younger individuals with paranoid symptoms, older adults with paranoia rarely seek treatment on their own and often don't come to clinical attention unless their symptoms cause severe functional impairments and others, such as family or neighbors, seek help on their behalf (Fennig, Fochtmann, & Bromet, 2005). Most studies suggest that paranoid illness in those over age 60 is more likely to be diagnosed in women than men (Jorgensen & Munk-Jorgensen, 1985; Walker & Brodie, 1985). However, it should be noted that women live longer than men and therefore the difference may be partly due to the fact that there are simply more elderly women than men alive after age 65 to be diagnosed. A number of terms have been suggested to refer to paranoid syndromes in late life, for example, *transitional paranoid reaction*, *paranoid hallucinosis*, *paranoid reaction*, and *paraphrenia*, but none of these has been included in the *DSM* and, so far, there is no classification system for describing the unique paranoid states in old age that has been universally accepted.

Etiology of and risk factors for paranoia in late life

A review of the literature reveals a number of precipitating, risk, and premorbid factors commonly associated with the development of paranoid symptoms in late life. First is having a positive family history of schizophrenia and paranoid or schizoid premorbid personality disorders or traits. Second, individuals who have experienced stressful life events involving some kind of trauma and/or significant loss that serve to confirm the individual's previous suspicions or resentments or expectations of deception and hostile treatment from others are at risk for developing a paranoid reaction. In addition, other losses, both interpersonal as well as biological, can play a role in the etiology of paranoid symptoms in late life. Loss of a spouse, sensory losses such as hearing or vision loss, or the deaths of important members of the individual's social support network can trigger paranoid symptoms (Fisher, Ziess, & Carstensen, 2001). Individuals living independently whose health is beginning to fail and who fear losing independence and autonomy are also at risk for developing paranoid symptoms. Example:

> Esther, 84, lived alone in the family home that she had occupied for the past forty years. Up until Esther's husband died six years ago, she functioned well and was active in community activities, enjoying a large social support network. After the loss of her husband, however, Esther's functioning began to rapidly deteriorate, including an acceleration of hearing loss. While he was alive, Esther's husband kept a regular schedule and made sure that the house was kept clean, that meals were eaten at regular times, and that the household ran smoothly. He did this in a supportive manner, never making Esther feel that she was being controlled at all. After his death, however, it became clear that Esther's husband had been compensating for his wife's developing dementia. Esther became increasingly confused, sometimes forgetting to eat dinner or bathe. Mail piled up in the living room, the house became disheveled, and Esther began to have minor accidents when driving her car. When her adult children suggested that she consider selling her home and car and moving into an assisted living facility, Esther became very upset. Soon afterwards, she began accusing her family of plotting against her to take her assets, and accused them of stealing her jewelry and surreptitiously moving things around in the house deliberately to confuse her. Esther prized her independence highly and was terrified of

> losing it. One day, Esther's daughter came to visit her and could not open the door. Subsequently, she discovered that her mother had pushed furniture against the door in an effort to keep her family and any other intruders from coming in and forcing her to leave her home. (Newhill, 1995).

It is generally agreed that sensory losses are especially associated with the development of late-life paranoia, with impairment in hearing presenting the highest risk (Cooper, 1974; Cooper & Porter, 1976; LaRue, Dessonville, & Jarvik, 1985). In fact, studies have shown that a paranoid reaction can be experimentally induced in normal people who experience a temporary loss of hearing, supporting the hypothesis that there is a social-cognitive mechanism for the clinically observed association between paranoia and hearing loss in older adults (Zimbardo, Andersen, & Kabat, 1981). Berger & Zarit (1978) also report that the early lives of non-deaf paranoid older adults usually reveal a history of emotional coldness, problems with interpersonal relations, and sexual difficulties. Paranoid elderly with hearing loss are less likely to report such problems as frequently, suggesting that hearing loss itself constitutes a significant factor in the development of paranoid illness.

Gurian, Wexler, and Baker (1992), in a study of 39 individuals with late-life onset of paranoid symptoms without hearing loss, 36 of whom were women, reported that all but one had no children, more than half were refugees or holocaust survivors and, surprisingly, most showed no evidence of any form of sensory loss. The authors concluded that in late life, some paranoid individuals evidence what may be viewed as a late-life delusional state, qualitatively different from individuals with paranoia related to schizophrenia or dementia. Further, the paranoia in these delusionally disordered individuals cannot be accounted for exclusively by social isolation or sensory loss, rather, the paranoid state is related to an interaction among early trauma, the absence of children, and the appearance of paranoid ideation later in life.

Psychoses in later life may also involve a continuation or exacerbation of a chronic disorder first evident earlier in adulthood or, more commonly, the development of psychotic symptoms is associated with an underlying medical condition and/or its treatment (Cummings & Kropf, 2011). Common underlying medical conditions include delirium; various forms of dementia, for example, Alzheimer's disease; and other neurological conditions (Ballard, Chithiramohan, Bannister, Handy, & Todd, 1991; Ballard & Oyebode, 1995; Forsell & Henderson, 1998; Groch, 2005). Such neurological impairment, when coupled with social isolation and sensory loss, elevates risk for developing paranoid symptoms even further (Thorpe, 1997).

Paranoid symptoms that are associated with dementia almost always involve cognitive decline. Cognitive decline is not associated with non-dementia-related paranoia in old age, and day-to-day functioning for such individuals is less impaired, although the person may become withdrawn and isolated from others (Fisher, Ziess, & Carstensen, 2001). This can be very problematic for elderly individuals who depend on daily caregiving from others, such as family, because the paranoid delusions and other symptoms often focus on the caregivers since they typically have the most frequent contact with the individual. For example, Margaret, whose 92-year-old mother is in the moderate to severe stage of Alzheimer's disease, talks about the emotionally painful aspects of caregiving:

> My mother often doesn't recognize me and thinks I am her younger sister, who died decades ago. She lives in what is considered to be an excellent Alzheimer's care facility, but I will visit in the early evening after work and her diaper will need to be changed and her dinner will be sitting there, forgotten. I don't mind helping out with that—I know they are short staffed—but what is hardest for me are her accusations that I am stealing her personal things and poisoning her food. I explain

> over and over that I am not hiding her jewelry and am not poisoning her food but then she accuses me of being an imposter and starts pushing and hitting me, demanding I bring her "real daughter" back. It is so exhausting and I don't know how many more years this is going to go on—other than her dementia, my mother is very healthy physically. I guess I sound terrible, but I wish God would just take her so she could be with my dad again.

Accusations toward family members, such as the situation with Margaret's mother, can elicit strong feelings of painful guilt and anger, and providing caregiving to loved one in such a situation can be extremely taxing and stressful for the caregiver. Providing the family with psychoeducation about their relative's particular form of paranoia and particular type of dementia and its cause and prognosis can be helpful, along with a referral to a caregiver support group, such as those sponsored by the Alzheimer's Association (www.alz.org).

General Profile of the Older Person with Paranoia

Paranoid illness is most likely to affect individuals who are socially isolated, that is, who are single or widowed, have few close friends or relatives, and who have lived alone for many years prior to the onset of illness (Newhill, 1989; Swanson et al., 1970). In general, social isolation is a prominent feature and, with advancing age, individuals who may have always been loners or considered strange or eccentric by their community can develop progressive suspiciousness that can evolve into a full-blown late-onset delusional disorder (Munro, 1999).

The typical elderly paranoid client is female, over the age of 65, and living alone (Berger & Zarit, 1978). She may be self-referred, but in most cases she is referred for psychiatric help by family, neighbors or clergy, law enforcement, or other community agency personnel following persistent complaints from the client about people stealing her belongings, men making unwanted sexual comments, bugs in her house, or harassment from neighbors. She is usually divorced or never married and often does not have a good history of sustained interpersonal relationships, although she may have a good work history.

The development of paranoid symptoms in an elderly person is usually the result of an increased use of projection as a defense against perceived loss of autonomy, control, and independence (Molinari & Chacko, 1983). Common age-related losses related to autonomy and control include loss of a spouse, job, status or prestige, sensory acuity, and/or physical strength or attractiveness. Developing paranoid symptoms may adaptively protect the person from the painful anxiety and depression that some individuals experience with the impact of certain losses, such as physical decline, that are common as part of the process of growing older. Depression is avoided by externalizing the narcissistic injuries created by such losses. Often there is a kind of seesaw course with the depressive symptoms receding as the person becomes more paranoid and then with a decrease in paranoid symptoms, the depression becomes more prominent.

Paranoid states in late-life can have a particularly disturbing effect on family, friends, and community agencies. Symptoms that involve repeated unfounded accusations, hostility, and delusional complaints can sometimes lead to the afflicted individual being labeled "crazy" or "loony" and subsequently rejected with little attempt to secure treatment. There is an unfortunate, and empirically unsubstantiated, stereotype that psychiatric disturbance in older adults is untreatable and that custodial care is the best that can be offered, and that is unfortunate (Berger & Zarit, 1978; Cummings & Kropf, 2011). Appropriate timely intervention including crisis intervention or psychotherapy can, in fact, be extremely effective, as illustrated in the following case.

The Case of Ms. D

A referral was made to the county mental health crisis team by one of the agricultural scientists at the local agricultural extension testing service. For the past year the scientist had been receiving persistent calls from a Ms. D complaining of strange hairy bugs in her house. He had repeatedly gone out to her home, examined the interior and exterior, taking soil samples and testing them but finding no evidence of any bugs. In exasperation, he turned to the mental health crisis clinic because he had reached the point of concluding Ms. D was "dotty." Upon evaluation at her home, Ms. D was initially quite guarded, but soon relaxed with the crisis social worker, talking quite animatedly about her bugs. A psychosocial history revealed that she had never married, had retired from work as a librarian two years previously and her concern about the bugs currently comprised her primary activity. After much gentle probing by the social worker, Ms. D admitted that she often felt sad and lonely but had no idea how to help herself feel better. After several sessions of counseling and some low doses of antipsychotic medication, Ms. D improved considerably, commenting one day that the bugs had miraculously disappeared (Newhill, 1989).

In this case, the crisis social worker provided a quick response to the request by the agricultural scientist for help, which immediately allayed his anxiety about the situation. The choice of utilization of an outreach mode, that is, the client's own home as the intervention site, was ideal for such a client because it allowed her to feel safe and in control. The crisis social worker also did not directly confront Ms. D about her delusions, but rather worked to establish a trusting supportive relationship. This enabled Ms. D to eventually accept medication and counseling that helped alleviate her agitation over the bugs in her house. Engaging Ms. D's participation in appropriate social interactions with others at the local senior citizens center also helped in meeting her emotional and social needs in more constructive ways and thus helped to relieve her underlying depression and loneliness.

Assess your comprehension of ***the prevalence, etiology, and risk factors associated with paranoid symptomatology and conditions in older adults*** **by completing this quiz.**

TREATMENT OF PARANOID SYMPTOMS AND CONDITIONS

Appropriate treatment for a psychiatric condition depends upon a good assessment and an accurate diagnosis. However, with paranoid conditions other than schizophrenia, clinicians often miss the presence of the paranoid symptoms, particularly the less overt symptoms of paranoid personality disorder, in part because such individuals often are not immediately forthcoming with information about their fears and inner thinking patterns. One tool that can be helpful in identifying the presence of paranoid symptoms is the mental status exam.

The Mental Status Exam

Administering a mental status exam is often part of a typical psychosocial assessment. However, for many paranoid clients, administration of a mental status exam is interpreted as a challenge or even as an interrogation that must be met with increased hyperalertness and mistrust. During a mental status exam, a paranoid client may suspiciously ask why he or she should answer a particular question, or may simply say it is "nobody's business." The mental status exam may be perceived by the client as disguised trickery, so the clinician should either calmly explain the purpose of a particular question in easily understandable language or drop the question and go on to the next if the client seems too threatened and resistant. It is important that the clinician answer any appropriate questions the client has honestly and directly, although it is perfectly acceptable to decline an inappropriately intrusive personal question and explain why in a matter-of-fact manner.

Findings from a mental status exam often reveal the paranoid client's remarkable knowledge of details but, in spite of a phenomenal memory in some areas, there will be noticeable gaps in areas the client thinks are unimportant or which are threatening to remember (Walker & Cavenar, 1983). For example, attempts by the clinician to clarify vaguely presented information may be met with hostility and belligerence. Interpretation of proverbs, which is one component of the mental status exam, can be upsetting for many paranoid clients because of the open-endedness of such tasks, and their responses are often highly personal. For example, a typical response by a paranoid client when asked to interpret the proverb "You can lead a horse to water but you can't make him drink" might be "People think they can trick me but I know what's happening here." Thus, a good initial assessment is important; however, even when the correct diagnosis is made, it is often very challenging to engage such individuals in treatment.

Barriers to Treatment for People with Paranoid Conditions

Paranoid clients rarely seek help on their own but, instead, are often forced into treatment against their will. As a result, such clients may begin their treatment experience with angry, resentful, and anxious feelings. The clinician who recognizes that the client is trying to defend against the fear of being controlled and taken advantage of will have a better chance at establishing rapport and, eventually, a therapeutic alliance. Even once established, the alliance may be a fragile one and complicated by a range of barriers that get in the way of the paranoid individual fully engaging in treatment.

The following is a summary of common barriers to treatment for this population, which can help a social worker to better understand why people with paranoid symptoms only rarely seek out treatment and why, when they are in treatment, they can find it threatening and often drop out. Furthermore, those therapists who are knowledgeable and understand these barriers to treatment also understand the very real dangers in treating individuals who are paranoid, and so may be reluctant to take them on as clients. As a result, such individuals often do not receive the treatment they so desperately need. Even worse, when they have therapists who do not have the knowledge, skills, or professional discipline to treat people with paranoid disorders, the therapeutic relationship can become destructive for both (Yudofsky, 2005).

One of the first barriers to treatment for individuals with a paranoid condition is that clinicians may not recognize, even after a good assessment, that the person has paranoid symptoms. For example, in a study of individuals seeking treatment at the Columbia University Psychoanalytic Center, Oldham and Skodol (1994) compared the diagnostic assessments generated by clinicians with the findings from structured diagnostic instruments administered by the researchers. The authors found that for all of the patients who met diagnostic scale criteria for paranoid personality disorder, the clinicians completely missed identifying any paranoid symptoms. Even if an accurate diagnosis is made, however, there are additional barriers that get in the way of paranoid clients accessing, accepting, and engaging in appropriate treatment (Yudofsky, 2005).

The second barrier to treatment is that individuals with paranoid conditions have fundamental problems with trust (Yudofsky, 2005). To address this barrier, the basic strategy is to take an honest, direct approach that is affectively neutral. Being "too friendly" can be as destructive to achieving rapport with the paranoid client as being unfriendly. This is because friendliness and warmth may be perceived by the client as an effort to manipulate him or her, thus invoking immediate suspiciousness. The clinician should also be careful not to stand or sit too close to the client or touch the client, and arrange for an interview environment with plenty of personal space. Even a normal handshake of greeting may be perceived negatively.

Another barrier is that paranoid individuals often fervently believe they are completely self-sufficient in life and think they are smarter and already know all the answers to their concerns (Yudofsky, 2005). This assumption of self-sufficiency covers over a deep fear of dependency, which is threatening because dependency can make the individual feel vulnerable to attack. To address this, the clinician must give a clear and unambiguous message that they will support the individual's self-determination and will not make attempts to control or manipulate him or her. The clinician's role is presented as that of a *consultant* who will serve as a partner or ally in treatment. Framing treatment as "consultation with an expert" helps deflect fears of dependency and helps the client lower his or her guard a bit. It is also important that the clinician avoid becoming defensive if the client behaves in an arrogant and condescending way. Answer appropriate questions honestly but maintain appropriate boundaries at the same time. Example:

Client: So you're only a social worker. (said disdainfully) What kind of training do you have?

SW: That's a good question. I received my undergraduate degree from Penn State in sociology and my master's degree in social work from the University of Pittsburgh. My clinical training was at Western Psychiatric Institute and Clinic.

Client: Hmmm. . . . Is that a real diploma on your wall?

SW: Yes, would you like to see it?

Client: I just want to confirm that there is a watermark on it so I know it's for real. You wouldn't believe the number of quacks out there.

SW: Sure. Here, you can take a look. (the social worker hands the framed diploma to the client, who begins to remove it from the frame)

SW: It is fine for you to examine it, but I would prefer that you not take it out of the frame.

Client: (reluctantly) Okay, fine.

Another barrier to treatment is that people with paranoid symptoms tend to blame others for their problems and are unable to see their own role in their difficulties. Their symptoms are what is called "alloplastic," that is, they view their problems as molded by external forces and factors (Perry & Vaillant, 1989) and, therefore, are unable to see the need for treatment. The client may state emphatically, "I am not the problem here." Example:

SW: (first meeting with the client) Can you tell me what brought you here today?

Client: It really isn't anybody's business, but I got fired from my job.

SW: Can you tell me why you were fired?

Client: I didn't do anything wrong. I was doing a good job. I was told by my supervisor that I had problems getting along with my co-workers, but that's a bunch of baloney. My co-workers plotted to get me fired, and they finally got their way.

Paranoid individuals' inability to see the part that they play in their problems is often compounded by a lack of insight into the connection between their feelings and their mistrustful beliefs. This is sometimes referred to as "not being psychologically minded," but it more reflects the power of the defense mechanism of projection, which is the central psychodynamic feature in all forms of paranoia. Recall that projection can be defined as a form of displacement in which one attributes to others those objectionable character traits, attitudes, motives, and desires one wishes to disclaim in oneself (Perry & Vaillant, 1989). Essentially, the client attributes his or her own unacknowledged feelings to others. Projection can be very effective in enabling a person to remain blind to his or her own feelings and desires, while distorting the person's perception of the outside world. Projection is protective, but it also serves as a barrier to identifying and understanding feelings and motives and it reinforces untrue and distorted paranoid beliefs.

Projection leads to a number of problematic behaviors such as excessive faultfinding, hypersensitivity to criticism, vigilant injustice collecting, holding grudges, and litigiousness. This leads to another barrier to treatment engagement, which is inflexibility and argumentativeness. Paranoid rigidity and inflexibility stems from fears of loss of autonomy, but understanding this doesn't always make it easier to deal with. For example, the client may argue about fees or appointment times or accuse the clinician of "only being in it for the money." For the client with borderline personality, such accusations usually represent concerns the clinician doesn't care about him or her; for the paranoid client, it usually relates to issues of control.

The final barrier to treatment is that paranoid clients can become dangerous. This danger may manifest as a lawsuit but also may involve threats and even violence. The client may suddenly fear having revealed too much to the social worker and that the social worker might use that information against him or her. Or the client may experience a "paranoid illumination," in which suddenly everything makes sense, the pieces of the puzzle fit together to explain the person's suspicions, and that last puzzle piece may be the clinician, that is, "my social worker is the cause of all this—she is at the root of the conspiracy," and at that point, the client may strike out in self-defense, including an aggressive defense, "I'll get him before he gets me." At this point, the clinician should follow basic guidelines for dealing with threats and violence (see, e.g., Newhill, 2003).

As this review of barriers to treatment suggests, paranoid clients can be challenging to engage and work with. What can be helpful is to remember the basic dynamics of paranoid thinking patterns and how it feels to be paranoid—to be frightened and feel under threat—and then be aware of some of the unique barriers to treatment these conditions present and some general knowledge about how to respond effectively. Next, interventions that can be helpful in working with paranoid clients are discussed.

Hospitalization

Unlike individuals with other forms of serious mental illness, many people with paranoid disorders, including delusional disorder, can manage reasonably well independently in the community and can avoid the need for hospitalization. Because paranoid disorders, outside of those associated with dementia, generally do not result in severe cognitive deterioration, emotion dysregulation, or behavioral dysregulation, such clients are often able to maintain adequate psychosocial functioning within a structured regulated lifestyle even if they have a strong delusional system. Kaplan and Sadock (1971) comment that the closer the client's clinical presentation is to true paranoia and the further away it is from schizophrenia, the less need there usually is for hospitalization. Those paranoid individuals with schizophrenia, however, may require hospitalization occasionally, although their psychosocial functioning is often better between episodes of illness than those with other forms of schizophrenia.

Unless the paranoid client is dangerous to self or others, it is advisable to make all attempts necessary to avoid hospitalization. The removal of civil liberties and loss of control inherent in being hospitalized, especially involuntary commitment, is frightening to the client and can serve to reinforce the individual's delusional system and stimulate the client's hostility and resistance to further treatment (Walker & Brodie, 1985). However, people with paranoia can become dangerous and, if that is the case, then hospitalization may be necessary (Yudofsky, 2005). To reduce risk of violence and need for hospitalization, it can be helpful to allow the client to control the decisions about his or her own care as much as possible, support client-directed choices and self-determination, and avoid backing the person into a corner, psychologically or physically, in which he or she may feel trapped. It is important to try to offer the client options in order to save face and avoid punitive actions if possible (Yudofsky, 2005). In other words, allow the client to feel in control and build in avenues of safe escape.

Although violence risk and potential for dangerousness are not easy issues to assess, careful evaluation of the client's history can reveal if he or she has been motivated to engage in violent behavior in response to delusions or other provocation in the past. Comparing such past history with the client's current clinical state can provide some estimation of the presence of potential danger. It is even more helpful if the client is willing to reveal and discuss his or her delusions and his or her current emotional state in response to them. If, after a careful review of all this, the conclusion is in favor of hospitalization, then an effort should be made to persuade the client to enter the hospital willingly. Often firm supportive insistence within the context of this being in the client's best interest will work, but if that fails, then commitment should be executed without delay. Equivocating about such a decision will only serve to exacerbate the client's anxiety and elevate the potential for an aggressive response (Newhill, 2003).

Psychotherapy and Other Forms of Treatment for Paranoid Clients

Whether the paranoid client is to be treated as an inpatient or as an outpatient, certain transference and countertransference issues must be kept in mind. In general, paranoid clients are suspicious and mistrustful, deeply believing from long experience that the spoken word does not reveal actual intent. The social worker or other clinician will be viewed by the client as just another potential persecutor until a feeling of trust toward the therapist can be established. Establishing trust is a difficult task for the therapist, because he or she will be met initially with acute suspicion, hostility, and defensiveness (Kaplan & Sadock, 1971; Newhill, 1989; Yudofsky, 2005). Therefore, in order for treatment to be successful, the clinician should keep certain therapeutic guidelines in mind. First, the therapist must be scrupulously honest and dependable and make sure that words and deeds convey the same message. Second, both the client and the client's family must understand and agree to uphold client–therapist confidentiality. Initial contacts with the client's family should be made with the client present to avoid the client feeling that the clinician and family are "operating behind his or her back." When approaching the client about signing a waiver of confidentiality so that the clinician can confer with the family without the client present, the clinician should take a collaborative stance with the client about exactly what information will be shared and what will be kept confidential and why the waiver is in the client's best interest. Example:

SW: Mr. Smith, I think that we should talk about the idea of signing a limited waiver of confidentiality to allow me to talk with your family occasionally so we can all work together more effectively.

Client: Why do they have to know anything about my treatment?

SW: Well, in my experience working with people and their families, as we have been doing, the work usually goes better when we can all talk openly and honestly together about some of the issues.

Client: Like what?

SW: Well, right now you are living with your mother and sister, am I right about that?

Client: Yeah, so what?

SW: A limited waiver of confidentiality will allow us to all sit down together and talk about things collaboratively, like how your family can be more helpful to you. For example, I can help by explaining to them why you are on the medication you are on and how they can help you remember to take your pills. When families understand the purpose of medication, everything usually goes more smoothly.

Client: Well, okay, I get that, but you're not just going to turn my whole record over to them, are you?

SW: Absolutely not. You can decide what information can be shared and what information will be kept confidential. You are in control of that and I will support you in your decisions about confidentiality.

Client: Well, okay, I'll think about it.

In general, it is recommended that the clinician maintain a stance of neutral distance toward the client and, instead of directly confronting and/or arguing with the client's delusions and paranoid thinking patterns, the therapist should listen empathically, focus on how the delusional beliefs interfere with a constructive life, and help the client manage life demands by working around the paranoia (Walker & Brodie, 1985). For most delusional paranoid clients, medication is an essential adjunct to psychosocial intervention. Paranoid clients are notoriously wary of medication, however, because they view it as an invasive, mind-altering treatment and may incorporate the administration and effects of drugs into their delusional system. However, if the anxiety level of a client is acute and the delusions are particularly bothersome, low doses of antipsychotic medication can be quite helpful (Fennig, Fochtmann, & Bromet, 2005; Walker & Brodie, 1985). Although some paranoid clients are not reliable about taking oral medications, injections should be avoided if possible. Because they are particularly physically intrusive, injections can precipitate a panic reaction in some paranoid clients.

In addition to medication, certain forms of psychosocial treatment can help modify and buffer the effect of the paranoid symptoms. Cognitive therapy, for example, can be very helpful in modifying paranoid beliefs and schemas (Chadwick, Birchwood, & Trower, 1996; Freeman, Freeman, & Garety, 2008), while behavioral treatment can involve the manipulation of environmental variables to encourage modification of a client's behavior and perceptions (Brink, 1980; Gitterman & Germain, 2008; Mattimore-Knudson, 1985). Although not every paranoid client is receptive to receiving psychotherapy, many paranoid clients can be helped successfully to improve their lives and their suspicious thinking to some extent with therapy. Therapy may not "cure" the individual's paranoid condition, but appropriate therapy can enhance psychosocial functioning and help such individuals achieve recovery.

Environmental intervention based on the life model approach (Gitterman & Germain, 2008) can be a helpful tool for working with paranoid clients, particularly those who are socially isolated. Such interventions capitalize on strengths and can include working with the client's family, friends, and neighbors to mobilize social supports, work for changes in the client's living conditions to facilitate health and well-being, and encourage the client to become involved with community resources to the extent that he or she is willing and able. In the case of Ms. D described above, the crisis worker took this approach to helping and, instead of focusing on the psychiatric pathology, the worker mitigated Ms. D's paranoid symptoms by helping her connect to a new environment. The crisis worker's effort to involve Ms. D with the local senior citizens center was a form of environmental manipulation that proved helpful to her.

Encouraging a paranoid individual to get a pet can be another effective environmental manipulation technique to relieve loneliness and social isolation. Pets can be less emotionally threatening than another human being, and many paranoid clients are able to form a trusting attachment to a cat or dog that can serve as an important source of social support. As a former client once stated to the author: "I like animals better than people. Animals don't tell your secrets and, unlike people, they don't stab you in the back."

Self-Help Strategies

As with other serious mental illnesses, individuals with paranoid conditions can also use self-help strategies. Such strategies are designed to help manage and even overcome paranoid and suspicious thoughts by employing cognitive-behavioral techniques aimed at promoting understanding of and change in paranoid thinking and behavior patterns. These strategies first focus on helping the individual sort out justifiable anxieties from unfounded paranoid fears and understand where suspicious thoughts come from. CBT self-help models for the treatment of paranoia postulate that the origins of many suspicious thoughts often lie in internal and external events that are stressful and that affect emotions, perceptions, and interpretations of the events (Freeman, Freeman, & Garety, 2008).

To overcome how suspicious and paranoid beliefs and behaviors affect an individual's life, Freeman, Freeman, and Garety (2008) suggest six self-help steps. Each step is accompanied by a number of self-help exercises that walk the individual through the process. The first step is to track the suspicious thoughts week by week, similar to how individuals with mood disorders are encouraged to keep a chart to track fluctuations in mood. Each day, the individual writes down the suspicious thoughts that are most troubling and then rates each one on the basis of how strong it is, how distressing it is, and how often the thought occurs. The second step involves evaluating the effect that the suspicious thoughts have, to understand them better and what factors drive the thoughts. Keeping a diary or a journal can help in sorting out the thoughts and reflecting on their effects. The third step involves reality testing and asks the individual to review and assess the evidence, if any, that exists to support the paranoid thoughts. This reality-testing step also helps the individual step back and gain perspective about the thoughts. Once the evidence has been assessed, the next step is to test the suspicious thoughts to see if the evidence holds up. This step helps determine whether the individual really is in danger or whether he or she has reached the wrong conclusion about what is going on, that is, the thoughts represent distortions of reality. The fifth step in this self-help model is to move forward and deal with the suspicious thoughts as they occur by continuing to follow the first four steps to avoid getting back into the suspicious frame of mind. Strategies for doing this include not fighting suspicious thoughts when they occur, learning how to let the thoughts go; employing supportive techniques like encouraging self-talk phrases and thoughts that are empowering; and maintaining focus on what is actually going on in the current situation to distance oneself from the thoughts so that they dissipate. Finally, the sixth step involves dealing with and getting control over chronic worrying. The key strategy for overcoming chronic worrying is writing the worries down on paper and determining the "worst-case scenario consequences" of the worry, which enhances empowerment and decreases the power of the worry. Self-help is not a substitute for clinical care, but it can be an important adjunct to maintaining wellness and recovery.

Assess your comprehension of the *treatment of paranoid symptoms and conditions* by completing this quiz.

CONCLUSION

This chapter has addressed social work practice with individuals with paranoid symptoms, and paranoid conditions and disorders. It has emphasized the point that paranoid thinking patterns are ubiquitous across individuals and groups in our society and are not confined to psychiatric disorders but, rather, are more widely seen in varying degrees. We can all relate to certain elements of the experience of being paranoid and all of us have experienced aspects of paranoid symptoms to a minor degree, and recognizing this can serve to improve our understanding of the clients we serve and can enhance our empathy for the suffering of those who experience paranoid thinking patterns and behavior in more severe forms.

Appreciating the role of culture, race, ethnicity, socioeconomic status, and age is critical for a culturally competent understanding of paranoia. Paranoid symptoms are best viewed on a continuum with milder forms of mistrust often emanating from cultural issues, while more severe forms are more likely to stem from psychopathology. As seen in the case examples in this chapter, both can coexist in an individual, and thus, providing appropriate interventions depends on competent differential diagnosis.

Although paranoid individuals are often reluctant to seek treatment and may be forced into clinical care by others, the good news is that we do have intervention approaches that can be effective in mitigating symptoms and facilitating recovery. Cognitive-behavioral therapies and self-help approaches based on CBT principles can be very helpful for many individuals with paranoid symptoms. For those people with more severe paranoid disorders, psychosocial treatment may be combined with antipsychotic medication and more structured treatment, such as inpatient care. The chapter also addressed in detail the clinical strategies for effectively engaging paranoid clients, which are slightly different from the usual recommended engagement strategies.

Read *"Engagement, Assessment, and Intervention with Violent/Aggressive Clients and Practitioner Safety"* for more information on guidelines for violence risk assessment and safety in both office and community settings.

Kraepelin (1921) maintained that true classical paranoia was incurable. Current psychiatric thinking has moved beyond that conclusion, and studies have shown that many paranoid people are able to adjust fairly well in society, achieve meaningful recovery, and live productive lives in spite of their symptoms. Taking an ecological life model approach, which bypasses directly focusing on the psychopathology and, instead, focuses on strengths and environmental manipulation, can be helpful for some paranoid clients. Although most individuals with paranoid symptoms can be helped to learn how to achieve recovery, even in the face of continuing symptoms, others unfortunately never come to clinical attention or refuse treatment and end up living lives of fear, mistrust, and social isolation.

Assess your application and analysis of this chapter's contents by completing the *Chapter Review*.

Chapter 12

Social Work Practice with Individuals with Major Mood Disorders and their Families, and Suicide Assessment

INTRODUCTION: THE TYPES AND SYMPTOMS OF THE VARIOUS DISORDERS OF MOOD

This chapter addresses social work practice with individuals with serious mood disorders, specifically focusing on the various forms of depression and bipolar disorder, practice with the ill person's family and, finally, understanding and assessing suicide risk.

The two primary mood states in the various types of mood disorders are various forms of elevated mood and depressed mood. Bipolar disorder, formerly termed "manic depression," causes dramatic mood swings from overly high and/or irritable, to sad and hopeless, and then back again to an elevated mood, often with periods of normal mood in between. Extreme changes in energy and behavior go along with these changes in mood. The periods of highs and lows are called *episodes* of mania or hypomania and *episodes* of depression. Such abnormal moods, however, may or may not affect the individual's ability to function socially or occupationally, and thus, many individuals who might meet criteria for a mood disorder never end up receiving treatment or receive it after having lived with their disorder for a while.

The DSM System of Diagnosing Mood Disorders

To understand the rather complicated DSM criteria for the various mood syndromes and disorders, some definitions are in order. A manic episode is diagnosed if an elevated mood occurs with three or more of the other symptoms most of the day, nearly every day, for one week or longer (APA, 2013). If the mood is irritable, rather than elevated, then four additional symptoms must be present.

The signs and symptoms of mania (or a manic episode) include increased energy, activity, and restlessness; an excessively "high," overly good, euphoric mood; extreme irritability; racing thoughts evidenced by talking very fast and jumping from one idea to another; distractibility in which the individual has difficulty focusing attention and concentrating; a lessened need for sleep; unrealistic beliefs in one's abilities and powers; poor judgment; spending sprees or other reckless use of money or other assets; a lasting period of behavior that is different from usual; increased sexual drive and impulsive reckless sexual behavior; abuse of drugs, particularly cocaine, alcohol, and sleeping medications; provocative, intrusive, or aggressive behavior; and, finally, denial that anything is wrong—with irritability if someone suggests it.

A mild to moderate level of mania is called *hypomania*. Hypomania may feel good to the person who experiences it, and may even be associated with good functioning and enhanced productivity, and, thus many times people with it may not want to change it and refuse treatment that could stabilize the hypomanic mood. Thus even when family and friends learn to recognize the mood swings as possible bipolar disorder, the person may deny that anything is wrong. Part of that may be the presence of *anosognosia*, or lack of insight (see Chapter 4 for detail), but part may be simply not wanting to lose the high mood. Daniel, a car salesman, describes it this way:

> For a long time, I didn't want treatment even though I knew my moods weren't exactly normal. When I was hypomanic, boy did I sell cars! I would be Salesman-of-the-Month two, three months running, with the big bonuses that went with that. I felt great, didn't get into trouble because I never was manic and I didn't want that feeling to end. What got me to accept treatment, though, were the episodes of bad depression. I have bipolar II disorder. So, in order to get rid of the depression, I had to give up the hypomania. I know this may sound weird, but I miss being hypomanic—it's better than being high on cocaine.

Without proper treatment, however, hypomania can evolve into severe mania in some people or can switch into major depression. In bipolar I disorder, the individual has to have had at least one manic or mixed episode (a mixed episode is characterized by symptoms that meet criteria for both a manic episode and for a major depressive episode nearly every day for a week), usually accompanied by episodes of major depression. In bipolar II disorder, the individual has at least one episode of hypomania and at least one episode of major depression but no manic episodes. Finally, in cyclothymic disorder, the individual has fluctuating moods between hypomania and depression, but no episodes of mania or major depression.

An episode of major depression is diagnosed if five or more of the symptoms in the DSM criteria for major depression are present and last most of the day, nearly every day, for a period of 2 weeks or longer. People with depressive illnesses do not all experience the same symptoms. The type, number, severity, frequency, and duration of symptoms vary across individuals depending on the particular depressive illness they have and differences related to gender, age, culture, and other factors. In general, symptoms of depression include a persistent sad or anxious mood accompanied by feelings of emptiness, hopelessness, or pessimism; guilt, worthlessness, or helplessness; difficulty concentrating, remembering details, and making decisions; loss of interest in activities or hobbies once pleasurable, including sex; and fatigue and decreased energy. Depression is also characterized by "vegetative symptoms," which classically include persistent insomnia, early-morning wakefulness, worsened mood in the morning, decreased libido, and decreased appetite with weight loss (Turnbull, 1986). More recently, it has been recognized that many individuals with depression have *reverse* vegetative symptoms, in which they sleep excessively and overeat with weight gain. Other symptoms some people evidence with depression include aches or pains, headaches, cramps, or digestive problems that do not ease even with treatment, along with irritability and restlessness. Finally, people with depression are at elevated risk for experiencing suicidal thoughts or suicide attempts.

To make things even more complicated, and challenging in terms of the assessment and treatment of mood disorders, severe episodes of mania or depression sometimes include symptoms of psychosis. Such psychotic symptoms may include hallucinations and delusions, but not the negative symptoms that are seen in schizophrenia. Absence of negative symptoms is one of the primary characteristics distinguishing schizophrenia from mania or psychotic depression. Also, the psychotic symptoms seen in bipolar disorder tend to reflect the extreme mood state at the time. For example, delusions of grandiosity, such as believing one is the president or has special powers or wealth, may occur during mania;

while delusions of guilt or worthlessness, such as believing that one is ruined and penniless or has committed some terrible crime may appear during an episode of major depression. Such symptoms are described as *mood-congruent*, meaning that the content is consistent with the nature of the individual's current mood state, that is, elevated or depressed.

It is these psychotic symptoms that can cause people with bipolar disorder to be misdiagnosed as having schizophrenia, or vice versa, particularly in settings where accurate diagnosis can be difficult, such as the emergency room (McElroy, Keck, & Strakowski, 1996). Recall the case of Velma in Chapter 7, who was diagnosed with schizophrenia in the emergency room, but later her diagnosis was changed to bipolar disorder once she was in the hospital and observed over time. Clients who are members of racial/ethnic minority groups are particularly at risk for being misdiagnosed (Ali, 2004). To help counter this, it can be useful to think of the various mood states as existing on a *spectrum* or continuous range. At one end is severe depression, above which is moderate depression and then mild low mood, which many people call "the blues" when it is short-lived, but is termed "dysthymia" when it is chronic. Then there is normal or balanced mood, above which comes hypomania (ranging from mild to moderate), and then severe mania. At either end of the continuum, psychotic symptoms may occur. In some people, however, symptoms of mania and depression may occur together in what is called a mixed bipolar state. An individual may have a very sad, hopeless mood, while at the same time feeling extremely energized or irritable. Evidence of the existence of bipolar disorder may also be exhibited through problems that don't seem to be indicative of mental illness to the person's family or friends. Examples include alcohol or drug abuse, poor school or work performance, or strained interpersonal relationships.

Clinical Assessment of Mood Disorders

The accurate diagnosis of a mood disorder requires a good clinical assessment addressing the following clinical questions:

- Does the client have a history of . . .
  - financial difficulties or failed business investments?
  - increased sexual activity, reckless indiscreet sexual behavior, and/or engaging in unsafe sex?
  - any previous episodes of depression, hypomania, or mania?
  - rapid switches in mood?
  - substance abuse?
  - medical illness?
  - suicide ideation, threats, or attempts?
- What is the client's current mood or emotional state?
- Does the client express feelings of guilt, poor self-esteem, worthlessness, or hopelessness?
- Does the client *currently* evidence . . .
  - hallucinations or delusions?
  - suicidal ideation, threats, or behavior?
  - change in level of energy or fatigue?
  - change in pattern of sleep or eating?

Quick screening tools

Simple mnemonics have also been developed for use by primary care and emergency room clinicians to quickly screen for the presence of a mood disorder in response to studies showing that 25 to 30 percent of patients presenting to primary care physicians have psychiatric disorders and 30 to 80 percent of these go undetected (see, e.g., Schulberg & Burns,

1988). For example, a screen for depression originally developed by Dr. Carey Gross for the psychiatry residents at Massachusetts General Hospital (Carlat, 1998) uses a mnemonic that refers to a prescription a clinician might write for a depressed, anergic patient, that is, SIG: Energy CAPSules—SIG:ECAPS. Each letter refers to one of the major diagnostic criteria for major depressive disorder as follows (Carlat, 1998):

- S - Sleep increase or decrease
- I - Decrease in interest or pleasure in activities once enjoyed
- G - Feelings of guilt, worthlessness, or helplessness
- : - Decreased colonic activity—constipation
- E - Decreased energy, a feeling of fatigue or of being "slowed down"
- C - Concentration lapse, difficulty remembering and making decisions
- A - Appetite loss with weight loss
- P - Psychomotor retardation
- S - Suicide risk—thoughts of death or suicide, or suicide attempts

Another screening mnemonic for the hallmark symptoms of a manic episode is "DIG-FAST" (Carlat, 1998):

- D - Distractibility
- I - Indiscretion (reflecting the DSM-IV-TR's criterion of "excessive involvement in pleasurable activities that have high potential for painful consequences")
- G - Grandiosity
- F - Flight of ideas
- A - Activity increase
- S - Sleep deficit (reflecting the DSM-IV-TR's criterion of decreased need for sleep)
- T - Talkativeness (reflecting the DSM-IV-TR's criterion of pressured speech)

Let's now take a closer look at depression.

DEPRESSION

The most common subtype of mood disorder is depression. There are many types or forms of depression, some triggered by life events while others may seem to evolve independent of what is going on in the individual's life. Most depression, however, occurs in response to a combination of factors related to biology, environment, and psychological issues. Let's begin with the case of Debbie, who eloquently describes her decades-long experience with depression and how it evolved over the course of her life.

Debbie: A Self-Reflection of the Evolution of Depression

I am 60 years old now, am married with two grown children, and work as a registered nurse in a public urban trauma center. As I look back on my life, depression has been a part of it from the time I was a teenager. I had a very happy childhood, though. We lived in a small town in a neighborhood that was full of stay-at-home mothers and plenty of children. On days when we didn't have school, our mothers would shoo us out of the house after breakfast and we would run around the neighborhood all morning until our mothers called us in for lunch. Then we'd go back out to play until we were called in for dinner. There were no video games or scheduled playdates or even much that was of interest for children on TV. Life as a child then was a life of exploration of the outdoors, playing with other children and figuring out our own games and entertainment. Our parents didn't hover like parents do today and that was fine with us! I remember I always had lots of pets—kittens, a puppy, bunnies in a bunny hutch, turtles, frogs, you name it. I would spend hours in the woods behind our house collecting garter snakes in a jar, then I would count up how many I had collected and then I'd let them all go in the woods. The only thing I remember from that time that was indicative of the depression to come was that I told my mother many times that I liked animals better than people "because animals don't hurt your feelings." I was a sensitive child and my feelings were easily hurt if another child said something I thought was mean. But I was never lonely, I had enough friends and also enjoyed playing alone.

Things began to change when I reached adolescence, however. Around the time I turned 15, I began to have feelings of sadness—not really sadness exactly, but feelings of worthlessness. I began to feel that although I was a good person on the outside, I was a bad person on the inside and I began to fear that I would be "found out" if I wasn't careful. Nobody talked about "depression" then and it was just assumed that all teenagers were moody and that was that. I hated high school, I was bored and, as a teenager, tired of our small town. I couldn't wait to get out and go to college out of state. However, although I got into a good school and was doing well academically and socially, I began to feel more depressed and there were days I just couldn't shake it. I thought of going to the university's counseling center but this was the early 1970s, and the counseling center had its hands full with drug problems and other issues related to the social upheaval of the times. I thought my bouts of sadness were puny by comparison, so I just soldiered on, having good days and bad days, but it was like the spectre of depression was always hanging over me.

After college, I worked at a Planned Parenthood clinic in a poor neighborhood and discovered that I liked providing care for women in a health care setting, so a year later, I enrolled in nursing school. Then the depression really hit, and this time I went to the university counseling center and had my first appointment with a psychiatrist. She was a psychoanalyst and did psychoanalytically oriented psychotherapy. We delved into my childhood—but, as I said, I was happy as a child so there wasn't much to "mine" there in terms of understanding my current depression. The issue of medication never came up and although I liked my psychiatrist very much, we just didn't get anywhere, although I felt a little less depressed because she was supportive and it was good to have an empathic ear. After graduating with my BSN and getting my license as an RN, I found what I thought was my "dream job" working as a nurse in a trauma center. The problem with that job, however, was that I had to do "swing shift," working graveyard shift for a few days, then the day shift, then evenings, and then back to graveyard. This constantly changing schedule began to affect my sleep patterns and that, I think, was the tipping point for my depression.

One week, I suddenly couldn't sleep—I mean at all—I was awake for 24 hours three nights in a row and became more and more anxious and depressed. I went to my family doctor and he prescribed a sleeping pill, Halcion (triazolam). I got sleep with the Halcion, but my depression got worse and for the first time, I began to have thoughts of suicide. Then one day, when I was at work in the trauma center, I came across a bottle of Tofranil (imipramine) that a patient had discarded. I knew that Tofranil was an antidepressant, and I was desperate, so I took the bottle home, looked it up in my copy of the *PDR (Physician's Desk Reference)* and learned what dose to start taking, and I began dosing myself. Why didn't I seek psychiatric help? I guess I was ashamed—ashamed of the stigma of being depressed and so I thought I would first see if antidepressants worked for me. It was one thing to seek help as a student, it is another to risk having your employer find out somehow that you have a mental illness. Well, the Tofranil turned out to be helpful—not only did it help me to sleep, but my anxiety dissipated and my mood began to lift for the first time in years. At that point, I contacted a psychiatrist privately and, after an evaluation, he agreed that I should stay on the Tofranil plus begin reality-oriented problem-solving psychotherapy. He was extremely helpful, as was the medication, and I have been taking imipramine now regularly for the past 35 years.

After I had been on my medication for about 10 years, I tried to go off it because the side effects are annoying, but the depression came back, including suicidal feelings, insomnia, loss of appetite, and agitation, so I had to go back on the medication. Later, my psychiatrist suggested switching me to an SSRI, since the side effects of imipramine, in particular the dry mouth, was

(continued)

and is annoying, but I hated the Prozac he put me on—it made me so restless I felt like I would jump out of my skin. My psychiatrist explained that imipramine is most helpful in treating "agitated depressions" like mine, while SSRIs usually work best for "sedated depression," in which people sleep too much and have low energy.

I may have to take medication for the rest of my life, and I hate the side effects but I look at it this way—dry mouth is better than being depressed. I think that, today, the stigma associated with depression has lifted, and people today know more about depression, that it is treatable and that there is hope. That is a good thing. Depression has been called the "common cold of mental illness" but it is much more serious than a cold. I consider myself extraordinarily lucky in that I got treatment and it worked. Depression is very treatable but, unfortunately, many don't know this and continue to suffer needlessly.

WHAT DEPRESSION IS AND HOW IT IS TREATED

Everybody has days when they feel sad or blue, and such "down in the dumps" moods usually pass within a day or so. That is not clinical depression. True clinical depression is much more than the blues. Depression interferes with one's daily life and ability to function and causes significant pain and distress not only for the person with depression, but also for his or her friends and family members (Coiro, Riley, Broitman, & Miranda, 2012). Depression, as Debbie noted above, is often described as the "common cold of mental illness," meaning that it is a common affliction, but it also is a serious though highly treatable illness. Many people with depression never seek treatment or, like Debbie, suffer for years before getting treatment that works. The good news is that the majority of individuals who meet criteria for a depressive disorder, even the most severe depression, can be helped with treatment. For some individuals, specific psychotherapies designed to treat depression prove sufficient to relieve their symptoms. For other people with depression, medication alone is helpful, and for many the combination of medication and psychotherapy works best. In Debbie's case, psychoanalytically oriented psychotherapy alone was not sufficient to adequately treat her depression. Medication was an essential component for Debbie's recovery, with intermittent problem-solving psychotherapy providing additional help. For most of her life, however, Debbie has only needed antidepressant medication to keep her symptoms under control.

Signs and Symptoms of Depression

There are many signs and symptoms of depression, and people with the various forms of depression do not all experience the same symptoms. In addition, the severity, frequency, and duration of symptoms vary depending on the individual and his or her particular illness. To recap, the symptoms of depression include the following (NIMH, n.d.):

- Persistent sad, anxious, or "empty" feelings
- Feelings of hopelessness or pessimism
- Feelings of guilt, worthlessness, or helplessness
- Irritability, restlessness
- Loss of interest in activities or hobbies once pleasurable, including sex
- Fatigue and decreased energy
- Difficulty concentrating, remembering details, and making decisions
- Insomnia, early-morning wakefulness, or excessive sleeping
- Overeating, or appetite loss
- Thoughts of suicide, suicide attempts
- Aches or pains, headaches, cramps, or digestive problems that do not ease even with treatment

Types or Forms of Depression

Debbie experienced many of the symptoms of depression described above during her long history of depression and was diagnosed with two different forms of depression: *recurrent major depressive disorder* and *dysthymic disorder*, which has been renamed *persistent depressive disorder* in the *DSM-5*. Major depressive disorder (MDD) is characterized by a combination of symptoms that interfere with an individual's ability to work, sleep, study, eat, and enjoy once-pleasurable activities. Major depression can be highly disabling and prevents a person from functioning normally. Some people may experience only a single episode within their lifetime, but more often, like Debbie, a person may have multiple episodes. Some people develop MDD *with psychotic features*. Major depression with psychotic features occurs when a person has severe depression plus some form of psychosis, such as experiencing delusions or hallucinations. An example would be the delusion that one's internal organs are being eaten away by worms.

The trigger for Debbie's first episode of major depression was her erratic work schedule, which threw her sleep pattern off kilter, resulting in her depression shifting from the chronic symptoms she had lived with for years to an episode of major depression. Her second episode occurred when she tried to go off her medication; her symptoms returned and she had to go back to taking the antidepressant. Debbie also met criteria for persistent depressive disorder (dysthymic disorder at the time it was diagnosed), which is the disorder that first appeared when she was an adolescent. Persistent depressive disorder is characterized by long-term (2 years or longer) symptoms that may not be severe enough to disable a person but can prevent normal functioning or feeling well. People with persistent depressive disorder may also experience one or more episodes of major depression during their lifetimes, as was the case for Debbie.

What may be called *minor depression* is characterized by having symptoms of depression for 2 weeks or longer that are more severe than "the blues" but the symptom picture does not meet full criteria for major depression or persistent depressive disorder. Without treatment, however, people with minor depression are at high risk for developing persistent depressive disorder or major depressive disorder. Some forms of depression, which may be mild to severe, develop under unique circumstances. These include *postpartum depression* and *seasonal affective disorder (SAD)*.

Postpartum depression

Postpartum depression is much more serious than the "baby blues" that many women experience after giving birth, when hormonal and physical changes and the new responsibility of caring for a newborn can be overwhelming. It is estimated that 10 to 15 percent of women experience postpartum depression after giving birth (Altshuler, Hendrich, & Cohen, 1998). A small group of women who experience postpartum depression also develop psychotic symptoms, and this serious condition is called *postpartum psychosis* (Doucet, Letourneau, & Blackmore, 2012) with a significant proportion of such women meeting criteria for bipolar disorder (Munk-Olsen, Laursen, Meltzer-Brody, et al., 2012). Postpartum depression and depression during pregnancy can have serious negative consequences to the mother, such as insufficient maternal weight gain, underutilization of health care, preeclampsia, smoking, and substance use (Wisner et al., 2010). This is compounded by a number of potential negative consequences for the developing infant, including lower birth weight, premature birth, increased infant irritability and crying, and other adverse cognitive and emotional outcomes (Wisner et al., 2010).

Unfortunately, due to lack of awareness, poor screening procedures, and stigma, many women suffering from postpartum depression do not receive the treatment they need. For example, Chaudron, Kitzman, Peifer, et al. (2005) found that as many as half of women with postpartum depression go undetected by health care providers and, furthermore, most women with postpartum depression do not recognize they have it and attribute other reasons for what they are experiencing. Screening for postpartum depression could easily be improved given that it occurs following a definable event, that is, childbirth, and the risk factors for developing postpartum depression are well established. These risk factors include having low income, being a member of a racial/ethnic minority group, and having previous experiences with depression, poor or negative social support, and multiple chronic life stresses (Grote, Bledsoe, Larkin, & Brown, 2007; Wisner et al., 2010).

Seasonal affective disorder

Another form of depression that has received increasing clinical and public attention is *seasonal affective disorder* (Rabin, 2011; Rohan, Lindsey, Roecklein, & Lacy, 2004). Seasonal affective disorder (SAD) is characterized by the onset of depression during the winter months, when there is less natural sunlight, shorter daylight hours, and drearier weather. Such depression generally lifts during spring and summer when the days get longer and provide more sunlight. SAD may be effectively treated with bright-light therapy, but nearly half of those with SAD do not get better with light therapy alone. Antidepressant medication and psychotherapy can reduce SAD symptoms, either alone or in combination with light therapy (Rohan, Lindsey, Roecklein, & Lacy, 2004).

Light therapy or bright-light therapy involves daily exposure to intensive (10,000 lux of light intensity) artificial light for 30–45 minutes per session. During the session, the person sits directly facing the light box that emits the prescribed level of light. Such boxes are usually square shaped with the bright light emanating from the flat surface of the box. There have been few well-controlled studies of the effectiveness of light therapy in the treatment of depression; however, one well-designed study (Lam, Levitt, Levitan, et al., 2006) that compared the effectiveness of bright-light therapy with the antidepressant fluoxetine (Prozac) demonstrated that bright-light therapy is equally effective as fluoxetine in treating the symptoms of SAD. The Internet websites of the Society for Light Treatment and Biological Rhythms at www.sltbr.org and Center for Environmental Therapeutics at www.cet.org provide detailed information about bright-light treatment for seasonal affective disorder.

Other Conditions That Often Coexist with Depression

It is common for depression to coexist with symptoms of anxiety and anxiety disorders, such as post-traumatic stress disorder (PTSD), obsessive-compulsive disorder, panic disorder, social phobia, and generalized anxiety disorder (Devane, Chiao, Franklin, & Kruep, 2005; Regier, Rae, Narrow, Kaebler, & Schatzberg, 1998). PTSD can, although not always, occur after an individual experiences an event that is terrifying and threatening to their well-being and safety, such as a violent physical or sexual assault, a natural disaster, a serious accident, or military combat (APA, 2000). People who develop PTSD are at high risk for having coexisting depression. For example, one study of 18,305 U.S. Army combat veterans reported prevalence rates of PTSD and depression after returning from combat that ranged from 9 to 31 percent, depending on the level of reported functional impairment (Thomas, Wilk, Riviere, et al., 2010).

Recent work by Omalu, Hammers, Bailes, et al. (2011) suggests that PTSD may be more than a psychological anxiety disorder, having a physical component to it as well. The epidemic of suicides and other problems experienced by Iraq and Afghanistan war veterans, in particular, may be caused by chronic traumatic encephalopathy (CTE), a degenerative brain condition that has been well documented in boxers, football players, and other individuals who have experienced repeated blows to the head (McKee, Stein, Nowinski, et al., 2012). Unlike Vietnam veterans or veterans from earlier wars, Iraq and Afghanistan veterans are more likely to have been exposed to blasts from explosive devices, resulting in shock waves that cause the brain to crash repeatedly into the skull. Helmets and other protective gear do not seem to prevent this. CTE results from such trauma and specifically affects the frontal and temporal lobes, areas of the brain that regulate impulse control, judgment, multitasking, memory, and emotions (Kristof, 2012). Individuals who develop CTE seem to be at higher risk for depression, PTSD, and suicide, although further study is needed (Omalu, Hammers, Bailes, et al., 2011).

Because of the growing recognition that comorbid depression and anxiety is more of an expectation than an exception, a new mood disorder category reflecting conditions in which depression coexists with anxiety (see www.dsm5.org) has been proposed, although the reliability of the proposed criteria requires further study. For this new mixed anxiety/depression syndrome, the individual must exhibit at least three of the symptoms of major depression, which must include depressed mood and/or anhedonia, simultaneously with symptoms of "anxiety distress," defined as having two or more of the following symptoms: irrational worry, preoccupation with unpleasant worries, having trouble relaxing, motor tension, and/or fear that something awful may happen. This change reflects current research demonstrating that many, if not most, individuals meeting criteria for a depressive disorder also exhibit anxiety distress (Leckman, Weissman, Merikangas, et al., 1983). In addition, comorbidity with anxiety is associated with longer episodes of depression (see, e.g., Fava, Alpert, Carmin, et al., 2004) and a higher risk for suicide (see, e.g., Boden, Fergusson, & Horwood, 2007). Example:

> Sheila, 37 years old, was first diagnosed with dysthymia at age 21. A year later, she had her first panic attack and, over time, developed severe agoraphobia. The agoraphobia worsened to the point where Sheila could not leave her home. As a result, she was unable to work or take care of any of her two children's outside activities. This created significant marital stress and eventually Sheila's husband told her he was considering filing for divorce and taking the children with him. The idea of being completely alone sent Sheila into a spiral of panic and, for the first time, she considered suicide. However, thinking of her children's welfare, Sheila called the local crisis service and asked for help. Initially, Sheila's social work therapist had to make a series of home visits and eventually was able to coax Sheila to come to the clinic to see the psychiatrist. A combination of treatment with paroxetine (Paxil) and cognitive-behavioral therapy (CBT) enabled Sheila to achieve recovery. Sheila's CBT treatment involved psychoeducation to teach her about agoraphobia, panic attacks, and depression and how to manage her symptoms through avoiding panic triggers and learning relaxation techniques. Sheila also benefitted from behavioral techniques, such as desensitization, that helped her face the places and situations that caused anxiety and fear. Sheila's husband also participated in the psychoeducation sessions to help him understand her illnesses and treatment, along with couples therapy, and their marriage survived, strengthened, and remained intact.

Depression also commonly occurs with various serious medical illnesses such as heart disease, diabetes, stroke, traumatic brain injury, cancer, HIV/AIDS, and Parkinson's disease. Individuals who have a serious medical illness plus depression tend to have more severe symptoms of both their depression and the medical illness, more difficulty adapting to and managing their medical illness(es), and higher medical costs than those who do not have coexisting depression (Cassano & Fava, 2002). Because treating the depression can also help improve the outcome of treating the coexisting medical illness, it is critical that primary care doctors screen for depression among their medically ill patients, particularly those with chronic disabling illnesses.

Other New Depressive Conditions Introduced in DSM-5

The controversial diagnosis of *premenstrual dysphoric disorder (PDD)* has been moved from the *DSM-IV-TR*'s Appendix B, "Criteria Sets and Axes Provided for Further Study" into the "Depressive Disorders" section of *DSM-5* (APA, 2013). PDD is characterized by marked affective lability (mood swings, feeling suddenly sad or tearful, increased sensitivity to rejection), marked irritability, anger, depression and anxiety, and symptoms that result in significant impairment of functioning. Another new diagnosis introduced in the "Depressive Disorders" section of *DSM-5* is *disruptive mood dysregulation disorder*, included for children up to 18 years of age who exhibit persistent irritability and frequent episodes of extreme behavioral dyscontrol, and represents an attempt to address concerns about the overdiagnosis and overtreatment with medication of bipolar disorder in children and adolescents (APA, 2013; Egan, 2008).

Causes of Depression

The cause of depression probably lies in a combination of factors related to genetics, biology, environment, and psychology that differ from individual to individual. Most researchers and clinicians believe that, at its core, depression is a disorder of the brain, but theories about that are difficult to prove. Imbalances in the neurotransmitters believed to be responsible for emotions and mood are probably central to developing depression, but the evidence for this is murky. Brain-imaging technology, such as fMRI, shows that the brains of individuals suffering from depression look different from the brains of people without depression, particularly the parts of the brain believed to be responsible for regulating mood, thinking, sleep, appetite, and behavior; however, this doesn't tell us why the depression has occurred nor can such imaging technology help in the diagnosing of depression (NIMH, n.d.).

Family history also seems to play a role in depression. Some families are more "loaded" with family members who currently have or have a history of depression, or who have attempted or completed suicide. Such family histories probably reflect a combination of genetics and environmental factors, a kind of generational transmission of risk factors (Tsuang, Bar, Stone, & Faraone, 2004; Tsuang & Faraone, 1990). However, stressful life events can also play an important role in triggering depression, and some people with no known family history of depression develop a depressive disorder.

Gender Differences in the Experience and Expression of Depression

Depression is diagnosed more frequently, and probably does occur more commonly, among women than among men. This difference in incidence and prevalence is likely due to gender differences in biology, life cycle, hormonal effects, and psychosocial factors. Hormonal changes during pregnancy, the postpartum period, during the premenstrual phase of the menstrual cycle, and during menopause are times when risk for depression increases (Eskandari, Martinez, Torvik, et al., 2007; Hartlage, Freels, Gotman, & Yonkers, 2012). Although the cyclical rise and fall of estrogen and other hormones may affect a woman's risk for developing depression, it also must be recognized that many women face the additional stresses of work and home responsibilities, caring for children and aging parents, intimate partner abuse, poverty, and other relationship strains, all of which can impact mood (Grote, Bledsoe, Larkin, & Brown, 2007; Rubinow, Schmidt, & Roca, 1998). In other words, many women experience multiple-role strain plus acute and chronic stress (Hochschild & Machung, 2012). However, it remains unclear how and why some women faced with significant stresses and challenges develop depression, while others with similar challenges do not.

Although we believe that women are more likely to experience depression than men are, there are other factors that play a role in why men are less likely to be diagnosed with depression and less likely to receive treatment. One factor is that many men with depression don't seek help because of shame and stigma that is gender related, for example, the belief that it is not "manly" to feel sad and to need and seek help. Also, many men have been socialized to shut down their emotions and be "strong" and "in control" of emotions, especially emotions that might connote weakness. Even the very early socialization of boys in many cultures emphasizes that toughness is important, and sensitivity and feeling emotions is equated with weakness (Kindlon & Thompson, 2000). This results in boys and men not being able to identify depression when it occurs and, if depression is recognized, that seeking help should be avoided and, instead, one should just "man up" and "soldier on." Men also often experience and express depression differently than women. Although many men experience the symptoms of depression listed earlier in this chapter, the three most common symptoms that men, in particular, experience when depressed include pain, risk-taking, and anger.

Many men experience depression somatically as literal physical pain, including constant headaches, stomach problems, or pain that doesn't seem to be from other causes or that doesn't respond to regular medical treatments (Cochran & Rabinowitz, 2000; Pollack, 1998; Watts, 2008). Depressed men often start taking risks like engaging in extreme sports, driving recklessly, gambling, engaging in casual unsafe sexual activities, and abusing recreational and/or prescription drugs. Men are also more likely to express feelings of irritability and anger rather than sadness or crying. Such irritability can manifest as "road rage," being short-tempered, being overly sensitive to criticism, and lashing out at others under little or no provocation. Some men are violent and abusive when depressed, even toward those who care about them, which erodes important sources of social support. Other symptoms of depression commonly found in men include feeling guilty, worthless, or like a failure as a man; having no energy; having problems concentrating or getting things done,; feeling "flat," blank, and empty; and missing work or other commitments. The negative consequences of these symptoms, such as reprimands at work or marital problems, may serve to make the man's depression worse, and rather than receiving help, he may experience punishment. In response to such symptoms of depression, some men may turn to alcohol or drugs to feel better. Other men may become irritable, angry, and even aggressive or abusive. Finally, although more women attempt suicide, many more men than women die by suicide in the United States (Kochanek, Murphy, Anderson, & Scott, 2004).

Like with women who have depression, depression in men can be triggered by stressful life events. Common types of events that trigger depression in men include money problems, job problems including being fired from one's job, marital problems, questions about one's sexuality, military combat, and relationship losses (Watts, 2008). Men tend to not have large flexible networks of social support, as many women do, and so loss of just one friend or colleague may carry a lot of weight emotionally. Also, many men don't have others in their social support network to whom they can turn to outside of family for emotional support and help. For example, Ted talks about his experience with depression:

> I first got depressed after my wife left me for another man. My wife was the only one I really talked to about things that mattered, you know, feelings, things that upset me and so on. With my buddies—and I have some good buddies—we'd talk about sports or politics or just do stuff together—go hunting or fishing or to a ballgame. I couldn't imagine going to one of them and saying I was depressed. No way. I'd have felt like an idiot. (Newhill, 1995)

Men who seek help for depression are likely to first go to their primary care doctor, and thus, it is critical for primary care physicians and nurses to know how to screen for

Newhill, C.E. (1995). A crisis casebook. (unpublished manuscript)

depression in men and how their symptoms differ from women's, particularly those evidencing risk factors for suicide (Shiels, Gabbay, & Dowrick, 2004; USPSTF, 2002).

Cultural Differences in the Experience and Expression of Depression

Depression can have very different meanings and consequences depending on the culture, and culture affects how depression is experienced, expressed, and communicated. How one views the "self" affects the experience of depression, and views of the self and how that relates to mood are impacted by the extent to which a culture is individualistic (Western) versus collectivist (Eastern). For example, in many Eastern cultural groups, the concept of self actually includes significant others, a concept known by various names, such as collateral, diffuse, or undifferentiated self. While the "undifferentiated self" is the norm in some Eastern cultures, Western culture and Western psychiatry often views this state as pathological, labeling it as "codependency" (Marsella, Sartorius, Jablensky, & Fenton, 1985).

Underdiagnosis or misdiagnosis can be avoided if the clinician is sensitive to ethnic and cultural differences in how depression is experienced and described. For example, in many cultures, depression is expressed largely in somatic, or physical, terms rather than complaints of sadness or feelings of worthlessness (Simon, von Korff, Piccinelli, et al., 1999). Depressed individuals of Latino and Mediterranean cultures may complain of "bad nerves" and headaches; in Chinese and other Asian cultures, depression is generally experienced as weakness, tiredness, or "imbalance"; problems of the "heart" depicts the depressive experience in Middle Eastern cultures, while the Hopi speak of being "heartbroken" (APA, 2000; Tseng, 2001). Such presentations combine features of the depressive, anxiety, and somatoform disorders (Tseng, 2001). There are also cultural differences with regard to which symptoms cause concern, and which are less likely to attract attention. In some cultures, for example, becoming sad and withdrawn is seen as a normal part of certain developmental transitions, while irritability and aggressiveness is viewed as problematic. Also, sadness is a normal human emotion and does not necessarily mean the person has depression (Horwitz & Wakefield, 2007). Some individuals may present at an emergency room or primary care physician's office with culturally distinctive experiences that may not indicate the presence of psychopathology, although they may be troubling to the individual and those around him or her. Examples include fear of being hexed or bewitched (see the case of "Mr. and Mrs. A", Chapter 11), feelings of "heat in the head" or crawling sensations of worms or ants, or dramatic experiences of being visited by deceased loved ones. Such experiences must be distinguished from actual psychotic symptoms, and input from friends or family can help distinguish whether the person's experiences fall within the norm for his or her culture (see Chapter 11 for more detailed discussion of cultural differential diagnosis).

Differences in cultural belief systems about mental health and illness

The way mental health, health, and illness are viewed is another important cultural difference. In the Western view of self as an object, health and mental health are often expressed in disease metaphors or analogies, whereas Eastern cultures view the self as a process considering the many levels of human functioning as one harmonious blend.

Among the causes of mental illness, Chinese Americans include organic disorders, supernatural intervention, genetic vulnerability or hereditary weakness, physical or emotional exhaustion caused by situational factors, metaphysical factors such as the imbalance between yin and yang, fatalism, and character weakness. Chinese Americans, Japanese Americans, and Filipino Americans also often believe that they can control their mental illness through willpower.

The type of care one seeks for what is called depression is also closely associated with cultural beliefs about mental health and illness. Some cultural groups seek folk healers and spiritual healers, or they look for help within their family community support systems.

Religious and spiritual beliefs

Although Western culture tends to view depressed mood and emotional pain from an illness perspective, other cultures perceive these same experiences within the context of religion. Some theorists view religious beliefs, among other cultural factors, as ways of providing a safe outlet for emotions. For example, some religions incorporate a belief in the existence of a soul. These groups tend to speak of loss in terms of loss of soul—often associated with death—which is described as feeling empty, dispirited or, often, depressed; other groups express loss as existential despair. Now, let's turn to discussing bipolar disorder, which involves episodes of depression but also episodes of mania or hypomania.

Assess your comprehension of the *causes, symptoms, and treatment of depression* by completing this quiz.

BIPOLAR DISORDER

One of the author's more memorable moments as a social worker was meeting a client who will be referred to as Rosie. The situation unfolded as follows:

Rosie

Rosie, a 25-year-old Italian American woman, was first diagnosed with manic depression when she was 18 years old. Rosie had a lengthy history of hospitalizations and poor adherence to taking her medication. One day, the police brought Rosie to the psychiatric emergency service (PES) for evaluation.

Since her last hospitalization 2 months prior, Rosie had refused to take her medication and, as a result, had decompensated. She was manic, not sleeping, running around her neighborhood barely clothed, taking large amounts of money out of the bank, planning to go to Las Vegas and "win big." Her family reported that she went down to the city park the night before, took her clothes off, and was running around nude. They believe that she was then sexually assaulted.

As the police were escorting Rosie to the interviewing room, she suddenly broke away from their grasp and ran into the women's bathroom, yelling, "You can't catch me!" I was in the hallway with the two police officers, both men, and the other three PES workers, who were also all men. One of the police officers turned to me and said, "Okay, you're the only woman here—you'll have to go get her."

I went into the women's bathroom calling, "Rosie? Rosie, it's Christina Newhill. We met a couple months ago—do you remember? I would like to talk to you—could you come out and talk with me?"

Rosie called out, "Ha, ha, you can't find me!" I looked under all the stalls but didn't see any feet.

"See, I'm hiding!" said Rosie. "Where do you think I could be?" I knocked lightly on each of the bathroom stall doors. When I knocked on the third one, it flew open and there was Rosie, with a large jar of Oil of Olay face cream.

"Holy cow, your skin looks *terrible*," Rosie exclaimed. "Here, I'll fix it!!" Upon which she scooped out a handful of pink face cream, reached over, and smeared it all over my face and then rubbed it in my hair. "This cream works as hair conditioner, too! There you go—you'll really see a difference!"

I grabbed Rosie's arm and led her out of the bathroom. When I emerged, the police officers and PES workers looked at me and then burst out laughing. After thanking me for getting Rosie out of the bathroom, it was suggested I just go home, wash up, and take the rest of the day off.

Rosie was subsequently hospitalized on an involuntary commitment by one of my PES colleagues after I left to go home. Before being taken to the psychiatric inpatient unit, Rosie was evaluated at the medical emergency room for the sexual assault reported by her family. The rape kit was positive and there were physical signs of assault. Rosie was discharged from our psychiatric hospital 3 weeks later, and she stopped by to see me. She apologized for the face cream incident and I told her it was okay, "and you know, Rosie, I do think my skin looked better afterwards." Rosie smiled.

Although I look back on this incident with some amusement, the impact of Rosie's illness on her life was far from amusing. Rosie had bipolar I disorder, and her particular form of bipolar disorder is what is called "rapid cycling," which can be challenging to treat. The *DSM* defines rapid cycling as the occurrence of four or more mood episodes (manic, depressive, mixed, or hypomanic) during the previous 12 months (APA, 2000). Another aspect to the difficulty in treating Rosie's symptoms was the fact that at that time, the only mood-stabilizing medication available was lithium, and some people, like Rosie, have difficulty in achieving and maintaining a stable blood level of the medication, which makes symptom reduction and stability difficult. In addition, we only had first-generation antipsychotic medications available for the treatment of psychotic symptoms in bipolar disorder, and those individuals with bipolar disorder who need antipsychotic medication usually fare better with the second-generation medications (Scherk, Pajonk, & Leucht, 2007; Wegmann, 2012). Rosie was a very bright and very likeable client, and when she was stable, she was able to work, live independently, and maintain positive interpersonal relationships but, too often, such stability did not last for very long and her life became a roller coaster of one episode of mania or depression after another.

Watch the video *"Speaking out: Ann: Bipolar disorder."* What is the experience of living with bipolar disorder?

Some of the Facts about Bipolar Disorder

Bipolar disorder, formerly known as manic-depressive illness, is a brain disorder that causes unusual and extreme shifts in a person's mood, energy, and ability to function. Different from the normal ups and downs that everyone goes through, the symptoms of bipolar disorder are severe and can result in impaired relationships with other people and poor or erratic job and school performance, and bipolar disorder carries a high risk for suicide. But there is good news—today, bipolar disorder can be effectively treated, and people with this illness can lead full and productive lives provided they receive the right treatment, receive it as early in the illness as possible, and learn how to manage their symptoms and achieve wellness and recovery (Kahn, Keck, Perlis, et al., 2004; Kahn, Ross, Printz, et al., 2000; NIMH, 2012).

More than 2 million American adults, or about 1.2 percent of the population age 18 and older in any given year, have bipolar disorder—about the same rate as for schizophrenia (Regier, Narrow, Rae, et al., 1993). Bipolar disorder most typically develops in late adolescence or early adulthood, however, some people have their first symptoms during childhood, and some even develop them late in life. It is not unusual for the onset of the disorder to not be recognized as an illness, and people may suffer for years before it is properly diagnosed and treated. Problems like substance abuse, reckless behavior, and poor school or work performance may be symptoms of an underlying mood disorder but not recognized as such until much later (NIMH, 2012). Like diabetes, high blood pressure, or heart disease, bipolar disorder is a serious long-term illness that must be carefully managed throughout a person's life to achieve recovery.

Causes of Bipolar Disorder

Like many other serious mental illnesses, there is no single cause for bipolar disorder, rather, it probably develops as a result of the interaction of multiple causal factors involving genetics, biology, and environment. Although bipolar disorder tends to run in families, suggesting a genetic component, studies of identical twins, who share all the same genes, indicate that both genes and other factors must play a causal role. This is because if one identical twin has the disorder, the other twin is at high risk but that risk isn't 100 percent (NIMH Genetics Workgroup, 1998). In addition, the genetic factors probably involve multiple genes acting together or in combination with environmental factors to cause bipolar disorder rather than the cause lying in a single gene (Hyman, 1999). Researchers are continuing to search for more specific information about the genetic causes for bipolar disorder to guide the development of better treatments for those living with the illness (NIMH, 2012).

One potentially fruitful area for investigation into the causes of bipolar disorder is using brain-imaging techniques to examine the living brains of individuals with the illness to determine what goes on in their brains that is different from the brains of people without the illness (Soares & Mann, 1997a; Soares & Mann, 1997b). Such brain-imaging technology allows researchers to take pictures of the living brain at work, to examine its structure and activity, without the need for surgery or other invasive procedures (NIMH, 2012). As researchers are more able to identify the specific differences in the brains of individuals with bipolar disorder as compared to the brains of healthy individuals, they will achieve a better understanding of the underlying causes of the illness and use such information to better understand how treatment works as well as predict which types of treatment will work most effectively for which individuals.

Symptoms of Bipolar Disorder

Let's go over the symptoms associated with bipolar disorder, and then some thoughts of those who live with the disorder will be presented. Bipolar disorder causes dramatic mood swings from overly euphoric and/or irritable, to sad and hopeless, and then back again, often with periods of normal mood in between. Extreme changes in energy and behavior go along with these changes in mood, having significant impact on the person's ability to function (Kahn et al., 2000; Kahn et al., 2004). These periods of highs and lows are called *episodes* of mania, hypomania, and depression. The signs and symptoms of mania (or a manic episode) include the following (APA, 2013):

- A distinct period of abnormally and persistently elevated, expansive, or irritable mood and abnormally and persistently increased activity or energy, lasting at least 1 week and present most of the day, nearly every day (or any duration if hospitalization is necessary).
- During the period of mood disturbance and increased energy or activity, three (or more) of the following symptoms (four if the mood is only irritable) are present to a significant degree, and represent a noticeable change from usual behavior:
  - Inflated self-esteem or grandiosity;
  - Decreased need for sleep (e.g., feels rested after only 2–3 hours of sleep);
  - More talkative than usual or feels pressure to keep talking;
  - Flight of ideas or subjective experience that thoughts are racing;
  - Distractibility (i.e., attention too easily drawn to unimportant or irrelevant external stimuli), as reported or observed;
  - Increase in goal-directed activity (either socially, at work or school, or sexually) or psychomotor agitation (i.e., purposeless, non-goal-directed activity);
  - Excessive involvement in activities that have a high potential for painful consequences (e.g., engaging in unrestrained buying sprees, sexual indiscretions, or foolish business investments).
- The mood disturbance is sufficiently severe to cause marked impairment in social or occupational functioning or to necessitate hospitalization to prevent harm to self or others, or there are psychotic features.
- The episode is not attributable to the direct physiological effects of a substance (e.g., a drug of abuse, a medication, or other treatment).

Returning to the case of Rosie, Rosie clearly met criteria for a manic episode at the time of my evaluation of her, even by today's proposed DSM-5 criteria. She had a distinct period of abnormally and persistently elevated mood along with increased activity or energy that her family reported had occurred consistently over the previous 2 weeks. She had decreased need for sleep, reported and showed evidence that her thoughts were racing, and had an increase in activity level. She also was involved in activities with a high potential for painful consequences, for example she took large amounts of money out of the bank with intent to gamble, she dressed provocatively and took her clothing off in public, which sometimes resulted in sexual assault, and she inappropriately smeared skin cream on the social worker's face and hair. Her symptoms prevented her from working and created great stress on her relationships with family members. Finally, there was no evidence that her symptoms could be attributable to substance use or abuse. Rosie was clearly experiencing a manic episode, distinctly different from her normal mode of functioning.

Watch the video *"Feliziano: Bipolar disorder."* What are the experience and the range of symptoms associated with bipolar disorder, including depression, self-harming behaviors, psychotic symptoms, and hypomania?

Consumer Perspectives on Bipolar Disorder

The voices of those living with bipolar disorder are important for social workers to hear, because what they have to say offers valuable insights into the various mood states associated with the illness and the impact of the illness on a person's life and those who love him or her. There have been a number of articles and books written by individuals living with bipolar disorder that describe how they experience the disorder and its impact on their lives and the lives of their families (see, e.g., Duke, 1988; Duke, 1992; Harvey, 2006; Jamison, 1995b; Jamison, 2009; Johnson & Johnson, 2012; Lewis, 2000; Yager, 2000). For example, clinical psychologist Kay Redfield Jamison, an international authority and researcher on mood disorders, has a unique insight into the world of mental illness, specifically bipolar disorder, because she has lived the experience herself. Currently a professor of psychiatry at Johns Hopkins University School of Medicine and co-director of the Johns Hopkins Mood Disorders Center, Dr. Jamison shocked her colleagues by going public with her own struggle with manic depression in a 1995 *Washington Post* article (Jamison, 1995a) and subsequent book, *An Unquiet Mind* (Jamison, 1995b). The book became a *New York Times* bestseller and was cited by several major publications as one of the best nonfiction books of 1995, and Dr. Jamison soon became a trusted spokesperson on behalf of the millions of people who live with one or more mood disorders, particularly bipolar disorder. She describes her experience living with manic depression this way:

> Manic-depression distorts moods and thoughts, incites dreadful behaviors, destroys the basis of rational thought, and too often erodes the desire and will to live. It is an illness that is biological in its origins, yet one that feels psychological in the experience of it; an illness that is unique in conferring advantage and pleasure, yet one that brings in its wake almost unendurable suffering and, not infrequently, suicide. I am fortunate that I have not died from my illness, fortunate in having received the best medical care available, and fortunate in having the friends, colleagues, and family that I do. Because of this, I have in turn tried, as best I could, to use my own experiences of the disease to inform my research, teaching, clinical practice, and advocacy work. (Jamison, 1995b, p. 6)

Because encountering clients who have depression is more common in their field placements or jobs than encountering clients who are manic, social work students often think they have a good sense of how it feels to be depressed, but are less certain about understanding the experience of mania or hypomania. As a result, social work students often ask their field instructors or professors: "What is it like to be manic?" Simply reviewing the DSM criteria doesn't adequately capture the real-life experience of living with bipolar disorder and, in particular, experiencing the symptoms of a manic episode.

Jamison, K.R. (1995b). An unquiet mind. New York: Knopf, p. 6.

Many years ago, during one of my first-year MSW classes, "Human Behavior: Mental Health," a student asked me what it is like to be manic. I answered her question as best I could, based on my practice experience, but knew that, lacking direct personal experience, my answer was somewhat limited in its ability to fully describe what mania is like. The next day, I found an anonymous note slipped under my office door from one of the students in the class where the question was asked. The letter read as follows:

> When I was seventeen, I was diagnosed with Bipolar I Disorder. Someone asked in class what was meant by "manic"—what would a description of mania sound like, beyond what is described in the DSM-IV. I thought I would give it a shot.
>
> Being manic is a lot like being buzzed—that feeling of having a bit too much alcohol and suddenly sitting on top of the world, except when you are manic, you don't need any alcohol whatsoever to feel this way. You are funny, intelligent, you can do anything. You are attractive, you find others very attractive. You feel generous—buy the next round, or a car, or a vacation trip for your family. Because you are on top of the world, you don't need to worry about money. Ideas just flow into your head, so quickly that it is hard to get them all out. But you must, because otherwise you feel like you are going to explode. Speech is often slurred, because of the inability of the tongue to keep up with the rapidity of ideas. You become boisterous, invincible. Nothing can stop you. You try to accomplish all the ideas you have had, but always another, better idea lures you away from what you were doing. Your body language changes—you become more flamboyant, use hand gestures more. Sometimes sexuality is stressed. But, always, everything is exaggerated. You stay awake until the ideas stop flowing, because you don't want to miss anything. This is sometimes for days. Being manic is a great feeling, mainly because you have no idea of what is really going on around you. You are so wrapped up in the feeling and the ideas that you miss your deadlines, your appointments, everything. And then when the feelings and ideas end, you are left with nothing.

These two consumers—one a mental health professional, one a social work student—describe well how the symptoms of bipolar disorder are experienced. Next, let's look at another personal account, by a social work professional, who describes how having bipolar disorder can impact one's life over time:

Living with Bipolar Disorder

I am a 45-year-old man diagnosed with bipolar II disorder. Living with this illness has been both a blessing and a curse. I have celebrated as many successes as I have failures. I have attained an undergraduate degree and four master's degrees, all from accredited and highly ranked universities. I have been employed by Fortune 500 companies and by an array of well-established organizations. I am a 32nd degree, Scottish Rite/Shrine Mason and have been an officer in eight parts of the fraternity. I sit on the boards of several charitable organizations and have a great deal of visibility in my community. I write and perform my own music. I have recorded over twenty music CDs and written three books. I have mastered twelve instruments. I have received a black belt in kung fu and proficiency in tai chi and yoga practices. I have had a string of beautiful women in my life and am surrounded by the most intelligent, creative, and supportive friends and family one could ever hope for. I have traveled to seventeen foreign countries and a large part of the United States. But there is the downside of my illness, the traumas and dramas of having bipolar II disorder.

I was academically suspended from my undergraduate program and only returned under a period of probation. I was threatened with suspension from three of my four master's programs for various reasons stemming from acts of impulsivity. I have been terminated from almost every

(continued)

Anonymous, 2003.

professional position I've held. I have forgone major responsibilities to benefit my music career and directed my life along the lines of my artistic needs. I have broken the law and been arrested (but never prosecuted), thus potentially jeopardizing my career. I have had more than thirty professional positions in my life. I have been involved in brutal fights and have been faced with guns and other weapons on several occasions. I have traveled as far away as Scotland to meet a girl and driven ten hours to see a concert and home the same night. I have had more than 280 failed sexual relationships. I have impregnated eleven women, resulting in eight abortions, two miscarriages, and one unplanned birth. I have been suicidal on several occasions, with a plan and the means to carry it out. I have been impulsive in many areas of my life and have suffered the consequences of rash decision-making. I am 45 and I do not own a home, a decent vehicle, or a bank account worth mentioning. Conversely, I do have twenty guitars, five keyboards, a drum set, and a storage locker full of all my collected belongings.

When I am hypomanic, there are a thousand thoughts rushing through my head at any given second and they all seem crucial. Every idea seems like a life altering opportunity and the energy that I have to accomplish these things is endless. I never get tired and I am aware of everything going on around me. The smallest gestures, sights, and sounds are so obvious and they all have hidden meaning that only I can pick up upon. The people around me all seem to move so slowly and with unnecessary caution. They don't understand my brilliant ideas nor do they agree with my methods of accomplishing the same. I get an incredible number of things done but rarely get anything completely done as I come up with a new and better idea before the previous one is finished. My sex drive goes through the roof and everyone seems to be attractive. My powers of coercion are finely tuned when I am hypomanic and I act on every impulse. All of this is the fun part. After the hypomania has been in effect for a few weeks, it becomes problematic. The repercussions of my impulsive acts start to haunt me. I become irritable and argumentative with everyone. Lights and various sounds bother me and my skin feels like it is crawling. I don't want to be touched and I definitely don't want to be told that I am hypomanic. I lose my appetite and I begin to fatigue but still can't manage to sleep or slow down my brain enough to relax. My heart races and I get phantom pains in my chest and extremities. Sometimes I become so uncomfortable that I want to die and unlike having depression, when I'm hypomanic I have the energy and the ability to plan it out.

When I'm depressed, I am just a mess. I still can't sleep but I lay in bed for most of the day, ruminating about my losses and fantasizing about the horrible things that have happened to me, replaying them in my mind over and over again. I don't always remember to eat and I hide from the world. I vacillate between preying on friends to tell me that things will get better and avoiding them and watching endless sad movies and listening to countless sad songs. My ideas are fewer but still good yet I lack the energy to carry any part of them out. If I'm lucky I can write some music, but it takes everything that I have to do it. I become so miserable that again I want to die but I don't have the energy to carry it out. Everything moves so slowly and I have no patience but plenty of apathy. Physically I am sick to my stomach and my body feels heavy and somehow alien. I have been medicated for the past sixteen years and have made considerable strides toward remission if not recovery. I am fortunate to have a therapist who specializes in bipolar disorder and who has gone the extra mile for me to the point of treating me pro bono when I lost my health insurance. Through my adventures, I have mourned the loss of friends and family, all victims of my bipolar II disorder. This illness has cost me dearly over the course of my life. It has been a constant struggle, dealing with this disease. I have been relatively stable for a few years now but I am constantly worried about subtly shifting back into a hypomanic or, even worse, a depressive episode despite my vigilance with regard to my medication regimen. I am always on guard for the slightest indications of either extreme. I have learned to question almost every thought that I have, especially when things don't seem to be going my way. I exist in a place where I often feel squashed creatively and sedated when I want to be feeling something more intensely. I also live in fear of those around me finding out that I suffer from this disorder, a fear of rejection and being judged for that which I cannot help.

I have, in the past, been running to stand still. I am grateful for the creativity and energy that my bipolar mind has afforded me but I curse it for the tragedies I have endured, both personally and professionally. I can remember a time before this thing took over, a much happier, more free time. Now I am relegated to a constant vigilance. This is my bipolar life.

by Eric Cohen

Eric Cohen

Treatments for Bipolar Disorder

Fortunately, bipolar disorder is a very treatable illness and most individuals with the disorder, even in its more severe forms, can achieve mood and symptom stability and recovery with appropriate treatment (Huxley, Parikh, & Baldessarini, 2000; Sachs, Printz, Kahn, et al., 2000; Sachs & Thase, 2000; White & Preston, 2009). As with schizophrenia, wellness and recovery are best achieved with bipolar disorder via a combination of mood-stabilizing medication, sometimes in combination with antipsychotic medication, various targeted psychosocial treatments, and support from family and friends. The Depression and Bipolar Support Alliance (DBSA), formerly called the National Depressive and Manic-Depressive Association, identifies a number of keys to recovery. First, the DBSA notes that most people can be effectively treated with appropriate medication. Second, guidance, education, and support from a mental health professional can help the individual with the disorder to deal positively with interpersonal relationships, maintain a healthy self-image, and ensure adherence to recommended treatments. Third, support and self-help groups can be an invaluable resource for learning coping skills, feeling acceptance, and coping with stigma. Finally, as with other severe and persistent mental illnesses, friends and family should also consider joining a support group (e.g., Depression & Bipolar Support Alliance [DBSA]: www.dbsalliance.org, the National Alliance on Mental Illness [NAMI]: www.nami.org, or Mental Health America (formerly the Mental Health Association) at www.mentalhealthamerica.net to help understand the illness and offer encouragement and support to their ill loved ones. Thus, an approach combining medication, psychosocial treatment, family support, and self-help is the best strategy for managing bipolar disorder over time (NIMH, 2012); furthermore, bipolar disorder is much better controlled if treatment is continuous rather than if it is on and off.

Role of the social worker

As with other severe and persistent mental illnesses, social workers play an important key role in helping the client with bipolar disorder manage the illness, achieve wellness, and move forward in the journey of recovery. Because you, as your client's social worker, will likely meet with the client and the client's family more frequently than other members of the treatment team, you may be in the best position to detect beginning mood changes or early signs of relapse, and you can teach the individual to detect such changes in him or herself. This is important, because early detection of signs of relapse may be able to prevent a full-blown episode via making adjustments to the treatment plan. Working closely with the individual, the family, and the treatment team in order to facilitate open communication about treatment concerns and options can make a huge difference in how effective the treatment is. In addition, relapse prevention strategies, such as keeping a chart of daily mood symptoms, medication effects and side effects, sleep patterns, and life events may help people with bipolar disorder and their families to understand the illness better. Such a chart can also help the doctor track and treat the symptoms of the illness more effectively with medications (see example of a Mood Chart below).

Medication Treatments

The two categories of medication primarily prescribed for treating the symptoms of bipolar disorder are mood stabilizers and antipsychotic medications, primarily second-generation antipsychotics. While primary care physicians who do not specialize in psychiatry may prescribe these medications, it is strongly recommended that people with bipolar disorder see a psychiatrist for treatment, because medication treatment can be very complicated in terming of monitoring therapeutic effects and managing side effects.

Several different types of mood stabilizers are available. In general, people with bipolar disorder continue treatment with mood stabilizers for extended periods of time and other medications, such as antipsychotics, antidepressants, and benzodiazepines, are added when necessary. As a cautionary note, antidepressants can trigger manic episodes and benzodiazepines have a high potential for addiction, therefore, close monitoring by the doctor and social worker is critical. Detailed information about all of these medications is provided in Chapter 8 on psychopharmacology.

Psychosocial Treatments for Bipolar Disorder

In addition to medication, psychosocial treatment for the ill person and for the family is a critical component to optimal outcomes for people with bipolar disorder. Multiple studies have shown that psychosocial interventions specifically targeted to treat bipolar disorder can lead to increased mood stability, fewer hospitalizations, and improved psychosocial functioning (Huxley, Parikh, & Baldessarini, 2000). Typically, the social worker or other counselor provides these therapies and works together with the psychiatrist and other members of the treatment team to monitor the client's overall progress. The number, frequency, and type of sessions are, of course, based on the treatment needs of the particular individual. Psychosocial interventions commonly used for bipolar disorder include cognitive-behavioral therapy, psychoeducation, and family therapy, along with somewhat newer approaches such as interpersonal therapy and social rhythm therapy (Frank, 2005). Researchers continue to study how these interventions compare to one another in combination with medication (see, e.g., Frank, Kupfer, Thase, et al., 2005).

How do these approaches differ? Similar to how cognitive-behavioral therapy is used with other disorders, CBT for bipolar disorder helps people learn to change inappropriate or negative thought patterns and behaviors associated with the illness specifically to ameliorate the symptoms produced by manic episodes and, especially, the depressive episodes (see, e.g., Basco & Rush, 1996). Similar to the approaches used with families with a loved one with schizophrenia, family-focused therapy for bipolar disorder includes family members in the treatment. Family-focused therapy helps to enhance family coping strategies, such as recognizing early symptoms of relapse and helping their loved one stay well. Such therapy also teaches families strategies to reduce the level of stress and distress within the family that may either contribute to or result from the ill person's symptoms. For example, families learn how to keep regular predictable schedules, which is essential to maintaining stability with bipolar disorder, and how to keep stress levels down and communication clear (Miklowitz, Richards, George, et al., 2003).

Psychoeducation for families and their relatives who have bipolar disorder

Similar to its use for individuals with schizophrenia (see Chapter 10 for a detailed discussion of psychoeducation intervention strategies), psychoeducation for bipolar disorder involves teaching clients about the illness and its treatment and how to recognize signs of relapse so that early intervention can be sought before a full-blown illness episode occurs (Miklowitz, George, Richards, et al., 2003; Smith, Jones, & Simpson, 2010). Psychoeducation is also very helpful for family members in terms of understanding the illness and how to help their loved one stay well.

In psychoeducation for bipolar disorder, as with schizophrenia, individuals and their families learn about the signs and symptoms of bipolar disorder, the types of episodes the individual experiences, and the types of treatments that are helpful and how they help. Understanding the vulnerability-stress model is important along with identifying specific stresses associated with relapse. For example, for many individuals with bipolar disorder, drug or alcohol abuse, poor sleep, or irregular daily routines are risk factors for relapse. Another important issue is encouraging and learning strategies for medication adherence.

The medications used to treat bipolar disorder are hard to take over the long term in large part because managing side effects can be difficult. Thus, it is important to strategize with clients about how to stick with their prescribed medication routine and how to deal with side effects by adjusting dosages and utilizing lifestyle changes. Keeping the family environment low key and low stress is also very important, which is very similar to recommendations made for families with a loved one with schizophrenia. Environments characterized by high levels of expressed emotion are associated with elevated relapse rates for many individuals with bipolar disorder. Thus, keeping expressed emotion low is helpful.

Another helpful strategy is conducting a "relapse prevention drill," which involves helping the client identify someone he or she can depend on and with that "help mate" talk about the early warning signs of relapse and identify who will contact the client's doctor or social worker. A period of wellness and stability is also a good time to develop an advanced directive (see Chapter 3 for details about what an advance directive consists of) that can provide protection against harmful consequences, particularly regarding manic or hypomanic episodes. Example:

> Toni, who has bipolar II disorder, has never had a manic episode but has had several hypomanic episodes along with episodes of major depression. When she is hypomanic, Toni will run up her credit cards to the maximum, and then it takes months to pay off the balances. During one of her well periods, Toni and her family developed an advance directive under the guidance of Toni's social worker that specifies that when Toni (who has learned to recognize early triggers for relapse) and/or her family notice beginning symptoms of hypomania, her sister Jody takes custody of Toni's credit cards and locks them up in her safety deposit box at the bank, to which Toni does not have access. The first time Jody had to take away Toni's credit cards, Toni became very angry. In response, Jody pulled out the advance directive, showed it to Toni and where her signature of agreement was on the document and, although Toni fumed about it for a while, it avoided a fight and Toni turned over her credit cards to her sister. (Newhill, 1995)

Interpersonal and social rhythm therapy

Interpersonal and social rhythm therapy (IPSRT), developed by psychologist Ellen Frank and colleagues at Western Psychiatric Institute and Clinic at the University of Pittsburgh, helps people with bipolar disorder to both improve interpersonal relationships and to regularize their daily routines as a treatment adjunct to pharmacotherapy (Frank, 2005; Frank, Kupfer, Thase, et al., 2005). The main idea is that keeping regular daily routines, a regular sleep schedule, and positive interpersonal relationships can help protect against relapse in terms of triggering manic episodes and episodes of depression (Frank, 2005).

IPSRT is a form of behavioral therapy coupled with interpersonal psychotherapy (IPT) that treats the disruption in circadian rhythms that is related to triggering episodes of mania, hypomania, and depression in bipolar disorder. IPSRT takes a biopsychosocial approach and argues that although adherence to an appropriate medication regime is essential to wellness for individuals with bipolar disorder, pharmacotherapy alone is not sufficient. Frank and colleagues' research (Frank, Kupfer, Thase, et al., 2005) found that solving interpersonal problems and maintaining regular daily rhythms in activities such as sleeping, waking, eating, and exercise can increase quality of life, reduce symptoms, and help prevent relapse. In almost all cases, the patients in her study continued to receive medications on a regular basis.

IPSRT teaches clients to extensively track their moods every day using a mood chart that can detect the minor fluctuations in mood that may, without adjustment, lead to more

---

Newhill, C.E. (1995). A mental health casebook. Unpublished manuscript.

Assess your comprehension of *the causes, symptoms, and treatment of bipolar disorder* by completing this quiz.

major mood changes. Another component involves helping a client identify personal daily routines. Once the client identifies his or her daily routines, the therapist helps the client keep the routines consistent and address problems that may arise that could upset the routines, including building better, healthier, and more stable interpersonal relationships by improving interpersonal skills (Frank, Gonzalez, & Fagiolini, 2006).

Avoiding Relapse with Bipolar Disorder

The importance of good sleep patterns and "sleep hygiene"

One of the most critically important regular daily routines for individuals with bipolar disorder is maintaining a stable sleep pattern and practicing "good sleep hygiene" to assure quality sleep (Harvey, Schmidt, Scarnà, et al., 2005). This is important because poor sleep can trigger a vicious cycle in which the sleep disturbance promotes poor daytime regulation of affect which, in turn, interferes with nighttime sleep further, triggering more affect dysregulation, in particular, negative emotions, and in time this can lead to relapse (Harvey, 2008).

Good sleep hygiene means abiding by certain practices and habits routinely to enable good restful daily sleep and daytime alertness (Thorpy, 2012). Sleep hygiene practices include going to bed at the same time each night; getting up at the same time each morning, even on weekends; avoiding naps during the day; avoiding stimulants, such as coffee or tea after mid-afternoon; exercising daily but not before bedtime; avoiding large or heavy meals before bedtime; using the bed only for sleep and sexual activity, not for reading or watching TV, so the bed is associated with sleeping; ensuring exposure to natural light during the day, which can help in maintaining a healthy sleep-wake cycle (bright-light therapy can help in winter); and establishing a relaxing bedtime routine, including avoiding anything stimulating or upsetting before bedtime (Thorpy, 2012; White & Preston, 2009).

Other keys to avoiding relapse

Along with maintaining a regular sleep pattern, clients can help reduce mood swings and stresses that can lead to relapse by attending to some additional keys for recovery. Social workers or other therapists can share the following recommendations with their clients and discuss their importance and how to implement the suggestions into the client's daily life (Frances, Docherty, & Kahn, 1996; White & Preston, 2009):

1. Emphasize to your client the importance of maintaining a regular pattern of activity and to avoid being overly busy. Teach your client how to set limits at work and home, how to learn to say no, how to ease up on personal expectations for productivity, and to try not to drive him or herself too hard.
2. Caution your client to avoid using alcohol or illicit/recreational drugs because these substances can trigger mood episodes and interfere with the effectiveness of prescribed medication. Using drugs or alcohol to "self-medicate" his or her mood and relieve dysphoria almost always makes things worse and can lead to relapse and undermine recovery.
3. Advise your client to be careful about using even small amounts of caffeine and over-the-counter drugs that contain caffeine or alcohol because caffeine and the ingredients of nonprescription medications can interfere with sleep, mood, and the effectiveness of prescribed medications.
4. Emphasize the importance of keeping a regular eating schedule by eating healthy (protein, vegetables, fruit, whole grains, low-fat dairy) meals three times a day at regular times. It is important to avoid skipping meals and avoid eating large meals in the evening, because that can interfere with sleep.

5. Urge your client to enlist the help of family and friends to keep stress down and maintain regular daily routines. It is also important to try to avoid people—including family—who are upsetting and raise the individual's stress level.
6. Help your client to figure out strategies to reduce stress at work as much as possible and keep regular work hours. Jobs involving swing shift work or 24-hour work, in particular, can disrupt circadian rhythms and negatively affect mood stability. The case of "Debbie" described in the section on depression illustrates this well. If mood symptoms interfere with your client's ability to do his or her work, discuss whether it is better to "soldier on" or whether it might be wise to take some time off. It is important to discuss with your client the pros and cons of telling his or her employer about the illness and how much to tell (Wahl, 1999).
7. Teach your client to recognize early warning signs of relapse, paying particular attention to changes in sleep patterns. Keeping a mood chart can be a helpful tool to track even minor changes in mood. Here is an example of what a daily mood chart looks like:

Example of a Daily Mood Chart

Day of the week	Medications I took	Side effects I felt
Wednesday, June 13th	Lithium, 1,200 mg; I took 2 pills at 8 a.m. and 2 pills at 8 p.m. Klonopin, 1 mg at bedtime	Some nausea in the morning Discovered I gained 2 pounds! Mild tremor in my hands
0 = Most depressed	**My Symptoms 5 = Normal**	**10 = Most manic**
	5: I feel good today, no depression or high feelings	
How my life is going, good things, stresses, life events		
Work: Things are better because they hired a new staff person so I have less stress.	Home: No fights with my teenage daughter, things are pretty calm.	Slept better, the Klonopin helps; made a list of the good things that happened this week.

8. Demonstrate hope and build in strengths. Many people with bipolar disorder, even those who have a severe form of it, can achieve recovery and have happy and fulfilling lives. Hope is a key element to maintain when the going gets tough.

Helping Families of Individuals with Bipolar Disorder

People with bipolar disorder may need help from family or friends to get the help they need, and providing that caregiving over a long period of time can be challenging for the family. The following suggestions are things that families and friends can do for their loved one with bipolar disorder that can be helpful:

1. First, it is important that all family members agree to support and encourage the ill person to adhere to the treatment plan, including medication and psychosocial treatment, and to avoid using alcohol, illicit drugs, or over-the-counter drugs that could interfere with the effectiveness of the prescribed medication or affect mood or sleep patterns.

2. If side effects are a problem, family members should encourage the ill person to see a doctor immediately and offer to accompany the ill person to the appointment if that would be helpful. If the person is still not doing well, get a second opinion rather than stopping the medication abruptly without a doctor's advice.
3. Families must know that if their loved one suffers a relapse of depression or mania and rejects the family's efforts to help, calling such efforts interference, that rejection is not personal, rather it is just part of the illness. Joining a support group and getting support, encouragement, and insight from other family members in the same boat can be very helpful in keeping things in perspective.
4. Individuals with bipolar disorder are at extremely high risk for completing suicide. It is estimated that between 3 percent and 20 percent of people diagnosed with bipolar disorder die by their own hand. Because of this elevated risk, it is important that family members know the warning signs for suicide and take any threats the person makes very seriously. The next section of the chapter will review the basics of suicide assessment and what the warning signs for suicide are. If the loved one shows these warning signs, the family should call 911, take the person to the emergency room or, if the situation becomes a crisis of imminent harm, call the police. In such situations, privacy and interfering with self-determination are secondary considerations.
5. As in the case example above of Toni and her sister Jody, if the ill family member is prone to mania, arrange an advance directive (AD) during a period of wellness. In the AD, specify how and when to institute safeguards, such as withholding credit cards, car keys, and banking privileges, and when to call the person's therapist or doctor or take the person to the emergency room or hospital.
6. All personal caregiving can be stressful, and providing care to a loved one with bipolar disorder is no exception. Because of this, it is important that family members share caregiving responsibilities so that no individual caregiver is overly burdened and "burns out." Again, joining a family support group through NAMI or DBSA can be helpful.
7. Just as we give someone who has suffered a heart attack time to recover, a loved one who has recently had an episode of bipolar illness needs to be provided the opportunity to move forward in recovery at his or her own pace. However, it is important to encourage the person to be independent and do things *with* the person rather than *for* him or her as much as possible. Try to avoid expecting too much too soon or expecting too little too late. Be the person's cheerleader, communicate hope, and help him or her regain self-efficacy and self-confidence.
8. Family members, along with the ill loved one, need to learn to distinguish between having a really good day and early warning signs of mania, or having a bad day and depression. Just like everyone else, people with bipolar disorder can have good days and bad days and experience the normal ups and downs of life. Psychoeducation can help both the family and the person with bipolar disorder learn to tell the difference.
9. Families should work collaboratively with their ill loved one to find mental/behavioral and health care providers who are willing to build in strengths rather than only emphasizing pathology, who will work collaboratively with the family and ill person to seek recovery in the fullest sense, and who hold and communicate hope that the client can achieve recovery, not focus solely on learning to handle symptoms and avoid hospitalization.

Watch the video *"Speaking out: Feliziano: Living with Bipolar Disorder."* What is the experience of consumers and their families living with bipolar disorder? What tools and resources are available to them?

Improving the Treatments for Individuals with Bipolar Disorder

Researchers, many supported by the National Institute of Mental Health, are continuing to investigate new psychosocial and pharmacological therapies for the effective treatment of bipolar disorder. For example, the NIMH-funded Systematic Treatment Enhancement Program for Bipolar Disorder (STEP-BD) is a long-term outpatient study designed to find out which treatments, or combinations of treatments, are most effective for treating episodes of depression and mania and for preventing recurrent episodes in people with bipolar disorder. In one of the STEP-BD studies, which focused on psychotherapies, the researchers compared people in two groups. The first group was treated with collaborative care (three sessions of psychoeducation over 6 weeks). The second group was treated with medication and intensive psychotherapy (30 sessions over 9 months of CBT, interpersonal and social rhythm therapy, or family-focused therapy). The investigators found that the group provided with intensive psychotherapy had fewer relapses, lower hospitalization rates, and were better able to stick with their treatment plans (Miklowitz, Otto, Frank, et al., 2007). They were also more likely to get well faster and stay well longer. NIMH is continuing to support research that will illuminate which combinations of psychotherapy and medication work best and for whom. The goal of all these efforts is to help people living with bipolar disorder to achieve recovery, suffer fewer episodes of illness, and live symptom-free for longer periods and recover from the episodes they do experience more quickly (see http://www.nimh.nih.gov/trials/practical/step-bd/index.shtml for more information about the ongoing STEP-BD studies).

Assess your comprehension of *the key strategies that individuals with bipolar disorder and their families can use to avoid relapse and maintain wellness* by completing this quiz.

SUICIDE AND SUICIDE RISK ASSESSMENT

"There is but one truly serious philosophical problem and that is suicide."
(Albert Camus, 1913–1960)

One Night in the Psychiatric Emergency Room . . .

- 8:43 p.m.: 11-year-old Josie is brought to the emergency room by her parents after ingesting approximately 30 tablets of acetaminophen (Tylenol). Josie says she didn't want to live anymore because her best friend broke off their friendship. Because an overdose of acetaminophen can cause liver damage, Josie is admitted to the hospital for observation.
- 10:35 p.m.: 13-year-old Alan is brought to the emergency room by his older brother following a suicide threat. Alan is upset because his parents are getting a divorce. The crisis social worker meets with Alan, his brother and, later, their parents. Alan agrees to counseling and a safety contract and goes home with his parents with a counseling appointment for the next day.
- 11:30 p.m.: 15-year-old Maria is brought to the emergency room by paramedics after cutting her wrists with a razor blade following a fight with her boyfriend. The boyfriend says he can't deal with Maria's emotional problems any longer and doesn't want to see her anymore. "My life is over," Maria says, "I can't live without him." The crisis social worker on duty evaluates Maria, determines she is still highly suicidal, and arranges for psychiatric hospitalization.
- 1:48 a.m.: 46-year-old Carlos is brought to the emergency room following a third suicide attempt by carbon monoxide poisoning. Carlos is in financial debt due to gambling, and was just fired from his job. After his wife left for work, Carlos went into his garage, rigged up a hose from the exhaust pipe to the interior of his car, closed the windows and started the car. When his wife returned to the house to get the some papers for work she

(continued)

Albert Camus, 1913-1960

had forgotten and pulled her car into the garage, she found him unconscious and called the paramedics. Carlos is admitted to the hospital's intensive care unit.

- 3:21 a.m.: 55-year-old George is brought to the emergency room for treatment for a self-inflicted gunshot wound to the head. The social worker meets with his distraught family, who tell her that George has fought depression his whole life and had a setback at work a few days ago that had upset him. He had recently threatened to kill himself, but the family didn't think he was serious: "He always makes these kinds of threats—we just thought he wanted attention." George's 21-year-old son, Jack, was watching a late-night movie, heard the gun go off, and found his father upstairs lying on the floor. George is immediately taken to the OR for neurosurgery.

All of the above incidents actually occurred one memorable night during the author's practice with a psychiatric emergency service although, as always, identifying information has been altered to protect confidentiality. These cases represent different individuals of different genders, ages, and ethnic groups, in different situations, but all had one thing in common—they turned to suicidal behavior or threats in response to problems they felt they could not handle, overcome, or resolve. In none of the cases were the threats or attempts at suicide designed as simply bids for attention, rather, they were all expressions of each individual's extreme psychological and emotional distress.

Suicide is a major global public health problem that is different from many other public health problems in that it is highly preventable. In 2007, suicide was the tenth leading cause of death in the United States, accounting for 34,598 deaths with an overall rate of 11.3 suicide deaths per 100,000 people (CDC, 2007). For every completed suicide, it is estimated that 11 nonfatal attempts are made, with men and elderly individuals more likely to have fatal attempts than are women and youth (CDC, 2012). The most frequent methods of completed suicide are by firearms, suffocation, and poisoning (CDC, 2012).

Most people live under the assumption that suicide will never happen to them or their loved ones, yet in the United States each year, more than half a million families must face the reality that someone they love believed it was better to die than to continue living. Suicidal behavior is complex and many of the identified risk factors for suicide vary considerably in accordance with age, gender, culture, and racial/ethnic group, and these risk factors may occur in combination and/or change over time.

Risk Factors for Suicide

Research shows that there are certain individual and contextual risk factors that are associated with suicide attempts and completions. First, rarely does someone take his or her own life without concomitant mental illness of some kind; fully 90 percent of individuals who complete suicide have one or more psychiatric disorders (Moscickm, 2001), although they may not have received treatment for them. Depression, in particular, is a risk factor for suicide, as is having a substance abuse disorder, other mood disorders such as bipolar disorder, schizophrenia, and certain personality disorders, in particular borderline personality disorder and antisocial personality disorder. Other risk factors include having a history of prior suicide attempts; a family history of mental disorder or substance abuse; a family history of attempted or completed suicide; experiencing family violence, including physical or sexual abuse; having firearms in the home, which is the method used in more than half of completed suicides; being incarcerated; and exposure to the suicidal behavior of influential others, such as family members, peers, or celebrity media figures (Miller, Azrael, Hepburn, et al., 2006; Moscickm, 2001; Wasserman, 1984). Many individuals, however, evidence one, more, or even all of these risk factors and do not go on to engage in suicidal behavior. What research suggests is that risk for suicide is elevated if the individual has, in addition to the aforementioned risk factors, abnormalities in certain neurotransmitters, in particular, serotonin. Scientists still don't know exactly what the mechanism is, but research has shown that the brains of suicide victims who have a history of at-risk mental illness and prior suicide attempts show a decreased level of serotonin and, furthermore, this depletion may be evident at birth (Arango, Huang, Underwood, & Mann, 2003; Yates, 2001).

What Are Some of the Facts When It Comes to Suicide?

The first important fact is that most of the time, suicidal people are torn between wanting to live and wanting to die. Most suicidal individuals don't want death; they just want an end to the emotional pain that they are feeling. It is that ambivalence that the suicide prevention clinician can draw on and capitalize upon to work with individuals to help them move through and past the acute suicidal phase and into the side that wants to live.

Second, out of every ten people who complete suicide, eight give definite clues and warnings to others before their attempt, although the clues may be nonverbal or difficult to detect. Few people take their own lives without first letting someone know how they feel. Many individuals tell others directly that they want to kill themselves; others may begin to give away prized possessions in preparation for suicide; and others may provide clues via artwork or writings that reflect their depressed, distressed, and desperate feelings. Most suicidal people seek out or set it up for someone to rescue them, reflecting the ambivalence between wanting life and desiring death that most suicidal people have.

Third, people who have attempted suicide are very likely to try again. Four out of five individuals who complete suicide have made at least one previous attempt. Unfortunately, with each successive attempt, other people may become increasingly blasé about the potential for suicide and assume, erroneously, that the more attempts that are made, the less lethal the individual's intentions are. Every suicide attempt or threat must always be taken seriously and the individual should be provided with immediate mental health intervention and support (Roggenbaum, Christy, & LeBlanc, 2012).

Fourth, it is all right to talk directly with a person about whether the person is thinking of harming him or herself. Many depressed people have already considered suicide as an option, and thus, discussing it openly helps the suicidal person sort through the problems he or she is facing and generally provides a sense of relief and understanding. It doesn't "put the idea of suicide in someone's head," rather, it is one of the most helpful things that someone can do for the suicidal person. And, if someone is not suicidal, he or she will almost always tell you when asked.

Fifth, a person is not suicidal forever. Individuals who wish to kill themselves are acutely suicidal only for a limited period of time. Part of suicide prevention interventions involves getting the person to move safely through and past that acute period. Finally, one of the basic facts about suicide in the United States is that risk increases as a function of age (Shahal, 2007). Completed suicide is rare in children under 12, and becomes more common after puberty, with the incidence increasing in each adolescent year, reaching its peak among youth at age 23. The highest rates, however, are still among elderly White men. Although in the past 30 years the rate for young adults has tripled, 80-year-olds are still twice as likely to commit suicide as 20-year-olds. Why? Part of the answer lies in the nature of human development across the life cycle.

Adult Development and Suicide Risk

Examining ways in which adult development may affect suicide risk can suggest some answers—although univariate answers are not possible because suicide really represents a multifactorial phenomenon. Throughout the human life span, there are many fluctuating and competing risk factors as well as protective factors that affect the probability of suicide occurring (Blumenthal, 1990). Suicide essentially results from the unlikely convergence of predisposing and immediate risk factors together in the absence of sufficient protective factors. Thus, people can move in and out of elevated risk and suicidal crises at various points in their lives as the result of disruptions in homeostasis between the risk and protective factors (Blumenthal, 1990).

This begs the question as to whether suicide is the same phenomenon in childhood as it is in old age. Does it have different meaning? Are there different risk factors across the life span? Are the protective factors different across the life span? What remains a major obstacle to answering such questions definitively is the lack of longitudinal data on suicide risk and protective factors except for the very few countries that maintain longitudinal registers, such as Denmark (Qin, Agerbo, & Mortensen, 2002). Most current research, however, suggests that suicidal behavior throughout the life cycle is on a continuum, that is, similar risk factors operate across various stages of life but *their contributory weight differs* at different points in the life cycle, and the same is true for protective factors.

Certainly, some contributory factors do not change, such as genetic predisposition, race, or biological sex. For example, across age groups, males are more likely to die from suicide than females (CDC, 2012). In terms of race and ethnicity, the highest rates of completed suicide are among American Indians and Alaskan Natives (14.3 per 100,000) and non-Hispanic Whites (13.5 per 100,000), while the lowest rates are among Asian-Americans and Pacific Islanders (6.2 per 100,000), Hispanics (6.0 per 100,000), and non-Hispanic Blacks (5.1 per 100,000) (CDC, 2012, citing 2007 data).

Also, some factors impacting suicide rates are not directly affected by the developmental life cycle model. For example, one risk factor that is independent of development is the increased availability of handguns in the United States (Clarke & Jones, 1989; Miller, Lippmann, Azrael, & Hemenway, 2007). An example of a protective factor independent of development would be the British government's efforts in the early 1970s to reduce the carbon monoxide content of domestic coal gas in England, which reduced the national suicide rate by reducing the gas's toxic effects on brain function (Kreitman, 1976). Finally, longitudinal epidemiological data has shown that when conservative parties control government in ostensibly democratic countries, such as the United States, rates of violence and suicide increase, while during more liberal party rule, rates of violence and suicide decrease (Gilligan, 2011).

Furthermore, there are two additional protective factors in suicide that are relatively independent of life cycle issues. First is the availability of psychiatric and other social intervention and supports (Blumenthal, 1990). This factor is relatively independent of development, although certain individuals in need of help may experience barriers to access at certain developmental stages, such as lack of financial resources, access to transportation, or knowledge of appropriate resources and the impact of stigma. Also, children, young teens, and older adults may have to depend on others to access help for them.

The second protective factor relatively independent of life cycle issues is *hope*. One of the most important aspects in an individual's journey toward recovery with any mental illness is achieving and maintaining hope. But what is hope, exactly? Hope is generally defined as the desire for something accompanied by the expectation of obtaining it. We still don't know much about hope's determinants, biological correlates, or why some individuals can have hope in the most dire of circumstances while others in similar circumstances cannot achieve or maintain hope. What we do know is that lack of hope or *hopelessness* is often very detrimental to mental health and is often the key component in negative psychosocial outcomes, such as completed suicides. It is lack of hope, rather than depression, that is most significant for suicide. Thus, the development and maintenance of hope is important for suicide prevention.

Domains of Risk and Protection

When examining risk factors for suicide, such factors may be organized into four overlapping domains: psychosocial milieu, biologic vulnerability, psychiatric disorder, and personality factors (Blumenthal, 1990). The first domain is *psychosocial milieu.*

Psychosocial milieu

Stressful life events, depression, physical illness, and loss, even when they occur together, rarely result in completed suicide if a person has a solid and flexible positive social support system. Social support is probably the single most important protective factor against completed suicide. This is clearly emphasized in Erikson's model of life span development, that is, human growth and development is in continual movement toward an ever-widening social radius (Erikson, 1994). As individuals mature, their social network usually becomes more resilient and, consequently, more protective.

This leads to the question: who, then, would be at particular risk in this regard? In a potentially suicidal person, risk may peak if important others in the environment move away from the person and the person suffers significant interpersonal losses as a result. For example, two peak periods of suicide risk are *adolescence*, which is a time of leaving home and achieving independence, and *old age*, during which one typically begins to lose more friends and same-age family members, such as an intimate partner, to death or disability. Both of these life periods represent times of particular risk for losing important loved ones and caretakers faster than they can be replaced. Also in adolescence and old age, the cultural permission for suicide is highest. The fluid identity of adolescence promotes susceptibility to so-called "contagious" suicides, "romantic" suicides, and so-called "cluster suicides" (Gould, Wallenstein, & Davidson, 1989). Then as individuals reach old age, membership both literally and metaphorically in "Hemlock societies" has become increasingly culturally syntonic (Humphry, 2002). For example, many supported Dr. Jacob "Jack" Kevorkian's controversial stance and actions with regard to assisted suicide, particularly if an individual was suffering greatly, terminally ill, and older (Gurney, 2011). Others, of course, viewed him as nothing but a serial murderer. Most agree, however, that his legacy must be credited with helping to spur the growth of palliative and hospice care for terminally ill people and influenced many doctors to become more sympathetic to those in severe pain and more willing to engage in active pain management to alleviate suffering (Schneider, 2011). This brings us to the next domain for consideration in suicide risk, *biological vulnerability.*

Biological vulnerability

A major difference between suicide in adolescence versus suicide in old age is that, in adolescence, suicide tends to be an act of impulse driven by emotional factors, such as the cases of Josie, Alan, and Maria at the beginning of this section. Suicide in old age, in contrast, tends to be an act of reflective choice. Medical illness (in particular, cancer, coronary heart disease, stroke, chronic obstructive pulmonary disease, and osteoporosis) operates as a risk factor in adult suicides (Webb, Kontopantelis, Doran, Qin, et al., 2012). It plays less of a role with adolescents, with one exception—being diagnosed and living with AIDS. People who have AIDS have a much greater incidence of suicide than the general population primarily due to chronic pain, depression, and the cognitive impairments associated with AIDS-related dementia. Further, the protective buffer of social support may be absent for many individuals with AIDS due to rejection from some friends and family, friends dying from AIDS, and loss of social support because of periods of prolonged hospitalization. How can the differences in the importance of specific risk factors across the life cycle be explained? One hypothesis suggests that the impact of a particular risk factor (e.g., medical illness) depends on, first, the co-occurrence of other risk factors for suicide and, second, the extent to which protective factors are able to buffer the risk. Thus, someone may have terminal cancer, but if the person has a strong active social support network, he or she may avoid suicidal feelings and behavior. The third domain in our risk factor model is *psychiatric disorder.*

Psychiatric disorder

As already noted, very few people take their lives without concomitant psychiatric disorder, and which types of psychiatric illness are most commonly associated with suicide changes somewhat across the life span. Adolescence and young adulthood are the prime times for the emergence of mood disorders and schizophrenia. Access to drugs and alcohol and the development of a substance use disorder also commonly begins in adolescence or young adulthood. Personality pathology also becomes apparent in early adolescence. The key protective factor for psychiatric disorder as a risk factor for suicide is the availability of good mental/behavioral health intervention, although such intervention, particularly for low-income individuals, is often unavailable or inadequate in quality (Olfson, Marcus, & Bridge, 2012; Roggenbaum, Christy, & LeBlanc, 2012).

Research on adult and adolescent completed suicides suggest more than 90 percent suffered from one or more psychiatric disorders. There are five broad categories of psychiatric disorder that put individuals at particular risk. These include mood disorders, schizophrenia, mental disorders due to a medical condition, substance use disorders, and certain personality disorders, specifically antisocial personality disorder and borderline personality disorder. Comorbidity of these disorders with particular personality traits, such as impulsivity and aggression, increases the risk across the life span (Blumenthal, 1990). The final domain is *personality.*

Personality

There are certain key personality traits that constitute risk factors for suicide. These include an action orientation, depression, hostility, impulsivity, shame, and hopelessness. Individuals who evidence these personality traits are more at risk for substance abuse, and substance abuse is a risk factor for suicide, particularly alcohol abuse.

The degree to which personality changes over the life span is debatable, although clinicians and researchers agree that change does occur due to developmental changes and life events. We know, for example, that maturity can decrease suicidal risk to the extent that it decreases impulsivity, leads to the increasing ability to master and tolerate anger and dysphoria and, to some extent, the emotional dysregulation and behavioral dysregulation of personality disorders begins to settle down. With development from adolescence, patience increases, tolerance for hostile and sad feelings increases, perceived stress decreases, and perceived well-being and happiness increases (Cohen & Janicki-Deverts, 2012; Sostek, 2012). In essence, maturity brings ego strength, an important protective factor against suicide.

The Suicide Risk Continuum

An individual's suicidality may go unrecognized, even by skilled mental health professionals. However, there are some clear guidelines that can help social workers to identify and assess suicide risk (Roggenbaum, Christy, & LeBlanc, 2012). Often the first obstacle is that the clinician simply doesn't ask the client if he or she is experiencing suicidal feelings. Such clear and direct inquiry can lead to exploring the client's ideas about suicide and whether the client is experiencing suicidal feelings and gives the client permission to talk about it, providing understanding and relief. Such inquiry can also help to clarify what problems are going on with the individual that may be prompting the suicidal feelings or actions.

When considering suicide risk, it can be helpful to see it on a continuum ranging from the wish to live to the wish to die (Healey, 1993). At one end of the continuum, the individual poses no risk for suicide. These are people who have no history of suicide attempts, no suicidal ideation, and a strong desire to live. Next are those at low risk for suicide. Low-risk individuals have no history of previous suicide attempts and, if they express current suicidal ideation, it involves contemplating a method of low lethality. They have no specific plan to take their life and state clearly that they believe they can control their suicidal urges. The primary motivation of low-risk individuals is not to die; rather, they want to live, make changes in their life, and have hope for the future. Toward the other end of the continuum are the moderate-risk individuals. These clients have considered suicide with a highly lethal method but do not have a plan to put the method into action, or they have a plan with rescue, meaning that the plan involves setting up a situation in which they will be found and rescued. There may or may not be a history of low-lethality attempts, the individual does admit to family difficulties of some kind and, if there is a therapeutic alliance, the client and clinician may be able to work together on an outpatient basis. If, however, there is no therapeutic alliance, the risk is enhanced and may suggest the person falls into the final category, which is high risk.

The high-risk individual really does want to die. He or she currently has a highly lethal method and the means to follow through with it, there is a possible history of attempts, and the person currently is experiencing severe personal difficulties. The person may be isolated and depressed, cut off from any source of social support, and facing one more significant loss. Through the act of suicide, the person may seek to have an impact on his or her environment, but the goal isn't to solve a problem, rather, it is to induce guilt or seek revenge in some way in other, for example, "See what you made me do" (Yates, 2001). These individuals do not want to improve their situation—they want to die. A rescue plan is not present, and if they have been rescued from suicide attempts in the past, the rescue was purely accidental. These clients probably need hospitalization and may be seen by the mental health clinician after a serious attempt, or the clinician may see the distraught family after the suicide has been attempted or completed. The cases of Carlos and George, described at the beginning of this section of the chapter, are good examples of individuals who were high risk. Carlos used a lethal method and was rescued only by accident when his wife came home to pick up some forgotten papers for work, and in the case of George, the social worker met with the family after George had shot himself in the head with a gun, a highly lethal method. But no matter where someone fits on this continuum, all need to be taken seriously.

Conducting a Suicide Risk Assessment

When conducting a suicide risk assessment, it is important to consider all of the risk and protective factors that have been described above. The 16 primary risk factors include mental disorder, substance abuse, prior attempts, having a method or plan, social isolation, cognitive rigidity, being an older White male, having a family history of suicide, work problems, financial difficulties, marital problems, stress, experiencing aggression, having an action orientation, hopelessness, and physical illness (Healey, 1993). Protective factors that can balance out or buffer the risk factors for suicide include what is called *cognitive flexibility*. People who are highly suicidal often demonstrate *cognitive rigidity*, meaning that they are unable to see any options other than suicide to resolve their problems, and attempts to suggest alternatives are rejected. Cognitive flexibility, on the other hand, is the ability to see several sides to an issue and numerous possibilities for problem solving. Such individuals, with a strong therapeutic alliance, often can work out their problems and reduce their suicide risk on an outpatient basis. Other protective factors include strong social supports, no precipitating events, no significant losses, and a sense of hope. Considering these risk and protective factors can help one determine the risk level for a particular client and what interventions should be provided. In addition, the clinician should assess whether there is the presence of suicidal ideation, intent, and/or plan. *Suicidal ideation* refers to the extent to which the client wishes to die or "be dead"; *suicidal intent* refers to the level of motivation and ability to follow through with a suicide plan; *suicide plan* refers to the description the person provides of when and how the person will take his or her life. A basic suicide assessment addresses the following questions:

- Do you have thoughts that life is not worth living and you are thinking about killing yourself?
- Do you have a specific plan to kill yourself? If so, how and when?
- Have you ever attempted to harm or kill yourself in the past?
- What has kept you from acting on your thoughts and killing yourself this time?
- Have you told anyone else about your thoughts, your intent, or your plan to kill yourself?

The following dialogue with a depressed client illustrates risk assessment interviewing skills and how both risk and protective factors play a role in the client's situation and are identified through skillful questioning by the social worker.

The Case of John

John is a 60-year-old gay White man who is separated from his partner, Andrew, with whom he has been for over 30 years. John and Andrew adopted two babies from Vietnam, who are now teenagers, aged 14 and 15. The two daughters are living with Andrew since John lost his job as a software engineer in a corporate downsizing. John moved to a new town about 2 hours from his former home in order to take a new job, which is a step down in status and pay from his previous position. A longtime friend, with whom John is currently living until he can afford his own place, became concerned about John's apparent depression and recommended counseling. With the friend's persuasion, John set up an appointment with a licensed clinical social worker at the local community mental/behavioral health center. This is the initial evaluation.

SW: So, John, what brings you here today?

John: Well . . . (deep sigh) . . . the friend I'm staying with is concerned about me and suggested that I see someone.

SW: Could you tell me a little about why your friend suggested that you see someone?

John: Well . . . I just haven't been myself lately.

SW: Haven't been yourself?

John: Yes, I . . . I had to move in with my friend after my partner and I split up. I had lost my job, you see . . . I have a new one but it doesn't pay as well so I can't afford to get my own place.

SW: I see. Can you tell me a little more about what happened with you and your partner?

John: (after a lengthy silence) My partner, I guess I should say former partner, Andrew, and I have been together for a long time, over 30 years now. We have two children—they're teenagers now—that we adopted as babies from Vietnam. They're with him. We went through a really ugly breakup. We had been kind of drifting apart, the kids were having some problems that stressed us, I was having problems at work, and then he—Andrew—started coming home late. . . .

SW: Was that because of his work schedule?

John: No. . . . I thought so at first but, no, I found out through a mutual friend that Andrew was having an affair with a younger man. I confronted him, he denied it at first, but then admitted it, said he "wanted space," and things went downhill from there.

John continues, describing the breakup, the loss of his job, his daughters' problems in school that, for one, involved racist bullying and, with the other, problems with using marijuana and skipping school. Suspecting that John may be depressed, the social worker begins to inquire about how John is feeling emotionally.

SW: So, John, how have you been feeling lately? How has your mood been?

John: Not so good. I'm not sleeping well and I'm having a hard time concentrating at work. I'm there a lot, but I just can't seem to get the job done, which is ridiculous because it is an entry-level job. And I've been drinking more—it helps me sleep but then I wake up early and can't get back to sleep.

SW: It sounds like you've been going through a lot of changes, a lot of stress, and a lot of losses.

John: Yeah . . . (sighs) . . . but I'm sure things will get better, you know. . . . (sighs and slumps in chair)

SW: John, how are things really going? How are you *really* feeling these days?

John: I guess to be honest, not well. I miss my girls, I miss Andrew in spite of what he did, I miss my old job and my friends.

SW: What are your thoughts about life? Where do you think your life is at this point, and where do you think it is headed?

John: To tell you the truth, life hasn't turned out like I thought it would. I feel like I've just fallen short of things, that I've failed . . . in work, with my family . . . everything.

SW: Hmmm . . . it sounds like, perhaps, you feel almost like it's not worth going on?

John: Oh . . . sometimes I think that. (sighs) Sometimes I think my girls would just be better off without me. If I were gone, they would have my insurance money and that would provide for them since I'm not doing a very good job of being a dad.

SW: John, do you feel sometimes like life isn't worth living?

John: Something along those lines.

SW: Do you find yourself wishing you were dead?

John: Sometimes . . .

SW: Are you having these thoughts right now?

John: Yeah, I am . . . you know, my father took his life when he was about my age. . . . I was only 15 when it happened . . . I found him.

SW: That had to have been a terrible experience for you.

John: It was.

SW: Have you been feeling suicidal lately—feeling that you might take your own life?

John: Yes. . . . I guess that makes me seem pretty weak. . . .

SW: No, not weak . . . what it does tell me is that you are pretty depressed and you're burdened by a lot of worries and problems that seem overwhelming.

John: Yeah, well, there is no solution to any of this. I've screwed up my life and everyone would just be better off without me.

SW: Do you think you can control your feelings and urges about taking your own life?

John: No. . . . I guess that's really why I'm here. I admit I have a gun at home . . . it's loaded . . . I've really thought about using it.

SW: John, it sounds like things have reached a point where you feel like there aren't many options open for you, and your suicidal feelings seem to be kind of strong. I do believe that solutions can be found and I want to help you figure out what those solutions could be. Right now, however, I am concerned about your safety and I think it would be best if you came into the hospital for a few days. There, you can begin to get the help you need, you will be safe, and we'll have the time to sort things out.

John: (with a look of relief) Okay, I'm willing to do that.

As illustrated in the interview with the client "John," when talking with a depressed and possibly suicidal person, it is good to use a gradual graded approach (Healey, 1993). Once you find out what problems are troubling the client, you can then explore his or her desire for life or death, the extent to which the client is feeling suicidal, and whether there is the presence of hope. Of utmost importance is to communicate empathy and understanding. If you come across to the client as if you are afraid to talk about suicide and his or her suicidal feelings, that will only keep the person from opening up to you and you won't be able to do a good and complete assessment. As part of the assessment process it is, of course, important to use good basic clinical skills such as facilitation, communicating with empathy and authenticity, and the strategic use of open-ended questions that allow for the client to expand in his or her own words what is being discussed, and get at the deeper more troubling feelings the person may be experiencing. Also it is important to provide a sense of support, showing interest, concern, and a willingness to help the individual. A sense of empathy is very important, that is, your understanding and communication of the client's thoughts and feelings. The use of reflection, which mirrors what the client has said, and the appropriate and well-timed use of interpretation can validate the client's feelings, and the client will feel understood and supported. Finally, the availability of good consultation and supervision is critical when working with suicidal clients so that hospitalization or other more direct interventions can be provided if needed. Working with suicidal clients is highly stressful, and good consultation and supervision can help the social worker manage stress (Ting, Jacobson, & Sanders, 2011). Of note: This client was particularly responsive and articulate. Other clients may not be this way; they may be silent, agitated, under the influence of alcohol or drugs, psychotic, or recovering from a suicide attempt that may affect the nature and quality of the interview.

The risk factors revealed in the interview include John's symptoms of depression (lack of energy and ability to concentrate). He feels hopeless and helpless and demonstrates cognitive rigidity, that is, he sees suicide as the only option, with no possible solutions to his problems. John has few social supports and is estranged from his long-time partner and children. He has a very lethal means—a loaded gun—and does not feel he can control his suicidal urges. Although it seems as if he has established a good rapport with the social worker, overall, the risk factors present outweigh the protective factors available, therefore hospitalization is recommended. This interview and hospitalization will be the beginning of the process of helping John alleviate his distress and move him toward desiring life more than desiring death.

Assess your comprehension of *the risk factors for suicide and how to conduct a suicide risk assessment* by completing this quiz.

CONCLUSION

This chapter has addressed practice with individuals with serious mood disorders, specifically focusing on the various forms of depression and bipolar disorder, interventions that are helpful for the ill person and their family and, finally, understanding and assessing suicide risk. The two primary mood states in the various types of mood disorders are various forms of elevated mood and depressed mood.

The most common subtype of mood disorder is depression. There are many types or forms of depression, some triggered by life events while others may seem to evolve independent of what is going on in the individual's life. Most depression, however, occurs in response to a combination of factors related to biology, environment, and psychological issues. Everybody has days when they feel sad or blue, but that is not clinical depression. True clinical depression is much more than the blues. Depression interferes with one's daily life and ability to function and causes significant pain and distress not only for the person with depression, but also for his or her friends and family members. There are many distinct forms of depression including chronic mild depression, called dysthymia, depression triggered by the postpartum period, seasonal affective disorder, and major depressive disorder. All are very treatable with targeted psychosocial treatments and/or antidepressant or mood-stabilizing medications. Depression is diagnosed more frequently in women, however, we believe that depression in men, which evidences slightly different symptoms, may be underdiagnosed and undertreated.

Bipolar disorder, formerly known as manic-depressive illness, is a brain disorder that causes unusual and extreme shifts in a person's mood, energy, and ability to function. Different from the normal ups and downs that everyone goes through, the symptoms of bipolar disorder are severe and can result in impaired relationships with other people and poor or erratic job and school performance, and bipolar disorder carries a high risk for suicide. But, like depression, the good news is that bipolar disorder can be effectively treated, and people with this illness can lead full and productive lives provided they receive the right treatment, receive it as early in the illness as possible, and learn how to manage their symptoms and achieve wellness and recovery.

Having a mood disorder elevates risk for suicide, although mood disorders are not the only psychiatric illnesses that carry suicide risk. Knowing the facts and myths about suicide is important, and it is critical to ask all clients if they have ever had or are currently having thoughts of suicide. Having thoughts of suicide or making a feasible plan to carry it out elevates risk and must be assessed carefully. Behavioral changes, such as giving away prized possessions, may be an indicator of more serious risk, and any threats of self-harm must always be taken seriously. There are several organizations that can help clinicians, consumers, and families with resources to help someone who is at risk for suicide. These include:

- The National Hopeline Network; Telephone: 1-800-SUICIDE. This will connect the caller with a crisis center in the caller's area. Website: www.hopeline.com
- American Foundation for Suicide Prevention; Telephone: 1-212-363-3500; Website: www.afsp.org
- American Association of Suicidology; Telephone: 1-202-237-2280; Website: www.suicidology.org

Assess your application and analysis of this chapter's contents by completing the Chapter Review.

Chapter 13

Social Work Practice with Individuals with Personality Disorders

INTRODUCTION

Clients with personality disorders regularly demonstrate to us the limits of our knowledge, expertise, empathy, and patience (Perry & Vaillant, 1989). They drop out of treatment, tell us we're lousy therapists, and they are the very clients to whom we may unfortunately respond by referring them to another clinician or another agency. There is little doubt that the clinical management of such individuals can be exceptionally difficult, and many clinicians respond by simply refusing to treat them (Adler, 1990). On the positive side, however, the challenges faced when working with individuals with personality disorders can strengthen our skills as clinicians and teach us a lot about ourselves in terms of our own strengths, vulnerabilities, and inner conflicts. More so than any other type of client, the client with a personality disorder can truly challenge and push us to be the best that we can be as clinicians. In other words, we may find that we learn the most clinically from working with our clients who have a personality disorder or related personality traits.

Widiger and Trull (1993), in a comprehensive summary of epidemiological studies, concluded that about 10 to 13 percent of the population meets the criteria for a personality disorder at some point in their lifetime, and these individuals represent a disproportionate number of individuals in both inpatient and outpatient clinical settings, with the greatest general population frequency occurring among single individuals from lower socioeconomic classes in urban areas (de Girolamo & Dotto, 2000; Torgersen, Kringlen, & Cramer, 2001). What empirical data there is suggests that people with personality disorders make up a sizeable proportion of those in our jail and prison populations, those who are chronically unemployed and/or on public assistance, and those receiving services in substance abuse treatment programs (Perry & Vaillant, 1989). They are also the same people we may describe in lay terminology as bad, deviant, horrible, or "the client from heck." However we, as clinicians, cannot ignore, avoid, or reject clients with personality disorders, because they are coming to our agencies for help and are on our caseloads and we are obligated to provide the best quality care and services we can, just as we would do for any other client in need of assistance. In fact, clients with personality disorders are often much more disabled in terms of psychosocial functioning than many of the depressed and anxious clients many of us prefer to work with and may even have poorer psychosocial functioning than some of our clients with psychotic disorders. David Adler in his book *Treating Personality Disorders* refers to them as "the non-psychotic chronic patient" (Adler, 1990, p. 3). What such clients have, in essence, is a serious and enduring mental and emotional disability. At times we may not like or may become frustrated working with clients with personality disorders, but we need to understand why they are so challenging and, most importantly, recognize that they are clearly deserving of our help.

As a first step toward preparing to work effectively with clients with personality disorders, we must abandon the pejorative language that we often reserve to use when describing these clients, such as referring to them as "the antisocial, manipulative, borderline, med-seeking, sociopath" (Minkoff, 2000) and, instead, recognize that much of what is difficult about such clients is simply symptomatic of their particular mental illness. A good analogy for clarification is to look at a comparison with the infectious disease model. When one has an infection of some kind, the body reacts by developing certain symptoms, such as a fever, cough, or inflammation. The fever, cough, or inflammation are not the infection itself but, rather, constitute symptoms indicating that an underlying disorder exists. With the person with a personality disorder, manipulativeness or self-harming behaviors serve as symptoms indicative of underlying problems and conflicts (Perry & Vaillant, 1989). Just as the presence of a fever indicates an effort of the body to heal itself when it has been invaded by a virus, symptoms of a personality disorder reflect an individual's efforts to heal him or herself psychiatrically (Perry & Vaillant, 1989). Furthermore, it may be argued that just as with people who are depressed or have an anxiety disorder, individuals with personality disorders have potentially treatable underlying mechanisms. Recognizing this can help us to be more willing to try to understand and respond to their distress empathically.

Understanding and empathizing with clients who have personality disorders is, admittedly, not always easy. Clients suffering from depression or an anxiety disorder typically see that they have a problem and, in response, seek out help to resolve their problems and relieve their suffering. In technical terminology, their symptoms are *autoplastic*, that is, they perceive that their problems are caused by internal factors, they "own" their problems, and their symptoms are experienced as ego-dystonic, that is, seen as incompatible with coping well with the demands of everyday life (Fenichel, 1945). The client essentially says: "I have a problem and I need help." In contrast, people with personality disorders often don't see they have or are a problem, often come to treatment via the pressure of others, are likely to reject psychiatric help, and view everyone else as the problem. The client essentially says: "I am not the problem here!" Their symptoms are what we call, in technical terminology, *alloplastic*, that is, they perceive their distress as being caused and molded by external factors and their symptoms are experienced as ego-syntonic, that is, they think their behaviors and their symptoms as perfectly justified (Fenichel, 1945). As a client with antisocial personality disorder once stated to the author during an interview: "Yeah, I killed a couple people—but they deserved it. They double-crossed me."

Another difference is that so-called neurotic symptoms in the form of phobias, obsessions, anxiety, and depression are generally highly distressing to the person experiencing the symptoms, but such symptoms may not really affect other people significantly. In contrast, expressions of personality disorder, for example, passive-aggressive behavior and narcissism, are often seen as harmless or justified by the person exhibiting it, but can be extremely upsetting to others. For example, people with passive-aggressive personalities will behave in ways that give the message, "I'm going to do whatever I want and if you don't like it, that's your problem." These are individuals who are always late for appointments, don't do their fair share of work on group projects, grab credit surreptitiously for the accomplishments of others, sabotage other people's work for their own gain, and behave in ways that suggest passive obstinacy, angry kindness, and compliant defiance. Although the parties who are targeted by the behavior are upset by it, they often feel like they can't quite put a finger on what is going on and, thus, the behavior is difficult to confront (Carey, 2004; Kantor, 2002; Long, Long, & Whitson, 2009). The following is a case vignette depicting a client who has a long-existing personality disorder, and it was a traumatic loss that brought him into treatment for the first time, rather than his personality disorder.

The Case of Bob

Bob, a 55-year-old asparagus farmer, came in to the community mental health center one morning asking to talk to somebody. A few weeks before, his cat had been crushed to death by a hay bale that had come untied and fell to the floor in his barn. Since the death of his cat, Bob has had problems sleeping and concentrating and, because he feels tired all the time, he has had problems getting all of his farm work completed each day. Bob has a small asparagus farm with a few chickens and a cow, and lives alone and simply. For years, Bob has had no contacts with other people beyond minimal interactions when he goes into town to buy supplies or sell his asparagus and eggs, and occasional contacts by telephone with his family. Bob has always preferred to be by himself, never enjoyed conversations with other people, and felt awkward if anyone tried to form a relationship with him. Although Bob only completed high school, he reads constantly and is an avid consumer of nonfiction books, particularly those related to history. However, he makes no efforts to connect with any people around him, including the many family members who live in the area. His older sister finally gave up trying to get Bob to join in and attend various family holiday events and, although it hurt her feelings, accepted the fact that he just doesn't want to be around other people, including family. Bob lives his life alone in his own sphere of existence without any close relationships except for the relationship he had with his cat Charlie.

Bob has always liked cats because cats are independent, aren't emotionally demanding, yet are willing to curl up on the couch and be companionable. At Christmas time, Bob always bought his cat expensive gifts including an elaborate scratching post, a large supply of catnip, and imported toy mice. In return, Bob would receive a wrapped bottle of bourbon that he bought for himself as a gift from the cat. The loss of his pets have been the only events in Bob's life that have caused him sadness. When his younger sister was diagnosed with terminal cancer, Bob felt little emotion, and even the deaths of his parents elicited little feeling and he did not even attend their funerals, considering it too much of a bother. Bob considers himself smarter than other people and prefers to live within his own mind and his own thoughts. However, the death of his cat filled him with unbearable sadness.

As depicted in this vignette, Bob sought treatment because he felt depressed over his cat's death, and his depression was affecting his ability to function in his daily life. And, although many of us are pet lovers, most clinicians would probably conclude that Bob also has some sort of mental disorder because of the extreme intensity of his reaction to the death of his cat and the time the reaction lasted, especially in comparison to his lack of emotional reaction to other losses in his life, such as his sister's cancer diagnosis and the deaths of his parents. As we look at Bob's life over the course of his adulthood, we see that Bob evidences significant impairments in personality functioning and shows a number of unusual personality traits. Bob shows a pronounced difficulty in understanding the impact of his behavior on others and he lacks empathy for others, for example, he refuses to attend family holiday events even though it hurts his sister's feelings. He has exceptionally restricted affectivity including a long-standing pattern of little reaction to normally emotionally arousing situations, for example, the deaths of his parents; constricted emotional experience and expression; and indifference or coldness toward other people. He has an extreme preference for being alone rather than being with others, is reticent in social situations, avoids social contacts and activities (e.g., family holiday events), and does not initiate social contact with others. These impairments in personality functioning are of long standing and seem to be relatively stable across time and consistent across situations. Furthermore, they are not better understood as normative for Bob's developmental stage or sociocultural environment or due to the direct physiological effects of a substance (e.g., a drug of abuse, medication) or a general medical condition (e.g., severe head trauma) (APA, 2013).

The most appropriate DSM-5 Axis I diagnosis for Bob's clinical presentation would probably be adjustment disorder with depressed mood because his distress is clearly linked to an identifiable stressor, that is, the sudden unexpected death of his cat as the result of a traumatic accident. However, this diagnosis alone does not completely capture all of the features of Bob's life and his current clinical presentation. His lifelong pattern of always choosing solitary activities and only rarely experiencing strong emotions is indicative of having a schizoid personality disorder, and it was the presence of his personality disorder that made Bob particularly vulnerable to experiencing extreme stress following the death of his cat. In fact, there is abundant clinical evidence suggesting that having a personality disorder adversely affects the course, duration, and response to treatment for any co-existing Axis I disorder that a client may have (Reich & Vasile, 1993). Next, this chapter examines some of the general characteristics that cut across all of the personality disorders.

OVERVIEW OF CROSS-CUTTING CHARACTERISTICS OF PERSONALITY DISORDERS

Personality Traits versus Personality Disorder

Before addressing the four characteristics all individuals with personality disorders have in common, a distinction must be made between personality *traits* and personality *disorder*. Personality traits "are enduring patterns of perceiving, relating to and thinking about the environment and oneself, and are exhibited in a wide range of important social and personal contexts" (APA, 2013, p. 647). Everyone has personality traits—personality traits make each person who they are as a unique individual and are usually in place from a very early age. If someone is asked to describe another person, that description almost always includes identification of personality traits, for example, "she is optimistic, hard-working, flexible, and kind." A personality *disorder*, however, is indicated when the individual's personality traits are inflexible and maladaptive, and cause significant impairment in self, social, interpersonal, and/or occupational functioning that is relatively stable across time and consistent across situations (APA, 2013). The following is a hypothetical example to illustrate the difference between personality traits that are flexible and adaptive versus personality traits that are inflexible and maladaptive and may constitute a personality disorder:

> Dean and George work as middle managers for a construction company, each in a different division of the company. They have both been employed full-time at this particular company for over 10 years, and both are described by their co-workers as optimistic, assertive, and hard-working. One day, a rumor begins to circulate that company layoffs may be occurring in the near future. Dean thinks to himself: "Well, I hope I won't be laid off, I like working for this company but, in case I end up getting a pink slip, I better at least dust off my resume. I'll hope for the best, but prepare for the worst." George thinks: "I won't be laid off—I'm too important to this company. It is to my credit that the company has been so successful." Two weeks go by and then the layoffs come through and both Dean and George get pink slips and are asked to clean out their desks by 5 p.m. Dean is very disappointed, but he spends the afternoon asking key supervisors for recommendations, saying goodbye to co-workers, and packing up the contents of his desk. As he is about to leave, the vice president of the company stops by, shakes his hand, and tells Dean how much they hate to lose him, adding that Dean will get 3 months' severance pay and a guarantee of an excellent job reference.
>
> When George gets his pink slip, however, he becomes enraged, storms into the office of the president of the company, and bellows, "Who the hell do you think

> you are? You want to lay me off? I'll hit you with the biggest wrongful termination lawsuit this company has ever seen!" When the president orders him to leave, George punches him in the face, breaking his nose. Security officers are called to escort him out only to be met by the city police because the injured company president decided to press charges for assault. George is hauled off to jail and now is facing criminal charges. He has lost any hope of a good job reference and has burned bridges with other co-workers, who were shocked by his behavior.

Why did Dean and George react so differently to the stressor of being laid off from their jobs? Both had been successful managers, both were described by co-workers as having the personality traits of optimism and assertiveness, and both experienced the very same stressor. The difference is that Dean's personality traits of optimism and assertiveness were flexible and adaptive. His optimism caused him to hope for the best but he also prepared for the reality that he might be laid off. Before leaving for the day, he appropriately and assertively approached everyone who could support him in seeking new employment and, although he was disappointed about being laid off, he handled the stress well. George, however, reacted very differently. His normal optimism morphed into narcissistic entitlement and his assertiveness turned into aggression. George's personality traits were inflexible and significantly maladaptive, resulting in a negative outcome socially, interpersonally, and occupationally. Under normal non-stressful circumstances, the symptoms of George's personality disorder remained hidden, but under stress, the symptoms emerged.

The Four Cross-Cutting Characteristics All Personality Disorders Have in Common

There are four general characteristics that cut across all of the personality disorders regardless of subtype. These include the following (Perry & Valliant, 1989):

1. An inflexible and maladaptive response to stress;
2. A disability in working and achieving intimacy with others that is generally serious and pervasive;
3. Elicitation of symptoms by interpersonal conflict;
4. A peculiar capacity to "get under the skin" of others.

The first characteristic is *an inflexible and maladaptive response to stress*. People with personality disorders exhibit repetitious self-detrimental responses to stressors in their lives. When stress occurs, the individual repeatedly responds in ways that cause significant impairment in their relationships with others, their social life, and their school or job performance. The inability to handle stress without behaving in ways that cause problems result in their being repeatedly fired from jobs, experiencing multiple interpersonal relationship problems, and basically "burning bridges" with other people, resulting in loss of social supports. Furthermore, without treatment, the consequences of their behavior often have little impact upon modifying future behavior—it is as if they are unable to learn from experience and make different choices. The self-detrimental behavior is repeated over and over again, which frustrates and exasperates others, including helping professionals. It also may eventually frustrate the individual him or herself, and it is at this juncture that the individual may voluntarily seek treatment. Example:

> Jack, 50 years old, on parole after a lengthy sentence for armed robbery, seeks counseling at the local behavioral health clinic. During the intake evaluation, the social worker asks Jack why he is seeking treatment now for the first time. Jack says: "One thing about prison is that you have a lot of time to think. I have been in and out of

jail and prison my whole life, even as a juvenile. I'm just tired of it. I'm tired of wasting my life, I'm tired of being locked up and I want to change how things are going for me. While I was in prison, I had problems with my nerves and with always getting into fights with other people. The prison doctor put me on Sinequan* and for the first time I was able to think before I acted. That was a good thing—that gave me hope that maybe I can change my life for the better." (Newhill, 1995).

The second characteristic, *having a disability in working and achieving intimacy with others that is generally serious and pervasive*, addresses the degree of psychosocial disability exacted by having a personality disorder. The two components that primarily drive this psychosocial disability are emotional and behavioral dysregulation, with the dysregulated emotions driving the behavioral problems. For example, in the hypothetical case vignette above, the incident of George assaulting the president of the company was driven by the rage and indignation that overwhelmed him as a result of the narcissistically perceived insult of being laid off.

People with personality disorders are often more impaired in their interpersonal relations and general ability to function socially, psychologically, and occupationally than those who might be referred to as neurotic, that is, those whose primary problems involve depression and anxiety.

Many individuals with personality disorders, particularly certain subtypes, are individuals who do not modulate anger or any really strong negative emotion in a flexible and appropriate manner. They have what is called *emotional dysregulation*. This means that the person has (1) a low threshold or high sensitivity to emotional stimuli, particularly negative emotional stimuli such as stimuli that might provoke anger or depressed feelings; (2) when emotionally provoked, they have a high amplitude/level of emotional response; and, finally, (3) they have a slow return to emotional baseline, that is, a hard time calming or settling down (Linehan, 1993). Emotional dysregulation is particularly pronounced with negative affects, such as anger, dysphoria, sadness, or panic, and is probably biologically based. This will be discussed in more detail later when this chapter addresses borderline personality disorder in depth.

The third characteristic seen across all types of personality disorder is *elicitation of symptoms by interpersonal conflict*. Unlike psychotic disorders or neurotic conditions, the symptoms of a personality disorder almost always manifest within an interpersonal context. It is as if they need someone else to interact with in order to bring their symptoms forth. Also, universally, people with personality disorders lack empathy toward others and cannot see themselves as others do (Perry & Vaillant, 1989). As was the case with Bob, in the vignette above, such individuals are unable to perceive how their behavior may hurt other people. In fact, they may exhibit toward others the very behaviors they complain about others exhibiting toward them (Zanor, 2010). Example:

> Margaret, a senior vice president at a credit union, complained continually to her co-workers about the shabby treatment she believed she endured from the president of the company: "He bullies me," Margaret would lament, "and treats me like dirt. He disrespects me and discounts the work I do. How can someone treat another person that way and not care?" Meanwhile, Margaret had a reputation for bullying the workers she supervised, including criticizing and sabotaging their work and taking credit for other people's accomplishments. Margaret was unable to make any connection between the behavior she detested from her boss and how that was similar to the way she treated those under her supervision and control.

* *Sinequan is the trade name for doxepin, a tricyclic antidepressant that has anti-anxiety properties.*

Margaret's behavior involves a different form of anosognosia, or lack of insight. She is unable to see herself as others do or see how her behavior negatively affects others. Instead, she sees it as justified. This is particularly pronounced in people with narcissistic personality disorders.

Finally, the last major cross-cutting characteristic of people with personality disorders is *an uncanny ability to get under the skin of others*. Central to this is the notion of the merging of personal boundaries, which is manifested in the profound effect people with personality disorders have on the other people around them (Perry & Vaillant, 1989). These are people who can literally invade other people's lives and psychologically engulf them. Because of this, a cornerstone to the effective treatment of individuals with personality disorders, as well as living and working with them in one's personal life, is to *always employ structure and set limits with empathy and fairness*. It is also critical not to lose professional objectivity and judgment, because not maintaining appropriate objectivity may result in simply labeling the person with a personality disorder as difficult and untreatable and the client, then, may be rejected, and not receive the help he or she needs. It is important to recognize that our own negative countertransference reactions, if not recognized and dealt with appropriately, have the potential for undermining the possibility of treatment success.

Assess your comprehension of *the four cross-cutting characteristics all personality disorders have in common* by completing this quiz.

WHAT BRINGS THE PERSON WITH A PERSONALITY DISORDER INTO TREATMENT

Given that people with personality disorders often don't see that they have a problem, even though they may make life miserable for those around them, what brings such an individual into treatment? There are several common triggers that can push a person with a personality disorder (PD) into seeking treatment. One trigger is suffering a significant loss, such as being fired from a job, breaking up with a significant other, or a death in the family. For example, Bob, the client with schizoid personality disorder depicted in the case vignette above, entered treatment following the traumatic death of his cat. People with PDs also seek treatment because they are experiencing major mood or anxiety symptoms. It is very common for individuals with a PD to have a comorbid Axis I condition—for example, a mood or anxiety disorder, a substance abuse disorder, or a psychotic disorder—and in the course of treatment for the precipitating condition, the presence of a PD may be detected.

Experiencing what is called a "developmental dyssynchrony" can also push an individual with an underlying personality disorder into treatment (Budman & Gurman, 1988). One has a developmental dyssynchrony when one's life is out of sync with where the majority of one's age peers are in terms of maturation milestones. For example, a person may present for treatment and say that the problem is that he or she is 40 years old, single, still living in his or her parents' basement, and working part-time in a grocery store. Meanwhile almost all of the person's peers are living independently, in stable relationships with a partner, and working full-time. Or clients might say that they have never been able to actualize their potential and don't know why or they have never been happy and can't figure out how to change that. Another form of developmental dyssynchrony is illustrated by the case of John in the vignette above. Here, the person—usually upon reaching mid-life—realizes that his or her life hasn't been going well and, for the first time, is motivated to make the changes needed to improve his or her life in the future, including embarking upon difficult characterological changes. Although, by definition, personality disorders are chronic lifelong conditions (Paris, 2003), the maturity that goes along with reaching mid-life often brings with it a muting of the individual's externalizing symptoms along with a capacity to be reflective about one's life and the beginnings of the development of insight.

Interpersonal conflict can also trigger someone with a PD into seeking treatment. Examples include ongoing marital discord, a long history of involvement in abusive relationships, repeatedly being fired from jobs because of discord with co-workers, repeated involvement with law enforcement and engaging in violations of the law, and/or other repetitive patterns of interpersonal conflict. In these kinds of cases, treatment may be sought via the pressure from others with whom the person is having conflict, for example, a spouse, employer, other family member, or the legal system. An example of this would be the high-powered executive with a narcissistic personality whose wife has threatened to file for divorce unless he gets counseling to help him become less self-centered and critical. Individuals with personality disorders who present for treatment secondary to interpersonal conflict may be, essentially, *socially involuntary clients* (see Chapter 5), and angry and indignant about being forced to comply with someone else's request. In this kind of situation, the clinician is wise to follow the principles laid out in Chapter 5 on working with involuntary clients.

Somatic problems for which no medical cause has been found can also result in a referral for psychiatric treatment for someone with a personality disorder. There also is some evidence that certain persistent conditions such as chronic fatigue syndrome are associated with maladaptive personality features, although maladaptive personality features may also be a consequence of dealing with the condition rather than causal (Nater, Jones, Lin, et al., 2010). Some personality disorders also show a high comorbidity with certain medical illnesses. For example, medical illnesses that often occur with borderline personality disorder include chronic back pain, arthritis, and fibromyalgia (Frankenburg & Zanarini, 2006; Sansone & Hawkins, 2004).

Finally, individuals with personality disorders commonly enter treatment because of various forms of addiction. Through the course of treatment for the addiction, the presence of a personality disorder may be identified. For such clients, motivational interviewing or motivational enhancement therapy is often the treatment of choice for engagement. This is discussed in more detail in the next chapter on co-occurring disorders.

Because many of the triggers that send someone with a personality disorder into treatment are problems that have been going on for some time, a key initial question for the social worker or other clinician to ask is: "Why are you seeking treatment *now*?" The answer to this can provide important information about what has changed in the ongoing saga of the person's life to prompt them to seek treatment at this particular time, and where their motivation for accepting treatment and change lies. Now that the person has come through the "treatment door," the next question is: What do you do with them? The next section will review some basic strategies that are useful in the early stages of treatment with individuals with personality disorders, look at some later-stage treatment approaches and, finally, discuss concretely how to deal with some of the common behavior challenges such individuals present with during treatment.

General Early and Late-Stage Intervention Strategies

Helpful strategies in the early stages of treatment

The first step for the clinician to take is to address the client's presenting problem. This facilitates the development of rapport and trust because you are starting where the client is and where the probable source of highest motivation lies. Helpful strategies for achieving this include basic active listening skills, including ample use of open-ended questions; strategic use of empathic communication; and early-stage exploratory cognitive-behavioral interventions. It is important to assess and provide appropriate treatment for any Axis I psychopathology, with the most common conditions comorbid with personality disorders including mood disorders, anxiety disorders, and substance use disorders (Paris, 2003).

The next step is to help the client identify *patterns* of feelings, perceptions, and behaviors that seem to be causing problems for the person and other people in his or her life via the use of gently probing questions. As the maladaptive behavior patterns are identified, ask the client how these patterns are working out in his or her life. Do the patterns result in problems? What is the client losing as a result of continuing these patterns? What are the costs to the client of maintaining the patterns? And, finally, are these patterns of behavior getting the client what the client wants out of life? As Dr. Phil McGraw often puts it to guests on his show: "So, how's that working out for you?" Asking this question puts both the choice to change and responsibility for change back in the client's hands, makes it the client's responsibility, and supports the client's control and self-determination.

Next, it can be helpful to collaborate with the client in drawing a connection between the client's presenting problem(s) and the more pervasive patterns of behavior that you and the client have identified. Then, collaborate with the client in exploring ways to challenge and change these more enduring problematic (maladaptive) patterns. At this point, the client has to make a decision whether he or she wants to move forward and commit to treatment or not; however, it is the client's decision. It can be helpful to employ some of the strategies outlined in Chapter 5 on working with involuntary clients, such as weighing the advantages and disadvantages of entering treatment versus not entering treatment.

Helpful strategies in the later stages of treatment

Cognitive-behavioral treatment (CBT) or its derivatives, such as dialectical behavioral therapy (DBT), can be helpful in treating individuals with personality disorders if they are motivated and committed to treatment (Linehan, 1993; Young, 1990). If using CBT, identify the client's core schemas that may underlie the patterns of maladaptive behavior and the underlying painful feelings. Then standard CBT techniques can be employed to challenge and change these core beliefs (Bowers, 1999). Individuals with personality disorders, however, tend to react to such challenges with anger rather than insight and, thus, the clinician must be prepared for this. Using CBT derivatives explicitly developed for working with individuals with personality disorders, such as DBT, can sometimes be more effective than standard CBT because DBT emphasizes the importance of maintaining the dialectic balancing validation of the client as he or she is with opportunity for change. The emphasis is on challenging maladaptive behaviors while also reinforcing adaptive behaviors.

If using psychodynamic strategies, combine challenging problematic defenses (discussed in more detail below), such as splitting, denial, passive-aggressive, and projection, with support of mature adaptive defenses (altruism, suppression, sublimation, and humor) while facilitating insight and providing support. Encourage the client to begin to test out new behaviors in real-life situations by giving homework assignments that take small "baby steps" one at a time so that the client has a high probability of success. The therapist can also serve as a "coach" via telephone consultation sessions in between group or individual sessions to provide support and guidance for the homework. Group treatment can also be a very effective modality in treating personality disorders because the group can reinforce behavior change, enhance social support, and challenge resistant and evasive behaviors. It can be helpful to also supplement formal treatment with participation in self-help groups, including appropriate 12-step groups, drop-in centers, and consumer peer support.

For some individuals with borderline, antisocial, and narcissistic personality disorders, psychotropic medication may be helpful to reduce impulsivity, self-harm, and aggression and improve emotion regulation. Selective serotonin reuptake inhibitor antidepressants, mood stabilizers, and atypical antipsychotic medication in low doses can be helpful for some clients. An important final point is that working with individuals with personality disorders can be extraordinarily stressful for the clinician. Clinical supervision is critically important to have in place for the therapist for managing countertransference, safety issues, and to avoid burnout. It is important to always remember that it took years for the client's personality and behavior patterns to develop, thus, these behavior patterns will not change overnight or even by the next week or month. However, with patience, empathy, structure, limits, and supportive help, clients with personality disorders can improve, and many can achieve success in recovery.

Assess your comprehension of *what brings someone with a personality disorder into treatment and what strategies are helpful at the beginning of treatment* by completing this quiz.

KEY DEFENSE MECHANISMS, ASSOCIATED BEHAVIORS, AND CLINICAL RESPONSES

The Theory behind the Role of Defense Mechanisms

When thinking about the assessment and treatment of individuals with personality disorders, it is important to understand and appreciate the contribution that a psychodynamic understanding of personality functioning can provide, even if one doesn't use the psychodynamic approach directly in treatment (Alliance of Psychoanalytic Organizations, 2006). Clinicians can become very exasperated and frustrated by the repetitive self-detrimental and destructive behaviors of their clients with personality disorders, and such feelings can erode the preservation of empathy and the therapeutic alliance, and undermine a successful outcome. Psychodynamic theory, particularly the theory of the role of defense mechanisms in driving behavior, can provide good explanations for where these behaviors come from, and such understanding can inform how one approaches treatment and can serve to enhance empathy for the client's suffering. Recognizing the role of defense mechanisms in driving behavior does not provide an "excuse" for the behavior, but it does provide an explanation. This section will address some of the key defense mechanisms commonly exhibited by individuals with the various personality disorders and discuss how clinicians can appropriately and effectively intervene when the action of such defenses manifests in treatment. Let's begin with a quick overview of Sigmund Freud's and his daughter, psychoanalyst Anna Freud's, original thinking about defense mechanisms and their function in mental life.

The Theory of Defense Mechanisms

Freud's earliest thinking was termed "the topographic era," in which he theorized that mental life is characterized by three layers: the unconscious, the preconscious, and the conscious. Because Freud continually modified his theories based on his experiences with patients, his later clinical experiences caused him to revise his topographic theory into what he called the "structural model," composed of three entities: the id, the ego, and the superego. In this new structural theory, Freud believed that some forces of repression were relegated to the unconscious part of the mind, and he proposed the existence of a new entity, which he termed the "ego." The role and function of the ego is to mediate between the demands of the id (the repository of unconscious drives), the superego (defined as, roughly, morality and conscience), and reality, and had both a conscious part and an unconscious part. These three major structures of the mind—the id, ego, and superego—were seen as three separate groups of related functions that operated in an integrated manner (Freud, 1911, 1923, 1926).

Freud, and later Wilhelm Reich (1949), postulated that there is an unconscious part of the ego within which lies the "character armor" of the individual, that is, the person's psychological defenses. If something happens in the person's life to cause anxiety to well up, the anxiety triggers the defenses to "kick into action" to protect the individual from consciously feeling the pain produced by experiencing the anxiety. To Freud, the most painful affects a person can experience are anxiety and depression. Individuals with personality disorders have exceptionally powerful defenses against feeling anxiety and depression—which are the treatable conditions in the individual's personality—and, thus, to help clients with personality disorders, we must have a clear understanding of these underlying defenses. In treatment, the therapist must get past or through the defenses in order to treat the underlying depression and anxiety, so the theory goes, which are the affects at the core of all personality disorders.

Defense mechanisms are defined as the unconscious mental processes that the ego uses to resolve conflicts among the four focal points of mental life: (1) instinct (the id); (2) reality (the ego); (3) important objects (people); and (4) moral conscience (the superego) (A. Freud, 1936/1966; Perry & Vaillant, 1989). Defense mechanisms are important for all of us to function as human beings and do not necessarily cause psychopathology to develop. In fact, good mature defenses, such as altruism, positively and constructively serve and support good mental health. This is because healthy defenses can be very powerful mechanisms for buffering and even abolishing anxiety and depression and helping a person cope with the ups and downs of everyday life. This is the major reason why clients with personality disorders are so reluctant to alter their behavior, because to abandon a defense—no matter how problematic it may be—means experiencing an increase in anxiety and depression. I used to tell my clients with personality disorders that "you will feel worse before you feel better." That was true, but a "hard sell" to the client.

However, the good news is that defenses, and the patterns of behavior driven by them, are not set in stone. Rather, defenses are both dynamic and reversible, as clients learn new ways of handling problems and develop new patterns of behavior that help them to function better. The job of a person's defenses, even those that are problematic, is to serve health and maintain psychic balance. Through treatment, the individual with a personality disorder can learn to abandon problematic defenses and try out new defenses promoting new healthier patterns of behavior, but it is not easy and can be a frightening prospect for the client. Although each type of personality disorder has a most dominant or pervasive defense—for example, projection is the key defense in all paranoid disorders including paranoid personality disorder—all types of personality disorders actually use several defenses, and these defenses represent ongoing dimensions of the client's life history. They have shaped the person into who he or she is today. However, while an individual without a personality disorder but with, let's say, depression or an anxiety disorder values insight and values the interpretation of his or her defenses, the client with a personality disorder bristles at such efforts and meets addressing defenses with anger (Perry & Vaillant, 1989). Clumsy attempts to tackle defenses head-on usually don't work and can rupture the relationship with the client and undermine mutual trust. An important therapeutic rule of thumb is: When challenging defenses and changing behaviors is part of the treatment, provide a buffer by mobilizing strong social supports, such as including group treatment or self-help groups as part of the treatment package in combination with helping the client develop healthier alternative defenses. For example, dialectical behavioral therapy for the treatment of borderline personality disorder explicitly requires both individual and group treatment, which provides social support and skills development as clients move through the challenges that change poses for them (Linehan, 1993).

Specific Defenses Found in the Various Personality Disorders

Perry and Vaillant (1989) point out that when working with clients who deny they have a problem yet are presenting for treatment, as is the case for many clients with personality disorders, the clinician is in the position of having to identify problematic patterns of behavior and infer what underlying psychodynamics are driving the behavior. Whether one believes these forces are defense mechanisms, from the psychodynamic perspective, or cognitive schemas, from the CBT perspective, they need to be identified and understood by the clinician to inform the most productive way of interacting with the client.

There are ten primary defense mechanisms used by individuals with personality disorders. These include fantasy, dissociation, denial, hypochondriasis, splitting, passive aggression, isolation, projection, acting out, and devaluation. It is beyond the scope of this chapter to address all ten defenses, thus, the discussion will be limited to the five defenses that drive some of the most problematic behavior that clinicians are faced with when working with clients with personality disorders: denial, projection, splitting, passive aggression, and devaluation.

Denial

Freud called denial the most primitive defense because it develops very early in life. It is also the most commonly used defense across all of the subtypes of personality disorder. Denial is an easily understood defense because it functions by pushing out of consciousness all emotions, impulses, or shameful desires that might be upsetting and cause anxiety if experienced consciously. Pushing such troubling affects out of consciousness doesn't mean they aren't apparent to others, however, and the clinician may have no difficulty observing indicators that the client is angry, for example, although the client indignantly denies it. Perry and Vaillant (1989) explain that "denial is the callus that has supplanted the hurt the individual experienced growing up, when honest self-awareness and expression repeatedly brought down the wrath and punishing comments of caretakers" (p. 1360). An example would be the client who can't openly express any feelings of anger because when she did so as a child, her mother literally washed her mouth out with soap, stating, "We do not get angry in this family!" Although denial may be the only choice when one is a child with few alternatives, denial does not work well in the long run. The problem with denial is that it keeps oneself and others at a distance from one's real emotional experiences and, equally important, it doesn't make problems disappear. In fact, problems that are denied are more likely to get worse than get better. Clients using denial as a defense may hotly protest that they are fine, but their anger, depression, and anxiety is obvious to others via their behavior. How does the clinician handle such a situation?

One technique that can help break through the denial and allow the client to experience the feared affects is the technique of *displacement*. In using displacement, one talks about the same emotional issue but in a less threatening context (Perry & Vaillant, 1989). Then, the clinician can express empathy for the denied affect, which gives the client the message that such feelings are acceptable. This provides support and validation for the client, and then he or she may be able to openly talk about the original issue. Let's return to the example of the woman whose mother washed her mouth out with soap when she expressed anger as a child:

SW: It sounds like your mother's constant demands for attention may make you feel a little angry. . . .

Client: No! I am not angry at my mother. I have never been angry with my mother.

SW: Never?

Client: Never. I learned long ago that was not okay.

SW: That feeling anger is not okay?

Client: Of course it isn't okay—we're talking about my mother here. I love my mother and she loves me. Look, I don't want to talk about this anymore. I do not have a problem with anger toward my mother.

In a low-key manner, using the technique of displacement, the social worker goes on to discuss other ongoing difficulties the client has been having that may involve anger, such as difficulties in being assertive when being treated unfairly at work.

SW: Can you think of an example when you felt you were being treated unfairly at work?

Client: Okay, like last week, I had worked eight straight days in a row before I had a day off and then my boss left a message on my cell, telling me to come in on my day off. It was okay, though.

SW: Gee, I think if that happened to me, I'd be pretty upset.

Client: Well . . . we were short staffed, though.

SW: Even so, that wasn't very fair.

Client: No, it wasn't! But I didn't say anything.

SW: Is feeling angry kind of scary for you?

Client: Yeah . . .

SW: Strong feelings, like anger, *can* be scary. But anger is a valid feeling when one is being treated unfairly.

Client: Would you be angry at your boss?

SW: I would freely *feel* the anger if it was justified. I would try not to blow up at my boss, but anger can be functional in helping us stand up for our rights at work, with friends, and even with family.

Client: Gee . . . I don't know. So, anger can be okay to feel?

SW: Absolutely.

At this point, with a lot of empathic support, the social worker encourages the client to talk about her fears over expressing anger and where that fear may be coming from. Eventually, the client may be able to connect the current situation at work with old issues and experiences with her mother and move toward being able and willing to address and work through those old issues that are continuing to affect her current maladaptive patterns of behavior, such as allowing herself to be treated unfairly at work along with her mother's continuing unfair demands.

Projection

Projection as a defense and projective thinking patterns have already been discussed in Chapter 11 on social work practice with individuals with paranoid disorders, thus it will only be briefly addressed here. Projection is defined as a form of displacement in which the person attributes to others those objectionable character traits, attitudes, motives, and desires one wishes to deny in him or herself. This enables the individual to remain unaware of his or her own important personality drives while distorting picture of the outside world. Essentially, the client attributes his or her own unacknowledged feelings onto others.

When faced with a client who utilizes the defense of projection, it is important to not react with anger or defensiveness but rather to respond with honesty and anticipate ahead of time, as much as possible, any future problems that might arise to avoid the client assuming there is a conspiracy against him or her. For example, let's say a clinician is making a referral on the client's behalf to an internist for a medical evaluation. The clinician can say: "I will refer you to Dr. Doe, but I cannot say for certain when he can see you. I have been told he is good but you must arrive at your own judgment about that." Strict honesty, presenting yourself as the client's ally and supporter of the client's rights, and maintaining a more formal demeanor, rather than being too warm or friendly, can be helpful in initiating trust and overcoming the barrier of projection.

Splitting

The defense mechanism known as splitting is seen most commonly with individuals who meet criteria for borderline, narcissistic, and antisocial personality disorders. When a client employs splitting, instead of relating to people as they are with both positive and negative qualities, the client divides people, particularly those for whom they hold ambivalent feelings, into good people and bad people. For example, in milieu treatment settings, such as residential treatment, partial hospitalization programs, or inpatient units, the client will idealize certain staff and highly dislike other staff. They will also do the same toward their peers in the program, and these uniform feelings toward others can switch quickly into the polar opposite. The effect of this can be extremely disruptive to the treatment program and destructive to treatment milieu by provoking staff to turn against each other and turn against the client.

Splitting can also occur with one person who is initially idealized and then disparaged later due to something that disappoints or upsets the client. The best way to manage splitting is to anticipate the process, discuss it openly in treatment sessions and at staff meetings, and present a uniform message to the client that nobody is all good or all bad, everyone contains degrees of both, and that is reality. During psychotherapeutic treatment, the clinician must aim to create a safe and validating atmosphere that allows clients to openly and safely experience both positive and negative aspects of themselves, of the therapist, and of the issues that are discussed. Through this, clients will learn to combine the good and the bad into an integrated whole, including a consolidated sense of their own identity and seeing the therapist as a person with contrasting aspects of their self.

Passive aggression

The behavior patterns driven by passive aggression as a defense can be found in all of the personality disorders to some degree but are most common in individuals with borderline personality disorder and passive-aggressive or negativistic personality disorder. Passive-aggressive personality disorder first appeared in the *DSM-II* (APA, 1968) as a separate category. The criteria were refined for the *DSM-III* (APA, 1980) and, subsequently, for the *DSM-III-R* (APA, 1987). However, passive-aggressive personality disorder was excluded as a formal Axis II diagnosis beginning with the *DSM-IV* (1994), relegated to the appendix called "Criteria Sets and Axes Provided for Further Study" (APA, 1994; APA, 2000), and completely disappeared with *DSM-5* (APA, 2013). There were two main reasons cited for this shift. First was the *structural reactivity* aspect, which means that while the characteristics of the other personality disorders were pervasive across contexts, passive-aggressive behavior might be seen in certain contexts but not in others. Second, it was argued, passive aggression as defined by the DSM criteria appears to be focused on only a single theme, that is, resistance to external demands (Robinson, 2005). As a result, the American Psychiatric Association concluded that there is not enough evidence to consider passive aggression to be a distinct disorder or even to warrant further study. The characteristic or defense mechanism of passive aggression, however, is clearly recognized, commonly seen in practice, and can be difficult to manage across family, school, and workplace settings (Long, Long, & Whitson, 2009).

Passive aggression may be defined as a defense mechanism in which rather than expressing them directly, feelings of anger are turned inward and then expressed in a passive, obstinate way. Behaviors indicative of passive aggression include repeated forgetfulness, intentional inefficiency or failure at assigned tasks, procrastination, chronic complaints about being mistreated or misunderstood, and self-destructive behavior such as repeated wrist-cutting and other self-harming behaviors that do not have suicidal intent (Millon, Grossman, Millon, et al., 2004). Underlying all of these behaviors is unacknowledged hostility that is often not even particularly well concealed.

For example, it is not uncommon for a clinician to see the family of an individual who is in the emergency room following a episode of wrist-cutting in which the family exclaims, "How could she have done this to us?" Although the cutting of the wrists was a self-harming behavior directed at the client, the hostility toward others conveyed by the self-harming action was clearly apparent to the family, so it is as if they had been assaulted.

The best way to deal with passive aggression is to try to get the person to express the underlying anger and hostility in words rather than actions. The relief that many clients feel after engaging in self-harm should be discussed in a matter-of-fact way, and then the clinician can ask the client: "Can you put what you are feeling into words?" and empathically support and validate the feelings that the client reveals. Sometimes clients are stubborn and refuse to talk about what they are feeling. In such cases, it is best to avoid a battle of wills and just take a "time out." This allows the client to reflect on the choice of not speaking up and also conveys the message that passive aggression will result in less attention rather than more attention. Example:

> Sandy, age 27, has been admitted to the county hospital emergency room 30 times over the past 2 years for treatment after cutting her wrists. The current evaluation takes place at 3 a.m. on a Saturday morning. Sandy is lying on a gurney, wrists bandaged, with her face to the wall. The social worker assigned to evaluate Sandy enters the room, introduces herself, and sits down.

SW: How are you doing, Sandy?

Sandy: Not so good . . .

SW: How are your wrists?

Sandy: They hurt.

SW: I imagine so. I talked with the doctor before I came in and he said that you cut your wrists pretty seriously, although he said you will be fine in terms of healing up. Can you tell me a little about what happened this evening?

Sandy: I don't want to talk about it.

SW: You must have felt very upset and desperate to get to the point where you decided to cut your wrists.

Sandy: Whatever . . . you're the professional, you should know how I feel.

SW: Sandy, I would like to help you. Can you put what you were feeling into words?

Sandy stays silent. The social worker waits for about a minute before speaking again.

SW: It sounds like you don't feel like talking now. Let's take a break. I'm going to go out to the nursing station to write some notes and I'll be back in 15 minutes.

The social worker returns to Sandy's room in 16 minutes and sits down.

Sandy: You're one minute late.

SW: I'm sorry. I guess I lost track of time. Now, where were we? (putting the responsibility back on the client)

Sandy: You wanted to know why I did this.

SW: Yes. Can you put what you are or were feeling into words? What were you feeling before you cut your wrists?

Sandy: Okay, I'm pissed off, all right? My dad told me to get off my butt and get a job, but he doesn't understand that I can't work! I'm too depressed and my life is a mess. . . .

In this scenario, the social worker addresses the wrist-cutting in a matter-of-fact manner, expresses empathy for what the client may be feeling, and inquires if the client can put the feelings underlying the wrist-cutting into words. The client balks and won't talk about what is going on, so the social worker suggests a time out to break the contest of wills. When the social worker returns, the client reprimands her for being one minute late, which reveals that the client had been keeping track of the time and cared about when the social worker would return. The social worker apologizes for being late and again inquires about what the client is feeling, and this time the client reveals her angry feelings and the events that led up to the wrist-cutting.

Although passive aggression can be exasperating for clinicians and family members, it is important not to respond to the behavior with anger or punishment because that only serves to reinforce and even escalate the behavior. It is also important not to take actions that will humiliate the client, rather, respond in ways that will set limits on the behavior and encourage the client to take responsibility and develop alternative healthy ways of dealing with the underlying feelings that are driving the passive-aggressive behavior. The last defense mechanism to be discussed is devaluation.

Devaluation

One kind of devaluation occurs with splitting—as discussed previously. Another type of devaluation occurs as an aspect of the narcissism seen in narcissistic personality disorder, antisocial personality disorder, and borderline personality disorder. Narcissistic clients, on the surface, see themselves as powerful and all-important. Underneath this facade, however, are often feelings of low self-worth and poor self-esteem. This poor self-esteem is shored up by an assumption of omnipotence, grandiosity, and entitlement. When these assumptions are threatened, however, some narcissistic clients may respond by becoming critical and belittling toward the clinician. In reaction to being disparaged, some clinicians may become angry, defensive, and rejecting toward the client. What can set such a client off? It is important to understand that the simple fact the client is there for help makes the client feel helpless and vulnerable, which causes anxiety to well up and kicks in the defense of devaluation (Perry & Vaillant, 1989).

Developing a therapeutic alliance with a narcissistic client can be achieved if the clinician takes certain strategic steps. First, the clinician should avoid becoming defensive, belittling, or rejecting toward the client in response to the client's provocations, and recognize the dynamics of the client's behavior for what it is and where it stems from. This can support empathy toward the client. Narcissistic individuals generally don't experience much empathy from others due to their behavior, and so responding to them empathically can be disarming. Second, actively affirm the client's worth and dignity, and convey that the client is a person who deserves respect. Finally, to help the client feel less vulnerable and decrease defensiveness, frame treatment as an offer for consultation with competent experts rather than therapy (Perry & Vaillant, 1989). Example:

SW: Mr. Smith, I'm Esther Rubenstein, and I am a licensed clinical social worker here in the outpatient department. How can I be of help?

Client: You're just a *social worker*? (said with disdain) I would prefer to see a doctor.

SW: We do have doctors here at the clinic. However, since we are here together now, would you like to tell me more about why you came in today?

Client: I am here for some advice about a personal matter. So, where did you get your training? At some *state* school?

SW: I got my MSW at a state school, California State University, Sacramento, and I did my doctoral work at Smith College.

Client: Smith . . . well, that's an acceptable school.

SW: I appreciate your interest in getting assurance that the professionals you see are competently trained. You deserve to have the best.

Client: I do deserve the best. Well, okay, this is what I want to get some advice about . . .

As can be seen in the scenario, the client first belittles the social worker's discipline and then questions her training. However, she provides a matter-of-fact response, avoids getting defensive, and then affirms the client's right to competent treatment. This reduces the client's assumption of entitlement and provides reassurance about the clinician's competence, and he becomes willing then to talk about what advice he wants.

DIAGNOSING PERSONALITY DISORDERS: THE DSM APPROACH

The diagnostic criteria for personality disorders address maladaptive behaviors or traits that are characteristic of the person's long-term functioning since adulthood. For the newly released *Diagnostic and Statistical Manual of Mental Disorders, Fifth Edition (DSM-5)* (APA, 2013), the essential characteristics of a personality disorder involve impairments in personality, both in terms of self and interpersonal functioning, along with the presence of pathological personality traits and, similar to previous editions of the *DSM*, emphasizes the importance of not diagnosing a personality disorder unless the characteristic features are typical of the person's long-term functioning and are not limited to discrete periods of another mental illness. An example would be a person with paranoid schizophrenia who during an acute psychotic episode is assaultive and engages in illegal activities that result in arrest, but when stable is law-abiding and nonviolent. In such a case, the clinician would not give the person a diagnosis of antisocial personality disorder because the antisocial behavior is only in evidence when the individual is psychotic.

The *DSM-5* (APA, 2013) originally proposed a complex Alternative DSM-5 Model for Personality Disorders that was radically different from the traditional diagnostic approach used through all of the previous successive editions of the DSM. The new model, which takes a dimensional approach to viewing personality pathology, is very different conceptually from the traditional categorical approach, which is the approach used in most systems of medical diagnosis. After the proposed model was posted on the APA's DSM-5 website for public comment, the public and clinical feedback to the APA about the model was so uniformly negative (Carey, 2012) that after the public comment period was closed, the APA decided to return to the old model and criteria employed in the *DSM-IV-TR* for personality disorder (the Alternative Model is provided in an appendix toward the back of the DSM-5 manual on pages 761–781).

Most of the negative reactions related to concern that clinicians had about the practical utility of the new model and potential problems in using it. As Jonathan Shedler, a psychologist at the University of Colorado Medical School, noted (Zanor, 2010): "Clinicians are accustomed to thinking in terms of syndromes, not de-constructed trait ratings. Researchers think in terms of variables, and there's just a huge schism," adding that the DSM-5 Personality Disorders Work Group was comprised primarily of academic researchers "who really don't do a lot of clinical work. We're seeing yet another manifestation of what's called in psychology the science-practice schism" (quoted in Zanor, 2010). What the "science-practice schism" means is that academic researchers generally approach evaluating and understanding psychopathology phenomena differently than clinicians do. Academic researchers have the luxury of time and control and can develop complex systems to explain something. Clinicians, on the other hand, must consider all aspects of how a client presents, must base their assessment on what information they can obtain, and are working within a system of competing demands (from agency, insurance company, community) over which they have limited control.

Ten Personality Disorders within Three Clusters

As in the *DSM-IV-TR*, the *DSM-5* identifies ten separate personality disorders, which are grouped into three clusters. Each cluster has overarching dimensional characteristics common to all the disorders included within the particular cluster, but dissimilar to the other clusters. For example, Cluster A includes paranoid, schizoid, and schizotypal personality disorders and, as a collective, people with these disorders appear generally odd, isolative, and/or eccentric. Cluster B includes antisocial, borderline, histrionic, and narcissistic personality disorders and, as a collective, people with these disorders are generally dramatic, emotional, and erratic. Finally, Cluster C includes avoidant, dependent, and obsessive-compulsive personality disorders and, as a collective, people with these disorders appear anxious and/or fearful.

The *DSM-5* did initiate two changes, however. The DSM-IV-TR diagnosis of "Personality Disorder Not Otherwise Specified (NOS)" has been eliminated and replaced by the DSM-5 diagnosis of "Personality Disorder—Trait Specified," based on moderate or greater impairment in personality functioning and the presence of pathological personality traits, providing a more informative diagnosis for individuals who do not meet full criteria for one of the specific personality disorders. Also, the diagnosis of "personality change due to another medical condition" is provided to account for situations in which a general medical condition is a direct physiological cause for a change in personality function.

SPECIFIC CULTURE, AGE, AND GENDER FEATURES TO BE CONSIDERED WITH PERSONALITY DISORDERS

Culture

Judgments about personality functioning must take into account an individual's ethnic, cultural, and social background. As discussed in Chapter 11, careful differential diagnosis must be made so that diagnosing personality pathology is not confounded by the challenges people face in the process of immigration or the expression of cultural or religious practices or political actions. If a social worker or other clinician is evaluating someone from a culture other than his or her own, it can be very useful to obtain information from others who are familiar with the client's cultural background to sort out what represents normal personality functioning versus abnormal functioning within the parameters of the individual's culture. Certain cultural practices and expressions are sometimes vulnerable to being stereotyped by those outside the culture and such stereotypes may seem to fit certain personality disorder criteria. This must be avoided. So, for example, how emotions are expressed differs significantly across cultures. In some cultures, emotions are expressed freely and strongly to others and individuals from such cultures may be misdiagnosed with histrionic personality traits. Or, in some cultures, women are required to be submissive and are forbidden to travel independently outside the home without accompaniment by a male relative. A woman who is a member of such a culture could be misdiagnosed as having dependent personality traits. Or, some individuals who live in poverty-stricken, high-crime neighborhoods may join a gang and engage in criminal activities as a means of survival and, thus, might be misdiagnosed as having antisocial personality disorder. Example:

> Su-Hwa, a 22-year-old Korean graduate student, sought counseling at her university's counseling center because she was feeling overwhelmed by school demands and not sure whether she wanted to continue the chemical engineering doctoral program that she was enrolled in. Su-Hwa had always dreamed of being a journalist but her father, an engineer in Korea, wanted her to follow in his footsteps. Su-Hwa and the counseling center therapist had a good session, however, the therapist noted the following in the clinic record: "Client says she is afraid of angering her father if she switches majors and wants to talk with her mother before making any decisions. Impression: Dependent personality disorder."

What the therapist did not understand is that in Korean culture, children—including adult children—are expected to obey and please their parents. Su-Hwa's concerns were culturally syntonic, and the fact she sought counseling for some career guidance actually demonstrated a considerable level of assertiveness rather than dependency.

Age

Childhood and adolescence

The general recommendation is to *not* diagnose a personality disorder in childhood or adolescence, unless the individual's particular maladaptive personality traits appear to be pervasive (across a range of contexts), persistent (i.e., present for at least 1 year), and unlikely to be explained by a particular developmental stage or an episode of an Axis I disorder (APA, 2000). In such a case, diagnosing the client as having a personality disorder may be appropriate and justified, but clinicians should be extremely careful and conservative on this. The exception to this is antisocial personality disorder, which cannot be diagnosed under age 18 because the same behaviors in a child or adolescent under age 18 is called conduct disorder.

One primary reason that it is recommended that one use caution in diagnosing a personality disorder in a child or adolescent is the risk of stigma. Studies have shown that individuals with personality disorders are particularly affected by stigma and are often the object of negative patronizing attitudes from others, although they may not have experienced overt discrimination (Dinos, Stevens, Serfaty, et al., 2004). Another reason that caution is advised is because it can be difficult to differentiate the tumultuousness of normal adolescence from features suggesting a personality disorder. When one is 13 years old, has little independence, and must suffer through one's parents still picking out one's clothes, it is normal to stamp up to one's room and behave in a passive-aggressive manner. It is developmentally appropriate and probably not an indicator of passive-aggressive personality.

Old age

Although, by definition, a personality disorder diagnosis requires an onset no later than early adulthood with a relatively stable course and long duration, some clients may not come to clinical attention until much later in life. For example, symptoms of a previously unrecognized personality disorder may be unveiled following the loss of a significant other or the loss of a previously stabilizing situation, for example, a job. However, this is unusual. The development of a change in personality in middle to late adulthood warrants a thorough evaluation to determine whether another condition may be present, such as Personality Change Due to a General Medical Condition or an unrecognized substance-related disorder.

Gender

Research has shown that certain personality disorders, such as narcissistic and antisocial personality disorders, are diagnosed more frequently in men. Other personality disorders, specifically borderline, histrionic, and dependent personality disorders, are more frequently diagnosed in women. It is still unclear to what extent this reflects real gender differences in the prevalence of such patterns and to what extent it reflects gender bias on the part of clinicians reflecting stereotypes about gender roles and behavior.

SUBTYPES OF PERSONALITY DISORDER

This section of the chapter will discuss six of the ten specific personality disorder subtypes included in *DSM-5*. Schizotypal, obsessive-compulsive, avoidant, narcissistic, and antisocial/psychopathic personality disorders will be described more briefly and then the borderline personality type will be examined in more depth, since individuals who meet criteria for the borderline personality disorder type can be quite challenging to treat and are commonly seen across a number of social work practice settings, placing a significant burden on society in large part because of their emotional, dramatic, and erratic behaviors. The four personality disorders that will not be addressed include *schizoid personality disorder*, which involves a pattern of detachment from social relationships and a restricted range of emotional expression, and was illustrated in the case of Bob above; *paranoid personality disorder*, which involves a pattern of distrust and suspiciousness such that others' motives are interpreted as malevolent, and has already been described in detail in Chapter 11; *histrionic personality disorder*, which involves a pattern of excessive emotionality and attention-seeking; and, finally, *dependent personality disorder*, which involves a pattern of submission and clinging behavior related to an excessive need to be taken care of (APA, 2013, p. 645).

Schizotypal Personality Disorder

Schizotypal personality is a very interesting personality disorder type, and when seeing such a client initially, one may think that the client has schizophrenia. Such individuals, however, do not have a psychotic disorder, but they experience many of the perceptual abnormalities one finds in schizophrenia and have a certain measure of the pathological personality trait called *psychoticism*. Psychoticism is characterized by odd, unusual, or bizarre appearance or behavior. The person may have odd or unusual thought processes and say odd, unusual, or inappropriate things. They often answer questions vaguely, provide highly circumstantial descriptions, and report odd sensory abilities, for example, they may say they are clairvoyant or have extrasensory perception. Furthermore, it is not uncommon for clients with schizophrenia to evidence the symptoms of schizotypal personality disorder prior to their first psychotic break.

Individuals with schizotypal personality disorder show a pervasive (across multiple contexts) pattern of impairments in self and interpersonal functioning. The impairments in self-functioning involve a confused rather than consolidated sense of identity, inappropriate reactions to social cues from others, and unrealistic, vague, or incoherent life goals. In terms of impairments in interpersonal functioning, individuals with schizotypal personality have difficulty empathizing with others or appreciating the effect their behavior has on others, and often misinterpret others' motivations and behaviors. Such individuals also often have great discomfort and feelings of inadequacy in relationships with other people and, as a result, may be isolated with few social contacts outside of family.

People with schizotypal PD also have cognitive and perceptual distortions, and eccentricities of behavior that are clearly different from what is seen in schizoid personality disorder (see the case of Bob above). For example, people with schizotypal personality disorder often report having ideas of reference. *Ideas of reference* is defined as incorrect interpretations of innocuous incidents and perceiving external events as having a particular and unusual meaning specifically for the person. Example:

Client: I believe that I have special sensory gifts. Just the other night I thought about my mother feeding the cat and then she got up and fed him. I believe that my thought moved her to feed him.

SW: Have you had any other experiences like that?

Client: Well, (with a small secretive smile) Mary Costanza makes references to me.

SW: Mary Costanza on Channel 11?

Client: Yes . . . when she gives the news, I feel she is sending me special messages.

SW: Why would she do that?

Client: We have a special relationship. It's special, not something most people would understand, but I know she is speaking to me.

SW: Do you hear voices—Mary's voice, for instance?

Client: I don't hear voices—I'm not psychotic, if that's what you mean. I hear her voice when she is telling the news. You see, embedded in the news are messages I can discern that are meant for me. Most people can't understand that.

In this example, the client is reporting *ideas of reference*, that is, believing that the newsperson on television is making personal references to him, although the ideas are not to delusional proportion nor do they constitute hallucinations. People with schizotypal personality may be preoccupied with paranormal phenomena that are outside the norms of their culture. They may also feel that they have special powers or sense events before they happen or can read or influence other people's thoughts, such as the client above, who believed that his thought about his mother feeding the cat influenced her to feed the cat. Such individuals with schizotypal personality may look and act very oddly. Example:

> One day a young man spontaneously walked into the crisis clinic when he saw the mental health sign while walking down the street, and asked to speak to someone "for a dose of mental health." He wore three baseball caps, two pairs of sunglasses and had attached all kinds of unusual ornaments to his jacket. When asked about the ornaments, he said they held special powers but was vague about what kind of powers they were exactly. After talking about his life in a very detailed circumstantial manner that actually didn't provide much real information, he stood up, said he had to go, and walked out of the clinic and down the street. This client returned to the clinic several times, never with any particular request, but as the staff got to know him better, their conclusion was that he probably had schizotypal personality and his visits to the clinic were probably spurred by loneliness. He never evidenced any overt psychotic symptoms, mood problems, or other indicators of another mental illness and no evidence of substance use was present. He was mostly just very eccentric and odd.

The prevalence of schizotypal personality is about 3 percent in the general population, with a higher risk among first-degree relatives of individuals with schizophrenia (Siever, Silverman, Horvath, et al., 1990), and appears to be slightly more common in males. The disorder is relatively stable but, even with treatment, not very malleable to change.

Obsessive-Compulsive Personality Disorder

The Scientist

John, age 50, is a research scientist at the local university. He is extremely successful at getting federal research grants and runs a large laboratory with many graduate students and post-doctoral fellows working on his studies. His lab, however, is not a happy place. John insists on micromanaging everyone's work, has great difficulty delegating work to others, and his research associates complain that his demands on them are excessive. John is at the lab or in his office working on papers or writing more grants 6–7 days per week, which his family is unhappy about. Every Sunday evening, John holds a "family meeting," the purpose of which is to draw up elaborate "to do" lists for the coming week for every member of the family, even including his 6-year-old daughter. These lists are then converted into charts and each family member is expected to cross off items as they are completed throughout the week, and then the charts for the previous week are reviewed at the meeting. If his wife or children protest this arrangement, John becomes furious and says that having a well-run household is as important as a well-run research lab. One day, as a group, the research associates draw up a letter outlining complaints about John's behavior. This letter is given to the dean of his department, who sternly advises John to ease up on his demands although, the dean adds, he is very happy about all the money John brings in to the department. The same day, John's wife tells him that she is very unhappy in their marriage because of his cold and controlling ways, and wants to get some couples counseling. John is annoyed, primarily because a counseling appointment will take time away from his lab, however he reluctantly agrees to his wife's request.

People with obsessive-compulsive personality disorder (OCPD) are preoccupied with rules, details, and organization in many aspects of their life. They tenaciously manage their lives by always trying to make them predictable and safe—"spontaneity" is not in their vocabulary. Rigidly committed to the minute details of life, people with OCPD tend to lack a larger perspective on most activities. That is, they lose sight of the forest because they are so focused on the individual trees. They often hoard worthless possessions, usually out of a conviction that "some day I might need it." This pack-rat mentality is also reflected in stinginess with money. Other people sometimes use derogatory language in describing such individuals, for example, calling them bean counters, nitpickers, or worrywarts.

Many people with OCPD are so perfectionistic about every task that they end up making little or no progress on them and they take so long at them that they miss important deadlines, and it is in this area where they can get into trouble at work. At the same time, they are unwilling to delegate tasks to others for fear that the work won't be done to their standards. In such individuals, conscientiousness becomes so extreme as to constitute a liability. For all their concern about doing things perfectly, many such folks end up being ineffective and indecisive, often worrying themselves into mediocre performance.

People with obsessive-compulsive personalities also tend to be inflexible about moral and ethical matters and, in personal and romantic relationships, to be controlling and aloof, almost as if emotional spontaneity were too threatening to tolerate. What happens is that they appear cold and insensitive to others.

Engaging a client with OCPD in treatment can be challenging, but creating a friendly, collaborative atmosphere in which the clinician supports client choice and self-determination can be helpful. Cognitive therapy that focuses on exploring the consequences of the typical OCPD client's automatic assumptions, for example, "everything has to be perfect" or "if I don't do it, it won't be done right" can be useful in changing firmly

---

Newhill, C.E. (1995). A mental health casebook. Unpublished manuscript.

held schemas along with encouraging and supporting the client in identifying and expressing feelings. Group therapy is also often useful because the conscientiousness of the OCPD client can be a model for other clients and other clients can model spontaneity, relaxation, and expression of feelings (Shapiro, 1965).

OCPD is not the same as, and should be clearly distinguished from, obsessive-compulsive disorder (OCD). Obsessive-compulsive personality disorder is a chronic personality style governed by worried busyness, obstinacy, and rigid habits and does not evidence the specific intrusive obsessive thoughts and compulsive rituals that are the hallmarks of obsessive-compulsive disorder, which is classified as an anxiety disorder. The prevalence of obsessive-compulsive personality disorder has been reported to be about 1 percent of the general U.S. population, and 3 to 10 percent of those in outpatient psychiatric settings. It is diagnosed about twice as often in men as in women.

Avoidant Personality Disorder

Shy

Jenny, a 30-year-old successful culinary writer, lived alone with her cat named Precious and had only a few acquaintances and no close personal friends with the exception of her younger sister, Annie. From early childhood, Jenny has always been shy, and any kind of social event, even another child's birthday party, would fill her with anxiety beginning several days before the event. Often, on the day of the party, Jenny would develop a tummy ache or a headache and beg her mother not to make her go. Jenny's mother, who was very sociable and always eager to go out to social events or entertain others, could not understand Jenny's shyness and thought that if she just pushed Jenny into being more sociable, she would get over it. Jenny remembers how she constantly felt criticized by her mother because she was not sociable, and after attending a social event at her mother's urging, she would be so exhausted and emotionally drained afterwards that she would have to go to bed for a day. The heart of Jenny's shyness was a great fear that she would not be liked by other people, that she would be criticized by other people, or that she would be stuck with someone to talk to and not know what to say and be embarrassed. As a child, Jenny recalls being embarrassed by her alcoholic father who, when drunk, would behave obnoxiously in front of others. By the time Jenny turned 30, she realized she was "getting older" and, fearing that she might end up alone for the rest of her life, she finally sought psychotherapy. With therapy, Jenny learned social skills and how to be assertive, which helped improve her ability to approach and talk with other people. Finally, Jenny was able to develop a couple of friendships.

The main characteristics of avoidant personality disorder are constant feelings of inadequacy and ineptitude, especially in social situations. Persons with this disorder are afraid of being embarrassed, ridiculed, or criticized by others and, consequently, they avoid social situations whenever possible. If forced into a social situation, as Jenny was by her mother, they are usually very inhibited and afraid of making a mistake that will bring social rejection. Avoidant individuals often seek constant reassurance that others will like them and tend to avoid occupations requiring a lot of social interaction. For example, as a culinary writer, Jenny was able to work at home and was much more comfortable interacting with co-workers over the computer than if she had to work in an office and interact with people face to face.

If they, like Jenny, can obtain an occupation in which they can avoid social interaction, people with avoidant personalities may function quite well at work. However, unlike people with schizoid personality disorder, who don't care about social interaction, those with avoidant personality disorder often long for affection and social acceptance and are distressed by not having it. It was the fear she might always be alone that prompted Jenny to seek treatment.

People with avoidant personality are quite inhibited and overly cautious—fearful that any new situation "may throw them a social interaction curve" for which they aren't prepared. Because of this, people with avoidant personality tend to follow a set routine and try to stay out of any situation that would require them to act spontaneously.

These are folks who typically have been timid and shy from the time they were children, as was the case with Jenny. As substitutes for the real interpersonal contacts they crave but avoid, they may often fantasize about "perfect relationships" that await them in the future but aren't in the present. In terms of diagnosis, it can be difficult to distinguish between avoidant personality disorder and social phobia, which is an anxiety disorder and, in fact, the two conditions may be the same disorder. The prevalence of the avoidant personality type has been reported to be about 0.5%–1.0% of the general U.S. population and 10% of those in outpatient psychiatric settings and is diagnosed with the same frequency in males as females.

Narcissistic Personality Disorder

Mr. Wonderful

Sitting in the waiting room, Nick clearly stood out from the crowd. Unlike the other clients sitting in the waiting area of this urban public mental health center, Nick was extremely well dressed and groomed, and sat somewhat away from the others, as if not wanting to risk having any contact with the other people in the room. The social worker called Nick from the waiting room, exchanged mutual introductions, and then invited him to accompany her to her office. Nick immediately began the conversation.

Nick: Well, here I am! You probably don't realize it, but you are about to have the best experience of your professional life.

SW: (a bit startled) Okay, um, I'm not sure what you mean?

Nick: I'm giving you a chance to be my counselor. And . . . (leaning forward intently) . . . this is a chance of a lifetime.

SW: I'm still not clear what you're saying.

Nick: (sitting back in his chair) I'm giving you the chance to counsel me. Me! I have never offered this to anyone before and, believe me, you are really going to learn a lot. In fact, and—well—I came up with this idea while I was sitting in the waiting room—and, by the way, you should really clean that place up—anyway, quite frankly, I think it would not be unreasonable to suggest that we make an arrangement for you to pay me for the privilege of seeing me.

SW: (after a brief moment of stunned silence) I don't think it is possible to do that.

Nick: Why not? It'll be worth your while and worth your money.

SW: Let's step back a bit, if that's okay. Can you tell me what brought you here today?

Nick: (looks around the room and frowns) There is nothing I need from you, you see, it's my wife that thinks I need therapy, which is, of course, ridiculous. I don't need therapy but I came in just to make her happy. What would you like to talk about? I can talk about anything—anything you like.

It is certainly unusual for a client to suggest that a therapist pay for the privilege of seeing him, but this exchange actually occurred in the author's practice. Reading the dialogue, the reader may think that this scenario couldn't possibly have happened in real life but, in fact, it did. This particular client had a narcissistic personality disorder and as the interview progressed, it became quite clear why his wife had insisted that Nick get some counseling. Throughout their marriage, Nick's wife had been forced to cater to him and accommodate his every whim although, in his view, this was perfectly acceptable and justified. He expected her to provide him with unwavering admiration and insisted on always being the center of attention. He viewed his children as an extension of his own ego, and their accomplishments provided positive reflections on him and their failures constituted unforgivable personal insults. Nick's family life completely revolved around him and, finally, they had had enough.

The essential feature of someone with a narcissistic personality is a pervasive pattern of grandiosity, need for admiration, and a profound lack of empathy for others. Such individuals have a grandiose sense of their own self-importance, and routinely overestimate their abilities and overpromote and inflate their accomplishments along with underestimating and devaluing the accomplishments of others. Such folks believe that they are superior, special, and unique, and they expect others to recognize them as such. Like Nick, they believe that just being in their company is an honor like no other.

Individuals with narcissistic personalities may feel that they can only be understood by, and should only associate with, people whom they view as special or of high status. Because they believe that their needs are special and, therefore, beyond the understanding of ordinary people, they are likely to insist on having only the "top" person (doctor, therapist, hairstylist) or being affiliated with the "best" institutions, but may devalue the credentials of those who disappoint them. As the college-aged daughter of a narcissistic CEO father stated:

> Thank god I got into Princeton. I was so anxious during the whole college admissions process that I couldn't sleep, I developed constant gastrointestinal problems, and chewed my nails to nubs. If I hadn't gotten in to my father's alma mater, I know he would have disowned me. My brother goes to SUNY Geneseo, which is the State University of New York honors college, but it's a public school and not Ivy League so my father stopped speaking to him and cut him off financially.

Now, one has to bear in mind that for many individuals with the non-psychopathic form of narcissistic personality, underneath all the grandiosity and airs of entitlement lies very fragile self-esteem. Because of this, such people are often preoccupied with how well they are doing and how favorably they are regarded by others, and immediate family members function as extensions of their own egos. These are people with a strong sense of entitlement, and if they are not provided favorable treatment in the fashion they believe they are entitled to, rage and indignation results.

Individuals with narcissistic personality disorder also have a severe lack of empathy for others and have difficulty recognizing and caring about the desires, needs, and feelings of others including family members, employees, and co-workers. This, in combination with their sense of entitlement, can result in their exploiting other people and treating them insensitively. In sum, these are individuals who generally present as arrogant, haughty, snobbish, disdainful, and condescending. They're tough to work with clinically, and generally don't present for treatment unless forced to by others, such as a spouse or an employer.

Stone (1989) conducted a longitudinal study of patients with different forms of narcissistic, borderline, and antisocial personalities and was able to identify certain factors associated with better treatment outcomes and certain factors associated with poorer outcomes. Client factors associated with good outcomes included perseverance, courage, a sense of humor, the ability to take responsibility, artistic talent, high intelligence, attractiveness, self-discipline, and likeableness. In other words, they possessed healthy ego strengths. Client factors associated with a poor outcome included a history of parental abuse and neglect, incest experiences, and features of clinical psychopathy (discussed in more detail below) including extreme exploitation of others and extreme lack of empathy. Thus, how "treatable" an individual with narcissistic personality is largely depends on the extent to which there is evidence of comorbidity with antisocial personality disorder and, most importantly, the level of psychopathy present. The more psychopathic the individual's personality is, the poorer the treatment outcome tends to be. The prevalence of narcissistic personality disorder has been reported to be less than 1 percent of the general U.S. population, although that may be rising, but about 2 to 16 percent of clinical populations, and most individuals who meet criteria (50%–75%) are male (APA, 2000; Stinson, Dawson, Goldstein, et al., 2008).

The role of modern society in facilitating and rewarding narcissism

The hallmark perspective of the social work profession is the ecological paradigm, which views individuals within the context of their environment. When looking at personality pathologies, such as narcissism, an individual's environment plays a critical role. Many have argued that we now live in an age of narcissistic entitlement (Bruni, 2012; Friesen, 2009; Twenge & Campbell, 2009), but how did that come to be? Let's look back in time.

From post–World War II up until the mid-1960s, American society was more conforming and concerned about the common good than it is now. Influenced by the philosophy of the New Deal, government and the American people agreed that regulation of corporate excess and providing opportunities to facilitate the common good were important to the health of our society as a whole. For example, major infrastructure projects were undertaken at taxpayer expense, including our vast interstate highway system, and a comprehensive system of public education from kindergarten through higher education was developed. Americans believed collectively that access to avenues of transportation and the opportunity for all to obtain a good education were examples of public investments to ensure the strength of the country for the current generation and generations to come. Beginning in the mid-1960s, however, many recognized that opportunities were not as equal as many assumed, and certain groups were excluded from all that society had to offer due to discrimination, blocked opportunities, and economic inequality. Such groups included people of color, women, gays and lesbians, certain religious minorities—essentially almost anyone who was not a White Anglo-Saxon Protestant male. So, during the late 1960s, American society erupted into upheaval as groups who had been disenfranchised began to demand civil rights. These efforts occurred over the backdrop of the war in Vietnam, which many opposed, many were forced to fight, and many of the privileged were able to escape.

At the end of the 1960s, as we moved into the 1970s, monumental changes occurred in our country politically, economically, culturally, and socially as civil rights were won for many. The ideals associated with equal rights in some sectors of society, however, began to change in form to what might be called radical individualism, with commitment to the common good receding into the background (Andersen, 2012). Radical individualism fully embraced the second line of our Declaration of Independence, "Life, Liberty and the Pursuit of Happiness," with the baby boomer "Me" generation successfully reframing allegiance to our Declaration of Independence into a preoccupation with self (Wolfe, 1976). Granted, there had been previous eras of heightened self-gratification in America—for example, the 1840s, the Gilded Age, the Roaring Twenties—but many began to notice that something was different in the 1970s. Social critic and historian Christopher Lasch termed this new preoccupation with self-gratification "the culture of narcissism" (Lasch, 1979), arguing that America was becoming a society of "dangerously self-absorbed individuals, fixated on personal goals, fearful of their impulses and easily controlled by power elites" (Grimes, 1994). Lasch argued that narcissism was no longer merely a psychiatric condition, but was also a social condition.

Today, our culture of narcissism has broadened and deepened with technology providing a range of options to feed it. For example, Facebook, Twitter, YouTube, and the Internet in general provide avenues for packaging, branding, and marketing ourselves in unprecedented ways (Twenge & Campbell, 2009). Does the Internet age cause narcissism? No, but it can serve to encourage and reinforce it, particularly for young people whose identities are still forming (Buffardi & Campbell, 2008).

The *DSM-5* argues that maladaptive personality traits such as narcissism are on a continuum, and there are many degrees of narcissism that don't meet threshold for narcissistic personality disorder but which profoundly affect interpersonal relationships, our political climate, our economic system, and the very core values of our society. Narcissism often drives taking risks, and was the backdrop for the 2008 national, and later global, financial meltdown. Many of the financiers and bankers who promoted subprime mortgages and created and sold exotic derivatives, losing billions of their shareholders' and investors' dollars, showed little to no empathy for their victims, maintaining remarkable arrogance even under congressional investigations. Narcissism is almost a job requirement today for politicians, corporate CEOs, and hedge fund managers, but it also drives reckless, dangerous behavior and, without the checks and balances of regulation, can lead to disaster. Banking regulations, for example, were not designed to artificially control the invisible hand of the free market, they were designed to set limits on reckless, greedy human behavior. We currently have a society that rewards narcissism, doesn't always punish the consequences of behavior driven by it and, some have argued, has generally led to less empathy and concern for others, especially those who are less advantaged. Twenge and Campbell (2009) argue that to counter this trend, significant changes must be made. Such changes include changes in how we parent and educate our children, changes in the laws that regulate corporate behavior, changing the role of money in politics and government, and changing some of America's more narcissistically oriented core values in order to "quiet the ego" (p. 282). This is certainly a tall order. However, changing the culture of narcissism is essential if our democracy is to survive.

ANTISOCIAL PERSONALITY DISORDER AND PSYCHOPATHY IN DEPTH

Bobby

From the time he was a young child, Bobby exhibited callous aggressive behavior toward others. When he was 6 years old, he pushed his younger brother down the cellar stairs, breaking his arm, because his brother had touched Bobby's toy action figures. When he was 7, he rode his bike deliberately over a neighbor child's kitten, killing it. He was suspended from school numerous times for beating up other children and was repeatedly caught lying and stealing from family members and schoolmates. He was placed in juvenile hall approximately 30 times as a youth and, at age 20, was placed in a correctional state hospital for 2 months following stealing a car and shooting a police officer. After discharge from the hospital, Bobby was admitted for outpatient therapy, both group and individual treatment, at the local county mental health center, but there was little improvement in his behavior. The outpatient intake diagnosis was explosive personality and antisocial personality disorder, moderate; however, that was soon revised to a diagnosis of solely antisocial personality disorder, severe.

(continued)

Following 2 months of unsuccessful outpatient treatment, Bobby was arrested for rape and placed in the county jail. Angry that he was unable to post bail, Bobby telephoned his therapist from the jail and stated he was planning to kill his wife, others he was angry at including the woman he allegedly raped, and then himself upon his release. The therapist issued a *Tarasoff* warning to Bobby's wife and the rape victim and alerted the jail officials about the threat, upon which a judge decided to revoke the bail option. After Bobby was informed of the judge's decision, he called his therapist and threatened to kill him. Throughout his life, Bobby never felt any remorse for his actions, seeming to feel no mercy for his victims, and no one around him felt safe whenever he was out of the various institutions to which he had been sent during much of his adolescence and adult life. Bobby did succeed in one thing, however—he achieved the status of being a career criminal.

In this composite case vignette from the author's practice, it is clear that Bobby's behavior is highly aggressive and shows complete disregard for the rights and welfare of others. He seems to have no empathy for his victims' suffering at his hands, and attacks people who have tried to help him, such as his therapist, as readily as strangers, acquaintances, or those he considers to be his enemies. Despite the punishment he has received and the attempts at treatment that have been made in the institutions he has been sent to, Bobby's behavior has evidenced little change; if anything, it has become more vindictive. As a youth, Bobby was appropriately diagnosed as having severe conduct disorder and, since his pattern of antisocial behavior continued unabated into adulthood, he met criteria for the diagnosis of antisocial personality disorder with a severity level of "severe."

The Nature of Antisocial Personality Disorder

The individual with antisocial personality disorder (ASPD) demonstrates a pervasive pattern of disregard for, and violation of, the rights of others. This pattern usually begins in early childhood or adolescence and then continues into adulthood. In childhood or adolescence, however, the same pattern of behavior is called "conduct disorder," thus antisocial personality disorder cannot be diagnosed in someone under the age of 18. The prevalence of antisocial personality disorder has been reported to be about 3 percent for males and 1 percent for females in the general U.S. population; this varies from 3 to 30 percent within clinical settings depending on the population served by the clinic, and rises to 50 percent or greater in substance abuse and forensic settings (APA, 2000).

Antisocial personality disorder emphasizes the individual's relationship to social norms and rules of conduct. Social norms are essentially ideal standards that bind the members of a group and serve to guide, control, or regulate proper and acceptable behavior (Goode, 2011). Some norms are implicit or related to common courtesy, others are codified in our penal laws. Thus, in antisocial personality disorder we are focusing on behavior that runs counter to societal norms, meaning primarily aggressive or antisocial behavior that may or may not break the law. For the individual with antisocial personality, it is as if they have turned the Judeo-Christian moral code inside out. What are seen as strengths by society in general are viewed negatively by the antisocial individual. Thus, sensitivity and empathy is viewed as weakness to them; exploiting others is a strength; honesty and hard work is devalued. Although most individuals with antisocial personality disorder, particularly at moderate or severe levels, were or could have been diagnosed with conduct disorder as child, many children meeting criteria for conduct disorder do not go on to develop antisocial personality disorder in adulthood. This is largely dependent on and shaped by when the onset of the conduct disorder symptoms begin (a later onset bodes a better prognosis), how severe the symptoms are, and whether the child and family receive appropriate, adequate, and timely treatment.

The essential symptomatic behavior of antisocial personality disorder involves the persistent, repetitive violation of rules and a profound disregard for the rights of others, which is clearly illustrated in the case of Bobby. In addition, such individuals may be deceitful, manipulative, and exploit others for their own gain with, typically, an inability to feel empathy for the victims of their antisocial acts or to feel remorse. They are also often impulsive and fail to anticipate, or don't care about, the consequences of their behavior. As a prison inmate, incarcerated for shooting a man in a drug deal gone wrong, stated to the author many years ago: "That night I just wanted to go get high, I wanted to get loaded, and I didn't think about the consequences or, if I did, I didn't care. I certainly didn't think I'd wind up in here in prison."

The Nature of Psychopathy and the Psychopathic Personality

Related to but different from ASPD in important ways is the maladaptive personality condition called *psychopathy*. Psychopathy is characterized by superficial charm, egocentricity, lack of a capacity for empathy, guiltlessness, lack of remorse and shame, lack of insight, and an amassment of externalizing behaviors, strained interpersonal relationships, impulsivity, anger, and proneness for engaging in interpersonal conflicts and fights (Cleckley, 1976; DeLisi & Vaughn, 2008; Hare & Neumann, 2008; Millon, Simonsen, Birket-Smith, & Davis, 1998; Newhill, Vaughn, & DeLisi, 2010). Studies that have looked at prison inmates and the extent to which they meet criteria for antisocial personality versus psychopathy have found that about 70 to 80 percent of inmates meet criteria for ASPD, but only about 25 to 30 percent meet criteria for psychopathy (Patrick, 2005). What this means is that a significant number of inmates exhibit the antisocial and aggressive criminal behaviors essential for a diagnosis of ASPD but most do not evidence the selfish, callous, and remorseless personality characteristics essential for a diagnosis of psychopathy (Hare et al., 1999; Widiger, 2006). Furthermore, many psychopathic individuals, the so-called "successful psychopaths," manage to stay out of prison, although they may inflict significant harm upon many individuals and to society (Hall & Benning, 2006; Schouten & Silver, 2012).

Modern approaches to the clinical understanding of psychopathy began with Cleckley's (1941/1976) conceptualization in his 1941 book *The Mask of Sanity*. His conceptualization of psychopathy came to be known as *primary psychopathy*. Cleckley's colleague, psychiatrist Benjamin Karpman (1941), identified another form of psychopathy, which he termed *secondary psychopathy*. More recent empirical study and classification of psychopathic criminal offenders has been led by the work of Blackburn (1971, 1975, 1998). Blackburn's early work classified such offenders as falling into four groups: two of which consisted of "overcontrolled personality" offenders, and the other two consisting of "undercontrolled personality" offenders (Blackburn, 1971). Further study of the two "undercontrolled" groups led to a classification of one group as "primary psychopaths" and the second group as "secondary psychopaths," a refinement of Cleckley's and Karpman's earlier work.

Primary psychopaths are extroverted, impulsive, aggressive, confident, dominant, narcissistic, and low to average in anxiety, whereas secondary psychopaths are impulsive, aggressive, socially anxious, moody, more submissive, and low in self-esteem (Blackburn, 1998). Blackburn (1996) argues that secondary psychopaths actually have predominantly borderline personalities, although he stops short of saying that borderline personality and the secondary form of psychopathy are synonymous. It is important to note that Blackburn's work has primarily employed samples of personality disordered incarcerated offenders, not civil or non-forensic psychiatric populations. However, in a 1-year follow-up study of 220 individuals with borderline personality disorder in the community, Newhill, Eack, and Mulvey (2009) found that 73 percent of the sample engaged in violence during the 1-year study period, and these violent subjects with BPD also frequently exhibited comorbid ASPD along with elevated levels of psychopathy. Skeem, Poythress, Edens, et al. (2003) suggest that secondary psychopathy typically includes many borderline personality traits along with narcissism, and that such traits may be useful in distinguishing between subtypes of psychopathy, which has implications for treatment and management in both forensic and non-forensic settings.

Measuring Psychopathy

The gold standard for measuring psychopathy is the Psychopathy Checklist-Revised (PCL-R), developed by psychologist Robert Hare and colleagues (Hare, 1980; Hare, 1991; Hare, 2003). Hare's research suggests that psychopathy and ASPD are related, and psychopathy, in particular, may be viewed as having two dimensions, each associated with and predictive of different behaviors. The first dimension involves the affective and interpersonal core of the disorder, which includes certain personality traits such as lack of remorse or guilt, callousness and lack of empathy, glibness and superficial charm, a grandiose sense of self-worth (narcissism), and pathological lying and is reflected in the new DSM-V ASPD criteria. People whose personality is primarily characterized by this dimension may exploit others by, for example, deliberately selling defective or counterfeit merchandise, conducting financial con games such as Ponzi schemes, gambling with other people's money, and so forth, but may stop just short of breaking the law so they succeed in avoiding prison. These are the people who rationalize their morally reprehensible behavior by saying, "Look, it's legal," conveniently ignoring the ethical or moral problems and the fact their behavior harms other people.

The second dimension of psychopathy reflects antisocial behaviors, and has a greater overlap with the traditional criteria for antisocial personality disorder. Aspects of this dimension include having an antisocial, impulsive, and socially deviant lifestyle, needing excessive stimulation via risk taking, poor behavioral controls, irresponsibility, and a parasitic lifestyle. For example, an individual with predominantly this dimension in his personality may father many children with different women but refuse to provide financial support for any of them, may live on other people's couches and refuse to work and figure out how to defraud the government for ill-gotten benefits, use illicit drugs and alcohol, force others to engage in unsafe sexual practices with him, and be involved in gambling and other activities that involve excitement and risk. It should be noted that both ASPD and psychopathy are diagnosed most frequently in men, although the nature of female antisocial behavior is somewhat different from men's and, therefore, women may be underdiagnosed to some degree.

Causes of Psychopathy

Most violent crimes are committed by a small group of repeat offenders who were or could have been diagnosed with conduct disorder as a child or adolescent and meet criteria for ASPD, often with evidence of psychopathy (Kratzer & Hodgins, 1997; Loeber & Stouthamer-Loeber, 1998; Moffitt, 2003). Evidence from twin and adoption studies suggests that such long-term antisocial behavior is probably heritable (Moffitt, 2005; Rhee & Waldman, 2002) as well as being influenced by environment. In addition, evidence from a structural MRI study of antisocial male violent offenders shows that such individuals evidence reduced gray matter volume in the brain, and this may account for problems in empathy processing, moral reasoning, and possession of prosocial emotions such as guilt, all of which are found in psychopathy (Gregory, Ffytche, Simmons, et al., 2012).

The DSM Conceptualization and Criteria

Our ideas about how to diagnose ASPD, and to what extent aspects of psychopathy are included, has differed across the various editions of the *DSM* and, in particular, for *DSM-5*. Considerable research has shown that the presence of psychopathy is far more predictive of criminal recidivism (Patrick, 2006), thus, the DSM-IV-TR criteria has been revised for *DSM-5* to reflect many of the components of psychopathy.

As with the other defined types of personality disorder, the criteria for ASPD in *DSM-5* specifies impairments in personality (self and interpersonal) functioning and the presence of pathological personality traits. The self-functioning area in ASPD involves impairments in identity, manifested by egocentrism and reliance on sources of self-esteem that stem from personal gain, power, or pleasure. In addition, there is impairment in self-direction, for example, the individual chooses goals for him or herself that are based on self-gratification rather than concern for others and are often associated with failure to conform to social norms and established laws.

In addition, the individual must evidence at least one of two types of impairment in interpersonal functioning. The first is lack of empathy and concern for the suffering of others coupled with lack of remorse after engaging in behavior that harms others. Second, the person is unable to engage in mutually positive intimate relationships, instead, the individual exploits others for his or her own benefit by means of coercion and deceit, or dominates and controls others via threats and intimidation. In addition, to meet criteria for ASPD, the individual must evidence certain pathological personality traits, including (1) antagonism, characterized by manipulative behavior, deceitfulness, callousness, and hostility; and (2) disinhibition, characterized by being irresponsible, impulsive, and risk taking. Finally, as with the other personality disorder types, the impairments must show stability across time and social contexts, and not be better understood as normative for the individual's developmental stage or sociocultural environment, or due to use of substances or the presence of a general medical condition. And, exclusive for ASPD, the individual must be at least 18 years of age; under 18, the diagnosis for the same behavior patterns is called conduct disorder (APA, 2013).

Treatment for Antisocial Personality Disorder

Individuals with antisocial personality disorder are most likely to be engaged in treatment if they perceive treatment as being to their advantage. Such individuals usually come to treatment on an involuntary basis—either via the criminal justice system or civil commitment procedures—and thus principles for engagement of involuntary clients are recommended. For example, one strategy that can be effective with antisocial clients is the "quid pro quo" or "let's make a deal" strategy (Murdach, 1980; Rooney, 1992), in which the clinician offers some small benefit in exchange for the client agreeing to try treatment. Furthermore, to be effective the clinician must maintain clear boundaries and keep the responsibility for change and consequences squarely on the client. Motivational enhancement therapy can often be effective in doing this. Hopefully, as the client learns new skills, takes responsibility for his or her actions, gives up some of the destructive behaviors, and his or her life improves (e.g., avoiding jail), the client will begin to "buy into" treatment, and real engagement can occur. For antisocial clients, treatment is more likely to show some success if they do not show traits of psychopathy and if they are moving toward or already in their middle-age years when there may be dampening of some of the most problematic antisocial and aggressive behaviors.

Assess your comprehension of *the nature, symptoms, and treatment of antisocial personality disorder and psychopathy* by completing this quiz.

BORDERLINE PERSONALITY DISORDER IN DEPTH

What Borderline Personality Disorder Is

Borderline personality disorder (BPD) is characterized by significant impairment in self and interpersonal functioning, and those with the disorder face considerable difficulties achieving successful community adjustment (Skodol, Gunderson, Pfohl, et al., 2002). Individuals with BPD have a pervasive pattern of instability in a variety of areas including interpersonal relationships, sense of self, emotions, and behavior. The core disturbance and central feature of BPD is problems in emotion regulation, particularly the management and regulation of negative emotions, such as intense anger. Some researchers and clinicians have even suggested renaming the disorder "emotion regulation disorder" since this characteristic is key not only to the nature of the disorder but also to its treatment (Skodol, 2005). These problems in emotion regulation are associated with the other features of the disorder including marked reactivity of mood, chaotic and unstable relationships, problems with impulsivity, an unstable sense of self, suicide attempts along with repetitive self-harming behavior, feelings of profound shame, fears of abandonment, and chronic feelings of emptiness or boredom (Kreisman & Straus, 1989). One fact that comes through clearly in clinical work with clients with the disorder is that many individuals with BPD have experienced significant physical or sexual abuse in childhood (Goldberg, D'Angelo, DeMaso, et al., 1992). However, there are many people who experience such abuse and don't develop BPD, suggesting that causes involve more than just experiencing trauma. Today, we believe that the causes of BPD probably lie in a combination of biological vulnerability coupled with environmental stressors.

Prevalence and Comorbidity

The majority of individuals with BPD meet criteria for additional psychiatric illnesses, most commonly substance use disorders, eating disorders, anxiety disorders, mood disorders, and other personality disorders, such as antisocial personality disorder. In terms of prevalence, more than 14 million American adults, distributed equally between men and women, have BPD. Approximately 11 percent of outpatients, 20 percent of psychiatric inpatients, and 6 percent of primary care visit patients meet the criteria for the disorder (Gunderson, 2011). BPD exacts a heavy toll on the individuals with the disorder, their family members, and society—in other words, BPD represents a significant public health burden. The good news, however, is that recent treatment development efforts have proved beneficial for many living with the disorder, and we now have several evidence-based treatments effective in treating the symptoms of BPD and helping people with the disorder achieve recovery. Longitudinal research has also shown that the majority of individuals with BPD get better over time; however, long-term functioning is variable, and 3 to 10 percent commit suicide (Zanarini, 2005).

Watch the video *"Janna: Borderline Personality Disorder."* What are the challenges a client with borderline personality disorder faces in relationships with others?

The Symptoms of BPD

People with BPD often have highly unstable and intense interpersonal relationships. The quality of such intense attachments, however, may suddenly shift from idealization ("You're the most wonderful friend/therapist/lover I have ever had") to strong devaluation manifested by intense anger, dislike, or aggression ("You don't love/care for me! You're lower than pond scum"). These shifts in attitude and behavior are often referred to as "splitting" (discussed previously), and occur even with those the individual has had a long-term trusting relationship with, such as close family members. Splitting may be triggered by seemingly minor events, such as a sudden change in a friend's plans, that are interpreted by the individual with BPD as signifying rejection or other negative attribution (Porr, 2010). Example:

> *(When you feel very negative toward someone or something, how do you usually behave in response to the emotions?)* Nobody really cares about me. Nobody. (*What do you mean?*) Like, I broke up with my boyfriend. I didn't want to break up but I knew he'd be breaking up with me so, like, I did it first, you know, so I'd hurt less. But, anyway, I got really angry, I threw things, I wanted to hit him. I wanted him to hurt like I was hurting. I felt worthless and then like I was spiraling down this hole. I couldn't stand it. I wanted to cut myself or cut him. I couldn't stand the pain, I just wanted the pain to stop. So I hit him, kept hitting him. Then I cut myself . . . I wanted him to hurt, to know it was his fault. (*How did you feel then?*) I felt better then, I don't know why. (*Were either of you drinking at the time?*) Well, yeah, I had a couple of beers. Sometimes that helps. (*Helps?*) Helps to deal with my feelings. I wasn't drunk though . . . (Newhill & Mulvey, 2002, p. 166)

Distortions in thinking and sense of self can lead to frequent changes in long-term goals, career plans, jobs, friendships, gender identity, and values. Along with the devaluation that may be exhibited toward others, many people with BPD direct devaluation toward themselves and see themselves as fundamentally bad, or unworthy. They may feel unfairly misunderstood or mistreated, bored, empty, and have little idea who they are, for example, "I'm just an empty shell" (Spitzer, Gibbon, Skodol, et al., 2002, p. 236). This is related to the core feature called identity disturbance, which involves markedly and persistently unstable self-image or sense of self. These symptoms are exacerbated if the person is isolated and lacking in social support, and may result in frantic efforts to avoid being alone (Gunderson & Hoffman, 2005).

Individuals with BPD are in a constant quest to avoid real or imagined abandonment. Thus, when the individual perceives that there is any impending separation or loss, frantic efforts to avoid abandonment kick in including acting out through impulsive behavior, suicide attempts, or aggressive behavior. These are individuals who are very sensitive to environmental circumstances. They may experience intense abandonment fears and inappropriate anger even when faced with a realistic time-limited separation or when there are unavoidable changes in plans, for instance, sudden despair in reaction to a clinician announcing the end of a session or panic or fury when someone important to them is a few minutes late. Why such an extreme reaction? Because, to them, such "abandonment" means they are "bad," a.k.a. a "bad person," which is intolerable.

Watch the video "*Speaking out: Liz: Borderline Personality Disorder.*" How do the symptoms of borderline personality disorder converge and lead to an individual making a suicide attempt and being hospitalized as a result?

Watch the video "*Sarah: Depression and Deliberate Self-Harm.*" From a client's perspective, how and why does she engage in self-harming behavior in response to, and to cope with, feelings of depression?

Many, although not all, clients with borderline personality disorder engage in parasuicidal or self-harming behaviors. Also, some clients engage in self-harm although they do not meet criteria for BPD but, rather, may suffer from depression. Sarah, for example, has depression and engages in repetitive self-harming behavior as a way to relieve her painful feelings; cutting provides her with temporary relief although it is not a positive constructive solution to resolving her difficulties.

The Nature and Causes of Emotion Regulation Problems in BPD

The central and most problematic feature of BPD is problems with emotion regulation (Putnam & Silk, 2005). Emotion regulation can be defined as the process of initiating, maintaining, and modulating the occurrence, intensity, or duration of internal feeling states,

---

Newhill, C.E. & Mulvey, E.P. (2002). Emotional dysregulation: The key to a treatment approach for violent, mentally ill individuals. Clinical Social Work Journal, 30, 157–171.

emotion-related cognition, emotion-related behaviors, and the physiological processes related to emotions (Gross, 2002; Thompson, 1994). Emotion *dysregulation* may be defined as a low threshold, or high sensitivity/vulnerability, to emotional stimuli coupled with a high amplitude of emotional response and a slow return to emotional baseline, that is, difficulty in calming down after an emotional upset (Linehan, 1993). Negative emotions such as sadness, shame, guilt, humiliation, and anger are the most difficult emotions for individuals with BPD to manage and tolerate and are the most prone to dysregulation (Linehan, 1993).

Where does emotion regulation capacity originate? Emotions and associated behaviors appear to be regulated by a complex neurobiological circuitry involving the parts of the brain called the prefrontal cortex and the amygdala (Davidson, Jackson, & Kalin, 2000; Davidson, Putnam, & Larson, 2000). Research suggests that this emotion regulatory neuronal system functions abnormally in individuals with BPD, serving as an underlying biological predisposition for many of the symptoms seen in the disorder, such as self-harming behavior and aggression toward others (Putnam & Silk, 2005). Cutting or burning oneself, for example, can serve as an effective strategy for focusing attention and decreasing overwhelming psychic pain. The etiology of emotion regulation problems is believed to lie in an interaction of inherent susceptibility and learned maladaptive coping responses. Emotion regulation problems are probably neurologically based, and abnormalities of the central serotonergic systems are likely involved in the dysregulation of mood, affect, and impulse control seen in BPD (Coccaro, Siever, Owen, & Davis, 1990). Emotional dysregulation, thus, is thought to result from a combination of this biological diathesis or underpinning, coupled with learned responses to affectively laden early experiences combined with poor coping skills (Linehan, 1993). Fortunately, clients with BPD can learn emotion regulation skills, a key component to dialectical behavioral treatment (DBT), to learn how to regulate and manage their overwhelming negative emotions (Butler, 2001).

The Borderline Client in Crisis

Because of the nature of their symptoms, many clients with borderline personality disorder lurch from one crisis to another, sometimes for years, thus addressing the topic of the borderline client in crisis is germane to learning how to work effectively with such clients and to understand some of the formidable barriers to achieving good outcomes.

The following case vignette describes a client whom the author saw off and on for many years in the psychiatric emergency service. She will be referred to as "Terry." Terry's clinical presentation is, in many ways, very typical of the kinds of situations in which clients with borderline personality disorder can become involved in a crisis. Such complex scenarios are either initially triggered by a crisis and/or an escalation of symptoms serves to create a crisis situation. Below is a verbatim excerpt from progress notes describing event by event what happened during the very first contact with Terry, and illustrates well many of the common dynamics such clients present with.

Terry

Terry is a 19-year-old single White female referred to the crisis service by the city police after they brought her to the county's locked inpatient unit admissions area from St. Elizabeth Hospital's crisis intervention unit. [St. Elizabeth was a local general hospital with a private psychiatric inpatient unit.] This client has been in their crisis intervention unit under the care of Dr. C for the past 2 months. According to the unit staff, everyone, including Dr. C, was becoming increasingly frustrated with treating Terry on the unit because she refused to consistently cooperate with the treatment program. Finally, they decided to discharge her the morning of October 6th with the recommendation that she be followed by county mental health.

(continued)

This decision upset Terry, and around 10 p.m. she cut her wrist and then left the crisis intervention unit AMA [against medical advice]. Around midnight, she called us [the county psychiatric emergency service], stating that she would like to go back to St. Elizabeth's at least for tonight but was afraid they would not accept her back—at that time she was calling from a friend's house. I called St. Elizabeth's and after a conference between staff and Dr. C, he agreed to accept Terry back for the night provided she was cooperative, and then he would discharge her in the morning. I advised Terry of this and she said she would go to St. Elizabeth's ER for treatment of the cut wrist and then ask for admission back to the crisis intervention unit. The friend called about an hour and a half later, stating Terry was still at her house and was having a seizure—she had not gone to St. Elizabeth's yet. I advised the friend to call the paramedics and have her taken to the hospital.

According to the police report, Terry then went to the ER, a Bandaid was put on her cut wrist (the cut was very superficial), the crisis intervention unit staff came down to escort her to the unit but she refused to go. They convinced her to go with them anyway but when they got to the unit she began to scream and thrash her arms and legs, stating she did not want to stay because she knew they "really didn't want her." She became so out of control that the city police were called and directed to take her to the county unit. She was combative with the police officers, so they cuffed her hand and foot.

Upon evaluation, Terry presented as a very angry young woman, lying face down on the floor of the admissions unit, with both wrists and ankles cuffed. She agreed to cooperate, so I asked the police to take the cuffs off. Terry told me that she was very angry with the St. Elizabeth crisis intervention unit staff because she felt they had, in the course of her stay there, opened up a lot of painful issues for her but didn't help her to resolve her pain, i.e., "they just left me hanging." She stated that she wanted to go back to St. Elizabeth's but I informed her that they had made it clear they would not admit her again. She did not want hospitalization on our unit and refused placement at our transitional care facility.

Terry stated she was fearful she "would not make it" outside a hospital setting but was not sure exactly what might happen except that she perceives herself as having overall difficulty coping and controlling her impulses. She admitted she has alienated all her friends and family, feels very abandoned, and is scared. She wants a place to live, a job, and some supports.

I told her I would be willing to help her work on her problems and she agreed to try. I set up two appointments for her—one at 8:00 a.m. this morning to see the triage crisis worker [at the time of our interview, it was 3:00 a.m.], and one the following morning to see me. I advised Terry that she only really had 4 hours to cope until she could come into the crisis clinic and she said she would try but was afraid she would lose control—but added she didn't know what might happen, although she denied having any suicidal plans. I gave Terry our emergency numbers and she agreed to call if she felt she was losing control. It was left she would try to contact her friend—I offered to call her or have Terry call before she left, but she refused.

Follow-up: Terry did not show up for the 8 a.m. appointment but she did show for the appointment with me the following day and said, "I know you can help me. You're so kind, not like my other therapists." I knew how quickly such sentiments could change but I took advantage of the positive transference to work on engaging Terry in some short-term crisis intervention counseling while setting her up with ongoing outpatient treatment.

One of the main problems encountered by emergency services in working with borderline clients in crisis situations is the simple lack of viable options for solving the immediate problems. This is due to two main categories of factors. First are the characteristics of the individual's common clinical picture and second is the lack of available resources and providers willing to work with the client.

Characteristics of the individual's common clinical picture

Borderline clients often show a number of common characteristics when they are in a crisis situation. First is impulsivity and unpredictability that is potentially or actually self-destructive. Often the individual herself will say that she cannot maintain control or "doesn't know" if she can. (Note: I am using the female pronoun but, of course, BPD occurs equally frequently in males, although it may be underdiagnosed or misdiagnosed in males). She may engage in actual dangerous behavior toward self or others that may include the use of weapons; for example, cutting tools, such as knives, razor blades, or glass are common choices.

Secondly, the ongoing pattern of unstable, chaotic, and/or intense interpersonal relationships may include an underlying tendency to use others for one's own needs. Unfortunately, this serves to weaken or wreck social supports. Using or exploiting others usually occurs in clients who also meet or partially meet criteria for antisocial personality disorder or have symptoms of psychopathy, both of which are commonly comorbid with borderline personality disorder (Newhill, Eack, & Mulvey, 2009).

Third, borderline clients often experience inappropriate, intense, unmanageable anger, which reflects problems with emotion regulation (Newhill, Eack, & Mulvey, 2012). This anger, along with other negative affects, may escalate into physical altercations with other people or self-harming behavior. A fourth characteristic present with many borderline clients is chronic uncertainty about goals, choices, wants, or needs, which makes resource mobilization and contracting for treatment or safety very challenging.

As noted previously, the hallmark characteristic of BPD is emotion regulation problems and, in crisis, this emotional instability can even include transient psychotic symptoms. This makes the individual's behavior more unpredictable, because emotion dysregulation drives behavioral dysregulation. A sixth characteristic present with some, although not all, clients with BPD is an intolerance to being alone yet often requesting to be "left alone." The title of the book *I Hate You—Don't Leave Me* captures this dynamic. Essentially, what is going on is that the client wants to avoid abandonment and loneliness, but the person or people who are there at the time aren't meeting the client's needs, so the client vacillates between wanting to connect but also feeling anger about the nature or quality of that connection.

The final characteristic common to BPD clients' clinical presentation during a crisis that can make effective emergency intervention challenging are the chronic feelings of emptiness and boredom. Clients often express these feelings through statements such as "I'm not whole without you" or, simply, "I don't know who I am." This lack of a consolidated sense of identity impairs the client's ability to make decisions and set goals and means to achieve the goals. They don't know what they want, and this is often quite genuine, not manipulative, albeit frustrating to clinicians. The second category of factors challenging clinicians as they attempt to work out a crisis intervention plan is lack of resources.

Lack of resources

Similar to clients with other types of personality disorders, clients with BPD may have shaky financial supports to meet their basic needs. Their illness may have interfered with being able to complete high school, college, or vocational training. The illness may also have interfered with getting and keeping a job, so their employment history may be checkered and show gaps in employment. Although this is changing a little bit, many clients with BPD don't qualify for disability and may not qualify for any form of public assistance except the most meager, such as general relief. Given today's weak economy, many states, however, are eliminating or moving to eliminate general relief. So, lack of financial support is one problem, and some clients with BPD end up homeless.

When people are down on their luck, or ill, or have lost their home or job, many can turn to friends and family members for help—at the very least, for provision of a hot meal and a couch for the night. Many clients with BPD, however, have ruptured such sources of social support due to repeated crises that have served to alienate their friends and family. Over time, friends and family members simply "burn out" and may refuse to take the client into their home or help them in other ways any longer. The client has, to put it bluntly, "burned their bridges."

In spite of the behavioral problems individuals with BPD exhibit when they are in a crisis, they usually haven't broken any laws, so jail may not be an option, even temporarily. Although nobody wants to go to jail, sometimes a short jail stay can provide some benefits, such as structure and imposition of consequences for one's actions that can have a therapeutic impact. Sometimes the individual has broken a minor law but nobody is willing to press charges because "they need help." They are seen as mentally ill by all those they have come in contact with, consequently, there is pressure for mental health services to "do something," usually stated along the lines of "Can't you people do something about him/her?" Finally, many individuals with BPD have only marginal internal resources due to their fluctuating symptoms and, in crisis, are unable to utilize therapeutic intervention effectively in terms of traditional crisis intervention techniques because they are too emotionally and behaviorally dysregulated. Ascertaining the level of risk in terms of dangerousness to self and others and deciding about hospitalization is often very difficult and, in today's world of shrinking resources, structured settings like inpatient care are in short supply. Clients with BPD in a crisis also often have difficulty contracting for safety because, like Terry, they feel chronically not in control of their impulses and can't say for sure whether they can control their behavior or not, and any perception of abandonment can send the person into a spiral of self-destructive behavior.

Another problem for crisis and emergency services is that many clients with personality disorders, including those with BPD, are not reliable about following through with appointments or other aspects of traditional treatment. Brenda, a client with BPD depicted in the dialogue below, rarely kept her appointments and so her mental health "treatment" was almost solely provided through 24-hour emergency services, which resulted in poor continuity of care. Unfortunately, when such clients don't keep their appointments and "fall through the cracks" some clinicians secretly feel relief and don't follow up to reengage the client, thus feeding into the lack of follow-through.

Finally, other social service agencies, such as emergency housing facilities, private psychiatric units, shelters, or other housing options may refuse to accept the client with BPD. Many of these individuals become well known to such services and, based on previous negative experiences, the doors to admission become shuttered. Plus, even if an agency does agree to help in a crisis situation, such alternatives are often not structured enough to safely contain the person's dysregulated behavior and affect. As a psychiatric emergency worker, one often finds oneself in a bind and taking on the role of "marketing" the client to an agency in an attempt to get services. Example:

> Brenda, 27 years old, was first diagnosed with borderline personality disorder and schizophrenia, paranoid type, 3 years ago when she was hospitalized following a serious suicide attempt. Brenda also has alcohol dependence and has been in the county detoxification unit several times and twice has gone through the 28-day program at Recovery House, the local residential alcohol rehabilitation center. During the last Recovery House stay, however, Brenda cut her wrists and had to be hospitalized. Tonight, she is intoxicated, has been drinking steadily for the past 2 weeks, and wants to go back to Recovery House. The crisis worker calls on Brenda's behalf to see if Recovery House will readmit her; however, they refuse. (RC: Recovery House staff person; CW: crisis worker; B: Brenda)

CW: I understand that you're concerned about readmitting Brenda, but she is *really* committed to following through with her recovery and is adamant she won't harm herself.

RH: The last time she was here, she cut her wrists—we can't take that chance.

CW: Brenda, could you talk to the Recovery House staff member?

B: Hi, this is Brenda. I won't hurt myself—I really, really promise. I've been drinking—I admit it—but I want help. I promise I won't do anything. Please take me back.

RH: We've given you two chances. That's it.

B: Please—I will do my 12 steps, just please give me a chance.

RH: Let me talk to the crisis worker.

RH: (to crisis worker) Look, we don't like dealing with borderlines, you know. You can't trust them.

CW: I understand your concerns, but I know Brenda well, and I think she is very serious about both wanting to get clean and sober and contracting for safety.

RH: I don't know . . . what guarantee can you give us?

CW: I'll tell you what. I promise that if there are any problems, you can call us and we will come and get Brenda and work something else out. Just give her a chance.

RH: Well, all right. But this is her last chance.

In this particular example, the crisis worker advocated on behalf of the client, the client herself engaged in self-advocacy, the referral agency reluctantly agreed to admit the client to the program, and the outcome turned out to be successful. Brenda completed the program, there were no problems with suicidal behavior or self-harm during her stay, and she stayed clean and sober for 2 years before relapsing. This positive outcome not only helped Brenda, it helped future clients with BPD and substance use problems, because that positive experience influenced the agency to be more willing to accept substance-using clients with BPD into their program.

Treatment for Borderline Personality Disorder

In the past few decades, treatments for borderline personality disorder have changed and improved to a great extent. We have developed evidence-based treatments specifically targeted to their symptoms and needs and, as a result, both the course and prognosis for individuals living with the disorder has significantly improved.

In decades past, treatment for BPD often involved lengthy inpatient stays, including state hospital care, the impact of which has been documented in well-known memoirs (see e.g., Kaysen, 1994). Inpatient care today for BPD is usually limited to the management of crises in which the individual is at risk for harming self or others. Curtailing inpatient care has certainly been the product of the impact of managed care but, in addition, we have increasingly recognized that lengthy hospital care can cause many clients with BPD to regress, and it can encourage unhealthy dependency, thus outpatient care is preferable as long as the person is safe.

Ongoing psychotherapy is the key to successful treatment for the borderline client. One of the big challenges for both clients and their families, however, is finding a good therapist. Many clinicians are unwilling to work with clients with BPD and/or don't have the right training or sufficient clinical experience working with this population. The more experience in working with borderline clients that the therapist has, the better are the chances that therapy will work (Gunderson, 2011). In addition, it is critical that the therapist and client are able to develop a strong positive therapeutic alliance with good empathic communication and a collaborative approach. A secure therapeutic attachment is essential for success in psychotherapy with the client with BPD, but it is not easy because of such clients' intense needs and fears about relationships (Gunderson, 2011). Gunderson (2011) notes, however, that even when therapy episodes appear to have "failed," for example, the client drops out, therapy still may have served a useful purpose in providing the client with a positive therapeutic experience and helping the client navigate a difficult period in his or her life. This can make the client more amenable to seeking help in the future. When working with clients with BPD, it is important to leave an "open door" so that the client feels he or she can come back to therapy even after having dropped out. Brenda, the client depicted in the dialogue above, rarely kept her appointments, but she knew that, in a crisis, she could contact me.

There are many different therapies that have proven efficacy in treating BPD. These include schema-focused cognitive therapy (Young, 1990); dialectical behavioral therapy, which can be successfully provided on an outpatient basis (Linehan, 1993, 1993b) or inpatient (Bloom, Woodward, Susmaras, & Pantalone, 2012); developmental/ego psychology therapy (Goldstein, 1990); psychodynamically oriented therapy (Clarkin, Levy, Lenzenweger, & Kernberg, 2007; Clarkin, Yeomans, & Kernberg, 1999); structural analysis of social behavior (Benjamin, 2002); mentalization-based therapy (MBT) (Bateman & Fonagy, 2010); and general psychiatric management (GPM) (McMain, Guimond, Streiner, et al., 2012; McMain, Links, Gnam, et al., 2009). All of these treatments work in terms of decreasing suicidality, self-harm, and use of hospitals, emergency rooms, substances, and medications; however, certain approaches are more or less effective with different individual clients. In addition, support by the client's family for his or her treatment is very important for treatment adherence and success. This can be achieved better if the family receives support via psychoeducation (see, e.g., Kreger & Mason, 2010; Kreger & Shirley, 2002) and joins a self-help advocacy group, such as the National Alliance on Mental Illness (NAMI) (www.nami.org).

Dialectical behavioral therapy

Dialectical behavioral therapy is the most well-known and practiced treatment for BPD, although unfortunately, sometimes the full model is not offered in many communities. The reason is that the full package of formal DBT training is expensive and time consuming and many clinicians and agencies cannot afford the training or don't have access to it. In addition, DBT requires several treatment components, including individual treatment, group skills treatment, and therapist consultation and support that, together, require considerable resources. However, DBT has been shown to be highly effective in reducing suicidality and inpatient care and helps clients learn skills to achieve recovery (Bloom et al., 2012; Linehan, Comtois, Murray, et al., 2006).

DBT focuses on teaching the borderline client emotion regulation skills and tools to reduce self-destructive behaviors. DBT employs the concept of mindfulness, which refers to learning how to be self-aware in the moment, and to how to balance cognitive and emotional states, so that one moves from the emotional mind to what DBT refers to as the "wise mind." DBT also emphasizes skills for tolerating distress and improving interpersonal skills so that interpersonal relationships are more stable and lasting. DBT is proactive, validating, supportive of self-determination, and uses an active problem-solving approach. The group treatment component also enhances social support for participants, and encourages altruism as clients help each other solve problems and learn skills.

What Clients with BPD Say Is Helpful in Treatment

The big question at this juncture is: What do borderline clients themselves say is truly helpful to them in treatment? To answer this question, the author asked individuals living with borderline personality disorder who have achieved successful recovery to describe what they have found to be helpful in their treatment experiences. The following summarizes what they said.

- The first thing that is helpful is for the therapist to work with the client to make sure he or she is safe and, when in a crisis, help the client pull out of the crisis mode and into stability. In the case scenario with Terry (see above), this was achieved by immediate intervention, assurance of help, and immediate follow-up appointments.

- Second, build a trusting relationship by being honest, straightforward, and genuine.
- Third, use empathy—not by just saying you understand but rather by reflecting to the client that you perceive his or her feelings accurately. That provides the validation the client desperately needs.
- Fourth, realize and accept that "testing is what they do." Clients with BPD will test their therapist repeatedly to provide assurance about the genuineness of the relationship. Deal with testing by providing structure and setting clear limits with follow-through. This is explicitly built into dialectical behavioral treatment. For example, in DBT, if you miss treatment sessions so many times, you're out.
- Don't give up on your client with BPD! Treatment takes time and is a long process.
- Help your clients learn to be aware of their emotions and learn to describe their emotions in words rather than expressing painful emotions in destructive actions such as cutting. Help your client to know what his or her "self" is about, who he or she is.
- Help your clients to be aware of what their emotional pain is about and where it is coming from so they can understand the pain and have it validated.
- Help your clients to build their identity and sense of consolidated "self."
- Teaching skills for coping with stress and emotions is very important, for example, emotion regulation skills and distress tolerance skills.
- If your client acts out and, for example, throws a book across the room, ask, "Why did you do it (throw the book)? What are your feelings? Is there a healthier way to express your feelings?" If your client is cutting him or herself, ask, "Why do you cut? What does it do for you? Is there a healthier way to achieve the same goals?"
- Journaling can be a very helpful therapeutic tool for many clients, that is, "Can you write down what you are feeling inside?"
- Spirituality and faith can also be a very helpful adjunct to therapy for many clients.

Living with Borderline Personality Disorder: A Consumer Perspective

Throughout this book, the importance of listening to clients' and families' voices has been strongly emphasized. Individuals who have borderline personality disorder are keenly aware of the many unfortunate stereotypes about BPD, in particular, that the illness is hopeless, untreatable, and people with BPD cannot achieve recovery. This is far from the actual truth. It is true that clinical work with borderline clients can be very challenging and sometimes the long-term outcomes are poor, with some individuals continuing to struggle with managing their symptoms and even taking their own lives. Far more individuals, however, get better and do achieve recovery. Many are our co-workers, neighbors, friends, and family members. The following is a personal account written by a young woman who is a recent MSW graduate and who, after years of hard work, has achieved recovery while living with BPD.

Living with BPD

I was diagnosed with bipolar II disorder and borderline personality disorder at the same time, at the age of 20. Although I had problems controlling my mood from puberty on, the blow of receiving a diagnosis, especially that of borderline personality disorder, hit me harder than expected. I sat in my psychiatrist's office with my mother by my side, and I screamed and cried, "Anything but borderline! I don't want to be a borderline!" I was blatantly aware of the stigma that surrounded borderline personality disorder, being in midst of my psychology undergraduate degree. I also knew a girl who had the same diagnosis, who untreated eventually committed suicide, and all of a sudden I saw my grim future there in my psychiatrist's office.

(continued)

My psychiatrist continued to ask me to name three things I liked about myself before I was allowed to leave her office in tears with my mother, and finally I left her office after I named superficial traits such as my hair as things I liked about myself. It turned out that later, I figured out that a more aggressive therapy style worked for me in terms of how I would get better.

I was a happy child, with a controlling mother and an alcoholic father, but as any child may be, unaware of the turmoil around me. I excelled in school until my first mental break at the age of 20. A ballet dancer and music enthusiast at heart, I spent a lot of my time as an adolescent with the arts, in band and color guard, on dance teams, and in a ballet company.

When I started to first show symptoms of bipolar II disorder, my parents and I assumed I was a sullen, moody teenager around the age of 15. Later, I began spending excessive money that wasn't mine, losing jobs, having long-term depressive episodes lasting up to 6 months, and self-injurious behavior starting at the end of high school. When I was bailed out of jail for driving 115 miles per hour on a 55 mile an hour road during a manic episode, my parents knew that there was something wrong with me and sent me to therapy.

My first break, and dissociative episode, came due to an interpersonal relationship issue. I remember listening to music in my car, and dissociated for about four to five hours after that. Apparently friends came to my aid as I attempted to jump off the top of my apartment complex, cut myself in front of them, and wept the entire time. That was my first of four hospitalizations.

The stigma surrounding borderline personality disorder was apparent to me, a psychology major, and to other clinicians that refused to treat me due to my axis II diagnosis. Some stated "borderlines are too aggressive" or "they are all liars" or finally, my favorite, "I can't treat you due to insurance."

After finally finding a combination of medicines that worked for me, a psychiatrist who specialized in my axis I and II disorders, and a DBT therapist that did not have stigma towards me, I decided to apply for a graduate degree in social work. I wanted to combat the stigma surrounding mental illness that both society and individuals placed upon themselves, specifically with borderline personality disorder. Due to the relationship hazards that sometimes accompany borderline personality disorder and bipolar II disorder, I decided to move away from my hometown of Austin, Texas, and move to the balmy northeast Pittsburgh, Pennsylvania. I also wanted to leave Texas because, although my father and brother were supportive of my recovery, my mother often threw the "borderline" card out in arguments, and imposed full-on stigma towards me due to my diagnosis. I felt stable enough to leave, and have done well thus far (with a couple of bumps in the road like medication changes and therapist woes) in Pittsburgh at the University of Pittsburgh's social work program.

Debating on whether or not to disclose the reality of my borderline personality disorder in this essay for students caused some tension and apprehension on my part. Stigma surrounds mental illness, no matter the diagnosis. Rather than feel classified and ashamed of my BPD, through recovery I decided to embrace it. My journey through BPD and the recovery process not only led me to the field of social work, but also helped me grow and change as a student, friend, volunteer, and family member.

Before my diagnosis, I believed all borderlines to be deceitful liars who were simply craving attention. I worked with a young girl at a sandwich shop, during my college years, who proclaimed herself (through help of her psychiatrist) as BPD. One incident with this girl stands out in my mind. She showed up for work distraught and crying. Something obviously wrong, she refused to discuss her problem. She moved straight to the knife rack in the back of the store and cut her wrists in the restaurant. Tearfully displaying her wounds to customers, she was quickly escorted away by the manager while blood dripped across the tile floor. In my view, she displayed a textbook version of BPD, completely unlike my secret cutting, depressive nature, and lying. Hacking up half of my leg as a young adult, fighting with family members claiming they didn't love me enough, and sabotaging interpersonal relationships filled my life from age 16 until my diagnosis at age 20. I knew I had the disorder and lived in denial because of the shame and disgrace I associated with BPD. Breaking through my own biases proved difficult.

After my diagnoses, I launched my first therapy session with an MSW therapist that specialized in DBT. Visiting my therapist once a week, we discussed my interpersonal relationships,

(continued)

school, and everything in between. Due to the bias I held about BPD, after some time in therapy I seemed to hit a wall. Our conversations grew stale and therapy stagnated. On a day in a session like any other, I continued to complain about how I did not desire the diagnosis of borderline anymore. My therapist then stated something that caused a breakthrough both with therapy and my treatment of my BPD. She simply pronounced, "You just have traits of the disorder. The disorder doesn't make you the person you are." Suddenly, it clicked. I didn't have to be the girl from the sandwich shop, the example from my school textbooks, or my distorted version of BPD. I was me, and I had these traits. I needed to deal with them. Carol helped me remove the burden I placed on myself, so I could finally begin to deal with my diagnosis and treatment. Changing my perspective opened my mind to many different types of treatment such as DBT, peer groups, and utilizing one-on-one therapy, for me, in a novel way. Beginning to deal with the disorder, rather than stigmatizing myself, started me on the road to recovery. My work ethic at my job improved, I stayed out of the hospital, and stopped self-injury.

I decided to disclose this personal story about my recovery to address the issue of stigmatizing persons with mental illness. Those who are diagnosed with mental illnesses (whether it is BPD, bipolar disorder, or schizophrenia) struggle with the issue of self-deprecation, which spurs from the biases of others on a day-to-day basis. I disclose this personal story to represent someone who achieved an undergraduate degree, stopped self-injury, and functioned in society, rather than the habitually hospitalized BPD person that clinicians often think of.

My best advice to the future social worker is to practice with as little stigmatization of clients as possible, and help them to remove some of the shame and self-consciousness they place on themselves. By having this unique outlook on social work practice, and this problem, you can help change attitudes and minds one person at a time.

What Families of Individuals with Borderline Personality Disorder Need

Working with individuals who have borderline personality disorder can be challenging for clinicians. For families, however, the struggle of trying to help someone one loves who is suffering from BPD can be extraordinarily difficult. Parents, children, siblings, and spouses often bear considerable objective and subjective burdens and find themselves "walking on eggshells" as they try to help their ill loved one while trying to keep the peace and avoid crisis (Kreger & Mason, 2010). The sudden mood changes, unpredictable behavior and, in particular, self-harming behavior and aggression can be highly stressful for family members, particularly if they don't know that their loved one has BPD and don't know the best way to help.

Although the prevalence of BPD in clinical settings has been well recognized since the 1980s, only recently have the enormous public health costs been acknowledged and attention given to the needs of families. In the past, similar to the situation with schizophrenia, it was believed that families were culpable in causing borderline personality disorder, and now we know that the cause of BPD is probably primarily genetic, although environment matters (Gunderson, 2011). Also, similar to old ideas about schizophrenia, BPD is no longer seen as a treatment-resistant generally hopeless diagnosis that requires monumental therapeutic efforts to effect change. Instead, clinical researchers have developed a range of effective treatments and longitudinal studies have elevated hope for recovery, and such information can provide families with reassurance and relief. Family-blaming still occurs, unfortunately, but strides are being made through family advocacy groups like NAMI to raise public awareness about the fallacies in blaming families for BPD and, instead, advocating for families to play an important role as partners in treatment.

The principles outlined in Chapter 7 on working with families apply equally to working with families with loved ones with BPD and, as with other serious mental illnesses, psychoeducation is the key intervention that families need most at the beginning.

Megan Marshall

Learning about the illness, available treatments and their effectiveness, and how the family can contribute to helping their loved one can be very useful. Although families don't cause BPD, the quality of the family's environment, especially in terms of level of stress, matters. As with schizophrenia, families of loved ones with BPD can learn how to communicate more effectively, how to keep stress levels down to avoid crises, and how to not have to walk on eggshells. Support and advocacy organizations that can help families include the National Alliance on Mental Illness (NAMI), the National Education Alliance for Borderline Personality Disorder (NEA-BPD), and family training and support programs such as NAMI's Family-to-Family Program and NEA-BPD's Family Connections (www.neabpd.org).

Unfortunately, even today, many mental health providers still are not welcoming toward input from family members of individuals with BPD, which is very frustrating for family members, particularly those who are providing caregiving and financial support for their ill loved one. NAMI and other advocacy organizations can help families and consumers to find mental health professionals who are inclusive and who approach treatment as a partnership among the provider, the consumer, and the family. The following is a listing of some of the resources available for families and consumers about BPD:

1. Behavioral Technology LLC, which provides DBT referral, training, and resources: www.behavioraltech.com;
2. Borderline Personality Disorder Resource Center, which provides referrals to BPD resources and treatment: www.bpdresourcecenter.org;
3. The National Education Alliance for Borderline Personality Disorder (NEA-BPD), which offers BPD conferences, publications, videos, and education: www.borderlinepersonalitydisorder.com;
4. NEA BPD Family Connections, which offers a 12-week course for families that provides education, coping skill strategies, and support: www.borderlinepersonalitydisorder.com;
5. New England Personality Disorder Association (NEPDA), which provides BPD family workshops, regional conferences, education, advocacy, and support: www.nepda.org;

Assess your comprehension of *the nature, symptoms, and treatment of borderline personality disorder and how families of individuals with BPD can be supported as well* by completing this quiz.

CONCLUSION

I would like to end the chapter by reviewing some general suggestions for what social workers and other clinicians should do and what they should avoid doing when working with clients with personality disorders (Perry & Vaillant, 1989). In general, once clients have aired their complaints about their problems, including problems other people are causing them or their indignation about being forced into treatment, avoid allowing them to keep going over the same complaints again and again. Repetition serves to reinforce the complaints, not resolve them, and can result in both client and therapist getting "stuck" and not moving forward in treatment. After responding empathically to the feelings the client is experiencing, move on to another topic with the goal of keeping the responsibility for problem solving and change in the client's court.

It is inevitable that a therapist who works with clients with personality disorders will be, from time to time, lied to or tricked or manipulated by the client. It goes with the territory. Try not to get defensive when this happens or feel anger or shame, rather, remember that this is part of what clients with personality disorders do, and the job of the clinician is to understand the client, not engage in a battle with the client (Perry & Vaillant, 1989).

Although the cornerstone to treating clients with personality disorders is structure, and setting limits with empathy, one has to be reasonable with expectations and limits or the clients will be set up for failure. For example, insisting that clients with BPD must agree to no missed appointments, no alcohol use, no crisis calls, and no extra sessions as a precondition to treatment is essentially requiring them to solve their problems before treatment begins. The exception to this is violent or self-destructive behavior. Safety contracts are very important and appropriate, and requiring the client to seek help, such as going to the crisis service or emergency room, before acting on destructive impulses is important (Perry & Vaillant, 1989).

Structure and limits combined with empathy help clients move away from maladaptive behavior patterns, provides a safe holding environment, and can help clients reflect on what they are doing and reacting to and reflect on what they really want for themselves. Setting limits can incite anger and produce anxiety and depression, thus good social support should be in place. Perry and Vaillant (1989) note that the success of authoritarian organizations, such as military service, in mitigating personality disorders is a direct demonstration of the power of structure coupled with social support.

Don't rescue or punish the client when the client is distressed or new problems develop; rather, help the client learn the skills he or she needs to develop responsibility for managing and solving problems, and allow the client to set the pace for change. The therapist can't and shouldn't control the client's life. The therapist can, however, help the client improve his or her life and move toward recovery.

Avoid giving the client with a personality disorder mixed messages either verbally or nonverbally. Many clients with personality disorders have repeatedly experienced relationships with others in which trust has been violated and their needs have not been appropriately met. Be authentic, honest, and direct in communication—that will enhance the therapeutic alliance and the development of trust. Show in words and deeds that you will stick with the client through the good times and bad times as the client goes through the difficult process of giving up old familiar maladaptive patterns and adopting new healthy patterns. Now, let's turn to what the therapist *should* do.

Perry and Vaillant (1989) recommend when working with clients with personality disorders to emphasize the "consultation model" of treatment, which stresses that the work done by the clinician and client is a collaborative partnership. This is less threatening for clients who are paranoid or narcissistic because it minimizes the imbalance of power often inherent in the psychotherapeutic relationship.

Recognize and accept that the maladaptive behavior patterns of clients with personality disorders will take time to change, just as they took time to develop. Change is a gradual process and won't happen overnight; however, with time, patience, and skilled interventions, many clients with personality disorders can improve. It is also important to accept the reality that some clients won't change due to lack of motivation, problems in engagement, and/or fear. However, even if a client isn't ready for change now, he or she may be ready later on.

When confronting the maladaptive behavior patterns and defenses of a client with a personality disorder, do so in the context of a strong therapeutic alliance coupled with social support in place. Many of the evidence-based treatments for personality disorders include a group component, which can provide both peer support and a forum for learning skills. It is amazing how clients with "hear" the same feedback from peers more readily than those perceived as superiors or authority figures.

Help clients learn to step back and think through the consequences of their actions before they act, instead of impulsively moving from whim to action. As the client progresses and his or her life begins to improve, celebrate these positive steps with the client and take pleasure in the client's attempts to learn and grow. This rewards both the client and the clinician and helps both to persevere in their work together (Perry & Vaillant, 1989). As the client improves with treatment, the clinician's skills will be enhanced as well.

In conclusion, individuals with personality disorders are challenging to work with, but if a clinician has appropriate training and uses the right targeted treatments, such clients can improve and truly achieve recovery. The costs to society of not treating individuals with personality disorders is simply too great. Many of our society's most vexing problems are not caused by accidents or mistakes, rather they are caused by the decisions made by individuals with personality pathology who are in positions of power. This is seen from the micro level with individuals involved in interpersonal violence, abuse toward others, and criminal activity to the macro level as seen in the behavior of some members of plutocratic oligarchies. Finally, however, there are all the individuals and families who suffer from the psychological and interpersonal pain that untreated personality disorders can cause. We, as social workers, must make a commitment to do our part to ease these burdens.

Assess your application and analysis of this chapter's contents by completing the *Chapter Review*.

Chapter 14

Practice with Individuals with Serious Mental Illness and Substance Use Problems and Their Families

INTRODUCTION

Jack

Jack, aged 40, has a long history of alcoholism and major mental illness. He has made several suicide attempts in the past, often while intoxicated. Today, he came to the crisis clinic with suicidal feelings, was having visual hallucinations, and was quite paranoid, and staff concluded that he might be going into delirium tremens due to alcohol withdrawal. He was sent to the County General Hospital—they cleared him medically and sent him back to the county's psychiatric inpatient admissions unit. The County General Hospital ER was contacted, and they stated that Jack was not going into the DTs, but was very tremulous, so they administered vitamins and chlordiazepoxide (Librium).

Upon evaluation at the admissions unit, Jack is a long-haired, bearded, downcast, unkempt man who is quite despondent. He states he has been seeing Mexican gang members in front of his eyes and that these people are following him and are going to kill him. He states that if he leaves the hospital, he knows this will happen and so he is planning to kill himself by cutting his stomach open with a knife. Attempts were made to encourage him to postpone such action, for example, to try some medication or a stay in our transitional care facility, but to no avail—Jack insisted he could not postpone killing himself, and that it would be better to commit suicide than to be killed by others. Diagnostic impression: Axis I: Alcohol withdrawal hallucinosis; Alcohol abuse, chronic; Schizophrenia, paranoid type, chronic. Axis II: Borderline personality disorder. Disposition: 72-hr involuntary civil commitment on the basis of danger to self and grave disability.

(Two weeks later . . .) This is a 40-year-old White male, who came to crisis with the complaint that he has been drinking four fifths of wine a day and is now hearing voices and afraid of going into delirium tremens (DTs). He states that after he was discharged from the psychiatric unit, he dropped out of treatment here and went to Los Angeles. He states he fell apart down there and was admitted to Metropolitan State Hospital in January. He left against medical advice in early May and has been in San Francisco ever since. He is presently exhibiting some tremulousness in his upper extremities and complains of hearing voices calling him an informant and a snitch. I called Good Beginnings (detox center) and the Honor Farm detox program, but Jack is no longer welcome at these facilities due to his frequent use and abuse of their services, for example, 6 times at Honor Farm over the past 3 months; once he was there twice in one day. He refuses to stay long enough to benefit from the program. Disposition: Salvation Army Rescue Mission.

(continued)

(One week later . . .) Jack, a 40-year-old White male with a long history of chronic alcohol abuse and schizophrenia, was brought to the county hospital emergency room via ambulance this evening. He made multiple razor blade and knife cuts on his arms, chest, and abdomen. While in the ER, he broke a glass IV bottle and used that to cut himself. He had been drinking wine before all of the self-harming behavior started. Upon evaluation, he was coherent and oriented. Jack denied suicidal feelings or intent, stating that if he wanted to die he wouldn't just cut himself. In the past, he has also been given a diagnosis of borderline personality disorder. Currently, he is future oriented, wants his SSI straightened out (he hasn't been getting his checks), and wants to go down to the Social Security office today once he is discharged from the hospital. Client refused to consider any treatment options for his alcoholism or for treatment of his mental illnesses.

Jack is a "dually diagnosed" client, meaning that he has a substance use problem (both alcohol abuse and alcohol dependence) and mental illness, in his case, both schizophrenia and borderline personality disorder. Jack has had multiple contacts with all of the systems of care that should be able to help him —the mental health system, the addiction treatment system, and the health care system—but it hasn't worked. Jack has not received the help he needs and none of the various services he has had contact with seem to be able to work out a way to coordinate the services he needs and wants into an integrated treatment plan. Why has this happened? Granted, Jack has his own set of problems and challenges, but the system ought to be able to address them and work collaboratively to help him achieve recovery with both his addiction problems and his mental illnesses.

There is no question that people with co-occurring disorders are a difficult group to work with. For one thing, they generally have poorer treatment outcomes in all areas than people who have only one disorder or one disorder at a time (Minkoff, 1999). They are more likely to relapse from the disorders they have, they are more likely to be rehospitalized, be treatment resistant, treatment non-adherent, medically involved, incarcerated or otherwise criminally involved, HIV positive, impoverished, and homeless (Drake, Essock, Shaner, et al., 2001; Minkoff, 1999; Prince, 2012; Prince, Walkup, Akincigil, et al., 2012; Sun, 2012). Furthermore, individuals with co-occurring disorders are more likely to engage in self-destructive and aggressive behavior (Yang, Mulvey, Loughran, & Hanusa, 2012) and, finally, they tend to use a lot of the most expensive services, such as emergency rooms and inpatient care, but often without positive outcomes. Part of this is because they are "system misfits" (Minkoff, 1999). They are individuals with more than one disorder who are trying to get services from systems basically designed to treat only one disorder at a time. Jack, for example, would go to the mental health center and be told he couldn't get treatment until he sobered up. So, he would dutifully go over to the local addiction treatment center and be told by their staff that they could not treat him until his psychiatric disorders were stabilized. At that point, Jack would say "to heck with it" and go out and get drunk, and then end up in the kinds of situations described in the case vignettes above.

Individuals who use and/or abuse certain types of legal, illicit, and prescription drugs, including alcohol, and who have mental disorders present special challenges for social workers and other mental health professionals. Although the co-occurrence of mental health and substance abuse problems is not a new phenomenon, only in the past 30 years or so has it received serious and widespread attention by professionals in both the substance abuse and mental health fields (Evans & Sullivan, 1990).

Terminology

A number of terms have been used for persons who abuse substances and have mental disorders. The terms *dually diagnosed* and *co-occurring disorders* are the most commonly used terms but can be confusing because these terms are sometimes used for co-occurrence of other disorders, for example, mental disorder and mental retardation or mental retardation and substance abuse. *Comorbidity* is the term used by the federal Department of Health and Human Services and the National Institute of Mental Health (the NIMH Epidemiological Catchment Area study used this term), as well as commonly used in the field of psychiatry. *Co-existing problems* is another term—although less common—and there are a variety of commonly used acronyms, such as MISA, mentally ill substance abuser, or MICAA, mentally ill and chemically abusing or addicted. None of these terms is inherently preferable; the important thing is to make sure it is clear that both substance abuse and mental illness are the foci of concern. Of course, even the terms *mental illness* and *substance abuse* can be vague, because "mental illness" refers to a diverse range of psychiatric disorders, and "substance abuse," also called *drug abuse* or *chemical dependency*, can refer to a wide variety of substances. For the purpose of this chapter, two terms will be used interchangeably. The first is the traditional term *dual-diagnosis* and the other is the term currently used by the Substance Abuse and Mental Health Services Administration (SAMHSA), which is *co-occurring disorders*. In order to understand the challenges faced by a client with a co-occurring disorder, one has to have a basic understanding of the substances that people commonly use and abuse. The next section provides a brief overview of the various categories of psychoactive drugs commonly used and abused.

SUBSTANCES OF ABUSE

Alcohol and other drugs are used and abused because of their psychoactive properties, that is, their effect on the brain and on mood. The most vexing problem in the area of substance abuse research and treatment is the simple fact that most drugs that are abused *make people feel good*. As Elwood Bernas, a chemical dependency counselor at the Hazelden Addiction Treatment Center, described it: "People use drugs and alcohol because they work, they're powerful, they're satisfying. It feels good to be high. It feels great to be stoned. When people ingest mood-altering chemicals, usually, rather innocently at first, they experience what would appear to be a desirable outcome, they work. Alcohol is probably the most famous—it's legal, it's available, people use it all the time because it does what it's intended to do" (Bernas, 1999). This is pretty much what addicts will say—drugs reliably do what they are supposed to do and, at least temporarily, they "fix" what needs to be fixed, for example, a bad mood, chronic feelings of emptiness, painful loneliness, or stress.

Data from the NIMH Epidemiological Catchment Area Study (Regier, Farmer, Rae, et al., 1990) reports that, overall, the lifetime prevalence of mental disorders other than alcohol and other drug abuse dependency is 22.5 percent. Alcohol abuse has a lifetime prevalence of 13.5 percent, while drug abuse-dependence disorders have a 6.1 percent lifetime prevalence. About one out of eight people who tries a potentially addictive drug becomes addicted. Why that happens to some people but not others is very complex, representing a mixture of psychological factors, environmental factors, and brain chemistry. Here is what addiction looks like in an individual person—a woman named Abby Stevens:

> Abby knew things were spinning out of control her junior year at college when one night she embarked on a beer drinking contest at the college's on-campus pub and managed to drink two male friends who were large football players over twice her size "under the table." Her roommate, Bekka, tried to keep up with her, but a couple hours into the contest, Bekka gave up and, on her way back to the dorm, passed out on the grass in the middle of the quad. Abby had been practicing for this drinking contest since age 11 when she had her first drink. In high school she always carried a water bottle with her to school but it didn't contain water, it was full of coconut rum. By now, at age 30, Abby was a putting a pint of scotch, a 12-pack of beer,

and a couple bottles of wine into her 125-pound body every day. She preferred drinking to any other activity and, although she was still able to work, she didn't know how much longer she could keep it up. "I've never gone to work without a buzz on," Abby admits ruefully. Abby has tried and failed to quit alcohol on her own multiple times, but went into delirium tremens each time as a consequence of severe alcohol withdrawal. Although for many years Abby could have been described as a "functioning alcoholic," she isn't functioning very well any more. She now had reached the point that she knew she had no choice but to sign herself into rehab, although she dreaded facing the potential stigma that would go along with that. (Newhill, 1995)

For a long time, addicts like Abby were seen as morally deficient individuals who simply lacked willpower, an assumption that provides little help in guiding treatment and achieving sobriety. Today, in the terminology of the modern addiction recovery movement, addiction to alcohol or other drugs is less a character flaw than it is a "bio-psycho-social-spiritual disorder," a phrase that emphasizes how complex and multifaceted the problem, and its treatment, is (Interlandi, 2008).

The word *addiction* comes from the Latin word *addictus*, which refers to a person who has been bound as a slave to another person he or she owes money to and is, therefore, indentured to work off what is owed (Interlandi, 2008). The meaning of *addictus* is quite relevant to the position of someone who is addicted to a substance, that is, the power of an addiction is so great, it can enslave a person. The first step of Alcoholics Anonymous, "We admitted we were powerless over alcohol: that our lives had become unmanageable," reflects the dynamic of being enslaved to one's addiction (Alcoholics Anonymous, 1952). For individuals with a severe addiction, like Abby, the initial pleasure that the substance used to provide soon gives way to a simple struggle to feel somewhat normal and avoid withdrawal, which speaks to the biological aspects of addiction. With the current emphasis on understanding behavioral health problems from a medical or biological standpoint, current research efforts on addiction are focused primarily on the biology of addiction and searching for medications that can help in achieving sobriety.

Addiction is much more than a brain disease, however. It involves behavioral issues as well. Addicts make choices and decisions about whether or not they ingest substances, and relapse is not an inevitable consequence of a diseased brain. Calling addiction a "disease" serves several useful purposes, including reducing stigma, which can help in getting addicted individuals into treatment—it also enhances the probability of insurance coverage and can serve to increase research funding—but addiction really isn't the same as diseases such as diabetes or heart disease (Satel, 1998). Addiction psychiatrist Sally Satel comments that "the message that addiction is chronic and relapse inevitable is demoralizing to patients and gives the treatment system an excuse if it doesn't serve them well" (Satel, 1998). She argues that it is better to view addiction as a behavioral condition and the addicted person as an empowered, rather than powerless, individual who can be an active partner in recovery. Yes, all addicts are vulnerable to relapse, but our treatment system needs to do better in the kinds of messages we give to people about their hope for recovery.

Many experts agree that there is simply no magic bullet for treating addiction, and because addiction is more than a disease of the brain, treatment must be holistic and ecological in nature (Rosenthal, 2008; Sun, 2012). Certainly, advances in neuroscience have given us new information and insights about addiction and its neurological basis and have led to the development of several drugs to curb the cravings of addiction. However, similar to the treatment of serious mental illness, drugs alone are not the sole answer for addiction. Drugs don't address and provide answers for the myriad psychosocial factors and problems that both cause and sustain addiction. These issues must also be addressed for an individual to achieve and maintain recovery. And for the dually diagnosed individual, that road is even more complicated and challenging. To understand the problems of drug and alcohol addiction and the situation of dually diagnosed clients, one first has to have a basic understanding of substances of abuse. These substances can be grouped into five categories: (1) central nervous system (CNS) depressants; (2) central nervous system (CNS) stimulants; (3) opioids or narcotics; (4) hallucinogens; and (5) over-the-counter drugs. The first four categories describe chemicals that are controlled substances and therefore are either illegal or can only be obtained via a doctor's prescription. Let's take a brief look at the first category, central nervous system (CNS) depressants.

Central Nervous System (CNS) Depressants

CNS depressants, also referred to as sedative-hypnotic drugs, include alcohol, barbiturates and methaqualone, benzodiazepines, and inhalants. All CNS depressants, including alcohol, are particularly dangerous drugs because consumption of high doses and withdrawal effects in those who are physically addicted can result in serious medical complications including death.

The number one CNS depressant in terms of availability and level of use is *alcohol*. Alcohol is the most widely used and abused drug in the United States because it can be obtained legally, it is relatively inexpensive, and it is easy to obtain, with even underage drinkers having little difficulty obtaining alcohol. In 2003, 22.6 percent of Americans aged 12 and older reported binge drinking and 6.8 percent were found to be heavy drinkers (SAMHSA, 2004). A national representative survey of high school students (Johnston, O'Malley, & Bachman, 1993) found that nearly 90 percent of American high school seniors report using alcohol, and over a quarter of the high school seniors reported having five or more drinks on at least one occasion in the 2 weeks before the survey was conducted. Alcohol use by teens increases the risk of addiction and can change the developing brain for life. In fact, a 1998 study by the National Institute on Alcohol Abuse and Alcoholism reports that if a teen starts to drink at age 15, he or she has a 40 percent chance of alcoholism or alcohol dependence as an adult.

For individuals of all ages who have little money, alcohol is frequently shared on the streets. In fact, certain cheap, high-alcohol-content wines and malt liquors, known by names such as "Thunderbird" and "Night Train," are particular substances for street abuse. Malt liquor is heavily marketed in poorer socioeconomic areas, is specifically marketed to appeal to young people, and is associated with excessive drinking, alcohol problems, and the use of illicit drugs, particularly marijuana (Collins, Bradizza, & Vincent, 2007). If beer, wine, or distilled spirits containing ethanol or ethyl alcohol are not readily available, the individual with alcohol dependence may misuse common products that contain alcohol, such as vanilla or other extracts, NyQuil, or mouthwash. When really desperate, they may resort to types of alcohol not intended for human consumption, such as perfume, aftershave lotion, or rubbing (isopropyl) alcohol. The complications of alcohol withdrawal can be extremely serious and can include a type of delirium that is life threatening, called *delirium tremens*.

Delirium tremens

The symptoms of all forms of delirium include relatively global cognitive impairment, disorientation, and confusion. When a person is delirious, he or she has difficulty mobilizing, focusing, shifting, and sustaining attention. Such individuals often evidence a wide and changeable range of strong emotions that do not seem related to environmental events. Delirium can occur as a result of either an acute brain condition or a chronic brain condition (Trzzepacz, Meagher, & Wise, 2002). The four general causes of delirium include (1) brain disease (e.g., an infection or tumor); (2) a disease or infection in another part of the body that affects the brain (e.g., a metabolic condition); (3) intoxication from drugs or alcohol; and (4) withdrawal from a substance to which an individual is addicted, such as alcohol or drugs. The biological mechanisms underlying all cases of delirium are an imbalance in the brain's system of neurotransmitters coupled with a general derangement of brain metabolism. Although everyone has the potential to develop delirium, there appear to be wide variations in susceptibility. Delirium is what is known as a *threshold phenomenon*, meaning that every individual probably has a specific threshold for developing the condition. Preexisting brain damage, addiction, and certain chronic medical disorders can bring an individual closer to this threshold so that relatively small metabolic changes are sufficient to push the person over the threshold into a delirium state.

One of the most dramatic examples of delirium can be seen in the acute brain condition known as delirium tremens, or "the DTs." Delirium tremens results from cessation from alcohol following excessive alcohol consumption over a long period of time, and occurs in about 5 percent of individuals with alcoholism. Delirium tremens is characterized by tremors and vivid visual, tactile and, sometimes, auditory hallucinations, which result in a state of acute terror. For example, a person in the throes of delirium tremens will believe that spiders are burrowed under his or her skin and then scratch the skin until it bleeds, trying to get the spiders out.

One of the best descriptions of delirium tremens can be found in the classic book *The Adventures of Huckleberry Finn*, by Mark Twain, in a scene in which Huck describes DTs as experienced by Pap, who was a heavy user of alcohol for years. Huck says:

> I don't know how long I was asleep, but all of a sudden there was an awful scream and I was up. There was Pap, looking wild, and skipping around every which way and yelling about snakes. He said they was crawling up his legs; and then he would give a jump and scream, and say one had bit him on the cheek—but I couldn't see no snakes. He started and run round and round the cabin, hollering "Take him off, take him off; he's biting me on the neck!" I never see a man look so wild in the eyes. Pretty soon he was all fagged out, and fell down panting; then he rolled over and over wonderful fast, kicking things every which way, striking and grabbing the air with his hands, and screaming and saying there was devils a-hold of him. He wore out by and by, and laid still awhile, moaning. Then he laid stiller, and didn't make a sound. I could hear the owls and wolves away off in the woods, and it seemed terrible still. He was laying over by the corner. By and by he raised up part way and listened, with his head to one side. He says, very low: "Tramp—tramp—tramp; that's the dead; tramp—tramp—tramp—they're coming after me; but I won't go. Oh, they're here, don't touch me—don't! Hands off—they're cold; let go. Oh, let a poor devil alone." Then he went down on all fours and crawled off, begging them to let him alone, and he rolled himself up in his blanket and wallowed in under the old pine table, still a-begging; and then he went to crying. I could hear him through the blanket. (Twain, 1884, pp. 47–48)

The symptoms of delirium tremens usually are not evident until the person has stopped drinking. Several aspects of the mechanism that causes its symptoms are not well understood, but the DTs seem to be due to the prolonged interference of alcohol with the metabolism of neurons in the brain. Delirium tremens can last for a week or longer and constitutes a clear medical emergency. The affected person must usually be hospitalized, and tranquilizing drugs and a quiet and orderly environment are essential to recovery. However, complete recovery depends on restoration of metabolic equilibrium and, in some cases, metabolic equilibrium cannot be restored and the person dies.

The second type of CNS depressant is *barbiturates*. Clinically, barbiturates are used as sedatives, hypnotics, anesthetics, and anticonvulsants. How these drugs act, for example, as a sedative or an anesthetic, depends on how much is taken: the larger the dose, the greater the effect (Smith & Riskin, 1991; Truog, Berde, Mitchell, & Grier, 1992). The barbiturate called

---

Mark Twain, Huckleberry Finn, 1884

secobarbital (trade name Seconal; street names, reds or devils) used to be commonly prescribed to treat insomnia although, today, it has been largely replaced by other drugs more effective in treating the underlying conditions associated with insomnia, such as anxiety, depression, or pain. Secobarbital also can leave users with a "barbiturate hangover" due to its long half-life, while more recently developed sleep medications, such as zolpidem (Ambien) and eszopiclone (Lunesta), have shorter half-lives and so users feel more rested and alert in the morning. Another well-known barbiturate is phenobarbital. This barbiturate is used clinically to prevent seizures in epilepsy and to treat detoxification patients whose withdrawal from other drugs (e.g., cocaine) may result in seizures. Another well-known barbiturate not available legally, but which can be found on the streets, is methaqualone (trade names Quaalude and Sopor; street names: ludes, sopors, quads). This drug received so much bad press in the 1970s (see, e.g., Pascarelli, 1973) that its production was discontinued in the United States, although it continues to be imported illegally (Parry, 1997).

The third type of CNS depressant is *benzodiazepines*. There are several subtypes of benzodiazepines, and three of the most well known are diazepam (Valium), chlordiazepoxide (Librium), and alprazolam (Xanax). Benzodiazepines are antianxiety agents and are also referred to as "minor tranquilizers," in contrast to "major tranquilizers" (antipsychotic medications). They have clear beneficial properties in easing anxiety, however, they have been prescribed in large quantities in the United States, particularly during the 1970s to 1980s, and are highly addictive, thus many people end up abusing them. Medical professionals have been criticized for being too quick to prescribe these drugs before thoroughly investigating the causes of a particular client's anxiety and seeking nondrug alternatives.

In addition to overdose and withdrawal problems, combining more than one CNS depressant can be dangerous because one drug can potentiate the other, resulting in a multiplier rather than additive effect. *Cross-tolerance* can also occur, in which tolerance developed for one drug in this class results in tolerance to other drugs in the class. Cross-tolerance then can lead to *cross-addiction*, which means that when the drug of choice is not available, the addicted person may substitute another drug in the same class, for example, Librium instead of Valium, and the addiction will carry over to the substitute drug. Sometimes, physicians or dentists prescribe benzodiazepines before checking a client's record for drug interactions or a history of addiction, and a client who is in recovery from addiction may be inadvertently sent into relapse. In this arena, social workers can educate clients about the importance of honestly communicating with medical personnel about their diagnoses and medications to prevent such problems from occurring.

The final type of CNS depressant is *inhalants* (street names include: whippets, poppers, snappers). All inhalant substances emit breathable chemical vapors that users intentionally inhale because of the chemicals' mind-altering effects. Inhalant substances include common household products that contain volatile solvents, aerosols, or gases, such as gasoline, nail polish remover, PAM cooking spray, and paint. Most inhalants produce a rapid high that resembles alcohol intoxication. If sufficient amounts are inhaled, nearly all inhalants produce a loss of sensation, and even unconsciousness and death from heart failure or suffocation (inhalants displace oxygen in the lungs). Other irreversible effects can be hearing loss, limb spasms, central nervous system or brain damage, or bone marrow damage (Johnston, O'Malley, Bachman, & Schulenberg, 2012; National Institute on Drug Abuse, n.d.). Example:

> Moses was first seen at the county mental health clinic when he was 14 years old. Moses and his family immigrated to the United States from Mexico 3 years prior so his parents could secure farmwork in the central valley of California. For the first 2 years, Moses did not go to school because his family was undocumented and feared deportation, also his parents needed his help at home caring for younger siblings

while the parents worked in the fields. Moses's life was very hard; he was lonely and sad much of the time. One Saturday, his parents allowed him to go into town with the son of another farm worker, and the two of them met some other teenagers who introduced them to inhalants, specifically huffing paint and gasoline fumes. Moses didn't like using inhalants at first and so after one time using, refused to use any more. The following year, Moses's parents summoned the courage to enroll him in middle school and it was immediately apparent to his teachers that he was intellectually gifted. Testing revealed his IQ to be 135, in the superior range. The school made special efforts to support Moses in his education and within a short period of time, he was fluent in English and doing well in all of his subjects. Then the following summer he began hanging out with the same kids he knew before and tried using inhalants again. This time, he found he liked the feeling of being high and so he continued to use. The next year, Moses did not do as well in school and the teachers suspected drug use and possible depression, and referred him to mental health services for an evaluation. We determined that he was experiencing depression, but this was compounded by ongoing inhalant use. Moses was treated for his depression and referred to a teen addiction program. However, Moses refused to stop using inhalants. Three years later, an IQ test revealed that Moses's IQ had dropped from 135 to 80 as a result of brain damage sustained from repeated use of inhalants. Moses's once hopeful future was shattered by his use of drugs. (Newhill, 1995)

In 2009, 2.1 million Americans aged 12 and older reported that they had abused inhalants (SAMHSA, 2011). The NIDA-funded 2010 Monitoring the Future study showed that 8.1 percent of 8th graders, 5.7 percent of 10th graders, and 3.6 percent of 12th graders had abused inhalants at least once in the year prior to being surveyed (Johnston, O'Malley, Bachman, & Schulenberg, 2012). Inhalant use and abuse constitutes a serious public health problem that disproportionately affects youth because inhalants are inexpensive and are easily obtained at home. Now let's turn to the second category of substances of abuse, which is central nervous system (CNS) stimulants.

Central Nervous System (CNS) Stimulants

The two main subtypes of CNS stimulates are amphetamines and cocaine and their respective derivatives. Although caffeine and nicotine are stimulants, and nicotine in particular can be physically harmful, attention here will be primarily on the former two.

Amphetamines

Amphetamines were prescribed widely by doctors in the 1960s and 1970s as diet pills (street names include: robin's eggs, Christmas trees, black beauties, bennies). Because amphetamines are highly effective in suppressing appetite, they worked well to help many people lose weight quickly but, over time, weight loss doctors began to realize that weight loss and, in particular, weight loss maintenance, is complex and pills do not help people learn good nutrition, handle "emotional eating" problems, and make the lifestyle changes necessary for weight loss to be maintained. In addition, it became clear that amphetamines are highly addictive and so using them medicinally for weight loss grew out of favor among most doctors.

Today, the most prominent drug closely related to amphetamine that is manufactured and used illicitly is methamphetamine (meth). What started as a fad among motorcycle gangs in the 1970s has become a big global business, largely due to the efforts of two Mexican drug runners who began smuggling ephedrine into California's central valley by the ton. Ephedrine is a key ingredient in manufacturing methamphetamine, and is the same chemical used to make over-the-counter cold remedies.

Meth is a highly addictive stimulant drug that is long lasting and toxic to dopamine nerve terminals in the central nervous system. It is a white, odorless, bitter-tasting powder taken orally or by snorting or injecting, or formed into a rock "crystal" that is heated and smoked (NIDA, n.d.). Street names include speed, meth, chalk, ice, crystal, and glass. Methamphetamine elevates a person's mood, induces euphoria, increases alertness, reduces fatigue, increases energy, decreases appetite, increases movement and speech, and provides a sense of increased personal power and prowess. Unlike a cocaine or crack high, which is relatively brief, the effect of meth lasts for 6 to 8 hours or more depending upon how much is ingested.

Hundreds of illegal meth labs are now operating in the Western and Midwestern United States, and the effects have spread across the states, hitting rural areas particularly hard. The implications of this situation for social workers is profound, because the manufacture, sale, and ingestion of meth has ruined communities and countless lives, with the most innocent victims being the children of meth users, and this has had a huge impact on the nation's child welfare system (Zernike, 2005).

Cocaine

Cocaine is a powerfully addictive CNS stimulant that makes people feel euphoric and energetic. Street names for cocaine include coke, C, snow, flake, and blow. Cocaine comes in many forms and can be snorted, injected, or smoked. All three methods of cocaine abuse can lead to addiction and other severe health problems, including increasing the risk of contracting HIV/AIDS and other infectious diseases (NIDA, n.d.2). Crack is cocaine hydrochloride powder that has been processed to form a rock crystal that is then usually smoked. The term *crack* originates from the crackling sound the drug makes when it is heated. "Freebasing" cocaine involves heating it in a particular way using certain chemicals before it is smoked which both purifies and makes the drug more potent for an intense high.

Both crack and crank (which is injected) have particular dangers. First, both are more purified and therefore more potent and intense than powder cocaine and, second, both are cheap and easily obtained on the street. And what goes with the brief intense high both of them produce is an equally intense "crash" with profound feelings of depression, irritability, and desire for more of the drug. On the street, people will sometimes take narcotics to mitigate the effects of the crash; clinically, antidepressants or benzodiazepines can sometimes be helpful to ease the crash. Researchers have found that the human liver combines cocaine and alcohol, manufacturing a third substance, cocaethylene, that intensifies cocaine's euphoric effects. The mixture of cocaine and alcohol is the most common two-drug combination that results in drug-related death.

Cocaine increases body temperature, blood pressure, and heart rate and, thus, carries the risk of heart attacks, respiratory failure, strokes, seizures, abdominal pain, and nausea even in otherwise healthy individuals. Other physical effects include destruction of the nasal passages if cocaine is snorted, and eventual vein collapsing if it is injected. The primary psychological withdrawal effect from cocaine is depression. Long-term or heavy use of cocaine can result in psychosis, particularly paranoid psychosis, and even death. In 2009, 4.8 million Americans aged 12 and older had abused cocaine in its various forms, and 1.0 million had abused crack at least once in the year prior to being surveyed (SAMHSA, 2011).

Opioids or Narcotics

The major types of opioids or narcotics include heroin, morphine, fentanyl, and prescription opioids such as hydrocodone (Vicodin), oxycodone (OxyContin), propoxyphene (Darvon), hydromorphone (Dilaudid), and codeine. Since 1924, heroin has been classified as a drug with a high potential for abuse and deemed without medical value. Other drugs in this class, for example, fentanyl, oxycodone, and morphine, continue to be prescribed primarily for their analgesic (pain-relieving) properties. However, these drugs are also likely to be abused, and many people have become addicted to them after having been prescribed such drugs for pain.

Heroin is processed from morphine and usually appears as a white or brown powder or as a black, sticky substance. It is injected, snorted, or smoked. Street names include smack, H, ska, and junk, which is where the term *junkie* comes from. The short-term effects of heroin include an initial surge of euphoria and clouded thinking followed by alternately wakeful and drowsy (nodding) states. Heroin depresses breathing, thus overdose can be fatal, and users who inject the drug risk infectious diseases such as HIV/AIDS and hepatitis. Although for many decades the aggregate number of heroin users remained relatively stable, recently heroin has become popular with individuals not traditionally in the high-risk pool, such as White affluent suburban youth.

Long-term use of opioids or narcotics can result in physical dependence and addiction. Narcotics and opioids can produce feelings of well-being initially, then drowsiness and, depending on amount taken, can depress breathing, which, in overdose, can be fatal. CNS depressants overall slow down brain function and can be dangerous if combined with other CNS depressants. Withdrawal from narcotics is difficult because the acute withdrawal phase lasts longer than for other classes of drugs and it is very difficult for someone who is addicted to go through withdrawal on their own.

One strategy for managing addiction to and gradual withdrawal from heroin is the supervised use of methadone. Methadone is a synthetic narcotic used as a substitute drug for those addicted to heroin, although it is not a cure for addiction. Methadone maintenance programs were instituted for two main reasons: (1) to provide legal access to methadone in order to assist addicts in the process of getting help, and (2) to curtail the criminal activity associated with getting money to support the addict's habit. Another advantage to methadone programs is that methadone is administered orally, thus providing an alternative to needle use and reducing exposure to HIV and hepatitis B. Methadone can be abused, however, and some have criticized methadone programs as a poor substitute for a drug-free life. In addition, many methadone programs are underfunded and no longer provide counseling, a component necessary to move towards a drug-free life. As a result, many users end up taking methadone for life.

One of the largest growing substance abuse problems in the United States is the abuse of prescription drugs, particularly prescription painkillers, such as oxycodone (OxyContin) (Cave & Schmidt, 2012). Prescription drug abuse is defined as taking a prescription medication that is not prescribed for the person taking it, or taking it for reasons or in dosages other than as prescribed (NIDA, n.d.). Abuse of prescription drugs can produce serious health effects, including addiction.

Besides prescription painkillers, other prescription drugs commonly abused include benzodiazepines, barbiturates, and CNS stimulants, such as dextroamphetamine (Dexedrine), methylphenidate (Ritalin and Concerta), and amphetamines (Adderall). According to the National Survey on Drug Use and Health (SAMHSA, 2011), in 2009, 16 million Americans aged 12 and older had taken a prescription pain reliever, tranquilizer, stimulant, or sedative for nonmedical purposes at least once in the year prior to being surveyed.

Hallucinogens

The following is a description of the author's experience working as a volunteer for a university campus drug counseling program:

> During the first half of the 1970s, use of hallucinogenic drugs, particularly LSD (lysergic acid diethylamide, a.k.a. "acid"), was rampant, particularly on college campuses. I worked for 2 years as a volunteer for our campus drug counseling center, aptly named "High Hopes." My job was to drive the blue VW van called "The Magic Bus" on weekend nights around campus to pick up students having bad LSD

> trips and take them to the emergency room. I recall one student who was standing catatonically on one foot in the middle of the quad. He told us he couldn't move because he was surrounded by a "wall of orange" and had lost all sense of orientation. Another student believed he could fly and took a dive out of his fourth-floor dormitory window. In that case, paramedics were called and he was taken to the hospital. He survived but suffered multiple broken bones and a concussion. Some students flunked out of school because their use of LSD had impaired their ability to function. As people said at the time, "It was a bad scene."

The category of hallucinogens involves a number of substances, including LSD (lysergic acid diethylamide) or "acid," PCP (phencyclidine) or "angel dust," Psilocybin or "magic mushrooms," and peyote. Hallucinogens have been used by people for centuries, usually as part of religious ceremonies. All hallucinogens, however, have potential for severely adverse side effects. For example, LSD can produce distorted perceptions of reality and vivid hallucinations (the wall of orange) and delusions (believing that one can fly), and the effects can be frightening and cause panic. LSD produces unpredictable psychological effects, with the drug's effects, called "trips," lasting about 12 hours. Physical effects include increased body temperature, heart rate, and blood pressure; sleeplessness; and loss of appetite. One user described her trip as the following:

> After I took the acid, I drove through the woods in the fall—the leaves had never been so bright and colorful. I went back to my apartment and sat looking at my kitchen floor, which had tiles with pictures of rabbits holding carrots. Suddenly I saw the rabbits hopping and juice came out of the carrots. I walked to the bathroom but it was hard because the floor was undulating and the walls were "breathing," moving back and forth as if alive. I was talking to a friend and everything he said was funny and deeply philosophical at the same time. The experience was wonderful—but I was one of the lucky ones—I had a good trip. I never did it again, though.

Another hallucinogen is PCP, which was developed in the 1950s as an intravenous anesthetic but use in humans was discontinued in 1965 because of documented adverse effects. PCP is a "dissociative drug," meaning that it distorts perceptions of sight and sound and produces feelings of detachment (dissociation) from the environment and self (NIDA, n.d.2).

In the late 1960s to 1970s people began to use PCP recreationally, but it soon gained a reputation as a drug that could cause bad reactions and was not worth the risk. However, PCP can produce feelings of superhuman strength, power, and invulnerability as well as a numbing effect on the mind that some users find attractive. Example:

> One night I saw a young man in the emergency room who had been brought in by the police because he was trying to direct traffic in a busy intersection and seemed to be psychotic and possibly experiencing an acute episode of schizophrenia. Because he had been combative with the police, he was placed in four-point leather restraints on a gurney. I entered the examination room and introduced myself. The man looked at me and gave a yell and suddenly reared up, still tied to the gurney, stood, and started to walk out the door, carrying the gurney with him. At that point, the emergency room doctor yelled, "He's on PCP," and the police managed to push the gurney back down and moved the man to a gurney that was bolted to the floor. I asked the emergency room doctor to hold him until he was cleared from the effects of the drug and then I could evaluate him. (Newhill, 1995)

PCP can produce symptoms that mimic schizophrenia, such as delusions, hallucinations, paranoia, disordered thinking, anxiety, and a sensation of being separate from one's

---

Newhill, C.E. (1995). A mental health casebook. Unpublished manuscript.

environment (Yago, Pitts, Burgoyne, et al., 1981). Long-term use of PCP can produce memory loss, difficulty with speech and thinking, and depression.

Mescaline, the active ingredient in peyote, is obtained by drying the disc-shaped buttons in the crown of the peyote cactus and then the buttons are chewed or soaked in water and made into a tea. Psilocybin is the active ingredient in certain fresh or dried mushrooms and is quite bitter in taste and, thus, is usually brewed into a tea or added to other foods. The hallucinatory effects of peyote and psilocybin are similar to those associated with LSD.

Over-the-Counter (OTC) Drugs

In addition to the drugs and prescription medications already identified, over-the-counter drugs—that is, those that can be purchased without a prescription—can also be abused. Those with greatest potential for abuse include over-the-counter sedatives that people buy to help them sleep, cough and cold preparations containing drugs such as alcohol, and other nonprescription drugs to ease pain. It is important to note that many individuals use, abuse, or are addicted to more than one drug. Such a situation is called polysubstance abuse or polysubstance dependence.

Assess your comprehension of *the five categories of substances of abuse* by completing this quiz.

ETIOLOGICAL THEORIES OF SUBSTANCE ABUSE

Although the exact causes of substance abuse and dependence are still unclear, there are a variety of biological, psychological, and sociological theories that suggest explanations for the occurrence of these problems. These etiological theories include the moral model, the biological model, the sociological model, the psychological model, and the multi-causal model.

The oldest explanations for substance abuse fall under the moral model. According to this perspective, substance abuse is a result of an individual's personal weaknesses, character flaws, or shortcomings, and occurs because one fails to exercise enough willpower. The moral model is also reflected in the perception of alcohol and other drug use as a crime deserving of punishment. This stance was well illustrated during Prohibition in the United States (1920–1933), which made the manufacture, sale, and transportation of alcoholic beverages a crime (Sajatovic, 2012). Drinking, of course, continued but simply shifted to the private and underground arenas. There was also a significant increase in organized crime activity involving the trafficking of alcohol. It wasn't until the 1950s that the American Medical Association formally espoused the disease model as a contrasting view to the moral model, and state governments began to consider the treatment needs of individuals addicted to alcohol and other drugs. Despite this formal recognition of the need for treatment, the moral model persists in our society in myriad ways, including our emphasis on the "war on drugs" and relying on legal enforcement and punishment as the primary responses to substance use and abuse. Thus, today, we find long waiting lists for treatment centers, and it is clear that treatment needs are not being met (Fisher & Harrison, 2008).

Next, we have the biological model. This model essentially argues that addiction to alcohol or drugs is caused by a genetic predisposition for developing the disease. Twin studies, adoption studies, and family studies have suggested, for example, that alcoholism occurs more frequently in some families than others. This was bolstered by the identification, in 1990, of a gene that may provide a link to one form of alcoholism (Blum, 1991). However, most researchers argue that the role of environment must also be considered (West, 2001).

This brings us to the third model, which is the sociological model. This model considers a variety of social, cultural, and societal factors and has been used to study differences in levels of substance abuse problems across societies or across subgroups in a culture. Factors that appear to have some influence include the degree of stress in a culture and cultural norms that encourage, permit, or inhibit substance abuse. Such factors have provided some explanation of why certain cultural groups have higher rates of alcoholism and drug abuse than others.

The fourth model is the psychological model. This model argues that people become dependent on alcohol or drugs because such substances act to reduce stress or provide some kind of positive reinforcement. Many attempts have been made to isolate a particular personality profile that has a significant association with drug abuse but with little success. As researcher Mark Keller famously stated in 1972: "The investigation of any trait in alcoholics will show that they have either more or less of it" (Keller, 1972).

Finally, we have the multi-causal model. This model argues that the etiology of addiction is multifactorial and must take into account a variety of influences including the biological, environmental, psychological, and cultural or sociological. Such a combination suggests a multi-causal or multivariate model of substance abuse, which acknowledges that causes may vary across individuals and certain causal theories, may be more relevant than others for a particular individual. Given current knowledge, the multi-causal model is the most sound and holistic and represents the bio-psycho-social-spiritual perspective of substance abuse the best.

Now that this chapter has provided a relatively brief introduction to some theories about why people use drugs, let's consider the challenges involved in having both a substance use problem and psychiatric disorder.

THE FACES OF COMORBIDITY

Ever since the problem of comorbidity was recognized in the early 1980s and subsequently investigated (Caton, 1981; Pepper, Krishner, & Ryglewicz, 1981), researchers have consistently found that comorbidity of mental illness and substance use is common, with about 50 percent of individuals with severe mental disorders affected by substance abuse. The NIMH Epidemiologic Catchment Area Study (Regier, Farmer, Rae, et al., 1990) reports that individuals with a lifetime history of an alcohol abuse-dependence disorder are twice as likely to have a comorbid mental disorder than individuals without a history of an alcohol disorder. Individuals with a lifetime history of a drug abuse-dependence are six times more likely to have a mental disorder when compared with individuals with no history of drug abuse or dependence. Among those with a lifetime history of a drug abuse-dependence disorder, more than half have also been affected by a mental disorder and are at more than four times the risk of having such a mental disorder compared with those with no history of drug abuse-dependence. Other conclusions from the ECA study include the following:

- Fifty percent (50%) of individuals with drug abuse-dependence disorders meet criteria for at least one mental disorder diagnosis;
- During the study period, 64 percent (64%) of drug users who sought treatment during the previous 6-month period met criteria for at least one comorbid mental disorder;
- Almost 20 percent of individuals with mental illness who are in treatment have a comorbid drug or alcohol disorder;
- Twenty-nine percent (29%) of all persons with mental disorders had a lifetime diagnosis of alcohol and other drug abuse;
- For individuals with schizophrenia, the lifetime rate of alcohol or other drug abuse-dependence is 47 percent, almost half;
- For individuals with bipolar disorder, the lifetime rate of alcohol and other drug abuse-dependence is 56 percent, over half.

What one can conclude from these statistics is that comorbidity of mental disorders with alcohol and drug disorders is not the exception, rather it is almost an expectation (Kessler, McGonagle, Zhao, et al., 1994; Robins & Regier, 1991). As a result, treatment professionals in both systems must routinely investigate both categories of disorder, that is, mental health professionals must routinely inquire about alcohol and drug use, and addiction specialists must routinely screen for the presence of symptoms of mental illness. The earlier that integrated treatment begins for all of the disorders an individual has, the better the prognosis is. However, this often doesn't happen in real life. The reality is that substance abuse professionals sometimes minimize mental health problems, for example, "It'll clear up with sobriety," and mental health professionals may overlook substance abuse problems, for example, "Everybody drinks." Also, administrative rules and regulations, including the nature of insurance reimbursement rules and regulations, have discouraged accurate reporting. This is why it is often difficult to obtain accurate data about comorbidity outside of rigorous studies such as the ECA investigation.

Trends Affecting the Prevalence and Our Understanding of Comorbid Conditions

The problem of comorbidity has emerged over the past 3–4 decades due to several evolving trends (Minkoff, 1999). The first involves one of the unintended consequences of deinstitutionalization. As noted in Chapter 2, deinstitutionalization came about, in part, due to the influence of civil libertarian ideology, which emphasized the importance of giving individuals with mental illness self-determination and free choice. To achieve this, thousands of individuals with serious mental illness were relocated from the more controlled institutional environment of the state hospital to more open community settings. One of the things we've discovered as deinstitutionalization has proceeded is that among the choices that people may make in the community is using and abusing alcohol and other drugs. Although clinicians often explain the use of drugs and alcohol by individuals with mental illness as an effort to "self-medicate" their psychiatric symptoms, the evidence we have suggests that isn't really the case with most people (Mueser, Drake, & Wallach, 1998). Instead, what consumers generally say about their drug use is that using substances helps to relieve painful feelings of isolation, loneliness, and boredom; helps to facilitate interaction with peers and social engagement; and helps in generating feelings of well-being or escape from lives that are experienced as being bleak or hopeless (Minkoff, 1999). These reasons are not all that different from reasons often given for substance use by non-mentally ill people, except that individuals with mental illness tend to have these painful feelings in greater measure, and have fewer alternative, healthier resources with which to cope (Minkoff, 1999).

Another trend that has occurred over the past few decades that impacts the picture of comorbidity is a trend seen generally in our society with regard to how people use substances. In the past, we would see individuals who abused one drug and one drug only. Some people were alcohol abusers, others were addicted to heroin. Increasingly, however, people who use substances are polysubstance users, and many of the substances available today are much stronger in terms of the psychoactive components than similar drugs used in the past. For example, the marijuana that is sold today generally has a much higher THC (delta-9-tetrahydrocannabinol) content than was the case with marijuana generally available in the 1960s (Wanjek, 2002). Over the past few decades, people have also developed new and creative ways of combining different drugs (e.g., PCP infused in marijuana) and cooking up new derivatives of existing drugs (e.g., the various club drugs), and this has complicated the picture of substance use today.

The third and final trend involves the significant advances and changes in our understanding of the nature of the most serious mental illnesses and how the symptoms of such illnesses interact with substance use. Many illnesses that were, in the past, categorized as "functional," that is, not biologically based, such as depression and schizophrenia, are now recognized as biologically based brain disorders. This has completely changed our understanding of how mental illness and substance use interact, and this has led to new advances in treatment. In particular, it has led to the development of evidence-based treatments, such as integrated treatment for co-occurring disorders, described later in this chapter (SAMHSA, 2010).

Dilemmas in Service Provision

Having a dual diagnosis is associated with a number of negative outcomes, including higher rates of relapse, hospitalization, violence, incarceration, homelessness, and serious infections such as HIV and hepatitis. Because the mental health and substance abuse systems in the United States are parallel but separate, the care that is delivered is fragmented and ineffective (Ridgely, Osher, Goldman, et al., 1987). Consumers are unable to navigate the separate systems or make sense of disparate messages about treatment and recovery. Clients with serious mental illness and substance abuse problems tend to be "system misfits," that is, to not fit well with traditional mental health and substance abuse treatment programs. In fact, many programs intentionally exclude such clients via rigorous screening criteria. Grounds for denying drug treatment services to mentally ill clients include arguing that such clients are so different that they would be ostracized by others in the program; or that they do not have the proper cognitive skills to benefit from treatment; or that they have been psychologically unstable or suicidal too recently for the program to take that risk, like the case of Brenda in the previous chapter; or that they appear unmotivated to participate and generally have poor outcomes (Watkins, Lewellen, & Barrett, 2001).

What can happen is that the dually diagnosed client may be offered minimal help. So, for example, he or she might be admitted to a detox unit for a few days, but then released quickly, without adequate plans for long-term treatment. Part of this, admittedly, is due to substance abuse programs having negative experiences with dually diagnosed clients, such as premature termination, treatment noncompliance, extreme acting-out episodes, suicide attempts, and/or verbal or physical aggression (Drake & Wallach, 1989; O'Hare, 1992). Addiction program staff may argue that dually diagnosed clients often can't accomplish their treatment goals, and jeopardize the treatment goals of their peers by getting into fights or bringing drugs into the program. Likewise, traditional community mental health programs primarily focus on the treatment of psychiatric disorders. Sometimes careful psychosocial assessments and client histories are not constructed and questions about drug or alcohol abuse are not asked or, if asked, any problems revealed are ignored or minimized. The reality is that we tend to inquire about areas where we have confidence in our expertise and ignore those areas where we don't. Furthermore, if the presence of comorbidity is identified, residential or halfway house programs for mentally ill clients may specifically screen out the drug-abusing client. The client may then be directed to a drug/alcohol detox or rehabilitation program, but then be denied admission by that program because of their mental illness. The client ends up in a never-ending shuffle between systems, not getting the help he or she needs, and eventually falling through the cracks and often ending up on the streets, in the emergency room, or in jail, like what happened to Jack in the opening vignette.

An additional note must be made in order to understand how comorbidity has emerged as a significant public health concern. In the first couple waves of deinstitutionalization, the mentally ill released into the community were primarily older clients, who had spent many years in the state hospital and did not have access to drugs and alcohol. Some of these clients did choose to use substances, however, today we have severely mentally ill young adult clients who have not been protected by confinement to a state hospital, and who present a different picture because of the ready availability of drugs and alcohol. These younger noninstitutionalized clients often demand yet reject services for their problems. They often have extensive histories of drug and alcohol abuse, and such use exacerbates their symptoms of mental illness and vice versa. Example:

Brad

Brad is a 20-year-old single White male who was referred to the partial hospitalization program by his intensive case manager, Connie. He has a history of multiple hospitalizations for paranoid schizophrenia and, each time, admits to using drugs, specifically smoking "Sherman" ("Sherman" is marijuana laced with PCP), which seems to be a precipitating factor. Brad is known for his resistance to treatment and has little to no insight into his illness and the role of drug abuse in exacerbating his psychiatric symptoms. When decompensated, he has a history of antisocial behavior such as burglary and auto theft. The presenting problem now is that Brad does not want to attend the partial hospital program, does not want to take his medication, and wants people to leave him alone so he can sit in his apartment by himself. However, when he does this, he becomes extremely psychotic and has to be hospitalized. An example of this client's behavior is the following: On the first day of admission to the partial hospitalization program, he came to his intake conference stating that he did not want to be there and that he thought everybody here was immature and that he didn't want to hang around with any mentally ill people. He was sullen and hostile and, following attempts to engage him, said he was "out of here." Two weeks later, he was brought in by the police and had to be rehospitalized.

Although Brad's treatment team was well aware of his drug use and that such use played a role in his instability and precipitating hospitalization, many mentally ill individuals who also use substances may end up misdiagnosed and treated inappropriately because effects of the substance abuse on their mental illness is not recognized. Given all this, the first challenge for clinicians is recognizing comorbidity when they see it. Careful histories, including talking with family and friends rather than just depending on patient self-report, are critical. Toxicology screens can help confirm use of drugs or alcohol and can reveal the extent and types of substances used.

Assess your comprehension of *the trends affecting the prevalence of comorbid conditions and some of the dilemmas in service provision with this population* by completing this quiz.

TREATING CLIENTS WITH COMORBID CONDITIONS

Understanding the Cyclical Nature of Comorbidity

Although mental disorders and substance abuse disorders may have separate etiologies and courses, epidemiologic evidence, such as the findings from the NIMH Epidemiological Catchment Area study, suggests that mental illness and substance abuse occur together more frequently than chance would predict. Furthermore, exacerbation of one illness can exacerbate the other and lead to combined relapse and hospitalization. Part of the reason for this is the cyclical nature of the problems of dually diagnosed clients. The cycle usually begins when individuals stop taking their psychotropic medication, which is targeted to control the symptoms of their mental illness, and the symptoms return, as was the case with Brad. Vulnerable because of recurring symptomatology, the next step in the cycle is when the person experiences a life crisis or problem of some kind, which causes discomfort and dysphoria. The person desires relief from these feelings but doesn't possess adequate coping skills to manage the distress, such as recognizing he or she should restart taking medication. The discomfort builds and, more desperate for relief, the individual begins to crave alcohol or drugs to provide a temporary "fix." The person obtains the substance, uses and abuses the substance, and this provides the person with a desired "high," which feels much better than the distressful feelings he or she had been experiencing. In Brad's case, he would begin to smoke Sherman. But the "high" provided by the substance leads to more psychological stress, which leads to more use of the substance, the person's psychiatric symptoms get worse, and the cycle goes round and round until the individual decompensates and must receive emergency care or hospitalization (Bennett, Woolf, & Vourackas, 1983). More concisely, the process is the following:

Step 1 Psychological crisis and/or not taking prescribed psychotropic medication leads to dysphoria and discomfort.

Step 2 Desire for relief plus poor coping skills lead to craving for alcohol or illicit drugs.

Step 3 Use of alcohol or drugs leads to a "high" and temporary psychological relief, but then leads to problem behavior or exacerbation of the psychological stress . . . back to Step 1. . . .

Minkoff's Model of Integrated Treatment

Research and clinical evidence have clearly shown that traditional treatments without modifications don't meet the needs of most dually diagnosed clients. Hybrid and novel approaches to treatment have been developed, because to practice successfully with clients who have co-occurring conditions, one must attain specialized knowledge, methods, and skills concerning both mental illness and substance abuse (Drake, Essock, Shaner, et al., 2001; Minkoff, 1991; Minkoff, 2001).

One of the first models for treating dually diagnosed clients, developed by Kenneth Minkoff, M.D., is a good example of a program specifically designed to concurrently treat both a mental illness and a substance use problem (Minkoff, 1989, 1991, 1999, 2001). Minkoff's model is based on several guiding principles for the effective treatment of dually diagnosed clients. The first principle, as noted above, is that in today's world, comorbidity is not the exception, rather it is an expectation for the majority of the clients we serve who have an identified mental illness or substance use problem. Second, for treatment to be successful, there must be a strong empathic, hopeful, and ongoing therapeutic relationship between the client and clinician that will be sustained throughout the course of multiple treatment episodes. Third, within this strong therapeutic alliance, the clinician makes strategic well-timed use of case management skills and empathic confrontation as the client moves through the stages of recovery. Fourth, rather than trying to figure out which disorder is "primary," the clinician and treatment team treat *both* disorders as primary so that *integrated dual primary treatment* is continuously provided and, within this framework, the specific treatments chosen are diagnosis specific, that is, which psychosocial interventions are used and which medications are employed is determined by the particular illnesses the individual has. For example, a client with schizophrenia and cannabis abuse would have a different set of interventions than a client with antisocial personality disorder and alcoholism. The final principle is that one size does not fit all. The integrated dual primary treatment for each individual is designed according to the person's diagnosis, phase of recovery, stage of readiness to change and motivation, level of psychosocial functioning and disability, recovery supports available, and level of acuity, which takes into account safety, health status, and capacity for treatment adherence (Minkoff, 1999).

What Minkoff argues is that rather than treating the problems of mental illness and substance abuse in tandem, one treatment program can address both disorders concurrently via four phases of treatment. The first phase, "stabilization," involves detoxification for the substance use problem and stabilization of the acute symptoms of mental illness, which may be provided via intensive crisis intervention or outpatient care, residential treatment, or inpatient care. Throughout the stabilization phase, both disorders are continually assessed simultaneously until the acute symptoms of both disorders are stable. The second phase, "engagement/motivational enhancement," addresses engagement in treatment through the strategic use of empathy, education about both disorders, and motivational interviewing techniques. For legally or socially involuntary clients, involuntary engagement strategies should be employed (see Chapter 5). In this phase, the client may experience multiple relapses of any of the disorders he or she has before solid engagement is achieved. The third phase, "prolonged stabilization," includes abstinence from substances and control of the symptoms of mental illness and lasts for at least one year. The final phase, "recovery and rehabilitation," addresses continued sobriety with regard to the substance use problem(s) and continued stability of the individual's psychiatric symptoms.

Educating Clients about Dual Diagnoses

One of the first steps in Minkoff's model is providing the client and family with education about dual diagnoses and comorbidity, essentially a form of psychoeducation but specifically for clients who have both a mental illness and a substance use problem. Although many clients have families who have remained involved, other clients may have "burned their bridges" with family and friends through repeated crises and relapses. These families need strong efforts by the social worker and treatment team to try to reengage them by providing education and support (Clark, 2001). It is absolutely critical for clinicians to be empathic and understanding about what such families have gone through and, for some families, reengagement may not occur until the ill relative is more stable and has shown commitment to ongoing treatment and recovery.

Good educational materials are available from SAMHSA, NAMI, and other organizations, and all psychoeduational materials emphasize that messages to clients must be clear and consistent. For example, it is critical to inform clients consistently that the use and/or abuse of alcohol and/or other nonprescribed drugs can be harmful or lethal, and that interactions of nonprescribed and prescribed drugs can be harmful or lethal. Popular slogans such as "just say no to drugs" or "a drug is a drug is a drug" can be confusing for the dually diagnosed client. The social worker and doctor must clearly differentiate between *medications*, that is, drugs prescribed by the psychiatrist and used as directed by the person they are prescribed for, versus *recreational or street drugs* including over-the-counter drugs, alcohol, and improperly used prescription drugs.

An important outcome in providing psychoeducation for dually diagnosed clients is for the clients to be able to make the connection between use of drugs and exacerbation of their mental illness. What can help is to sit down with the client and do a time-line follow-back (Sobell & Sobell, 1992) tracking of the client's history of times of wellness, decompensations, and the use of drugs to help the client to see the role of drug use in triggering episodes of illness. Example:

SW: It sounds like what I am telling you about how your substance use interacts with your symptoms of bipolar disorder is kind of confusing—I know it is hard to put everything together. Let's try something that might be helpful. I'm going to tape together a couple pieces of paper and we're going to draw a time line and, together, see if we can track what's been happening with you over the past couple years.

Client: Okay.

SW: As you can see, I have drawn a time line and have divided it into two parts—one part covers the year 2011 and one part of the line covers 2012. Now what I'd like you to do is to divide each year into 12 sections and label each section according to the 12 months of the year.

Client: Okay . . . I'm done.

SW: Now, let's think back over the past couple years to the times you were well and living on your own, working, and feeling good. Can you pinpoint on the time line when those periods were?

Client: Yes—I felt good all summer of 2011, then I got sick, then I was well from—oh, around the beginning of October through New Year's, then I was in the hospital, and then from February through the end of the summer I was doing well.

SW: Great—mark those times down using brackets. Label them "wellness" or something like that—whatever you want to call those times. Now, using this red pen, so we can distinguish it better, mark down the periods when you were in the hospital.

Client: Okay, let's see . . . September 2011 for 2 weeks; end of January 2012 for 1 week; and then September 2012 I was in the hospital for 3 weeks.

SW: Just before each of those times, what was going on?

Client: Um . . . well, I wasn't getting along with my boyfriend—I think that was the case all of those times—and I was feeling depressed each of those times.

SW: And what did you do when you felt depressed?

Client: Um . . . well . . . I stopped taking my lithium and . . . I guess I started using cocaine. I don't do that anymore but I guess I used each time before I got sick and ended up in the hospital. I never thought about it, but, maybe there is a connection?

SW: Yes, there probably is. Let's talk about that. . . .

Writing something down on paper is a useful strategy for organizing one's thoughts, and using a written time line can be helpful by providing a tool to visualize one's life and when periods of wellness occurred and when periods of illness occurred, including identifying triggers for illness. Then, once the client grasps that, the social worker can move the conversation forward to talking more about the connection between substance use and exacerbation of psychiatric symptomatology.

Group treatment can also be very helpful for clients with co-occurring disorders in supporting recovery, and several models have been described in the literature. For example, Bellack and DiClemente (1999) describe a social skills training approach to co-occurring disorders treatment and Bellack, Mueser, Gingerich, and Agresta (1997) provide a step-by-step guide on how to conduct social skills training for dually diagnosed consumers, including providing a specific curriculum that can help consumers learn how to say no to substances and teach skills for dealing with substance abuse situations. Using brief clinical vignettes to illustrate different group treatment methods, Mueser and Noordsy (1996) describe four different types of group interventions for co-occurring disorders, including educational groups, stage-wise (persuasion and active treatment) groups, social skills training groups, and self-help groups.

Employing the support of peers, for example, a "peer persuasion group," can also help in encouraging clients to seek help when substance cravings or use occurs. Minkoff (1999) suggests that it can also be useful to teach clients to recognize the parallels or similarities between their two types of problems. For example, with both substance use disorders and mental illness, denial is common regarding having the disorder(s), there is usually a loss of control over behavior and emotions, and there is a need for ongoing formal treatment. Self-help groups, such as 12-step recovery groups, can also be helpful but can pose special challenges for participants with co-occurring disorders. For example, studies have shown that consumers with co-occurring disorders often experience the use of 12-step philosophy and jargon by mental health professionals as alienating, "in your face," and unempathic (Noordsy, Schwab, Fox, & Drake, 1996). Hard-line 12-step members may also be critical of consumers for taking medication, that is, "a drug is a drug is a drug." Social workers can help clients manage this, if the 12-step group is helpful otherwise, by counseling consumers about how to be assertive about their individual need to take medication to stay well or to just keep quiet about it during 12-step meetings.

Integrated Treatment for Co-occurring Disorders

After almost 30 years of intervention research effort, effective treatments for dually diagnosed clients have emerged that are tailored to their complex needs (Drake et al., 2001). In one of the first comprehensive reviews on integrated treatment, Drake et al. (2001) identified several critical components of effective programs, which include comprehensiveness, a long-term view, a staged approach to recovery, assertive outreach, motivational interventions, helping clients in acquiring skills and supports to manage both illnesses and to pursue functional goals, and cultural sensitivity and competence (p. 469).

Integrated treatment for co-occurring disorders is an evidence-based (i.e., research-proven) practice model of treatment for people with serious mental illnesses and co-occurring substance use disorders that incorporates these key components (SAMHSA, 2010). In this model, consumers receive combined treatment for mental illnesses and substance use disorders from the same practitioner or treatment team. As a result, they receive one consistent message about treatment and recovery. Integrated treatment for co-occurring disorders is based upon the following seven practice principles (SAMHSA, 2010):

- Mental health and substance abuse treatment are integrated to meet the needs of people with co-occurring disorders;
- Integrated treatment specialists are trained to treat both substance use and serious mental illnesses;
- Co-occurring disorders are treated in a stage-wise fashion with different services provided at different stages;
- Motivational interventions are used to treat consumers in all stages, but especially in the persuasion stage;
- Substance abuse counseling, using a cognitive-behavioral approach, is used to treat consumers in the active treatment and relapse prevention stages;
- Multiple formats for services are available, including individual, group, self-help, and family;
- Medication services are integrated and coordinated with psychosocial services.

The most important central component of the practice is that treatment is *integrated*, meaning that both the mental health and substance use treatments are evaluated and addressed by the same team at the same location at the same time. Treatment targets the individual needs of the consumers and is integrated on organizational and clinical levels.

Research has shown that the most effective programs for treating co-occurring disorders or dual diagnoses are programs that are delivered to consumers by stages. Thus, integrated treatment for co-occurring disorders is designed to be provided in a stage-wise fashion. The first stage, "Precontemplation—Engagement," employs assertive outreach, practical help with things like housing and entitlements, and an introduction to individual, family, group, and self-help treatment formats. The second stage, "Contemplation and Preparation—Persuasion," emphasizes psychoeducation about mental illness and substance abuse, goal setting, and building awareness of problem through motivational enhancement therapy. The third stage is "Action—Active Treatment." This is the stage in which a lot of hard work takes place and consumers receive ongoing counseling and treatment based on cognitive-behavioral techniques, skills training, and support from families and self-help groups, such as 12-step programs specifically for the dually diagnosed client. Finally, the fourth stage is "Maintenance—Relapse Prevention," in which counseling and treatment continues but the emphasis is on relapse prevention techniques, more advanced skill building, and ongoing support to promote integrated holistic recovery (Drake et al., 2001; SAMHSA, 2010).

Communicating, encouraging, and maintaining hope is a critical component in the integrated treatment recovery model. Services and treatment goals are consumer-driven and consumers are provided with unconditional respect and compassion from all members of the treatment team. Integrated treatment specialists are responsible for engaging consumers and supporting their recovery, and the primary focus is on consumers' goals and functioning, not on adhering to treatment or a particular framework of treatment. Consumer choice, shared decision making, and consumer/family education are important throughout each stage of treatment.

Integrated treatment is associated with a number of positive outcomes including reduced substance use, improvement in psychiatric symptoms and functioning, decreased hospitalization, increased housing stability, fewer arrests, and improved quality of life (Drake et al., 2001). In summary, integrated treatment for co-occurring disorders is effective in the recovery process for consumers with co-occurring disorders. The goal of this evidence-based practice is to support consumers in their recovery process. In integrated treatment programs, the same practitioners, working in one setting, provide mental health and substance abuse interventions in a coordinated fashion so that consumers receive one consistent message about treatment and recovery (SAMHSA, 2010).

Other Treatment Options

Integrated treatment is the best option for optimal treatment outcomes for clients with co-occurring disorders, however, such treatment may not be available for some consumers or they may not want to participate. However, there are a number of other treatment options that can be helpful. First are detoxification programs for individuals physically addicted to one or more substances. Detoxification programs are either inpatient or outpatient. Inpatient programs are generally of two types: (1) hospital-based programs; or (2) free-standing community facility programs. Most commonly, detox programs are for people who have alcoholism only. For those who are psychologically addicted to substances, there are social setting programs that offer peer and emotional support. Unfortunately, dually diagnosed clients are sometimes refused admission to social setting programs because of their mental illness and, even if admitted, many cannot tolerate the confrontational atmosphere of such programs, and many programs limit the number of admissions and screen out so-called "revolving door clients," illustrated in the case of "Jack", at the beginning of the chapter. Some clients can be detoxed on an outpatient basis, which can be more cost-effective but provides little supervision.

Next, we have missions and shelters. Mentally ill persons, substance abusers, and dually diagnosed clients often spend time in missions and shelters when they have nowhere else to go, like the situation with "Jack" in the vignette. Sometimes clients find their own way there, sometimes social workers refer clients to missions or shelters, or sometimes the police may take them to a mission or shelter as an alternative to arresting individuals for loitering, vagrancy, and the like. Such programs can be helpful, and some can even provide structured help, however, participation in religious services or activities is often a requirement, which can be a problem for some clients.

Next we have intensive inpatient treatment programs. Intensive inpatient programs are available in most areas if the client has the resources to pay for it. However, many of the clients we serve as social workers do not have the necessary financial resources, so such services aren't a feasible alternative. For dually diagnosed clients, sufficient time on the unit for recovery from both disorders is a must, although programs that offer simultaneous or parallel treatment for both conditions remain in short supply, particularly in resource-poor areas. To be effective, such programs must be able to provide a range of services including psychoeducation, group therapy, individual therapy—including medication for the mental illness, if needed—family psychoeducation, and an introduction to self-help programs. Finally, we have other modalities. Other modalities include supervised living arrangements, day treatment/partial hospitalization programs, outpatient treatment, social skills training, and sober peer groups, including MISA or dual diagnosis 12-step programs.

Assess your comprehension of *the issues related to treating clients with co-occurring disorders* by completing this quiz.

WHAT FAMILIES NEED TO KNOW ABOUT CO-OCCURRING DISORDERS

Clients with co-occurring disorders who have good social support generally have better treatment outcomes. One of the most important sources of good social support is the client's family. However, as noted previously, coping with the challenges brought to bear by a loved one with both a mental illness and a substance use problem can be very burdensome for families. By the time the loved one receives appropriate treatment, the family may have endured years of hardship as they have tried to get services for their family member and many may have provided years of financial and other support. The first task for the clinician is to engage the family and ask them what they need. The clinician can then work out a plan with the family. It is important to provide information and support and allow the family time to share their story of what they have gone through. Then, it can be helpful to share with the family certain strategies that can be useful in coping with a relative who is dually diagnosed.

The first strategy is to be informed, and such information is available through psychoeducation and through organizations such as the National Alliance on Mental Illness. It is important for the family to be aware of how common co-occurring disorders are and why they are so common, particularly in young male clients. Next, the family needs to learn about the signs of alcohol or drug problems in a family member. The following are some of the behaviors that can alert families to the possibility of a substance use problem in their mentally ill loved one (www.nami.org): the relative suddenly has money problems; the relative stops seeing old friends and suddenly has new friends; valuables, including money, begin disappearing from the house; the family discovers drug paraphernalia in the house (needles, pipes, roach clips); the relative begins to spend long periods of time in the bathroom; the relative seems unusually euphoric or drowsy and has dilated or pinpointed eyes; and/or the family notices needle marks on the relative's body or he or she has persistent nose bleeds. Families also must be aware that even small amounts of a licit or illicit drug, including alcohol, can cause significant changes in a mentally ill individual due to interactions with symptoms and prescribed psychotropic medications. Even over-the-counter drugs can have negative interactions (Clark & Drake, 1992; Strickland, 1993).

In collaboration with other families via organizations such as NAMI, families can advocate and keep pressure on politicians and behavioral health services to offer integrated treatment to consumers with co-occurring disorders. SAMHSA has an evidence-based toolkit (www.samhsa.gov) that has free materials designed for agencies to help start new programs, and there are other resources available to bring the newest and best treatments to the community from the National Institute of Mental Health. Families can also advocate for more service development research on co-occurring disorders. To do effective advocacy, however, families must become educated about co-occurring disorders including the nature of substance abuse as a relapsing disorder, the effects of substances on psychiatric symptomatology, patterns of recovery when one has co-occurring disorders, and interactions between prescribed medications and substances (Clark & Drake, 1992; Strickland, 1993). Let's turn now to looking at one group of clients at particularly high risk for developing a substance abuse-dependence problem: individuals with personality disorders.

PERSONALITY DISORDERS AND SUBSTANCE ABUSE

Behavioral health staff generally consider dually diagnosed individuals with personality disorders to be some of the most difficult individuals to manage in most treatment settings (Watkins, Lewellen, & Barrett, 2001). Data from many studies, however, clearly demonstrates that the association between personality disorders and substance abuse is particularly strong, particularly with antisocial personality disorder (ASPD), borderline personality disorder (BPD) and, to a somewhat lesser extent, with avoidant personality disorder (Compton, Conway, Stinson, et al., 2005; Links, Heslegrave, Mitton, et al., 1995; Trull, Sher, Minks-Brown, et al., 2000). For example, data from the Epidemiologic Catchment Area study showed that males with alcoholism are four times more likely to have antisocial personality disorder than non-alcoholic males. Women with alcoholism are 12 times more likely to have antisocial personality disorder than non-alcoholic females. These rates are for the general population; the rates are even higher in clinical or forensic samples. It is important to note that the rates of the diagnosis of both antisocial personality and alcoholism are much lower in females than in males. Substance abuse is not strongly associated with all personality disorders, however. For example, alcoholism is rare in schizoid or paranoid personality disorders.

Degree of abuse is also an issue; the greater the degree of abuse, the higher the probability of comorbidity with BPD, ASPD, or avoidant personality disorder. Finally, within the substance-dependent and abusing population, 50 percent of individuals could be diagnosed with personality disorder. An obvious question emerges from these statistics: Why does having a personality disorder predispose a person to developing a substance use problem?

Why There Is a High Comorbidity of Certain Personality Disorders and Substance Abuse

Let's specifically consider antisocial personality disorder and borderline personality disorder, the two personality disorders with the highest comorbidity rates with substance abuse. If we consider these two personality disorders in the generic sense, two broad areas of dysfunction stand out. The first is a dysfunction in the regulation of behavior. This dysfunction manifests in poor impulse control, reckless behavior, and ongoing failure to anticipate consequences. When such features are dominant, experimentation with drugs is expected because a realistic concern about the consequences of one's behavior won't be present; the inability to delay gratification will compromise efforts to resist taking drugs; and, finally, self-centeredness and lack of empathy will function as blinders to the effects on others of using substances. The second area of dysfunction is the inability to appropriately regulate emotions, that is, the ability to recognize, regulate, and tolerate emotions is limited. Rather than experiencing focused feelings, which can serve as indicators of well-being and sources of initiative, a vague sense of dysphoria is chronically present both with individuals with ASPD and individuals with BPD. Given this, the appeal of drugs for such folks is easily understood, that is, the euphoric or stimulating properties of drugs serve to alter this vague discomfort and can provide affective focus. Getting high is also a goal, but not necessarily the sole goal. Example:

> I recall a young female client diagnosed as having borderline personality disorder who experienced mild to moderate anxiety whenever she was high on marijuana. When I asked why she continued to use marijuana, she explained that the anxiety induced by the drug made her more cautious and thus less likely to act in an impulsive manner. The marijuana, in effect, served as a kind of safety valve for her usual impulsive behavior. (Newhill, 1995)

Substances, thus, can temporarily correct the individual's problems with regulating and tolerating certain emotions via the drug's ability to buffer painful emotions and compensate for defects in ego function, that is, difficulties in coping with the demands and realities of everyday life. For such individuals, drugs really do represent an effort to self-medicate or buffer emotional pain. Other examples would include the individual who uses cocaine to buffer chronic feelings of dysphoria, emptiness, or boredom; or the person who uses heroin because it provides relief from chronic feelings of anger and rage. Thus, the subjective effect of drugs has a wide range, from the relatively simple brief period of achieving a "high"; to escape from, or serving as a buffer for, painful feelings; to actual ego support or repair similar to intrapsychic defenses. Thus, for the individual with a personality disorder, drug use can represent more than simply wanting to get high.

How Having a Personality Disorder Complicates the Course of Substance Use

The course and duration of a substance use disorder is complicated by presence of a personality disorder in three ways. First, the onset of the individual's substance abuse problems is likely to occur at an earlier age in a person with a personality disorder. Second, individuals who have ASPD or BPD have an increased likelihood of polysubstance abuse. Finally, the presence of a personality disorder in someone who also has a problem with substance abuse elevates the risk of developing additional psychiatric symptoms, for instance, a significantly high proportion of individuals addicted to heroin have depression along with meeting criteria for one or more personality disorders (Khantzian & Treece, 1985; Linehan, Dimeff, Reynolds, et al., 2002). Furthermore, such comorbidity both complicates and exacerbates the symptoms and course of each of the disorders.

Treatment of Substance Abuse and Its Impact on Symptoms of Personality Disorder

There are two basic approaches to treating individuals with personality disorders: (1) interventions that emphasize improvement in adaptation and psychosocial functioning, which generally utilize some form of cognitive-behavioral strategy, or (2) interventions that aim for structural intrapsychic character change, which generally utilize some form of psychodynamically oriented psychotherapy. In both cases, change is slow to occur and the clinician and client must be persistent and patient. Fortunately, for the dually diagnosed client with a personality disorder and a substance abuse problem, traditional addiction treatment for substance abuse disorders sometimes can result in modification of maladaptive personality traits, provided that the treatment is slightly modified, from the

---

Newhill, C.E. (1995). A mental health casebook. Unpublished manuscript.

traditional confrontational "in your face" approach to one of confrontation mixed with empathic support. This is particularly important for clients with BPD for whom traditional high-confrontation models can be too much and "blow such clients away" and they are then lost to treatment. On the other hand, traditional confrontational approaches can work well for clients with ASPD.

How traditional addiction programs can be helpful

Let's look at the process of recovery in a traditional substance abuse rehabilitation program. Typically, in such programs, the environment is highly structured, that is, time is ordered, activities are tightly scheduled, and participants' behavior is governed by rules and regulations with consequences. Setting limits is usually a constant feature of such programs. For example, complete abstinence from any drug/alcohol use is required, there are limits on visits from outsiders, medications used only include those absolutely necessary, and there are strict prohibitions against acting out. Traditional drug and alcohol (D&A) programs also emphasize a reality orientation that stresses coping and discourages regressive behaviors, and development of emotional self-care skills is emphasized, for example, learning how to anticipate consequences and curb impulsive behavior. These functions—structure, limit setting, and an emphasis on adaptation—shore up and strengthen ego functions. Furthermore, an emphasis on recognizing and tolerating emotions, rather than buffering or avoiding feelings via use of alcohol or drugs, serves as an integrating process essential to learning self-control.

Traditional substance abuse programs emphasize abstinence, which, for the client with a personality disorder, serves as paradigm for other issues besides avoiding drugs. Achieving and maintaining abstinence depends on developing frustration tolerance, patience, impulse control, and the ability to manage and regulate emotions. All of these abilities and skills are central to treatment of personality pathology. Thus, learning how to maintain a drug-free lifestyle can positively influence the individual's maladaptive personality traits. For the client with BPD, the structure and limit setting must include support and empathy; for the client with ASPD, little modification is needed from the traditional D&A approach.

How 12-step groups can be helpful

The steps that participants go through in 12-step program self-help groups can also be helpful for individuals with personality disorders for both their substance abuse problems and their personality challenges. For example, Alcoholics Anonymous (AA) requires that each member work through 12 specific steps that focus not only on the individual's addiction but extend the process of recovery to addressing the individual's relationships with others.

Looking specifically at AA as an example, the initial focus is on the member's relationship to alcohol, expressed in Step 1 as: "We admitted we were powerless over alcohol—that our lives had become unmanageable" (Alcoholics Anonymous, 1952). Thus, first, the individual with an alcohol problem must accept the limitation of his or her relationship to alcohol. The next step then examines the person's relationship to others and to "a higher power." The next four steps then address spiritual relationships and, in Step 5, relationships to other people are emphasized. The next few steps address the process of self-examination, and challenge the individual to examine how his or her alcoholism has caused problems for others. This forces the person to look at the consequences of his or her behavior and challenges the person to move from a self-centered stance to one of empathy toward others and then take action by making amends for harm to others that the person may have caused. This is very central to the dynamics of both addiction and personality disorders.

Twelve-step groups, like Alcoholics Anonymous, can in fact have a therapeutic impact on the person with both a substance use problem and a personality disorder. The first three steps may be categorized as "surrender steps," that is, the individual begins to overcome feelings of helplessness and gains an internal locus of control; steps 4 and 5 are "inventory steps," which parallel the process of psychotherapy by encouraging self-reflection and self-examination; steps 6 and 7 are what could be called "personality disorder treatment steps" because they specifically address defects of character; steps 8 and 9 promote honest relationships, step 10 requires taking responsibility for one's actions, step 11 addresses accepting a higher power however one conceptualizes it and, finally, step 12 is a "sharing step." Together the 12 steps utilize power of facing limitations, self-examination, confession, and restitution, which are issues commonly reflected in various forms of psychotherapy as well as the conceptualization of alcoholism by AA. Thus, recovery from alcoholism is more than not drinking alcoholic beverages; it also can have an impact on character structure, which enables the alcoholic person to cope with the absence of the drug upon which he or she was dependent. This allows the formation of a new identity based on sobriety and recovery and, from this, integrity and positive character change can emerge. This does not imply treatment of the personality disorder is complete by any means, but a start has been made via treatment for the substance abuse disorder. There is, thus, some compatibility of treatment strategies for both the personality disorder and the substance abuse problem that can help support recovery.

Assess your comprehension of *the issues specifically related to personality disorders and substance abuse* by completing this quiz.

CONCLUSION

This chapter has addressed practice with individuals who are dually diagnosed with mental illness and a substance abuse-dependence problem. Although individuals with co-occurring disorders may be described as a challenging group, and on many indicators have poorer outcomes than people who have only one disorder or one disorder at a time, much of this is because of the way we have traditionally offered services via parallel but separate service streams. Individuals with co-occurring disorders can achieve recovery if all of their disorders are treated at the same time in an integrated fashion. Integrated treatment for co-occurring disorders is a model that has shown positive outcomes including reduced substance use, improvement in psychiatric symptoms and functioning, decreased hospitalization and incarceration rates, and improved quality of life. Families are important partners in this treatment and must be provided with accurate information about co-occurring disorders as well as support from providers and advocacy organizations.

Assess your application and analysis of this chapter's contents by completing the *Chapter Review*.

In summary, the comorbidity of mental illness and substance abuse is an increasingly serious issue and one affecting the majority of clients we see as social workers in behavioral health settings. The interaction of both conditions can be thought of as a cyclical process with each potentially exacerbating the other. To successfully treat such clients, treatment must be offered simultaneously by individuals well trained in both areas, and with treatment approaches modified to take into account the unique needs of this population.

Read some *closing thoughts* about how to maintain competence in practice, the importance of good clinical supervision, how to avoid burnout, boredom and frustration in one's practice and, finally, strategies to improve behavioral health services and ensure a good future for our clients and their families.

References

CHAPTER 1

Adler, J. (2006, March 27). Freud in our midst. *Newsweek*, 43–51.

American Psychiatric Association. (1952). *Diagnostic and statistical manual of mental disorders*. Washington, DC: Author.

American Psychiatric Association. (1968). *Diagnostic and statistical manual of mental disorders* (2nd ed.). Washington, DC: Author.

American Psychiatric Association. (1980). *Diagnostic and statistical manual of mental disorders* (3rd ed.). Washington, DC: Author.

Beers, C. (1913). *A mind that found itself: An autobiography*. New York: Longmans Green & Co.

Bleuler, E. (1911). *Dementia praecox or the group of schizophrenias* (Zinkin, J., Trans., with foreword by Lewis, N. D. C., 1950). New York: International Universities Press.

Bockhoven, J. S. (1972). *Moral treatment in community mental health*. New York: Springer.

Browne, E. G. (1921). *Arabian medicine*. New York: MacMillan.

Butcher, J. N., Mineka, S., & Hooley, J. M. (2007). *Abnormal psychology* (13th ed.). New York: Pearson.

Charland, L. C. (2007). Benevolent theory: Moral treatment at the York Retreat. *History of Psychiatry, 18*, 61–80.

Colp, R. (2005). History of psychiatry. In B. J. Sadock & V. A. Sadock (Eds.), *Kaplan & Sadock's comprehensive textbook of psychiatry* (8th ed., Vol. II, pp. 4013–4047). Philadelphia: Lippincott Williams & Wilkins.

Corsini, R. J., & Marsella, A. J. (1983). *Personality theories, research and assessment*. Itasca, IL: Peacock.

DaCosta, J. M. (1871). On irritable heart: A clinical study of a form of functional cardiac disorder and its consequences. *The American Journal of the Medical Sciences, 61*, 18–52.

Danto, E. A. (2008). Psychoanalysis. In T. Mizrahi & L. E. Davis (Eds.), *The encyclopedia of social work* (20th ed., Vol. 3, pp. 158–165). Washington, DC: NASW Press; New York: Oxford.

Deutsch, A. (1948). *The shame of the states*. New York: Harcourt Brace.

Deutsch, A. (1949). *The mentally ill in America*. New York: Columbia University Press.

Felix, R. H. (1949). Mental disorders as a public health problem. *American Journal of Psychiatry, 106*, 401–406.

Fishbein, L. (1979). "The Snake Pit (1948)": The sexist nature of sanity. *American Quarterly, 31(5),* 641–655.

Foucault, M. (1972). *Histoire de la folie a l'age classique*. Paris: Gallimard.

Franciscan Mission Associates. (n.d.). *St. Dymphna's story*. The St. Dymphna Devotion, Franciscan Mission Associates, P.O. Box 598, Mount Vernon, NY.

Freud, S. (1915). *The interpretation of dreams* (3rd ed.) (Brill, A. A., Trans.). New York: MacMillan.

Freud, S. (1923). *The ego and the id*. New York: Norton.

Freud, S. (1930). *Civilization and its discontents*. New York: DeVinne & Hallenbeck.

Gay, P. (1988). *Freud: A life for our time*. New York: Norton.

Goldberg, H. S. (2006). *Hippocrates: Father of medicine*. New York: Authors Choice.

Grob, G. N. (1983). *Mental illness and American society, 1875–1940*. Princeton, NJ: Princeton University Press.

Grob, G. N. (1994). *The mad among us*. New York: Free Press.

Hinshaw, S. P. (2007). *The mark of shame: Stigma of mental illness and an agenda for change*. New York: Oxford University Press.

Karnosh, L. J. (with Tucker, E. M.). (1945). *A handbook of psychiatry*. St. Louis, MO: C. V. Mosby Company.

Keck, P. E., Pope, H. G., Hudson, J. I., McElroy, S. L., & Kulick, A. R. (1988). Lycanthropy: Alive and well in the twentieth century. *Psychological Medicine, 18*(1), 113–120.

Kinzie, J. D. (1989). Post-traumatic stress disorder. In H. I. Kaplan & B. J. Sadock (Eds.), *Comprehensive textbook of psychiatry* (5th ed., pp. 1000–1008). Baltimore, MD: Williams & Wilkins.

Kraepelin, E. (1902). *Lehrbuch der Psychiatrie* [Clinical psychiatry; A text-book for students and physicians, abstracted and adapted from the 6th German edition]. New York: Macmillan.

Krafft-Ebing, R. von. (1892). *Psychopathia sexualis, with especial reference to contrary sexual instinct: A medico-legal study*. Philadelphia: F. A. Davis.

Levison, J. R. (2003). Elizabeth Parsons Ware Packard: An advocate for cultural, religious, and legal change. *Alabama Law Review, 54*, 985–1076.

Lindemann, E. (1944). Symptomatology and management of acute grief. *American Journal of Psychiatry, 101*, 141–148.

Maher, B. A., & Maher, W. R. (1985). Psychopathology: From ancient times to the eighteenth century. In G. A. Kimble & K. Schlesinger (Eds.), *Topics in the history of psychology* (pp. 251–294). Hillsdale, NJ: Erlbaum.

Martin, M. (1976) *Hostage to the Devil: The possession and exorcism of five living Americans.* San Francisco: Harper Collins.

McCoubrey, C. (2000, November 12). Dr. Gerard Chrzanowski, innovative psychoanalyst, dies at 87. *The New York Times.*

Menting, A. M. (2007). Root of the matter: Genes controlling the growth of the brain's white matter are suspects in the development of schizophrenia. *Harvard Medical Alumni Bulletin, Spring/Summer*, 1.

Millon, T. (2004). *Masters of the mind.* Hoboken, NJ: Wiley.

Mondale, S., & Patton, S. (Producers), & Mondale, S. (Director). (1990). *Asylum: A history of the mental institution in America* [Motion picture documentary]. Distributed by United States Direct Cinema Limited.

Moselhy, H. F. (1999). Lycanthropy: New evidence of its origin. *Psychopathology, 32*(4), 173–176.

Neely, S. (2008). *A concise history of the French Revolution.* New York: Rowman & Littlefield.

Nemec, J. (1974). *Witchcraft and medicine (1484–1793)* (DHEW Publication No. (NIH) 76-636). Washington, DC: U.S. Department of Health, Education and Welfare, Public Health Service, National Institutes of Health.

Newhill, C. E. (1995). *A mental health casebook.* Unpublished manuscript.

Newhill, C. E. (2003). *Client violence in social work practice: Prevention, intervention and research.* New York, NY: Guilford.

Okasha, A., & Okasha, T. (2000). Notes on mental disorders in Pharaonic Egypt. *History of Psychiatry, 11*, 413–424.

Packard, E. P. W. (1868). *Insane asylums unveiled.* Chicago: Author. (A.B. Case, 189 Monroe St. Chicago, Illinois, 2 v in 1).

Pernoud, R. (1969). *Joan of Arc: By herself and her witnesses.* London: Scarborough House.

Pinel, P. (1806). *A Treatise on insanity: In which are contained the principles of a new and more practical nosology of maniacal disorders than has yet been offered to the public.* London: Oxford University Press.

Plato. (n.d.). *The laws* (Vol. 5) (G. Burges, Trans.). London: George Bell and Sons.

The Public Hospital 1773-1885, (n.d.). The Colonial Williamsburg Foundation. Rockney, H. M., & Lemke, T. (1992). Casualties from a junior-senior high school during the Persian Gulf War: Toxic poisoning or mass hysteria? *Developmental and Behavioral Pediatrics, 13*, 339–342.

Rohrbaugh, M., Tennen, H., Press, S., & White, L. (1981). Compliance, defiance, and therapeutic paradox: Guidelines for strategic use of paradoxical interventions. *American Journal of Orthopsychiatry, 51*, 454–467.

Rothman, D. J. (1990). *The discovery of the asylum: Social order and disorder in the New Republic.* Boston: Little Brown.

Sarton, G. (1993). *Ancient science through the golden age of Greece.* New York: Dover.

Schoeneman, T. J. (1984). The mentally ill witch in textbooks of abnormal psychology: Current status and implications of a fallacy. *Professional Psychology, 15*(3), 299–314.

Schorow, S. (2005). *The Cocoanut Grove fire—New England remembers.* Beverly, MA: Commonwealth Editions.

Schutt, R. K., & Goldfinger, S. M. (2011). *Homelessness, housing, and mental illness.* Cambridge, MA: Harvard University Press.

Selling, L. S. (1943). *Men against madness.* New York: Greenberg.

Sharfstein, S. S. (2012). Taking issue: Status of stigma, 2012. *Psychiatric Services, 63*(10), 953.

Shore, J. H. (1989). Community psychiatry. In H. L. Kaplan & B. J. Sadock (Eds.), *Comprehensive textbook of psychiatry* (5th ed., Vol. 2, pp. 2063–2067). Baltimore: Williams & Wilkins.

Slaikeu, K. (1984). *Crisis intervention: A handbook for practice and research.* Boston, MA: Allyn & Bacon.

Stone, S. (1937). Psychiatry through the ages. *The Journal of Abnormal and Social Psychology, 32*, 131–160.

Sulloway, F. J. (1979). *Freud, biologist of the mind: Beyond the psychoanalytic legend.* New York: Basic.

Tuchman, B. (1978). *A distant mirror: The calamitous 14th century.* New York: Knopf.

Van Wyhe, J. (2004). *Phrenology and the origins of Victorian scientific naturalism.* Burlington, VT: Ashgate.

Viney, W., & Bartsch, K. (1984). Dorothea Lynde Dix: Positive or negative influence on the development of treatment for the mentally ill. *Social Science Journal, 21*, 71–82.
Walker, A. A. (1997). Neolithic surgery. *Archeology, 50*, 9.
Wang, S. (2006). Contagious behavior. *Psychological Science, 19*, 22–26.
Ward, M. J. (1946). *The snake pit*. New York: Random.
Warner, M. (1981). *Joan of Arc: The image of female heroism*. New York: Knopf.
Weyer, Johann. (1563). *De praestigiis daemonum et incantationibus, ac veneficiis, libri quinque* [On the illusions of the demons and on spells and poisons] (Zilboorg, G., Trans.). Basileae: Per Joannem Oporinum.
Zillboorg, G., & Henry, G. W. (1941). *A history of medical psychology*. New York: Norton.
Zwelling, S. S. (1985). *Quest for a cure: The public hospital in Williamsburg, Virginia, 1773–1885*. Williamsburg, VA: The Colonial Williamsburg Foundation.

CHAPTER 2

Aisenberg, E. (2008). Evidence-based practice in mental health care to ethnic-minority communities: Has its practice fallen short of its evidence? *Social Work, 53*, 297–306.
Amador, X. (2000). *I am not sick—I don't need help!* Peconic, NY: Vida.
American Association of Social Workers. (1929). *Social case work: Generic and specific*. New York: Author.
Aron, L., Honberg, R., Duckworth, K., et al. (2009). *Grading the states 2009: A report on America's health care system for adults with serious mental illness*. Arlington, VA: National Alliance on Mental Illness.
Bachrach, L. L. (1976). *Deinstitutionalization: An analytical review and sociological perspective* (DHEW Publication No. ADM 76-351). Washington, DC: U.S. Government Printing Office.
Bambauer, K. Z. (2005). Proposition 63: Should other states follow California's lead? *Psychiatric Services, 56*, 642–644.
Bandura, A. (1997). *Self-efficacy: The exercise of control*. New York: Worth Publishers.
Barber, M. E. (2012). Recovery as the new medical model for psychiatry. *Psychiatric Services, 63*(3), 277–279.
Barton, R. (1966). *Institutional neurosis* (with a forward by Noel Gordon Harris). Bristol, UK: John Wright & Sons, Ltd.
Bhavnani, R. (2009, February 4). Don't touch Prop. 63 funds. *Ventura County Star*.
Butterfield, F. (1998, March 05). Asylums behind bars: A special report. Prisons replace hospitals for the nation's mentally ill. *The New York Times*.
Center for Mental Health Services (CMHS). (2006). *Mental health: United States, 2004* (R. W. Manderscheid & J. T. Berry, Eds.) (DHHS Pub No. SMA-06-4195). Rockville, MD: Substance Abuse and Mental Health Services Administration.
Clarkin, J. F., Levy, K. N., Lenzenweger, M. F., & Kernberg, O. F. (2007). Evaluating three treatments for borderline personality disorder: A multiwave study. *American Journal of Psychiatry, 164*, 922–928.
Coleman, D. (1985, April 30). Social workers vault into a leading role in psychotherapy. *The New York Times*.
Colp, R. (2005). History of psychiatry. In B. J. Sadock & V. A. Sadock (Eds.), *Kaplan & Sadock's comprehensive textbook of psychiatry* (8th ed., Vol. II, pp. 4013–4047). Philadelphia: Lippincott Williams & Wilkins.
Committee on Psychiatry and the Community, Group for the Advancement of Psychiatry. (2009). Jailing is failing people with mental illness. *Psychiatric Services, 60*, 723.
Corcoran, J., & Walsh, J. M. (2008). *Mental health in social work: A casebook on diagnosis and strengths-based assessment*. Boston, MA: Allyn & Bacon.
Coyle, G. (1930). *Social process in organized groups*. New York: Richard R. Smith.
Cross, T., Bazron, B., Dennis, K., & Isaacs, M. (1989). *Towards a culturally competent system of care: A monograph on effective services for minority children who are severely emotionally disturbed* (Vol. I). Washington, DC: Georgetown University Child Development Center.
Eack, S. M. (2012). Cognitive remediation: A new generation of psychosocial interventions for people with schizophrenia. *Social Work, 57*(3), 235–246.
Eack, S. M., & Newhill, C. E. (2008). What influences social workers' attitudes toward working with clients with severe mental illness? *Families in Society, 89*, 418–427.
Editorial. (2012, December 13). The cost of solitary confinement. *The New York Times*.
Fahy, J. (2007, November 19). Mayview suspends downsizing in wake of ex-patient's death: Fatality raises concern over discharges. *Pittsburgh Post-Gazette*.
Fitzpatrick, M. J. (2009). Letter from NAMI executive director. In L. Aron, R. Honberg, K. Duckworth, et al. (Eds.), *Grading the states 2009: A report on America's health care system for adults with serious mental illness*

(pp. vii–viii). Arlington, VA: National Alliance on Mental Illness.

Feuer, A. (2009, March 12). A house halfway to Hades. *The New York Times.*

Flexner, A. (1915, May). *Is social work a profession?* Paper presented at the National Conference on Charities and Correction, Baltimore.

Foucault, M. (1965). *Madness and civilization: A history of insanity in the age of reason.* New York: Vintage.

Frontline. (2005). *The new asylums.* [Motion picture documentary transcript]. United States: Public Broadcasting Corporation.

Gambrill, E. (2006). Evidence-based practice and policy: Choices ahead. *Research on Social Work Practice, 16,* 338–357.

Gambrill, E. (2012). *Critical thinking in clinical practice: Improving the quality of judgments and decisions* (3rd ed.). New York: Wiley.

Geller, J. L. (2012). Patient-centered, recovery-oriented psychiatric care and treatment are not always voluntary. *Psychiatric Services, 63*(5), 493–495.

Gibbs, L. (2003). *Evidence-based practice for the helping professions.* Pacific Grove, CA: Brooks/Cole.

Goffman, E. (1961). *Asylums: Essays on the social situation of mental patients and other inmates.* Garden City, NY: Anchor.

Goode, E. (2012, March 10). Rethinking solitary confinement. *The New York Times.*

Grob, G. N. (1994). *The mad among us: A history of the care of America's mentally ill.* New York: Free Press.

Handler, A. (2006). Personal communication.

Hawthorne, W. B., Folsom, D. P., Sommerfeld, D. H., Lanouette, N. M., & Lewis, M. (2012). Incarceration among adults who are in the public mental health system: Rates, risk factors, and short-term outcomes. *Psychiatric Services, 63*(1), 26–32.

Healy, D. (2004). *The creation of psychopharmacology.* Cambridge, MA: Harvard University Press.

Hepworth, D. A., Rooney, R. H., Rooney, G. D., Strom-Gottfried, K., & Larsen, J. A. (2009). *Direct social work practice: Theory and skills* (8th ed.). Pacific Grove, CA: Brooks/Cole.

Hinshaw, S. P. (2007). *The mark of shame: Stigma of mental illness and an agenda for change.* New York: Oxford.

Hohmann, A. A., & Shear, K. (2002). Community-based intervention research: Coping with the "noise" of real life in study design. *American Journal of Psychiatry, 159,* 201–207.

Holden, G., Rosenberg, G., Barker, K., & Onghena, P. (2006). An assessment of the predictive validity of impact factor scores: Implications for academic employment decisions in social work. *Research on Social Work Practice, 16(6),* 613–624.

Hopps, J. G., & Lowe, T. B. (2008). Social work profession: Overview. In T. Mizrahi & L. E. Davis (Eds.), *The encyclopedia of social work* (20th ed., Vol. 4: S–Y, pp. 144–155). Washington, DC: NASW Press; New York: Oxford.

Hubbard, L. R. (1969, June 23). *Crime and psychiatry.* Retrieved from http://freedom.lronhubbard.org/page080.htm

Human Rights Watch. (2003). *Ill-equipped: U.S. prisons and offenders with mental illness.* New York: Author.

Interlandi, J. (2012, June 24). A madman in our midst. *The New York Times.*

International Association of Schools of Social Work (IASSW). (2001). *International definition of social work.* Retrieved March 31, 2009, from http://www.iassw-aiets.org

Jenson, J., & Howard, M. O. (2008). Evidence-based practice. In T. Mizrahi & L. E. Davis (Eds.), *The encyclopedia of social work* (20th ed., Vol. 2, pp. 158–165). Washington, DC: NASW Press; New York: Oxford.

Johnson, C. K. (2009, March 22). Mentally ill a threat in nursing homes. *The Associated Press.*

Judge David L. Bazelon Center for Mental Health Law. (2003). *Criminalization of people with mental illness: The role of mental health courts in system reform.* Washington, DC: Author.

Kennedy, J. F. (1963). *Special message to the Congress on mental illness and mental retardation.* Public papers of the Presidents of the United States: John F. Kennedy, 1963, GPO. Washington, DC.

Lacasse, J. R. & Gomory, T. (2003). Is graduate social work education promoting a critical approach to mental health practice? *Journal of Social Work Education, 39(3),* 383–408.

Laing, R. D. (1960). *The divided self: An existential study in sanity and madness.* Harmondsworth, UK: Penguin.

Lamb, H. R., & Weinberger, L. E. (1998). Persons with severe mental illness in jails and prisons: A review. *Psychiatric Services, 49,* 483–492.

Langsley, D. G. (1985a). Community psychiatry. In H. I. Kaplan & B. J. Sadock (Eds.), *Comprehensive textbook of psychiatry/IV* (4th ed., pp. 1878–1884). Baltimore: Williams & Wilkins.

Langsley, D. G. (1985b). Prevention in psychiatry: Primary, secondary, and tertiary. In H. I. Kaplan & B. J. Sadock (Eds.), *Comprehensive textbook of psychiatry/IV* (4th ed., pp. 1885–1888). Baltimore: Williams & Wilkins.

Leadbetter, M. (2002). Empowerment and advocacy. In R. Adams, L. Dominelli, & M. Payne (Eds.), *Social work: Themes, issues and critical debates*. Basingstoke, UK: Palgrave in association with the Open University.

Marcuse, H. (1964). *One-dimensional man: Studies in the ideology of advanced industrial society*. Boston: Beacon.

McNiel, D. E., & Binder, R. L. (2007). Effectiveness of a mental health court in reducing criminal recidivism and violence. *American Journal of Psychiatry, 164*, 1395–1403.

Mechanic, D. (2008). *Mental health and social policy: Beyond managed care* (5th ed.). Boston: Pearson.

Mechanic, D., & Rochefort, D. A. (1990). Deinstitutionalization: An appraisal of reform. *Annual Review of Sociology, 16*, 301–327.

Mental Health Services Act, Proposition 63. Retrieved from http://www.dmh.ca.gov/prop_63/MHSA/docs/Mental_Health_Services_Act_Full_Text.pdf

National Association of Social Workers. (2009a). *Issue fact sheets: Mental health*. Washington, DC: Author. Retrieved from http://www.socialworkers.org/pressroom/features/issue/mental.asp?print=1

National Association of Social Workers. (2009b). *What is the National Social Work Public Education Campaign?* Retrieved March 31, 2009, from http://www.naswfoundation.org/imageCampaign/campaign/default.asp

National Mental Health Consumers' Self-Help Clearinghouse. (n.d.). *Technical assistance guide: History of the mental health self-help and advocacy movement*. Retrieved March 9, 2009, from http://www.mhselfhelp.org

New Freedom Commission on Mental Health. (2003). *Achieving the promise: Transforming mental health care in America—final report* (DHHS Pub. No. SMA-03-3832). Rockville, MD: U.S. Department of Health and Human Services.

Newhill, C. E., & Harris, D. (2007a). African-American consumers' perceptions of racial disparities in mental health services. *Social Work in Public Health, 23*, 107–124.

Newhill, C. E., & Harris, D. (2007b). *African-American consumer project field notes*. Unpublished manuscript.

Newhill, C. E., & Korr, W. S. (2004). Practice with people with severe mental illness: Rewards, hallenges, burdens. *Health and Social Work, 29*, 297–305.

O'Hagan, M. (2001). *Recovery competencies for New Zealand mental health workers*. Wellington, NZ: Mental Health Commission.

O'Neill, J. V. (1999, June). Profession dominates in mental health. *NASW News, 44*, 1, 8.

Payne, M. (2005). *Modern social work theory* (3rd ed.). Chicago: Lyceum.

Pennsylvania Office of Mental Health and Substance Abuse Services. (2005). *A call for change: Toward a recovery-oriented mental health service system for adults*. Pennsylvania Department of Public Welfare.

Perrin, B., & Nirje, B. (1985). Setting the record straight: A critique of some frequent misconceptions of the normalization principle. *Australia and New Zealand Journal of Developmental Disabilities, 11*, 69–72.

Repeal of the Institutions for Mental Disease Exclusion briefing paper. (2013). Treatment Advocacy Center. Retrieved September 3, 2013, from http://www.treatmentadvocacycenter.org/storage/documents/Institution_for_Mental_Diseases_IMD_Exclusion.pdf

Richmond, M. (1917). *Social diagnosis*. New York: Russell Sage Foundation.

Rissmiller, D. J., & Rissmiller, J. H. (2006). Evolution of the antipsychiatry movement into mental health consumerism. *Psychiatric Services, 57*, 863–866.

Roberts, R. C., & Tamminga, C. A. (2005). Schizophrenia: Neuropathology. In B. J. Sadock & V. A. Sadock (Eds.), *Kaplan & Sadock's comprehensive textbook of psychiatry* (8th ed., Vol. I, pp. 1408–1416). Philadelphia: Lippincott Williams & Wilkins.

Robinson, V., & Taft, J. J. (1930). *A changing psychology in social casework*. Chapel Hill: University of North Carolina Press.

Rosenheck, R. A. (2012). Introduction to the special section: Toward social inclusion. *Psychiatric Services, 63*(5), 425–426.

Rothman, D. J. (2002). *Conscience and convenience: The asylum and its alternatives in progressive America*. Piscataway, NJ: Aldine Transaction.

Sackett, D. L., Rosenberg, W., Gray, J. A. M., Haynes, R. B., & Richardson, W. S. (1996). Evidence-based medicine: What it is and what it isn't. *British Medical Journal, 312*, 71–72.

Sackett, D. L., Straus, S. E., Richardson, W. S., Rosenberg, W., & Haynes, R. B. (2000). *Evidence-based medicine: How to practice and teach EBM* (2nd ed.). New York: Churchill Livingstone.

Sands, R. G. (1991). *Clinical social work practice in community mental health*. New York: Maxwell MacMillan.

Sands, R. G. (2001). *Clinical social work practice in behavioral mental health: A postmodern approach to practice with adults* (2nd ed.). Boston: Allyn & Bacon.

Saraceno, B., & Barbui, C. (1997). Poverty and mental illness. *Canadian Journal of Psychiatry, 42*, 285–290.

Sarteschi, C. M. (2009). *Assessing the effectiveness of mental health courts: A meta-analysis of clinical and recidivism outcomes* (Doctoral dissertation). Retrieved from Dissertation Abstracts International. (UMI No. 3384946)

Sarteschi, C. M., Vaughn, M. G., & Kim, K. (2011). Assessing the effectiveness of mental health courts: A quantitative review. *Journal of Criminal Justice, 39*(1), 12–20.

Satel, S. (2003, November 1). Out of the asylum: Into the cell. *The New York Times*, p. A-29.

Satel, S. L., & Redding, R. E. (2005). Sociopolitical trends in mental health care: The consumer/survivor movement and multiculturalism. In B. J. Sadock & V. A. Sadock (Eds.), *Kaplan & Sadock's comprehensive textbook of psychiatry* (8th ed., Vol. I, pp. 644–655). Philadelphia: Lippincott Williams & Wilkins.

Schutt, R. K., & Goldfinger, S. M. (2011). *Homelessness, housing, and mental illness*. Cambridge, MA: Harvard University Press.

Segal, S. P. (2008). Deinstitutionalization. In T. Mizrahi & L. E. Davis (Eds.), *The encyclopedia of social work* (20th ed., Vol. 2, pp. 10–20). Washington, DC: NASW Press; New York: Oxford.

Segal, S. P., & Baumohl, J. (1980, September). Engaging the disengaged: Proposals on madness and vagrancy. *Social Work*, 358–365.

Shore, J. H. (1989). Community psychiatry. In H. I. Kaplan & B. J. Sadock (Eds.), *Comprehensive textbook of psychiatry* (5th ed., pp. 2063–2098). Baltimore: Williams & Wilkins.

Smith, M. J. W. (2003). *Behavioral health practice update, October 2003*. Washington, DC: NASW.

Specht, H., & Courtney, M. (1994). *Unfaithful angels: How social work has abandoned its mission*. New York: Free Press.

Stack, B. W., & Rial, M. (1995). Prisoner of the mind. *Pittsburgh Post-Gazette*, November 26: pp. A-1, A-12, and A-14; November 27: A-6–A-9.

Steadman, H. J., Osher, F. C., Robbins, P. C., Case, B., & Samuels, S. (2009). Prevalence of serious mental illness among jail inmates. *Psychiatric Services, 60*, 761–765.

Steinberg, P. (2012, December 25). Our failed approach to schizophrenia. *The New York Times*.

Substance Abuse and Mental Health Services Administration. (1994). *Resident patients in state and county mental hospitals, 1994 survey*. Washington, DC: Survey and Analysis Branch, Center for Mental Health Services, SAMHSA, U.S. Department of Health and Human Services.

Szasz, T. S. (1961). *The myth of mental illness*. New York: Delta.

Szasz, T. S. (1974). *The second sin*. Garden City, NY: Anchor.

Teplin, L. (1984). Criminalizing mental disorder: The comparative arrest rate of the mentally ill. *American Psychologist, 39*, 794–803.

Thase, M. E. (2005). Mood disorders: Neurobiology. In B. J. Sadock & V. A. Sadock (Eds.), *Kaplan & Sadock's comprehensive textbook of psychiatry* (8th ed., Vol. I, pp. 1408–1416). Philadelphia: Lippincott Williams & Wilkins.

Thyer, B. A. (2004). What is evidence-based practice? *Brief Treatment and Crisis Intervention, 4*, 167–176.

Torrey, E. F. (1997a). *Out of the shadows: Confronting America's mental illness crisis*. New York: John Wiley & Sons.

Torrey, E. F. (1997b, July 18). Stop the madness. *The Wall Street Journal*, p. A-14.

Torrey, E. F. (2008). *The insanity offense*. New York: Norton.

Torrey, E. F., Stieber, J., Ezekiel, J., Wolfe, S. M., Sharfstein, J., Noble, J. H., et al. (1992). *Criminalizing the seriously mentally ill: The abuse of jails as mental hospitals*. Washington, DC: A joint report of the National Alliance for the Mentally Ill and Public Citizen's Health Research Group.

Treffert, D. A. (1973). Dying with their rights on. *American Journal of Psychiatry, 130*, 1041.

U.S. Bureau of the Census. (2000). *Total population in households and group quarters by sex and selected age groups, for the United States: 2000*.

Weil, A. (1972). *The natural mind: A new way of looking at drugs and the higher consciousness*. Boston: Houghton Mifflin.

Wickham, D. S. (1999, October 31). Society criminalizes their mental illness. *The Orlando Sentinel*.

Windell, E., Norman, R., & Malla, A. K. (2012). The personal meaning of recovery among individuals treated for a first episode of psychosis. *Psychiatric Services, 63*(6), 548–553.

Winerip, M. (1999, May 23). The crisis of the mentally ill. *The New York Times Magazine, Section 6*, pp. 42–49, 56, 65–66, 70.

Wolfensberger, W., & Nirje, B. (1972). *The principle of normalization in human services*. Toronto: Toronto National Institute on Mental Retardation.

CHAPTER 3

Adair, C. E., McDougall, G. M., Beckie, A., Joyce, A., Mitton, C., Wild, C. T., et al. (2003). History and measurement of continuity of care in mental health services and evidence of its role in outcomes. *Psychiatric Services, 54*, 1351–1356.

American Psychiatric Association. (2013). *Diagnostic and Statistical Manual of Mental Disorders* (5th ed.). Washington, DC: Author.

American Psychological Association. (2009). *Facts: Emerich v. Philadelphia Center for Human Development*. Retrieved February 15, 2013, from http://www.apa.org/about/offices/ogc/amicus/emerich.aspx

Amering, M., Stastny, P., & Hopper, K. (2005). Psychiatric advance directives: Qualitative study of informed deliberations by mental health service users. *British Journal of Psychiatry, 186*, 247–252.

Appelbaum, P. S. (1985). Tarasoff and the clinician: Problems in fulfilling the duty to protect. *American Journal of Psychiatry, 142*, 425–429.

Appelbaum, P. S. (2004). Psychiatric advance directives and the treatment of committed patients. *Psychiatric Rehabilitation, 55*(7), 751–763.

Appelbaum, P. S. (2008). Privilege in the federal courts: Should there be a "dangerous patient exception"? *Psychiatric Services, 59*, 714–716.

Aron, L., Honberg, R., Duckworth, K., et al. (2009). *Grading the states 2009: A report on America's health care system for adults with serious mental illness.* Arlington, VA: National Alliance on Mental Illness.

Ault-Brutus, A. A. (2012). Changes in racial-ethnic disparities in use and adequacy of mental health care in the United States, 1990–2003. *Psychiatric Services, 63*(6), 531–540.

Bachrach, L. (1981). Continuity of care for chronic mental patients: A conceptual analysis. *American Journal of Psychiatry, 138*, 1449–1456.

Backlar, P., McFarland, B., Swanson, J., & Mahler, J. (2001). Consumer, provider, and informal caregiver opinion of psychiatric advance directives. *Administration and Policy in Mental Health, 28*, 427–441.

Barton, R. (1966). *Institutional neurosis* (with a forward by Noel Gordon Harris). Bristol, UK: John Wright & Sons, Ltd.

Baum, H. (2000, July 18). Crisis of mental illness: Replace the stigma of disease with compassion and aid. *Pittsburgh Post-Gazette*, Perspectives section, p. F4.

Becker, M. H., Drachman, R. H., & Kirscht, J. P. (1974). A field experiment to evaluate various outcomes of continuity of physician care. *American Journal of Public Health, 64*, 1062–1070.

Beigler, J. S. (1984). Tarasoff vs. confidentiality. *Behavioral Sciences and the Law, 2*, 272–286.

Biestek, F. P. (1957). *The casework relationship.* Chicago: Loyola University Press.

Blashfield, R. K., & Draguns, J. G. (1976). Evaluative criteria for psychiatric classification. *Journal of Abnormal Psychology, 85(2)*, 140–150.

Callahan, J. (1994). The ethics of assisted suicide. *Health and Social Work, 19*, 237–244.

Caplan, G. (1964). *Principles of preventive psychiatry.* New York: Basic Books.

Cocozza, J. J., & Steadman, H. J. (1978). Prediction in psychiatry: An example of misplaced confidence in experts. *Social Problems, 25*, 265–278.

Cohen, R. (1996). Supreme Court ruling supports confidentiality principle for clinical social workers. *The Pennsylvania Social Worker, 17*(4), 1, 3.

Commonwealth of Pennsylvania. (1976). *Mental Health Procedures Act.* (P.L.817, No.143).

Corrigan, P. W. (2007). How clinical diagnosis might exacerbate the stigma of mental illness. *Social Work, 52*, 31–39.

Covington v. Harris, 410 F.2d 617, 623 (D.C. Cir. 1969).

Davis, N. J. (1972). Labeling theory in deviance research: A critique and reconsideration. *Sociological Quarterly, 13*, 447–474.

Dolgoff, R., Loewenberg, F. M., & Harrington, D. (2009). *Ethical decisions for social work practice* (8th ed.). Belmont, CA: Thomson/Brooks/Cole.

Eack, S. M., Newhill, C. E., & Watson, A. C. (2012). Effects of severe mental illness education on MSW student attitudes toward individuals with schizophrenia. *Journal of Social Work Education, 48*(3), 425–438.

Emerich v. Philadelphia Center for Human Development, Inc., 554 Pa. 209, 720 A.2d 1032 (1998).

Erickson, P. E., & Erickson, S. K. (2008). *Crime, punishment, and mental illness: Law and the behavioral sciences in conflict.* New Brunswick, NJ: Rutgers University Press.

Erickson, S. K. (2005). Beyond overt violence: Wisconsin's progressive civil commitment statute as a marker of a new era in mental health law. *Marquette Law Review, 89*, 359–405.

Fahy, J. (2005, March 8). Pennsylvanians can now prepare advance mental health directives. *Pittsburgh Post-Gazette*, pp. C-1, C-2.

Fauman, M. A. (2002). *Study guide to the* DSM-IV-TR. Washington, DC: American Psychiatric Press.

Fuoco, M. A. (2007, September 5). Mental health law balances danger and rights. *Pittsburgh Post-Gazette*, pp. A1, A6.

Gambrill, E. (2006). *Social work practice: A critical thinker's guide.* New York: Oxford.

Geller, J. L. (2001). Taking issue: You must read this. *Psychiatric Services, 52*, 265.

Geller, J. L. (2006). The evolution of outpatient commitment in the USA: From conundrum to quagmire. *International Journal of Law and Psychiatry, 29*, 234–248.

Gibbs, J. (1972). Issues in defining deviant behavior. In R. A. Scott & J. D. Douglas (Eds.), *Theoretical perspectives on deviance* (pp. 39–68). New York: Basic.

Gilman, P. (2012, December 17). Don't blame autism for Newtown. *The New York Times.*

Goffman, E. (1961). *Asylums: Essays on the social situation of mental patients and other inmates.* Garden City, NY: Anchor.

Gordon, R. A. (1977). A critique of the evaluation of Patuxent Institution, with particular attention to the issues of dangerousness and recidivism. *Bulletin of the American Academy of Psychiatry and the Law, 5*, 210–255.

Green, G. (2009). *The end of stigma? Changes in the social experience of long-term illness.* London: Routledge.

Green, S. (1997). Silence and violence. *Psychiatric Services, 48*, 175–176.

Greenhouse, L. (1995, October 17). Supreme Court roundup: Justices to decide case on establishing therapist-client privilege. *The New York Times.*

Grob, G. N. (2005). Policy and mental illnesses: Jimmy Carter's Presidential Commission on Mental Health. *Milbank Quarterly, 3*, 425–456.

Herbert, P. B., & Young, K. A. (2002). *Tarasoff* at twenty-five. *Journal of the American Academy of Psychiatry and Law, 30*, 275–281.

Hogarty, G. E., & Flesher, S. (1999). Practice principles of cognitive enhancement therapy for schizophrenia. *Schizophrenia Bulletin, 25*, 693–708.

Hogarty, G. E., Greenwald, D. P., & Eack, S. M. (2006). Durability and mechanism of effects of cognitive enhancement therapy. *Psychiatric Services, 57*, 1751–1757.

Huber, G. A., Roth, L. H., Appelbaum, P. S., & Ore, T. M. (1982). Hospitalization, arrest and discharge: Important legal and clinical issues in the emergency evaluation of persons believed to be dangerous to others. *Law and Contemporary Problems, 45*, 99–123.

Jaffee v. Redmond, 518 U.S. 1 (1996).

Joshi, K. (2003). Psychiatric advance directives. *Journal of Psychiatric Practice, 9*, 303–306.

Kagle, J. D., & Kopels, S. (1994). Confidentiality after *Tarasoff. Health and Social Work, 19*, 217–222.

Kalson, S. (2002, August 1). Views heard on bill to commit mentally ill. *Pittsburgh Post-Gazette*, p. B-7.

Kapp, M. B. (1988). Forcing services on at-risk older adults: When doing good is not so good. *Social Work in Health Care, 13*, 1–13.

Kendra's law. (1999). The New York State Office of Mental Health's (OMH) interim Report on Kendra's Law. Retrieved from OMH website: http://www.omh.ny.gov/omhweb/Kendra_web/interimreport

Kentucky revised statutes annotated. (1988).

Kirk, S. A., & Kutchins, H. (1988). Deliberate misdiagnosis in mental health practice. *Social Service Review, 62*, 225–237.

Kozol, H. L. (1982). Dangerousness in society and law. *The University of Toledo Law Review, 13*, 241–267.

Kutchins, H., & Kirk, S. A. (1988). The business of diagnosis: DSM-III and clinical social work. *Social Work, 33*, 215–220.

Lake v. Cameron, 364 F.2d 657 (D.C. Cir. 1966).

Langsley, D. G. (1985). Community psychiatry. In H. I. Kaplan & B. J. Sadock (Eds.), *Comprehensive textbook of psychiatry* (4th ed., pp. 1885–1888). Baltimore: Williams & Wilkins.

Lanterman-Petris-Short Act (LPS Act) (Cal. Welf & Inst. Code, sec. 5000 et seq.). The full act can be found at http://www.leginfo.ca.gov

Lessard v. Schmidt, 349 F.Supp. 1078 (E.D. Wis 1972).

Levy, C. S. (1976). *Social work ethics.* New York: Human Sciences Press.

Levy, C. S. (1979). *Values and ethics for social work practice.* Washington, DC: National Association of Social Workers.

Lidz, C. W. (1998). Coercion in psychiatric care: What have we learned from the research? *Journal of the American Academy of Psychiatry and the Law, 26*, 631–637.

Loewenberg, F., & Dolgoff, R. (1988). *Ethical decisions for social work practice* (3rd ed.). Itasca, IL: F. E. Peacock.

McQuaide, S. (1999). A social worker's use of the *Diagnostic and Statistical Manual. Families in Society, 80*, 410–416.

Meyers, C. J. (1984). The legal perils of psychotherapeutic practice (Part II): Coping with *Hedlund* and

Jablonski. The Journal of Psychiatry and Law, Spring, 39–47.

Miller, R. D. (1982). The least restrictive alternative: Hidden meanings and agendas. *Community Mental Health Journal, 18,* 46–55.

Miller, R. D. (1988) Outpatient civil commitment of the mentally ill: An overview and an update. *Behavioral Sciences & the Law, 6*(1), 99–118.

Mosby's Medical Dictionary (8th ed.). (2009). St. Louis, MO: Elsevier, Inc.

Murdach, A. D. (2011). What happened to self-determination? *Social Work, 56*(4), 371–373.

National Association of Social Workers (NASW). (1996). *Code of ethics.* Washington, DC: Author.

National Association of Social Workers (NASW). (1997, April). Treatment bill of rights issued. *NASW News, 42,* 1, 8.

National Association of Social Workers. (2009). *HIPAA 101 for health care providers' offices.* Retrieved May 20, 2009, from http://www.socialworkers.org/hipaa

National Mental Health Association (NMHA). (n.d.) *Psychiatric advance directives: Issue summary.* Alexandria, VA: NMHA Advocacy Resource Center.

New York State Office of Mental Health (NYOMH). (2005). *Kendra's law: Final report on the status of assisted outpatient treatment.* Albany: New York State Office of Mental Health.

Newhill, C. E. (1989). *Validation of a scale to assess danger to others in psychiatric emergency room patients* (Doctoral dissertation, University of California at Berkeley). Microfiche, Ann Arbor, MI: University Microfilms International.

Newhill, C. E. (1990). The role of culture in the development of paranoid symptomatology. *American Journal of Orthopsychiatry, 60,* 176–185.

Newhill, C. E. (1995). *A mental health casebook.* Unpublished manuscript.

Newhill, C. E. (2003). *Client violence in social work practice: Prevention, intervention and research.* New York: Guilford.

Newhill, C. E., & Harris, D. (2007). African-American consumers' perceptions of racial disparities in mental health services. *Social Work in Public Health, 23,* 107–124.

O'Connell, M., & Stein, C. (2005). Psychiatric advance directives: Perspectives of community stakeholders. *Administration and Policy in Mental Health, 32,* 241–265.

O'Connor v. Donaldson, 422 U.S. 563 (1975). Retrieved April 15, 2009, from http://supreme.justia.com/us/422/563/case.html

Office of Field Education. (2003). *HIPAA information for social work students.* Pittsburgh: Office of Field Education, School of Social Work, University of Pittsburgh.

Pone, D. A. (2009). *Summary of grave disability criteria.* Retrieved February 21, 2009, from http://pai-ca.org/pubs/508301.htm

Poulin, A. B. (1998). The psychotherapist-patient privilege after *Jaffee v. Redmond*: Where do we go from here? *Washington University Law Review, 76,* 1341–1409.

President's Commission on Mental Health. (1978). *Report to the president from the President's Commission on Mental Health* (4 vols.). Washington, DC: U.S. Government Printing Office.

Public Broadcasting Corporation (PBS). (2009). *The tragic cycle.* Retrieved April 29, 2009 from http://www.pbs.org/wgbh/pages/frontline/released/cycle/

Reamer, F. G. (1983). The concept of paternalism in social work. *Social Service Review, 57,* 254–271.

Reamer, F. G. (2003). *Social work malpractice and liability* (2nd ed.). New York: Columbia University Press.

Reamer, F. G. (2006). *Social work values and ethics* (3rd ed.). New York: Columbia University Press.

Ridgely, S. M., Borum, R., & Petrila, J. (2001). *The effectiveness of involuntary outpatient treatment: Empirical evidence and the experience of eight states.* Santa Monica, CA: RAND Law and Health Initiative.

Rosenthal, J. M., & Miller, D. B. (1979). Providers have failed to work for continuity. *Hospitals, 53,* 79–83.

Sands, R. G. (1991). *Clinical social work practice in community mental health.* New York: Maxwell MacMillan.

Sands, R. G. (2001). *Clinical social work practice in behavioral mental health: A postmodern approach to practice with adults* (2nd ed.). Boston: Allyn & Bacon.

Scheff, T. (1975). The labeling theory of mental illness. In T. Scheff (Ed.), *Labeling madness.* Englewood Cliffs, NJ: Prentice-Hall.

Scheyett, A., Kim, M., Swanson, J., Swartz, M., Elbogen, E., Van Dorn, R., et al. (2008). Social workers' familiarity with psychiatric advance directives: Implications for education, practice and research. *Families in Society, 89,* 228–236.

Schwartz, L. H. (1974). Litigating the right to treatment: *Wyatt v. Stickney. Hospital and Community Psychiatry, 25,* 460–463.

Shah, S. (1978). Dangerousness: Some definitional, conceptual and public policy issues. In B. D. Sales

(Ed.), *Perspectives in law and psychology* (Vol. 1). New York: Plenum.

Shelton v. Tucker, 364 U.S. 479 (1960).

Sherrill v. Wilson, 653 S.W.2d 661, 664 (Mo. 1983).

Slaikeu, K. A. (1984). *Crisis intervention: A handbook for practice and research.* Boston: Allyn & Bacon.

Srebnik, D., Russo, J., Sage, J., Peto, T., & Zick, E. (2003). Interest in psychiatric advance directives among high users of crisis services and hospitalization. *Psychiatric Services, 54*, 981–986.

Stavis, P. F. (1995, August–September). Civil commitment: Past, present, and future. *Quality of Care Newsletter, 64*.

Steadman, H. J. (1980). The right not to be a false positive: Problems in the application of the dangerousness standard. *Psychiatric Quarterly, 52*, 84–93.

Steadman, H. J. (1982). A situational approach to violence. *International Journal of Law and Psychiatry, 5*, 171–186.

Straub, K. M., & Parker, K. S. (Eds.). (1966). *Continuity of patient care: The role of nursing.* Washington, DC: Catholic University Press.

Swanson, J., Swartz, M., Ferron, J., Elbogen, E., & Van Dorn, R. (2006). Psychiatric advance directives among public mental health consumers in five U.S. cities: Prevalence, demand, and correlates. *American Academy of Psychiatry and Law, 34*(1), 43–57.

Szasz, T. S. (2002). *Fatal freedom: The ethics and politics of suicide.* Syracuse, NY: Syracuse University Press.

Tarasoff v. The Regents of the University of California, 551 P.2d 334 (Cal. 1974/1976).

U.S. Department of Health and Human Services (DHHS). (1999a). *Mental health: Culture, race and ethnicity—A supplement to mental health: A report of the Surgeon General.* Rockville, MD: U.S. Department of Health and Human Services, Public Health Service, Office of the Surgeon General.

U.S. Department of Health and Human Services (DHHS). (1999b). *Mental health: Culture, race, and ethnicity—A supplement to mental health: A report of the Surgeon General: Executive summary.* Rockville, MD: U.S. Department of Health and Human Services, Public Health Service, Office of the Surgeon General.

U.S. Department of Health and Human Services (DHHS). (2009). *The Health Insurance Portability and Accountability Act of 1996.* Retrieved September 12, 2013, from http://www.hhs.gov/ocr/privacy/index.html

Watson, A., Hanrahan, P., Luchins, D., & Lurigio, A. (2001). Mental health courts and the complex issue of mentally ill offenders. *Psychiatric Services, 52*(4), 477–481.

Williams, J. B. W. (2008). Diagnostic and statistical manual of mental disorders. In T. Mizrahi & L. E. Davis (Eds.), *The encyclopedia of social work* (20th ed., Vol. 2: D–I, pp. 26–31). Washington, DC: NASW Press; New York: Oxford.

Winerip, M. (1999, May 23). Bedlam in the streets. *The New York Times.*

Wise, T. P. (1978). Where the public peril begins: A survey of psychotherapists to determine the effects of *Tarasoff. Stanford Law Review, 31*, 165–190.

Wyatt v. Stickney, 325 F. Supp. 781, *aff'd, 344* F. Supp. 1341 (M.D. Ala. 1971), and 344 F. Supp. 373 (M.D. Ala. 1972), *aff'd sub nom*, Wyatt v. Aderholt, 503 F.2d 1305 (5th Cir. 1974).

CHAPTER 4

Acker, G. M. (1999). The impact of client's mental illness on social workers' job satisfaction and burnout. *Health & Social Work, 24*(2), 112–119.

Acker, G. M. (2004). The effect of organizational conditions (role conflict, role ambiguity, opportunities for professional development, and social support) on job satisfaction and intention to leave among social workers in mental health care. *Community Mental Health Journal, 40*(1), 65–73.

Amador, X. F. (with Johanson, A. L.) (2000). *I'm not sick, I don't need help!* Peconic, NY: Vida.

Amador, X. F. (2007). *I'm not sick, I don't need help!* (2nd ed.). Peconic, NY: Vida.

Amador, X. F. (2011). *I'm not sick, I don't need help! How to help someone with mental illness accept treatment* (10th anniversary ed.). Miami: Vida.

Amador, X. F. & David, A. S. (Eds.). (1998). *Insight and psychosis.* New York: Oxford.

Amador, X. F., & Shiva, A. A. (2001). Insight into schizophrenia. *Civil Rights Law Journal, 12*, 401–415.

Amador, X. F., Strauss, D. H., Yale, S. A., Flaum, M. M., Endicott, J., & Gorman, J. M. (1993). Assessment of insight in psychosis. *American Journal of Psychiatry, 150*, 873–879.

American Psychiatric Association. (2013). *Diagnostic and statistical manual of mental disorders* (5th ed.). Washington, DC: Author.

Americans with Disabilities Act of 1990 (ADA), Pub. L No.101–336, 104, Stat. 327. See www.ada.gov

Anonymous. (2007). Why having a mental illness is not like having diabetes. *Schizophrenia Bulletin, 33*(4), 846–847.

Associated Press. (2005, January 13). "Crazy" teddy bear prompts protest. *The Boston Globe.*

Associated Press. (2012, December 5). House approves eliminating "lunatic" from federal law. *The New York Times.*

Atwood, N. (1982). Professional prejudice and the psychotic client. *Social Work, 27,* 172–177.

Bachrach, L. L. (1988). Defining mental illness: A concept paper. *Hospital and Community Psychiatry, 39,* 383–388.

Ball, R. A., Moore, E., & Kuipers, L. (1992). Expressed emotion in community care staff: A comparison of patient outcome in a nine month follow-up of two hostels. *Social Psychiatry & Psychiatric Epidemiology, 27*(1), 35–39.

Barrowclough, C., Haddock, G., Lowens, I., Connor, A., Pidliswyj, J., & Tracey, N. (2001). Staff expressed emotion and causal attributions for client problems on a low security unit: An exploratory study. *Schizophrenia Bulletin, 27*(3), 517–526.

Bender, K. G. (2001). Social problems in Pakistani psychiatric patients. *International Journal of Social Psychiatry, 47,* 32–41.

Bjorklund, R. (1996). Psychiatric labels: Still hard to shake. *Psychiatric Services,* 47(12): 1329–1330.

Bogardus, E. S. (1926). Social distance in the city. *Proceedings and Publications of the American Sociological Society, 20,* 40–46.

Busko, M. (2007). Asian-Americans' reluctance to seek or use mental health services explored. *Medscape.* Retrieved September 5, 2007, from http://www.medscape.com/viewarticle/562290

Chang, T. (2007). Quote from M. Busko, Asian-Americans' reluctance to seek or use mental health services explored. *Medscape.* Retrieved September 5, 2007, from http://www.medscape.com/viewarticle/562290

Cohen, N. L. (1990). Stigma is in the eye of the beholder: A hospital outreach program for treating homeless mentally ill people. *Bulletin of the Menninger Clinic, 54,* 255–258.

Corrigan, P. W. (2007). How clinical diagnosis might exacerbate the stigma of mental illness. *Social Work, 52,* 31–39.

Corrigan, P. W. (2012). Where is the evidence supporting public service announcements to eliminate mental illness stigma? *Psychiatric Services, 63*(1), 79–82.

Corrigan, P. W., Edwards, A., Green, A., Thwart, S., & Penn, D. (2001). Prejudice, social distance, and familiarity with mental illness. *Schizophrenia Bulletin, 27,* 219–225.

Corrigan, P. W., & Gelb, B. (2006). Three programs that use mass approaches to challenge the stigma of mental illness. *Psychiatric Services, 57,* 393–398.

Corrigan, P. W., Morris, S. B., Michaels, P. J., Rafacz, J. D., & Rusch, H. (2012). Challenging the public stigma of mental illness: A meta-analysis of outcome studies. *Psychiatric Services, 63*(10), 963–973.

Covarrubias, I., & Han, M. (2011). Mental health stigma about serious mental illness among MSW students: Social contact and attitude. *Social Work, 56*(4), 317–325.

Crane, M. (2009). Best ways to deal with noncompliant patients. *Medscape Business of Medicine.* (Originally published June 6, 2009). Retrieved June 9, 2009, from www.medscape.com/viewarticle/703674?src=mp&spon=17&uac=6343AZ

Dell'Osso, L., Pini, S., Cassano, G. B., Mastrocinque, C., Seckinger, R. A., Saettoni, M., et al. (2002). Insight into illness in patients with mania, mixed mania, bipolar depression and major depression with psychotic features. *Bipolar Disorders, 4,* 315–322.

Diefenbach, D. L. (1997). The portrayal of mental illness on prime-time television. *Journal of Community Psychology, 25,* 289–302.

Duke, P., & Hochman, G. (1992). *A brilliant madness: Living with manic-depressive illness.* New York: Bantam.

Eack, S. M., Bahorik, A., Newhill, C. E., Neighbors, H., & Davis, L. E. (2012). Interviewer-perceived honesty mediates racial disparities in the diagnosis of schizophrenia. *Psychiatric Services, 84*(9), 875–880.

Eack, S. M., & Newhill, C. E. (2008a). An investigation of the relations between student knowledge, personal contact, and attitudes toward individuals with schizophrenia. *Journal of Social Work Education, 44,* 77–95.

Eack, S. M., & Newhill, C. E. (2008b). What influences social workers' attitudes toward working with clients with severe mental illness? *Families in Society: The Journal of Contemporary Social Services, 89,* 418–427.

Eack, S. M., Newhill, C. E., & Watson, A. C. (2012). Effects of severe mental illness education on MSW student attitudes toward individuals with schizophrenia. *Journal of Social Work Education, 48*(3), 425–438.

Eisenberg, L. (2005). Violence and the mentally ill. *Archives of General Psychiatry, 62,* 825–826.

Elinson, J., & Padella, E. (1967). *Public image of mental health services.* New York: Mental Health Study Center.

Falk, G. (2001). *Stigma: How we treat outsiders.* New York: Prometheus.

Fisher, C. (2008). *Wishful drinking.* New York: Simon & Schuster.

Ford, B. (2003). *Healing and hope.* New York: Putnam.

Friedman, R. A. (2008, October 21). When all else fails, blaming the patient often comes next. *The New York Times,* p. B-4.

Goffman, E. (1963). *Stigma: Notes on the management of spoiled identity.* New York: Simon & Schuster.

Goldstein, H. (1983). Starting where the client is. *Social Casework, 64,* 267–275.

Green, G. (2009). *The end of stigma? Changes in the social experience of long-term illness.* London: Routledge.

Group for the Advancement of Psychiatry. (1986). *A family affair: Helping families cope with mental illness: A guide for the professionals.* New York: Brunner/Mazel.

Hafner, K. (2009, May 26). Texting may be taking a toll. *The New York Times.*

Hatfield, A. G., & Lefley, H. P. (1987). *Families of the mentally ill: Coping and adaptation.* New York: Guilford.

Hepworth, D. H., Rooney, R. H., Rooney, G. D., Strom-Gottfried, K., & Larsen, J. A. (2010). *Direct social work practice: Theory and skills* (8th ed.). Belmont, CA: Brooks/Cole Cengage Learning.

Heresco-Levy, U., Ermilov, M., Giltsinsky, B., Lichtenstein, M., & Blander, D. (1999). Treatment-resistant schizophrenia and staff rejection. *Schizophrenia Bulletin, 25*(3), 457–465.

Hinshaw, S. P. (2007). *The mark of shame: Stigma of mental illness and an agenda for change.* New York: Oxford.

Hromco, J. G., Lyons, J. S., & Nikkei, R. E. (1995). Mental health case management: Characteristics, job function, and occupational stress. *Community Mental Health Journal, 31,* 111–125.

In our own voice. (2009). Retrieved June 8, 2009, from http://www.nami.org/Template.cfm?section=In_Our_Own_Voice

Juvva, S. (2007, March 18). Personal communication.

Kadushin, A. (1992). *Supervision in social work* (3rd ed.). New York: Columbia University Press.

Kim, H., Ji, J., & Kao, D. (2011). Burnout and physical health among social workers: A three-year longitudinal study. *Social Work, 56*(3), 258–268.

Krugman, P. (2012, February 16). Moochers against welfare. *The New York Times.*

Lamb, H. R. (1979). Staff burnout in work with long-term patients. *Hospital and Community Psychiatry, 30,* 396–398.

Lamb, H. R. (1982). *Treating the long-term mentally ill.* San Francisco: Jossey-Bass.

LeCroy, C. W., & Holschuh, J. (2012). *First person accounts of mental illness and recovery.* New York: Wiley.

Lefley, H. P. (2009). *Family psychoeducation for serious mental illness.* New York: Oxford.

Ly, N., & Peterson, C. (1993). Depressive symptoms among Vietnamese-American college students. *Journal of Social Psychology, 133,* 65–71.

Markham, D. (2003). Attitudes towards patients with a diagnosis of "borderline personality disorder": Social rejection and dangerousness. *Journal of Mental Health, 12,* 595–612.

Martin, J. K., Pescosolido, B. A., & Tuch, S. A. (2000). Of fear and loathing: The role of "disturbing behavior," labels, and causal attributions in shaping public attitudes toward people with mental illness. *Journal of Health and Social Behavior, 41,* 208–223.

Mason, K., Olmos-Gallo, A., Bacon, D., McQuilken, M., Henley, A., & Fisher, S. (2004). Exploring the consumer's and provider's perspective on service quality in community mental health care. *Community Mental Health Journal, 40*(1), 33–46.

Merton, R. (1957). Some preliminaries to a sociology of medical education. In R. K. Merton, G. G. Reader, & P. L. Kendall (Eds.), *The student physician* (pp. 71–79). Cambridge, MA: Harvard University Press.

Meyerson, A. T. (1978). What are the barriers or obstacles to treatment and care of the chronically mentally disabled? In J. A. Talbott (Ed.), *The chronic mental patient: Problems, solutions, and recommendations for a public policy* (pp. 129–134). Washington, DC: American Psychiatric Association.

Minkoff, K. (1987). Resistance of mental health professionals to working with the chronic mentally ill. In A. T. Meyerson (Ed.), *Barriers to treating the chronic mentally ill* (Spring, pp. 3–20). New Directions for Mental Health Services, 33, San Francisco: Jossey-Bass.

Minkoff, K., & Stern, R. (1985). Paradoxes faced by residents being trained in the psychosocial treatment of people with chronic schizophrenia. *Hospital & Community Psychiatry, 36,* 859–864.

Mirabi, M., Weinman, M. L., Magnetti, S. M., & Keppler, K. N. (1985). Professional attitudes toward the chronic

mentally ill. *Hospital and Community Psychiatry, 36*, 404–405.
Moore, E., & Kuipers, L. (1992). Behavioural correlates of expressed emotion in staff–patient interactions. *Social Psychiatry & Psychiatric Epidemiology, 27*(6), 298–303.
Nakazawa, D. J. (2009, February). Ill in a day's work: Chronic illness in the workplace. *More*, 42–48.
Newhill, C. E. (1993). Short-term treatment of a severely suicidal Japanese-American client with schizoaffective disorder. *Families in Society, 74*, 503–507.
Newhill, C. E., & Harris, D. (2007). *African-American consumer project field notes.* Unpublished manuscript.
Newhill, C. E., & Korr, W. S. (2004). Practice with persons with severe mental illness: Rewards, challenges and burdens. *Health and Social Work, 29*, 297–305.
Nielsen, A. C., Stein, L. I., Talbott, J. A., Lamb, H. R., Osser, D. N., & Glazer, W. M. (1981). Encouraging psychiatrists to work with chronic patients: Opportunities and limitations of residency education. *Hospital & Community Psychiatry, 32*, 767–775.
Nuland, S. (2009). *The soul of medicine.* New York: Kaplan.
Owen, P. R. (2012). Portrayals of schizophrenia by entertainment media: A content analysis of contemporary movies. *Psychiatric Services, 63*(7), 655–659.
Paul Wellstone and Pete Domenici Mental Health Parity and Addiction Equity Act, 29 U.S.C.A. § 1185a(a)(3)(A). (2009).
Phelan, J. C., Link, B. G., Stueve, A., & Pescosolido, B. A. (2000). Public conceptions of mental illness in 1950 and 1996: What is mental illness and is it to be feared? *Journal of Health and Social Behavior, 41*, 188–207.
Pini, S., Cassano, G. B., Dell'Osso, L., & Amador, X. F. (2001). Insight into illness in schizophrenia, schizoaffective disorder, and mood disorders with psychotic features. *American Journal of Psychiatry, 158*, 122–125.
Pini, S., Dell'Osso, L., Amador, X. F., Mastrocinque, C., Saettoni, M., & Cassano, G. B. (2003). Awareness of illness in patients with bipolar I disorder with or without comorbid anxiety disorders. *Australian and New Zealand Journal of Psychiatry, 37*, 355–361.
Pintard, P., D'Sa, A., & Sciascia, S. (2012). Medical students' attitudes about mental illness. *Psychiatric Services, 63*(8), 836.
Phelan, J. C., Link, B. G. & Dovidio, J. F. (2008). Stigma and prejudice: One animal or two? *Social science & medicine, 67(3)*, 358–367.
Pratt, L. A. (2012). Characteristics of adults with serious mental illness in the United States household population in 2007. *Psychiatric Services, 63*(10), 1042–1046.
Puhl, R., & Brownell, K. D. (2001). Bias, discrimination, and obesity. *Obesity Research, 9*, 788–805.
Rabkin, J. (1974). Public attitudes toward mental illness: A review of the literature. *Schizophrenia Bulletin, 1*(10), 9–33.
Raths, L., Harmin, M., & Simon, S. (1966). *Values and teaching.* Columbus, OH: Merrill.
Richmond, M. (1917). *Social diagnosis.* New York: Free.
Ryan, W. (1976). *Blaming the victim.* New York: Vintage.
Sartorius, N. (1998). Stigma: What can psychiatrists do about it? *The Lancet, 352*, 1058–1059.
Satel, S. (2009, April 21). To fight stigmas, start with treatment. *The New York Times.*
Savava, R. (2012). Social worker burnout in Israel: Contributions of daily stressors identified by social workers. *British Journal of Social Work, 42*(8), 1–16.
Schofield, W. (1986). *Psychotherapy: The purchase of friendship.* Piscataway, NJ: Transaction.
Schwartz, S., Krieger, M., & Sorenson, J. (1981). Preliminary survey of therapists who work with chronic patients: Implications for training. *Hospital and Community Psychiatry, 32*, 799–800.
Schwarz, J. (2009). *UW [University of Washington], state launch project to improve understanding, coverage of mental illness.* Retrieved August 31, 2013, from http://www.washington.edu.
Sharfstein, S.S. (2012). Status of stigma, 2012. *Psychiatric Services, 63(10)*, 953.
Shaw, F. (1998). Mistaken identity. *The Lancet, 352*, 1050–1051.
Shaw, G. M. (2007). *The welfare debate: Historical guides to controversial issues in America.* Santa Barbara, CA: Greenwood.
Shepherd, S. (n.d.). *They're possessed?* Retrieved June 2, 2009, from http://www.medhunters.com/articles/theyrePossessed.html
Shera, W., & Delva-Tauiliili, J. (1996). Changing MSW students' attitudes towards the severely mentally ill. *Community Mental Health Journal, 32(2)*, 159–169.
Simon, S. B., Howe, L. W., & Kirschenbaum, H. (1972). *Values clarification: A handbook of practical strategies for teachers and students.* New York: Hart.
Simon, S. B., Howe, L. W., & Kirschenbaum, H. (1995). *Values clarification: A handbook of practical strategies for teachers and students.* New York: Warner.
Smith, D. M., Damschroder, L. J., Kim, S. Y. H., & Ubel, P. A. (2012). What's it worth? Public willingness to

pay to avoid mental illnesses compared with general medical illnesses. *Psychiatric Services, 63*(4), 319–324.

Snyder, K. S., Wallace, C. J., Moe, K., & Liberman, R. P. (1994). Expressed emotion by residential care operators and residents' symptoms and quality of life. *Hospital & Community Psychiatry, 45*(11), 1141–1143.

Snyder, K. S., Wallace, C. J., Moe, K., Ventura, J., & Liberman, R. P. (1995). The relationship of residential care-home operators' expressed emotion and schizophrenic residents' symptoms and quality of life. *International Journal of Mental Health, 24*(3), 27–37.

Specht, H., & Courtney, M. (1994). *Unfaithful angels: How social work has abandoned its mission*. New York: Free Press.

Springer, I. (1992). Patients doctors hate. *Cosmopolitan, 213*, 160, 162.

Steadman, H. J., Mulvey, E. P., Monahan, J., Robbins, P. C., Appelbaum, P. S., Grisso, T., et al. (1998). Violence by people discharged from acute psychiatric inpatient facilities and by others in the same neighborhood. *Archives of General Psychiatry, 55*, 393–401.

Steinberg, P. (2012, December 25). Our failed approach to schizophrenia. *The New York Times.*

Stiglitz, J. E. (2012). *The price of inequality: How today's divided society endangers our future.* New York: Norton.

Strauss, J. S., & Carpenter, W. T. (1977). Prediction of outcome in schizophrenia. *Archives of General Psychiatry, 43*, 159–163.

Stuart, H. (2003). Stigma and the daily news: Evaluation of a newspaper intervention. *Canadian Journal of Psychiatry, 48*, 651–656.

Substance Abuse and Mental Health Services Administration (SAMHSA). (2012). *Mental health, United States: 2010* (HHS Publication No. (SMA) 12–4681). Rockville, MD: Author.

Talbott, J. A. (Ed.). (1978). *The chronic mental patient: Problems, solutions, and recommendations for a public policy.* Washington, DC: American Psychiatric Association.

Teplin, L. A., McClelland, G. M., Abram, K. M., & Weiner, D. A. (2005). Crime victimization in adults with severe mental illness: Comparison with the National Crime Victimization Survey. *Archives of General Psychiatry, 62*, 911–921.

Theriot, M. T., & Lodato, G. A. (2012). Attitudes about mental illness and professional danger among new social work students. *The Journal of Social Work Education, 48*(3), 403–423.

Torrey, E. F. (1997). *Out of the shadows: Confronting America's mental health crisis.* New York: Wiley.

Townsend, L., Gearing, R. E., & Polyanskaya, O. (2012). Influence of health beliefs and stigma on choosing Internet support groups over formal mental health services. *Psychiatric Services, 63*(4), 370–376.

Trattner, W. I. (2007). *From poor law to welfare state: A history of social welfare in America* (6th ed.). New York: Free.

Tringo, J. L. (1970). The hierarchy of preference toward disability groups. *Journal of Special Education, 4*, 295–306.

U.S. Department of Health and Human Services (DHHS). (1999). *Mental health: A report of the Surgeon General: Executive summary.* Rockville, MD: U.S. Department of Health and Human Services, Substance Abuse and Mental Health Services Administration, Center for Mental Health Services, National Institutes of Health, National Institute of Mental Health.

Vaughn, G., & Hansen, C. (2004). "Like minds, like mine": A New Zealand project to counter the stigma and discrimination associated with mental illness. *Australasian Psychiatry, 12*, 113–117.

Wahl, O. F. (1999). *Telling is risky business: Mental health consumers confront stigma.* New Brunswick, NJ: Rutgers University Press.

Warner, R. (2005). Local projects of the world psychiatric association programme to Reduce Stigma and Discrimination. *Psychiatric Services, 56*, 570–575.

Werrbach, G. B., & DePoy, E. (1993a). Social work students' interest in working with persons with serious mental illness. *Journal of Social Work Education, 29*, 200–211.

Werrbach, G. B., & DePoy, E. (1993b). Working with persons with serious mental illness: Implication for social work recruitment and retention. *Community Mental Health Journal, 29*, 305–319.

White, H. S., & Bennett, M. B. (1981). Training psychiatric residents in chronic care. *Hospital and Community Psychiatry, 32*, 339–343.

Williams, C. L., & Berry, J. W. (1991). Primary prevention of acculturative stress among refugees: Applications of psychological theory and practice. *American Psychologist, 46*, 632–641.

Zippay, A., & Lee, S. K. (2008). Neighbors' perceptions of community-based psychiatric housing. *Social Service Review, 82*(3), 395–417.

CHAPTER 5

Arkowitz, H., Westra, H. A., Miller, W. R., & Rollnick, S. (Eds.). (2007). *Motivational interviewing in the treatment of psychological problems.* New York: Guilford.

Bandura, A. (1994). Self-efficacy. In V. S. Ramachaudran (Ed.), *Encyclopedia of human behavior* (Vol. 4, pp. 71–81). New York: Academic Press.

Brehm, J. W. (1972). *Responses to loss of freedom: A theory of psychological reactance.* Morristown, NJ: General Learning Press.

Brehm, J. W. (1976). *A theory of psychological reactance* (2nd ed.). New York: Academic Press.

Brehm, J. W., & Brehm, S. S. (1981). *Psychological reactance: A theory of freedom and control.* San Diego: Academic Press.

Brehm, S. (1976). *The application of social psychology to clinical practice.* New York: Wiley.

Davis, M. H. (1983). Measuring individual differences in empathy: Evidence for a multidimensional approach. *Journal of Personality and Social Psychology, 44,* 113–126.

Fischer, J. (1973). An eclectic approach to therapeutic casework. In J. Fischer (Ed.), *Interpersonal helping: Emerging approaches for social work practice* (pp. 317–335). Springfield, IL: Charles C. Thomas.

Hepworth, D. H., & Larsen, J. A. (1990). *Direct social work practice: Theory and skills* (3rd ed.). Belmont, CA: Wadsworth.

Hepworth, D. H., Rooney, R. H., Rooney, G. D., Strom-Gottfried, K., & Larsen, J. A. (2010). *Direct social work practice: Theory and skills* (8th ed.). Belmont, CA: Wadsworth.

Lindenberg, R. E. (1958). Hard to reach: Client or casework agency? *Social Work, 3*(4), 23–29.

Lundahl, B. W., Kunz, C., Brownell, C., Rollefson, D., & Burke, B. L. (2010). A meta-analysis of motivational interviewing: Twenty-five years of empirical studies. *Research on Social Work Practice, 20*(2), 137–160.

Maluccio, A., & Marlow, W. (1974). The case for contract. *Social Work, 19*(1), 28–35.

Merton, R. K. (1968). *Social theory and social structure.* New York: Free Press.

Miller, W. R. (2000). Motivational enhancement therapy: Description of counseling approach. In J. J. Boren, L. S. Onken, & K. M. Carroll (Eds.), *Approaches to drug abuse counseling* (pp. 89–93). Washington, DC: National Institute on Drug Abuse.

Miller, W. R., & Rollnick, S. (1991). *Motivational interviewing: Preparing people to change addictive behavior.* New York: Guilford.

Miller, W. R., & Rollnick, S. (Eds.). (2002). *Motivational interviewing: Preparing people for change* (2nd ed.). New York: Guilford.

Miller, W. R., Sovereign, R. G., & Krege, B. (1988). Motivational interviewing with problem drinkers: II. The drinker's check-up as a preventive intervention. *Behavioral Psychotherapy, 16,* 251–268.

Mitchell, W. C. (1973). Bargaining and public choice. In H. J. Leavitt & L. R. Purdy (Eds.), *Readings in managerial psychology* (2nd ed., pp. 588–590). Chicago: University of Chicago Press.

Murdach, A. D. (1980). Bargaining and persuasion with nonvoluntary clients. *Social Work, 25*(6), 458–461.

Prochaska, J. O., & DiClemente, C. C. (1983). Stages and processes of self-change of smoking: Toward an integrative model of change. *Journal of Consulting and Clinical Psychology, 51,* 390–395.

Prochaska, J. O., DiClemente, C. C., & Norcross, J. C. (1992). In search of how people change: Applications to addictive behavior. *American Psychologist, 47,* 1102–1114.

Raynor, P. (1978). Compulsory persuasion: A problem for correctional social work. *British Journal of Social Work, 8*(4), 411–424.

Rogers, C. (1961). *On becoming a person: A therapist's view of psychotherapy.* Cambridge, MA: Riverside.

Rooney, R. H. (1988). Socialization strategies for involuntary clients. *Social Casework, 69*(2), 131–140.

Rooney, R. H. (1992). *Strategies for work with involuntary clients* (1st ed.). New York: Columbia University Press.

Rooney, R. H. (Ed.). (2009). *Strategies for work with involuntary clients* (2nd ed.). New York: Columbia University Press.

Sagarin, E. (1975). *Deviants and deviance.* New York: Praeger.

Saltmarsh, R. E. (1976). Client resistance in talk therapies. *Psychotherapy: Research and Practice, 13*(1), 34–39.

Saunders, D. G. (1982). Counseling the violent husband. In P. A. Keller & L. G. Ritt (Eds.), *Innovations in clinical practice.* Sarasota, FL: Professional Resource Exchange.

Seabury, B. A., Seabury, B. H., & Garvin, C. D. (2011). *Foundations of interpersonal practice in social work: Promoting competence in generalist practice* (3rd ed.). Los Angeles: Sage.

Simons, R. L. (1982). Strategies for exercising influence. *Social Work, 27*(3), 268–274.

Simons, R. L. (1985). Inducement as an approach to exercising influence. *Social Work, 30*(1), 56–62.

Videka-Sherman, L. (1985). *Harriet M. Bartlett Practice Effectiveness Project: Report to NASW board of directors.* Silver Spring, MD: National Association of Social Workers.

West, R. (2005). Editorial. *Addiction, 100*, 1036–1039.

Wicklund, R. A. (1974). *Freedom and reactance.* Potomac, MD: Erlbaum.

CHAPTER 6

Abe-Kim, J., Takeuchi, D. T., Hong, S., Zane, N., Sue, S., Spencer, M. S., et al. (2007). Use of mental health-related services among immigrant and US-born Asian Americans: Results from the National Latino and Asian American Study. *American Journal of Public Health, 97*(1), 91–98. doi: 10.2105/ajph.2006.098541

Abraido-Lanza, A. E., Viladrich, A., Florez, K. R., Cespedes, A., Aguirre, A. N., & De La Cruz, A. A. (2007). Commentary: Fatalismo reconsidered: A cautionary note for health-related research and practice with Latino populations. *Ethnic Disparities, 17*(1), 153–158.

Agency for Healthcare Research and Quality. (2005). *National healthcare disparities report.* Rockville, MD: Author.

Agyemang, C., Bhopal, R., & Bruijnzeels, M. (2005). Negro, Black, Black African, African Caribbean, African American or what? Labelling African origin populations in the health arena in the 21st century. *Journal of Epidemiology and Community Health, 59*(12), 1014–1018. doi: 10.1136/jech.2005.035964

Akutsu, P. D., & Chu, J. P. (2006). Clinical problems that initiate professional help-seeking behaviors from Asian Americans. *Professional Psychology: Research and Practice, 37*(4), 407–415. doi: 10.1037/0735-7028.37.4.407

Alegria, M., Canino, G., Shrout, P., Woo, M., Duan, N., Vila, D., et al. (2008). Prevalence of mental illness in immigrants and non-immigrants U.S. Latino groups. *American Journal of Psychiatry, 165*, 359–369.

Alegria, M., Mulvaney-Day, N., Torres, M., Polo, A., Cao, Z., & Canino, G. (2007). Prevalence of psychiatric disorders across Latino subgroups in the United States. *American Journal of Public Health, 97*(1), 68–75.

Alegria, M., Woo, M., Takeuchi, D., & Jackson, J. (2009). Ethnic group differences in mental health and service use: Findings from the Collaborative Psychiatric Epidemiology Surveys. In P. Ruiz & A. Primm (Eds.), *Disparities in psychiatric care: Clinical and cross-cultural perspectives.* Bethesda, MD: Wolters Kluwer Lippincott Williams and Wilkins.

Alexander, M. (2012). *The new Jim Crow: Mass incarceration in the age of colorblindness.* New York: New Press.

Anderson, M. J., & Ellis, R. (1995). On the reservation. In N. A. Vacc, S. B. DeVaney, & J. Wittmer (Eds.), *Experiencing and counseling multicultural and diverse populations.* Bristol, PA: Accelerated Development.

Anez, L. M., Paris, M. J., Bedregal, L. E., Davidson, L., & Grilo, C. M. (2005). Application of cultural constructs in the care of first generation Latino clients in a community mental health setting. *Journal of Psychiatric Practice, 11*(4), 221–230.

Arnold, L. M. (2003). Gender differences in bipolar disorder. *The Psychiatric Clinics of North America, 26*(3), 595–620.

Bae, S.-W., & Kung, W. W.-M. (2000). Family intervention for Asian Americans with a schizophrenic patient in the family. *American Journal of Orthopsychiatry, 70*(4), 532–541. doi: 10.1037/h0087789

Baker, F. M. (1988). Afro-Americans. In L. Comas-Diaz & E. E. H. Griffith (Eds.), *Clinical guidelines in cross-cultural mental health* (pp. 151–181). New York: John Wiley.

Baker, F. M., & Lightfoot, O. B. (1993). Psychiatric care of ethnic elders. In A. C. Gaw (Ed.), *Culture, ethnicity, and mental illness* (pp. 517–552). Washington, DC: American Psychiatric Press.

Barcus, C. (Ed.). (2003). *Recommendations for the treatment of American Indian populations. Council of National Psychological Associations for the Advancement of Ethnic Minority Interests.* Washington, DC: Association of Black Psychologists.

Barksdale, C., & Molock, S. (2009). Perceived norms and mental health help seeking among African American college students. *The Journal of Behavioral Health Services and Research, 36*(3), 285–299. doi: 10.1007/s11414-008-9138-y

Barnett, M. C., Cotroneo, M., Purnell, J., Martin, D., Mackenzie, E., & Fisherman, A. (2003). Use of CAM in local African-American communities: Community-partnered research. *Journal of the National Medical Association, 95(10)*, 943–950.

Barnett, R. C., & Baruch, G. K. (1985). Women's involvement in multiple roles and psychological distress. *Journal of Personality and Social Psychology, 49*(1), 135–145. doi: 10.1037/0022-3514.49.1.135

Battle, C. L., Zlotnick, C., Najavits, L. M., Guttierrez, M., & Winsor, C. (2003). Posttraumatic stress disorder and substance use disorder among incarcerated women. In P. C. Ouimette & P. J. Brown (Eds.), *Trauma and substance abuse: Causes, consequences, and treatment of comorbid disorders* (pp. 209–225). Washington, DC: American Psychological Association.

Baugh, J. (1999). *Out of the mouths of slaves: African American language and educational malpractice.* Austin: University of Texas Press.

Beals, J., Manson, S. M., Whitesell, N. R., Spicer, P., Novins, D. K., & Mitchell, C. M. (2005). Prevalence of DSM-IV disorders and attendant help-seeking in 2 American Indian reservation populations. *Archives of General Psychiatry, 62*, 99–208.

Beals, J., Novins, D. K., Whitesell, N. R., Spicer, P., Mitchell, C. M., Manson, S. M., & American Indian Service Utilization Psychiatric Epidemiology Risk and Protective Factors Project Team. (2005). Prevalence of mental disorders and utilization of mental health services in two American Indian reservation populations: Mental health disparities in a national context. *American Journal of Psychiatry, 162*, 1723–1732.

Berg, I. K., & Jaya, A. (1993). Different and same: Family therapy with Asian-American families. *Journal of Marital and Family Therapy, 19*(1), 31–38. doi: 10.1111/j.1752-0606.1993.tb00963.x

Birmingham, C. L., Su, J., Hlynsky, J. A., Goldner, E. M., & Gao, M. (2005). The mortality rate from anorexia nervosa. *International Journal of Eating Disorders, 38*(2), 143–146. doi: 10.1002/eat.20164

Black, L. (1996). Families of African origin: An overview. In M. McGoldrick, J. Giordano, & J. K. Pearce (Eds.), *Ethnicity and family therapy* (pp. 57–65). New York: Guilford.

Boyd-Franklin, N. (2006). *Black families in therapy: Understanding the African American experience* (2nd ed.). New York: Guilford.

Brammer, R. (2004). *Diversity in counseling.* Belmont, CA: Brooks/Cole.

Brennan, E. (2011, November 25). The unbelievers. *The New York Times.*

Breslau, J., Aguilar-Gaxiola, S., Kendler, K. S., Su, M., Williams, D., & Kessler, R. C. (2006). Specifying race-ethnic differences in risk for psychiatric disorder in a US national sample. *Psychological Medicine, 36*(1), 57–68.

Breslau, J., Kendler, K. S., Su, M., Gaxiola-Aguilar, S., & Kessler, R. C. (2005). Lifetime risk and persistence of psychiatric disorders across ethnic groups in the United States. *Psychological Medicine, 35*(3), 317–327.

Bromberger, J. T., Meyer, P. M., Kravitz, H. M., Sommer, B., Cordal, A., Powell, L., et al. Psychologic distress and natural menopause: A multiethnic community study. *American Journal of Public Health, 91*(9), 1435–1442. doi: 10.2105/ajph.91.9.1435

Brown, E. R., Ojeda, V. D., Wyn, R., & Levan, R. (2000). *Racial and ethnic disparities in access to health insurance and health care.* Los Angeles: UCLA Center for Health Policy Research and the Henry J. Kaiser Family Foundation.

Burt, V. K., & Rasgon, N. (2004). Special considerations in treating bipolar disorder in women. *Bipolar Disorders, 6*(1), 2–13. doi: 10.1046/j.1399-5618.2003.00089.x

Burton, E. (1983). Surviving the flight of horror: The story of refugee women. *Indochinese Issues, 34*, 1–7.

Cahill, L., Uncapher, M., Kilpatrick, L., Alkire, M. T., & Turner, J. (2004). Sex-related hemispheric lateralization of amygdala function in emotionally influenced memory: An fMRI investigation. *Learning & Memory, 11*(3), 261–266. doi: 10.1101/lm.70504

Campbell, L. (2000). *American Indian languages: The historical linguistics of Native America.* New York: Oxford University Press.

Case, A., & Reid, R. (2001). Menstrual cycle effects on common medical conditions. *Comprehensive Therapy, 27*(1), 65–71. doi: 10.1007/s12019-001-0010-8

Castellanos, F., Giedd, J. N., Berquin, P. C., Walter, J. M., Sharp, W., Tran, T., et al. (2001). Quantitative brain magnetic resonance imaging in girls with attention-deficit/hyperactivity disorder. *Archives of General Psychiatry, 58*(3), 289–295. doi: 10.1001/archpsyc.58.3.289

Chapman, L. K., & Steger, M. F. (2010). Race and religion: Differential prediction of anxiety symptoms by religious coping in African American and European American young adults. *Depression & Anxiety, 27*(3), 316–322.

Chatters, L. M., Taylor, R. J., Bullard, K. M., & Jackson, J. S. (2009). Race and ethnic differences in religious involvement: African Americans, Caribbean Blacks and non-Hispanic Whites. *Ethnic and Racial Studies, 32*(7), 1143–1163. doi: 10.1080/01419870802334531

Chatters, L. M., Taylor, R. J., Jackson, J. S., & Lincoln, K. D. (2008). Religious coping among African Americans, Caribbean Blacks and non-Hispanic Whites. *Journal of Community Psychology, 36*(3), 371–386.

Chow, J. C., Jaffee, K., & Snowden, L. (2003). Racial/ethnic disparities in the use of mental health services in poverty areas. *American Journal of Public Health, 93*, 792–797.

Chu, J. P., & Sue, S. (2011). Asian American mental health: What we know and what we don't know. *Online Readings in Psychology and Culture, Unit 3.*

Retrieved from http://scholarworks.gvsu.edu/orpc/vol3/iss1/4/
Chua, A. (2011). *Battle hymn of the tiger mother.* New York: Penguin.
Chung, H. (2002). The challenges of providing behavioral treatment to Asian Americans. *Western Journal of Medicine, 176*(4), 222–223.
Cohen, L. S., Altshuler, L. L., Harlow, B. L., Nonacs, R., Newport, J., Viguera, A. C., et al. (2006). Relapse of major depression during pregnancy in women who maintain or discontinue antidepressant treatment. *The Journal of the American Medical Association, 295*(5), 499–507. doi: 10.1001/jama.295.5.499
Cohen, L. S., Soares, C. N., Poitras, J. R., Prouty, J., Alexander, A. B., & Shifren, J. L. (2003). Short-term use of estradiol for depression in perimenopausal and postmenopausal women: A preliminary report. *The American Journal of Psychiatry, 160*, 1519–1522.
Comas-Diaz, L. (1988). Cross-cultural mental health treatment: The evolution of identity. *Cultural Diversity and the Ethnic Minority Psychology, 7*, 115–120.
Conner, K. O., Copeland, V. C., Grote, N. K., Koeske, G., Rosen, D., Reynolds, C. F., et al. (2010). Mental health treatment seeking among older adults with depression: The impact of stigma and race. *The American Journal of Geriatric Psychiatry: Official Journal of the American Association for Geriatric Psychiatry, 18*(6), 531–543.
Cooper-Patrick, L., Gallo, J. J., Powe, N. R., Steinwachs, D. M., Eaton, W. W., & Ford, D. E. (1999). Mental health service utilization by African Americans and Whites: The Baltimore Epidemiologic Catchment Area Follow-Up. *Medical Care, 37*(10), 1034–1045.
Cowen-Fletcher, J. (1999). *It takes a village.* New York: Scholastic.
Dana, R. H. (1993). *Multicultural assessment perspectives for professional psychology.* Needham Heights, MA: Allyn & Bacon.
David, R. J., & Collins, J. W. (1997). Differing birth weight among infants of U.S.-born Blacks, African-born Blacks, and U.S.-born Whites. *New England Journal of Medicine, 337*(17), 1209–1214. doi: 10.1056/NEJM199710233371706
Dayer-Berenson, L. (2011). *Cultural competencies for nurses: Impact on health and illness.* Sudbury, MA: Jones and Bartlett Publishers.
Day-Vines, N. L., Patton, J. M., & Baytops, J. L. (2003). Counseling African American adolescents: The impact of race, culture, and middle class status. *Professional School Counseling, 7*(1), 40–51.
Dennerstein, L., Judd, F., & Davies, B. (1983). Psychosis and the menstrual cycle. *Medical Journal of Australia, 1*(11), 524–526.
Deyhle, D., & Swisher, K. (1997). Research in American Indian and Alaska Native education: From assimilation to self-determination. *Review of Research in Education, 22*, 113–194.
Diala, C., Muntaner, C., Walrath, C., Nickerson, K. J., LaVeist, T. A., & Leaf, P. J. (2000). Racial differences in attitudes toward professional mental health care and in the use of services. *American Journal of Orthopsychiatry, 70*(4), 455–464. doi: 10.1037/h0087736
Diamond, J. (1999). *Guns, germs and steel: The fates of human societies.* New York: Norton.
Dickerson, D. J. (2004). *The end of blackness.* New York: Anchor.
Du, N., & Lu, F. G. (1997). Assessment and treatment of posttraumatic stress disorder among Asian Americans. In E. Lee (Ed.),*Working with Asian Americans: A guide for clinicians.* New York: Guilford Press.
DuBard, C. A., & Gizlice, Z. (2008). Language spoken and differences in health status, access to care, and receipt of preventive services among US Hispanics. *American Journal of Public Health, 98*(11), 2021–2028. doi: 10.2105/ajph.2007.119008
Dube, S. R., Anda, R. F., Whitfield, C. L., Brown, D. W., Felitti, V. J., Dong, M., et al. (2005). Long-term consequences of childhood sexual abuse by gender of victim. *American Journal of Preventive Medicine, 28*(5), 430–438. doi: 10.1016/j.amepre.2005.01.015
Duncan, B., Hotz, V. J., & Trejo, S. J. (2006). Hispanics in the U.S. labor market. In National Research Council (Ed.), *Hispanics and the future of America* (pp. 228–290). Washington, DC: National Academies Press.
Eaton, W. W., & Muntaner, C. (1999). Socioeconomic stratification and mental disorder. In A. V. Horwitz & T. K. Scheid (Eds.), *A handbook for the study of mental health: Social contexts, theories and systems* (pp. 259–283). New York: Cambridge.
Edwards, V. J., Holden, G. W., Felitti, V. J., & Anda, R. F. (2003). Relationship between multiple forms of childhood maltreatment and adult mental health in community respondents: Results from the Adverse Childhood Experiences Study. *The American Journal of Psychiatry, 160*, 1453–1460.
Eisenberg, D., Golberstein, E., & Gollust, S. E. (2007). Help-seeking and access to mental health care in a university student population. *Medical Care, 45*(7),

594–601. doi: 510.1097/MLR.1090b1013e31803bb318 04c31801

Ellison, C. G., Musick, M. A., & Henderson, A. K. (2008). Balm in Gilead: Racism, religious involvement, and psychological distress among African-American adults. *Journal for the Scientific Study of Religion, 47*(2), 291–309. doi: 10.1111/j.1468-5906.2008.00408.x

Espinosa, G., Elizondo, V., & Miranda, J. (2003). *Hispanic churches in American public life: Summary of findings.* Notre Dame, IN: Institute for Latino Studies, University of Notre Dame.

Evans-Campbell, T., Lindhorst, T., Huang, B., & Walters, K. L. (2006). Interpersonal violence in the lives of urban American Indian and Alaska Native women: Implications for health, mental health, and help-seeking. *American Journal of Public Health, 96*(8), 1416–1422.

Fang, J., Madhavan, S., & Alderman, M. H. (1996). The association between birthplace and mortality from cardiovascular causes among Black and White residents of New York City. *New England Journal of Medicine, 335*(21), 1545–1551. doi: 10.1056/NEJM199611213352101

Flemming, C. M. (1990). American Indians and Alaska Natives: Changing societies past and present. In M. A. Orlandi (Ed.), *Cultural competence for evaluators: A guide for alcohol and other drug abuse prevention with ethnic/racial communities.* Rockville, MD: U.S. Department of Health and Human Services.

Fletcher, M. L. M. (2010). *Consent and resistance: The modern struggle between American Indian tribes and the United States.* Legal Studies Research Paper Series. East Lansing: Michigan State University College of Law.

Flores, G. (2006). Language barriers to health care in the United States. *New England Journal of Medicine, 355*(3), 229–231. doi: 10.1056/NEJMp058316

Fong, R. (2002). Culturally competent social work practice: Past and present. In R. Fong & S. Furuto (Eds.), *Culturally competent practice: Skills, interventions and evaluations,* Boston, MA: Pearson.

Freeman, E. W., Sammel, M. D., Liu, L., Gracia, C. R., Nelson, D. B., & Hollander, L. (2004). Hormones and menopausal status as predictors of depression in women in transition to menopause. *Archives of General Psychiatry, 61*(1), 62–70. doi: 10.1001/archpsyc.61.1.62

Friedman, A. R. (1992). Rape and domestic violence: The experience of refugee women. In E. Cole, O. M. Espin, & E. D. Rothblum (Eds.), *Refugee women and their mental health: Shattered societies, shattered lives* (pp. 65–78). New York: Haworth Press, Inc.

Fujii, J. S., Fukushima, S. N., & Yamamoto, J. (1993). Psychiatric care of Japanese Americans. In A. C. Gaw (Ed.), *Culture, ethnicity and mental illness* (pp. 305–345). Washington, DC: American Psychiatric Press.

Fuligni, A. J., Tseng, V., & Lam, M. (1999). Attitudes toward family obligations among American adolescents with Asian, Latin American, and European backgrounds. *Child Development, 70*(4), 1030–1044.

Gallo, L. C., Penedo, F. J., Espinosa de los Monteros, K., & Arguelles, W. (2009). Resiliency in the face of disadvantage: Do Hispanic cultural characteristics protect health outcomes? *Journal of Personality, 77*(6), 1707–1746. doi: 10.1111/j.1467-6494.2009.00598.x

Gallup, G., & Lindsay, D. M. (1999). *Surveying the religious landscape: Trends in U.S.* Harrisburg, PA: Morehouse Pub.

Gannotti, M. E., Kaplan, L. C., Handwerker, W. P., & Groce, N. E. (2004). Cultural influences on health care use: Differences in perceived unmet needs and expectations of providers by Latino and Euro-American parents of children with special health care needs. *Journal of Developmental & Behavioral Pediatrics, 25*(3), 156–165.

Garcia, B., & Petrovich, A. (2011). *Strengthening the DSM.* New York: Springer Publishing Company.

Garland, A. F., Lau, A. S. L., Yeh, M., McCabe, K. M., Hough, R. L., & Landsverk, J. A. (2005). Racial and ethnic differences in utilization of mental health services among high-risk youths. *The American Journal of Psychiatry, 162*(7), 1336–1343.

Gaw, A. C. (1993). Psychiatric care of Chinese Americans. In A. C. Gaw (Ed.), *Culture, ethnicity and mental illness* (pp. 245–280). Washington, DC: American Psychiatric Press.

Gearon, J. S., Kaltman, S. I., Brown, C., & Bellack, A. S. (2003). Traumatic life events and PTSD among women with substance use disorders and schizophrenia. *Psychiatric Services, 54,* 523–528.

Ghosh, C. (2010). A national health agenda for Asian Americans and Pacific Islanders. *Journal of American Medical Association, 304*(12), 1381–1382.

Golding, J. M. (1999). Intimate partner violence as a risk factor for mental disorders: A meta-analysis. *Journal of Family Violence, 14*(2), 99–132. doi: 10.1023/a:1022079418229

Gordon, S. M. (1994). Hispanic cultural health beliefs and folk remedies. *Journal of Holistic Nursing, 12*(3), 307–322. doi: 10.1177/089801019401200308

Grant, B. F., Stinson, F. S., Dawson, D. A., Chou, S. P., Ruan, W. J., & Pickering, R. P. (2004). Co-occurrence of 12-month alcohol and drug use disorders and personality disorders in the United States: Results from the National Epidemiologic Survey on Alcohol and Related Conditions. *Archives of General Psychiatry, 61*, 361–368.

Grant, B. F., Stinson, F. S., Hasin, D. S., Dawson, D. A., Chou, S. P., & Anderson, K. (2004). Immigration and lifetime prevalence of DSM-IV psychiatric disorders among Mexican Americans and non-Hispanic Whites in the United States: Results from the National Epidemiologic Survey on Alcohol and Related Conditions. *Archives of General Psychiatry, 61*, 1226–1233.

Guarnaccia, P. J., Pincay, I. M., Alegria, M., Shrout, P., Lewis-Fernandez, R., & Canino, G. (2007). Assessing diversity among Latinos: Results from the NLAAS. *Hispanic Journal of Behavioral Science, 29*(4), 510–534. doi: 10.1177/0739986307308110

Guilamo-Ramos, V., Dittus, P., Jaccard, J., Johansson, M., Bouris, A., & Acosta, N. (2007). Parenting practices among Dominican and Puerto Rican mothers. *Social Work, 52*(1), 17–30.

Gurung, R. A. R. (2012). A multicultural approach to health psychology. *American Journal of Lifestyle Medicine, 7*, 4–12. doi: 10.1177/1559827612444548

Hallonquist, J. D., Seeman, M. V., Lang, M., & Rector, N. A. (1993). Variation in symptom severity over the menstrual cycle of schizophrenics. *Biological Psychiatry, 33*(3), 207–209. doi: 10.1016/0006-3223(93)90141-y

Hamilton, D. (1993, July 29). Chinese-American leaders call for action on "parachute kids": Taiwan is urged to cut the flow of children sent alone to attend U.S. schools. *The Los Angeles Times.*

Harris, K. M., Edlund, M. J., & Larson, S. (2005). Racial and ethnic differences in the mental health problems and use of mental health care. *Medical Care, 43*(8), 775–784.

Heinrich, R. K., Corbin, J. L., & Thomas, K. R. (1990). Counseling Native Americans. *Journal of Counseling and Development, 69*, 128–133.

Hickey, G. C. (1964). *Village in Vietnam.* New Haven, CT: Yale University Press.

Ho, M. K. (1992). *Minority children and adolescents in therapy.* Newbury Park, CA: Sage.

Holzer, C. E., Goldsmith, H. F., & Ciarlo, J. A. (1998). Effects of rural-urban country type on the availability of health and mental health care providers. In R. W. Manderscheid & M. J. Henderson (Eds.), *Mental health, United States.* Rockville, MD: Center for Mental Health Services.

Howell, W. (1973). *The Pacific Islanders.* New York: Scribner's.

Huer, M. B., Saenz, T. I., & Diem Doan, J. H. (2001). Understanding the Vietnamese American community. *Communication Disorders Quarterly, 23*(1), 27–39. doi: 10.1177/152574010102300105

Huntington, S. P. (2004). *Who are we: The challenges to America's national identity.* New York: Simon & Schuster.

Ishii-Kuntz, M. (2004). Asian American families: Diverse history, contemporary trends, and the future. In M. Coleman & L. Ganong (Eds.), *Handbook of contemporary families: Considering the past, contemplating the future* (pp. 369–384). Newbury Park, CA: Sage.

Ito, K. L., Chung, R. C.-Y., & Kagawa-Singer, M. (1997). Asian/Pacific American women and cultural diversity: Studies of the traumas of cancer and war. In S. B. Ruzek, V. L. Olesen, & A. E. Clarke (Eds.), *Women's health: Complexities and differences* (pp. 300–328). Columbus: Ohio State University Press.

Iwamasa, G. Y., Hsia, C., & Hinton, D. (2006). Cognitive-behavioral therapy with Asian Americans. In P. A. Hays & G. Y. Iwamasa (Eds.), *Culturally responsive cognitive-behavioral therapy: Assessment, practice, and supervision* (pp. 117–140). Washington, DC: American Psychological Association.

Jacobs, E. A., Shepard, D. S., Suaya, J. A., & Stone, E.-L. (2004). Overcoming language barriers in health care: Costs and benefits of interpreter services. *American Journal of Public Health, 94*(5), 866–869. doi: 10.2105/ajph.94.5.866

Johnson, T. M., Fenton, B. J., Kracht, B. R., Weiner, M. F., & Guggenheim, F. G. (1988). Providing culturally sensitive care: Intervention by a consultation-liaison team. *Hospital and Community Psychiatry, 39*, 200–202.

Kales, H. C., Blow, F. C., Bingham, C. R., Roberts, J. S., Copeland, L. A., & Mellow, A. M. (2000). Race, psychiatric diagnosis, and mental health care utilization in older patients. *American Journal of Geriatric Psychiatry, 8*(4), 301–309.

Kearney, L. K., Draper, M., & Barón, A. (2005). Counseling utilization by ethnic minority college students. *Cultural Diversity and Ethnic Minority Psychology, 11*(3), 272–285. doi: 10.1037/1099-9809.11.3.272

Kendler, K. S., Kuhn, J. W., Vittum, J., Prescott, C. A., & Riley, B. (2005). The interaction of stressful life events and a serotonin transporter polymorphism in the prediction of episodes of major depression: A replication. *Archives of General Psychiatry, 62*(5), 529–535. doi: 10.1001/archpsyc.62.5.529

Kessler, R., McGonagle, K., Zhao, S., Nelson, D., Hughes, M., Eshleman, S., et al. (1994). Lifetime and 12-month prevalence of DSM-III-R psychiatric disorders in the United States. *Archives of General Psychiatry, 51*, 8–19.

Kessler, R. C., Chiu, W. T., Demler, O. & Walters, E. E. (2005a). Prevalence, severity, and comorbidity of twelve-month DSM-IV disorders in the National Comorbidity Survey replication (NCS-R). *Archives of General Psychiatry, 62*(6), 617–627.

Kessler, R. C., Demler, O., Frank, R. G., Olfson, M., Pincus, H. A., Walters, E. E., et al. Prevalence and treatment of mental disorders, 1990 to 2003. *New England Journal of Medicine, 352*(24), 2515–2523. doi: 10.1056/NEJMsa043266

Keyes, K. M., Hatzenbuehler, M. L., Alberti, P., Narrow, W. E., Grant, B. F., & Hasin, D. S. (2008). Service utilization differences for Axis-I psychiatric and substance use disorders between White and Black adults. *Psychiatric Services, 59*(8), 893–901.

Kim, K. C., & Hurh, W. M. (1985). The wives of Korean small businessmen in the U.S.: Business involvement and family roles. In I. S. Lee (Ed.), *Korean American women: Toward self-realization* (pp. 1–41). Mansfield, OH: The Association of Korean Christian Scholars in North America.

Kim, K. C., & Hurh, W. M. (1988). The burden of double roles: Korean wives in the USA. *Ethics and Racial Studies, 11*(2), 151–167.

Kim-Ju, G. M., Maeda, W., & Maffini, C. (2009). A historical and contemporary overview of Asian American and Pacific Islander experiences: Immigration, racialization, and liminality. *Aggression and Violent Behavior, 14*, 437–444.

Kinzie, D., & Fleck, J. (1987). Psychotherapy with severely traumatized refugees. *American Journal of Psychotherapy, 41*, 82–93.

Kinzie, J. D., Boehnlein, J. K., Leung, P. K., Moore, L. J., Riley, C., & Smith, D. (1990). The prevalence of posttraumatic stress disorder and its clinical significance among Southeast Asian refugees. *The American Journal of Psychiatry, 147*(7), 913–917.

Kinzie, J. D., & Leung, P. K. (1993). Psychiatric care of Japanese Americans. In A. C. Gaw (Ed.), *Culture, ethnicity and mental illness* (pp. 281–304). Washington, DC: American Psychiatric Press.

Kinzie, J. D., Sack, W., Angell, R., Clarke, G., & Ben, R. (1989). A three-year follow-up of Cambodian young people traumatized as children. *Journal of the American Academy of Child and Adolescent Psychiatry, 28*(4), 501–504.

Krause, N. (1983). Conflicting sex-role expectations, housework dissatisfaction, and depressive symptoms among full-time housewives. *Sex Roles, 9*(11), 1115–1125.

Krause, N. (1984). Employment outside the home and women's psychological well-being. *Social Psychiatry, 19*, 41–48.

Krause, N., & Chatters, L. M. (2005). Exploring race differences in a multidimensional battery of prayer measures among older adults. *Sociology of Religion, 66*(1), 23–43. doi: 10.2307/4153114

LaVeist, T. A. (2005). *Minority populations and health: An introduction to health disparities in the United States*. San Francisco: Jossey-Bass.

Le, C. N. (2012). Adopted Asian Americans. *Asian-Nation: The Landscape of Asian America*. Retrieved June 20, 2011, from http://www.asian-nation.org/adopted.shtml

Lee, E. (2000). *Working with Asian Americans: A guide for clinicians*. New York: Guilford.

Lee, H. A (2001). *Korean women in America: Gender-role attitude and depression* (Doctoral dissertation). Retrieved from University of Pittsburgh library website: https://sremote.pitt.edu/,DanaInfo=proquest.umi.com+pqdlink?Ver=1&Exp=09-03-2016&FMT=7&DID=725941511&RQT=309&attempt=1

Lee, I. S. (1988). *Korean-American women's experience: A study in the cultural and feminist identity formation process*. New York: Teacher's College, Columbia University.

Lee, J. (1999). Retail niche domination among African American, Jewish, and Korean entrepreneurs. *American Behavioral Scientist, 42*(9), 1398–1416. doi: 10.1177/00027649921954967

Lee, S. J., Wong, N. W. A., & Alvarez, A. N. (2009). The model minority and the perpetual foreigner: Stereotypes of Asian-Americans. In N. Tewari & A. N. Alvarez (Eds.), *Asian American psychology: Current perspectives* (pp. 69–84). New York: Taylor & Francis.

Lee, W. M. L. (1999). *An introduction to multicultural counseling*. Ann Arbor, MI: Taylor & Francis.

Leong, F. T. L. (1986). Counseling and psychotherapy with Asian-Americans: Review of the literature. *Journal of Counseling Psychology, 33*(2), 196–206. doi: 10.1037/0022-0167.33.2.196

Leong, F. T. L., & Lau, A. S. L. (2001). Barriers to providing effective mental health services to Asian Americans. *Mental Health Services Research, 3*(4), 201–214. doi: 10.1023/a:1013177014788

Lin, K.-M., & Cheung, F. (1999). Mental health issues for Asian Americans. *Psychiatric Services, 50*(6), 774–780.

Lincoln, E. C., & Mamiya, L. H. (1990). *The Black church in the African American experience*. Durham, NC: Duke University Press.

Lincoln, K., Taylor, R., Chatters, L., & Joe, S. (2012). Suicide, negative interaction and emotional support among Black Americans. *Social Psychiatry and Psychiatric Epidemiology, 47(12)*,1–12. doi: 10.1007/s00127-012-0512-y

Lopez, M. H., & Minushkin, S. (2008). *2008 national survey of Latinos: Hispanic voter attitudes*. Washington, DC: Pew Hispanic Center.

Marbley, A. F. (2011). *Multicultural counseling: Perspectives from counselors as clients of color*. New York: Taylor and Francis Group.

Markides, K. S., & Coreil, J. (1986). The health of Hispanics in the southwestern United States: An epidemiologic paradox. *Public Health Reports, 101*, 253–265.

Martin, T., & Bumpass, L. (1989). Recent trends in marital disruption. *Demography, 26*(1), 37–51. doi: 10.2307/2061492

Matsuoka, J. K., Breaux, C., & Ryujin, D. H. (1997). National utilization of mental health services by Asian Americans/Pacific Islanders. *Journal of Community Psychology, 25*(2), 141–145. doi: 10.1002/(sici)1520-6629(199703)25:2<141::aid-jcop3>3.0.co;2-0

Mazure, C. M., Keita, G. P., & Blehar, M. C. (2002). *Summit on women and depression: Proceedings and recommendations*. Washington, DC: American Psychological Association.

Merikangas, K. R., He, J.-P., Burstein, M., Swendsen, J., Avenevoli, S., Case, B., et al. (2011). Service utilization for lifetime mental disorders in U.S. adolescents: Results of the National Comorbidity Survey–Adolescent Supplement (NCS-A). *Journal of the American Academy of Child & Adolescent Psychiatry, 50*(1), 32–45. doi: 10.1016/j.jaac.2010.10.006

Mieder, W. (1993). *The only good Indian is a dead Indian: History and meaning of a proverbial stereotype*. Retrieved August 10, 2012, from http://www.dickshovel.com/ind.html#Note49

Min, P. G. (1988). Korean immigrant entrepreneurship: A multivariate analysis. *Journal of Urban Affairs, 10*(2), 197–212. doi: 10.1111/j.1467-9906.1988.tb00537.x

Min, P. G. (1996). Korean immigrant wives' increased economic role and unequal social rewards. In E. Higginbotham & M. Romero (Eds.), *Women and work: Race, ethnicity, and class*. Newbury Park, CA: Sage Publications.

Miranda, J., McGuire, T. G., Williams, D. R., & Wang, P. (2008). Mental health in the context of health disparities. *American Journal of Psychiatry, 165*(9), 1102–1108.

Mohanty, J., & Newhill, C. E. (2008). A theoretical framework for understanding ethnic socialization among international adoptees. *Families in Society, 89*, 543–550.

Mohanty, J., & Newhill, C. E. (2011). Asian adolescent adoptees' psychological well-being: Examining the mediating role of marginality. *Children and Youth Services Review, 33*(7), 1189–1195.

Mollica, R. F., Lavelle, J., & Khoun, F. (1985). *Khmer widows at highest risk*. A paper presented at the Cambodian Mental Health Conference: A Day to Explore Issues and Alternative Approaches to Care, New York.

Mollica, R. F., Wyshak, G., & Lavelle, J. (1987). The psychosocial impact of war trauma and torture on Southeast Asian refugees. *American Journal of Psychiatry, 144*, 1567–1572.

Montalvo, F. F., & Codina, G. E. (2001). Skin color and Latinos in the United States. *Ethnicities, 1*(3), 321–341. doi: 10.1177/146879680100100303

National Alliance on Mental Illness (NAMI). (2003). *American Indian and Alaska Native resource manual*. Retrieved from National Alliance on Mental Illness website: www.nami.org

National Alliance on Mental Illness (NAMI). (2009). *Women and depression*. Retrieved from National Alliance on Mental Illness website: http://www.nami.org/Content/NavigationMenu/Mental_Illnesses/Women_and_Depression/Depression_and_Asian_American_Women_Fact_Sheet.htm

National Institute of Justice and Centers for Disease Control. (2000). *Findings from the National Violence against Women Survey*

National Institute of Mental Health (NIMH). (2012, August 6). *Women and mental health*. Retrieved July 20, 2012, from http://nimh.nih.gov/health/topics/women-and-mental-health/index.shtml

National Research Council. (2006). *Hispanics and the future of America*. Washington, DC: National Academies Press.

Neighbors, H. W., Musick, M. A., & Williams, D. R. (1998). The African American minister as a source of help for serious personal crises: Bridge or barrier to mental health care? *Health Education & Behavior, 25*(6), 759–777. doi: 10.1177/109019819802500606

Neighbors, H. W., Woodward, A. T., Bullard, K. M., Ford, B. C., Taylor, R. J., & Jackson, J. S. (2008). Mental health service use among older African Americans: The

National Survey of American Life. *American Journal of Geriatric Psychiatry, 16*(12), 948–956. doi: 910.1097/JGP.1090b1013e318187ddd318183
Newhill, C. E. (1990). The role of culture in the development of paranoid symptomatology. *American Journal of Orthopsychiatry, 60*(2), 176–185. doi: 10.1037/h0079170
Newhill, C. E. (1993). Short-term treatment of a severely suicidal Japanese-American client with schizoaffective disorder. *Families in Society, 74*, 503–507.
Newhill, C. E., & Harris, D. (2008). African-American consumers' perceptions of racial disparities in mental health services. *Social Work in Public Health, 23*(2–3), 107–124.
Nguyen, S. (1982). Psychiatric and psychosomatic problems among Southeast Asian refugees. *Psychiatric Journal of Ottawa, 7*, 163–172.
Norris, D. M. (1999). African Americans and mental illness: Impasses to care. *The Journal of the California Alliance for the Mentally Ill, 10*, 22–23.
Norton, I. M., & Manson, S. M. (1996). Research in American Indian and Alaska Native communities: Navigating the cultural universe of values and process. *Journal of Consulting and Clinical Psychology, 64*(5), 856–860. doi: 10.1037/0022-006x.64.5.856
Novins, D. K., Bechtold, D. W., Sack, W. H., Thompson, J., Carter, D. R., & Manson, S. M. (1997). The DSM-IV outline for cultural formulation: A critical demonstration with American Indian children. *Journal of the American Academy of Child & Adolescent Psychiatry, 36*(9), 1244–1251. doi: 10.1097/00004583-199709000-00017
Office of Minority Health. American Indian/Alaska Native profile. Retrieved September 17, 2013 from http://minorityhealth.hhs.gov
O'Hare, W. P. (1996). A new look at poverty in America. *Population Bulletin, 51*, 1–48.
Ong, P., & Scott, M. E. (2008). Asian American projection by nativity. In P. Ong (Ed.), *The state of Asian America: Trajectory of civic and political engagement.* Los Angeles: LEAP.
Paniagua, F. A. (2005). *Assessing and treating culturally diverse clients: A practical guide* (3rd ed.). Thousand Oaks, CA: Sage.
Pascoe, E. A., & Smart Richman, L. (2009). Perceived discrimination and health: A meta-analytic review. *Psychological Bulletin, 135*(4), 531–554. doi: 10.1037/a0016059
Perez-Escamilla, R. (2010). Health care access among Latinos: Implications for social and health care reforms. *Journal of Hispanic Higher Education, 9*(1), 43–60. doi: 10.1177/1538192709349917
Pinkerton, J. V., Guico-Pabia, C. J., & Taylor, H. S. (2010). Menstrual cycle-related exacerbation of disease. *American Journal of Obstetrics and Gynecology, 202*(3), 221–231. doi: 10.1016/j.ajog.2009.07.061
Pinn, A. B. (2002). *The Black church in the post-civil rights era.* Maryknoll, NY: Orbis Books.
Proctor, E. K., & Davis, L. E. (1994). The challenge of racial difference: Skills for clinical practice. *Social Work, 39*, 314–323.
Rank, M. R. (2004). *One nation underprivileged: Why American poverty affects us all.* New York: Oxford.
Rapaport, M. H., Clar, C., Fayyad, R., & Endicott, J. (2005). Quality of life impairment in depressive and anxiety disorder. *The American Journal of Psychiatry, 162*(6), 1171–1178.
Religionlink. (2007, April 2). *Race and religion in America.* Retrieved July 31, 2012, from http://www.religionlink.com/tip_070108.php#stats
Rhee, S. (1995). Separation and divorce among Korean immigrant families. In Y. S. Kim & A. Moon (Eds.), *Korean American women from tradition to modern feminism.* Binghamton, NY: Haworth Press.
Richardson, E. H. (1999). Cultural and historical perspectives in counseling American Indians. In D. W. Sue (Ed.), *Counseling the culturally different: Theory and practice.* New York: John Wiley.
Robson, D., & Gray, R. (2007). Serious mental illness and physical health problems: A discussion paper. *International Journal of Nursing Studies, 44*(3), 457–466. doi: 10.1016/j.ijnurstu.2006.07.013
Sandoval, M. C., & De La Roza, M. C. (1986). A cultural perspective of Hispanic clients. In H. P. Lefley & P. B. Pedersen (Eds.), *Cross-cultural training for mental health professionals* (pp. 151–181). Springfield, IL: Charles C Thomas.
Schmidt, P. J., Haq, N., & Rubinow, D. R. (2004). A longitudinal evaluation of the relationship between reproductive status and mood in perimenopausal women. *The American Journal of Psychiatry, 161*, 2238–2244.
Senior, P. A., & Bhopal, R. (1994). Ethnicity as a variable in epidemiological research. *BMJ, 309*(6950), 327–330. doi: 10.1136/bmj.309.6950.327
Shore, J. H., & Manson, S. M. (2009). American Indians and Alaska Natives. In P. Ruiz & A. Primm (Eds.), *Disparities in psychiatric care: Clinical and cross-cultural perspectives* (pp. 52–61). Philadelphia: Lippincott Williams & Wilkins.
Sigelman, L., Tuch, S. A., & Martin, J. K. (2005). What's in a name? Preference for "Black" versus

"African-American" among Americans of African descent. *The Public Opinion Quarterly, 69*(3), 429–438.
Singh, G. K., & Siahpush, M. (2002). Ethnic-immigrant differentials in health behaviours, morbidity, and cause-specific mortality in the United States: An analysis of two national data bases. *Human Biology, 74*, 83–109.
Smith, S. S., & Moore, M. R. (2000). Intraracial diversity and relations among African Americans: Closeness among Black students at a predominantly White university. *American Journal of Sociology, 106*(1), 1–39.
Smith, T. W. (1992). Changing racial labels: From "Colored" to "Negro" to "Black" to "African American." *Public Opinion Quarterly, 56*(4), 496–514. doi: 10.1086/269339
Smitherman, G. (1995). Introduction. In G. Smitherman (Ed.), *African American women speak out on Anita Hill–Clarence Thomas* (pp. 7–10). Detroit: Wayne State University Press.
Sobralske, M. (2006). Machismo sustains health and illness beliefs of Mexican American men. *Journal of the American Academy of Nurse Practitioners, 18*(8), 348–350. doi: 10.1111/j.1745-7599.2006.00144.x
Stier, H. (1991). Immigrant women go to work: Analysis of immigrant wives' labor supply for six Asian groups. *Social Science Quarterly, 72*, 67–82.
Substance Abuse and Mental Health Services Administration (SAMHSA). (2000). *Summary of findings from the 1999 National Household Survey on Drug Abuse.* Rockville, MD: U.S. Department of Health and Human Services.
Substance Abuse and Mental Health Services Administration (SAMHSA). (2009). *Family psychoeducation: Getting started with evidence-based practices* (HHS Pub. No. SMA-09-4422). Rockville, MD: Center for Mental Health Services, Substance Abuse and Mental Health Services Administration U.S. Department of Health and Human Services.
Sue, D. W., & Sue, D. (1990). *Counseling the culturally different: Theory and practice* (2nd ed.). Oxford, England: John Wiley & Sons.
Sue, D. W., & Sue, D. (2003). *Counseling the culturally diverse: Theory and practice* (5th ed.). New York: John Wiley & Sons.
Sue, S., & Morishima, J. K. (1982). *The mental health of Asian Americans.* San Francisco: Jossey-Bass.
Sue, S., & Zane, N. (1987). The role of culture and cultural techniques in psychotherapy: A critique and reformulation. *American Psychologist, 42(1)*, 37–45.
Szymusiak, M. (1986). *The stones cry out: A Cambodian childhood, 1975–1980.* New York: Hill and Wang.
Taft, J. (1987). *Issues and options for refugee women in developing countries.* Washington, DC: Refugee Policy Group.
Taylor, R. J., Ellison, C. G., Chatters, L. M., Levin, J. S., & Lincoln, K. D. (2000). Mental health services in faith communities: The role of clergy in Black churches. *Social Work, 45*(1), 73–87. doi: 10.1093/sw/45.1.73
Telzer, E. H., & Vazquez Garcia, H. A. (2009). Skin color and self-perceptions of immigrant and U.S.-born Latinas. *Hispanic Journal of Behavioral Sciences, 31*(3), 357–374. doi: 10.1177/0739986309336913
Thompson, J., Walker, R. D., & Silk-Walker, P. (1993). Psychiatric care of American Indians and Alaska Natives. In A. C. Gaw (Ed.), *Culture, ethnicity, and mental illness.* Washington, DC: American Psychiatric Press.
Thompson, V. L. S., & Bazile, A. A. (2004). African Americans' perceptions of psychotherapy and psychotherapists. *Professional Psychology: Research and Practice, 35*, 19–26.
Thornton, R. (1987). *American Indian holocaust and survival.* Norman: University of Oklahoma Press.
Tseng, W. (2003). *Clinician's guide to cultural psychiatry.* New York: Academic.
Tseng, W., & Streltzer, J. (2008). *Cultural competence in health care.* New York: Springer.
Tsui, P., & Schultz, G. L. (1985). Failure of rapport: Why psychotherapeutic engagement fails in the treatment of Asian clients. *American Journal of Orthopsychiatry, 55*(4), 561–569. doi: 10.1111/j.1939-0025.1985.tb02706.x
Tyler, K. A. (2002). Social and emotional outcomes of childhood sexual abuse: A review of recent research. *Aggression and Violent Behavior, 7*(6), 567–589. doi: 10.1016/s1359-1789(01)00047-7
U.S. Census Bureau. (1999). *Statistical abstract of the United States.* Washington, DC: Author.
U.S. Census Bureau. (2001). *Profiles of general demographic characteristics: 2000 census of population and housing.* Washington DC: Department of Commerce.
U.S. Census Bureau. (2003a). *Language use and English-speaking ability: 2000. Census 2000 brief.* Washington DC: Department of Commerce.
U.S. Census Bureau. (2003b). *Marital status: 2000. Census 2000 brief.* Retrieved June 30, 2012, from http://www.census.gov/hhes/socdemo/language/
U.S. Census Bureau. (2006a). *Hispanics in the United States.* Washington, DC: Ethnicity and Ancestry Branch Population Division.
U.S. Census Bureau. (2006b). *We the people: American Indians and Alaska Natives in the United States.*

Census 2000 special reports. Washington, DC: Department of Commerce.

U.S. Census Bureau. (2008). *Income, earnings, and poverty data from the 2007 American Community Survey*. Washington, DC: Department of Commerce.

U.S. Census Bureau. (2010a). *Income, poverty, and health insurance coverage in the United States: 2009*. Washington, DC: Department of Commerce.

U.S. Census Bureau. (2011a). *Overview of race and Hispanic origin: 2010*. Washington, DC: U.S. Department of Commerce.

U.S. Census Bureau. (2011b). *The Black population: 2010. 2010 census briefs*. Washington, DC: Department of Commerce.

U.S. Census Bureau. (2012a). *Detailed language spoken at home and ability to speak English for the population 5 years and older by states: 2006–2008 (ACS)*. Retrieved June 30, 2012, from http://www.census.gov/hhes/socdemo/language/

U.S. Census Bureau. (2012b). *Income, poverty, and health insurance coverage in the United States: 2009*. Washington, DC: Department of Commerce.

U.S. Census Bureau. (2012c). *The American Indian and Alaska Native population: 2010. 2010 census briefs*. Washington, DC: Department of Commerce.

U.S. Census Bureau. (2012d). *The Asian population: 2010. 2010 census briefs*. Washington, DC: Department of Commerce.

U.S. Department of Health and Human Services (DHHS). (2001a). *Mental health: Culture, race and ethnicity—A supplement to mental health: A report of the Surgeon General*. Rockville, MD: U.S. Department of Health and Human Services, Public Health Service, Office of the Surgeon General.

U.S. Department of Health and Human Services (DHHS). (2001b). *Mental health: Culture, race and ethnicity—A supplement to mental health: A report of the Surgeon General: Executive summary*. Rockville, MD: U.S. Department of Health and Human Services, Public Health Service, Office of the Surgeon General.

U.S. Department of Homeland Security (DHS). (2011). *2010 yearbook of immigration statistics*. Washington, DC: Office of Immigration Statistics.

U.S. Department of Justice. (2011). *Correctional population in the United States, 2010*. Washington, DC: Office of Justice Programs.

Van Boemel, G. B., & Rozee, P. D. (1992). Treatment for psychosomatic blindness among Cambodian refugee women. In E. Cole, O. M. Espin, & E. D. Rothblum (Eds.), *Refugee women and their mental health: Shattered societies, shattered lives* (pp. 239–266). New York: Haworth Press, Inc.

Van Fossen, B. E. (1981). Sex differences in the mental health effects of spouse support and equity. *Journal of Health and Social Behavior, 22*, 130–143.

Van Overhagen, M. (1990). Introduction. In M. van den Engel (Ed.), *VENA newsletter: Refugee and displaced women* (V2, n2, pp. 3–6). The Netherlands.

Vega, W. A., Alderete, E., Kolody, B., & Aguilar-Gaxiola, S. (1998). Illicit drug use among Mexicans and Mexican Americans in California: The effects of gender and acculturation. *Addiction, 93*, 1839–1850.

Vega, W. A., Kolody, B., Aguilar-Gaxiola, S., Alderete, E., Catalano, R., & Caraveo-Anduaga, H. (1998). Lifetime prevalence of DSM-III-R psychiatric disorders among urban and rural Mexican Americans in California. *Archives of General Psychiatry, 55*, 771–778.

Waldram, J. B. (2004). *Revenge of the windigo: The construction of the mind and mental health of North American aboriginal peoples*. Toronto: University of Toronto Press.

Walker, R. D., & LaDue, R. (1986). An integrative approach to American Indian mental health. In C. B. Wilkinson (Ed.), *Ethnic psychiatry*. New York: Plenum Medical.

Walters, K. L., & Simoni, J. M. (2009). Decolonizing strategies for mentoring American Indians and Alaska Natives in HIV and mental health research. *American Journal of Public Health, 99*, S71–S76.

Wan, K. W. (2008). Mental health and poverty. *The Journal of the Royal Society for the Promotion of Health, 128*(3), 108–109. doi: 10.1177/14664240081280030902

Weaver, A. J., Flannelly, K. J., Flannelly, L. T., & Oppenheimer, J. E. (2003). Collaboration between clergy and mental health professionals: A review of professional health care journals from 1980 through 1999. *Counseling and Values, 47*(3), 162–171. doi: 10.1002/j.2161-007X.2003.tb00263.x

Welch, M. (2003). Care of Blacks and African Americans. In J. A. Bigby (Ed.), *Cross-cultural medicine* (pp. 29–60). Philadelphia: American College of Physicians.

Whaley, A. L., & Hall, B. N. (2009). Effects of cultural themes in psychotic symptoms on the diagnosis of schizophrenia in African Americans. *Mental Health, Religion & Culture, 12*(5), 457–471. doi: 10.1080/13674670902758273

Wilkinson, C. B., & Spurlock, J. (1986). The mental health of Black Americans: Psychiatric diagnosis and treatment. In C. B. Wilkinson (Ed.), *Ethnic psychiatry* (pp. 31–54). Littleton, MA: Wright.

Williams, D. R., González, H. M., Neighbors, H. W., Nesse, R., Abelson, J. M., Sweetman, J., et al. (2007). Prevalence and distribution of major depressive disorder in African Americans, Caribbean Blacks, and non-Hispanic Whites: Results from the National Survey of American Life. *Archives of General Psychiatry, 64*(3), 305–315. doi: 10.1001/archpsyc.64.3.305

Wong, E. C., Palaniappan, L. P., & Lauderdale, D. S. (2010). Using name lists to infer Asian racial/ethnic subgroups in the healthcare setting. *Medicare, 48*(6), 540–546.

Wong, M. M., Klingle, R. S., & Price, R. K. (2004). Alcohol, tobacco, and other drug use among Asian American and Pacific Islander adolescents in California and Hawaii. *Addictive Behaviors, 29*(1), 127–141. doi: 10.1016/s0306-4603(03)00079-0

Wu, F. (2003). *Yellow: Race in America beyond Black and White.* New York: Basic.

Yamamoto, J. (1986). Therapy for Asian Americans and Pacific Islanders. In C. B. Wilkinson (Ed.), *Ethnic psychiatry* (pp. 89–141). New York: Plenum.

Yeh, C. J., Kim, A. B., Pituc, S. T., & Atkins, M. (2008). Poverty, loss, and resilience: The story of Chinese immigrant youth. *Journal of Counseling Psychology, 55*(1), 34–48.

Yellow Horse Brave Heart, M., & Chase, J. (2005). Social work practice with First Nations peoples. In D. Lum (Ed.), *Cultural competence, practice stages, and client systems: A case study approach.* Belmont, CA: Brooks/Cole.

Yen, I., & Syme, S. L. (1999). The social environment and health: A discussion of the epidemiologic literature. *Annual Review of Public Health, 20*(1), 287–309.

Ying, Y.-W., & Han, M. (2007). Familism and mental health: Variation between Asian American children of refugees and immigrants. *International Journal of Applied Psychoanalytic Studies, 4*(4), 333–348. doi: 10.1002/aps.106

Zhou, H.-H., Koshakji, R. P., Silberstein, D. J., Wilkinson, G. R., & Wood, A. J. J. (1989). Racial differences in drug response. *New England Journal of Medicine, 320*(9), 565–570. doi: 10.1056/NEJM198903023200905

Zinn, M. C. (1994). Adaptation and continuity in Mexican-origin families. In R. L. Taylor (Ed.), *Minority families in the United States.* Englewood Cliffs, NJ: Prentice Hall.

CHAPTER 7

American Mental Health Fund (Producer). (1987). *Mental illness: Awareness and hope [VHS].* Retrieved from www.nmha.org

Anderson, C. M., Reiss, D. J., & Hogarty, G. E. (1986). *Schizophrenia and the family.* New York: Guilford.

Bateson, G., Jackson, D. D., Haley, J., & Weakland, J. (1956). Toward a theory of schizophrenia. *Behavioral Science, 1,* 251–264.

Butler, K. (2006, February 28). Beyond rivalry, a hidden world of sibling violence. *The New York Times.*

Cardno, A. G., Marshall, E. J., Coid, B., Macdonald, A. M., Ribchester, T. R., Davies, N. J., et al. (1999). Heritability estimates for psychotic disorders: The Maudsley twin psychosis series. *Archives of General Psychiatry, 56*(2), 162–168.

Colom, F., & Vieta, E. (2006). *Psychoeducation manual for bipolar disorder.* Cambridge, UK: Cambridge University.

Dickerson, F., & Lehman, A. (2006). Evidence-based psychotherapy for schizophrenia. *Journal of Nervous and Mental Disease, 194,* 3–9.

Dixon, L., Lucksted, A., Stewart, B., Burland, J., Brown, C. H., Postrado, L., et al. Outcomes of the peer-taught 12-week family-to-family education program for severe mental illness. *Acta Psychiatrica Scandinavica, 109,* 207–215.

Dixon, L., McFarlane, W., Lefley, H., Lucksted, A., Cohen, M., Falloon, I., et al. (2001). Evidence-based practices for services to families of people with psychiatric disabilities. *Psychiatric Services, 52,* 903–910.

Emrick, C. D. (1987). Alcoholics Anonymous: Affiliation processes and effectiveness as treatment. *Alcoholism: Clinical and Experimental Research, 11*(5), 416–423. doi: 10.1111/j.1530-0277.1987.tb01915.x

Falloon, I. R. H., Boyd, J. L., & McGill, C. W. (1984). *Family care of schizophrenia.* New York: Guilford.

Falloon, I. R. H., Held, T., Coverdale, J. H., Roncone, R., & Laidlaw, T. M. (1999). Family intervention for schizophrenia: A review of long-term benefits of international studies. *Psychiatric Rehabilitation Skills, 3,* 268–290.

Ferreira, A. J., & Winter, W. D. (1965). Family interaction and decision making. *Archives of General Psychiatry, 13*(3), 214–223.

Frank, E. (2005). *Treating bipolar disorder: A clinician's guide to interpersonal and social rhythm therapy.* New York: Guilford.

Freud, S. (1914). *The psychopathology of everyday life.* New York: Macmillan.

Fromm-Reichmann, F. (1948). Notes on the development of treatment of schizophrenics by psychoanalytic psychotherapy. *Psychiatry, 11*, 263–273.

Gross, J. (2004, December 10). For siblings of the autistic, a burdened youth. *The New York Times.*

Gunderson, J. G., & Hoffman, P. D. (2005). *Understanding and treating borderline personality disorder: A guide for professionals and families.* Washington, DC: American Psychiatric Press.

Hooley, J. (1985). Expressed emotion: A review of the critical literature. *Clinical Psychology Review, 5*(2), 119–139.

Johnson, J. T. (1988). *Hidden victims: An eight-stage healing process for families and friends of the mentally ill.* New York: Doubleday.

Johnson, J. T. (2007). *Hidden victims hidden healers: An eight-stage healing process for families and friends of the mentally ill.* Everett, MA: Pema.

Kopelowicz, A., Zarate, R., Wallace, C. J., Liberman, R. P., Lopez, S. R., & Mintz, J. (2012). The ability of multifamily groups to improve treatment adherence to Mexican-Americans with schizophrenia. *Archives of General Psychiatry, 69*(3), 265–273.

Kottgen, C., Mollenbauer, K., Sonnischen, I., Jurth, R., & Hand, I. (1983). *The Camberwell Family Interview as a diagnostic and therapeutic tool.* Paper presented to the 7th International World Congress of Psychiatry, Vienna, Austria.

Kuipers, L. (1979). Expressed emotion: A review. *British Journal of Social and Clinical Psychology, 18*, 237–243.

Kuipers, L., Sturgeon, I., Berkowitz, R., & Ixff, J. (1983). Characteristics of expressed emotion: Its relationship to speech and looking in schizophrenic patients and their relatives. *British Journal of Clinical Psychology, 22*, 257–264.

Lefley, H. P. (2009). *Family psychoeducation for serious mental illness.* New York: Oxford.

Lidz, R. W., & Lidz, D. (1949). The family environment of schizophrenic patients. *American Journal of Psychiatry, 106*, 332–345.

Lidz, T., Fleck, S., & Cornelison, A. R. (1965). *Schizophrenia and the family.* New York: International Universities Press.

Lin, W., Mack, D., Enright, R. D., Krahn, D., & Baskin, T. W. (2004). Effects of forgiveness therapy on anger, mood, and vulnerability to substance use among inpatient substance-dependent clients. *Journal of Consulting and Clinical Psychology, 72*(6), 1114–1121. doi: 10.1037/0022-006X.72.6.1114

Marsh, D., & Dickens, R. M. (1997). *Troubled journey: Coming to terms with the mental illness of a sibling or parent.* New York: Tarcher.

Marsh, D. T., Appleby, N. F., Dickens, R. M., Owens, M., & Young, N. O. (1993). Anguished voices: Impact of mental illness on siblings and children. *Innovations and Research, 2*, 26–34.

Marsh, D. T., & Lefley, H. P. (2003). Family interventions for schizophrenia. *Journal of Family Psychotherapy, 14(2)*, 47–67.

Mason, P. T., & Kreger, R. (1998). *Stop walking on eggshells: Taking your life back when someone you care about has borderline personality disorder.* Oakland, CA: New Harbinger.

McFarlane, W. R., Dixon, L., Lukens, E., & Lucksted, A. (2003). Family psychoeducation and schizophrenia: A review of the literature. *Journal of Marital and Family Therapy, 29*(2), 223–246.

Mental Health America (MHA). (n.d.). *Mental illness in the family. Part 1: Recognizing the warning signs & how to cope.* Retrieved June 2, 2011, from http://www.mentalhealthamerica.net

Mental Illness Education Project (Producer). (2000). *Dual diagnosis: An integrated model for the treatment of people with co-occurring psychiatric and substance disorders [VHS].* Retrieved from www.miepvideos.org

Miller, S. B. (1995). *When parents have problems: A book for teens and older children with an abusive, alcoholic, or mentally ill parent.* Springfield, IL: Charles C. Thomas.

National Alliance on Mental Illness (NAMI). *Family-to-family education program.* (2011). Retrieved June 2, 2011, from http://www.nami.org

Newhill, C. E. (1995). *A mental health casebook.* Unpublished manuscript.

Nuechterlein, K. H., & Dawson, M. E. (1984). A heuristic vulnerability/stress model of schizophrenic episodes. *Schizophrenia Bulletin, 10*(2), 300–312.

Nuechterlein, K. H., Dawson, M. E., Ventura, J., Gitlin, M., Subotnik, K. L., Snyder, K. S., et al. (1994). The vulnerability/stress model of schizophrenic relapse: A longitudinal study. *Acta Psychiatrica Scandinavica Supplement, 382*, 58–64.

Reed, G. L., & Enright, R. D. (2006). The effects of forgiveness therapy on depression, anxiety, and posttraumatic stress for women after spousal emotional abuse. *Journal of Consulting and Clinical Psychology, 74*(5), 920–929.

Rosen, L. E., & Amador, X. F. (1996). *When someone you love is depressed: How to help your loved one without losing yourself.* New York: Free.

Rotondi, A. J., Anderson, C. M., Haas, G. L., Eack, S. M., Spring, M. B., Ganguli, R., Newhill, C. E., & Rosenstock, J. (2010). Web-based psychoeducational intervention for persons with schizophrenia and their supporters: One-year outcomes. *Psychiatric Services, 61*(11), 1099–1105.

Rubin, A., Cardenas, J., Warren, K., Pike, C. K., & Wambach, K. (1998). Outdated practitioner views about family culpability and severe mental disorders. *Social Work, 43*(5), 412–422.

Sharan, S. N. (1966). Family interaction with schizophrenics and their siblings. *Journal of Abnormal Psychology, 71*(5), 345–353.

Solomon, A. (2012). *Far from the tree: Parents, children and the search for identity.* New York: Scribner.

Substance Abuse and Mental Health Services Administration (SAMHSA). (2009). *Family psychoeducation: Getting started with evidence-based practices* (HHS Pub. No. SMA-09-4422). Rockville, MD: Center for Mental Health Services, Substance Abuse and Mental Health Services Administration U.S. Department of Health and Human Services.

Substance Abuse and Mental Health Services Administration (SAMHSA). (2010). *Mental health, United States, 2008* (HHS Publication No. SMA-10-4590). Rockville, MD: Center for Mental Health Services, Substance Abuse and Mental Health Services Administration.

Tecce, J. J. & Cole, J. O. (1976). The distraction-arousal hypothesis, CNV and schizophrenia. In D. I. Mostofsky (Ed.), *Behavior control and modification of physiological activity.* Englewood Cliffs, N.J.: Prentice-Hall.

Torrey, E. F. (2006). *Surviving schizophrenia: A manual for families, patients, and providers* (5th ed.). New York: Harper.

Torrey, W. C., Drake, R. E., Dixon, L., Burns, B. J., Flynn, L., Rush, A. J., et al. (2001). Implementing evidence-based practices for persons with severe mental illnesses. *Psychiatric Services, 52*, 45–50.

University of Iowa Hospitals and Clinics (Producer) & Nancy Andreasen (Primary Contributor and Director). (1995). *Negative symptoms in schizophrenia [VHS].* Retrieved from www.amazon.com

Walsh, J. (2010). *Psychoeducation in mental health.* Chicago: Lyceum.

Warner, J. (2011). *We've got issues: Children and parents in the age of medication.* New York: Riverhead.

Williams, C. A. (1989). Patient education for people with schizophrenia. *Perspectives in Psychiatric Care, 25*(2), 14–21.

Yank, G. R., Bentley, K. J., & Hargrove, D. S. (1993). The vulnerability-stress model of schizophrenia: Advances in psychosocial treatment. *American Journal of Orthopsychiatry, 63*(1), 55–69.

CHAPTER 8

Altshuler, L. L., Cohen, L., Szuba, M. P., Burt, V. K., Gitlin, M., & Mintz, J. (1996). Pharmacologic management of psychiatric illness during pregnancy: Dilemmas and guidelines. *American Journal of Psychiatry, 153*, 592–606.

Austrian, S. G. (2005). *Mental disorders, medications, and clinical social work* (3rd ed.). New York: Columbia University Press.

Ayuso-Gutierrez, J. L., & del Rio Vega, J. M. (1997). Factors influencing relapse in the long-term course of schizophrenia. *Schizophrenia Research, 28*, 199–206.

Bavley, A. (2009, July 19). Medication errors harm millions of Americans each year. *Kansas City Star.*

Bender, E. (2004, November). Clinical and research news: Ethnicity shouldn't determine dosage decisions. *Psychiatric News, 39*. Retrieved September 7, 2009, from http://pn.psychiatryonline.org/cgi/content/full/39/22/22

Bentley, K. J., & Walsh, J. F. (2001). *The social worker and psychotropic medication: Toward effective collaboration with mental health clients, families, and providers* (2nd ed.). Belmont, CA: Brooks-Cole/Thomson Learning.

Bentley, K. J., & Walsh, J. F. (2005). *The social worker and psychotropic medication: Toward effective collaboration with mental health clients, families, and providers* (3rd ed.). Belmont, CA: Brooks-Cole/Thomson Learning.

Bentley, K. J., & Walsh, J. F. (2013). *The social worker and psychotropic medication* (4th ed.). Belmont, CA: Brooks-Cole/Thomson Learning.

Benzer, T. I. (2007). Neuroleptic malignant syndrome. *Medscape*. Retrieved July 22, 2009, from http://emedicine.medscape.com/article/816018-overview

Council on Social Work Education (CSWE). (1990). *Psychopharmacology in social work education: A contract report.* Alexandria, VA: Author.

De La Rosa, M. (1988). Puerto Rican spiritualism: A key dimension for effective social casework practice. *International Social Work, 31*, 273–283.

Diamond, R. J. (2009). *Instant psychopharmacology* (3rd ed.). New York: Norton.

Dziegielewski, S. (2009). *Social work practice and psychopharmacology* (2nd ed.). New York: Springer.

Dziegielewski, S. F., & Leon, A. M. (2001). *Social work practice and psychopharmacology.* New York: Springer.

Ettorre, E., & Riska, E. (1995). *Gendered moods.* London, UK: Routledge.

Galanter, M., & Kleber, H. D. (Eds.). (2008). *The American Psychiatric Publishing textbook of substance abuse treatment.* Washington, DC: American Psychiatric Publishing.

Gray, F. D. (2002). *The Tuskegee syphilis study: The real story and beyond.* Montgomery, AL: NewSouth.

Gray, M., Coates, J., & Yellow Bird, M. (Eds.). (2008). *Indigenous social work around the world.* Hampshire, UK: Ashgate.

Guy, W. (1976). *Assessment manual for psychopharmacology* (Rev. ed.). Washington, DC: U.S. Department of Health, Education and Welfare.

Hall-Flavin, D. K. (2009). Antidepressants and alcohol: What is the concern? *Mayo Clinic website.* Retrieved July 22, 2009, from www.mayoclinic.com

Heller, J. (1972, July 26). Syphilis victims in U.S. study went untreated for 40 years: Syphilis victims got no therapy. *The New York Times.*

Johnson, H. C. (1999). *Psyche, synapse, and substance: The role of neurobiology in emotions, behavior, thinking, and addiction for non-scientists.* Greenfield, MA: Deerfield Valley.

King, W. D. (2003). Examining African-Americans' mistrust of the health care system: Expanding the research question. *Public Health Reports, 118,* 366–367.

Kleinfield, N. R. (2006, June 12). In diabetes, one more burden for the mentally ill. *The New York Times.*

Lacro, J. P., Dunn, L. B., Dolder, C. R., Leckband, S. G., & Jeste, D. V. (2002). Prevalence of and risk factors for medication nonadherence in patients with schizophrenia: A comprehensive review of recent literature. *Journal of Clinical Psychiatry, 63,* 892–909.

Lin, K. M., Cheung, F., Smith, M., & Poland, R. E. (1997). The use of psychotropic medications in working with Asian patients. In E. Lee (Ed.), *Working with Asian Americans: A guide for clinicians* (pp. 388–399). New York: Guilford.

Mackay, A. V. (1994). High-dose antipsychotic medication. *Advances in Psychiatric Treatment, 1,* 16–23.

Mahmood, T., Silverstone, T., & Spittle, B. (1996). Risperidone appears safe in patients with antipsychotic-induced blood dyscrasias. *International Journal of Clinical Psychopharmacology, 11,* 53–54.

Melin, G. J. (2009). Pristiq: New antidepressant medication approved. *Mayo Clinic website.* Retrieved July 24, 2009, from http://www.mayoclinic.com/health/pristiq/MY00538

Munetz, M. R., & Benjamin, S. (1988). How to examine patients using the Abnormal Involuntary Movement Scale. *Hospital and Community Psychiatry, 39,* 1172–1177.

Nair, P., & Lippman, S. (2005). Blood dyscrasia with quetiapine and ziprasidone. *Psychosomatics, 46,* 89–90.

National Institute of Mental Health (NIMH). (2005). *Medications for mental illness* (NIH Publication No. 05-3929). Washington, DC: U.S. Department of Health and Human Services, National Institutes of Health.

National Institute of Mental Health (NIMH). (2009). *Bipolar disorder* (NIH Publication No. 09-3679). Washington, DC: U.S. Department of Health and Human Services, National Institutes of Health.

Newham, J. J., Thomas, S. H., MacRitchie, K., McElhatton, P. R., & McAllister-Williams, R. H. (2008). Birth weight of infants after maternal exposure to typical and atypical antipsychotics: Prospective comparison study. *British Journal of Psychiatry, 192,* 333–337.

Newhill, C. E. (1990). The role of culture in the development of paranoid symptomatology. *American Journal of Orthopsychiatry, 60,* 176–185.

Newhill, C. E. (1995). *A mental health casebook.* Unpublished manuscript.

Newhill, C. E. & Cahalane, H. G. (2003). *Client perceptions of medication treatment: An informational video for social workers.* Pittsburgh, PA: University of Pittsburgh School of Social Work.

Newhill, C. E., & Harris, D. (2007). *African-American consumer project field notes.* Unpublished manuscript.

Oberlander, T. F., Warburton, W., Misri, S., Aghajanian, J., & Hertzman, C. (2008). Effects of timing and duration of gestational exposure to serotonin reuptake inhibitor antidepressants: Population-based study. *British Journal of Psychiatry, 192,* 338–343.

Paton, C. (2008). Prescribing in pregnancy. *British Journal of Psychiatry, 192,* 321–322.

Petersen, M. (2004, February 1). Making drugs, shaping the rules. *The New York Times.*

Physician's Desk Reference staff. (2007). *PDR drug guide for mental health professionals* (3rd ed.). Des Moines, IA: Thomson Reuters.

Physician's Desk Reference staff. (2009). *Physician's desk reference* (63rd ed.). Des Moines, IA: Thomson Reuters.

Piepho, R. W. (2002). Cardiovascular effects of antipsychotics used in bipolar illness. *Journal of Clinical Psychiatry, 63*(suppl. 4), 20–23.

Preston, J., & Johnson, J. (2012). *Clinical psychopharmacology made ridiculously simple* (7th ed.). Miami: Medmaster.

Preston, J. D., O'Neal, J. H., & Talaga, M. C. (2005a). *The consumer's guide to psychiatric drugs* (new updated edition). Oakland, CA: New Harbinger.

Preston, J. D., O'Neal, J. H., & Talaga, M. C. (2005b). *Handbook of clinical psychopharmacology for therapists* (4th ed.). Oakland, CA: New Harbinger.

Ramos, E., St-André, M., Évelyne, R. E., Oraichi, D., & Bérard, E. (2008). Duration of antidepressant use during pregnancy and risk of major congenital malformations. *British Journal of Psychiatry, 192*, 344–350.

Rampulla, J. (n.d.). Hyperthermia and heat stroke: Heat related conditions. *Health Care of Homeless Persons: Part II*. Retrieved September 1, 2009, from http://www.nhchc.org/Hyperthermia.pdf

Sachs, G. S., Nierenberg, A. A., Calabrese, J. R., Marangell, L. B., Wisniewski, S. R., Gyulai, L., et al. (2007). Effectiveness of adjunctive antidepressant treatment for bipolar depression. *The New England Journal of Medicine, 356*(17), 1711–1722.

Samuels, S. C., & Neugroschl, J. A. (2005). Delirium. In B. J. Sadock & V. A. Sadock (Eds.), *Kaplan & Sadock's comprehensive textbook of psychiatry* (8th edition, Vol. II, pp. 1054–1068). Philadelphia: Lippincott Williams & Wilkins.

Sue, D. W., & Sue, S. (1999). *Counseling the culturally different: Theory and practice* (3rd ed.). New York: Wiley.

The TalkingDrum. (2009). Retrieved August 11, 2009, from www.thetalkingdrum.com/tus.html

Thase, M. E., & Sachs, G. S. (2000). Bipolar depression: Pharmacotherapy and related therapeutic strategies. *Biological Psychiatry, 48*(6), 558–572.

Tohen, M., Sanger, T. M., McElroy, S. L., Tollefson, G. D., Chengappy, K. N., Daniel, D. G., et al. (1999). Olanzapine versus placebo in the treatment of acute mania. *American Journal of Psychiatry, 156*(5), 702–709.

U.S. Department of Health and Human Services (DHHS). (1999). *Mental health: Culture, race and ethnicity—A supplement to mental health: A report of the Surgeon General*. Rockville, MD: U.S. Department of Health and Human Services, Public Health Service, Office of the Surgeon General.

Wegmann, J. (2012). *Psychopharmacology: Straight talk on mental health medications*. Eau Claire, WI: Premier Publishing & Media.

Weiden, P. J., Kozma, C., Grogg, A., & Locklear, J. (2004). Partial compliance and risk of rehospitalization among California Medicaid patients with schizophrenia. *Psychiatric Services, 55*, 886–891.

Weiden, P. J., Scheifler, P. L., Diamond, R. J., & Ross, R. (1999). *Breakthroughs in antipsychotic medications: A guide for consumers, families, and clinicians*. New York: Norton.

Weiden, P. J., & Zygmunt, A. (1996). The road back: Working with the severely mentally ill: Medication noncompliance in schizophrenia: Part 1. Assessment. *Journal of Psychiatric Practice, 2*, 106–110.

Wolf, M. E., & Mosnaim, A. D. (Eds.). (1988). *Tardive dyskinesia*. Washington, DC: American Psychiatric Press.

Yonkers, K. A., & Ellison, J. M. (1996). Anxiety disorders in women and their pharmacological treatment. In M. F. Jensfold, U. Halbreich, & J. A. Hamilton (Eds.), *Psychopharmacology and women* (pp. 261–285). Washington, DC: American Psychiatric Press.

CHAPTER 9

Allen, M. (1996). Separate and unequal: The struggle of tenants with mental illness to maintain housing. *Clearinghouse Review, 30*, 720–739.

Andersen, A., & Sherwood, K. E. (2000). *Connecticut supportive housing demonstration program: Final program evaluation report*. New Haven: Connecticut Corporation for Supportive Housing.

Bailey, E. L., Ricketts, S. K., Becker, D. R., Xie, H., & Drake, R. E. (1998). Do long-term day treatment clients benefit from supported employment? *Psychiatric Rehabilitation Journal, 22*(1), 24–29.

Becker, D. R., & Drake, R. E. (2003). *A working life for people with severe mental illness*. New York: Oxford University Press.

Becker, D. R., & Drake, R. E. (n.d.). *Supported employment for people with severe mental illness: A guideline developed for the Behavioral Health Recovery Management Project*. Retrieved June 30, 2011, from http://www.bhrm.org/guidelines

Bond, G. R. (2004). Supported employment: Evidence for an evidencebased practice. *Psychiatric Rehabilitation Journal, 27*(4), 345–359.

Bond, G. R., Becker, D. R., Drake, R. E., Rapp, C. A., Meisler, N., Lehman, A. F., et al. (2001). Implementing supported employment as an evidencebased practice. *Psychiatric Services, 52*(3), 313–322.

Bond, G. R., Dietzen, L. L., & McGrew, J. H. (1995). Accelerating entry into supported employment for persons with severe psychiatric disabilities. *Rehabilitation Psychology, 40*, 91–111.

Bond, G. R., Drake, R. E., Mueser, K. T., & Latimer, E. (2001). Assertive community treatment for people with severe mental illness: Critical ingredients and impact on patients. *Disease management and health outcomes, 9*(3), 141–159.

Bond, G. R., McGrew, J. H., & Fekete, D. M. (1995). Assertive outreach for frequent users of psychiatric hospitals: A meta-analysis. *Journal of Mental Health Administration, 22*, 4–16.

Burns, B. J., & Santos, A. B. (1995). Assertive community treatment: An update of randomized trials. *Psychiatric Services, 46*(7), 669–757.

Chandler, D., Meisel, J., Hu, T., McGowen, M., & Madison, K. (1997). A capitated model for a cross-section of severely mentally ill clients: Employment outcomes. *Community Mental Health Journal, 33*, 501–516.

Chow, W., Law, S., & Andermann, L. (2009). ACT tailored for ethnocultural communities of metropolitan Toronto. *Psychiatric Services, 60*(6), 847.

Coldwell, C. M., & Bender, W. S. (2007). The effectiveness of assertive community treatment for homeless populations with severe mental illness: A meta-analysis. *American Journal of Psychiatry, 161*(3), 393–399.

Consensus Conference on Mental Health Recovery. (2004). Sponsored by the Center for Mental Health Services of the Substance Abuse and Mental Health Services Administration. Washington, DC: U.S. Department of Health and Human Services.

Corrigan, P. W., & McCracken, S. G. (2005). Place first, then train: An alternative to the medical model of psychiatric rehabilitation. *Social Work, 50*, 31–39.

Culhane, D. P., Metraux, S., & Hadley, T. (2002). Public service reductions associated with placement of homeless persons with severe mental illness in supportive housing. *Housing Policy Debate, 13*(1), 107–163.

De Beer-Wunderink, C., Visser, E., Sytema, S., & Wiersma, D. (2012). Social inclusion of people with severe mental illness living in community housing programs. *Psychiatric Services, 63*(11), 1102–1107.

Dillon, C. (2003). *Learning from mistakes in clinical practice.* Pacific Grove, CA: Brooks/Cole.

Drake, R. E., Becker, D. R., Biesanz, J. C., Torrey, W. C., McHugo, G. J., & Wyzik, P. F. (1994). Rehabilitative day treatment vs. supported employment: I. Vocational outcomes. *Community Mental Health Journal, 30*, 519–532.

Drake, R. E., Becker, D. R., Biesanz, J. C., Wyzik, P. F., & Torrey, W. C. (1996). Day treatment versus supported employment for persons with severe mental illness: A replication study. *Psychiatric Services, 47*, 1125–1127.

Drake, R. E., McHugo, G. J., Bebont, R. R., Becker, D. R., Harris, M., Bond, G. R., & Quimby, E. (1999). A randomized clinical trial of supported employment for inner-city patients with severe mental illness. *Archives of General Psychiatry, 56*, 627–633.

Drake, R. E., McHugo, G. J., Becker, D. R., Anthony, W. A., & Clark, R. E. (1996). The New Hampshire study of supported employment for people with severe mental illness: Vocational outcomes. *Journal of Consulting and Clinical Psychology, 64*, 391–399.

Eack, S. M., Anderson, C. M., & Greeno, C. G. (2012). *Mental health case management: A practical guide.* Thousand Oaks, CA: Sage.

Erickson, S. K., Lamberti, J. S., Weisman, R., Crilly, J., Nihalani, N., Stefanovics, E., et al. (2009). Predictors of arrest during forensic assertive community treatment. *Psychiatric Services, 60*(6), 834–837.

Flynn, R. J., & Nitsch, K. E. (Eds.). (1980). *Normalization, social integration and community services.* Baltimore: University Park Press.

Fukui, S., Goscha, R., Rapp, C. A., Mabry, A., Liddy, P., & Marty, D. (2012). Strengths model case management fidelity scores and client outcomes. *Psychiatric Services, 63*(7), 708–710.

Gervey, R., & Bedell, J. R. (1994). Supported employment in vocational rehabilitation. In J. R. Bedell (Ed.), *Psychological assessment and treatment of persons with severe mental disorders.* Washington, DC: Taylor & Francis.

Gold, P. B., Meisler, N., Santos, A. B., Keleher, J., Becker, D. R., Knoedler, W. H., et al. (2003). The program of assertive community treatment: Implementation and dissemination of an evidence-based model of community-based care for persons with severe and persistent mental illness. *Cognitive and Behavioral Practice, 10*, 290–303.

Greenwood, R. M., Schaefer-McDaneil, N. J., Winkel, G., & Tsemberis, S. J. (2005). Decreasing psychiatric symptoms by increasing choice in services for adults with histories of homelessness. *American Journal of Community Psychology, 36*, 223–238.

Henwood, B. F., Padgett, D. K., & Nguyen, D. (2011). Consumer and case manager agreement on needs assessments in programs for homeless adults with serious mental illness. *Journal of the Society for Social Work and Research, 2*, 143–148.

Hepworth, D. H., Rooney, R. H., Rooney, G. D., & Strom-Gottfried, K. (2010). *Direct social work practice: Theory and skills.* Belmont, CA: Brooks/Cole.

Herdelin, A. C., & Scott, D. L. (1999). Experimental studies of the program of assertive community treatment (PACT): A meta-analysis. *Journal of Disability Policy Studies, 10*(1), 53–89.

Holschuh, J., & Segal, S. P. (2002). Factors related to multiplexity in support networks of persons with severe mental illness. In J. A. Levy & B. A. Pescosolido (Eds.), *Advances in Medical Sociology: Vol. 8. Social networks and health* (pp. 293–321). Emerald Group Publishing Limited.

Institute of Medicine (IOM). (2011). *The health of lesbian, gay, bisexual, and transgender people: Building a foundation for better understanding.* Washington, DC: The National Academies Press.

Kanter, J. (1989). Clinical case management: Definition, principles, components. *Hospital and Community Psychiatry, 40*(4), 361–368.

Larimer, E. L., Malone, D. K., Garner, M. D., Atkins, D. C., Burlingham, B., Lonczak, H. S., et al. (2009). Health care and public service use and costs before and after provision of housing for chronically homeless persons with severe alcohol problems. *JAMA, 301*(13), 1349–1357.

Latimer, E. A. (1999). Economic impacts of assertive community treatment: A review of the literature. *Canadian Journal of Psychiatry, 44,* 443–454.

Leff, H. S., Chow, C. M., Pepin, R., Conley, J., Allen, I. E., & Seaman, C. A. (2009). Does one size fit all? What we can and can't learn from a meta-analysis of housing models for persons with mental illness. *Psychiatric Services, 60*(4), 473–482.

Marx, A. J., Test, M. A., & Stein, L. L. (1973). Extrohospital management of severe mental illness: Feasibility and effects of social functioning. *Archives of General Psychiatry, 29,* 505–511.

McFarlane, W. R., Dushay, R. A., Deakins, S. M., Stastny, P., Lukens, E. P., Toran, J., et al. (2000). Employment outcomes in family-aided assertive community treatment. *American Journal of Orthopsychiatry, 70,* 203–214.

McGrew, J. H., & Bond, G. R. (1997). The association between program characteristics and service delivery in assertive community treatment. *Administration and Policy in Mental Health, 25,* 175–189.

McHugo, G. J., Drake, R. E., Teague, G. B., & Xie, H. (1999). Fidelity to assertive community treatment and client outcomes in the New Hampshire dual disorders study. *Psychiatric Services, 50,* 818–824.

Mondello, M., Gass, A. B., McLaughlin, T., & Shore, N. (2007, September). *Cost of homelessness, cost analysis of permanent supportive housing, state of Maine-greater Portland.* Portland, ME: Corporation for Supportive Housing, Maine Housing, Maine Department of Health and Human Services.

Monroe-DeVita, M., Morse, G., & Bond, G. R. (2012). Program fidelity and beyond: Multiple strategies and criteria for ensuring quality of assertive community treatment. *Psychiatric Services, 63*(8), 743–750.

National Alliance for the Mentally Ill Board of Directors. (2001). *NAMI Strategic Plan, 2001–2003.* Alexandria, VA: National Alliance for the Mentally Ill.

National Institute of Mental Health. (1999). *Bridging science and service: A report by the National Advisory Mental Health Council's Clinical Treatment and Services Research Workgroup.* Rockville, MD: Author.

New Freedom Commission on Mental Health. (2003). *Achieving the promise: Transforming mental health care in America: Final report* (DHHS Pub. No. SMA-03-3832). Rockville, MD: Department of Health and Human Services.

Nogaski, A., Rynell, A., Terpstra, A., Edwards, H. (2009). *Supportive housing in Illinois: A wise investment.* Heartland Alliance Mid-America Institute on Poverty, Supportive Housing Providers Association, Corporation for Supportive Housing. Retrieved January 4, 2012, from www.heartlandalliance.org/research

Phillips, S., Burns, B., Edgar, E., Mueser, K. T., Linkins, K. W., Rosenheck, R. A., et al. (2001). Moving assertive community treatment into standard practice. *Psychiatric Services, 52*(6), 771–779.

Raiff, N., & Shore, B. K. (1993). *Advanced case management: New strategies for the nineties.* Newbury Park, CA: Sage.

Rapp, C. A., & Goscha, R. J. (2011). *The strengths model: A recovery-oriented approach to mental health services.* New York: Oxford.

Rose, S. M. (1992). *Case management and social work practice.* New York: Longman.

Sands, R. G., & Gellis, Z. D. (2012). *Clinical social work practice in behavioral mental health: Toward evidence-based practice* (3rd ed.). Boston: Pearson/Allyn & Bacon.

Schutt, R. K., & Goldfinger, S. M. (2011). *Homelessness, housing and mental illness.* Cambridge, MA: Harvard University Press.

Stein, L. I., & Santos, A. B. (1998). *Assertive community treatment of persons with severe mental illness.* New York: W. W. Norton.

Stoesen, L. (2008, April). Teaming up for case management. *NASW News,* p. 53.

Stroul, B. A. (1988). *Community support systems for persons with long-term mental illness: Questions and answers.* Rockville, MD: National Institute of Mental Health.

Substance Abuse and Mental Health Services Administration (SAMHSA). (2008). *Assertive community treatment: The evidence* (DHHS Pub. No. SMI-08-4344).

Rockville, MD: Center for Mental Health Services, Substance Abuse and Mental Health Services Administration, U.S. Department of Health and Human Services.

Substance Abuse and Mental Health Services Administration (SAMHSA). (2010). *Permanent supportive housing: EBP toolkit* (HHS Pub. No. SMA-10-4509). Rockville, MD: Center for Mental Health Services, Substance Abuse and Mental Health Services Administration, U.S. Department of Health and Human Services.

Summers, N. (2011). *Case management practice: Skills for the human services* (4th ed.). Belmont, CA: Brooks-Cole Cengage Learning.

Surber, R. W. (1994). *Clinical case management: A guide to comprehensive treatment of serious mental illness.* Thousand Oaks, CA: Sage.

Teague, G. B., Bond, G. R., & Drake, R. E. (1998). Program fidelity in assertive community treatment: Development and use of a measure. *American Journal of Orthopsychiatry, 68*, 216–232.

U.S. Department of Health and Human Services (DHHS). (n.d.). *Supported employment: An evidence based practice.* Substance Abuse and Mental Health Services Administration, Center for Mental Health Services. Retrieved June 30, 2011, from www.samhsa.gov

U.S. Department of Health and Human Services (DHHS). (n.d.). *What is supportive employment?* Substance Abuse and Mental Health Services Administration, Center for Mental Health Services. Retrieved June 30, 2011, from www.samhsa.gov

U.S. Public Health Service Office of the Surgeon General. (1999). *Mental health: A report of the Surgeon General.* Rockville, MD: Department of Health and Human Services, U.S. Public Health Service.

Walsh, J. (2000). *Clinical case management with persons having mental illness: A relationship-based perspective.* Belmont, CA: Brooks-Cole/Thomson Learning.

Wehman, P., & Moon, M. S. (1988). *Vocational rehabilitation and supported employment.* Baltimore: Paul Brookes.

Wholey, D. R., Zhu, X., Knoke, D., Shah, P., Zellmer-Bruhn, M., & Witheridge, T. F. (2012). The teamwork in assertive community treatment (TACT) scale: Development and validation. *Psychiatric Services, 63*(11), 1108–1117.

WPATH. (2011). *World professional association for transgender health standards of care* (7th ed.). Retrieved December 26, 2011, from http://www.wpath.org/publications_standards.cfm

Zippay, A., & Lee, S. K. (2008). Neighbors' perceptions of community-based psychiatric housing. *Social Service Review, 82*(3), 395–417.

CHAPTER 10

American Psychiatric Association. (2000). *Diagnostic and statistical manual of mental disorders* (4th ed., text rev.). Washington, DC: Author.

American Psychiatric Association. (2013). *Diagnostic and statistical manual of mental disorders* (5th ed.). Washington, DC: Author.

Anderson, C. M., Reiss, D. J. & Hogarty, G. E. (1986). *Schizophrenia and the family.* New York: Guilford.

Andreasen, N. C. (Ed.) (1994). *Schizophrenia: From mind to molecule.* American Psychopathological Association Series. Washington, DC: American Psychiatric Press.

Anthony, W. A., Cohen, M. R., & Cohen, B. F. (1983). Philosophy, treatment process and principles of the psychiatric rehabilitation approach. In L. L. Bachrach (Ed.), *Deinstitutionalization: New Directions for Mental Health Services, 17.* San Francisco, CA: Jossey-Bass.

Bachrach, L. L. (1992). Psychosocial rehabilitation and psychiatry in the care of long-term patients. *American Journal of Psychiatry, 149*(11), 1455–1463.

Beard, J. H., Propst, R. N., & Malamud, T. J. (1982). The Fountain House model of psychiatric rehabilitation. *Psychosocial Rehabilitation Journal, 5*(1), 47–53.

Beck, J. S. (2011). *Cognitive behavior therapy: Basics and beyond* (2nd ed.). New York: Guilford.

Becker, D. R., & Drake, R. E. (n.d.) *Supported employment for people with severe mental illness: A guideline developed for the Behavioral Health Recovery Management Project.* Retrieved June 30, 2011, from http://www.bhrm.org/guidelines

Benton, M. K., & Schroeder, H. E. (1990). Social skills training with schizophrenics: A meta-analytic evaluation. *Journal of Consulting and Clinical Psychology, 58*(6), 741–747.

Bhugra, D., & Bhui, K. (2001). African-Caribbeans and schizophrenia: Contributing factors. *Advances in Psychiatric Treatment, 7*, 283–291.

Blanchard, J. J., Horan, W. P., & Collins, L. M. (2005). Examining the latent structure of negative symptoms: Is there a distinct subtype of negative symptom schizophrenia? *Schizophrenia Research, 77*, 151–165.

Bond, G. R., Becker, D. R., Drake, R. E., Rapp, C. A., Meisler, N., Lehman, A. F., et al. (2001). Implementing supported employment as an evidence based practice. *Psychiatric Services, 52*(3), 313–322.

Buckley, P. F., Miller, B. J., Lehrer, D. S., & Castle, D. J. (2009). Psychiatric comorbidities and schizophrenia. *Schizophrenia Bulletin, 35*(2), 383–402. doi: 10.1093/schbul/sbn135

Bustillo, J. R., Lauriello, J., Horan, W. P., & Keith, S. J. (2001). The psychosocial treatment of schizophrenia: An update. *American Journal of Psychiatry, 158*, 163–175.

Cannon, M., Jones, P., Huttunen, M. O., Tanskanen, A., Huttunen, T., Rabe-Hesketh, S., et al. (1999). School performance in Finnish children and later development of schizophrenia: A population-based longitudinal study. *Archives of General Psychiatry, 56*, 457–463.

Cohen, C. I. (1993). Poverty and the course of schizophrenia: Implications for research and policy. *Hospital and Community Psychiatry, 44*, 951–958.

Conte, H. R., & Plutchik, R. (1986). Controlled research in supportive psychotherapy. *Psychiatric Annals, 16*, 530–533.

Corrigan, P. W. (1991). Social skills training in adult psychiatric populations: A meta-analysis. *Journal of Behaviour Therapy and Experimental Psychiatry, 22*, 203–210.

Cubelli, G. E., & Havens, L. L. (1969). The expanding role of psychiatric rehabilitation. In L. Bellak & H. H. Barren (Eds.), *Progress in community mental health* (Vol. 1). New York: Grune & Stratton.

Daniels, J. (2009). Catatonia: Clinical aspects and neurobiological correlates. *The Journal of Neuropsychiatry and Clinical Neurosciences 21*, 371–380.

Davidson, L., O'Connell, M., Tondora, J., Styron, T., & Kangas, K. (2006). The top ten concerns about recovery encountered in mental health system transformation. *Psychiatric Services, 57*, 640–645.

Dickerson, F. B. (2004). Update on cognitive behavioral psychotherapy for schizophrenia: Review of recent studies. *Journal of Cognitive Psychotherapy, 18*, 189–205.

Dickerson, F. B. (2006). Disquieting aspects of the recovery paradigm. *Psychiatric Services, 57*, 647.

Dickerson, F. B., & Lehman, A. F. (2006). Evidence-based psychotherapy for schizophrenia. *The Journal of Nervous and Mental Disease, 194*(1), 3–9.

Dohrenwend, B. P., & Dohrenwend, B. S. (1974). Social and cultural influences on psychopathology. *Annual Review of Psychology, 25*, 417–452.

Drake, R. E., Becker, D. R., Biesanz, J. C., Torrey, W. C., McHugo, G. J., & Wyzik, P. F. (1994). Rehabilitation day treatment vs. supported employment: I. Vocational outcomes. *Community Mental Health Journal, 30*, 519–532.

Drake, R. E., Becker, D. R., Biesanz, J. C., Wyzik, P. F., & Torrey, W. C. (1996). Day treatment versus supported employment for persons with severe mental illness: A replication study. *Psychiatric Services, 47*, 1125–1127.

Drake, R. E., McHugo, G. J., Bebont, R. R., Becker, D. R., Harris, M., Bond, G. R., & Quimby, E. (1999). A randomized clinical trial of supported employment for inner-city patients with severe mental illness. *Archives of General Psychiatry, 56*, 627–633.

Drake, R. E., McHugo, G. J., Becker, D. R., Anthony, W. A., & Clark, R. E. (1996). The New Hampshire study of supported employment for people with severe mental illness: Vocational outcomes. *Journal of Consulting and Clinical Psychology, 64*, 391–399.

Eack, S. M. (2012). Cognitive remediation: A new generation of psychosocial interventions for people with schizophrenia. *Social Work, 57*(3), 235–246.

Eack, S. M., Bahorik, A., Newhill, C. E., Neighbors, H., & Davis, L. E. (2012). Interviewer-perceived honesty mediates racial disparities in the diagnosis of schizophrenia. *Psychiatric Services, 84*(9), 875–880.

Eack, S. M., Greenwald, D. P., Hogarty, S. S., Cooley, S. J., DiBarry, A. L., Montrose, D. M., et al. (2009). Cognitive enhancement therapy for early-course schizophrenia: Effects of a two-year randomized controlled trial. *Psychiatric Services, 60*(11), 1468–1476.

Eack, S. M., Greenwald, D. P., Hogarty, S. S., & Keshavan, M. S. (2010). One-year durability of the effects of cognitive enhancement therapy on functional outcome in early schizophrenia. *Schizophrenia Research, 120*(1), 210–216.

Eack, S. M., Hogarty, G. E., Cho, R. Y., Prasad, K. M. R., Greenwald, D. P., Hogarty, S. S., et al. (2010). Neuroprotective effects of cognitive enhancement therapy against gray matter loss in early schizophrenia: Results from a two-year randomized controlled trial. *Archives of General Psychiatry, 67*(7), 674–682.

Erlenmeyer-Kimling, L., Rock, D., Roberts, S. A., Janal, M., Kestenbaum, C., Cornblatt, B., et al. (2000). Attention, memory, and motor skills as childhood predictors of schizophrenia-related psychoses: The New York High-Risk Project. *American Journal of Psychiatry, 157*, 1416–1422.

Faris, R. E. L., & Dunham, H. W. (1939). *Mental disorders in urban areas: An ecological study of schizophrenia and other psychoses.* Chicago: Chicago University Press.

Fenton, W., & McGlashan, F. (1991). Natural history of schizophrenia subtypes: I. Longitudinal study of paranoid, hebephrenic, and undifferentiated schizophrenia. *Archives of General Psychiatry, 48*(11), 969–977.

Fine, S. B. (1980). Psychiatric treatment and rehabilitation: What's in a name? *National Association of Private Psychiatric Hospitals, 11,* 8–13.

Fish, B., Marcus, B., Hans, S. L., Auerbach, J. G., & Perdue, S. (1992). Infants at risk for schizophrenia: Sequelae of a genetic neurointegrative defect: A review and replication analysis of pandysmaturation in the Jerusalem Infant Development Study. *Archives of General Psychiatry, 49,* 221–235.

Freeman, H. (1994). Schizophrenia and city residence. *British Journal of Psychiatry, 164,* 39–50.

Fukui, S., Goscha, R., Rapp, C. A., Mabry, A., Liddy, P., & Marty, D. (2012). Strengths model case management fidelity scores and client outcomes. *Psychiatric Services, 63*(7), 708–710.

Fuller, R., Nopoulos, P., Arndt, S., O'Leary, D., Ho, B.-C., & Andreasen, N. C. (2002). Longitudinal assessment of premorbid cognitive functioning in patients with schizophrenia through examination of standardized scholastic test performance. *American Journal of Psychiatry, 159,* 1183–1189.

Galanter, M. (1988). Zealous self-help groups as adjuncts to psychiatric treatment: A study of Recovery, Inc. *American Journal of Psychiatry, 145,* 1248–1253.

Gara, M. A., Vega, W. A., Arndt, S., Escamilla, M., Fleck, D. E., Lawson, W. B., et al. (2012). Influence of patient race and ethnicity on clinical assessment in patients with affective disorders. *Archives of General Psychiatry, 69*(6), 593–600.

Gingerich, S., & Mueser, K. T. (2005). Illness management and recovery. In R. E. Drake, M. R. Merrens, & D. W. Lynde (Eds.), *Evidencebased mental health practice: A textbook* (pp. 395–424). New York: Norton.

Gottesman, I. I. (1991). *Schizophrenia genesis: The origin of madness.* New York: Freeman.

Grady, D. (1998, January 20). Studies of schizophrenia vindicate psychotherapy. *The New York Times.*

Grant, P. M., Huh, G. A., Perivoliotis, D., Stolar, N. M., & Beck, A. T. (2012). Randomized trial to evaluate the efficacy of cognitive therapy for low-functioning patients with schizophrenia. *Archives of General Psychiatry, 69*(2), 121–127.

Gunderson, J. G., & Mosher, L. R. (Eds.). (1975). *Psychotherapy of schizophrenia.* New York: Aronson.

Haas, G. L., Sweeney, J. A., Hien, D. A., Goldman, D., & Deck, M. (1991, April). *Gender differences in schizophrenia.* Presented at the International Congress on Schizophrenia Research, Tucson, AZ.

Heinssen, R. K., Liberman, R. P., & Kopelowicz, A. (2000). Psychosocial skills training for schizophrenia: Lessons from the laboratory. *Schizophrenia Bulletin, 26,* 21–46.

Hoff, A. L., & Kremen, W. S. (2003). Neuropsychology in schizophrenia: An update. *Current Opinion in Psychiatry, 16,* 149–155.

Hogarty, G. E. (2001). Personal communication.

Hogarty, G. E. (2002). *Personal therapy for schizophrenia and related disorders: A guide to individualized treatment.* New York: Guilford.

Hogarty, G. E., Anderson, C. M., Reiss, D. J., Kornblith, S. J., Greenwald, D. P., Javna, C. D., et al. (1986). Family psychoeducation, social skills training, and maintenance chemotherapy in the aftercare treatment of schizophrenia. *Archives of General Psychiatry, 43,* 633–642.

Hogarty, G. E., & Flesher, S. (1999a). Developmental theory for a cognitive enhancement therapy of schizophrenia. *Schizophrenia Bulletin, 25*(4), 677–692.

Hogarty, G. E., & Flesher, S. (1999b). Practice principles of cognitive enhancement therapy for schizophrenia. *Schizophrenia Bulletin, 25*(4), 693–708.

Hogarty, G. E., Flesher, S., Ulrich, R., Carter, M., Greenwald, D., Pogue-Geile, M., et al.(2004). Cognitive enhancement therapy for schizophrenia. Effects of a 2-year randomized trial on cognition and behavior. *Archives of General Psychiatry,* 61, 866–876.

Hogarty, G. E., Goldberg, S. C., Schooler, N. R, & the Collaborative Study Group. (1974). Drug and sociotherapy in the aftercare of schizophrenic patients III: Adjustment of nonrelapsed patients. *Archives of General Psychiatry, 31*(5), 609–618.

Hogarty, G. E., & Greenwald, D. P. (2006). *Cognitive enhancement therapy: The training manual.* Pittsburgh: University of Pittsburgh Medical Center. Retrieved from www.CognitiveEnhancementTherapy.com

Hogarty, G. E., Greenwald, D. P., Ulrich, R. F., Kornblith, S., DiBarry, A. L., Cooley, S., et al. (1997). Three-year trials of personal therapy among schizophrenic patients living with or independent of family, II: Effects on adjustment of patients. *American Journal of Psychiatry, 154*(11), 1514–1524.

Hogarty, G. E., Kornblith, S. J., Greenwald, D., DiBarry, A. L., Cooley, S., Flesher, S., et al. (1995). Personal therapy: A disorder-relevant psychotherapy for schizophrenia. *Schizophrenia Bulletin, 21,* 379–393.

Hogarty, G. E., Kornblith, S. J., Greenwald, D., DiBarry, A. L., Cooley, S., Ulrich, R. F., et al. (1997). Three-year trials of personal therapy among schizophrenic patients living with or independent of family, I: Description of study and effects on relapse rates. *American Journal of Psychiatry, 154*(11), 1504–1513.

Holschuh, J., & Segal, S. P. (2002). Factors related to multiplexity in support networks of persons with severe mental illness. In J. Levy & B. Pescosolido (Eds.), *Advances in Medical Sociology: Vol. 8. Social networks and health* (pp. 293–321). Bingley, UK: Emerald Group Publishing.

Hopper, K., Harrison, G., Janca, A., & Sartorius, N. (2007). *Recovery from schizophrenia: An international perspective: A report from the WHO Collaborative Project, the International Study of Schizophrenia.* New York: Oxford University Press.

Hornstra, R. K., Bruce-Wolfe, V., Sagduyu, K., & Riffle, D. W. (1993). The effect of intensive case management on hospitalization of patients with schizophrenia. *Hospital and Community Psychiatry, 44*, 844–847.

Hughes, C., Kumari, V., Soni, W., Das, M., Binneman, B., Drozd, S., et al. (2003). Longitudinal study of symptoms and cognitive function in chronic schizophrenia. *Schizophrenia Research, 59*, 137–146.

Jablensky, A., Sartorius, N., Ernberg, G., Anker, M., Korten, A., Cooper, J. E., et al. (1992). Schizophrenia: Manifestations, incidence and course in different cultures: A World Health Organization ten-country study. *Psychological Medicine: A Journal of Research in Psychiatry and the Allied Sciences, Supplement, 20*, 97.

Kantor, M. (2004). *Understanding paranoia: A guide for professionals, families, and sufferers.* Westport, CT: Praeger.

Karlsson, H., Bachmann, S., Schro, J., McArthur, J., Torrey, E. F., & Yolken, R. H. (2001). Retroviral RNA identified in the cerebrospinal fluids and brains of individuals with schizophrenia. *Proceedings of the National Academy of Science, 98*, 4634–4639.

Kates, J., & Rockland, L. H. (1994). Supportive psychotherapy of the schizophrenic patient. *American Journal of Psychotherapy, 48*, 543–561.

Katz, H. M., & Gunderson, J. G. (1990). Individual psychodynamically oriented psychotherapy for schizophrenic patients. In M. I. Herz, S. J. Keith, & J. P. Docherty (Eds.), *Handbook of schizophrenia: Psychosocial treatment of schizophrenia* (pp. 69–90). Amsterdam: Elsevier.

Kleinhaus, K., Harlap, S., Perrin, M. C., Manor, O., Weiser, M., Harkavy-Friedman, J. M., et al. (2012). Catatonic schizophrenia: A cohort prospective study. *Schizophrenia Bulletin, 38*(2), 331–337.

Krabbendam, L., & Aleman, A. (2003). Cognitive rehabilitation in schizophrenia: A quantitative analysis of controlled studies. *Psychopharmacology, 169*(3–4), 376–382.

Kurtz, L. F. (1997). *Self-help and support groups: A handbook for practitioners.* Thousand Oaks, CA: Sage.

Lamb, H. R., & Weinberger, L. E. (1998). Persons with severe mental illness in jails and prisons: A review. *Psychiatric Services, 49*(4), 483–492.

Leerhsen, C., Lewis, S. D., Pomper, S., Davenport, L., & Nelson, M. (1990, February 5). Unite and conquer. *Newsweek.*

Liberman, R. P. (1988). Coping with chronic mental disorders: A framework for hope. In R. P. Liberman (Ed.), *Psychiatric rehabilitation of chronic mental patients.* Washington, DC: American Psychiatric Press.

Liberman, R. P., & Mueser, K. T. (1989). Schizophrenia: Psychosocial treatment. In H. I. Kaplan & B. J. Sadock (Eds.), *Comprehensive textbook of psychiatry* (5th ed., pp. 792–806). London: Williams & Wilkins.

Liberman, R. P., & Phipps, C. C. (1987). Innovative treatment and rehabilitative techniques. In W. W. Menninger & G. Hannah (Eds.), *The chronic mental patient II.* Washington, DC: American Psychiatric Press.

Marsh, D. T., & Dickens, R. (1997). *How to cope with mental illness in your family: A self-care guide for siblings, offspring, and parents.* New York: Putnum.

Marsh, D. T., & Marks, M. J. (2009). *How to talk to families about child and adolescent mental illness.* New York: Norton.

McFarlane, W. R., Dixon, L., Lukens, E., & Lucksted, A. (2003). Family psychoeducation and schizophrenia: A review of the literature. *Journal of Marital and Family Therapy, 29*(2), 223–246.

McGlashan, T. H., & Fenton, W. S. (1993). Subtype progression and pathophysiologic deterioration in early schizophrenia. *Schizophrenia Bulletin, 19*, 71–84.

McGrath, J. J. (2006). Variations in the incidence of schizophrenia: Data versus dogma. *Schizophrenia Bulletin, 32*, 195–197.

McGurk, S. R., Twamley, E. W., Sitzer, D. I., McHugo, G. J., & Mueser, K. T. (2007). A meta-analysis of cognitive remediation in schizophrenia. *American Journal of Psychiatry, 164*, 1791–1802.

Mednick, S. A., Machon, R. A., Huttunen, M. O., & Bonett, D. (1988). Adult schizophrenia following prenatal exposure to an influenza epidemic. *Archives of General Psychiatry, 45*, 189–192.

Miller, R., & Mason, S. E. (2011). *Diagnosis: Schizophrenia* (2nd ed.). New York: Columbia University Press.

Mortensen, P. B., Pedersen, C. B., Westergaard, T., Wohlfahrt, J., Ewald, H., Mors, O., et al. (1999). Effects of family history and place and season of birth on the risk of schizophrenia. *New England Journal of Medicine, 340*, 603–608.

Mueser, K., & MacKain, S. (2008). *Illness management and recovery*. Retrieved June 28, 2011, from http://gainscenter.samhsa.gov/text/ebp/Illness-ManagementandRecovery.asp

Mueser, K. I., & Gingerich, S. (2006). *The complete family guide to schizophrenia*. New York: Guilford.

Mueser, K. T., & Berenbaum, H. (1990). Psychodynamic treatment of schizophrenia: Is there a future? *Psychological Medicine, 20*, 253–262.

Mueser, K. T., Corrigan, P. W., Hilton, D. W., Tanzman, B., Schaub, A., Gingerich, S., et al. (2002). Illness management and recovery: A review of the research. *Psychiatric Services, 53*, 1272–1284.

National Alliance for the Mentally Ill Board of Directors. (2001). *NAMI strategic plan, 2001–2003*. Alexandria, VA: National Alliance for the Mentally Ill.

National Institute of Mental Health (NIMH). (2009). *Schizophrenia*. Retrieved June 28, 2011, from www.nimh.nih.gov

New Freedom Commission on Mental Health. (2003). *Achieving the promise: Transforming mental health care in America: Final report* (DHHS Pub. No. SMA-03-3832). Rockville, MD: Department of Health and Human Services.

Newhill, C. E. (2003). *Client violence in social work practice: Prevention, intervention and research*. New York: Guilford.

Newman, L. S. (2001). What is social cognition? Four basic approaches and their implications for schizophrenia research. In P. W. Corrigan & D. L. Penn (Eds.), *Social cognition and schizophrenia* (pp. 41–72). Washington, DC: American Psychological Association.

Oransky, I. (2006). Wayne S. Fenton. *The Lancet, 368*(9547), 1568.

Ott, S. L., Roberts, S., Rock, D., Allen, J., & Erlenmeyer-Kimling, L. (2002). Positive and negative thought disorder and psychopathology in childhood among subjects with adulthood schizophrenia. *Schizophrenia Research, 58*, 231–239.

Owen, P. R. (2012). Portrayals of schizophrenia by entertainment media: A content analysis of contemporary movies. *Psychiatric Services, 63*(7), 655–659.

Pfammatter, M., Junghan, U. M., & Brenner, H. D. (2006). Efficacy of psychological therapy in schizophrenia: Conclusions from meta-analyses. *Schizophrenia Bulletin, 32*, S64–S80.

Pilling, S., Bebbington, P., Kuipers, E., Garety, P., Geddes, J., Martindale, B., et al. (2002). Psychological treatments in schizophrenia: II. Meta-analyses of randomized controlled trials of social skills training and cognitive remediation. *Psychological Medicine, 32*, 783–791.

Rapp, C. A. (1998). *The strengths model: Case management with people suffering from severe and persistent mental illness*. New York: Oxford.

Rector, N. A., & Beck, A. T. (2001). Cognitive behavioral therapy for schizophrenia: An empirical review. *Journal of Nervous and Mental Disease, 189*(5), 278–287.

Rector, N. A., & Beck, A. T. (2002). A clinical review of cognitive therapy for schizophrenia. *Current Psychiatry Report, 4*, 284–292.

Ronen, D. (2011). *The coping with psychosis and schizophrenia self help handbook* (Kindle ed.). Retrieved from www.amazon.com

Ruben, A. (1992). Is care management effective for people with serious mental illness? A research review. *Health and Social Work, 17*, 138–150.

Rund, B. R., Melle, I., Friis, S., Larsen, T. K., Midboe, L. J., Opjordsmoen, S., et al. (2004). Neurocognitive dysfunction in first-episode psychosis: Correlates with symptoms, premorbid adjustment, and duration of untreated psychosis. *American Journal of Psychiatry, 161*, 466–472.

Rutman, I. D. (1987). The psychosocial rehabilitation movement in the United States. In A. T. Meyerson & T. Fine (Eds.), *Psychiatric disability: Clinical, legal and administrative dimensions*. Washington, DC: American Psychiatric Press.

Saha, S., Chant, D., Welham, J., & McGrath, J. (2005). A systematic review of the prevalence of schizophrenia. *PLoS Medicine, 2*, e141. doi:10.1371/journal.pmed.0020141

Saleeby, D. (2008). *Strengths perspective in social work practice* (4th ed.). Boston: Allyn & Bacon.

Schiller, L., & Bennett, A. (1994). *The quiet room: A journey out of the torment of madness*. New York: Time Warner.

Segal, S. P., Silverman, C., & Temkin, T. (1995). Characteristics and service use of longterm members of selfhelp agencies for mental health clients. *Psychiatric Services, 46*, 269–274.

Segal, S. P., Silverman, C., & Temkin, T. (1997). Program environments of self-help agencies for persons with mental disabilities. *Journal of Mental Health Administration, 24*(4), 456–464.

Shepherd, G. (1978). Social skills training: The generalization problem—some further data. *Behaviour Research and Therapy, 16(4)*, 298–288.

Skodol, A. (1989). *Problems in differential diagnosis: From DSM-III to DSM-III-R in clinical practice.* Washington, DC: American Psychiatric Press.

Snowdon, J. (1980). Selfhelp groups and schizophrenia. *Australian and New Zealand Journal of Psychiatry, 14*(4), 265–268.

Steadman, H., Mulvey, E., Monahan, J., Robbins, P., Appelbaum, P., Grisso, T., et al. (1998). Violence by people discharged from acute psychiatric hospital facilities and by others in the same neighborhoods. *Archives of General Psychiatry, 55*, 393–401.

Steinberg, P. (2012, December 25). Our failed approach to schizophrenia. *The New York Times.*

Substance Abuse and Mental Health Services Administration (SAMHSA). (n.d.). *Illness management & recovery program.* Retrieved from store.samhsa.gov

Substance Abuse and Mental Health Services Administration (SAMHSA). (n.d.). *Illness management and recovery toolkit.* Retrieved June 11, 2011, from www.samhsa.gov

Swanson, J. W., Swartz, M. S., Van Dorn, R. A., Elbogen, E. B., Wagner, H. R., Rosenheck, R. A., et al. (2006). A national study of violent behavior in persons with schizophrenia. *Archives of General Psychiatry, 63*(5), 490–499.

Swartz, M. S., Perkins, D. O., Stroup, T. S., Davis, S. M., Capuano, G., Rosenheck, R. A., et al. (2007). Effects of antipsychotic medications on psychosocial functioning in patients with chronic schizophrenia: Findings from the NIMH CATIE Study. *American Journal of Psychiatry, 164*, 428–436.

Tandon, R., Keshavan, M. S., & Nasrallah, H. A. (2008). Schizophrenia, "just the facts": What we know in 2008. 2. Epidemiology and etiology. *Schizophrenia Research, 102*, 1–18.

Tarrier, N., Kinney, C., McCarthy, E., Wittkowski, A., Yusupoff, L., Gledhill, A., et al. (2001). Are some types of psychotic symptoms more responsive to cognitive-behavior therapy? *Behavioural & Cognitive Psychotherapy, 29*, 45–55.

Temes, R. (2002). *Getting your life back together when you have schizophrenia.* Oakland, CA: New Harbinger.

Torrey, E. F. (2002). Studies of individuals with schizophrenia never treated with antipsychotic medications: A review. *Schizophrenia Research, 58*, 101–115.

Torrey, E. F. (2006). *Surviving schizophrenia: A manual for families, patients, and providers* (5th ed.). New York: Harper.

Toseland, R. W., & Hacker, L. (1982). Self-help groups and professional involvement. *Social Work, 27*(4), 341–347.

Turetsky, B. I., Moberg, P. J., Mozley, L. H., Moelter, S. T., Agrin, R. N., Gur, R. C., et al. (2002). Memory-delineated subtypes of schizophrenia: Relationship to clinical, neuroanatomical, and neurophysiological measures. *Neuropsychology, 16*, 481–490.

Turkington, D., Kingdon, D., & Weiden, P. J. (2006). Cognitive behavior therapy for schizophrenia. *American Journal of Psychiatry, 163*, 365–373.

Turkington, D., & Morrison, A. P. (2012). Cognitive therapy for negative symptoms in schizophrenia. *Archives of General Psychiatry, 69*(2), 119–120.

U.S. Department of Health and Human Services (DHHS). (n.d.). *Supported employment: An evidence based practice.* Substance Abuse and Mental Health Services Administration, Center for Mental Health Services. Retrieved June 30, 2011, from www.samhsa.gov

U.S. Department of Health and Human Services (DHHS). (n.d.). *What is supportive employment?* Substance Abuse and Mental Health Services Administration, Center for Mental Health Services. Retrieved June 30, 2011, from www.samhsa.gov

U.S. Department of Health and Human Services, Substance Abuse and Mental Health Services Administration. (n.d.). *National consensus statement on mental health recovery.* Retrieved June 28, 2011, from http://store.samhsa.gov/product/National-Consensus-Statement-on-Mental-Health-Recovery/SMA05-4129

United States Psychiatric Rehabilitation Association (USPRA). (n.d.). *Defining psychosocial rehabilitation.* Retrieved June 29, 2011, from www.uspra.org

van Winkel, R., & Genetic Risk and Outcome of Psychosis (GROUP) Investigators. (2011). Family-based analysis of genetic variation underlying psychosisinducing effects of cannabis. *Archives of General Psychiatry, 68*(2), 148–157. doi:10.1001/archgenpsychiatry.2010.152

Walsh, M. (1985). *Schizophrenia: Straight talk for family and friends.* New York: Warner.

Watts, F. N., & Bennett, D. H. (1983). Introduction: The concept of rehabilitation. In F. N. Watts & D. H. Bennett (Eds.), *Theory and practice of psychiatric rehabilitation.* Chichester, UK: Wiley.

Wykes, T., Huddy, V., Cellard, C., McGurk, S. R., & Czobor, P. (2011). A meta-analysis of cognitive remediation for schizophrenia: Methodology and effect sizes. *American Journal of Psychiatry, 168*(5), 472–485.

Zhang, A. Y. & Snowden, L. R. (1999). Ethnic characteristics of mental disorders in five U.S. communities. *Cultural Diversity and Ethnic Minority Psychology, 5*(2), 134–146.

CHAPTER 11

Allison, D. B., De Oliveira, P., Roberts, M. S., & Weiss, A. S. (1988). *Psychosis and sexual identity: Toward a post-analytic view of the Schreber case.* Binghamton: State University of New York Press.

Alper, G. (2005). *The paranoia of everyday life: Escaping the enemy within.* Amherst, NY: Prometheus.

American Psychiatric Association (APA). (2000). *Diagnostic and statistical manual of mental disorders* (4th ed., text rev.). Washington, DC: Author.

Ashby, H. U. (1986). Mislabeling the Black client: A reply to Ridley. *American Psychologist, 41,* 224–225.

Ballard, C., & Oyebode, F. (1995). Psychotic symptoms in patients with dementia. *International Journal of Geriatric Psychiatry, 10,* 743–752.

Ballard, C. G., Chithiramohan, R. N., Bannister, C., Handy, S., & Todd, N. (1991). Paranoid features in the elderly with dementia. *International Journal of Geriatric Psychiatry, 6,* 155–157.

Berger, K. S., & Zarit, S. H. (1978). Late-life paranoid states: Assessment and treatment. *American Journal of Orthopsychiatry, 48,* 528–537.

Bernstein, R. (2010, March 10). Letter from America: An old essay used to explain a new movement. *The New York Times.*

Breslau, N., Kessler, R. C., Chilcoat, H. D., Schultz, L. R., Davis, G. C., & Andreski, P. (1998). Trauma and posttraumatic stress disorder in the community. *Archives of General Psychiatry, 55,* 626–632.

Brink, T. L. (1980). Geriatric paranoia: Case report illustrating betrayal management. *Journal of the American Geriatrics Society, 28,* 519–522.

Bronstein, P. (1986). Self-disclosure, paranoia, and unaware racism: Another look at the Black client and the White therapist. *American Psychologist, 41,* 225–226.

Cameron, N. (1943). The paranoid pseudo-community. *The American Journal of Sociology, 49*(1), 32–38.

Cameron, N. (1959). The paranoid pseudo-community revisited. *The American Journal of Sociology, 65*(1), 57–61.

Cannon, W. B. (1942). Voodoo death. *American Anthropology, 44,* 169.

Carpenter, L., & Brockington, I. F. (1980). A study of mental illness in Asians, West Indians and Africans living in Manchester. *British Journal of Psychiatry, 137,* 201–205.

Carter, S. L. (2009, February 25). We're not cowards, we're just loud. *The New York Times.*

Chadwick, P. D., Birchwood, M. J., & Trower, P. (1996). *Cognitive therapy for delusions, voices and paranoia.* Oxford, England: Wiley.

Christenson, R., & Blazer, D. (1984). Epidemiology of persecutory ideation in an elderly population in the community. *American Journal of Psychiatry, 141,* 1088–1091.

Chuang, H. T., & Addington, D. (1988). Homosexual panic: A review of its concept. *Canadian Journal of Psychiatry, 33*(7), 613–617.

Combs, D. R., Penn, D. L., Cassisi, J., Michael, C., Wood, T., Wanner, J., et al. (2006). Perceived racism as a predictor of paranoia among African-Americans. *Journal of Black Psychology, 32*(1), 87–104.

Cooper, A. (1974). Hearing loss in paranoid and affective psychoses of the elderly. *Lancet, 2,* 851–854.

Cooper, A., & Porter, R. (1976). Visual acuity and ocular pathology in the paranoid psychoses of later life. *Journal of Psychosomatic Research, 20,* 107–114.

Cooper, J. M. (1933). The Cree whitico psychosis. *Primitive Man, 6,* 24.

Crichton-Miller, H. (1968). Quoted in L. C. Kolb & A. P. Noyes (Eds.), *Modern clinical psychiatry* (7th ed., p. 403). Philadelphia: Saunders.

Cummings, S. M., & Kropf, N. P. (2011). Aging with a severe mental illness: Challenges and treatments. *Journal of Gerontological Social Work, 54*(2), 175–188.

Dohrenwend, B. P., & Dohrenwend, B. S. (1974). Social and cultural influences on psychopathology. *Annual Review of Psychology, 25,* 417–452.

Editorial. (1980). Paranoia and immigrants. *British Medical Journal, 281,* 1513–1514.

Eisenbruch, M. (1991). From post-traumatic stress disorder to cultural bereavement: Diagnosis of Southeast Asian refugees. *Social Science & Medicine, 33*(6), 673–680.

Eke, N. (1981). Paranoia and immigrants—a reply. *British Medical Journal, 282,* 226.

Erikson, E. H. (1950). *Childhood and society.* New York: Norton.

Faris, R. E. L., & Dunham, H. W. (1939). *Mental disorders in urban areas: An ecological study of schizophrenia and other psychoses.* Chicago: Chicago University Press.

Farrell, J. (2007). *Paranoia and modernity: Cervantes to Rousseau.* Ithaca, NY: Cornell University Press.

Fennig, S., Fochtmann, L. J., & Bromet, E. (2005). Delusional disorder and shared psychotic disorder. In B. J. Sadock & V. A. Sadock (Eds.), *Comprehensive textbook of psychiatry* (8th ed., Vol. 1, pp. 1525–1533). Philadelphia: Lippincott Williams & Wilkins.

Fisher, J. E., Ziess, A. M., & Carstensen, L. L. (2001). Psychopathology in the aged. In H. E. Adams & P. B. Sutker (Eds.), *Comprehensive handbook of psychopathology* (3rd ed., pp. 921–952). New York: Springer.

Forsell, Y., & Henderson, A. S. (1998). Epidemiology of paranoid symptoms in an elderly population. *British Journal of Psychiatry, 172*, 429–432.

Frank, T. (2009). *The wrecking crew: How conservatives ruined government, enriched themselves, and beggared the nation*. New York: Henry Holt.

Freeman, D., Freeman, J., & Garety, P. (2008). *Overcoming paranoid & suspicious thoughts: A self-help guide using cognitive behavioral techniques*. New York: Basic.

Freeman, H. (1994). Schizophrenia and city residence. *British Journal of Psychiatry, 164*, 39–50.

Freud, S. (1911/2003). *The Schreber case* (Webber, A., Trans.). New York: Penguin Classics.

Gitterman, A., & Germain, C. B. (2008). *The life model of social work practice: Advances in theory and practice* (3rd ed.). New York: Columbia University Press.

Goldberg, R. A. (2001). *Enemies within: The culture of conspiracy in modern America*. New Haven, CT: Yale University Press.

Goldberg, R. A. (2003). Conspiracy theories in America: An historical overview. In P. Knight (Ed.), *Conspiracy theories in American history: An encyclopedia* (Vol. 1, pp. 1–12). Santa Barbara, CA: ABC-CLIO.

Grier, W., & Cobbs, P. (1968). *Black rage*. New York: Bantam.

Groch, J. (2005, May 10). Old, afraid and gripped by demons. *The New York Times*.

Gurian, B. S., Wexler, D., and Baker, E. H. (1992). Late-life paranoia: Possible association with early trauma and infertility. *International Journal of Geriatric Psychiatry, 7*(4), 277–284. doi: 10.1002/gps.930070409

Hindelang, M., Gottfredson, M. R., & Garafalo, J. (1978). *Victims of personal crime*. Pensacola, FL: Ballinger.

Hofstadter, R. (1965). *The paranoid style in American politics*. New York: Knopf.

Jack, R. A., Nicassio, P. M., & West, W. S. (1984). Single case study: Acute paranoid disorder in a Southeast Asian refugee. *The Journal of Nervous and Mental Disease, 172*, 495–497.

Jorgensen, P., & Munk-Jorgensen, P. (1985). Paranoid psychosis in the elderly: A follow-up study. *Acta Psychiatrica Scandinavica, 72*, 358–363.

Kantor, M. (2008). *Understanding paranoia: A guide for professionals, families, and sufferers*. Westport, CN: Praeger.

Kaplan, H. I., & Sadock, B. J. (1971). The status of the paranoid today: His diagnosis, prognosis and treatment. *Psychiatric Quarterly, 45*, 528–541.

Kinzie, J. D., Boehnlein, J. K., Leung, P. K., Moore, L. J., Riley, C., & Smith, D. (1990). The prevalence of posttraumatic stress disorder and its clinical significance among Southeast Asian refugees. *American Journal of Psychiatry, 147*, 913–917.

Klein, M. (1952). Some theoretical conclusions regarding the emotional life of the infant. In J. Riviere (Ed.), *Developments in psychoanalysis* pp. 198–236. London: Hogarth.

Kraepelin, E. (1917). *Lectures on clinical psychiatry*. New York: Wood & Co.

Kraepelin, E. (1921). *Manic-depressive insanity and paranoia*. Edinburgh, UK: Livingstone.

Krugman, P. (2009, November 9). Paranoia strikes deep. *The New York Times*.

LaRue, A., Dessonville, C., & Jarvik, L. (1985). Aging and mental disorders. In J. E. Birren & K. W. Schaie (Eds.), *Handbook of the psychology of aging* (pp. 664–702). New York: Van Nostrand Reinhold.

Lester, D. (2009). Voodoo death. *Omega, 59*(1), 1–18.

Mattimore-Knudson, R. S. (1985). Reality therapy via proxy for paranoia and agoraphobia. *Clinical Gerontologist, 4*, 58–61.

Mehlman, R. D. (1961). The Puerto Rican Syndrome. *American Journal of Psychiatry, 118*, 328.

Meyer, A. (1913). The treatment of paranoic and paranoid states. In W. A. White & S. E. Jelliffe (Eds.), *The modern treatment of nervous and mental disease* (Vol. 1, pp. 614–661). New York: Lea & Febiger.

Mirowsky, J. (1985). Disorder and its context: Paranoid beliefs as thematic elements of thought problems, hallucinations, and delusions under threatening social conditions. *Research in Community and Mental Health, 5*, 185–204.

Molinari, V., & Chacko, R. (1983). The classification of paranoid disorders in the elderly: A clinical problem. *Clinical Gerontologist, 1*, 31–37.

Mortensen, P. B., Pedersen, C. B., Westergaard, T., Wohlfahrt, J., Ewald, H., Mors, O., et al. (1999). Effects of family history and place and season of birth on the risk of schizophrenia. *New England Journal of Medicine, 340*, 603–608.

Munro, A. (1999). *Delusional disorder: Paranoia and related illnesses*. Cambridge, UK: Cambridge University Press.

Naipaul, S. (1982). *Journal to nowhere: A new world tragedy*. New York: Penguin.

Nash, J. L. (1983). Delusions. In J. O. Cavenar & H. K. H. Brodie (Eds.), *Signs and symptoms in psychiatry*. Philadelphia: Lippincott.

Ndetei, D. M. (1986). Paranoid disorder—environmental, cultural or constitutional phenomenon? *Acta Psychiatrica Scandinavica, 74*, 50–54.

Newhill, C. E. (1989). Paranoid symptomatology in late life. *Clinical Gerontologist, 8*(4), 13–30.

Newhill, C. E. (1990). The role of culture in the development of paranoid symptomatology. *American Journal of Orthopsychiatry, 60*(2), 176–185.

Newhill, C. E. (1995). *A crisis casebook.* Unpublished manuscript.

Newhill, C. E. (2003). *Client violence in social work practice: Prevention, intervention and research.* New York: Guilford.

Oldham, J. M., & Skodol, A. E. (1994). Do patients with paranoid personality disorder seek psychoanalysis? In J. M. Oldham & S. Bone (Eds.), *Paranoia: New psychoanalytic perspectives* (pp. 151–166). Madison, WI: International Universities.

Parisi, N., Gottfredson, M. R., Hindelang, M., & Flanagan, T. (1979). *Sourcebook of criminal justice statistics—1978.* Washington, DC: U.S. Government Printing Office.

Perry, J. C., & Vaillant, G. E. (1989). Personality disorders. In H. I. Kaplan & B. J. Sadock (Eds.), *Comprehensive textbook of psychiatry* (5th ed., pp. 1352–1395). Baltimore: Williams & Wilkins.

Rack, P. (1982). *Race, culture and mental disorder.* London, UK: Tavistock.

Ramirez de Arellano, R., Ramirez de Arellano, M., & Garcia, L. (1956). *Attack, hyperkinetic type: The so-called Puerto Rican syndrome and its medical, psychological and social implications.* San Juan: Veteran's Administration Report.

Reagan, R. W. (1984). *Remarks accepting the presidential nomination at the Republican National Convention in Dallas, Texas.* Retrieved August 29, 2011, from http://www.reagan.utexas.edu/archives/speeches/1984/82384f.htm

Richter, C. P. (1957). On the phenomenon of sudden death in animals and man. *Psychosomatic Medicine, 19*, 191.

Ridley, C. R. (1984). Clinical treatment of the nondisclosing Black client: A therapeutic paradox. *American Psychologist, 39*(11), 1234–1244.

Rokeach, M. (1964). *The Three Christs of Ypsilanti.* New York: Knopf.

Ross, C. E., Mirowsky, J., & Pribesh, S. (2001). Powerlessness and the amplification of threat: Neighborhood disadvantage, disorder, and mistrust. *American Sociological Review, 66*(4), 568–591.

Saha, S., Chant, D., Welham, J., & McGrath, J. (2005). A systematic review of the prevalence of schizophrenia. *PLoS Medicine, 2*, e141. doi:10.1371/journal.pmed.0020141

Saint Martin, M. L. (1999). Running amok: A modern perspective on a culture-bound syndrome. *Primary Care Companion: Journal of Clinical Psychiatry, 1*(3), 66–70.

Salzman, L. (1960). Paranoid state—theory and therapy. *Archives of General Psychiatry, 2*, 101–115.

Sapolsky, R. (2004). *Why Zebras don't get ulcers.* New York: Henry Holt.

Schafer, R. (1954). *Psychoanalytic Rorschach interpretation.* London: Grune.

Schreber, D. P. (1955). *Memoirs of my nervous illness* (translated, edited with introduction, notes, and discussion by Macalpine, I., & Hunter, R. A.). London: W. Dawson.

Schwartz, D. A. (1963). A review of the paranoid concept. *Archives of General Psychiatry, 8*, 349–361.

Searles, Harold F. (1961). The sources of anxiety in paranoid schizophrenia. *British Journal of Medical Psychology, 34*, 129–141.

Shapiro, D. (1965). *Neurotic styles.* New York: Basic.

Shapiro, D. (1981). *Autonomy and rigid character.* New York: Basic.

Shapiro, D. (1994). Paranoia from a characterological standpoint. In J. M. Oldham & S. Bone (Eds.), *Paranoia: New psychoanalytic perspectives* (pp. 49–57). Madison, WI: International Universities Press.

Shrestha, L. B., & Heisler, E. J. (2011). *The changing demographic profile of the United States.* Congressional Research Service, released March 31. Retrieved September 23, 2011, from http://www.fas.org/sgp/crs/misc/RL32701.pdf

Spradley, J. P., & McCurdy, D. W. (1974). *Conformity and conflict: Readings in cultural anthropology.* Boston: Little Brown.

Sullivan, H. S. (1956). Clinical studies in psychiatry. In H. S. Perry, M. L. Gawel, & M. Gibbon (Eds.), *The collected works of Harry Stack Sullivan* (Vol. 2). New York: Norton.

Sutton, M. A. (2011, September 25). Why the Antichrist matters in politics. *The New York Times.*

Swanson, D. W., Bohert, P. J., & Smith, J. A. (1970). *The paranoid.* Boston: Little, Brown & Co.

Terrell, F., & Terrell, S. L. (1981). Race of counselor, client sex, cultural mistrust level, and premature termination from counseling among Black clients. *Journal of Counseling Psychology, 31*, 371–375.

Thorpe, L. (1997). The treatment of psychotic disorders in late life. *Canadian Journal of Psychiatry, 42*, 19S–27S.

Tobin, J. J., & Friedman, J. (1983). Spirits, shamans and nightmare death: Survivor stress in a Hmong refugee. *American Journal of Orthopsychiatry, 53*, 439–448.

Tolin, D. F., Robison, J. T., Gaztambide, S., Horowitz, S., & Blank, K. (2007). Ataques de nervios and psychiatric disorders in older Puerto Rican primary care patients. *Journal of Cross-Cultural Psychology, 38*(6), 659–669.

Triandis, H. C., Feldman, J. M., Weldon, D. E., & Harvey, W. M. (1975). Ecosystem distrust and the hard-to-employ. *Journal of Applied Psychology, 60*(1), 44–56.

U.S. Department of Health and Human Services (DHHS). (2001). *Mental health: Culture, race and ethnicity—A supplement to mental health: A report of the Surgeon General.* Rockville, MD: U.S. Department of Health and Human Services, Public Health Service, Office of the Surgeon General.

U.S. Department of Health and Human Services (DHHS), Administration on Aging. (2011). *Aging statistics.* Retrieved October 10, 2011, from http://www.aoa.gov/aoaroot/aging_statistics/index.aspx

Valdivieso, R., & Davis, C. (1988). U.S. Hispanics: Challenging issues for the 1990s. *Population Trends and Public Policy, 17*, 1–16.

Varner, R., & Gaitz, C. (1982). Schizophrenic and paranoid disorders of the aged. *Psychiatric Clinics of North America, 5*, 107–118.

Walker, J. I., & Brodie, H. K. H. (1985). Paranoid disorders. In H. I. Kaplan & B. J. Sadock (Eds.), *Comprehensive textbook of psychiatry* (4th ed., pp. 747–755). London: Williams & Williams.

Walker, J. I., & Cavenar, J. O. (1983). Paranoid symptoms and conditions. In J. O. Cavenar & H. K. H. Brodie (Eds.), *Signs and symptoms in psychiatry.* Philadelphia: J. B. Lippincott.

Waska, R. T. (2000). Hate, projective identification and the psychotherapist's struggle. *The Journal of Psychotherapy Practice and Research, 9*, 33–38.

Whaley, A. (2001). Cultural mistrust and mental health services for African-Americans. *The Counseling Psychologist, 29*(4), 513–531.

Wolfgang, G. (2001, July). *Cultural factors in psychiatric disorders.* Paper presented at the 26th Congress of the World Federation for Mental Health, Vancouver.

Worth, R. F. (2002, February 24). A nation defined by its enemies. *The New York Times.*

Yudofsky, S. C. (2005). *Fatal flaws: Navigating destructive relationships with people with disorders of personality and character.* Washington, DC: American Psychiatric Press.

Zimbardo, P. G., Andersen, S. M., & Kabat, L. G. (1981). Induced hearing deficit generates experimental paranoia. *Science, 212*(4502), 1529–1531. doi: 10.1126/science.7233242

CHAPTER 12

Ali, A. (2004). The intersection of racism and sexism in psychiatric diagnosis. In P. J. Caplan & L. Cosgrove (Eds.), *Bias in psychiatric diagnosis* (pp. 71–75). Lanham, MD: Jason Aronson.

Altshuler, L. L., Hendrich, V., & Cohen, L. S. (1998). Course of mood and anxiety disorders during pregnancy and the postpartum period. *Journal of Clinical Psychiatry, 59*(Suppl. 2), 29–33.

American Psychiatric Association. (2000). *Diagnostic and statistical manual of mental disorders* (4th ed., text rev.). Washington, DC: Author.

American Psychiatric Association. (2013). *Diagnostic and statistical manual of mental disorders* (5th ed.). Washington, DC: Author.

Arango, V., Huang, Y. Y., Underwood, M. D., & Mann, J. J. (2003). Genetics of the serotonergic system in suicidal behavior. *Journal of Psychiatric Research, 37*, 375–386.

Basco, M. R., & Rush, A. J. (1996). *Cognitive-behavioral therapy for bipolar disorder.* New York: Guilford.

Blumenthal, S. J. (1990). Introduction—suicide over the life cycle: Implications for clinical practice. In S. J. Blumenthal & D. J. Kupfer (Eds.), *Suicide over the life cycle: Risk factors, assessment, and treatment of suicidal patients* (pp. 685–733). Washington, DC: American Psychiatric Press.

Boden, J. M., Fergusson, D. M., & Horwood, L. J. (2007). Anxiety disorders and suicidal behaviours in adolescence and young adulthood: Findings from a longitudinal study. *Psychological Medicine, 37*(3), 431–440.

Carlat, D. J. (1998). The psychiatric review of symptoms: A screening tool for family physicians. *American Family Physician, 58*(7), 1617–1624.

Cassano, P., & Fava, M. (2002). Depression and public health, an overview. *Journal of Psychosomatic Research, 53*, 849–857.

Centers for Disease Control and Prevention, National Center for Injury Prevention and Control (CDC). (2007). *Web-based Injury Statistics Query and Reporting System (WISQARS).* Retrieved March 6, 2012, from www.cdc.gov/ncipc/wisqars

Chaudron, L. H., Kitzman, H., Peifer, K., Morrow, S., & Perez, L. (2005). Self-recognition and provider response to maternal depressive symptoms in low-income Hispanic women. *Journal of Women's Health, 14*, 331–338.

Clarke, R. V., & Jones, P. R. (1989). Suicide and increased availability of handguns in the United States. *Social Science and Medicine, 28*(8), 805–809.

Cochran, S. V., & Rabinowitz, F. E. (2000). *Men and depression: Clinical and empirical perspectives.* San Diego, CA: Academic Press.

Cohen, S., & Janicki-Deverts, D. (2012). Who's stressed? Distributions of psychological stress in the United States in probability samples from 1983, 2006, and 2009. *Journal of Applied Social Psychology, 42*(6), 1320–1334.

Coiro, M. J., Riley, A., Broitman, M., & Miranda, J. (2012). Effects on children of treating their mother's depression: Results of a 12-month follow-up. *Archives of General Psychiatry, 63*(4), 357–363.

Devane, C. L., Chiao, E., Franklin, M., & Kruep, E. J. (2005). Anxiety disorders in the 21st century: Status, challenges, opportunities, and comorbidity with depression. *American Journal of Managed Care, 11*(Suppl. 12), S344–S353.

Doucet, S., Letourneau, N., & Blackmore, E. R. (2012). Support needs of mothers who experience postpartum psychosis and their partners. *Journal of Obstetric, Gynecologic & Neonatal Nursing, 41*, 236–245. doi:10.1111/j.1552-6909.2011.01329.x

Duke, P. (1988). *Call me Anna: The autobiography of Patty Duke.* New York: Bantam.

Duke, P. (1992). *A brilliant madness: Living with manic-depressive illness.* New York: Bantam.

Egan, J. (2008, September 14). The bipolar puzzle. *The New York Times.*

Erikson, E. H. (1994). *Identity and the life cycle.* New York: W. W. Norton.

Eskandari, F., Martinez, P. E., Torvik, S., Phillips, T. M., Sternberg, E. M., Mistry, S., et al. (2007). Low bone mass in premenopausal women with depression. *Archives of Internal Medicine, 167* (21), 2329–2336.

Fava, M., Alpert, J. E., Carmin, C. N., Wisniewski, S. R., Trivedi, M. H., Biggs, M. M., et al. (2004). Clinical correlates and symptom patterns of anxious depression among patients with major depressive disorder in STAR*D. *Psychological Medicine, 34*(7), 1299–1308.

Frances, A., Docherty, J. P., & Kahn, D. A. (1996). Expert consensus treatment guidelines for bipolar disorder: A guide for patients and families. *Journal of Clinical Psychiatry, 57*(Suppl. 12A). Reprint, National Depressive and Manic-Depressive Association (NDMDA).

Frank, E. (2005). *Treating bipolar disorder: A clinician's guide to interpersonal and social rhythm therapy.* New York: Guilford.

Frank, E., Gonzalez, J. M., & Fagiolini, A. (2006). The importance of routine for preventing recurrence in bipolar disorder. *American Journal of Psychiatry, 163*, 677–685.

Frank, E., Kupfer, D. J., Thase, M. E., Mallinger, A. G., Swartz, H. A., Fagiolini, A. M., et al. (2005). Two-year-outcomes for interpersonal and social rhythm therapy in individuals with bipolar I disorder. *Archives of General Psychiatry, 62*(9), 996–1004. doi:10.1001/archpsyc.62.9.996

Gillian, J. (2011). *Why some politicians are more dangerous than others.* Boston: Polity.

Gould, M. S., Wallenstein, S., & Davidson, L. (1989). Suicide clusters: A critical review. *Suicide & Life Threatening Behavior, 19*(1), 17–29.

Grote, N. K., Bledsoe, S. E., Larkin, J., & Brown, C. (2007). Depression in African-American and White women with low-incomes: The role of chronic stress. *Social Work in Public Health, 23*, 59–88.

Gurney, M. (2011). Kevorkian's ghastly hubris undermined his worthy cause. *National Post.* Retrieved June 14, 2012, from http://fullcomment.nationalpost.com

Hartlage, S. A., Freels, S., Gotman, N., & Yonkers, K. (2012). Criteria for premenstrual dysphoric disorder. *Archives of General Psychiatry, 69*(3), 300–305.

Harvey, A. G. (2008). Sleep and circadian rhythms in bipolar disorder: Seeking synchrony, harmony and regulation. *American Journal of Psychiatry, 165*, 820–829. doi:10.1176/appi.ajp.2008.08010098

Harvey, A. G., Schmidt, A., Scarnà, A., Semler, C. N., & Goodwin, G. M. (2005). Sleep-related functioning in euthymic patients with bipolar disorder, patients with insomnia and subjects without sleep problems. *American Journal of Psychiatry, 162*, 50–57.

Harvey, B. (2006). Scaling Mount Rushmore: Cartography of a manic episode. *Psychiatric Services, 57*, 177–178.

Healey, B. (Narrator/actor), & Menninger Video Productions (Producers). (1993). *Suicide risk assessment* [Educational video recording]. Distributed by the Menninger Foundation, United States.

Hochschild, A., & Machung, A. (2012). *The second shift: Working families and the revolution at home* (2nd ed.). New York: Penguin.

Horwitz, A. V., & Wakefield, J. C. (2007). *The loss of sadness: How psychiatry transformed normal sorrow into depressive disorder.* New York: Oxford.

Humphry, D. (2002). *Final exit: The practicalities of self-deliverance and assisted suicide for the dying* (3rd ed.). El Dorado, AK: Delta.

Huxley, N. A., Parikh, S. V., & Baldessarini, R. J. (2000). Effectiveness of psychosocial treatments in bipolar disorder: State of the evidence. *Harvard Review of Psychiatry, 8*(3), 126–140.

Hyman, S. E. (1999). Introduction to the complex genetics of mental disorders. *Biological Psychiatry, 45*(5), 518–521.

Jamison, K. R. (1995a, March 19). Physician, know thyself. *The Washington Post.*

Jamison, K. R. (1995b). *An unquiet mind.* New York: Knopf.

Jamison, K. R. (2009). *Nothing was the same: A memoir.* New York: Knopf.

Johnson, L., & Johnson, C. (2012). *Perfect chaos: A daughter's journey to survive bipolar, a mother's struggle to save her.* New York: St. Martin's Press.

Kahn, D. A., Keck, P. E., Perlis, R. H., Otto, M. W., & Ross, R. (2004, December). Treatment of bipolar disorder: A guide for patients and families. *Postgraduate Medicine Special Report*, 109–116.

Kahn, D. A., Ross, R., Printz, D. J., & Sachs, G. S. (2000, April). Expert consensus treatment guidelines for bipolar disorder: A guide for patients and families. *Postgraduate Medicine Special Report*, 97–104.

Kindlon, D., & Thompson, M. (2000). *Raising Cain: Protecting the emotional life of boys.* New York: Ballantine.

Kochanek, K. D., Murphy, S. L., Anderson, R. N., & Scott, C. (2004). Deaths: Final data for 2002. *National Vital Statistics Reports, 53(5).* Hyattsville, MD: National Center for Health Statistics.

Kreitman, N. (1976). The coal gas story: United Kingdom suicide rates, 1960–71. *British Journal of Preventive & Social Medicine, 30*(2), 86–93.

Kristof, N. D. (2012, April 25). Veterans and brain disease. *The New York Times.*

Lam, R. W., Levitt, A. J., Levitan, R. D., Enns, M. W., Morehouse, R., Michalak, E. E., et al. (2006). The Can-SAD study: A randomized controlled trial of the effectiveness of light therapy and fluoxetine in patients with winter seasonal affective disorder. *American Journal of Psychiatry, 163*(5), 805–812.

Leckman, J. F., Weissman, M. M., Merikangas, K. R., Pauls, D. L., & Prusoff, B. A. (1983). Panic disorder and depression. *Archives of General Psychiatry, 40*, 1055–1060.

Lewis, L. (2000). A consumer perspective concerning the diagnosis and treatment of bipolar disorder. *Biological Psychiatry, 48*, 442–444.

Marsella, A. J., Sartorius, N., Jablensky, A., & Fenton, F. R. (1985). Cross-cultural studies of depressive disorders: An overview. In A. Kleinman & B. Good (Eds.), *Culture and depression: Studies in the anthropology and cross-cultural psychiatry of affect and disorder.* Berkeley: University of California Press.

McElroy, S. L., Keck, P. E., & Strakowski, S. M. (1996). Mania, psychosis and antipsychotics. *Journal of Clinical Psychiatry, 57*(Suppl. 3), 14–26.

McKee, A. C., Stein, T. D., Nowinski, C. J., Stern, R. A., Daneshvar, D. H., Alvarez, V. E., et al. (2012). The spectrum of disease in chronic traumatic encephalopathy. *Brain, 136*, 43–64.

Miklowitz, D. J., George, E. L., Richards, J. A., Simoneau, T. L., & Suddath, R. L. (2003). A randomized study of family-focused psychoeducation and pharmacotherapy in the outpatient management of bipolar disorder. *Archives of General Psychiatry, 60*, 904–912.

Miklowitz, D. J., Otto, M. W., Frank, E., Reilly-Harrington, N. A., Wisniewski, S. R., Kogan, J. N., et al. (2007). Psychosocial treatments for bipolar depression: A 1-year randomized trial from the Systematic Treatment Enhancement Program (STEP). *Archives of General Psychiatry, 64*(4), 419–426.

Miklowitz, D. J., Richards, J. A., George, E. L., Frank, E., Suddath, R. L., Powell, K. B., et al. (2003). Integrated family and individual therapy for bipolar disorder: Results of a treatment development study. *Journal of Clinical Psychiatry, 64*, 182–191.

Miller, M., Azrael, D., Hepburn, L., Hemenway, D., & Lippmann, S. J. (2006). The association between changes in household firearm ownership and rates of suicide in the United States, 1981–2002. *Injury Prevention, 12*, 178–182. doi:10.1136/ip.2005.010850

Miller, M., Lippmann, S. J., Azrael, D., & Hemenway, D. (2007). Household firearm ownership and rates of suicide across the 50 United States. *Journal of Trauma-Injury Infection & Critical Care, 62*(4), 1029–1035.

Moscickm, E. K. (2001). Epidemiology of completed and attempted suicide: Toward a framework for prevention. *Clinical Neuroscience Research, 1*, 310–323.

Munk-Olsen, T., Laursen, T. M., Meltzer-Brody, S., Mortensen, P. B., & Jones, I. (2012). Psychiatric disorders with postpartum onset. *Archives of General Psychiatry, 69*(4), 423–434.

National Institute of Mental Health. (2012). *Bipolar disorder.* Retrieved June 11, 2012, from http://www.nimh.nih.gov/health/publications/bipolar-disorder/nimh-bipolar-adults.pdf

National Institute of Mental Health. (n.d.). *Depression.* Retrieved March 4, 2012, from http://www.nimh.nih.gov

National Institute of Mental Health (NIMH) Genetics Workgroup. (1998). *Genetics and mental disorders* (NIH Publication No. 98-4268). Rockville, MD: National Institute of Mental Health.

Newhill, C. E. (1995). *A crisis casebook.* Unpublished manuscript.

Olfson, M., Marcus, S. C., & Bridge, J. A. (2012). Emergency treatment of deliberate self-harm. *Archives of General Psychiatry, 69*(1), 80–88.

Omalu, B., Hammers, J. L., Bailes, J., Hamilton, R. L., & Kamboh, M. I. (2011). *Neurosurgery Focus, 31*(5), 1–10.

Pollack, W. (1998). Mourning, melancholia and masculinity: Recognizing and treating depression in men. In W. Pollack & R. Levant (Eds.), *New psychotherapy for men* (pp. 147–166). New York: Wiley.

Qin, P., Agerbo, E., & Mortensen, P. B. (2002). Suicide risk in relation to family history of completed suicide and psychiatric disorders: A nested case-control study based on longitudinal registers. *The Lancet, 360*(9340), 1126–1130.

Rabin, R. C. (2011, November 14). A portable glow to help melt those winter blues. *The New York Times.*

Regier, D. A., Narrow, W. E., Rae, D. S., Manderscheid, R. W., Locke, B. Z., & Goodwin, F. K. (1993). The de facto mental and addictive disorders service system. Epidemiologic Catchment Area prospective 1-year prevalence rates of disorders and services. *Archives of General Psychiatry, 50*(2), 85–94.

Regier, D. A., Rae, D. S., Narrow, W. E., Kaebler, C. T., & Schatzberg, A. F. (1998). Prevalence of anxiety disorders and their comorbidity with mood and addictive disorders. *British Journal of Psychiatry, 173*(Suppl. 34), 24–28.

Roggenbaum, S., Christy, A., & LeBlanc, A. (2012). Suicide assessment and prevention during and after emergency commitment. *Community Mental Health Journal, 48*(4), 741–745.

Rohan, K. J., Lindsey, K. T., Roecklein, K. A., & Lacy, T. J. (2004). Cognitive-behavioral therapy, light therapy and their combination in treating seasonal affective disorder. *Journal of Affective Disorders, 80,* 273–283.

Rubinow, D. R., Schmidt, P. J., & Roca, C. A. (1998). Estrogen-serotonin interactions: Implications for affective regulation. *Biological Psychiatry, 44*(9), 839–850.

Sachs, G. S., Printz, D. J., Kahn, D. A., Carpenter, D., & Docherty, J. P. (2000). The expert consensus guideline series: Medication treatment of bipolar disorder. *Postgraduate Medicine, Spec No,* 1–104.

Sachs, G. S., & Thase, M. E. (2000). Bipolar disorder therapeutics: Maintenance treatment. *Biological Psychiatry, 48*(6), 573–581.

Scherk, H., Pajonk, F. G., & Leucht, S. (2007). Second-generation antipsychotic agents in the treatment of acute mania: A systematic review and meta-analysis of randomized controlled trials. *Archives of General Psychiatry, 64*(4), 442–455.

Schneider, K. (2011, June 3). Dr. Jack Kevorkian dies at 83: A doctor who helped end lives. *The New York Times.*

Schulberg, H. C., & Burns, B. J. (1988). Mental disorders in primary care: Epidemiologic, diagnostic, and treatment research directions. *General Hospital Psychiatry, 10*(2), 79–87.

Shahal, A. (2007). The relationship between suicide rates and age: An analysis of multinational data from the World Health Organization. *International Psychogeriatrics, 19*(6), 1141–1152.

Shiels, C., Gabbay, M., & Dowrick, C. (2004). Depression in men attending a rural general practice: Factors associated with prevalence of depressive symptoms and diagnosis. *The British Journal of Psychiatry, 185,* 239–244.

Simon, G. E., von Korff, M., Piccinelli, M., Fullerton, C., & Ormel, J. (1999). An international study of the relation between somatic symptoms and depression. *New England Journal of Medicine, 341*(18), 1329–1335.

Smith, D., Jones, I., & Simpson, S. (2010). Psychoeducation for bipolar disorder. *Advances in Psychiatric Treatment, 16,* 147–154. doi:10.1192/apt.bp.108.006403

Soares, J. C., & Mann, J. J. (1997a). The anatomy of mood disorders: Review of structural neuroimaging studies. *Biological Psychiatry, 41*(1), 86–106.

Soares, J. C., & Mann, J. J. (1997b). The functional neuroanatomy of mood disorders. *Journal of Psychiatric Research, 31*(4), 393–432.

Sostek, A. (2012, June 16). As age goes up, stress goes down. *Pittsburgh Post-Gazette.*

Thomas, J. L., Wilk, J. E., Riviere, L. A., McGurk, D., Castro, C. A., & Hoge, C. W. (2010). Prevalence of mental health problems and functional impairment among Active Component and National Guard soldiers 3 and 12 months following combat in Iraq. *Archives of General Psychiatry, 67*(6), 614–623.

Thorpy, M. (2012). *Sleep hygiene.* Retrieved June 13, 2012, from http://www.sleepfoundation.org

Ting, L., Jacobson, J. M., & Sanders, S. (2011). Current levels of perceived stress among mental health social workers who work with suicidal clients. *Social Work, 56*(4), 327–336.

Tseng, W. S. (2001). *Handbook of cultural psychiatry.* New York: Academic Press.

Tsuang, M. T., Bar, J. L., Stone, W. S., & Faraone, S. V. (2004). Gene-environment interactions in mental disorders. *World Psychiatry, 3*(2), 73–83.

Tsuang, M. T., & Faraone, S. V. (1990). *The genetics of mood disorders.* Baltimore: Johns Hopkins University Press.

Turnbull, D. J. (1986). Diagnostic significance of vegetative symptoms in depression. *British Journal of Psychiatry, 148,* 442–446.

United States Preventive Services Task Force (USPSTF). (2002). Screening for depression: Recommendations and rationale. *Annals of Internal Medicine, 136,* 760–764.

Wasserman, I. H. (1984). Imitation and suicide: A reexamination of the Werther effect. *American Sociological Review, 49,* 427–436.

Wahl, O. F. (1999). *Telling is risky business.* New Brunswick, N.J.: Rutgers University Press.

Watts, G. (2008). *Men get depression.* Washington, DC: State of the Art. Retrieved May 9, 2012, from http://www.mengetdepression.com

Webb, R. T., Kontopantelis, E., Doran, T., Qin, P., Creed, F., & Kapur, N. (2012). Suicide risk in primary care patients with major physical diseases: A case-control study. *Archives of General Psychiatry, 69*(3), 256–264.

Wegmann, J. (2012). *Psychopharmacology: Straight talk on mental health medications* (2nd ed.). Eau Claire, WI: Premier Publishing & Media.

White, R. C., & Preston, J. D. (2009). *Bipolar 101: A practical guide to identifying triggers, managing medications, coping with symptoms, and more.* Oakland, CA: New Harbinger.

Wisner, K. (2010). SSRI treatment during pregnancy: Are we asking the right questions? *Depression and Anxiety, 27,* 695–698.

Yager, J. (2000). Charlie. *American Journal of Psychiatry, 157,* 1753–1754.

Yates, E. (Producer and Director). (2001). *Suicide.* [Motion picture documentary]. United States: Home Box Office.

CHAPTER 13

Adler, D. A. (1990). Personality disorders: Treatment of the nonpsychotic chronic patient. *Treating Personality Disorders: New Directions for Mental Health Services, 47,* 3–15.

Alliance of Psychoanalytic Organizations. (2006). *Psychodynamic diagnostic manual (PDM).* Bethesda, MD: Author.

American Psychiatric Association (APA). (1968). *The diagnostic and statistical manual of mental disorders* (2nd ed.). Washington, DC: Author.

American Psychiatric Association (APA). (1980). *The diagnostic and statistical manual of mental disorders* (3rd ed.). Washington, DC: Author.

American Psychiatric Association (APA). (1987). *The diagnostic and statistical manual of mental disorders* (3rd ed., rev.). Washington, DC: Author.

American Psychiatric Association (APA). (1994). *The diagnostic and statistical manual of mental disorders* (4th ed.). Washington, DC: Author.

American Psychiatric Association (APA). (2000). *Diagnostic and statistical manual of mental disorders* (4th ed., rev.). Washington, DC: Author.

American Psychiatric Association (APA). (2013). *Diagnostic and statistical manual of mental disorders* (5th ed.). Washington, DC: Author.

Andersen, K. (2012, July 3). The downside of liberty. *The New York Times.*

Bateman, A., & Fonagy, P. (2010). Mentalization based treatment for borderline personality disorder. *World Psychiatry, 9*(1), 11–15.

Benjamin, L. S. (2002). *Interpersonal diagnosis and treatment of personality disorders* (2nd ed.). New York: Guilford.

Blackburn, R. (1971). Personality types among abnormal homicides. *British Journal of Criminology, 11,* 14–31.

Blackburn, R. (1975). An empirical classification of psychopathic personality. *British Journal of Psychiatry, 127,* 456–460.

Blackburn, R. (1996). Replicated personality disorder clusters among mentally disordered offenders and their relation to dimensions of personality. *Journal of Personality Disorders, 10,* 68–81.

Blackburn, R. (1998). Psychopathy and the contribution of personality to violence. In T. Millon, E. Simonsen, M. Birketsmith, & R. D. Davis (Eds.), *Psychopathy: Antisocial, criminal and violent behavior* (pp. 50–68). New York: Guilford.

Bloom, J. M., Woodward, E. N., Susmaras, T., & Pantalone, D. W. (2012). Use of dialectical behavior therapy in inpatient treatment of borderline personality disorder: A systematic review. *Psychiatric Services, 63*(9), 881–888.

Bowers, W. A. (1999). *Cognitive behavior therapy for DSM-IV personality disorders: Highly effective interventions for the most common personality disorders.* New York: Brunner/Mazel.

Bruni, F. (2012, July 16). Individualism in overdrive. *The New York Times.*

Budman, S. H., & Gurman, A. S. (1988). *Theory and practice of brief therapy.* New York: Guilford.

Buffardi, L. E., & Campbell, W. K. (2008). Narcissism and social networking web sites. *Personality and Social Psychology Bulletin, 34*(10), 1302–1314.

Butler, K. (2001, May/June). Revolution on the horizon: DBT challenges the borderline diagnosis. *Psychotherapy Networker,* 26–39.

Carey, B. (2004, November 16). Oh fine, you're right. I'm passive-aggressive. *The New York Times.*

Carey, B. (2012, November 26). Thinking clearly about personality disorders. *The New York Times.*

Clarkin, J. F., Levy, K. N., Lenzenweger, M. F., & Kernberg, O. F. (2007). Evaluating three treatments for borderline personality disorder: A multiwave study. *American Journal of Psychiatry, 164,* 922–928.

Clarkin, J. F., Yeomans, F., & Kernberg, O. F. (1999). *Psychotherapy of borderline personality.* New York: Wiley.

Cleckley, H. (1976). *The mask of sanity.* St. Louis, MO: Mosby. (Original work published 1941)

Coccaro, E. F., Siever, L. J., Owen, K. R., & Davis, K. L. (1990). Serotonin in mood and personality disorders. In E. F. Coccaro & D. L. Murphy (Eds.), *Serotonin in major psychiatric disorders* (pp. 69–97). Washington, DC: American Psychiatric Press.

Davidson, R. J., Jackson, D. C., & Kalin, N. H. (2000). Emotion, plasticity, context, and regulation: Perspectives from affective neuroscience. *Psychological Bulletin, 126,* 591–594.

Davidson, R. J., Putnam, K. M., & Larson, C. L. (2000). Dysfunction in the neural circuitry of emotion regulation—a possible prelude to violence. *Science, 289,* 591–594.

de Girolamo, G., & Dotto, P. (2000). Epidemiology of personality disorders. In M. G. Gelder, J. J. Lopez-Ibor, & N. C. Andreasen (Eds.), *New Oxford textbook of psychiatry* (Vol. 1, pp. 959–964). New York: Oxford University Press.

DeLisi, M., & Vaughn, M. G. (2008). Still psychopathic after all these years. In M. DeLisi & P. J. Conis (Eds.), *Violent offenders: Theory, research, public policy and practice.* Boston: Jones & Bartlett.

Dinos, S., Stevens, S., Serfaty, M., Weich, S., & King, M. (2004). Stigma: The feelings and experiences of 46 people with mental illness. *The British Journal of Psychiatry, 184,* 176–181.

Fenichel, O. (1945). *The psychoanalytic theory of neurosis.* New York: Norton.

Frankenburg, F. R., & Zanarini, M. C. (2006). Obesity and obesity-related illnesses in borderline patients. *Journal of Personality Disorders, 20*(1), 71–80.

Freud, A. (1936/1966). *The ego and the mechanisms of defense* (Rev. ed.). New York: International Universities Press, Inc.

Freud, S. (1911). Formulations on the two principles of mental functioning. In *The standard edition of the complete psychological works of Sigmund Freud, Vol. 12* (Stachey, J., Trans.). London: Hogarth.

Freud, S. (1923). The ego and the id. In *The standard edition of the complete psychological works of Sigmund Freud, Vol. 19* (Stachey, J., Trans.). London: Hogarth.

Freud, S. (1926). Inhibitions, symptoms, and anxieties. In *The standard edition of the complete psychological works of Sigmund Freud, Vol. 20* (Stachey, J., Trans.). London: Hogarth.

Friesen, D. P. (2009). *The age of entitlement.* Oklahoma City, OK: Speir.

Goldberg, S. J., D'Angelo, E. J., DeMaso, D. R., & Mezzacappa, E. (1992). Physical and sexual abuse histories among children with borderline personality disorder. *American Journal of Psychiatry, 149,* 1723–1726.

Goldstein, E. (1990). *Borderline disorders: Clinical models & techniques.* New York: Guilford.

Goode, E. (2011). *Deviant behavior* (9th ed.). Boston: Pearson.

Gregory, S., Ffytche, D., Simmons, A., Kumari, V., Howard, M., Hodgins, S., et al (2012). The antisocial brain: Psychopathy matters. *Archives of General Psychiatry, 69(9),* 962–972.

Grimes, W. (1994, February 15). Christopher Lasch is dead at 61; Wrote about America's malaise. *The New York Times.*

Gross, J. J. (2002). Emotion regulation: Affective, cognitive, and social consequences. *Psychophysiology, 39*(3), 282–291.

Gunderson, J. G. (2011). *A BPD brief: An introduction to borderline personality disorder diagnosis, origins, course and treatment.* Retrieved July 10, 2012, from www.borderlinepersonalitydisorder.com

Gunderson, J. G., & Hoffman, P. D. (Eds.). (2005). *Understanding and treating borderline personality disorder: A guide for professionals and families.* Washington, DC: American Psychiatric Press.

Hall, J. R., & Benning, S. D. (2006). The "successful" psychopath: Adaptive and subclinical manifestations of psychopathy in the general population. In C. J.

Patrick (Ed.), *Handbook of psychopathy* (pp. 459–478). New York: Guilford.

Hare, R. D. (1980). A research scale for the assessment of psychopathy in criminal populations. *Personal and Individual Differences, 1*, 111–119.

Hare, R. D. (1991). *The Hare Psychopathy Checklist—Revised.* Toronto, ON, Canada: Multi-Health Systems.

Hare, R. D. (2003). *The Hare Psychopathy Checklist—Revised* (2nd ed.). Toronto, ON, Canada: Multi-Health Systems.

Hare, R. D., Cooke, D. J., & Hart, S. D. (1999). Psychopathy and sadistic personality disorder. In T. Millon, P. H. Blaney, & R. D. Davis (Eds.), *Oxford textbook of psychopathy* (pp. 555–584). New York: Oxford.

Hare, R. D., & Neumann, C. S. (2008). Psychopathy as a clinical and empirical construct. *Annual Review of Clinical Psychology, 4*, 217–246.

Kantor, M. (2002). *Passive-aggression: A guide for the therapist, the patient and the victim.* New York: Praeger.

Karpman, B. (1941). On the need for separating psychopathy into two distinct clinical types: Symptomatic and idiopathic. *Journal of Criminology and Psychopathology, 3*, 112–137.

Kaysen, S. (1994). *Girl, interrupted.* New York: Vintage.

Kratzer, L., & Hodgins, S. (1997). Adult outcomes of child conduct problems: A cohort study. *Journal of Abnormal Child Psychology, 25*(1), 65–81.

Kreger, R., & Mason, P. T. (2010). *Stop walking on eggshells: Taking your life back when someone you care about has borderline personality disorder* (2nd ed.). Oakland, CA: New Harbinger.

Kreger, R., & Shirley, J. P. (2002). *Stop walking on eggshells workbook: Practical strategies for living with someone who has borderline personality disorder.* Oakland, CA: New Harbinger.

Kreisman, J. J., & Straus, H. (1989). *I hate you—don't leave me: Understanding the borderline personality.* New York: Avon.

Lasch, C. (1979). *The culture of narcissism: American life in an age of diminishing expectations.* New York: W. W. Norton.

Linehan, M. M. (1993a). *Cognitive-behavioral treatment of borderline personality disorder.* New York: Guilford.

Linehan, M. M. (1993b). *Skills training manual for treating borderline personality disorder.* New York: Guilford.

Linehan, M. M., Comtois, K. A., Murray, A. M., Brown, M. Z., Gallop, R. J., Heard, H. L., et al. (2006). Two-year randomized controlled trial and follow-up of dialectical behavior therapy vs. therapy by experts for suicidal behaviors and borderline personality disorder. *Archives of General Psychiatry, 63*(7), 757–766.

Loeber, R., & Stouthamer-Loeber, M. (1998). Development of juvenile aggression and violence: Some common misconceptions and controversies. *American Psychologist, 53*(2), 242–259.

Long, N. J., Long, J. E., & Whitson, S. (2009). *The angry smile: The psychology of passive-aggressive behavior in families, schools, and workplaces* (2nd ed.). Austin, TX: Pro-Ed.

McMain, S. F., Guimond, T., Streiner, D. L., Cardish, R. J., & Links, P. S. (2012). Dialectical behavior therapy compared with general psychiatric management for borderline personality disorder: Clinical outcomes and functioning over a 2-year follow-up. *American Journal of Psychiatry, 169*, 650–661.

McMain, S. F., Links, P. S., Gnam, W. H., Guimond, T., Cardish, R. J., Korman, L., et al. (2009). A randomized trial of dialectical behavior therapy versus general psychiatric management for borderline personality disorder. *American Journal of Psychiatry, 166*, 1365–1374.

Mental Illness Education Awareness Project, Inc. (Producer). (1999). *Dual diagnosis: An integrated model for the treatment of people with co-occurring psychiatric and substance disorders. A lecture by Kenneth Minkoff, M.D.* [Educational video recording]. United States: Mental Illness Education Awareness Project, Inc.

Millon, T., Grossman, S., Millon, C., Meagher, S., & Ramnath, R. (2004). *Personality disorders in modern life.* Hoboken, NJ: Wiley.

Millon, T., Simonsen, E., Birket-Smith, M., & Davis, R. (1998). *Psychopathy: Antisocial, criminal and violent behavior.* New York: Guilford.

Moffitt, T. E. (2003). Adolescence-limited and life-course-persistent antisocial behavior: A developmental taxonomy. *Psychological Review, 100*(4), 674–701.

Moffitt, T. E. (2005). Genetic and environmental influences on antisocial behaviors: Evidence from behavioral-genetic research. *Advances in Genetics, 55*, 41–104.

Murdach, A. D. (1980). Bargaining and persuasion with nonvoluntary clients. *Social Work, 25*, 458–461.

Nater, U. M., Jones, J. F., Lin, J. M., Maloney, E., Reeves, W. C., & Heim, C. (2010). Personality features and personality disorders in chronic fatigue syndrome: A population-based study. *Psychotherapy and Psychosomatics, 79*(5), 312–318.

Newhill, C. E. (1995). *A crisis casebook.* Unpublished manuscript.

Newhill, C. E., Eack, S. M., & Mulvey, E. P. (2009). Violent behavior in individuals with borderline personality disorder. *Journal of Personality Disorders, 23*, 541–554.

Newhill, C. E., Eack, S. M., & Mulvey, E. P. (2012). A growth curve analysis of emotion dysregulation as a mediator for violence in borderline personality disorder. *Journal of Personality Disorders, 26*(3), 452–461.

Newhill, C. E., & Mulvey, E. P. (2002). Emotional dysregulation: The key to a treatment approach for violent, mentally ill individuals. *Clinical Social Work Journal, 30*, 157–171.

Newhill, C. E., Vaughn, M. G., & DeLisi, M. J. (2010). Psychopathy scores reveal heterogeneity among patients with borderline personality disorder. *Journal of Forensic Psychiatry and Psychology, 21*, 202–220.

Paris, J. (2003). *Personality disorders over time: Precursors, course and outcomes.* Washington, DC: American Psychiatric Press.

Patrick, C. J. (2005). Getting to the heart of psychopathy. In H. Herve & J. C. Yuille (Eds.), *Psychopathy: Theory, research and social implications* (pp. 207–252). Hillsdale, NJ: Erlbaum.

Patrick, C. J. (Ed.). (2006). *Handbook of psychopathy.* New York: Guilford.

Perry, J. C., & Vaillant, G. E. (1989). Personality disorders. In H. I. Kaplan & B. J. Sadock (Eds.), *Comprehensive textbook of psychiatry* (5th ed., pp. 1352–1395). Williams & Wilkins: London.

Porr, V. (2010). *Overcoming borderline personality disorder: A family guide for healing and change.* New York: Oxford.

Putnam, K. M., & Silk, K. R. (2005). Emotion dysregulation and the development of borderline personality disorder. *Development and psychopathology, 17*, 899–925.

Reich, J. H., & Vasile, R. G. (1993). Effect of personality disorders on the treatment outcome of Axis I conditions: An update. *Journal of Nervous and Mental Disorders, 181*(8), 475–484.

Reich, W. (1949). *Character analysis* (3rd ed.). New York: Orgone Press.

Rhee, S. H., & Waldman, I. D. (2002). Genetic and environmental influences on antisocial behavior: A meta-analysis of twin and adoption studies. *Psychological Bulletin, 128*(3), 490–529.

Robinson, D. J. (2005). *Disordered personalities* (3rd ed.). Port Huron, MI: Rapid Psychler Press.

Rooney, R. H. (1992). *Strategies for work with involuntary clients.* New York: Columbia University Press.

Sansone, R. A., & Hawkins, R. (2004). Fibromyalgia, borderline personality, and opioid prescription. *General Hospital Psychiatry, 26*(5), 415–416.

Schouten, R., & Silver, J. (2012). *Almost a psychopath: Do I (or does someone I know) have a problem with manipulation and lack of empathy?* Center City, MN: Hazelden.

Shapiro, D. (1965). *Neurotic styles.* New York: Harper & Row.

Siever, L. J., Silverman, J. M., Horvath, T. B., Klar, H., Coccaro, E., Keefe, R. S. E., (1990). Increased morbid risk for schizophrenia-related disorders in relatives of schizotypal personality disordered patients. *Archives of General Psychiatry, 47*(7), 634–640. doi:10.1001/archpsyc.1990.01810190034005

Skeem, J. L., Poythress, N. G., Edens, J. F., Lilienfeld, S. O., & Cale, E. M. (2003). Psychopathic personality or personalities? Exploring potential variants of psychopathy and their implications for risk assessment. *Aggression and Violent Behavior, 8*, 513–546.

Skodol, A. E. (2005). The borderline diagnosis: Concepts, criteria and controversies. In J. G. Gunderson & P. D. Hoffman (Eds.), *Understanding and treating borderline personality disorder: A guide for professionals and families* (pp. 3–19). Washington, DC: American Psychiatric Press.

Skodol, A. E., Gunderson, J. G., Pfohl, B., Widiger, T. A., Livesley, W. J., & Siever, L. J. (2002). The borderline diagnosis I: Psychopathology, comorbidity, and personality structure. *Biological Psychiatry, 51*, 936–950.

Spitzer, R. L., Gibbon, M., Skodol, A. E., Williams, J. B. W., & First, M. B. (2002). *The DSM-IV-TR casebook.* Washington, DC: American Psychiatric Publishing.

Stinson, F. S., Dawson, D. A., Goldstein, R. B., Chou, S. P., Huang, B., Smith, S. M., (2008). Prevalence, correlates, disability, and comorbidity of DSM-IV narcissistic personality disorder: Results from the wave 2 national epidemiologic survey on alcohol and related conditions. *Journal of Clinical Psychiatry, 69*(7), 1033–1045.

Stone, M. H. (1989). Long-term follow-up of narcissistic/borderline patients. *Psychiatric Clinics of North America, 12*(3), 621–641.

Thompson, R. A. (1994). Emotion regulation: A theme in search of definition. In N. A. Fox (Ed.), *The development of emotion regulation: Biological and behavioral considerations. Monographs of the Society for Research in Child Development, serial no. 240, 59*(2–3), 25–52.

Torgersen, S., Kringlen, E., & Cramer, V. (2001). The prevalence of personality disorders in a community sample. *Archives of General Psychiatry, 58*, 590–596.

Twenge, J. M., & Campbell, W. K. (2009). *The narcissism epidemic: Living in the age of entitlement.* New York: Free.

Widiger, T. A. (2006). Psychopathy and DSM-IV psychopathology. In C. J. Patrick (Ed.), *Handbook of psychopathy* (pp. 156–171). New York: Guilford.

Widiger, T. A., & Trull, T. J. (1993). Borderline and narcissistic personality disorders. In P. B. Sutker & H. E. Adams (Eds.), *Comprehensive handbook of psychopathology* (2nd ed., pp. 371–394). New York: Plenum.

Wolfe, T. (1976, August 23). The "Me" decade and the third great awakening. *New York Magazine.*

Young, J. E. (1990). *Cognitive therapy for personality disorders: A schema-focused approach.* Sarasota, FL: Professional Resource Exchange.

Zanarini, M. C. (2005). The longitudinal course of borderline personality disorder. In J. G. Gunderson & P. D. Hoffman (Eds.), *Understanding and treating borderline personality disorder: A guide for professionals and families* (pp. 83–101). Washington, DC: American Psychiatric Press.

Zanor, C. (2010, November 29). A fate that narcissists will hate: Being ignored. *The New York Times.*

CHAPTER 14

Alcoholics Anonymous. (1952). *Twelve steps and twelve traditions.* New York: AA World Services, Inc.

Bellack, A. S., & DiClemente, C. C. (1999). Treating substance abuse among patients with schizophrenia. *Psychiatric Services, 50*(1), 75–80.

Bellack, A. S., Mueser, K. T., Gingerich, S., & Agresta, J. (1997). *Social skills training for schizophrenia: A step-by-step guide.* Treatment manuals for practitioners. New York: Guilford.

Bennett, G., Woolf, D., & Vourackas, C. (1983). *Substance abuse: Pharmacologic, developmental and clinical perspectives.* Hoboken, NJ: Wiley.

Bernas, E. (1999). Interview. In 5759 Productions (Producers) & Zemeckis (Director), *Smoking, drinking, drugging in the 20th century: The pursuit of happiness.* [Motion picture documentary].

Blum, K. (1991). *Alcohol and the addictive brain.* New York: Free.

Caton, C. L. M. (1981). The new chronic patient and the system of community care. *Hospital and Community Psychiatry, 32*, 475–478.

Cave, D., & Schmidt, M. S. (2012, July 16). Rise in pill abuse forces new look at U.S. drug fight. *The New York Times.*

Clark, R. E. (2001). Family support and substance use outcomes for persons with mental illness and substance use disorders. *Schizophrenia Bulletin, 27*(1), 93–101.

Clark, R. E., & Drake, R. E. (1992). Substance abuse & mental illness: What families need to know. *Innovations & Research, 1*, 43–61.

Collins, R. L., Bradizza, C. M., & Vincent, P. C. (2007). Young-adult malt liquor drinkers: Prediction of alcohol problems and marijuana use. *Psychology of Addictive Behaviors, 21*(2), 138–146.

Compton, W. M., Conway, K. P., Stinson, F. S., Colliver, J. D., & Grant, B. F. (2005). Prevalence, correlates, and comorbidity of DSM-IV antisocial personality syndromes and alcohol and specific drug use disorders in the United States: Results from the National Epidemiologic Survey on Alcohol and Related Conditions. *Journal of Clinical Psychiatry, 66*(6), 677–685.

Drake, R. E., Essock, S. M., Shaner, A., Carey, K. B., Minkoff, K., Kola, L., et al. (2001). Implementing dual diagnosis services for clients with severe mental illness. *Psychiatric Services, 52*(4), 469–476.

Drake, R. E., & Wallach, M. A. (1989). Substance abuse among the chronically mentally ill. *Hospital and Community Psychiatry, 40*, 1041–1046.

Evans, K., & Sullivan, J. M. (1990). *Dual diagnosis: Counseling the mentally ill substance abuser.* New York: Guilford.

Fisher, G. L., & Harrison, T. C. (2008). *Substance abuse: Information for school counselors, social workers, therapists and counselors* (4th ed.). Boston: Allyn & Bacon.

Interlandi, J. (2008, March 3). What addicts need. *Newsweek*, pp. 37–42.

Johnston, L. D., O'Malley, P. M., & Bachman, J. G. (1993). *National survey results on drug use from the Monitoring the Future study, 1975–1992. Vol. I. Secondary school students.* Rockville, MD: National Institute on Drug Abuse.

Johnston, L. D., O'Malley, P. M., Bachman, J. G., & Schulenberg, J. E. (2012). *Monitoring the Future national results on adolescent drug use: Overview of key findings, 2011.* Ann Arbor: Institute for Social Research, University of Michigan.

Keller, M. (1972). The oddities of alcoholics. *Quarterly Journal Studies on Alcohol, 33*, 1147–1148.

Kessler, R. C., McGonagle, K. A., Zhao, S., Nelson, C. B., Hughes, M., Eshleman, S., et al. (1994). Lifetime and 12-month prevalence of DSM-III-R psychiatric disorders in the United States: Results from the National Comorbidity Survey. *Archives of General Psychiatry, 51*(1), 8–19.

Khantzian, E. J., & Treece, C. (1985). DSM-III psychiatric diagnosis of narcotic addicts. *Archives of General Psychiatry, 42*(11), 1067–1071.

Linehan, M. M., Dimeff, L. A., Reynolds, S. K., Comtoisa, K. A., Welch, S. S., Heagerty, P., et al. (2002). Dialectical behavior therapy versus comprehensive validation therapy plus 12-step for the treatment of opioid dependent women meeting criteria for borderline personality disorder. *Drug and Alcohol Dependence, 67*(1), 13–26.

Links, P. S., Heslegrave, R. J., Mitton, J. E., Van Reekum, R., & Patrick, J. (1995). Borderline personality disorder and substance abuse: Consequences of comorbidity. *The Canadian Journal of Psychiatry / La Revue canadienne de psychiatrie, 40*(1), 9–14.

Minkoff, K. (1989). An integrated treatment model for dual diagnosis of psychosis and addiction. *Hospital and Community Psychiatry, 40*(10), 1031–1036.

Minkoff, K. (1991). Program components of a comprehensive integrated care system for serious mentally ill patients with substance disorders. *Dual Diagnosis of Serious Mental Illness and Substance Disorder: New Directions for Mental Health Services, 50*, 13–27.

Minkoff, K. (1999, November). The Mental Illness Education Project, Inc. (Producer/Director). *Dual diagnosis: An integrated model for the treatment of people with co-occurring psychiatric and substance disorders. A lecture by Kenneth Minkoff, M.D.* [Educational video recording]. United States: Mental Illness Education Awareness Project, Inc.

Minkoff, K. (2001). Best practices: Developing standards of care for individuals with co-occurring psychiatric and substance use disorders. *Psychiatric Services, 52*(5), 597–599.

Mueser, K. T., Drake, R. E., & Wallach, M. A. (1998). Dual diagnosis: A review of etiological theories. *Addictive Behaviors, 23*(6), 717–734.

Mueser, K. T., & Noordsy, D. L. (1996). Group treatment for dually diagnosed clients. *New Directions for Mental Health Services, 70*, 33–51.

National Institute on Drug Abuse (NIDA). (n.d.). *Drugs of abuse.* Retrieved July 19, 2012, from http://www.drugabuse.gov/drugs-abuse/inhalants

National Institute on Drug Abuse (NIDA). (n.d.). *Drug facts.* Retrieved July 19, 2012, from http://www.drugabuse.gov/publications/drugfacts/cocaine

Newhill, C. E. (1995). *A crisis casebook.* Unpublished manuscript.

Noordsy, D. L., Schwab, B., Fox, L., & Drake, R. E. (1996). The role of self-help programs in the rehabilitation of persons with severe mental illness and substance use disorders. *Community Mental Health Journal, 32*(1), 71–81.

O'Hare, T. (1992). The substance-abusing chronically mentally ill client: Prevalence, assessment, treatment, and policy concerns. *Social Work, 37*, 185–187.

Parry, C. D. H. (1997). The illegal narcotics trade in southern Africa: A programme for action. *South African Journal of International Affairs, 5*(1), 38–70.

Pascarelli, E. F. (1973). Methaqualone abuse, the quiet epidemic. *Journal of the American Medical Association (JAMA), 224*(11), 1512–1514.

Pepper, B., Krishner, M. C., & Ryglewicz, H. (1981). The young adult chronic patient: Overview of a population. *Hospital and Community Psychiatry, 32*, 463–469.

Prince, J. D. (2012). Risk of inpatient stay for mental illness among individuals with substance use disorders. *Psychiatric Services, 63*(9), 938–941.

Prince, J. D., Walkup, J., Akincigil, A., Amin, S., & Crystal, S. (2012). Serious mental illness and risk of new HIV/AIDS diagnoses: An analysis of Medicaid beneficiaries in eight states. *Psychiatric Services, 63*(10), 1032–1038.

Regier, D. A., Farmer, M. E., Rae, D. S., Locke, B. Z., Keith, S. J., Judd, L. L., et al. (1990). Comorbidity of mental disorders with alcohol and other drug abuse: Results from the Epidemiologic Catchment Area (ECA) study. *Journal of the American Medical Association (JAMA), 264*(19), 2511–2518.

Ridgely, M. S., Osher, F. C., Goldman, H. H., & Talbott, J. A. (1987). *Executive summary: Chronic mentally ill young adults with substance abuse problems: A review of research, treatment and training issues.* Baltimore: University of Maryland School of Medicine, Mental Health Services Research Center.

Robins, L. N., & Regier, D. A. (Eds.). (1991). *Psychiatric disorders in America: The Epidemiologic Catchment Area study.* New York: Free.

Rosenthal, M. S. (2008, March 3). Sadly, there is no magic bullet: Addiction is not solely a disease of the brain. The case for holistic treatment. *Newsweek*, 43.

Sajatovic, M. (2012). The complicated lessons of Prohibition. *Psychiatric Services, 63*(7), 627.

Satel, S. (1998, April 4). Don't forget the addict's role in addiction. *The New York Times*, p. A-23.

Smith, M. C., & Riskin, B. J. (1991). The clinical use of barbiturates in neurological disorders. *Drugs, 42*(3), 365–378.

Sobell, L. C., & Sobell, M. B. (1992). Timeline followback: A technique for assessing self-reported ethanol consumption. In J. Allen & R. Z. Litten (Eds.), *Measuring alcohol consumption: Psychosocial and biological methods* (pp. 41–72). Totowa, NJ: Humana Press.

Strickland, M. (1993, October 9). What families need to know about substance abuse & mental illness. *AMI-Nevada Newsletter.*

Substance Abuse and Mental Health Services Administration. (2010). *Evidence-based practices kit: Integrated treatment for co-occurring disorders* (DHHS Publication No. SMA-08-4367). Rockville, MD: Author.

Substance Abuse and Mental Health Services Administration. (2011). *Results from the 2010 National Survey on Drug Use and Health: Summary of national findings* (NSDUH Series H-41, HHS Publication No. SMA-11-4658). Rockville, MD: Author.

Substance Abuse and Mental Health Services Administration, Office of Applied Studies. (2004). *Results from the 2003 National Survey on Drug Use and Health: National findings* (NSDUH Series H-25; DHHS Publication No. SMA 04-3964). Rockville, MD: Author.

Sun, A. P. (2012). Helping homeless individuals with co-occurring disorders: The four components. *Social Work, 57*(1), 23–37.

Trull, T. J., Sher, K. J., Minks-Brown, C., Durbin, J., & Burr, R. (2000). Borderline personality disorder and substance use disorders: A review and integration. *Clinical Psychology Review, 20*(2), 235–253.

Truog, R. D., Berde, C. B., Mitchell, C., & Grier, H. E. (1992). Barbiturates in the care of the terminally ill. *New England Journal of Medicine, 327*, 1678–1682.

Trzzepacz, P. T., Meagher, D. L., & Wise, M. C. (2002). Neuropsychiatric aspects of delirium. In S. C. Yudofsky & R. E. Hales (Eds.), *The American Psychiatric Publishing textbook of neuropsychiatry and clinical neurosciences* (pp. 525–564). Washington, DC: American Psychiatric Publishing.

Twain, M. (1884/1996). *The adventures of Huckleberry Finn.* Thorndike, ME: G. K. Hall & Co.

Wanjek, C. (2002, June 4). The real dope. *The Washington Post*, p. HE-01.

Watkins, T. R., Lewellen, A., & Barrett, M. C. (2001). *Dual diagnosis: An integrated approach to treatment.* Thousand Oaks, CA: Sage.

West, R. (2001). Theories of addiction. *Addiction, 96*(1), 3–13.

Yago, K. B., Pitts, F. N., Burgoyne, R. W., Aniline, O., Yago, L. S., & Pitts, A. F. (1981). The urban epidemic of phencyclidine (PCP) use: Clinical and laboratory evidence from a public psychiatric hospital emergency service. *Journal of Clinical Psychiatry, 42*, 193–196.

Yang, S., Mulvey, E. P., Loughran, T. A., & Hanusa, B. H. (2012). Psychiatric symptoms and alcohol use in community violence by persons with a psychotic disorder or depression. *Psychiatric Services, 63*(3), 262–269.

Zernike, K. (2005, July 11). A drug scourge creates its own form of orphan. *The New York Times.*

Index

E